STEEL CITY

STEEL CITY

*Entrepreneurship, Strategy, and
Technology in Sheffield
1743–1993*

GEOFFREY TWEEDALE

CLARENDON PRESS · OXFORD

This book has been printed digitally and produced in a standard specification
in order to ensure its continuing availability

OXFORD
UNIVERSITY PRESS

Great Clarendon Street, Oxford OX2 6DP

Oxford University Press is a department of the University of Oxford.
It furthers the University's objective of excellence in research, scholarship,
and education by publishing world-wide in

Oxford New York

Auckland Bangkok Buenos Aires Cape Town Chennai
Dar es Salaam Delhi Hong Kong Istanbul Karachi Kolkata
Kuala Lumpur Madrid Melbourne Mexico City Mumbai Nairobi
São Paulo Shanghai Taipei Tokyo Toronto

Oxford is a registered trade mark of Oxford University Press
in the UK and in certain other countries

Published in the United States
by Oxford University Press Inc., New York

ISBN 0-19-828866-2

Antony Rowe Ltd., Eastbourne

ACKNOWLEDGEMENTS

This book had its genesis in the multi-volume *History of Sheffield* project, which was launched by the History Department at Sheffield University to commemorate the city's centenary in 1993—a date which virtually coincided with the 250th anniversary of the discovery of crucible steelmaking. My research and writing was funded entirely by the Leverhulme Trustees, who awarded a three-year fellowship in 1991 for me to explore business strategies in Steel City after 1918. Since they had earlier supported work on an unrelated subject elsewhere, my debt to the Leverhulme Trust is great. At Sheffield, Clyde Binfield especially, and also Colin Holmes and Ian Kershaw (as head of department) provided the support for this project. Others who took an interest in my work included David Martin, David Higgins, Kenneth Warren, and Peter Payne; and I also received help along the way from Robert Gordon and Robert Kanigel in America. I owe a particular debt to Philip Hansen, whose labours at the photocopier and amongst dusty old newspapers saved me much drudgery and many trips to Sheffield. Bernard Callan greatly assisted in the final 'crinking' by meticulously reading this manuscript: he also kept me in touch with the Sheffield scene and ensured that living on the other side of the Peaks was not too great a disadvantage.

Most of the research was undertaken at two locations: Sheffield City Library Archives, where Richard Childs (and his successor, Margaret Turner), Ruth Harman, and others, gave every assistance; and in the Central Library's peerless Local Studies Department, where Doug Hindmarch, Sylvia Pybus, Martin Olive, and several others have kindly fetched books and documents for me over the years.

In locating and gaining access to other records, I was assisted by Peter Carnell at Sheffield University Library; Julie MacDonald at the Cutlers' Company; Michael Moss at Glasgow University Archives; Elizabeth Ogborn at the Bank of England Archives; Jenny Robinson at the British Steel Regional Records Centre, Middlesbrough; John Taylor at the Cammell-Laird Archives, Birkenhead; Nigel Watts at John Brown PLC, London; and N. Brown at the Rural History Centre, University of Reading.

Within the steel industry I received considerable help from many former and present company chairmen, directors, and metallurgists, who provided recollections (usually by interview) and documents, and commented on my early drafts. They are listed in the sources.

David Musson, my editor at Oxford University Press, was helpful in various ways, especially in gently urging upon me a sharper framework for this book. Paul Tweedale provided computer help; and Mary Titchmarsh, as ever, kept me cheerful during its writing.

CONTENTS

1. TEEMING CRUCIBLE STEEL

Teeming crucible steel at Andrews Toledo Ltd., a scene probably recorded between the Wars. As the teemer carefully pours the molten steel into the ingot mould — a job demanding great strength and careful judgement — an assistant holds back the floating layer of slag with a rod. The crucible process, devised by Benjamin Huntsman in the early 1740s, could still be seen in Sheffield over 200 years later. It was the basis for Sheffield's dominance of the special steel industry. (Courtesy Sheffield Newspapers Ltd.)

LIST OF PLATES

LIST OF FIGURES

LIST OF MAPS

LIST OF TABLES

ABBREVIATIONS

BDR   Balfour Darwin Records

BISF   British Iron & Steel Federation

BISPA   British Independent Steel Producers' Association

BLPES   British Library of Political and Economic Science

BSC   British Steel Corporation

ESC   English Steel Corporation

IMR   *Implement and Machinery Review*

JISI   *Journal of the Iron and Steel Institute*

JHMS   *Journal of the Historical Metallurgy Society*

R&D   Research and development

RMS   R. Mushet's Special Steel

SCL   Sheffield City Library

SDT   *Sheffield Daily Telegraph*

SI   *Sheffield Independent*

TES   *The Times Engineering Supplement*

THAS   *Transactions of the Hunter Archaeological Society*

Prologue

In terms of crude tonnage, the Sheffield steelmaking area (which statistically includes Rotherham, Stocksbridge and a works in Manchester) is not the most important in Great Britain. Sheffield, nevertheless, remains the most famous name in steel, and this pre-eminence is justified by the variety, the quality and the high value of its products. Although one may anticipate a murmur of protest from makers of deep-drawing sheet, it is broadly true to say that Sheffield specialises in those steel products that require the highest degree of metallurgical knowledge and practical skill.

British Steelmaker, 30 (1964), 282

It might seem boastful, but there's nothing as skilled as manipulating steel into shape.

Bill Winfield, an old Sheffield hand-forger, quoted in C. Jenkins and S. McClarence, *On the Knife Edge* (Sheffield, 1989), 168

Some fifteen years ago, when I first visited Sheffield, it still laid claim—somewhat tenuously, perhaps—to its soubriquet, 'Steel City'. At the end of the 1970s, it was still possible to walk along the main trunk roads in the River Don valley, along Savile and Carlisle Streets, between the giant steel mills that flanked the river, and find that the city's steel industry was still relatively intact. Although Sheffield's industries had been in marked decline once the steel boom of the 1950s was over (especially the cutlery and tool trades), the catastrophic closure of the large factories, the decline of the tool steel industry, and the bitter labour disputes still lay in the future.

In the 1970s the imprint of nineteenth- and early twentieth-century industrialization still lay heavy upon the city, slicing it into separate areas (see Maps). To the south were the better residential parts, such as Nether Edge and Ecclesall, stretching from the fringes of the city into picturesque Derbyshire. The steel-producing area started on the north side of the city at Neepsend, stretched alongside the River Don through the Wicker and then continued into the wide river valley towards Rotherham, several miles distant. Meanwhile, what was left of the cutlery and tool trades crowded surprisingly close to the city centre, in the vicinity of The Moor and West Street, two of the main thoroughfares in Sheffield.

At that time a brisk walk for an hour or two from the Midland Railway Station would give a surprisingly complete picture of the main phases of Sheffield's post-1800 industrial history. It would begin with a steep climb into the city centre, past Arundel Street and its string of old cutlery factories; on towards West Street and into the Solly Street area, where one could loiter amongst Victorian workshop courtyards and still hear the pound of forging hammers and throb of grinding wheels, turning out cutlery and tools. It would continue with a descent to the banks of the Don at Neepsend, where the river wound its way through one of the oldest manufacturing districts in Sheffield. The Kelham Island goit (which had long ago diverted water for gristmills), the furnaces, and the grimy factories with their famous frontages—Bedford's Lion Works, Hoole's of Green Lane, and James Dixon's Cornish Place Works—had changed little since the nineteenth century. Following the River Don out of Neepsend in the general direction of Rotherham would lead into the main industrial area, still one of Europe's leading centres of steel production. Here the

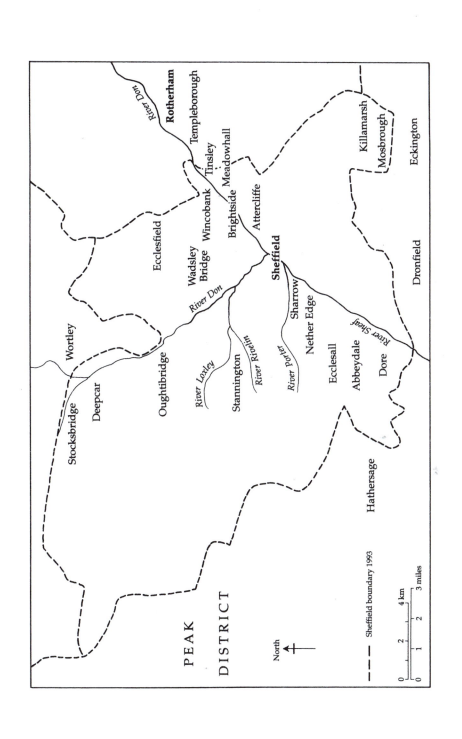

PEAK DISTRICT

Rotherham

Templeborough

Tinsley

Meadowhall

Brightside

Wincobank

Attercliffe

Wadsley Bridge

Sheffield

Ecclesfield

Sharrow

Nether Edge

Killamarsh

Mosbrough

Eckington

Dronfield

River Don

Wortley

Oughtibridge

River Loxley

Stannington

River Rivelin

River Porter

Ecclesall

Abbeydale

Dore

River Sheaf

Stocksbridge

Deepcar

Hathersage

North

– – – Sheffield boundary 1993

0   1   2   3 miles

0   2   4 km

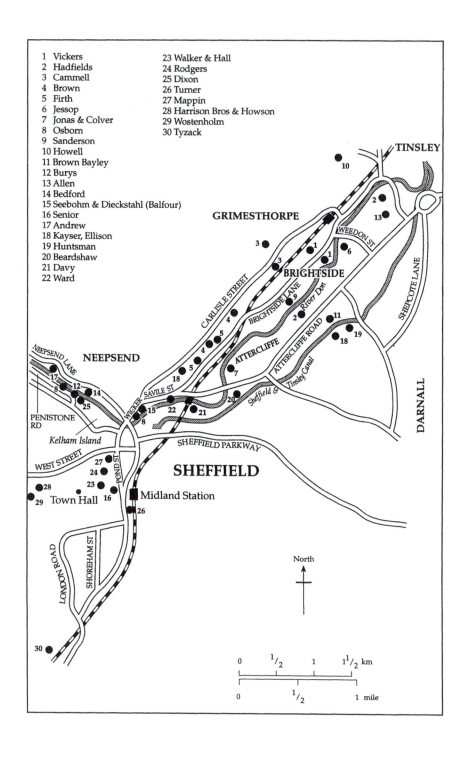

1 Vickers
2 Hadfields
3 Cammell
4 Brown
5 Firth
6 Jessop
7 Jonas & Colver
8 Osborn
9 Sanderson
10 Howell
11 Brown Bayley
12 Burys
13 Allen
14 Bedford
15 Seebohm & Dieckstahl (Balfour)
16 Senior
17 Andrew
18 Kayser, Ellison
19 Huntsman
20 Beardshaw
21 Davy
22 Ward
23 Walker & Hall
24 Rodgers
25 Dixon
26 Turner
27 Mappin
28 Harrison Bros & Howson
29 Wostenholm
30 Tyzack

TINSLEY

GRIMESTHORPE

WEEDON ST

BRIGHTSIDE

CARLISLE STREET

BRIGHTSIDE LANE

River Don

ATTERCLIFFE

ATTERCLIFFE ROAD

SHEPCOTE LANE

DARNALL

NEEPSEND LANE

NEEPSEND

WICKER

SAVILE ST

Sheffield & Tinsley Canal

PENISTONE
RD

Kelham Island

SHEFFIELD PARKWAY

WEST STREET

POND ST

SHEFFIELD

Town Hall

Midland Station

LONDON ROAD

SHOREHAM ST

North

0   ½   1   1½ km

0   ½   1 mile

scale of operations would begin changing dramatically, as the route led, in a steady and seemingly never-ending progression, past the locations of Sheffield's oldest and biggest firms. The companies that had carved out a place here would read like a *Who's Who* of British engineering and steelmaking: Vickers, John Brown, Cammell, Firth, Hadfields, and Jessop. For by the end of the nineteenth century this area of the Don, running three miles or so north-east of the city centre towards Rotherham, had been, along with Pittsburgh, the most concentrated centre for steel production in the world. These firms, although there had occasionally been a change of name, were still working at the end of the 1970s.

Sheffielders had once described this part of the valley, along Carlisle Street, as 'a long drawn horror of confluent damnation'; a street 'separated from Hell only by a sheet of tissue paper'.[1] In the late twentieth century, although its famous smoke had disappeared, the Don Valley had not entirely lost this aspect. When I first walked along these roads in 1978, under a suitably rainy and leaden sky, I wondered how anyone could work in such dirty and forbidding surroundings. Though I did not realize it at the time, my impressions were the same as almost every other visitor to Sheffield. One had written in 1870 that, such was its grimy character, 'an entire stranger . . . would need more than an average amount of philosophy to overcome the blues'.[2] 'Dingy hole', was the American artist John Singer Sargent's more succinct appraisal in 1884.[3]

Later my views began changing as I familiarized myself with the city and its industries. First came the realization that Sheffield, besides its more sombre industrial activities, was a place of hills and great natural beauty—the famous dirty picture in a golden frame. There was the character of Sheffielders themselves, which had appealed to the famous socialist and free-thinker, Edward Carpenter, who had written: 'From the first I was taken with the Sheffield people. Rough in the extreme, twenty or thirty years in date behind other towns, and very uneducated, there was yet a heartiness about them, not without shrewdness that attracted me.'[4] There was also the recognition that Sheffield's industrial heart lay not so much in its giant steelworks, important though these were, but in the scores of small workshops, which in the 1970s were still producing a surprising variety of products. Here could be seen that visible sign of the city's independence and creativity, which commanded respect above all

[1] Harry Brearley, *Knotted String* (London, 1941), 21.

[2] J. K. Hoyt, *SI*, 4 Jan. 1871.

[3] James Hamilton, *The Misses Vickers* (Sheffield, 1984), 43. For other visitors' views on Sheffield, see Sylvia Pybus, *'Damned Bad Place, Sheffield'* (Sheffield, 1994).

[4] E. Carpenter, *My Days and Dreams* (London, 1916), 92. Quoted in D. Hey, 'Continuities and Perceptions', in C. Binfield *et al.*, *The History of the City of Sheffield, 1843–1993* (Sheffield, 1993), iii. 15–16.

else—its craftsmanship; that sheer virtuosity in working steel, which en-
thralled even that sternest Victorian critic of capitalism, John Ruskin. In
the 1970s that craftsmanship could still be found by those with time to
look, and not only in the city's museums.

Twenty years later all that has changed. By the 1990s Sheffield's reputation was fading almost as fast as the demand for its products. Once at
the centre of the Industrial Revolution, Sheffield now found itself in the
front line of the devastation caused by British economic decline. Steel was
still produced in Sheffield, but the industry was no longer a leading
employer in the local economy. In 1920 the Sheffield steel industry had
employed about 70,000—to say nothing of the thousands in its allied
cutlery, edge tool, and engineering industries; but by the early 1990s this
had plummeted to well under 10,000 and the city council had become
easily the largest employer in the city. The decline showed no sign of
abating. In the early 1990s hardly a week seemed to pass without an
announcement of a factory closure or more job losses. In its heyday before
the First World War, the city had supported over 150 steel producers: by
1993 the number of large steelmakers in the area had fallen to not much
more than half a dozen. Occasionally, a sudden flurry of interest, such as
the publicity in 1990 over the Iraqi 'Supergun' affair, would remind
everyone that Sheffield was still producing steel. But for most, the steel
industry was part of the past. Some were even unaware that the city still
melted steel! In cutlery and tools, a once mighty industry had shrivelled
almost into insignificance. The number of large firms was certainly below
half a dozen, in an industry employing perhaps less than two thousand,
and the traditional craftsmen had declined to a handful. There, as in any
other British city, if one turned over a knife the chances were that it would
have 'Made in China' or 'Made in Japan' stamped on the blade.

By 1993 the visual impact of this on Sheffield was all too apparent. Steel
City would now have been unrecognizable to its Victorian inhabitants.
Sheffield was 'de-industrialized', the air clear and smokeless, and the old
trades had largely fled from the city centre. A retired cutlery worker had
remembered the centre of Sheffield at its peak, as 'one big boom, boom,
boom, like a big heart going. It was all exciting and alive.'[5] But the great
cutlery factories were mostly no more: the famous Sheffield houses of
Wostenholm, Rodgers, and Mappin were long ago reduced to piles of
rubble. Some old workshops survived, recognizable by their leaning walls
and old brickwork, but these were decreasing in number. Often they stood
marooned in the middle of car parks or waste ground, awaiting the arrival
of the demolition men who were clearing a way for new signs of progress.

[5] Doris Walsh, acid etcher, quoted in Clare Jenkins and Stephen McClarence, *On the Knife Edge* (Sheffield, 1989), 24.

Around the city centre, motorways and a new 'Supertram' system had cut wide swathes through the old manufacturing districts, accelerating the destruction of old Steel City. Sheffield city centre was still crowded and alive with noise and bustle: but the activity was generated by shoppers and office workers, not the sounds of factories and hammers. Around the city, high-rise tower blocks and ski-slopes dominated the skyline instead of plumes of smoke. Sheffield's urban landscape now looked much the same as any other English metropolis.

The decline was most evident in the industrial heartland of the Don Valley. Wrote one contemporary: 'For the visitor entering Sheffield from the northerly motorway at the turn of the 1990s the first impression was of a vast wasteland. The great sheds and rolling mills, which by night made Sheffield grander and more terrible than Dante's inferno and by day bathed Sheffield in impenetrable fogs, had gone.'[6] Here and there the bulldozers had been at work, opening up huge gaps and returning these industrial sites to their original green fields—except that often the greenery had not yet returned. Instead, the landscape lay scarred and lifeless, though some took heart from the fact that fish had again been found swimming in the Don; others saw hope for the future in the city's new flagship developments.

The old steelmasters would probably have been mystified by the city's replacements for its old smokestack industries. These have included Orchard shopping precinct in the city centre, Meadowhall shopping mall, Don Valley international athletics stadium, Sheffield Arena, and a sports complex at Ponds Forge. For the young, Sheffield was now more famous for snooker and the World Student Games than for steel. These developments had obliterated the old steelworks, though occasionally it had been thought fit to commemorate the past. In the middle of Orchard shopping precinct, an area of boutiques and piped music, stood a clock tower. When each hour chimed, visitors were treated to the Disneyesque appearance of a Sheffield grinder and buffer girl—waxworks dummies that revolved to the huffings and puffings of taped grinding and polishing sounds. It would be the closest most visitors would get to the Sheffield steel industry.

In 1993—some 250 years after the birth of the industry in the area—it was not difficult to imagine the day when Sheffield would no longer be synonymous with steel, perhaps even when the city would no longer produce steel at all. Standing on the hills that fringe the Don Valley, it is difficult to resist pondering the enormous changes that have occurred between 1743 and 1993. How has Sheffield's dramatic rise and fall occurred? The need to provide a chronology and an explanation presents a

---

[6] C. Binfield, *History of Sheffield*, ii. 1.

unique challenge to the industrial historian and lay behind the impetus to write this book.

One would expect some help from the work of earlier historians on the industry. Since steel was amongst the three most important manufacturing industries during the nineteenth century (behind textiles and engineering), it has attracted attention from some of the leading economic historians since the War. Among this roster are Philip Andrews and Elizabeth Brunner, T. S. Ashton, Alan Birch, James Carr and Walter Taplin, Duncan Burn, Charlotte Erickson, Donald McCloskey, Peter Payne, Peter Temin, Kenneth Warren, and Ulrich Wengenroth.[7] Compared with other industries, there is no lack of industry-wide studies on steel, detailed monographs on particular firms, and biographical materials. Indeed, library shelves sag beneath the weight of books describing various aspects of the history of the British (and world) steel industry.

Some of these studies have been content with a traditional chronology; others have described in detail particular firms or technological processes.[8] Within the last thirty years or so, many historians—reflecting contemporary concerns with Britain's failure to match the economic growth achieved by other nations—have examined various phases of British decline in steelmaking. The period between about 1880 and 1914, when Britain lost its lead (in terms of output) to America and then to Germany, has evoked particular interest. Indeed, the story of the alleged loss of British steelmaking superiority supplied some of the raw material from which historians such as David. S. Landes, Derek Aldcroft, and A. L. Levine, writing in the 1960s and 1970s, fashioned their accounts of United Kingdom industrial decline.[9] Thus began a lively and extended debate amongst historians over the reasons for Britain's loss of steelmaking leadership. By the 1990s steel manufacture was a much less fashionable subject amongst historians, whose interests had switched more towards 'new'

---

[7] P. W. S. Andrews and E. Brunner, *Capital Development in Steel* (Oxford, 1951); T. S. Ashton, *Iron and Steel in the Industrial Revolution* (Manchester, 2nd edn., 1951); A. Birch, *The Economic History of the British Iron and Steel Industry 1784–1879* (London, 1967); D. L. Burn, *The Economic History of Steelmaking 1867–1939* (Cambridge, 1940); J. C. Carr and W. Taplin, *A History of the British Steel Industry* (Oxford, 1962); Bernard Elbaum, 'The Steel Industry Before World War I', in B. Elbaum and William Lazonick (eds.), *The Decline of the British Economy* (Oxford, 1986), 51–81; C. J. Erickson, *British Industrialists: Steel and Hosiery 1850–1950* (Cambridge, 1959); D. M. McCloskey, *Economic Maturity and Entrepreneurial Decline: British Iron and Steel, 1870–1913* (Cambridge, 1973); P. L. Payne, *Colvilles and the Scottish Steel Industry* (Oxford, 1979); P. Temin, 'The Relative Decline of the British Steel Industry, 1880–1913', in Henry Rosovsky (ed.), *Industrialization in Two Systems* (New York, 1966); K. Warren, *The British Iron and Sheet Steel Industry since 1840* (London, 1970); U. Wengenroth, *Enterprise and Technology: The German and British Steel Industries, 1865–1895* (Cambridge, 1993).

[8] Joan Day and Ronald F. Tylecote, *The Industrial Revolution in Metals* (London, 1991).

[9] D. S. Landes, *The Unbound Prometheus* (Cambridge, 1970); D. H. Aldcroft, 'The Entrepreneur and the British Economy, 1870–1914', *Economic History Review*, 17 (Aug. 1964), 113–34; A. L. Levine, *Industrial Retardation in Britain, 1880–1914* (London, 1967).

industries such as computers and pharmaceuticals. Nevertheless, the task of bringing our knowledge of the industry up to contemporary times continued. Jonathan Boswell compared the management of the leading firms in the inter-war years; Steven Tolliday examined institutional factors governing the steel industry during the same period; and Kathleen Burk, Geoffrey Dudley, and Jeremy Richardson have recently begun exploring the industry during recent phases of government nationalization (and denationalization).[10]

Summarizing this literature is difficult and a detailed examination will not be attempted here (though the arguments in these books will be referred to at various points in this text). Two facts, however, immediately stand out. The first, is that much of this literature is suffused with the theme of British 'entrepreneurial failure'—a term used by historians to describe national shortcomings in economic growth and industrial efficiency (more popularly known as the 'British disease'). In steelmaking, the claim that British business leaders made a bad job of things is a dominant one. Specific criticisms have suggested that British steel owners were unscientific, too wedded to empirical methods; adopted the wrong locations for their works; were too slow to scrap old plant; lacked marketing skills, especially abroad; were reluctant to join cartels and co-operate overseas; and failed to adopt modern managerial hierarchies in place of the traditional family firm. In short, that British manufacturers only had themselves to blame for being overtaken by America and Germany. These arguments have not been accepted by every historian and even a cursory examination shows that there were several mitigating factors (for example, that Britain had the problem of its early start and as a free-trader faced highly protectionist competitors). Since virtually all the world's major steelmaking techniques were developed in Britain between 1743 and 1914, one might wonder how its steelmakers had suddenly become so backward. If the rapid loss of the country's pole position before the First World War was due to entrepreneurial failure of some kind, then surely it must have been a fairly massive one. Strangely, despite the number of studies on the subject, it is fair to say that no one has yet found one: though this has not prevented the idea of British business failure in steelmaking becoming the accepted wisdom in general studies of British economic history. Versions of the theme can be found, for example, in Alfred Chandler's work on big business;[11] and in Corelli Barnett's attempt

---

[10] J. Boswell, *Business Policies in the Making* (London, 1983); K. Burk, *The First Privatisation: The Politicians, the City, and the Denationalisation of Steel* (London, 1988); G. F. Dudley and J. J. Richardson, *Politics and Steel in Britain, 1967–1988: The Life and Times of the British Steel Corporation* (Aldershot, 1990); S. Tolliday, *Business, Banking and Politics: The Case of British Steel, 1918–1939* (Cambridge, Mass., 1987).

[11] A. D. Chandler, *Scale and Scope: The Dynamics of Industrial Capitalism* (Cambridge, Mass., 1990), 281–4, 321–32.

to explain United Kingdom decline since 1945. Barnett, for example, talks of Britain's 'defunct Victorian technological supremacy in iron and steel', which was apparent even by 1914 and was largely due to the conservatism of British manufacturers and their failure to adopt the scientific approach of the Germans. Although Barnett's position is perhaps more extreme than most economic historians would allow, he offers a good summary of the negative pronouncements on the steel industry. According to Barnett:

German deployment of science to serve her steel industry . . . [grew] . . . in the 1890s and 1900s; systematic investigations were to be undertaken into alloy steels, the thermal efficiency of production, in-plant transportation, and the mechanisation of steel mills; even more copious exchanges of ideas and personnel between universities and the industry were to take place. All this effort was to be closely related to parallel developments in the electrotechnical and mechanical engineering industries, so creating a multiplier effect throughout the German industrial economy. In Britain in 1890 no such deployment of science existed. . . .

Underlying [this] German deployment . . . lay a fundamentally new attitude of mind; a new concept of industry, industrial leadership and industrial progress. The Americans too shared in this mental revolution . . . [but] few indeed of British ironmasters in this period—or much later—were capable of such breadth of vision and scale of ambition, such a way of thinking. So technical conservatism went hand in hand with *entrepreneurial* conservatism. British iron and steel makers too often resembled small-town businessmen . . . [who adopted] . . . a cautiously defensive strategy conducing to less investment rather than more. So British iron and steel companies stayed small . . .[12]

A second feature of this literature becomes apparent when we attempt to fit Sheffield into the overall picture. The simple and surprising fact is that, despite Steel City's undoubted world-wide fame, few of these books discuss Sheffield in any detail. In 1978, when I first began studying the city, this was my first striking finding: the published material available was meagre, to say the least. T. S. Ashton and Alan Birch were perhaps the only historians to stress the importance of the early development of the Sheffield steel industry in the late eighteenth and early nineteenth centuries. Birch certainly placed Sheffield at the heart of things, in this earlier period at least (though he was guilty of underestimating the size of the industry in the early nineteenth century, believing that it was essentially a cottage industry, thriving in the 'orchards' of the town). The inference of most published work on the steel industry was unmistakable: by 1860 Sheffield no longer mattered much as a focus of the steel industry.

How has such a blind spot occurred? The main reason is undoubtedly the fact that historians have invariably devoted nearly all their attention to

---

[12] C. Barnett, *The Audit of War* (London, 1986), 93–4.

heavy steel manufacture, with the emphasis on blast furnace technology and the achievements of Sir Henry Bessemer and Sir William Siemens. For most economic historians the 'Age of Steel' begins with Bessemer: the era predating his invention is deemed hardly worthy of attention. This view can be seen at its most extreme in America, where the idea that American steel history begins with the exploits of Andrew Carnegie is almost universally held by historians. A massive, five-volume history of the American steel industry, for example, disposes of the (crucial and important) pre-1860 United States industry in a page or two, while the index does not even list Sheffield.[13] Happily for these scholars, business records for these aspects are relatively plentiful; a good run of tonnage data exists from the late nineteenth century; and the technology itself is easier to understand and was well publicized.

The corollary of this is that economic efficiency and success are usually defined entirely in terms of output, bigness, the adoption of academic science, and the ability to form giant industrial combines. Hardly surprising, then, that Sheffield's contribution over the centuries has been obscured. The city was characterized neither by large-scale enterprise, nor by its vast tonnages (though, interestingly, it did have its giant companies and for a time did lead the world in output). Sheffield's steel industry—which was established and beginning to thrive fifty years before Bessemer was born—was mostly characterized by small firms, producing small quantities of steel. Information on these firms is relatively hard to find, since it needs to be sought at a local level in obscure business records, trade directories, rate books, obituaries, and company histories. In fact, there are few easily accessible sources on the industrial history of Sheffield and finding data on the development of the steel industry can be a frustrating experience. No official figures exist on special steelmaking until at least the 1920s, and even after that date statistics on the city's specialities are often subsumed under the aggregate figures for tonnage products and for other regions.

Sheffield steel technology is also specialist, reflecting the city's place within the general scheme of things. Its industrial culture stemmed from an important fact that is not made explicit in most books on steel: the industry had two divisions—bulk (tonnage) and special steel production. The two sides operated in the same industry, but were highly distinctive, almost always involved separate firms, and did not usually compete in the same product areas. They had two entirely distinct cultures. Whereas

[13] W. T. Hogan, *Economic History of the Iron and Steel Industry in the United States* (Lexington, Mass., 1971), 5 vols. Historians who have devoted attention to the early history of American iron and steel before 1860 are rare birds. One of the most outstanding is Robert B. Gordon, with his work on the genesis of American iron- and metal-working technology. See R. B. Gordon and Patrick M. Malone, *The Texture of Industry* (New York, 1994).

the bulk steel producers sought economies of scale and speed, the special steel manufacturers (or batch or specialty producers, as they are known in America) thrived on economies of flexibility and opportunism, tailoring their production to fill highly specific niches in the market. Sheffield erected a complex alternative manufacturing organization, which complemented the much better known and much vaunted American mass-production system. It was owner-operated, rather than corporate and bureaucratic; agglomerated, rather than monolithic; craft-based, instead of machine-oriented. These were the characteristics that made Sheffield unique and, once they are accepted, we can begin altering the nature of the debate about Britain's steelmaking performance and restore Sheffield to its rightful position closer to the centre of the stage.

As this book will show, Sheffield at one time or another perfected (or tried) on a large scale almost every iron- and steelmaking process, and also produced almost every iron and steel product. This would be notable enough: but what really distinguished Sheffield from its rivals—as the leading quote to this chapter highlights—was not tonnage, but *quality*, *variety*, *added-value*, and, above all, the *metallurgical skill* needed to attain these ends. Sheffield's forte from the outset was producing:

special steel in a special form to meet a special order. Short runs must therefore frequently be used and the production costs which these dictate must be borne by the consumer. The difficulties of producing steel to an exact specification under close analytical control, the high fuel costs created by the limited range of working temperature of many alloy steels and the consequent need for constant and careful re-heating during rolling and forging, the complex heat treatment required by many of the steels, the high initial cost and rapid rate of deterioration of the steelworks plant and the cost of the research and testing constantly undertaken, are all reflected in the *value* of the products[14] [my italics].

Historians appear to have forgotten that the quantity of steel produced is only one economic indicator: value must also be taken into account. For much of the twentieth century, Sheffield's proportion of total United Kingdom steel output in terms of tonnage was never much more than about 10–15 per cent, but its share was considerably higher in terms of value by reason of the high average quality of a substantial part of its steel. This can be demonstrated in two ways: by Sheffield's share of the country's alloy steel output—which has averaged about 65 per cent since the War—and by a simple price comparison: in the 1950s, whereas mild steel sold for £33 per ton, Sheffield tool steels (especially its sophisticated high-speed and gas-turbine alloys) could sell for as much as £1,700 per ton.[15] Little wonder that Sheffield boasted in 1951 that, although its annual steel output was only about 1 million tons against 16 million in the United

[14] W. D. Hargeaves, 'Steel-Making and Engineering', in David L. Linton (ed.), *Sheffield and Its Region: A Scientific and Historical Survey* (Sheffield, 1956), 278–96, 282.
[15] Ibid. 283.

Kingdom, the value of that million was equal to the rest. This was un-doubtedly an exaggeration—Sheffield's share of United Kingdom prod-uct value was probably closer to a third or a half—but the point remains valid, especially since Sheffield's alloy steels could have further value added by the city's engineering sector. Complex forging, heat-treatment, and machining could transform a 20s. ingot of high-speed steel into a milling cutter that sold in the United Kingdom for about £13. Not only economic historians have failed to consider product value: when in 1967 the government nationalized steel along a line dictated solely by tonnage, it produced a far from neat division. Some of the most profitable sectors of the industry were left outside nationalization, creating a highly confused and disordered situation in Sheffield.

The *technological* impact of special steels must also be considered. Here again, we have strayed into a field that has been relatively neglected by historians of the steel industry. Far too often their accounts have been one-dimensional, portraying the industry as being somehow isolated from mainstream developments in the economy. Steel was not simply a passive product: it interacted directly with other industries, providing crucial inputs in industries as diverse as agriculture, coal mining, and mechanical and electrical engineering. Much of this impact is difficult to assess in strictly quantifiable terms, a fact which has led those historians who have been concerned with the more visible signs of economic growth and mass production to ignore it. But it was none the less real for that. Indeed, some of the more perceptive historians of technology, such as Nathan Rosenberg, have concluded that technological changes appear to have been far more important than has the mere growth in the supplies of capital and labour inputs.[16] If this is true, it makes more alarming the comparative neglect of Sheffield steels, since their impact on the produc-tivity and technology of other industries has always been so pronounced. As one Sheffield steelmaker noted in the 1970s:

Almost everything that the scientist and the engineer can devise and build today is in some way dependent on steel, either as a component part or as a medium of process or construction. Very little that we handle or consume, no matter whether metallic or non-metallic, has not at some point in its processing, manufacture, or distribution been in contact with steel and, in most cases, there will have been some stipulation or working condition which called for particular performance characteristics or properties in that steel. Indeed, the spectrum of engineering, embracing as it does both the spectacular and the commonplace, relies absolutely on a range of materials which is described collectively and somewhat over-simply as special steels.[17]

[16] N. Rosenberg, 'Technological Change in the Machine Tool Industry', 1840–1910', *Jour-nal of Economic History*, 23 (1963), 414–43.

[17] G. J. Polson, 'The Role of Special Steels and the Special Steelmaker', *Steel Times* (Aug. 1976), 637–45, 637.

Not surprisingly, technologists and metallurgists have always accorded Sheffield special steels more attention and respect than have historians. Taking only size as a variant, the scope of special steels is huge: it encompasses components whose weight is measured in grammes or parts of a gramme, and objects weighing tens or even hundreds of tonnes; everything from the minute surgical needle to the massive rotor forging. The common denominator is that in 'each case manufacture is governed by a specification built around the particular service condition of the end product'.[18]

Tool steel, for so long a Sheffield speciality (indeed the city pioneered its manufacture), is a classic example of the impact of small, incremental changes in one industry having an enormous impact in another. This is due to the simple fact that most tonnage steel needs machining by tougher steel, or is used in machines which would be useless without alloy steels. Quite literally, special steels are the tools that make the tools. Although insignificant in volume, 'tool steel worth less than £2 may be manufactured into a gear hob or cutter worth perhaps £7 to £15; in one week that gear cutter may be instrumental in converting forgings worth £1,200 into gears worth £3,300—essential parts in a vehicle or machine'.[19]

The uses of tool steel—defined simply, they are the steels which enable other materials to be formed, shaped, or cut—are wide-ranging. There are shapes and sections which can best be produced by hot extrusion, calling for hot-die steels which can withstand high temperature, high stress, and abrasion. Hot and cold sawing and shearing, drop-stamping, cold-rolling, cold-heading, deep-drawing, and many similar cutting and machining operations each demand a different type of tool steel. Carbon tool steels, the oldest of the special steels, are used for chisels, smith's tools, chuck jaws, files, hammers, and punches. More sophisticated alloy steels are used for wood tools, shear blades, burnishing rolls, cams, mandrels, rock drill pistons, and dies of many types. There are also steels which have been developed for pressure-die castings, extrusion, plastic moulding, and hot-working and maraging steels. For cutting steel itself, complex high-speed steels have been developed for use in twist drills, reamers, hobs, and in tools for turning, milling, and shaping.

New scientific discovery and engineering developments have naturally led to a demand for more specialist steels to withstand increasingly severe conditions. Special steels play a major role in the automotive industry, much of them being channelled through the drop-forging industry either as billet or forging bar. It has been estimated that by the 1970s, 65–70 per

18 Ibid.   19 BISF, *Tool Steels* (London, 1954), 3.

cent of the United Kingdom production of alloy steels was consumed by the automobile industry, especially commercial vehicles and tractors. The development of the modern aircraft industry is unimaginable without special steels. Alloy steels became extensively used in the inter-war period in engine shafts, turbines and compressor discs, bearings and casing rings. Sir Frank Whittle relied upon Sheffield for the steels used in his first jet engine: materials that could tolerate the high temperatures without deformation. The power-generating industry has also increasingly demanded high levels of integrity and performance in steels for both conventional fossil-fuelled and nuclear systems. This is particularly true in nuclear engineering, where safety factors have demanded impeccable performance, durability, and reliability.

Operating in all these areas, especially the chemical, food, and industrial processing equipment industries, are the corrosion-resistant steels—the so-called stainless steels. The widespread domestic and commercial use of stainless hollow-ware, the functional and hygienic use of stainless steel for sinks and kitchen equipment and for food-making machinery and containers—all show the usefulness of this material, which was unavailable before the First World War. It is also a favourite material in architecture, transportation (in motor car trim), and heavy industry.

Our reliance on special steels is apparent every day. We awake to switch on the light, using current that depends on alloys in electrical transformers and nuclear power plant. We shave with a stainless steel razor, eat our breakfast with stainless cutlery, and wash it in a stainless kitchen sink. Most of us will travel to work by either automobile, train, or aircraft—all masterpieces of alloy steel engineering. This is only the beginning of the day, during which we will come into contact with hundreds of alloy steel items, or be transported or accommodated in structures that are made of alloy steels or depend on them for their construction. Some of us will even have our lives saved (or perhaps ended) by alloy steels. Most of them were discovered and developed in Sheffield.

A crucial area of Sheffield steel's interaction with the general economy was in cutlery and tool manufacture. Although a few centres, such as Pittsburgh, emulated the English city's example by establishing powerful tool and engineering sectors that drew from the local supply of steel, no other manufacturing district did so as successfully as Sheffield. In its late nineteenth-century heyday, Sheffield had the world's largest cutlery industry and was the leading centre for saw, scythe, and file manufacture. It also had a major toolmaking sector, characterized by the immense variety of its products, which included: axes and adzes; braces, bits, augers, and gimlets; chisels and gouges; spanners; hammers; joiners' tools; measuring

instruments; planes; surgical instruments and trade knives.[20] The importance of these tools to a wide range of industries is self-evident, yet their
history has usually been considered too lowly for all but a few academic
historians. Godfrey Lloyd's study of the Sheffield cutlery industry, published in 1913, is still the standard text on the subject.[21] T. S. Ashton's work
on the Warrington filemaker, Peter Stubs, with its perceptive appreciation
of the importance of high-quality Sheffield steel for tools, also stands
alone.[22] Much of the best work on such industries has been done by local
historians and tool collectors. Naturally, their approach, though it has
considerable merits, is usually too antiquarian or encyclopaedic to offer
generalized insights into British industrial development.[23]

Enough has been said, perhaps, to show that Sheffield is something of
a square peg in a round hole in relation to current debates in British
business history. Nor does it sit comfortably with some of the prevailing
theoretical ideas in the discipline. In the 1990s the dominating voice is
Alfred D. Chandler, who more than any other business historian has
charted the rise in the United States of the large industrial corporations
equipped to exploit the economies of 'scale and scope' made possible by
parallel developments in transportation, communication, and new mass-
production methods. Chandler identified three sets of interrelated investments necessary for manufacturers—who previously had confined their
attention to restricted, local markets under the influence of the original
family owners—to benefit from the new, high-volume, mass-production
technologies:

The first was an investment in production facilities large enough to exploit a
technology's potential economies of scale and scope. The second was an investment in a national and international marketing and distributing network, so that
the volume of sales might keep pace with the new volume of production.
Finally . . . the entrepreneurs also had to invest in management. It was this three-
pronged investment . . . that brought the modern industrial organisation into
being.[24]

Building on the American example, Chandler has extended his analysis
to compare the industrial experience of the United States, Germany, and

[20] Ruskin Gallery, *The Cutting Edge: An Exhibition of Sheffield Tools* (Sheffield, 1992).
[21] G. I. H. Lloyd, *The Cutlery Trades: An Historical Essay in the Economics of Small-Scale Production* (London, 1913).
[22] T. S. Ashton, *An Eighteenth Century Industrialist: Peter Stubs of Warrington, 1756–1806* (Manchester, 1939).
[23] The number of collectors' books on tools is very large. Few match the scholarship of Raphael A. Salaman (1906–94), who, as Joseph Needham observed, was 'among those scholars and educated men who did not despise the manual crafts'. See Salaman, *Dictionary of Tools Used in the Woodworking and Allied Trades 1700–1900* (London, 1975); id., *Dictionary of Leather-Working Tools c.1700–1950, and the Tools of the Allied Trades* (London, 1986).
[24] Chandler, *Scale and Scope*, 8. See also id., *The Visible Hand: The Managerial Revolution in American Business* (Cambridge, Mass., 1977).

Britain as far as the 1940s. He notes that, while the modern corporate organization was triumphant in America by 1914 and beyond, its example was only hesitantly followed in the United Kingdom, where industrialists clung more to the traditional, family-owned organization (which Chandler labels 'personal', as opposed to 'managerial capitalism'). Applying his measure of industrial success, Chandler has no doubts why: it was because British industrialists 'failed to make the essential three-pronged investment in manufacturing, marketing and management in a number of the capital-intensive industries of the Second Industrial Revolution'. At the root of the problem, was the fact that in Britain 'the founders and their families continued to dominate the management of the enterprises'.[25]

Chandler's arguments are powerful, persuasive, and, in the 1990s, pervasive. Few business historians fail to give due consideration to his ideas, and 'strategy' and 'structure' have become the most popular words in their current vocabulary. Like most overarching explanations, however, Chandler's account of economic growth does not succeed in embracing every type of industrial experience. The attempt to contrast the development of the United States, Germany, and Britain by comparing their largest firms may itself be suspect (obviously the biggest American firms were much larger than their British counterparts), even though due allowance is made for this bias.[26] Certainly, old Sheffield steelmakers—had they been alive—would not have been impressed by the criticisms of an American academic, who hailed from the world's most highly protectionist steel-producing country, with its advantage of a vast internal market. Nor would they have found congenial Chandler's single-track approach, which firmly ties competitive performance to size, using mass production as the yardstick of industrial efficiency, and making the evolution of modern business follow an inevitable logic towards the triumph of a corporate type of industrial capitalism. Whatever the merits of this view, it obviously omits whole areas of economic behaviour, besides largely ignoring wider educational, social, and cultural factors. As the foregoing discussion has shown, mere size is only one measure of economic growth and technological success. Although Chandler's viewpoint can be applied to some of the largest Sheffield firms, especially those involved with armaments and the less 'special' of the special steels, it has a more limited relevance to the small-scale steel producers that proved such a fertile breeding-ground of innovation.

[25] Chandler, *Scale and Scope*, 253.

[26] One critic notes: 'Given their lower absolute size, the management problems of lower ranking British and German firms were of a different order of magnitude than those of the giants. Chandler sometimes appears to forget this in his more general judgements.' See Leslie Hannah, 'Scale and Scope: Towards a European Visible Hand?', *Business History*, 33 (Apr. 1991), 297–309, 298.

Clearly, other frameworks are needed to supplement Chandler's insights. In the 1970s and 1980s, studies in various national contexts argued for a better appreciation of the various economic, political, and social contributions made by the small-firm sector. There was interest in 'the possibility that economic success in the future may depend on the flexible use of multi-purpose or universal machines and skilled labour to make an ever changing assortment of semi-customized products: a system that reverses the principles of mass production'.[27] A few historians have recently begun to examine the evolution of small-business enterprise in this light—Philip Scranton in Philadelphia textiles, John Ingham in Pittsburgh iron and steel—and have discovered a far from negative picture. In Philadelphia before 1940, specialist (batch) producers developed a versatile manufacturing system, reliant on craft skills and partial processes, to generate a diverse array of seasonal specialities rather than staple textiles. The result was a 'proprietary capitalism [which] differed from the better known corporate and bureaucratizing form along virtually every parameter of comparison'.[28] In Pittsburgh, many of that city's iron and steel producers also hardly qualified as 'modern business enterprises', most of them being run in a personal, sometimes even idiosyncratic manner by family members with an occasional outsider. However, they were highly successful and profitable over a very long period, and the decision to remain relatively small and local involved a very clear choice on the part of the owners.[29]

Besides the large number of small-business units, another characteristic feature of Sheffield's industrial development which requires consideration was the huge diversity of its industries. Leafing through a turn-of-the-century Sheffield trade directory is a fascinating experience: page after page of steelmakers, cutlers, and toolmakers, engineering firms, to say nothing of the brewers, papermakers, printers, musical instrument makers, confectioners, snuff-makers, and so on.[30] Beyond Sheffield, the linkages of the steel industry spread far and wide, both nationally—particularly with centres of engineering in Birmingham, Leeds, Manchester, and Huddersfield—and internationally. This diversity was nevertheless closely clustered, leading to the generation of a self-

---

[27] Charles Sabel and Jonathan Zeitlin, 'Historical Alternatives to Mass Production: Politics, Markets and Technology in Nineteenth-Century Industrialization', *Past and Present*, 108 (1985), 133–76, 133. See also M. J. Piore and C. F. Sabel, *The Second Industrial Divide* (New York, 1984).

[28] P. Scranton, *Figured Tapestry: Production, Markets, and Power in Philadelphia Textiles, 1885–1941* (New York, 1989), 2.

[29] J. N. Ingham, *Making Iron and Steel: Independent Mills in Pittsburgh, 1820–1920* (Columbus, Ohio, 1991).

[30] For a listing of recent published work on industries other than steel, see Binfield, *History of Sheffield*, ii. 494.

reinforcing system: competitive, yet feeding upon itself to grow even larger. The economist Alfred Marshall appreciated Sheffield's importance and may have had it in mind when he wrote this classic passage (which describes the Sheffield experience perfectly):

When an industry has thus chosen a locality for itself, it is likely to stay there long: so great are the advantages which people following the same skilled trade get from near neighbourhood to one another. The mysteries of the trade become no mysteries; but are as it were in the air, and children learn many of them unconsciously. Good work is rightly appreciated, inventions and improvements in machinery, in processes and the general organization of the business have their merits promptly discussed: if one man starts a new idea, it is taken up by others and combined with suggestions of their own; and thus it becomes the source of further new ideas. And presently subsidiary trades grow up in the neighbourhood . . . conducing to the economy of its material.[31]

Others have been struck by the fact that competitive firms, especially internationally competitive ones, tend to cluster together in a few nations and often in a few regions within nations. Michael Porter has attempted to explain this clustering with reference to a dynamic system of four determinants of international competitive advantage, in his famous 'diamond'.[32] In Porter's view a successful national economy is based on industries which score highly across a wide range of features within these four broad determinants: factor conditions (such as human and physical resources, technological know-how, and capital stock); buoyant home demand (properly segmented, sophisticated, large and growing); the existence of supporting and related industries (themselves internationally competitive and innovative); and micro-level factors (such as corporate strategy, structure, and rivalry). These factors interact in a cumulative way and flourish best in clusters. As Porter highlights (echoing Marshall):

Once a cluster forms, the whole group of industries becomes mutually supporting. Benefits flow forward, backward and horizontally. Aggressive rivalry in one industry tends to spread to others in the cluster, through the exercise of bargaining power, spin-offs and related diversification by established firms. Entry from other industries within the cluster spurs upgrading by stimulating diversity in R&D approaches and providing a means for introducing new strategies and skills.[33]

Naturally, the 'diamond' can work the other way: failures across one or several of the determinants can lead to a complex unravelling of national and international competitiveness which is difficult to restore.

---

[31] A. Marshall, *Principles of Economics* (London, 1890, 8th edn., 1964), 225. The passage, brought to my attention by David Musson, is quoted in John Kay, *Foundations of Corporate Success* (Oxford, 1993), 81.

[32] M. E. Porter, *The Competitive Advantage of Nations* (London, 1990).

[33] Ibid. 151.

Although we should beware (as with Chandler) of accepting Porter's ideas as a universal formula—especially since his work is not primarily historical, but prescriptive, seeking to administer a management consultancy-style medicine to present-day industrial ills—it has direct relevance for the United Kingdom industrial experience, especially with regard to Sheffield. As we will see in this study, the view of Sheffield as a self-reinforcing cluster comes closer than most to describing its great success and I have found it helpful in drawing together both my own work and the new strands of research that are beginning to appear on Sheffield's history.

As with economies, so too perhaps with historians; for over the last decade a number of mainly Sheffield-based historians have at last begun examining in detail the economic and social history of Steel City. Our knowledge of the Sheffield steel and cutlery trades has thus increased greatly and, although recent work has yet to make an impact on the more general literature, some semblance of balance has been restored in the history of the British steel industry. We now have a good picture of the nineteenth-century Sheffield industrial scene, at least as regards steel. As it happened, archival sources on the early Sheffield industry did not prove to be so sparse and elusive as some historians had supposed. Nevertheless, much patient research has been needed to clarify the main commercial and technological developments.

In a pathbreaking unpublished survey, Geoffrey Timmins presented the results of a meticulous examination of statistical evidence from the Sheffield rate books. Using the rateable value of property and assets as a proxy for firm size (there were no other available continuous statistical data), he charted the rise of Sheffield's crucible steel industry in the nineteenth century. He demonstrated amongst other things that the industry was not entirely a back-street affair and that the small-scale crucible process was not incompatible with large-scale growth and integration.[34] Equally detailed work by Kenneth C. Barraclough has described the technology of eighteenth- and nineteenth-century cementation and crucible steel manufacture—the deceptively simple processes that provided the foundation for Sheffield (and world) steelmaking. By titling his two-volume work, *Steelmaking before Bessemer*, Barraclough pointedly restored Sheffield steel to centre-stage in early British steelmaking.[35] Sheffield's primacy was underlined in my own study of Steel City's trans-

---

[34] J. G. Timmins, 'The Commercial Development of the Sheffield Crucible Steel Industry' (Sheffield University MA, 1976). See also id., 'Concentration and Integration in the Sheffield Crucible Steel Industry', *Business History*, 24 (Mar. 1982), 61–78.

[35] K. C. Barraclough, *Steelmaking Before Bessemer: Blister Steel; Crucible Steel* (London, 1984), 2 vols.

atlantic influence, which demonstrated its unrecognized but crucial role in the emergence of the nineteenth-century American steel industry.[36]

More recently, historians have begun exploring in detail the evolution of small-scale business enterprise in Sheffield. Lucy Newton has documented the finance of manufacturing in Sheffield's economic region between 1850 and 1885, revealing a continuing pattern of very localized manufacturing, banks, and system of finance—all revolving around small-scale enterprise and operating at a parochial level.[37] Timmins's analysis of the rate books has been extended in another unpublished work by Mervyn Lewis, who has examined the industrial structure of Sheffield between 1880 and 1930, the period when the steel industry was at its height. This has highlighted the tenacity of small-scale business organization in the city.[38]

Nor have local historians neglected the cutlery trades. David Hey has examined the development of the Sheffield region's economy between 1660 and 1740, emphasizing the deeply rooted nature of its craft skills and the extent to which, even before the birth of steelmaking in the area, it had developed a specialized, industrial economy.[39] An unpublished study on the Sheffield cutlery industry by Sally Taylor, which scrutinizes in unprecedented detail the era between 1870 and 1914, also enriches our understanding of the craft ethos of Sheffield and provides an assessment of business performance at the critical moment when the industry was first facing the challenge of overseas competition.[40] Steel City's centenary year in 1993 provided an opportunity to unite much of this material in a substantial appraisal of Sheffield's industrial, political, and social past.[41]

Unfortunately, none of these studies is comprehensive or goes much beyond about the 1920s. What about the subsequent story? Up-dating the story has an added interest because of the decline (some might say collapse) of the industry in the 1980s, which effaced so many firms and placed a question mark over the future of the whole industry. We have

[36] G. Tweedale, *Sheffield Steel and America: A Century of Commercial and Technological Interdependence, 1830–1930* (Cambridge, 1987).

[37] Lucy Newton, 'The Finance of Manufacturing Industry in the Sheffield Area, c.1850–c.1885' (Leicester University Ph.D., 1993).

[38] M. J. Lewis, 'The Growth and Development of Sheffield's Industrial Structure, 1880–1930' (Sheffield Hallam University Ph.D., 1989). See also id. and R. Lloyd-Jones, 'Business Structure and Political Economy in Sheffield: The Metal Trades 1880–1920s', in Binfield, *History of Sheffield*, ii. 211–33.

[39] D. Hey, *The Fiery Blades of Hallamshire: Sheffield and Its Neighbourhood, 1660–1740* (Leicester, 1991).

[40] S. Taylor, 'Tradition and Change: The Sheffield Cutlery Trades 1870–1914' (Sheffield University Ph.D., 1988). See also ead., 'The Industrial Structure of the Sheffield Trades, 1870–1914', in Binfield, *History of Sheffield*, ii. 194–210.

[41] Binfield, *History of Sheffield*.

already noted, too, the fact that Sheffield has yet to be assimilated properly into most accounts of the steel industry.

This book, therefore, attempts a broadly chronological account of the
commercial and technological development of Steel City. In writing it, I
have kept in mind two types of reader: first, local historians and the
ordinary reader, who will expect to find basic information on the development of the Sheffield steel industry, its companies and businessmen;
second, economists and business historians, who will want to know how
Sheffield relates to current debates about entrepreneurship and British
economic performance. The study largely reflects my own interests and
concentrates on the overall industrial structure and technology of
special steelmaking, the historical evolution of firms, and particularly the
industry leaders and their strategies. It is divided into three parts, corresponding to my own view of Sheffield's evolution as a steel manufacturing centre. The first part examines Steel City in its heyday and identifies
those factors which determined its success. This period stretched from the
discovery of crucible steelmaking in about 1743 to the end of the First
World War, a landmark date which saw the city's steel industry at its
zenith in terms of size, market share, and impact on the local economy.
Part two looks at Sheffield between 1918 and the mid-1930s, when
Sheffield's competitive advantage began weakening in the face of the
world depression and foreign competition. The final part outlines Steel
City's subsequent history to the present day, a period which began with a
long boom up to 1960 and then culminated in rapid decline.

This division, it must be said, is not entirely satisfactory, since all these
periods contain elements of both 'rise' and 'decline', due partly to the
different pace of change within different sectors of the steel industry (the
contrast between steel and cutlery, as we shall see, being extremely
marked). However, I believe that this layout is the best that can be devised
to make comprehensible the business history of an extremely complex
and diverse region.

Reflecting Sheffield's diversity, I have widened my analysis to include
certain aspects of the cutlery and tool trades, and also attempted to give
some indication of how Sheffield functioned as an economic 'cluster' by
sketching in its relationship with other industries (such as engineering)
and other localities. However, this book makes no pretence to being
comprehensive. While writing it, I was struck again by how vigorous the
Sheffield region was industrially and by how much work remains to be
done on its history. Many industries—iron manufacture, silver plate and
precious metals, wire and rope, coal and refractories, engineering, the tool
trades, even cutlery—are still to be researched in detail. Naturally, to have
included these would have made for an even longer book and multiplied
the research effort required. I have also largely ignored interactions be-

tween capital and labour, partly because this was not deemed as important (at least in the period up to the 1960s) an element as my main interest,
businessmen and their actions; partly because the subject has been
covered in considerable detail up to 1940 by Sidney Pollard;[42] and partly,
again, because it would have made the study too unwieldy. One other
conundrum was less easily settled: the question as to what constitutes
'Sheffield', an area and administrative unit that, like others, has changed
over time. Suffice to say, that I have kept the focus on Sheffield, only
allowing my horizons to embrace Rotherham and Stocksbridge in any
great detail in the twentieth century, when these centres began to assume
an importance greater than that of Sheffield. (A fact which will perhaps
not please those in Rotherham, who often point out with justice that their
locality has produced far greater tonnages of steel than Sheffield ever has.)
For the moment, the Rotherham steel industry must remain another area
requiring further research.

The conclusion examines Steel City's experience in the light of current
thinking about British industrial history and especially economic decline.
The picture that emerges (with some important qualifications) is of a
remarkably successful and enduring industry; and also a highly complex
one, which cannot be fitted easily into present theories of mass production
and entrepreneurial failure.

[42] S. Pollard, *A History of Labour in Sheffield* (Liverpool, 1959).

PART I

ESTABLISHING COMPETITIVE SUPERIORITY 1743–1918

1

Determinants of Steel City

The factors which have led to [Sheffield's] remarkable progress, in competition with other districts in situations apparently more favourable to expansion, are not obvious at a first glance, and a more detailed examination shows that a purely material explanation is insufficient, and that certain human and social elements have to be taken into account in the discussion.

> Cecil H. Desch, 'The Steel Industry of South Yorkshire: A Regional Study', Paper read to the Sociological Society, 24 Jan. 1922, 131.

In the special crucible steel trade Sheffield has natural advantages which . . . no other town in the world possesses. It is easier in Sheffield to start the manufacture of crucible steel than it is anywhere else in the world. You have everything at hand. You can hire a furnace. You do not want much capital. You find the workmen there. You find the material—all that you want—and you find a market.

> BLPES, Tariff Commission Papers. Charles W. Kayser, Evidence to the Commission, 4 May 1904, 7.

Situated approximately four miles south-west of the centre of Sheffield is one of the city's industrial museums—Abbeydale Industrial Hamlet.[1] Donated to the city in 1935 by the local scythe-makers Tyzack Sons & Turner and lovingly restored over the decades as a monument to Sheffield's craftsmen, the museum is an integrated eighteenth- and nineteenth-century edge-toolmaking complex. The setting, at the bottom of the steeply wooded valley of the River Sheaf, is idyllic. The attractive grey stone buildings nestle amongst the trees, which (in the summer at least) conveniently hide twentieth-century intrusions, such as the main-line railway to London. A millpond with ducks, a slowly turning water wheel and the sound of falling water evoke a world that moved to a different industrial rhythm than our own.

At Abbeydale, visitors can tour the counting house, with its ledger-books and rows of gleaming scythes on the wall; there is a forge, with its swing-chairs on which the tilters rocked back and forth passing their blades beneath the water-driven hammers; and there is a grinding hull, where the workers sat on their 'horsing', holding their scythe blades

---

[1] Janet Peatman, 'The Abbeydale Industrial Hamlet: History and Restoration', *Industrial Archaeology Review*, 11 (Spring 1989), 141–54.

against the rapidly turning sandstone wheels—one of the most arduous and dangerous jobs in the steel trades.

Abbeydale is far less well known than Ironbridge Gorge Museum, yet its modest appearance belies its significance. In the corner of the Hamlet is a somewhat nondescript stone building, the only notable feature of which appears to be its unusual oblong chimney-stack. Not much bigger than a small stable, the interior contains a row of holes cut into the stone floor against the far wall; some shelves supporting a number of large, white, clay pots; and several odd-looking implements—a large rusty funnel, some long pairs of tongs, a narrow iron receptacle standing upright in the floor and held together by rings and wedges, some old steel ingots, a broom and pan, even an old pair of shoes. It is not an impressive scene. Yet in many ways this part of the Hamlet—which many visitors probably turn away from without appreciating its importance—is the most remarkable of all. Had a visitor been able to witness activity in the furnace earlier in the century (it had ceased regular production by the 1940s) or even before, then all would have been revealed. The holes in the floor hold the grates for firing the steel with coke; the clay pots are crucibles for melting steel; the funnel is for filling them with bar iron and alloying elements; the tongs are for retrieving pots of molten steel; and the iron receptacle is the ingot mould into which the teemer poured the incandescent metal. These are, in fact, the remains of the world's only extant furnace for melting crucible steel. This was the technique, devised by the Quaker clockmaker Benjamin Huntsman (1704–76), which produced Europe's first steel ingot in the early 1740s—a truly revolutionary development and the birth of the modern steel industry. It transformed Sheffield from a small, but vigorous, working town into an industrial player of the first rank.

As with most museums of its type, it is difficult for visitors to imagine the brutal and sometimes violent working existence at Abbeydale. Nor is it immediately apparent why it should be there at all. The hills and streams, providing water-power for the wheels, are one evident locational advantage. Yet it seems a strange place for a steelworks. The incongruity is the greater in the Don Valley, where the giant steel mills, surrounded by some of the most beautiful scenery in the country, are miles from blast furnaces and the major ports.

The first challenge, then, in writing about the development of the Sheffield steel industry is explaining how steel manufacture came about in what, at first glance, seems a somewhat unpromising locality. The second is in describing how Sheffield came to acquire its other unique attributes. By the nineteenth century the town was firmly coupled with cutlery (and steel) in the popular mind: contemporaries spoke of Sheffield cutlery in the same breath as Nottingham lace, Staffordshire pottery, Manchester cottons, Kidderminster carpets, and Coventry ribbons. Yet

Sheffield cutlery and steel were the oldest and most familiar of them all. Moreover, Sheffield dominated the production of these wares, especially steel, to an extent and for a longer period than any of these other centres. To help us, it is proposed to adopt Michael Porter's framework for ana-lysing the growth of the competitive advantage of nations.[2] Porter has conveniently split the determinants of this process into four main compo-nents: factor conditions (such as human and physical resources, capital stock, and infrastructure); demand conditions (especially in the home market); the existence of related or supporting industries; and the nature of company strategy and structure.

FACTOR CONDITIONS

Michael Porter has given pride of place to the human resources—the skills, attitudes, knowledge-base—that make competitive advantage a re-ality. Sheffielders would have heartily agreed. They had little doubt as to the chief factor in their commercial success: it was the skill in hand and eye in working what was probably the most intractable of all industrial materials that separated them from mere mortals. It invariably impressed contemporaries and visitors, too, one of whom stated: 'In dexterity of handling, rapidity of execution, perception of results, and honest zest, the Hallamshire forger and grinder are unapproached by any foreign work-men in the trade.'[3]

These skills had been long in the making—so long, in fact, that in Sheffield they were often talked of as 'hereditary'. The ancient roots of the cutlery trade in Hallamshire (the district that included Sheffield) are well known and have been elucidated in detailed studies by Joseph Hunter, Godfrey Lloyd, and David Hey.[4] Chaucer's reference in the 'Reeve's Tale' to a Sheffield 'thwytel' (whittle) is the example usually quoted to show that the trade had already become prominent by the fourteenth century; and by the reign of Elizabeth I there are numerous literary allusions to Sheffield's renown. Daniel Defoe commented on the increase in the hard-ware trade, 'so ancient in this town', when he visited Sheffield early in the eighteenth century.[5] By then the cutlery trade was large enough to require

---

[2] M. Porter, *The Competitive Advantage of Nations* (London, 1990), 68–130.

[3] Henry J. Palmer, 'Cutlery and Cutlers at Sheffield', *The English Illustrated Magazine* (Aug. 1884), 659–69, 665.

[4] J. Hunter, *Hallamshire: The History and Topography of the Parish of Sheffield in the County of York*. Rev. edn. by Arthur Gatty (Sheffield, 1869); G. I. H. Lloyd, *The Cutlery Trades* (London, 1913); D. Hey, *The Fiery Blades of Hallamshire* (Leicester, 1991). A still useful unpublished study is by Peter Garlick, 'The Sheffield Cutlery and Allied Trades and Their Markets in the 18th and 19th Centuries' (Sheffield University MA, 1951).

[5] D. Defoe, *A Tour Through the Whole Island of Great Britain* (London, 1724–6), 482.

regulation and in 1624 an Act of Parliament was passed enabling the formation of the Company of Cutlers in Hallamshire, giving it full authority over the quantity and quality of products and the number of apprentices. Membership of the Company grew from 2,000 in 1679 to more than double that number by 1800, signifying Sheffield's rise to cutlery supremacy.

Besides this long lineage, which allowed the steady accretion of skills, three factors stretched the capabilities of cutlers in Hallamshire. One was the fact that until after 1800 most of the cutlery and tool trades were rural in character. Cutlers needed to be all-round men, capable of forging, grinding, and assembling an article from start to finish. These were 'the ancient Hallamshire cutlers', who in the nineteenth century were to assume an almost folkloric status—the kind of craftsmen who 'prided themselves that they could go into a [cutlery] shop and go through the whole process'.[6] Some of their work was, even then, as good as any. Hunter believed that during the seventeenth century London was the place for high-quality cutlery and that Sheffield goods were of 'the coarser and inferior kind'. However, a more recent and critical survey of contemporary sources has modified this picture by showing that several Sheffield cutlers worked with precious metals, such as gold and silver, and expensive hafting materials, like ivory. The records of the Cutlers' Company in 1625 show that local knives worth five shillings or more had to be damasked, inlaid, or studded with nothing less than sterling silver; while the Company records and parish registers show that one Martin Webster was a goldbeater and Robert Downes was both a silversmith and goldsmith.[7] These men may not have been in the majority: nevertheless, they show that Sheffield's expertise in working metals was already considerable.

The second mainspring of craftsmanship stemmed from the fact that until the mid-nineteenth century, although water-powered grindstones and polishing wheels helped in some of the more routine tasks, blades and tools still needed to be physically wrought from iron and steel sheets and bars. No machine tools were available; nor was any tool steel sufficiently tough for machine-dies and punches until the 1860s. Therefore, what invariably struck visitors to the cutlery shops was an absence of machinery and the simple nature of the cutlers' tools. Commented one observer after touring Mappin's Queen's Cutlery Works: 'We cannot but be struck with the absence of patterns and moulds; but this is explained by the skill and tact of the workmen, who supply, by talent and ingenuity,

---

[6] Sally Taylor, 'The Industrial Structure of the Sheffield Cutlery Trades, 1870–1914', in C. Binfield *et al.*, *The History of the City of Sheffield, 1843–1993* (Sheffield, 1993), ii. 194–210, 205.
[7] Hey, *Fiery Blades*, 102–14.

the necessity of moulds.'[8] Forgers would heat up the bars of iron and steel in their hearths and then hammer them into the required shape, with tangs for handles, [finger] nail marks, and makers' stamps. There were no pyrometers—forgers simply judged hardening and tempering by the colour of the hot steel—and no measurement was involved. Yet, having handled boxes of old hand-forged blades, the present writer can testify that a wonderful accuracy was achieved. As one Sheffield forger put it: 'The eye was really where the skill lay. Out of a tempered steel you'd make three dozen knives of different sizes and shapes, yet when you put them all together all the shapes would fit. And they'd all be out of a plain piece of steel.'[9]

The third feature of the Sheffield hardware trades that should be emphasized here (later in this chapter we shall return to it in greater detail) was the diversity of the cutlery and tool crafts, which spurred a similar multiplicity of skills. Each tool demanded a slightly different approach, a particular skill, which allowed further scope for craftsmanship. Sawmaking, for example, needed not only the customary knowledge in handling steel, but also great physical strength. This was especially so with large circular saws, which in grinding sometimes required four men, who had to take great care to avoid fatal injury on the large stones. File-cutting was at the opposite end of the spectrum: the cutters using a hammer and chisel to mark individually each cut in the file at the rate of about 60 to 80 blows a minute. As one writer commented: 'The skill of the old hand file-cutter had to be seen to be believed . . . even under the microscope it would be difficult to detect irregularities in the teeth.'[10] Pocket-knife assembly, in which a multitude of blades, corkscrews, scissors, and punches would be squeezed into a knife only a couple of inches (or less) in length was regarded as the most skilled job of all in the cutlery trades: seven years' apprenticeship was the norm and it was said that even longer was necessary for cutlers to become fully conversant with the art.

This handicraft ethic bred a unique community: proud, independent, secretive, sometimes arrogant, which even had its own dialect. The attitude was one of 'surly independence and reserve':

Manufacturers have their own particular ways and trade secrets, which they guard jealously from observation; workmen hand down their little handicraft knacks from father to son . . . [and] . . . if you want to find out how those brilliant results that you have seen in the show-case are brought about, you must look for the secret in the workman's fingers—there is nothing else. They say they have it in

---

[8] *Official Illustrated Guide to the Great Northern Railway* (c.1857), 148.
[9] C. Jenkins and S. McClarence, *On the Knife Edge* (Sheffield, 1989), 168.
[10] Eric N. Simons, *Steel Files: Their Manufacture and Application* (London, 1947), 4.

their fingers which makes them independent of anybody, and which nobody can take from them.[11]

This sturdy independence fostered a rebelliousness and religious noncon-formity that runs like a thread through Sheffield's history. To George III Sheffield was a 'damned bad place', not so much because of its smoke, but because of its reputation as a bed of radical unrest. In politics the theme of independence and self-assertion can be found in Sheffield's emergence after the French Revolution as one of the strongest centres of popular radicalism, with the foundation of the first working-class political organ-ization, the Sheffield Society for Constitutional Information. The theme continued with Sheffield's bitter opposition to the Poor Law and with its involvement in Chartism, to an almost unique support for Anarchism at the end of the nineteenth century. In religion it runs from its strong early Puritanism and Nonconformity to the leadership of Radical Methodism.

In industry, the most visible manifestation was in trade-unionism, which turned Sheffield into the world's largest 'closed shop'. The unions took on the task of organizing the teaching of the trades by regularizing apprenticeship (thus helping the managers), raised the standard of living of their members, and organized sickness and unemployment benefits. They ensured that Sheffield was one of the first in the field with the Saturday half-holiday; and also created the climate which saw Sheffield's pioneer People's College (1842) and adult classes at the Mechanics' Institute.[12]

The arrival of crucible steel manufacture intensified some of these char-acteristics and further extended Sheffield's expertise. The skills involved, like those in cutlery, were also in a sense 'hereditary', dating from the beginnings of iron manufacture in the area. Primitive iron smelting had begun in the region before Roman times; and it is known that in 1160 the monks of Kirkstead, in Lincolnshire, had erected forges to the north of Sheffield. The Sheffield steel industry, therefore, was partly a develop-ment of the charcoal iron industry which had flourished in the region for centuries, nurturing skills in smelting, forging, and the use of water-power.

Crucible steel technology was surprisingly simple; and yet at the same time (and here was the beauty of it, as far as Sheffielders were con-cerned—or the curse of it, for foreigners), it was extremely complex. Essentially, it was a two-stage process. The raw material was Swedish bar iron, extremely low in impurities, but not 'clean' enough or sufficiently high in carbon for the manufacture of cutlery and edge tools. The Sheffield steelmakers packed the bars in layers of charcoal in so-called cementation

[11] Charles Hibbs, 'Cutlery', in *Great Industries of Great Britain* (London, 1886), iii. 190.
[12] S. Pollard, *A History of Labour in Sheffield* (Liverpool, 1959).

(or converting) furnaces, so that during the firing process the bars could absorb carbon. The result was a crude type of steel, which because of the characteristic irregularities on the bars was known as 'blister steel'. The quality of blister steel could be improved by various forging processes to produce such materials as 'shear' steel—an unsurpassed product for edge tools—or it could be *melted*. This was Huntsman's key breakthrough. It was a response to a problem: how could he prevent his clock springs from failing due to the impurities and lack of uniformity in the cemented steel he was using? Huntsman had the inspired idea of breaking blister bar and then melting the pieces in a clay crucible. This dispersed the carbon throughout the metal; freed the slag impurities, which could be skimmed off as a scum; and enabled the molten metal to be poured into an ingot mould. When tilted and rolled into bar, rod, or wire, this was the ideal raw material for Sheffield's cutlery industries. The crucible also—though it was not appreciated immediately—allowed the addition of 'physics' to improve the characteristics of the steel, pointing the way to the development of alloy steels.

The furnace at Abbeydale Industrial Hamlet contains all the essential equipment for manufacturing crucible steel: in fact, after the Museum was opened in 1970 the furnace was occasionally lit on 'open days' to show crucible steel melting in action. However, some 250 years after Huntsman's discovery, working the seven holes is no longer possible, since the most vital ingredient is missing—the metallurgical skills (and brute strength) of the old melters and teemers. These remarkable men have been immortalized, and partly romanticized, in Harry Brearley's *Steel-Makers*.[13] It is easy to see why. The brawny, hard-drinking melters, lifting and scrupulously pouring the white-hot steel into such narrow moulds, seem heroic figures—to say nothing of the 'pullers-out', potmakers, the 'oddmen', the beer-carrier, the cellar lads, and the rest of the crucible team. The fact that the job was dirty, brutal, and occasionally dangerous only seems to add to the glamour. As one manufacturer put it, with typical Sheffield matter-of-factness, mingled with pride:

crucible furnace work requires a special constitution and training. In fact, the men have to be caught while they are still young and brought up to it. It is not everyone who can take on the duties of 'puller-out', which consists of standing over the hole and lifting from a depth three feet below ground level a pot weighing 30 lbs with its contents of 80 lbs, the whole at a temperature of 1500° Centigrade.[14]

But the job was also highly skilled. At every stage in manufacture specialist knowledge and skills were required. Selection of the appropriate

---

[13] H. Brearley, *Steel-Makers* (London, 1933). Brearley was the Sheffield metallurgist who discovered stainless steel.
[14] William Jessop & Sons, *Visit to Steelworks* (Sheffield, 1913), 13.

bar iron was crucial; cementation demanded fine judgement and timing; the treading and moulding of the clay crucibles was an art; melting required strength and a knowledge of steel that took years of training; classifying the bars according to temper (by reading the crystalline fracture of the bar end) needed an expert eye; and hammer-forging could only be undertaken by the most trusted workmen. At any stage the steel could be ruined by false judgement or carelessness. As Sheffielders delighted in pointing out: 'The arts of melting, reheating, and hammering steel cannot be learnt from books or lectures, but only in the hard school of practical experience; and in these respects for decades or even centuries Sheffield had bred a race of artisans second to none in the world.'[15]

The melters were at the centre of things. Recalled one tool steel manufacturer: 'Each firm had its own head melter, who was a little autocrat in his own way. . . Some of these melters became very wealthy men; they certainly had a genius for melting steel correctly, and, without any chemical or technical knowledge at all, produced first-rate steel of even quality.'[16] Another believed that Sheffield's success depended on the steel trade being able to select, from a large number of more or less experienced steelmen, the few exceptional individuals in whom sound judgement, technical skill, and steady habits were combined.[17] The 'rule of thumb' skill of these men, especially in being able to 'read' the carbon content of steel from the 'topped' ingot was legendary and had an aura of black magic about it. It was said that when the melter 'knocked the end off the cold ingot [he] saw in the fractured surface more than a college full of analysts could tell him . . . [and since he] . . . could distinguish . . . a variation in hardness corresponding to a fiftieth part of one percent of carbon it may be concluded that this means of observation was developed to an extraordinary extent. It became in fact an art.'[18] This dependence on 'art' was inevitable, since metallurgy, with its theories, textbooks, and academic courses, did not exist for much of the nineteenth century.

Of course, there was another side to the coin. Sheffield was not only a place filled with Ruskinite craftsmen: it was also Disraeli's 'Wodgate', a district marked by its dreadful working conditions and dismal poverty. Foreign visitors were often appalled. A Boston merchant, who visited England in 1815, thought that by a savage irony of industrialism, Sheffield workers were worse off for the necessities of life than the American backwoodsmen they supplied with tools.[19] The Sheffield trades, like many

---

[15] J. O. Arnold, 'The Sheffield Steel Industry: Its Beginning and Development', *TES*, 22 Nov. 1911.

[16] Lord Riverdale, 'Sheffield Steel: Memories of Years', *Quality*, 7 (May 1936), 300.

[17] Henry Seebohm, 'On the Manufacture of Crucible Cast Steel', *JISI* 25/2 (1884), 372–96.

[18] H. Brearley, *Stainless Pioneer* (Sheffield, 1988), 38.

[19] Joseph Ballard, *England in 1815 as Seen by a Young Boston Merchant* (Boston, 1913), 24–5. Wodgate is described in Benjamin Disraeli's *Sybil* (1845), bk. 3, ch. 4. Reference courtesy David Jeremy.

English industries, were also steeped in drink, a practice encouraged by the observance of 'Saint-Monday', an unofficial holiday usually celebrated in the pub. 'A vast deal of ale is drunk in Sheffield,' noted another American disapprovingly in 1868—though he also noted that then (as now) 'to enjoy good ale and get good ale one must go to Sheffield for it'.[20] Besides benefits, unionism brought 'rattenings' and trade 'outrages', when both workers and masters could be terrorized if their actions bucked a tightly controlled handicraft system. In the nineteenth century this atmosphere was to contribute to the stifling of innovation and mechanization in the light trades.

Overall, though, the balance before the 1850s was a positive one. Labour skills made up for any lack of formal science; they also supplied the bedrock for entrepreneurship. In Birmingham (which was perhaps Sheffield's nearest equivalent in metal-working skills), it has been said that the drive and initiative of Birmingham businessmen were as important as any other factor;[21] but in Sheffield it was the reverse. The success of Steel City came from the ground upwards.

The process was helped by the relative ease of entry into the local trades and the availability of capital. In the light trades, while cutlery was a handicraft it was always possible for a man to take a chance and set up on his own as a 'little mester', employing perhaps a worker or two, with the possibility of even greater things as trade expanded.[22] The same ease of entry characterized the crucible steel industry. According to one Sheffielder: 'Any man willing to risk a few hundred pounds might become a steel manufacturer. Experienced workmen could be engaged for twenty shillings a week, and a highly talented and skilled man for less than sixty shillings a week. A team of such men brought all the expert technical knowledge with them.'[23] Repeatedly, when examining the careers of Sheffield steelmen, one comes across the same pattern of upward mobility: a start as a working cutler, little mester, or traveller to acquire the necessary expertise and capital, then transition to full-scale manufacturer, even perhaps major industrialist. (Sir) John Brown (1816–96) began his career in 1837 as a partner in a file and cutlery business in Rockingham Street, before launching into the manufacture of steel and railway materials. William Butcher (c.1791–1871) was a cutler before joining his brother Samuel in establishing a highly successful steel and tool firm. Charles Cammell (1810–79), after experience as a traveller for the Sheffield firm of Ibbotson Bros., by 1837 was partner in a steel, file, and merchanting business in Furnival Street. Samuel Osborn (1826–91), the

[20] *SI*, 5 Dec. 1868.

[21] Eric Hopkins, *Birmingham: The First Manufacturing Town in the World* (London, 1989), 39.

[22] Protocol dictated that a manufacturer was a Mister; hence the Sheffield dialect version of the term for small manufacturer, 'Little Mester'.

[23] H. Brearley, *Talks about Steelmaking* (Cleveland, Ohio, 1946), 44–5.

tool steelmaker, also began his career as a traveller and then in 1851 began his own business as a file dealer in Brookhill.

It is important not to overstate this 'rags to riches' element. We know that John Brown, for example, so often described as rising from relative poverty, raised £500 from his family (his father was a builder) to start his business. However, it is certainly true that almost all the capital was generated locally, by what Joseph Hunter called the 'legitimate results of patient industry'. As Hunter put it: 'Sheffield had never been a place to which the capitalist from a distance resorted for the investment of his treasure.'[24] Instead, Sheffield businessmen relied upon their own resources, or called upon local banks, in which Sheffielders were usually the main shareholders. Hunter emphasizes the importance of local banks, such as Parker, Shore & Co., which invariably had Sheffield cutlers and steelmakers on their boards. (The crucible steelman Thomas Jessop, for example, was a director of the Sheffield & Rotherham Bank, whilst the directors of the Sheffield Banking Co. included leading cutlers such as John Rodgers, and steelmakers from the Huntsman and Bedford families.) A recent study has confirmed the largely regional financial network in Sheffield which, along with invested profits, generally appears to have provided manufacturing with adequate funds.[25]

One other arrangement, apparently, greatly helped: the 'liberal conduct' of Swedish iron manufacturers, upon whom the town depended for its supplies of the high-grade Swedish bar iron used as the main ingredient for the crucible process. By the early nineteenth century, through long-term contracts with Swedish ironmasters, Sheffield converters and crucible melters were able to obtain the most prized grades of Swedish iron—such as 'Hoop L', 'Double Bullet', 'Gridiron', 'W and Crown'—at terms which gave them a virtual monopoly of the trade. The twelve months' credit that Swedish ironmakers often advanced was as good as cash to Sheffield steelmakers launching their businesses.

We can now turn to the physical advantages possessed by Sheffield, relating to land, water, minerals, and location. Here one is struck by how fortunate the town was in having at hand so many necessary raw materials. Almost the first impression of visitors to Sheffield is that it is a place of hills and streams: indeed the town is at the confluence of five rivers—the Don, the Sheaf, the Porter, the Loxley, and the Rivelin. The availability

[24] Hunter, *Hallamshire*, 175.

[25] For brief details on banking, see Alfred Gatty, *Sheffield Past and Present* (Sheffield, 1873), 135, 222–6, 268. According to Gatty, banking also showed that Sheffielders were 'imbued with the spirit of self-help'. See also Robert E. Leader, *The Sheffield Banking Company Ltd.: An Historical Sketch, 1831–1916* (Sheffield, 1916); *Sheffield and Rotherham Bank: A Banking Bicentenary, 1792–1992* (Sheffield, 1992). For the latest scholarly study of Sheffield finance, see Lucy Newton, 'The Finance of Manufacturing Industry in the Sheffield Area, c.1850–c.1885' (Leicester University Ph.D., 1993).

of so much falling water was crucial to the foundation of Sheffield's industry. On almost thirty miles of these five streams and their tributaries over 115 water-mills have been identified: some were employed for corn-milling, paper-making, or snuff-grinding, but most were used by the metal trades for grinding, forging, and rolling.[26] Perhaps no district in the country used water-power so intensively.

In iron manufacture, the region's natural advantages were great. Iron ore, although not of the highest quality, could be mined by open-cast techniques, or in 'bell-pits'; wood for charcoal was abundant; and, above all, water-power was available—first to work the bellows, then later (after about the 1580s) to drive the hammers. It was only in the second half of the eighteenth century that Sheffield began to make its name as a steel-producing area, by using the cementation process; and until then, the bulk of the cutlery produced in the town was made from imported materials. But once steel manufacture began—especially with the introduction of the Huntsman process—Sheffield's situation turned out to be even more advantageous. Coke had now replaced charcoal as a metallurgical fuel, and Sheffield, on the western edge of the large and productive coalfield that forms the eastern flank of the south Pennines, had no more than a few miles to look for its coal. Other minerals outcropped or could be mined nearby. Sandstone for the grinding wheels could be mined at the edge of the town (for example, at Brincliffe Edge) or hacked out of the Peak moors around Sheffield. The town was also des-tined to become the centre of the British refractories industry. When cementation and crucible melting were introduced, the ganister ('firestone') for the furnace-chests and holes came from local sources, in the Loxley Valley and around Oughtibridge. The clay for making the crucibles came from slightly further afield in Stourbridge, but such were the special qualities of this refractory material that it proved surprisingly hard for Continental and American competitors to find a satisfactory equivalent. Later, when the Bessemer process revolutionized the industry, the ideal material for lining the converters was Sheffield ganister and silica firebrick.[27]

Other factors underlay Sheffield's success, besides skill and physical resources. Communications were important. Historians have invariably described Sheffield as 'one of the most land-locked towns in the country and one of the most difficult to reach along the nation's highways. A remarkable feature of Sheffield's industrial growth is its success in over-

---

[26] David Crossley *et al.* (eds.), *Water Power on the Sheffield Rivers* (Sheffield, 1989).

[27] John Benson and Robert G. Neville (eds.), *Studies in the Yorkshire Coal Industry* (Manches-ter, 1976); F. S. Atkinson, 'Mining and Refractories', in David L. Linton (ed.), *Sheffield and Its Region* (Sheffield, 1956), 267–78. Information on the development of the refractories industry can be found in the *SDT Trade Supplement*, 29 Dec. 1922, 31 Dec. 1934.

coming these handicaps.'[28] The main artery in the first phase of the steel industry's development was the Don Navigation as far as Tinsley. In 1819 the extension of the canal from Tinsley to the town centre was realized and a number of steelmakers—Greaves, Sanderson, Jessop—had established melting shops along the canal. The completion of the Sheffield–Rotherham Railway in 1838 was a crucial event: it stimulated a wave of expansion into Sheffield's East End, along the valley of the Don towards Rotherham. This improved access to domestic markets, but more crucially it strengthened Sheffield's links with vital overseas markets, notably Sweden and America.

Nevertheless, it should be noted that some of the factors that had led to the settlement of the industry in Sheffield were lessening in importance by the 1850s: water-power was being superseded by steam (by the late nineteenth century there were between four and five hundred steam engines driving grinding workshops alone), whilst charcoal was disappearing from use in the industry. And though Sheffield soon found itself well endowed with raw materials for steel manufacture—coal and ganister, for example—it nevertheless remained heavily dependent on imported Swedish iron. Moreover, although not isolated, Sheffield was to trail in national road and rail development in the nineteenth century. In the early 1800s Sheffield supported an impressive manufacturing base in steel and cutlery (with the lighter trades still dominant), but it remained comparatively small. Steel manufacture was still confined to a town which, when compared with other large industrial centres, preserved something of a village atmosphere, with open countryside where later the heavy industry along the Don would be situated. In short, despite its early superiority in steel manufacture, few would have predicted the scale and extent of its nineteenth-century manufactures. That depended on other factors.

DEMAND CONDITIONS

In skilled Sheffield hands crucible steel (sometimes called cast steel), suitably forged and heat-treated after its manufacture, became a crucial raw material in Britain's rise as the first industrial nation. It was the product which made Sheffield synonymous with tool steel manufacture and also gave the town a head start over its rivals. The crucible process proved infuriatingly difficult to transplant to other countries, though there was certainly no shortage of foreign industrial visitors to Sheffield searching for its secrets. Lack of suitable raw materials and the requisite

---

[28] Hey, *Fiery Blades*, 9. See also id., *Packmen, Carriers and Packhorse Roads: Trade and Communication in North Derbyshire and South Yorkshire* (Leicester, 1980).

skills ensured that at first only the Germans offered Sheffield any serious rivalry—and that was only after the 1850s.

Crucible steel was almost a precious metal: expensive (costing anything up to £70 per ton in the nineteenth century), produced in small quantities and available only from Sheffield at first, it was used sparingly. The small tonnages involved make it harder to describe in detail the nature of the demand. Historians of metallurgy have often discussed steel manufacture as an end in itself and have neglected the interrelationship of steel with the consuming industries. The fact that so little business correspondence between steelmakers and their customers has survived from the period before about 1850 may partly explain this.

Not surprisingly, it was the cutting qualities of crucible steel that first attracted consumers. Cast steel's ability to take a hard cutting edge almost matched the legendary hand-forged shear steel (the serations of which, produced by the tiny slag inclusions in blister steel, provided an edge which many Sheffielders believed was unrivalled).[29] However, crucible steel was much more uniform than blister steel, making it far more robust, and so it could be used for tools as well as cutlery. In fact, as one nineteenth-century writer stated: 'the purposes to which cast steel is applied . . . include the whole range of every article that comes under the head of cutlery, not to speak of the tools of nearly every trade or handicraft in the civilised world'.[30] Naturally, it was soon wanted by the file, plane, axe, hammer, shovel, and chisel manufacturers of Sheffield. But it was soon in demand elsewhere: by filemakers, such as Peter Stubs;[31] by surgical and dental instrument makers in London;[32] by the button, needle, and pen makers in Birmingham;[33] and by masons', leatherworkers', and woodworkers' tools manufacturers.[34] It is also clear that there was an

---

[29] A retired Sheffield forger has stated: 'The hand-forged double shear steel stands out more than anything in cutlery. When you talk to so many abattoir people and butchers they all say you have a sharper knife if it's hand-forged . . . This double shear business toughened the steel, you see. Stainless is expensive but it can never keep the edge on the same as double shear will . . . Double shear had to be flogged.' Bill Winfield quoted in Jenkins and McClarence, *Knife Edge*, 166–7.

[30] William Dundas Scott-Montcrieff, 'Cementation—Cast Steel', in *Great Industries of Great Britain*, i. 279.

[31] T. S. Ashton, *An Eighteenth-Century Industrialist* (Manchester, 1939). In 1829 the Stubs firm acquired a crucible steel works in Rotherham to control its own supplies of steel. In 1842 it purchased another site in Rotherham, Holmes Hall, where an imposing new crucible steel works was erected.

[32] Elisabeth Bennion, *Antique Medical Instruments* (London, 1979); Audrey B. Davis and Mark S. Dreyfus, *The Finest Instruments Ever Made* (Arlington, Mass., 1986).

[33] Cast steel was used for pen nibs. The leading Birmingham maker, Joseph Gillott, was Sheffield-born and a user of the town's steel, which he usually bought from William Jessop & Sons. J. J. Habershon & Sons Ltd., the Rotherham steelmakers, also exploited the demand from the pen makers. See the article on Habershon in *Histories of Famous Firms* (1957), 8–9.

[34] See R. A. Salaman, *Dictionary of Tools Used in the Woodworking and Allied Trades 1700–1900* (London, 1975); id., *Dictionary of Leather-Working Tools c.1700–1950* (London, 1986).

enormous demand from the manufacturers of farm tools, implements, and agricultural machines—though, again, little detailed historical research has been done on this. We should remember that Yorkshire itself offered a large market for rural tools.[35]

As Michael Porter emphasizes, an important element in the demand for products is the existence of sophisticated and knowledgeable buyers. This is particularly important in special steel manufacture, since the material is not an 'off-the-shelf' product. Special steels are usually tailored to specific markets and tasks, making the customer almost a partner in the production process. As it happened, at that time an industrializing Britain had the most sophisticated and advanced buyers in the world, especially in its engineering industries. Boulton and Watt, Maudslay, Clement, Fox, Roberts, Nasmyth and Whitworth—only the names need citing to signify that the late eighteenth and early nineteenth centuries saw major developments in machine tool and metal-cutting technologies.[36] These engineers required crucible steel for their dies, rolls, plates, and also as a cutting-tool steel. They had no doubts about its significance, Nasmyth pronouncing that the discovery that a bar of tool steel could be heated, quenched, and so hardened to cut softer metals marked the dawn of a new epoch. Boulton & Watt, for example, were amongst the first customers for Huntsman's steel for tooling, mint dies, hammers, and, above all, for rolls. Cast steel's resistance to shock and deformation was valued highly. Several letters (now preserved in Birmingham City Library), dating from between the 1750s and 1800, document Boulton & Watt's transactions with the Huntsmans. They show how such customers tried to spur the steelmakers into greater efforts by a mixture of criticisms, unsolicited advice, and promises of orders.[37]

Cast steel was a major discovery, so the trade was relatively easily internationalized, especially since Sheffield cutlers and toolmakers had already opened up a large overseas trade by the late eighteenth century. Ironically, the conservatism of Sheffield cutlers meant that it was the French who proved the best customers for the new steel. They described Huntsman's steel as: 'without doubt the best of all the steels produced commercially; it is the hardest, the most uniform and the most compact'.[38]

There is a large collectors' literature on antique tools, which often contains information related to Sheffield steel. Tool displays at antique fairs invariably confirm the ubiquity of both Sheffield tools and cast steel.

[35] The frequency with which Sheffield appears in the pages of the *IMR* (London, 1875+) shows the close connection between Sheffield steel and agricultural tools. On the Yorkshire market for tools, see David Morgan Rees, *Yorkshire Craftsmen at Work* (Clapham, 1981).

[36] L. T. C. Rolt, *Tools for the Job* (London, 1965).

[37] K. C. Barraclough, *Steelmaking Before Bessemer* (London, 1984), ii. 3–6, 16–19.

[38] Jean-Jacques Perret, *Mémoire sur L'Acier, Dans Lequel on Traite des Différentes Qualités de ce Métal, de la Forge, du Bon Emploi et de la Trempe* (Paris, 1779), 7.

The steady stream of Swedish, French, German, Swiss, and American businessmen and technologists to Sheffield's crucible steelworks after the 1750s show that the reputation of its steel continued to grow. A worldwide trade had begun.

Undoubtedly the main overseas market was America, whose importance to Sheffield in the nineteenth century cannot be exaggerated. Jim Potter, in a pioneering study of the 'Atlantic Economy', has provided the data for the growth of Sheffield's trade with America in steel and tools, besides looking at that of other British towns.[39] It is unlikely, though, that the Anglo-American connection of other manufacturing centres was as intense as that of Sheffield's, at least not over such a long period. The trade had first flourished in the late eighteenth century and, after interruptions during the Napoleonic War, began gathering pace after 1815.[40] If the demand for steel and tools was likely to be large in Britain, then it was virtually guaranteed to be even bigger in the United States. In the words of a contemporary:

Wherever the dreary expanse of forest, swamp or prairie, has to be made the smiling abode of mankind and plenty, the axe, the saw, the spade, scythe, hoe, and all their adjuncts, in some form, cannot be dispensed with. An indifferent observer would at once indicate the United States of America as an inexhaustible mine of wealth, of certain and steady increase, to such a town as Sheffield.[41]

At first the main demand was for cutlery and every type of edge tool for the American farmer and frontiersman. By 1850 American industry had begun to make many of its own tools, but it still needed Sheffield steel since its own crucible steel industry had not yet been established. This fact has been forgotten by American economic historians, who invariably regard the so-called 'American System' of mass production as self-contained. It was not: the New England cutlery, arms, and engineering trades needed tool steel and files for their machine-shops and before 1860 these invariably came from Sheffield. The irony of this situation was noted by Sheffield steelmasters such as William Ibbotson, who admitted 'sending steel to cut himself out of the market, but he could not avoid doing so. He was obliged to sell what the Americans were willing to purchase.'[42]

The result was that America became the biggest overseas market for Sheffield steel before 1860: in good years a third or more of the town's

---

[39] J. Potter, 'Atlantic Economy, 1815–1860: The USA and the Industrial Revolution in Britain', in L. S. Pressnell (ed.), *Studies in the Industrial Revolution: Studies Presented to T. S. Ashton* (London, 1960), 236–80.

[40] Charles S. Parson, *New Hampshire Clocks and Clockmakers* (Exeter, NH, 1976), 44, refers to an advertisement in the *New Hampshire Gazette*, 5 Nov. 1816, for 'best blistered and cast steel . . . [and] . . . an extensive assortment of files'. This is the earliest reference to Sheffield steel I have found in America.

[41] *Sheffield Times*, 7 Apr. 1849.

[42] *Sheffield Mercury*, 20 Nov. 1841.

steel output was sent across the Atlantic, and this was aside from the vast trade in cutlery and edge tools. Sheffield firms seized the opportunities this offered with alacrity. It has been customary in recent years to decry the sales efforts of British industrialists, but no such charge can be levelled against nineteenth-century Sheffield traders as they streamed endlessly across the Atlantic (and to other overseas destinations). The Sheffield steelmaker, noted a contemporary, visits: 'the metropolis with almost as little anxious forethought as he goes to his warehouse; while a voyage to America, or a residence there, are undertakings talked of almost with indifference'.[43]

Here then was a great paradox. Land-locked, part of olde England, and apparently twenty or thirty years behind other towns, yet nevertheless Sheffield was a supreme New World trader.[44] It was the American trade which was responsible for the remarkable expansion of the Sheffield crucible steel industry between 1851 and 1862, when the number of melting holes is said to have increased from 1,333 to 2,437. With the American market still completely at its mercy, with United States tariffs at a relatively low level, and with transatlantic demand from hundreds of American cutlery and edge-tools businesses, the leading Sheffield firms—Sanderson, Jessop, Vickers, Greaves, Butcher, Cammell—made large fortunes in the trade.

RELATED AND SUPPORTING INDUSTRIES

Before examining the structure of the Sheffield steel and cutlery trades themselves, we can pause to look at the development of the numerous allied industries. It has been said that Birmingham manufacturing in the nineteenth century was twice as highly differentiated as that of Sheffield.[45] Nevertheless, one of the most striking of Sheffield's characteristics was the multitude of support trades, orbiting around the steel nucleus.

The growth of these allied trades began well before Huntsman appeared and was rooted in the 'cottage' industry of early Hallamshire.[46] Scissorsmiths and shearsmiths were active in the early seventeenth century; so too were filesmiths, nailmakers, forkmakers, and razormakers; and buttonmaking had also appeared as a sideline for the cutlers. The manufacture of small metal boxes for tobacco, snuff, and trinkets had begun as a specialist craft by the late seventeenth century. This spread of

[43] J. Holland, *Tour of the Don* (London, 1837), 262–3.
[44] G. Tweedale, *Sheffield Steel and America* (Cambridge, 1987).
[45] Dennis Smith, *Conflict and Compromise: Class Formation in English Society, 1830–1914* (London, 1982); Hopkins, *Birmingham*.
[46] Hey, *Fiery Blades*, 114–36.

Table 1.1. *Sheffield trades, 1824*

Augers	Engravers' tools	Rules
Anvils	Fenders	Saws
Awls	Ferrules	Scissors
Bayonets	Files	Screws
Bellows	Fire irons	Scythes
Boilers for steam	Forks	Shears
Bone scales [handles]	Hammers	Sheaths
Brace bits	Horn hafts [handles]	Silver plate
Brass bolsters	Inkstands	Silver plating
Brass (in general)	Ivory goods	Silver refining
Britannia metal	Joiners' tools	Skates
Butchers' steels	Lancets & phlemes [fleams]	Snuffers
Buttons	Locks	Spades and shovels
Button moulds	Magnets	Spindles and flies
Cabinet cases	Optical instruments	Spoons
Candlesticks	Pen- and pocket-knives	Steel
Clasps	Powder flasks and belts	Stove grates
Combs	Printing types	Surgeons' instruments
Corkscrews	Razors	Table knives
Dies	Razor strops	Wire, brass, and iron
Edge tools	Rolled iron	

Source: Thomas Ramsay, *The Picture of Sheffield* (Sheffield, 1824), 232–4.

related trades continued to grow, so that by the end of the eighteenth century, makers of, *inter alia*, saws, anvils, lancets, household metalware, and many other cutlery products can be found in Sheffield directories.

An early nineteenth-century enumeration of the Sheffield trades (Table 1.1) lists over sixty different trades. The development of many of these industries is not surprising. The production of cutlery, for example, needed the help of pearl, ivory, and horn suppliers and cutters for handle materials; it needed acid etchers to decorate the blades; mark makers to provide the punches to stamp them; buffers to polish them; paper manufacturers and case-makers to package goods; glassmakers to supply crystals for silverware; and so on.[47]

[47] Denis Ashurst, *The History of South Yorkshire Glass* (Sheffield, 1993); Gill Booth, *Diamonds in Brown Paper: The Colourful Lives and Hard Times of Sheffield's Famous Buffer Lasses* (Sheffield, 1988); Frederick Bradbury, *History of Old Sheffield Plate* (London, 1912), 67–70; articles on boxmakers Fox & Robinson and Greaves, in *Histories of Famous Firms* (1957); Herbert Housley, *Grinders and Buffers: A Boyhood in the Sheffield Cutlery Industry* (Sheffield, 1988); 'Doris Walsh [acid etcher]', in Jenkins and McClarence, *Knife Edge*, 20–32; Edward Pryor & Son Ltd., *Making a Mark* (Sheffield, 6th edn., 1957); Tanya Schmoller, *Sheffield Papermakers: Three Centuries of Papermaking in the Sheffield Area* (Wylam, 1992); Wilmot Taylor, *The Sheffield Horn Industry* (Sheffield, 1927).

The growth of the steel industry fostered the birth of firms dealing in refractories, located to the west of Sheffield around Stannington, Deepcar, Loxley, Oughtibridge. These included J. & J. Dyson Ltd., established in 1810, which specialized in crucible pot clays and ganister; and the Oughtibridge Silica Firebrick Co., founded in 1856, which also specialized in furnace linings. Besides the mining industry, there were firms dealing with the processing of coal. The Sheffield Coal Co., for example, which worked several seams around the area after 1819, installed one of the first coke-making plants in the district. Earl Fitzwilliam also managed several such works around Sheffield, which in 1919 were to become the South Yorkshire Chemical Works. Newton Chambers, the ironfounding and mining company located at Thorncliffe, in the early 1800s coked coal in old-fashioned beehive ovens and by 1815 had booked its first order for gasworks equipment. None of these industries has yet been researched in detail by historians.[48]

It must not be forgotten that in 'Steel City' iron manufacture remained an important industry, even after the Huntsman revolution. Iron was still the ideal material for certain engineering products and for agricultural tools and machines. Wrought-iron railway axles were made for much of the nineteenth century at Wortley Top Forge, near Stocksbridge (a site now restored as a museum).[49] The business of John Crowley & Co., founded in 1821 and located at Kelham Island, was one of the most important makers of malleable iron castings in the country. It grew to specialize in chaff-cutters, lawnmowers, spanners, textile-machine parts, and projecting zinc letters for shop fronts.[50] The manufacture of stove grates and fenders was carried on nearby by Hoole's Green Lane Works, which had been founded in 1795. The works was rebuilt in the mid-nineteenth century and its elegant gateway and clock tower, recently cleaned and repainted to house modern workshops and offices, is still impressive—a testimony to the importance of the trade in the nineteenth century.

Most of these industries served a primarily domestic market. However, there were other related industries that provided a springboard for international competitive advantage in the nineteenth century. Perhaps the most important of these were the production of 'Sheffield Plate' and other plated wares, the development of engineering plant, and the manufacture of certain steel products such as castings and wire.

The Sheffield plated and precious-metal trades are strictly a branch of non-ferrous metallurgy; however, the relationship with the steel and cutlery industry was a close one and the two had the same roots. The method

---

[48] For references on related Sheffield industries, see Table 3.3.
[49] C. Reginald Andrews, *The Story of Wortley Ironworks* (Nottingham, 2nd edn., 1956).
[50] *The Century's Progress* (London, 1893), 130.

of producing Sheffield Plate was discovered by Thomas Boulsover (1705–88) in about 1743—roughly the same time as Huntsman was devising the crucible process. A cutler, Boulsover is credited with inventions in the rolling and setting of saws. It is said that when reparing a knife haft, he found that if a thin sheet of silver was fused to a thicker sheet of copper, the metal could be rolled and shaped so that it looked like solid silver. This was the beginning of a small, but highly profitable trade for a number of Sheffield firms: Boulsover himself, Joseph Hancock, Sissons, Bradbury, Roberts & Cadman, Hutton, Dixon & Smith (later James Dixon & Sons), and many others.[51] Though obviously far less expensive than silver (which was, of course, its attraction), Sheffield Plate needed great skill in its manufacture to transform it into trays, tureens, candlesticks, salt cellars, and so forth. Skilled workers were brought in from places such as London and Birmingham to teach the Sheffielders raising techniques and other skills, which were unfamiliar in a town that specialized in cutlery. This was done successfully and by the 1760s a new industry had emerged in Sheffield: the silver trade, which developed as an offshoot of fused-plate manufacture. Another new business arose from the precious-metal scrap produced as waste in the workshops. In 1760, John Read, a gold refiner at Bewdley, settled in Sheffield and began refining silver-bearing wastes. In 1846 the name of the business was changed to the Sheffield Smelting Co., later to become the leading precious-metals smelting works in the country.[52]

By 1825 there were said to be about twenty-eight fused plate firms in Sheffield, and though Birmingham had more, Sheffield's reputation was greater since it specialized in higher-grade goods. A large export trade was already under way by the 1790s, with destinations that included Hamburg, Amsterdam, Lubeck, Altona, and America and the West Indies. It was said that the first Sheffield traveller in America sold plated goods. By the early nineteenth century, trade with America had expanded to such an extent that before 1860 James Dixon & Sons had a senior partner in permanent residence in America, besides four agents. The firm had 400 workers by 1840, placing it alongside the largest cutlery factories—a testimony to the importance of the trade in plated goods. By then Dixon's were also Sheffield's leading manufacturers of Britannia metal, an industry that had begun in about 1769. According to Frederick Bradbury, writing in his classic study of Sheffield Plate, this was a 'vigorous offshoot' of the Huntsman process, 'so closely allied to its greater

[51] Bradbury, *Sheffield Plate*; Anneke Bambery, *Old Sheffield Plate* (Aylesbury, 1988); James Dixon & Sons Ltd., *Centenary Souvenir* (Sheffield, 1905); John and Julia Hatfield, *The Oldest Sheffield Plater* (Huddersfield, 1974); J. Geoffrey Timmins, *Workers in Metal Since 1784: A History of W. & G. Sissons* (Sheffield, 1984).

[52] Ronald E. Wilson, *Two Hundred Precious Metal Years: A History of the Sheffield Smelting Co. Ltd., 1760–1960* (London, 1960).

parent and playing so large a part in metal ware for domestic use as to demand special notice ... What plated ware did for those not wealthy enough to furnish their tables with sterling silver, Britannia metal did for the classes unable to afford silvered copper.'[53] White metal, as Britannia became known, was mostly tin with an admixture of antimony and a little copper, and it was first manufactured by James Vickers. It was used for a similar range of products to Sheffield fused plate—teapots, candlesticks, cake dishes, and bowls.

The proximity to the steel industry was crucial, since these industries were linked with the mass-production technique of die-stamping. The die sinkers hollowed out the shape of the article required from a block of cast steel—another highly skilled job. This technology gave Sheffield the chance to dominate other branches of the luxury goods trades, such as shooting accessories. Powder flasks (the most advanced nineteenth-century patents on which were held by a Sheffield gunsmith, Thomas Sykes) were a particularly popular line. By the 1830s and 1840s, although Birmingham and London had a flask industry too, Sheffield makers enjoyed the highest reputation, and names like Sykes, Bartram, Hawksley, and Dixon became synonymous with quality.[54]

Sheffield Plate was made obsolete in 1840 when the Birmingham silversmiths, Elkington's, tied up the patents on the superior electroplate method. But Sheffield's reputation as a centre of plated ware was not to be so easily dislodged: although the Sheffield Plate industry was moribund by 1850, it was soon replaced by firms specializing in the new process. Electroplating was a technique to which fused-plate makers, such as Dixon's and Sisson's, could easily adapt. Walker & Hall, which was founded in 1845, became a leader in the field under its founder, George Walker, who electroplated goods with silver, gold, and bronze. The market for plated wares of all kinds was to grow enormously in the Victorian and Edwardian eras and it is noticeable that the firms which made either plate alone or both plate *and* cutlery dominated this sector by 1914 (see Table 1.2). It is perhaps a pity, therefore, that historians have yet to show much interest in these industries.

In engineering the real growth occurred after the 1860s, with the arrival of the bulk steel processes of Bessemer and Siemens (see Chapter 2). But even before then, demand from the steel trades for equipment and tools had triggered the growth of this sector. In the early nineteenth century, Sheffield was not as important as Manchester and Leeds for the production of machinery and engineers' tools, but local machine-tool specialists such as Drury Bros. & Walker had made a start. Particularly important

---

[53] Bradbury, *Sheffield Plate*, 494.
[54] Peter Smithurst and Nicola Moyle, *Lock, Stock and Barrel: Sheffield Craftsmanship in Shooting Accessories* (Sheffield, 1991).

Table 1.2. *Leading Sheffield cutlery, silver plate, and tool firms, 1914*

Name	Established	Employees	Major Products
Walker & Hall	1845	2,000	Silver plate
Joseph Rodgers	1724	1,500	Cutlery
Dixon's	1806	1,000	Silver plate
Thomas Turner	1802	1,000	Cutlery
Mappin & Webb	1810	600	Cutlery/silver plate
Harrison Bros. & Howson	1843	600	Cutlery
Wostenholm	1745	400	Cutlery
Tyzack, Sons, & Turner	1812	400	Scythes/tools

Sources: Contemporary trade press, local publications, and business records.

was the business of Davy Bros., founded in Pear Street by David Davy (1806–65) and his brother Dennis. It produced sawmills, wagon axles, iron and brass castings, slide lathes, and high-pressure and condensing steam engines. By 1850, when it moved to the Park Iron Works in Attercliffe, steel plant production and rolling mill design had become part of its service, laying the basis for this firm to become a world leader in steel plant construction and design in the twentieth century.[55]

Not every steel innovation came from Sheffield. Once the crucible process arrived on the scene, European steelmakers were the first to successfully manufacture good-quality steel castings. By this process, molten steel, instead of being poured into a narrow iron mould, was teemed into a refractory mould, so that more complex shapes could be produced. The German firm Krupp's soon had a big reputation for its steel castings, which were technically extremely difficult to make commercially. It was German melters who brought the art to Sheffield in the mid-1850s, when Vickers decided it was time to enter the field. By the 1860s the technology had been absorbed (Vickers' first success was in making cast steel bells) and Sheffield had another related industry.

Steel firms in and around Sheffield, though, were at the forefront in mastering the difficult problem of manufacturing wire. Cocker Bros., founded in 1752 and based at the Fitzalan Works in Nursery Street, were one of the leaders in the field by the 1850s: their predecessors at the Fitzalan Works (Marriott & Atkinson) having pioneered cast steel wire. Also important was the company founded by Samuel Fox (1815–87) in 1842. Born in Bradwell, Derbyshire, the son of a weaver's shuttle-maker, Fox had been apprenticed to a wire-drawing firm in Hathersage before starting his own business in Stocksbridge. His major innovation in 1848

[55] 'The Story of Davy and United', *SDT*, 24 Nov. 1949.

was the steel-ribbed umbrella frame, which he improved by 1851 with the fluted or trough-section wire for umbrella ribs named 'Paragon'. After his success with his umbrella frames (which were exported worldwide), in 1854 Fox began producing strip, cold-rolled from wire, which enabled him to make £80,000 from the craze for steel wire for crinoline skirts.[56] Fox's product, in turn, supported the growth of crinoline skirtmakers in Sheffield. By the 1860s R. & G. Gray was described as the largest crinoline makers in the world, with about 500–800 workers (mostly women), and at least two other firms were involved in the trade.[57] The way in which these innovations cascaded through these companies was helped by the structure of the Sheffield industry.

COMPANY STRUCTURE AND STRATEGY

The determinants we have discussed so far—local skill, advantages in natural resources, growing demand, and the presence of related industries—provide most of the explanation for Sheffield's superiority. However, other elements must be considered. After all, other areas had skilful workers and were equally well endowed with natural advantages. In the cutlery trades, especially, the French and Germans had more ancient craft traditions than Sheffield, and also had lower wages. Why, then, did Sheffield acquire such a formidable lead? The answer to this puzzle lies partly in certain technical advances that were available only in Sheffield (especially the manufacture of crucible steel), but particularly in the complex structure of the Sheffield cutlery and steel trades. We shall examine each, in turn.

By the mid-nineteenth century, Sheffield was beginning to dominate the manufacture of cutlery and tools. By 1841, some 60 per cent of British cutlers worked in Sheffield; and the town also had the largest concentrations of saw- and filemakers (80 per cent and 54 per cent of United Kingdom workers, respectively). Concentrated from without, however, the cutlery trades were extensively subdivided within: first by the diversity of products. The main branches of the trade in the late 1820s are shown in Table 1.3.

These divisions were then shivered into the producing units themselves, which in the early nineteenth century were typically the independent craftsmen—a reflection of the domestic roots of the industry, its

---

[56] Joseph Kenworthy, *The Early History of Stocksbridge and District* (Deepcar, 2 vols., 1915); Joseph Sheldon, *The Founders and Builders of Stocksbridge Works* (Stocksbridge, 1922); Hazel Stansfield, *Samuel Fox & Co. Ltd. 1842–1967* (Stocksbridge, 1967).

[57] See *Pawson & Brailsford's Illustrated Guide to Sheffield and Neighbourhood* (Sheffield, 1862), 158–61.

Table 1.3. *Employment in the cutlery trades, c.1828*

On table knives	2,240
On spring-knives (pocket-knives)	2,190
In the plated trades nearly	2,000
On files	1,284
On scissors	806
On edge-tools	541
On forks	480
On razors	478
On saws	400
In the country	130
About	10,549

Source: Thomas Allen, *A New and Complete History of the County of Yorkshire* (London, 1831), iii. 31.

deep-rooted customs and practices, and, perhaps above all, the fact that making cutlery was a hand-skill. Forging, grinding, hardening, tempering, hafting (handle-making), and cutlering (assembly) were all highly skilled subdivisions of the cutlery trade, often done by 'outworkers'—an arrangement which suited factors and manufacturers anxious to cope with fluctuating overseas demand and a wide product range.[58] 'The manufactures, for the most part', wrote one visitor, 'are carried on in an unostentatious way, in small scattered workshops, and nowhere make the noise and bustle of a great ironworks.'[59]

The extreme subdivision of the cutlery trade was the first aspect noted by outsiders. A foreign visitor to Joseph Elliott's razor works observed:

We found the workmen not altogether in one factory, but in different buildings. In one was where the rough process of forging was performed; from thence, perhaps across a street, the blades received further touches from other workmen, and so on till . . . they were carried to the grinding and polishing works, some distance off, and finally returned to a building near the warerooms, to be joined to the handles, after which they were papered and packed, immediately adjoining the warerooms proper, where sales were made and goods delivered. I was surprised in visiting the forges where the elastic metal was bent into graceful blades, to find them little dingy nooks and corners in a series of old rookeries of buildings, often badly lighted, cramped and inconvenient, and difficult of access.[60]

[58] See Lloyd, *Cutlery Trades*; Sally Taylor, 'Tradition and Change: The Sheffield Cutlery Trades' (Sheffield Ph.D., 1988). Less authoritative, but offering contrasts with Birmingham is Maxine Berg, 'Small-Producer Capitalism in Eighteenth Century England', *Business History*, 35 (Jan. 1993), 17–39.

[59] Thomas Allen, *A New and Complete History of the County of Yorkshire* (London, 1831), iii. 33.

[60] 'An American View of Sheffield', *SI*, 5 Dec. 1868.

Sheffield did have its large cutlery firms, such as Joseph Rodgers & Sons and George Wostenholm & Son. Rodgers had been working cutlers since at least 1724 and by 1800 were firmly established at an address they were to make world famous—No. 6 Norfolk Street. By the 1820s the firm employed about 300, a number that had surpassed 500 by 1840. Wostenholm's had been founded in 1745 and had achieved its greatest success in the American market in the 1830s and 1840s. In 1848 Wostenholm's took the unprecedented step of acquiring a large factory in Wellington Street, named appropriately the Washington Works, which was regarded by contemporaries as 'a definite indication of change'.[61] The firm employed about 350 in the 1840s and by the 1850s the number was probably over 500. However, neither the Norfolk Street Works nor the Washington Works were factories in the modern, mechanized sense. Within their walls, the division of labour was extreme: a cutler might make one kind of knife—say a sleeveboard pattern—all his life: 'ask him to do anything else and there'd be trouble. He'd get moody, throw off his apron and go and get drunk for the rest of the day.'[62] And even the 'cutler' would make few of the parts for that knife for himself: blades, corkscrews, scissors, and scales (handles) would be made by other craftsmen, often outworkers. Both Rodgers and Wostenholm, though achieving some economies of scale, still relied on the outwork system. Their cutlers, though nominally employed by the firm, had the status of tenants, coming and going at will and still working for other makers when it suited them. Even at Rodgers, observed one journal:

it would be impossible to trace the manufacturing history of a knife without following it to other workshops in Sheffield. And such may be said of the larger firms generally, as well as the smaller ones. Each class of manufacturers is so dependent on the others, and there is such a chain of links connecting them all, that we have found it convenient to speak of Sheffield as one huge workshop for steel goods.[63]

The wellspring of the workshop was the town's increasingly successful crucible steel firms. The commercial exploitation of Huntsman's process had been initially steady rather than spectacular, but crucible steel manufacture was well under way in Sheffield by the 1790s and by the 1830s and 1840s growth had begun to quicken. Ten steel producers were listed in a 1787 Sheffield directory; later figures from similar sources show that the number of steelmakers rose from 34 in about 1817 to 124 in 1856. Employment in the steel industry had passed 5,000 by 1850, though three times this number were employed in the light trades. By the early 1840s annual

---

[61] J. H. Stainton, *The Making of Sheffield 1865–1914* (Sheffield, 1924), 246.
[62] G. Tweedale, *Stan Shaw: Master Cutler* (Sheffield, 1993), 38.
[63] 'A Day at the Sheffield Cutlery Works', *Penny Magazine* (1844), 168.

Table 1.4. *Leading Sheffield steel firms, 1852*

Company	Converting furnaces	Crucible holes
Jessop	10	120
Sanderson Bros.	10	110
Naylor & Vickers	8	90
Firth	?	80
Beet & Griffiths	?	70
Turton & Sons	11	48
Johnson & Cammell	6	40
John Brown	4	40

Sources: 'Sheffield Manufactories' (letter), *SI*, 2 Oct. 1852. Re-produced in J. G. Timmins, 'Concentration and Integration in the Sheffield Crucible Steel Industry', *Business History*, 24 (Mar. 1982), 60–78. I have added the figures for Brown from a description of the Atlas Works, *SI*, 5 Jan. 1856.

production of cementation steel was approaching 20,000 tons; twenty years later there were over 200 cementation furnaces, producing annually nearly 80,000 tons of steel. Significantly, one authority mentioned that by the early 1840s the Sheffield area was producing about 90 per cent of the country's steel output and about one-half of world steel production.

Like cutlery, steel was pyramidal in structure, with a handful of relatively large firms resting on a broad base of small businesses. A few large, integrated firms began appearing early in the nineteenth century. Perhaps the first to make an impression on the popular consciousness was Greaves's Sheaf Works, which was built in 1823 in response to rising American orders. Costing £50,000, the Sheaf Works (later owned by Turton's) was recognized as something new in the town, since 'one grand end was kept in view, namely that of centralizing on the spot all the various processes through which the iron must pass . . . until fashioned into razor, penknife or other article of use'.[64] Whether this factory was quite so self-contained as this implies, may perhaps be doubted: nevertheless, it was the first large steel and tool works in Sheffield.

Other firms that grew appreciably during the prosperous 1840s and 1850s were Sanderson's, Jessop's, Butcher's, and Vickers. Jessop's, for example, briefly emerged in the early 1850s as the country's largest steel producer: its ten converting furnaces and 120 melting holes at the Brightside Works was the largest capacity in the town (see Table 1.4). Other firms also took the opportunity to expand along the Don Valley, where ample cheap land and the railway were the attractions. Cammell's

[64] Hunter, *Hallamshire*, 174.

Cyclops Works was opened in 1846, and it was soon followed by Firth's Norfolk Works in 1852, John Brown's Atlas Works in 1855 and by Vickers' River Don Works in 1863.

But these firms, though responsible for a large share of crucible steel output by the 1850s, were not in the majority. The typical crucible steel firm was a small-scale affair, with a few melting holes and perhaps (though not always) a cementation furnace or two. This is how many Sheffield steelmakers appear (with varying degrees of artistic licence) in contemporary billheads and engravings: a row of bottle-shaped converting furnaces, a plume of smoke, the melting shops with their characteristic oblong chimney stacks, offices and workshops, fronted by an arched entrance with horses and carts denoting a busy manufactory. The engravings in Pawson & Brailsford's *Illustrated Guide to Sheffield and Neighbourhood* (1862) catch the small-scale character of this industry perfectly. So, too, does a tour of Abbeydale Industrial Hamlet. Both show one of the main advantages of the process—it did not need a large capital input—and even the biggest firms had started out from very modest origins. Firth's business, for example, was launched in 1842 with six crucible holes and a few hands.

Each firm was highly individualistic and so generalizations about their activities are difficult. A few companies confined their attention purely to converting; others concentrated on melting (or as it was sometimes known, 'refining') steel. Jessop's and Firth's were both founded by expert crucible steel melters and their success and rapid expansion were based entirely on this product. There were specialists in blister steel, such as Daniel Doncaster & Sons (founded in 1778), which began converting and dealing in Swedish iron in 1800. Several firms had both cementation and melting capacity—Huntsman, for example—but only a few, such as Sanderson Bros., had extensive tilting facilities. Often firms converted and melted steel for their own cutlery and tools. The manufacture of the latter was logical for them, since they often had their roots in the ancient cutlery and tool trades. Marsh Bros. was typical. By the early nineteenth century the firm was located at the Ponds Works on Forge Lane, where they had spacious offices and a warehouse, a new steam-driven rolling mill, and converting and cast steel furnaces. Marsh Bros. made a name for themselves both for the excellent quality of their steel and the tools (such as files) they made from it.[65] W. K. & C. Peace had a similar spread of products: its trade mark had been granted to John Peace by the Cutlers' Company in 1710 and it was one of the first crucible steelmakers in the town. Throughout its existence, Peace was involved with the manufacture of steel, files, and edge tools.[66]

[65] S. Pollard, *Three Centuries of Sheffield Steel: The Story of a Family Business* (Sheffield, 1954).
[66] 'The Story of W. K. & C. Peace: Sheffield Firm's Bi-Centenary, 1710–1910', *IMR* 36 (1 May 1910), 71–2.

It was an owner-operated industry: in business history parlance, 'personal', 'proprietary', 'family' capitalism personified. Sometimes this was true in a quite literal sense. When the impressive Globe Works was built in 1824 by William Ibbotson & Co. for the manufacture of steel and tools, the works (which is now restored near Kelham Island) included a residential wing into which William Ibbotson moved his family. Almost every firm had its own 'dynasty' of owners that harked back to distant times. John Bedford & Sons, a prominent nineteenth-century crucible steel and tool firm, had sprung from the activities of the first John Bedford, who built a forge at Oughtibridge in 1792. But the Bedford family itself had been involved in commerce since the thirteenth century, when they were merchants and traders in Hull.[67] Joseph Gillott & Sons, who were involved with the tool steel business, traced their history to the Huguenots.[68] Marsh Bros.'s ancestry has been traced to 1631. Companies that advertised trade marks that were granted in the seventeenth century were commonplace.

Yet, as with cutlery, although firms were highly individualistic, few could manage without their competitors. As one Sheffield steelmaker put it: 'Only a few firms, whose names are registered in the local directory as steel manufacturers, do the job from A to Z. There is a community doing jobs for one another.'[69] This was partly because it was unusual for a firm to have the facilities for all the stages of steel production (see Fig. 1.1): converting, melting, forging, and rolling, to say nothing of the crucial final marketing. Few firms were big enough to own their own tilting and rolling facility, so even the largest firms usually sent their steel out to tilts. This was known in Sheffield as 'hire-work', a practice unique amongst steelmaking regions. It was soon fostered further by the increasing range of tool steels and the sheer complexity of the industry in Sheffield. Some firms found they could exist wholly on hire-work and marketing. By developing extensive contacts with tool steelmakers they could often beat the big firms for price and for delivery. As one manager remarked, hire-work was attractive because 'little outlay was involved, turnover was quick, and you could also pick and choose to fit things in with whatever you were doing'.[70] This made it possible for 'a name, scantily known at home, to be blazoned in a foreign market. Some amongst them might have a scarce existence as a manufacturer, and yet be a top-notcher when it came to shopkeeping abroad, where it directed a warehouse, stocked mainly with lines it did not make, but sold, smartly and profitably, with all the assurance of perfect understanding.'[71]

---

[67] 'John Bedford & Sons Ltd. of Sheffield: 150th Anniversary', *British Steelmaker*, 8 (July 1942), 146–54.

[68] Joseph Gillott & Sons, *The Gillotts of Sheffield* (Sheffield, 1951).

[69] H. Brearley, *Knotted String* (London, 1941), 147.

[70] Eric Stubbs interview, 13 Apr. 1992. [71] Brearley, *Knotted String*, 147.

1. UK **wrought iron**

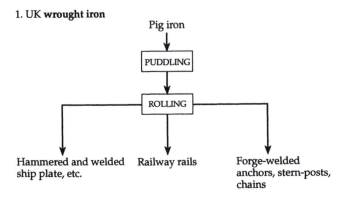

2. **Sheffield steel**

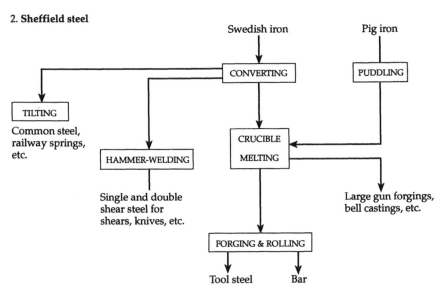

Fig. 1.1 *Iron and steel before Bessemer*

The picture, then, is of a classic 'cluster'. Sheffield's vast workshop of cutlery and steel firms was at once atomistic, yet at the same time closely interlocked; competitive and yet co-operative. The benefits of the cluster were many. As Marshall has stressed, the mysteries of the trade were 'in the air' and initiation into steel could begin early. The two real geniuses in Sheffield steelmaking—Harry Brearley and Robert A. Hadfield—are examples. Brearley, the grandson of a blacksmith and the son of a melter, was only eight when he tried forging nails in a fire. As a lad, he also wandered amongst the little mesters at work in the local 'wheels', and then found a job in the cellar of a crucible steel furnace, where he moulded clay lids and watched the melting of steel.[72] Hadfield, the son of a wealthy steelmaster, was experimenting with steel as a teenager, having persuaded his father to install a furnace in the basement of the family home in Broomhill. Both men later developed major alloy steels (see Chapters 2 and 3).

Sheffield was a breeding ground for innovation and also for business enterprise. Once a man had decided to become a manufacturer, the path was relatively easy. One toolmaker has described how 'it was possible to be a full-blown manufacturer with nothing more than a stamp with your name on it and a tiny office or a room in your house'.[73] A specialist markmaker would, with hand tools and a magnifying glass, cut your name into a punch; a forger would make the blades for you; a hardener would harden and temper the blades; and the next visit was to the organized chaos of the grinding wheel. 'Without looking at you or stopping work, [the grinder] would shout above the din "Purrendarntheer, si thi on Friday."'[74] When collected, the final trip was to the cutler to grind the bolster and fit the handle. The tools were ready for sale. Of course, not all manufacturers were like this, but even those that did many of the processes themselves were interdependent. The ledgers of the obscure, but fairly typical firm of John Littlewood, for example, reveal that it regularly made edge tools for some of the most famous makers, such as shearmakers Ward & Payne.[75]

Adaptability was the industry's watchword. Perhaps the most notable instance was in the cutlery trades, where the craftsmen in the era before mechanization and pattern-standardization revelled in the American demand for ornament and patriotic mottoes. Folding dirks, folding Bowies, and fixed-blade Bowie knives were manufactured by Sheffield between about 1830 and 1860, a period when the town dominated the American market for these items. American collectors find the 'Sheffield folding bowie . . . fascinating in its historical lore, mechanical workmanship and elegant beauty'.[76] Some were made with the 'half-horse, half-alligator' motif—a reference to the 'Hunters of Kentucky' song during the war of 1812. Others had crossguards stamped 'Liberty and Union', reflecting the sentiments of Daniel Webster's famous 'Constitution and Union' speech

[72] Brearley, *Knotted String*, 14–15; Brearley, *Stainless Pioneer*, 10, 20–2.
[73] Ashley Iles, *Memories of a Sheffield Tool Maker* (Mendham, NJ, 1993), 61.
[74] Ibid. 62.
[75] Ken Hawley, 'The Ledgers of John Littlewood, Sheffield Edge Tool Makers, 1900–1909', *Tools and Trades*, 7 (1992), 44–63.
[76] B. Levine, *Levine's Guide to Knives and Their Values* (Northbrook, Ill., 2nd edn., 1993), 196. See also W. Adams *et al.*, *The Antique Bowie Knife Book* (Conyers, Ga., 1990).

of 1850. Even more notable was the Bowie knife trade itself, which saw an astonishing variety of blade shapes, handle materials, and decoration by Sheffield makers. These knives were weapons—their lightness and sharpness leaving no doubt of that—but the best are often acid-etched with patriotic or frontier slogans, such as 'Death to Abolition', 'California Knife', and the 'Hunter's Companion', and worked in top-quality materials such as ivory and pearl. Virtuosity in die-stamping technology, acid-etching and metals manufacture made this possible: so too did the complex network of firms and trades. Neither could be emulated in America.

Rivalry, though, was keen, despite the extensive networking. Secrets were carefully guarded and firms were obsessive about their reputation. But as we shall see in the development of tool steel and other alloys, this did not prevent the stock of knowledge and skill in the industry steadily expanding as companies imitated each other and personnel moved between firms. The close proximity of firms seems to have acted as a spur to rivalry, even in the workplace. In Sheffield, noted one writer, 'where the ranks of every department of labour are so crowded, there seems to be an ambition as to who shall do the best work, who shall be he that turns out the most skilfully wrought article'.[77]

The structure and technology of Sheffield industry largely dictated company strategy, which was based on a wide product range; a dedication to quality; and a commitment to trade marks. The adaptability of the local industry and its almost monopolist position, which meant that demand was worldwide and extremely varied, fostered the proliferation of patterns. As Frederick Mappin, one of the town's leading cutlers, stated: 'The manufacturers of this town are required to suit the tastes of all countries—the means of every class of buyers. This at once calls forth an immense variety of goods.'[78] The first illustrated catalogue of Sheffield tools and cutlery—Joseph Smith's *Key*, published in 1816—gives a unique glimpse of the beginnings of this variety.[79] By the mid-nineteenth century, the manuscript pattern book of cutlers such as Wostenholm's and others show that the number of different styles was enormous—running into thousands—with pocket-knives differing in blade type and shape, handle material, the number of tools, degree of finish, and in almost every other conceivable way.[80] Explained one manufacturer:

A knife that would be popular in Scotland would not meet favour in the South of England, or *vice versa*, and certain makes of knives sent to the Colonies would

---

[77] *SI*, 5 Dec. 1868.
[78] F. T. Mappin, 'Sheffield Wares', *SI*, 19 Jan. 1856.
[79] J. Smith, *Explanation or Key, to the Various Manufactories of Sheffield, with Engravings of Each Article*, ed. J. S. Kebabien (Vermont, 1975).
[80] SCL Wostenholm Records. Pattern books.

probably find little or no sale here. As for the Colonies themselves, the Cape prefers knives with wooden handles and 'sheep foot' blades; Canada thinks more highly of knives with black horn, ivory, and pearl handles, and 'spear-pointed' blades, and so on with other parts of the world.[81]

The pride and dedication of an industry that was accustomed to using the best materials (such as crucible steel), bred a fierce belief in quality. In economic terms, this was simply a logical maximization of Sheffield's many advantages; however, in Sheffield this subject was never one of mere logic—it had deep cultural and emotional resonances. The quality of Sheffield's products, even its famous steel, did vary—especially in the early nineteenth century, when there was little science of metallurgy— and a few makers did produce for the cheaper end of the market. However, surviving tools and cutlery show that the general standard was surprisingly high, despite (or perhaps because of) the fact that the industries involved relied on handicrafts; and at its best it was superb.

Rodgers epitomized the quality ethos. Even amongst Sheffield cutlery firms its commitment to workmanship and the highest quality was unsurpassed, so that it was soon known as the 'King of Cutlers'. A family firm, its most successful member was John Rodgers (1779–1859), who did more than most to inculcate the need for quality. A brilliant marketing man, in the early nineteenth century John Rodgers launched the firm's business in America, secured the firm's Royal Warrants through contacts with the Prince Regent and opened Sheffield's first cutlery showroom in Norfolk Street. Here visitors could see Rodgers' superb exhibition pieces, such as the famous Year Knife, containing 1,822 blades in one knife—a number denoting its year of manufacture. Many collectors believe that the products made by this firm, especially its exhibition knives, are the finest ever made—a verdict Rodgers would have considered no more than its due. They stated that:

The principle on which the manufacture of cutlery is carried on by this firm is— quality first, and with this in view it is evident that their competition with other firms as to price comes second; it is the object of the firm to produce the finest quality of article both as regards material and workmanship, at a reasonable price, so that anyone who purchases one of this firm's productions bearing not only the name, *but also the trade mark, a star and Maltese cross*, can depend on the fact that he or she has obtained an article which can be relied upon, and if properly used will give complete satisfaction.[82]

Wostenholm's was no different. Of its leading light, the dynamic George Wostenholm (1800–76), it was said: '[his] whole thought and

---

[81] Turner & Wingfield Rowbotham, *Handicrafts that Survive: Centenary Souvenir 1802–1902* (Sheffield, 1902).

[82] Joseph Rodgers & Sons, *Under Five Sovereigns* (Sheffield, 1911), 25.

ideas—apart from realising a fortune—seemed to be centred in achieving in his cutlery the legend of his trade mark, I*XL'.[83] He made the most of Sheffield's high-quality shear and crucible steels (still in some ways the best materials for blades) and the availability of natural handle materials, such as pearl and ivory, to produce cutlery almost as fine as Rodgers'. A custom peculiar to Wostenholm's was 'drilling', by which each knife was critically examined. Wostenholm himself would strike the knife blades on an anvil to find out the smallest defect. When 'His Majesty' was in a genial mood, it was said, everyone rushed to get their work examined; 'but when the "Little Devil" was on the throne no one went unless forced'.[84]

For the steelmakers, the commitment to quality was no less important. It explains Sheffield's mostly rigid adherence to the finest melting materials, such as cemented Swedish iron. It also explains why many Sheffield tool firms (even some of the cutlers, such as Rodgers and Thomas Turner) preferred to melt their own steel. It was a way of controlling quality. Cost was a secondary consideration. Mistakes, when they occurred, could be costly not only in terms of lost business, but in other ways. Quality in other consumer goods was no doubt important—one only has to think of the drugs trade in the eighteenth and nineteenth centuries—but in steel, quality was of greater importance than in most products: the failure of a machine-part, tool, or weapon could, in certain circumstances, be catastrophic.

As the quality of products became paramount, so too did the importance of trade marks. The stamped letters, marks, and slogans on Sheffield blades denoted quality, history, and an all-important guarantee. One trade journal told its readers: 'When you buy look for good names and observe the trade-marks . . . Some firms have obtained a reputation by the experience of several generations in the trade, and their names and marks have a great value.'[85] Sheffield marks were extremely ancient. Of John Wilson, the cutlery manufacturer, it was said: '[he] was as well known to the town as the old church, and that he struck four pepper corns upon his ware as the old church strikes twelve'.[86] The two most famous marks in the cutlery industry were those of Rodgers and Wostenholm, granted in 1683 and 1787 respectively.

The earliest Sheffield cutlery marks were recorded and a few records have survived, but it was not until 1614 that a register of marks was kept and has since been preserved. From its foundation in 1624, the Cutlers'

---

[83] Sir Henry Coward, *Reminiscences of Henry Coward* (London, 1919), 40. According to another Wostenholm worker, 'the great leading aim of Mr. Wostenholm's ambition was quality'. See 'Presentation to G. Wostenholm', *SI*, 29 Dec. 1855. For details on Wostenholm, see also G. Tweedale, *Giants of Sheffield Steel* (Sheffield, 1986).

[84] Coward, *Reminiscences*, 41.

[85] *Ironmonger*, 20 (19 Oct. 1878), Paris Exhibition Supplement, 3.

[86] *Sheffield Times*, 7 Apr. 1849.

Company, besides its control of working cutlers, had always regarded quality control and the registering and defence of trade marks as an important area of its jurisdiction. In 1773 Sheffield's involvement in marking goods became even greater, when the Sheffield Assay Office opened in the town for the marking of silver, gold and precious-metal goods. In 1814 when most of its powers over the cutlery trade were abolished, the Cutlers' Company retained the right to supervise trade marks. Gradually, the Company was to become the centre for Sheffield's attempts to fight the false marking of goods in the nineteenth century.

Perhaps not surprisingly, given its reputation, Sheffield became the main victim of fraudulent marking—indeed, no other town appears to have suffered so much in the nineteenth century from so-called 'false wares'. This probably began almost as soon as the town attained prominence in the eighteenth century, but it was the period after 1840, when American and particularly German competition began, that trade mark defence became a serious issue in Sheffield. The result was that Sheffield became the 'very metropolis and headquarters of trademarks';[87] and it was to play a leading role in the late nineteenth-century adoption of international trade mark legislation. It was a legal manifestation of its belief in high-quality products.

SUMMARY

This chapter has described how individual determinants of Sheffield's industry contributed to its rapid rise in the early nineteenth century. Some will be seen to have been more important than others. Almost all the literature on Sheffield begins with a discussion of its situation and physical characteristics: the hills, water-power, coal, and other mineral resources. This account has given greater weight to factor conditions—local skills and knowledge—and the structure of Sheffield industry in facilitating networking and creating scope for rivalry (and co-operation). Pride and a belief in high quality were particularly important motivators.

Not surprisingly, these determinants were not isolated, but interacted in a dynamic way to produce something unique—a classic cluster, perhaps the most intense and successful in British industry at that time. By the early nineteenth century, the steel industry in the Sheffield area had generated its own momentum and 'the fact that a special, highly-skilled occupation had become localized in the district led to new inventions being brought [there] as a matter of course, for nowhere else could the

[87] *Great Industries of Great Britain*, iii. 189.

same reserve of skilled labour and supervision be found'.[88] It had all happened by chance and as yet without any major direct or indirect government support.

The question for the town's industry by the 1850s, however, was how this largely unplanned metropolis of steel was to sustain its lead when foreign competition and new technologies made their inevitable appearance. Already by the 1840s, American edge tool makers were steadily acquiring market share in their domestic market and were beginning to send their products abroad; and German steelmakers led by Krupp's had shown that with perseverance the crucible steel process could be made to work abroad. Sheffield's skilled workers, its highly specialized firms, and its dense texture of industries would need to adapt to these changes, and many others, across its range of determinants if they were to stay ahead of the competition. The extent to which they did so is examined in the subsequent chapters.

---

[88] C. H. Desch, 'The Steel Industry of South Yorkshire: A Regional Study', Paper read to the Sociological Society, 24 Jan. 1922, 135.

2

Factor Creation in Special Steels

The conservatism of Sheffield is not, perhaps, so absolute as some
people think.

Henry Seebohm, *Ironmonger*, 25 (5 March 1881), 290.

In the 1850s the Sheffield crucible steel and tool trades entered a golden
age. Sheffield's stranglehold on steel technology, the dominance of its
cutlery industry, coupled with the growth of overseas markets, led to a
decade of almost unlimited demand and opportunity. It is a commonplace, however, that economic competition is profoundly dynamic in
character. Improvement and innovation are continuous processes. No
sooner does one nation achieve superiority, than another nullifies or
supersedes it. Having gained an initial advantage, firms need to sustain it
by improving fast enough to stay ahead: 'This involves not only progress
in executing existing advantages but also widening and upgrading the
bases of competitive advantage over time. Often this involves the move to
more sophisticated industry segments.'[1]

No industry was more dynamic than steel from the 1850s onwards—a
period which saw the crucible steel industry at its peak and the introduction of new steelmaking technologies that were to set trends for the next
century. This chapter examines Sheffield's response to that challenge and
looks in detail at its adoption of new technologies. It also looks at its
record in innovation and the strategy and performance of firms in such a
highly competitive environment.

NEW TECHNOLOGY IN TONNAGE STEELS

The first problem Sheffield steelmakers had to overcome was the problem
of supply. One of the virtues of the crucible process was its size. The
smallness of the ingots allowed stringent quality control and ensured that
the process remained almost a handicraft. But obviously supply was
relatively inelastic, since higher output could only be achieved by increasing the size of the crucible or expanding the number of producing units—
a case of more men and/or bigger pots. As demand increased both were
tried: pot capacity was increased (up to about 70 lb with clay crucibles;

[1] M. Porter, *The Competitive Advantage of Nations* (London, 1990), 70.

100 lb or more with graphite), though the fact that the pot of steel still needed to be lifted by one man set limits to crucible size. The other alternative resulted in heroic efforts by large gangs of melters to produce large ingots by teeming the contents of scores of crucibles. An account of steel casting at Vickers' River Don Works in 1867 reports 'the almost military organisation' needed to produce a 25-ton casting from 576 pots, teemed (so it was said) at the rate of a pot every half-second.[2] These were impressive logistical feats, but they highlight the fact that the crucible process was now reaching the limits of its capabilities, at least as regards tonnage.

Moreover, a product that took (if we include cementation and melting) several weeks to make in such small quantities was obviously far too specialist and expensive for general engineering applications. At about £60 per ton crucible steel was not surprisingly reserved for cutlery and edge tools, springs, cutting tools and the critical parts in machinery. Some innovative attempts were made to produce mild (that is, low-carbon) steel in the crucible—indeed, in the 1850s, one Sheffield firm, Shortridge, Howell & Co., produced so-called 'homogeneous' steel for ship and boiler plates—but generally iron remained the mainstay in industrial Britain. By the end of the 1850s some two million tons a year of wrought iron were manufactured in Britain, with probably the same amount produced elsewhere in Europe and America. It served the need for railway axles, ships' shafts, crankshafts, and flywheels, as well as boiler plates, railway track, and armour-plate.

The first requirement, then, from the expanding engineering trades in the mid-nineteenth century was for a material better than wrought iron, but more economic than cast steel. A temporary solution was found by modifying the tried and trusted puddling process of making wrought iron.[3] By halting the oxidization of the carbon in the puddling furnace at an intermediate stage, a composition between pig iron and wrought iron was produced: stronger than wrought iron, but capable of being hardened and tempered.

Puddled steel was responsible for the first stirrings of the heavy steel industry in Sheffield, since it allowed the production of railway materials, tyres, and armour plates. In 1858 John Brown installed six puddling furnaces (alongside the appropriate forging and rolling equipment) to produce what was described appropriately as 'steel-iron'. Brown also puddled and sold iron as a melting base for some of the cheaper grades of crucible steel.[4] Contemporaries saw this as a 'natural extension of

---

[2] 'The River Don Steel Works', *Engineering*, 4 (24 Oct. 1867), 383–5.
[3] K. C. Barraclough, *Steelmaking 1850–1900* (London, 1990), 29–35.
[4] 'Introduction of the Manufacture of Iron, for Conversion into Steel, in Sheffield', *SI*, 17 Apr. 1858.

the Sheffield trade', which had the attraction of increasing Sheffield's independence, since as one newspaper pointed out, the town's makers drew their 'supplies of iron from distant places [Derbyshire, Shropshire, Staffordshire, and abroad], in a partially manufactured state. None of them purchased it in the pig and manufactured it for themselves; and even such of the processes as were performed in Sheffield were done at different places.'[5] It was calculated that Brown's six furnaces would enable him initially to produce about 60 tons of iron per week, consuming about 150 tons of hard coal and employing about seventy men. Within a few years Brown's puddling furnaces numbered 72; while Cammell's Cyclops Works had 60 by the 1860s and Firth's Whittington Works also began puddling steel with 18 furnaces.

But puddled steel still had drawbacks. Manufacturing it demanded as much skill and certainly more physical effort than the crucible process. In fact, the laborious 'rabbling', in which the puddler had to stir energetically a five-hundredweight mass of hot, glowing iron with a paddle was recognized as one of the most unpleasant and physically punishing jobs in the industry. One nineteenth-century British ironworker stated that in warm weather it was not unusual to see a puddler drop dead.[6] Moreover, puddled steel still contained slag, which affected its uniformity and so limited its application. Whenever large forgings were needed great lumps (up to a hundredweight) had to be brought at heat from the puddling furnace, for welding into the finished product.

A better answer to the problem of increasing production was found by (Sir) Henry Bessemer (1813–98) in the early 1850s. Using an egg-shaped furnace (a converter) open at one end, Bessemer's idea was simple, but unconventional—blowing air into molten pig iron. This was not entirely new (blowing air through molten pig iron was the basis of the charcoal-refinery process), but Bessemer's idea of blowing through iron in a vessel was bold, to say the least. Ignoring the obvious risks—molten metal might be blown out of the converter, or could run back into holes through which the air was supposed to enter—he watched the mass ignite into an inferno of unimagined intensity. Despite the fact that his scheme was *fuel-less*, the oxygen in the air blast rapidly burned out the carbon and other elements, so purifying the iron—all within about thirty minutes. In 1856 Bessemer was able to give a successful demonstration of the technique that bears his name, a process that almost overnight was to reduce the price of steel to about a fifth and make it available in unprecedented tonnages. In Sheffield, as elsewhere, the Bessemer converter was to transform the steelmaking scene, since the way was now open for the production of

[5] 'Atlas Steel and Spring Works', *SI*, 1 May 1858; 'Visit of the Lords of the Admiralty to Atlas Works', *SI*, 11 Apr. 1863.

[6] U. Wengenroth, *Enterprise and Technology* (Cambridge, 1994), 13.

large tonnages of mild steel—precisely the material that was required for the railways, ships, bridges, and other areas of heavy engineering. It meant that Sheffield's East End Works were now destined for an even more hectic round of expansion.

After various technical problems had been overcome relating to the chemistry of the process (Robert F. Mushet's fine-tuning of the carbon content and over-oxidation in the converter with additions of speigeleisen was a crucial breakthrough), the inventor himself came to Sheffield. In 1858 he opened the Bessemer Steel Works in Carlisle Street, intending 'not to work my process as a monopoly, but simply to force the trade to adopt it by underselling them in their own market . . . while still retaining a very high rate of profit on all that was produced'.[7] Bessemer succeeded brilliantly and Sheffield steelmakers began taking out licences. Bessemer pointed out with satisfaction that John Brown, next door to Bessemer's plant, was the first to be 'converted' in 1860. He was followed by Charles Cammell in 1861, then Samuel Fox in 1862.

Together these men launched a new industry, that struck a major chord. Although it was superimposed on a steel industry that had been in existence for about a hundred years, the bulk processes devised by Bessemer (and later Siemens) sent Sheffield's industry into a different trajectory. Compared with the older crucible steel trade, this new industry was large scale; it introduced new products; it broadened the steelmaking base to include areas outside Sheffield, such as Stocksbridge and Rotherham; and in doing so, it brought new capital and expertise into the region. In short, it brought a business, as well as a technological, revolution.

Almost everything about the Bessemer process was an order of magnitude larger than the crucible. By the end of the 1870s Bessemer production in the United Kingdom was almost a million tons, compared with about 100,000 tons or more from the crucible. While the older tool steel firms continued to ply their trade by melting steel in 60 lb pots, with a couple of hundred men (or less) and a few thousand pounds in capital, the Bessemer firms grew at an unprecedented rate. Table 2.1 shows the sudden gulf that appeared by 1864 between the biggest Bessemer steelmakers (Cammell and Brown) and even the largest crucible steel producers, such as Vickers.

An impressionistic idea of this transformation can be seen from the illustrative plates in a John Brown & Co. commemorative history published in 1924.[8] The first view of the Atlas Works is from a billhead of 1838: it shows the modest frontage of Brown's Orchard Street cutlery and tool premises, employing perhaps a dozen or so men. A later view shows the

---

[7] H. Bessemer, *An Autobiography* (London, 1905), 175–6.
[8] *John Brown & Co. Ltd, 1864–1924* (Sheffield, 1924).

Table 2.1. *Leading Sheffield steel firms, 1864*

Company	Issued Capital (£)	Workforce
Charles Cammell	800,000	3,000–4,000
John Brown	750,000	3,300
Vickers	155,000	1,000

Sources: Cammell-Laird Papers, Birkenhead; J. D. Scott, *Vickers: A History* (London, 1962); Joseph Hunter, *Hallamshire: The History and Topography of the Parish of Sheffield in the County of York*. Rev. edn., Arthur Gatty (Sheffield, 1869), 215.

Atlas Works in 1869, now covering 21 acres, filling the whole of the area between Savile and Carlisle Streets and dominating the Brightside skyline with dozens of chimneys and converting furnaces. Or, if we do not care to trust the accuracy of the industrial artist, as Brown's historian summarizes it: 'The number of men employed in 1857 was 200, and in 1867, 4,000. In the first year of his business, [Brown] turned over about £3,000, and in the last mentioned year nearly [£] one million.'[9] Cammell's, from similarly modest beginnings, also grew spectacularly: by 1864 it was keeping pace with Brown's and had net profits approaching £50,000 a year towards the end of the 1860s.

Ironically, Bessemer's own firm did not grow as fast or become as big: it appears to have stuck to its original intention of proving a point—the viability of the Bessemer process—rather than adopting a policy of unbridled expansion. The firm did not become a limited company until 1877, and its shares were not marketed until twelve years later. Nevertheless, after fourteen years Bessemer stated that each of the partners in the company had withdrawn in profits eighty-one times the amount of capital he originally subscribed.

Bessemer steel opened up new markets unavailable to the crucible. A major factor in the growth of the large firms was the suitability of Bessemer steel for rail production, for which there was an almost insatiable demand both in Britain and overseas. America was a major customer: Brown and Cammell alone exported to the United States some three times the whole domestic American output in 1871. All the pioneering Sheffield Bessemer steel works were built with an adjacent rail mill. John Brown, with his close connections with the railway firms through his spring buffer and his pioneering activities with puddled steel, was well placed to take advantage of this market. He had planned to use puddled steel for rails and was well aware of the deficiencies of wrought iron for trackwork (it wore out quickly, especially where traffic was heavy), so he

---

[9] Allan Grant, *Steel and Ships: The History of John Brown's* (London, 1950), 21.

had soon spotted the value of steel rails. Brown supplied his first rails in 1860 and for a time became the largest rail maker in the world. In 1861, Charles Cammell, whose works were almost adjacent to Brown, entered the same trade. The minutes books of the Cammell directors show the intense activity in rail manufacture in the 1870s, with the company supplying not only the British market, but also America, Canada, and South America. Such was the demand by the early 1870s (when the rail trade reached a peak) that the Cammell steelworks, despite major plant extensions, had difficulty in providing enough ingots and raw materials to feed its mills.

By 1873 the Sheffield district had a Bessemer rail capability of about a quarter of a million tons per annum.[10] This transformation in technology and scale of operation triggered a major locational change in the steel industry (the repercussions of which would last until the end of the twentieth century). Major steel works began moving outside the Sheffield town boundaries, so ending steelmaking as a purely *local* activity. The need for the giant rail firms to become integrated concerns was partly responsible. In the early 1870s Brown's joined forces with Bolckow Vaughan, of Middlesbrough, in a Spanish iron ore mining venture and also purchased for £142,000 the Aldwarke Main and Car House Collieries in Rotherham. In a similar move, Cammell's, which had already extended its Bessemer operations by taking over a works at Penistone, purchased the Oaks Colliery to gain access to 1,200 acres of the rich Barnsley coal seam. The Cammell board were also shareholders and directors in the Wilson-Cammell Patent Wheel Co. Ltd., built in 1873 at Dronfield to supply the market for steel rails. This was ostensibly an independent concern, but with the Wilson and Cammell families in control at Dronfield and the two companies engaged in the same trade, it was obviously no such thing—a fact underlined when Cammell's eventually took over the Dronfield works.[11]

Samuel Fox at Stocksbridge, building on his success in the metal finishing trades and his experience in steel manufacture (he had laid down 48 crucible holes in 1860), entered the Bessemer market in 1862 with two 5-ton converters. The locational disadvantages of the Stocksbridge location do not seem to have impaired Fox's growth (it became a limited liability company in 1871 with paid up capital of £240,000), despite the fact that for ten years it had no railway link and rails intended for export had to be taken the one and a half miles to Deepcar by horse-drawn carriage.

---

[10] See K. Warren, 'The Sheffield Rail Trade: An Episode in the Locational History of the British Steel Industry', *Insitute of British Geographers' Transactions*, 34 (1964), 131–57; Wengenroth, *Enterprise*.

[11] As the historians of the company note: 'It looked suspiciously as though the town families were using their connections to branch off independently of Charles Cammell & Co. in the pursuit of private gain.' See J. Austin and M. Ford, *Steel Town: Dronfield and Wilson Cammell 1873–1883* (Sheffield, 1983), 10.

Rotherham also emerged as an important steel centre. Amongst the entrants to the Bessemer trade were Owen's Patent Wheel, Tyre & Axle Co. and Hampton & Radcliffe, though both these concerns (which merged during the early 1870s) appear to have suffered from too rapid an expansion and under-capitalization. Their plant in the Ickles area of Rotherham was purchased in 1875 by William Peech and Henry Steel—one-time local victuallers who had made a fortune as 'agents of the turf'—to form Steel, Tozer, & Hampton (later Steel, Peech, & Tozer) with a capital of £70,000. Rail orders kept the firm busy and in the 1880s the manufacture of railway springs and tyres was added.

In Sheffield itself, besides Henry Bessemer's plant, there was one other new entrant to the trade. This was Brown, Bayley, & Dixon, founded in Attercliffe in 1871 by George Brown (a nephew of Sir John Brown), for the production of Bessemer steel and rails. In the late 1870s record outputs were achieved by the firm for rolling rails from two pairs of Bessemer converters. The firm seems to have been a close rival to the Cleveland steel works in being the first to introduce 'basic' Bessemer steelmaking, due to the work of its Bessemer steel department manager, Arthur Cooper (1849–1932).

Table 2.2 shows Bessemer steelmaking in the Sheffield area in the 1860s and 1870s.

The fact that bulk steelmaking was so capital intensive—a complete Bessemer converter plant could cost about £3,500, to say nothing of the cost of rolling mills and forging plant—and the fact that steelmaking was a national, as well as Sheffield, development injected new capital and entrepreneurial talent into the area. Bessemer himself—born near Hitchen and a London-based engineer and inventor—was again the symbol of this change. He was partnered by William Galloway, of the famous Manchester engineering firm; by Robert Longsden; and by his brother-in-law, William D. Allen—none of them Sheffielders. Even the Sheffield Bessemer licencees could not rely on local capital and talents. In John Brown's first phase of expansion in the mid-1850s he had taken two new partners: J. D. Ellis (1824–1906), the son of a Birmingham brass manufacturer and metal plater, and William Bragge, the son of a Birmingham jeweller. When Brown's became a limited company in 1864, the firm was promoted by the Manchester chemical manufacturer, Henry Davis Pochin; and another Manchester industrialist, Benjamin Whitworth, found a seat on the board. Brown's personal shareholding in the company of £125,000 was exactly counterbalanced by the shares of the Manchester group—a fact that was later to be of some significance for Brown's position at the company.[12] Similarly, three of the eight directors at Charles

[12] John Brown PLC, John Brown & Co., Minute Book No 1. List of shareholders, 1864. See also C. J. Erickson, *British Industrialists: Steel and Hosiery, 1850–1950* (Cambridge, 1959), 145.

Table 2.2. *Bessemer steel plant in Sheffield and district*

Firm	Location	Launch date	Converters 1871	Converters 1878
Bessemer	Sheffield	1859	5	4
Brown	Sheffield	1860	6	6
Cammell	Sheffield	1861	8	8
Fox	Stocksbridge	1862	2	2
Owens Patent Wheel	Rotherham	c.1870	2 ⎱ Steel, Tozer,	6
Hampton, Radcliffe	Rotherham	1872	2 ⎰ Hampton	
Brown, Bayley, Dixon	Sheffield	1871	2	4
Wilson-Cammell	Dronfield	1873	—	4

Sources: *JISI* 2/2 (1871), xv; J. S. Jeans, *Steel: Its History, Manufacture, Properties and Uses* (London, 1880), 87.

Cammell—Thomas Vickers, Alfred Peck, and James Harvey—were Manchester men, while Charles Vickers became a shareholder in Wilson-Cammell. Manchester (and London) capital was also influential in the launching of the Owen's Patent Wheel Co. in Rotherham.

Outside influence and the technological revolution in heavy steel-making continued with the work of Sir William Siemens (1823–83), who was responsible for that other great nineteenth-century breakthrough in steel production—the open-hearth furnace. Again the development of this technology is well-documented and stemmed originally from Siemens' attempts to utilize the waste heat from furnace exhaust gases. By 1870 the process, which involved the melting of blast furnace material and scrap in an open bath, was fully developed. The process was slower than Bessemer's converter (taking from four to twelve hours), but it had one great advantage: the molten steel could be analysed and modified during the melt. Sheffield firms were amongst the first commercial users of the process and open-hearth furnaces were at work in Sheffield by the early 1870s. Vickers installed eight furnaces (12 to 15 tons) in 1871. Cammell had sent a representative of the firm to the Siemens' plant at Landore, South Wales, in 1872, who was 'satisfied from what he had seen . . . that steel can be made by this process fully as cheaply as by the Bessemer and that no costly plant in the way of machinery is required for it'.[13] Cammell envisioned laying down four furnaces (at a cost approaching £1,000 each) at their Grimesthorpe works to remove bottlenecks in production, particularly a shortage of steel for rails, and boost turnover by £100,000 a year. By 1879 Cammell's had between six and eight open-hearth furnaces, compared with Vickers' ten, and production of open-hearth steel in

---

[13] Cammell-Laird Papers, Birkenhead. Directors' Minute Book, 3 Jan. 1872.

Sheffield was well over 20,000 tons. By 1900 the open-hearth process had largely supplanted the Bessemer converter in Sheffield, at least as regards tonnage (though some firms such as Hadfields and Edgar Allen retained the converter, or variants of it, for making steel for castings). This reflected wider developments: by the beginning of the twentieth century open-hearth tonnage was to surpass the output of Bessemer steel worldwide.

Heavy steelmaking, however, was not such a Sheffield monopoly as crucible steelmaking. For example, by 1878 the biggest Bessemer works was in Barrow-in-Furness, not in Sheffield—an indication that some of the town's disadvantages as a steelmaking centre were becoming apparent. Although the region had smelted pig iron for centuries and there were blast furnaces in operation in Rotherham in the nineteenth century (John Brown had also erected small blast furnaces in the 1870s), the Sheffield area has never been a major blast furnace centre. In bulk steelmaking the siting of raw materials—especially the non-phosphoric pig iron that was the staple of the Bessemer and Siemens furnaces until the discovery of the 'basic' processes—was crucial. In the rail trade, Sheffield was over a hundred miles from the haematite iron suppliers and blast furnaces, to say nothing of transport costs for the finished product. Sheffield's vulnerability was clearly demonstrated when the rail boom suddenly ended in 1873, caused initially by fluctuations in the American market and the growth of United States competition. By 1876 United Kingdom rail exports to America had ended. Demand recovered somewhat in the early 1880s, but as competition for the rail market in Britain and Europe intensified (Bessemer rail prices at the works fell from about £13 a ton in 1872 to about £5 a ton in 1879), Sheffield began to feel the pain. John Brown's soon dropped out of the market for rails completely, switching instead to armaments and engineering products. Although these products were bulky, their value was so high that freight costs were a secondary consideration. Brown, Bayley, & Dixon failed financially in 1881, hit by the fall in the demand for rails, especially from the United States and Europe, and fluctuations in pig iron prices. In 1888 it was re-formed as Brown, Bayley's Steel Works, with a Yorkshire ironmaster, W. J. Armitage, providing a quarter of the £160,000 capital. A 10-ton open-hearth furnace was added to the Bessemer converters: rails were eventually discontinued and other railway materials, such as springs and tyres, were introduced.[14]

Cammell's, so reliant on the rail business, commented frequently after 1874 on the drop in demand and the cut-throat competition. In 1878 the directors found that 'the price of steel rails continues extremely low, almost placing us for the time being outside the market'.[15] As prices fell,

[14] J. K. Almond, 'Sheffield's Historic Role', *Quality* (Jan./Feb. 1981), 49–51; *Brown Bayleys 1871–1971* (Sheffield, 1971).

[15] Cammell-Laird Papers, Birkenhead. Directors' Minute Book, 25 Sept. 1878.

producers of molten pig iron close to the ore supplies and nearer to the ports began to enjoy a marked superiority. As the Cammell directors explained: 'The costs of inland carriage are so great, and the probability of any appreciable reduction of it is so remote that rail manufacturers on the coast ... must command great advantages over the competitors whose works are inland.' They calculated that transporting iron into Sheffield and then sending out the finished rails for export cost about 18 shillings per ton (at a time when a ton of rails at the Dronfield Works sold for a little over £5). A rail works on the north-west coast would save at least 13s. a ton in carriage charges alone. Cammell's response was swift and dramatic: in 1882 the company took over the Derwent Hematite Iron Co. in Workington (with its three blast furnaces) and then in the following year transferred the whole of the Dronfield operation to Cumberland. Despite the estimated £35,000 removal costs, the directors believed that the new company, 'with its valuable and unique plant, its own pig iron, cheap labour, the opportunities for delivering rails for shipment to any part of the world at an almost nominal cost, and the established connection of the present firms combine ... every element which can contribute to a successful and profitable business'.[16]

Though there was an upturn in rail prices and domestic demand in the early 1880s, which boosted Sheffield rail production to over 300,000 tons in 1882, most of the other Bessemer rail plants in Sheffield had failed or been dismantled by 1890. Only Steel, Peech, & Tozer hung onto this market and were described in about 1910 as the 'only firm in the neighbourhood still supplying these'.[17]

Sheffield, as regards heavy steelmaking, thus lost its claim to be the world capital of steel. The Bessemer and open-hearth processes were great equalizers: they were more mechanical technologies, better publicized, more easily copied and understood than the mysterious crucible, and the specifications for mild steel were not quite so unforgiving as for tool steel. The result was that foreign competition appeared, particularly in America, where the output of Pittsburgh and other centres with their greater coal and ore resources soon dwarfed the efforts of the South Yorkshire town. This trend, however, merely reinforced Sheffield's role as a special steelmaking centre. Its relative position in world steel changed (at least as regards heavy steelmaking), but its expansion continued unchecked. Sheffield might not have been as productive as the Americans, but it could still excel in the skilful manipulation of molten steel. There were two important new lines of business: armaments and steel castings.

[16] Cammell-Laird Papers, Birkenhead. Directors' Minute Book, 2 Nov. 1881.
[17] *British Association Handbook & Guide to Sheffield* (Sheffield, 1910), 229.

The arms trade was of fundamental importance to Sheffield after the 1860s as the armies and, especially, navies of the 'civilized nations' demanded more efficient weapons of destruction and defence. As Anthony Sampson has written: 'It was in the mid-nineteenth century, in the wake of the first industrial revolution, that the modern armaments industry began to take shape, inspired and pressed forward by a handful of inventive entrepreneurs who developed the science of explosives and guns.'[18] We might also add that with explosives and guns came the need for steel forgings, armour plates, and projectiles. Crucible steel, of course, lent itself to warlike uses—in swords, bayonets, and rifles, for example. By 1855 there were even attempts to use *cast steel* for guns by Shortridge, Howell, & Jessop.[19] But essentially, the output of Sheffield's furnaces was destined for peaceable uses before the 1850s. Crucible steel was far too expensive to be used for naval armour-plate, for example. The bulk steelmaking processes and the arms industries were, however, made for each other. Whereas the Quaker Huntsman had discovered his steel searching for a better product for his clock springs, Bessemer's experiments with cast iron had stemmed directly from his interest in projectiles.

The subject of the Sheffield armaments industry—the significance of which may be appreciated by the simple fact that all but one (Armstrong-Whitworth) of the traditional arms firms originated in the town— demands a whole book in itself. Certainly it deserves closer attention than it has received in most studies about the industry. We are indebted to Clive Trebilcock and Richard Davenport-Hines for greatly deepening our knowledge of the Sheffield arms industry, especially with respect to Vickers.[20] The latter, in particular, has brought a refreshingly critical approach to the subject, when almost everything else written about Sheffield steel tends to underrate the impact of armaments. Historians of metallurgy, in particular, have neglected this area, perhaps because they have been reluctant to stress the destructive uses of steel, or because the technology itself is often so inscrutable. This was an area more secret than most that generated few books and papers; and even information on the commercial background is often scanty.

A capital-intensive, high-risk industry, but one that could be enormously profitable, the arms trade gave a new twist to the town's steel industry. When the local press reviewed the growth of the arms trade in 1863, it noted that it had raised Sheffield to the 'proud position of a manufacturing community upon which the country is mainly dependent

[18] A. Sampson, *The Arms Bazaar* (London, 1977), 35.
[19] 'Cast Steel Guns for the Government', *SI*, 22 Sept. 1855.
[20] R. P. T. Davenport-Hines, *Dudley Docker: The Life and Times of a Trade Warrior* (Cambridge, 1984); C. Trebilcock, *The Vickers Brothers: Armaments and Enterprise 1854–1914* (London, 1977).

for its protection as well as its power. More than that . . . a spirit of enterprise has sprung up which promises to raise the town to a position of
unprecedented prosperity, and convert war into a source of still greater
commercial activity.'[21]

It was this business that was mainly responsible for the sudden jump in
size of the industry leaders already noted—first Brown and Cammell,
then Vickers—who, having launched their large-scale businesses on the
back of the railways, now used the arms industry to take their companies
into an even higher orbit. This intensified Sheffield's industrial clustering
and specialization as steel companies found themselves pioneering and
competing for new lines of business. Sheffield firms (Brown's, Cammell's)
acquired a stranglehold in the British armour-plate trade in the late nineteenth century; supplemented this with a share of the market for projectiles and guns (where Firth's was well to the fore); and also catered for the
demand for other types of weaponry, so that companies such as Vickers
could supply virtually any type of ordnance. It stimulated metallurgical
innovation into new heat treatments, alloys, and production techniques.
It gave the town a far greater strategic importance, making Brown,
Cammell, and Vickers national names and bringing these firms into a
'special relationship' with the Government. They were transformed from
being merely steelmakers into integrated, if diverse, arms conglomerates
that were amongst the largest companies in the country, indeed in the
world (a trend examined in more detail in the next chapter). For above all,
the arms industry was global. This gave Sheffield opportunities for
greater international competitive advantage, even over countries such as
the United States, where military and imperial ambitions did not yet
dictate a large standing army or navy. Although foreign competitors in
France (Le Creusot) and Germany (Krupp's) occasionally made innovations ahead of Sheffield, the English town was the world's chief centre
for steel armaments manufacture in the late nineteenth century.

Here not much more than an impressionistic account can be given, but
the picture generally is one of intense experimentation and competition.
The battleground was armour-plate *versus* shell, with one Sheffield firm
devoting itself to producing a superior plate; whilst another tried to
destroy the results with more efficient projectiles. The fact that firms were
within walking distance of each other along the River Don intensified the
challenge.

In 1859–60 John Brown had led the way by pioneering the commercial
production of iron armour-plate in the United Kingdom—indeed his
puddling furnaces were built partly to satisfy this demand. By 1867 it was
reported that three-quarters of the British Navy ironclads were defended

---

[21] 'Enormous Casting at Sheffield', *SI*, 9 May 1863.

by armour-plates made at the Atlas Works. By then Brown's were said to be rolling some of the largest armour-plates in the world—21 tons—by a process that was clearly pushing the limits of available technology. A contemporary report describes how sixty men were needed to manipulate an ingot prior to rolling, who:

arranged themselves on each side of the furnace, as near to it as they could bear the heat. Then the doors were opened to their fullest and what had been a glare before and what had been a heat were quite eclipsed by the intense light and fervency with which the long tongues of flame leapt forth. In the midst of this great light lay a mass even whiter than the rest. To this some half-a-dozen men drew near. They were all attired in thin steel leggings, aprons of steel, and a thin curtain of steel wirework dropping over their faces like a long visor. All the rest of their bodies were muffled in thick, wet sacking. Thus protected, they managed, with the aid of a gigantic pair of forceps slung from a crane above, to work as it were amid the flames for a few seconds, and to nip the huge plate with the forceps. The signal was then given, and the whole mass of iron, fizzing, sparkling, and shooting out jets of lambent flame, was by the main force of chains attached to the steam rollers drawn forth from the furnace onto a long wrought-iron car.[22]

Cammell's, whose records survive for this period, also entered this market. Two things dominated the Cammell director's discussions by the 1860s—rails and armour—with the latter assuming increasing importance as the rail trade peaked in the early 1870s.[23] Its first orders were for English coastal defences: the use of more powerful guns increasing the need for the adoption of forts protected by massive casements of puddled iron and granite. By the late 1860s the armour-plate trade for ships was well under way, with orders not only from the Admiralty, but also from Denmark, Holland, Turkey, Russia, Spain, Japan, and Greece. By 1868 Cammell's had over 6,000 tons of plate on hand, with advance orders for nearly 5,000 tons.

The attractions of this business were obvious. When Brown's was founded as a limited company, armour-plate amounted to one-half of the firm's production and at least one-half of the turnover (see Table 2.3). This was the kind of trade that brought moderately prosperous businessmen like Brown unparalleled wealth. His stately pile, Endcliffe Hall, personal visits from Lord Palmerston and the Lords of the Admiralty, and the mayoralty and a knighthood were the visible signs of this success. But the arms trade also entailed risks. The companies operated in a market with monopsony conditions, serving a single, fickle, and often ruthless customer—Government. The leading arms firms soon found themselves tied to the ups and downs of a highly unpredictable weapons cycle. John

---

[22] 'Armour Plates at Atlas Works', *SI*, 12 Sept. 1867.

[23] Cammell-Laird Papers, Birkenhead. See also, 'The Cyclops Works Armour Plates', *SI*, 18 Nov. 1863; 'Opening of the Armour Plate Mill at Cyclops Works', *SI*, 21 Nov. 1863.

Table 2.3. *Turnover of John Brown & Co., 1865–1874 (£)*

	1865	1866	1867	1868	1869
General turnover	404,072	511,215	584,091	585,716	662,279
Armour-plate turnover	223,498	119,178	95,064	148,175	110,950
TOTAL	627,570	630,393	679,155	733,891	773,229
	1870	1871	1872	1873	1874
General turnover	751,719	797,358	1,159,999	1,353,021	1,055,011
Armour-plate turnover	177,436	152,721	251,691	212,513	211,245
TOTAL	929,155	950,079	1,411,690	1,565,534	1,266,256

Source: John Brown PLC, London. Transactions of Directors' Meetings, 1865+.

Brown had spent £200,000 in equipping his armour-plate mill—a colossal sum that unnerved his fellow Manchester-based directors, especially when plate orders suddenly fell. By 1871 they had forced him to resign. Cammell's, too, by 1868 was having to respond to Admiralty demands that the armour-plate makers be able to bend, fit, and drill even thicker plates for the shipyards. As it contemplated the expenditure of £7,000, the Cammell board found it was on a roundabout it dare not get off:

In this country [Brown] and ourselves are the only two houses now in the books of the Admiralty and the War Office . . . so that it may be truly said that the manufacture of armour plates is practically confined to the two houses, so far as the orders from our own Government are concerned, and it is of vital importance we preserve this position in order to maintain the good prices we are now getting and shall get for this class of work. To do this there is no alternative, but to meet the demands made upon us by adopting the means of finishing our armour as we are able to roll it, and thus keep faith with our deliveries, for unless this be done, the Admiralty will, we are assured, immediately proceed to encourage others to re-enter this trade and thus create anew a competition as will again result in loss and almost unremunerative prices. Again with such Governments as Russia, Austria, Greece, Turkey, Holland and Denmark, from all of whom we have good prospects of business, our established position with the English Government is of paramount importance to us . . .[24]

By the end of the 1870s, competition between Brown's and Cammell's had resulted in the next great English advance over foreign rivals—the mastering of the rolling of compound (steel-faced iron) plate. In 1877 Cammell's had 'no alternative but to place [itself] in competition with the other makers' here, too, laying down new planing shops in 1882, and

---

[24] Cammell, Directors' Minute Book, 5 Sept. 1868.

experimenting with various types of steel armour.[25] In 1884 Cammell's were contemplating a £45,000 hydraulic plant for steel forgings for guns and marine shafting, besides armour, so that the company should 'not lose the lead we have taken'.[26] By 1890 Brown and Cammell, alongside Vickers (who had entered the race in 1888 when the firm rolled its first plate), had developed the all-steel plate. The steady advance in metallurgical knowledge had made it possible to confer sufficient toughness on the solid steel plate through heat treatment, thus minimizing its liability to brittleness and cracking, while simultaneously increasing the resisting power with steel's higher tensile strength.

These improvements were spurred by corresponding developments in projectiles. Armour seems to have held an ascendancy over shells before about 1890, but innovations in this area were as plentiful as in plate. In armour-piercing projectile production—one of the most esoteric realms of the nineteenth-century steelmaker—the introduction of cast steel had produced shells with greater penetrative power.

A newcomer to the industry, Hadfield's Steel Foundry Co. (whose history is described below), began shell manufacture in 1880, when the Government needed shells to breach the new steel-faced armour-plate (made by the likes of Brown and Cammell) against which chilled iron Palliser shot was proving ineffective. French firms, such as Holtzer, were then leaders in armour-piercing shell manufacture. Robert Hadfield Sen. accepted the challenge and by 1885 had patented a cast steel 'compound armour-piercing shell', which had a combination of hardened steel point and resilient body. But not until 1888 was sufficient expertise acquired by the firm to execute a government order for 1,200 6-inch armour-piercing projectiles. Great technical difficulties were encountered in this pioneering use of crucible steel, which it was then believed would be unsuitable for these shells. Hadfield's eventual success was said to have been 'the result of chemical research into the action of often minute differences in proportions of alloys of iron and of the subsequent special heat-treatment the material receives'.[27] These new heat treatments led to sophisticated (and secret) ways of hardening the points of shells, allowing the production of more destructive missiles. By the 1880s, the leading Sheffield firms, such as Hadfield's and also Firth's, were moving rapidly ahead in this sphere and were to make even more advances after the 1890s.

Firth's were unstinting in their effort to cast the world's largest steel blocks for the most powerful guns. Their first steel gun was forged in 1852 at Claywheels Forge, Wadsley Bridge, which the firm rented throughout the later nineteenth century to roll its steel ingots. By the end of the 1850s,

[25] Ibid., 28 Dec. 1877.
[26] Ibid., Directors' Minute Book, 26 Nov. 1884.
[27] *The Times*, 21 Apr. 1904.

Firth's had installed two Nasmyth hammers, which were used to forge guns for Armstrong's and Whitworth's. In 1863 Firth's Norfolk Works were extended to include the West Gun Works and here 25-ton hammers were laid down in what was then considered a remarkable feat of engineering.[28] Prior to 1860, no gun was heavier than about 5 tons; by 1871, however, Firth's had cast the famous 'Woolwich Infant' gun of 35 tons, which reputedly involved the teeming of a thousand crucibles. In 1873 the construction of a 75-ton gun was proposed, and two years later the first 80-ton gun was actually completed. Once the Government had been persuaded that the inner tubes of guns should be made of steel instead of wrought iron, Firth's won the bulk of the orders and spent £100,000 on machinery for making steel tubes. The firm was also doing a good trade in Enfield steel rifle barrels, having installed several American boring machines in the 1860s, which enabled it to produce 300 rifle barrels a day.

Several of these armaments specialists also moved into the steel castings trade, which Sheffield began to exploit more fully after the 1870s. Despite the pioneei ng efforts of firms such as Vickers in the 1850s, the market for such castings had remained a small one, due to a widespread belief among customers that steel needed to be mechanically worked (forged) to impart the required qualities—a procedure impossible with casting. Evidently, some of the early hopes for steel castings had not been realized because of the persistent technical difficulties encountered in making complex steel shapes. One of the city's leading practitioners of steel casting later recalled that there was always 'a glamour over the practice of steel casting', but that, 'probably more heartbreaking and disappointment have occurred in the exercise of this art than in any branch of the steel industry'.[29] The experience of the Butchers, who were involved in an unsuccessful American steel castings works in Philadelphia in 1867, shows that the business was still a hit-or-miss affair.[30] Even in 1869, it was said, a sound steel casting was 'an object of considerable attraction and interest. It is a difficult thing to make, and there are but few makers who can produce it with an approach to perfection, even if all

---

[28] Firth's expansion stimulated other firms in the sector, such as J. M. Stanley & Co., which supplied Firth's with the large iron anvil blocks for its hammers. One involved a casting of 100 tons. See 'Enormous Casting at the Midland Works', *SI*, 20 Feb. 1863; 'Enormous Casting at Sheffield', *SI*, 9 May 1863.

[29] R. A. Hadfield, presidential address, *JISI* 67/1 (1905), 91–2.

[30] G. Tweedale, *Sheffield Steel and America* (Cambridge, 1987), 113–15. The Philadelphia venture was the William Butcher Steel Works, named (I once believed) after the noted Sheffield tool and steelmaker, William Butcher (*c*.1791–1870). But, confusingly, there appears to have been another William Butcher in the family—possibly a nephew of *the* William Butcher's brother, Samuel. It was William Butcher Jun., who was active in Philadelphia, and after whom the Works was christened (with the American interests making the most of the famous name). See Charles D. Wrege and Ronald D. Greenwood, *Frederick W. Taylor: The Father of Scientific Management* (Homewood, Ill., 1990), 9–29. I am grateful for Robert Kanigel for bringing this to my attention.

chances are favourable; whilst it is doubtful if any steelmaker can at this moment consider the process of casting steel fully at his command.'[31] It seems likely that in the 1850s and 1860s the Sheffield iron castings firms, such as John Crowley & Co., were as important in the town as the steel casters.[32]

The breakthrough in the steel castings industry came with a better understanding of the chemistry involved—in particular the addition of aluminium and silicon to prevent the 'honeycombing' that occurred when gases formed in the cooling steel—and the introduction of large-scale melting capabilities with the Bessemer and open-hearth furnaces. Sheffield firms were in the forefront. By 1873 one writer was surprised: 'to learn how many and varied are the uses these castings are applied to, from reaping machine fingers to screw propellers for steam ships . . . In fact, crucible steel castings are fast replacing metal work and wrought iron forgings, their superior qualities, viz., greater tenacity, strength and lightness, giving them special advantages over other metals.'[33]

These comments referred to Hadfield's Steel Foundry, the early history of which provides a perfect example of a highly innovative Sheffield firm responding to the fierce competitive environment of Sheffield steel after the 1860s.

The Foundry was started in 1872 in Newhall Road, Attercliffe, by Robert Hadfield (1832–88), a local rate-collector, who had acquired capital in property and land speculation. After acquiring the services of John Mallaband (1831–97), who had been a steel-moulder at Vickers, Hadfield launched his firm into the steel castings business. Cast steel mining-wheels for the South African diamond mines were amongst the first large orders. These were successfully executed, though the firm soon ran into a technical problem with the manufacture of large hydraulic cylinders for the presses that rammed down cotton bales. Mallaband later described the 'terrible fix' that the firm got into when making these cylinders, an episode that nearly broke his heart and ruined the company.[34] Despite using the tried and trusted crucible process, Mallaband had been unable to produce watertight cylinders that would hold the pressure. 'Thoroughly demoralised and utterly cast down', Robert Hadfield Sen. and Mallaband nevertheless surmounted the difficulty by a rule-of-thumb adjustment in the temper of the steel. With the production of these cylinders under way, Hadfield's turned the corner and began expanding rapidly: by 1878 a Bessemer converter had been installed; by 1885 Robert Hadfield had

[31] F. Kohn, *Iron and Steel Manufacture* (London, 1869), 216.

[32] 'John Crowley & Co.'s Concentration at Meadowhall', *IMR* 21 (1 Nov. 1895), 19693–4; 'The Late W. H. Crowley', *IMR* 24 (1 Sept. 1898), 23171–2.

[33] *Griffith's Guide to the Iron Trade of Great Britain* (1867: repr. Newton Abbot, 1967), 202.

[34] SCL Hadfield Papers. J. Mallaband to R. A. Hadfield, 6 May 1895. See also G. Tweedale, 'Pioneering in Steel Casting: A Melter's Reminiscences, ca. 1856–70s', *JHMS* (forthcoming).

patented his compound armour-piercing shell, signalling the beginning of a major involvement in armaments; and in 1888 the firm became a limited company with £110,000 capital and a workforce of 400–500, and with the son of the founder, Robert A. Hadfield, as chairman and managing director.[35]

Vickers, Brown's, and Jessop's also entered the steel castings trade, along with other firms. For example, the tool steelmakers, Samuel Osborn's, in 1885 purchased Samuel Butcher's old Rutland Works in Neepsend for the production of steel castings, so launching an important line of business for the firm. William Cook's began casting steel from crucibles in about 1886 at the Glasgow Steel & File Works in Washford Road (the name of the manufactory a reminder of the Scottish roots of this firm). In 1891 Joseph Trippett founded the Standard Steel Castings Works in Attercliffe and began manufacturing crucible steel castings, with the help of his son.

By now the steel castings industry had largely lived down the trials and tribulations of its early days and the Sheffield industry had emerged as a world leader. The castings from its foundries were now used in a number of increasingly critical applications, such as in ships' stems, rudders, and stern-pieces.

FURTHER EXPANSION IN SPECIAL STEELS

The arrival of heavy steelmaking in the 1860s meant that the industrial landscape of Sheffield became even more complex. As the town absorbed the latest bulk steelmaking technologies, and large-scale business spread into the East End along the Don Valley, its reputation as the major world steelmaking centre was enhanced. Across the Atlantic, Pittsburgh would soon challenge Sheffield's dominance, but even the American centre was unable to match the depth of industrial expertise in Sheffield. Meanwhile in Europe, Germany, and France were yet to make any serious inroads into Sheffield's special steel's market.

Bessemer believed (or perhaps hoped) that cheaper methods of making steel would eventually make the crucible process redundant. Convinced that his converter could make good-quality tool steel, he had little patience with the more conservative Sheffield steelmasters. According to Bessemer, 'we could, and did, produce commercially crucible cast steel of great purity, and of any precise and predetermined degree of carburisation, with greater accuracy than was obtained by the method employed

[35] G. Tweedale, 'The Metallurgist as Entrepreneur: The Career of Sir Robert Hadfield', *JHMS* 26 (1992), 19–30.

to produce crucible steel in Sheffield'.[36] Bessemer's confidence must have increased when he saw signs that the grip of the crucible on the lower-quality end of the market was slackening. The time-consuming process of converting Swedish iron into blister steel declined after the 1870s once it was found that bar iron and cast iron could be melted in one operation to achieve the same result (the cast iron providing the necessary carbon). The characteristic bottle-shaped converting furnaces remained part of the Sheffield landscape, but they had reached their maximum extent and henceforth began to disappear. Puddled steel, Russian iron, and even some of the better qualities of Yorkshire bar were substituted for the expensive Swedish grades, especially by firms such as Vickers, which were producing some of the lower qualities of crucible steel. Even the makers of top-quality crucible steel supplemented their output with the processing of Bessemer and Siemens steel in various ways. Bessemer billets were bought locally from firms such as John Brown, or they might be imported from abroad, from countries such as Sweden. Sanderson Brothers, for example, utilized bulk steels to keep their steam-powered hammers and rolling mills (which had a higher output than the old water-driven mills) at full stretch.[37]

After reaching a peak of approximately 130,000 tons in about 1870, Sheffield cementation and crucible steel production began declining to about a third of that amount by 1890 (though briefly in the early 1880s output again surpassed 100,000 tons). The reasons for this are complex. Bulk steelmaking took away some of the market for the lower qualities of tool steel; and the impact of the Great Depression may also be reflected in the decline. By the end of the 1860s the lucrative American market became increasingly difficult to penetrate by Sheffield steel and cutlery firms. An influential steel protectionist lobby, a high tariff, and a more rigorous United States customs administration served notice that Sheffield's steel 'monopoly' in America was about to end.[38] A sea change was taking place: Sheffield would need to adapt to new technologies and find new markets.

But this did not mean that the crucible process became redundant. Bessemer's claims not only proved exaggerated, but they also rebounded on him. The Bessemer and Siemens furnaces by dramatically increasing steel output simply expanded the market for tool steel. As one Sheffield manufacturer highlighted in 1884:

The commoner qualities of crucible cast steel have been to a large extent super-seded by Bessemer and Siemens steel, but the enormous quantities made by the latter processes have required . . . such a large quantity of the better qualities of crucible cast steel, that the total amount of the latter now produced in various

---

[36] Bessemer, *Autobiography*, 215, 180–8.
[37] G. B. Callan, *Secrets of Sheffield Steelmakers* (Sheffield, 1993), 28–9.
[38] Miles Taylor, 'The Sheffield Steel Inquiry of 1869', *THAS* 15 (1989), 38–47.

parts of the world is probably double that which was required before the birth of its rivals.[39]

In other words, the production of ships, bridges, and steam locomotives—or whatever—demanded more chisels, more drills, and ever more efficient turning tools. This was especially so, in view of the development of British engineering. Despite the 'genesis' of American competition in light engineering, in the heavy sectors of the industry—the building of railway locomotives and rolling stock, and textile-machine making—Britain still held a predominant position between the 1850s and 1870s.[40] And even the successes of the 'American System of Manufactures' were built partly on the best grades of Sheffield tool steel. Thus after 1890, Sheffield crucible steel production steadily began to grow again, reaching 80,000 tons by 1900.

Even the largest firms, such as Vickers and John Brown's, retained their interest in the Huntsman method. Edward Vickers noted that crucible steel 'had not only maintained itself against the opposition of all cheaper processes, but the production of crucible steel at [the River Don] Works was [in 1870] almost double of what it had been at the start of the company'.[41] John Brown's, though a pioneer in bulk steelmaking, also found that the crucible still held 'its own for the production of the finest classes of tool steel'.[42] The company's position as an integrated steel and engineering company (and therefore tool steel user) reinforced its involvement with every type and quality of tool steel.

With bulk steel production expanding so rapidly, far from destroying the base of Sheffield's fortunes, it stimulated further expansion, presented new openings, and allowed Sheffield to upgrade its competitive advantage. There would be new opportunities for special steels in Sheffield (and not only for firms such as John Brown's with established tool steelmaking capacity). The evidence for the period between about 1860 and 1893 shows this clearly, with both a significant number of new entrants to the tool steel trade itself, and with others keen to open up new lines of business.

One newcomer was William Edgar Allen (1837–1915), who had perhaps the most exotic background of any nineteenth-century Sheffield steelmaker. Born in London into poor circumstances, Allen was the illegitimate descendant of the wealthy Russian Rudelhoff family, who had fled

[39] H. Seebohm, *On the Manufacture of Crucible Cast Steel* (Sheffield, 1884), 4. Reprint of an Iron & Steel Institute address (*JISI* 25/2 (1884), 372–96. See also Seebohm's letter to *The Times*, 30 Sept. 1884, after Bessemer had contested his views. Seebohm doubtless enjoyed pointing out to Bessemer (and Siemens) that they were the Sheffield tool steel trades' 'greatest benefactors'.

[40] A. E. Musson, 'The Engineering Industry', in Roy Church (ed.), *The Dynamics of Victorian Business* (London, 1980), 87–106.

[41] J. D. Scott, *Vickers: A History* (London, 1962), 17.

[42] *John Brown & Company Ltd. 1864–1924*, 48.

at the time of Peter the Great. Brought up by an aunt (his mother died when he was an infant), Allen was educated in Paris and then began travelling in Europe to acquire languages and business experience. Whether due to his foreign roots or own inclinations, Edgar Allen became a remarkable linguist—an unusual quality in a Sheffield steel manufacturer. By 1862 he was the Continental representative for Ibbotson Bros., the Sheffield steel- and toolmakers. Here he met another traveller, George Rose Jones (*c*.1832–1902), and together they founded their own partnership in Well Meadow Street in 1868. Combining their own capital, they began manufacturing hand-cut files, a little tool steel, and circular saws. Allen concentrated on sales, especially in the European market, where 'he was away for ten months in the year . . . [accepting] orders whatever they were for. Pears' soap, patent remedies for sea sickness, steam-rollers, axes, files, saws, springs, bolts, nuts, rivets, shovels, hammers, picks, bicycles, salt water in barrels for the hardening of steel, glass tumblers, hatchets, all figured in the firm's order books'.[43] Not surprisingly, in an 1868 trade directory Allen was describing the firm as 'Manufacturers and Shipping Merchants'.

But Allen's steelmaking operations soon became paramount. In 1883 he and Jones quarrelled and the partnership ended: Jones set up his own steel and file business; Allen continued alone. In 1884, when the number of hands at Edgar Allen & Co. was about fifty, he acquired new crucible steelmaking capacity at Bridge Street (close to the River Don at Neepsend) and opened a large office in Savile Street. In 1886 Allen expanded further by buying a small crucible steelworks, originally owned by Hoole, Staniforth, & Co. In 1890 these developments culminated in the formation of a private limited company with a capital of £100,000, after Allen had taken Robert Woodward and Alfred Ernest Wells (both from Samuel Osborn's) into partnership under his own chairmanship. In the following year it was agreed that a new works should be built at Tinsley (then a small village about four miles from the centre of Sheffield), where Allen took over a deserted wagon works and begin centralizing the firm's steelmaking operations around a new foundry.

With his mysterious foreign background (which he took pains to hide), Allen was something of an 'outsider' in Sheffield steelmaking. So too were a number of German steel- and toolmakers, who decided to seek their fortunes in Sheffield. We have noted that German technologists were active in helping Sheffield launch its steel castings industry. Interestingly, Vickers' success at this time, especially in America, owed much to the talents of a German Jew, Ernst Benzon, who eventually became chairman of the company. But generally, the German component in the town's

---

[43] *Histories of Firms: Sheffield & District Survey* (1958), 6. On Allen, see also E. N. Simons, 'The Story of a Great Steel Firm', *Edgar Allen News* (Dec. 1953–Oct. 1958).

industry has rarely been commented upon, many Sheffielders past and present believing that making steel was an inborn talent. Yet in this period of expansion of the Sheffield steel trades, German immigrants exerted an influence that was—as in other branches of British industry—out of all proportion to their numbers. It was in tool steel manufacture that they made their greatest impact.

In 1865 a new crucible steelmaking business was founded by Henry Seebohm (1832–95) and George F. Dieckstahl, both men with German ancestry, who arrived in Sheffield in about the mid-1850s. The exact details are obscure, but Dieckstahl joined the crucible steel and tool firm of Moss & Gamble as a salesman in Russia and Germany. Seebohm was related to a prominent Bradford family of Quakers, his father having come to England from Germany in 1815. (His brother was the English economic historian, Frederic Seebohm.) Family connections with the Doncasters, the steelmakers and converters—who were also Quakers—led to practical and technical experience in the steel trade before Seebohm joined the small crucible steelmakers of George Fisher (founded in 1842). Seebohm and Dieckstahl began by acquiring an 18-hole furnace in Leadmill Street, a location within walking distance of the Midland Station. Dieckstahl's salesmanship proved indispensable to the business in its early days. A large export trade was built up (armaments and rifle steels featuring in the firm's early records), enabling the firm to move to its permanent base— the Dannemora Steel Works—in the Wicker in 1870. Another German, Robert Schott, who had been a Continental traveller for Vickers, also joined the firm at about this time. (It has been suggested that Benzon may have persuaded Schott to come to Sheffield originally.) Another German who worked for the firm was George Grafenhain (c.1865–1934), a near relative of Dieckstahl, who joined the firm aged 19 and whose linguistic abilities soon made him Continental representative and director.

Perhaps the most interesting character was Seebohm. While he built up a considerable reputation as a tool steelmaker, he became internationally recognized as an ornithologist. He undertook regular expeditions to Germany, Greece, Russia, and Japan in search of specimens and wrote a number of standard textbooks on British and Siberian birds. Later in life he preferred ornithology to steel and in 1889 retired to concentrate on his bird collections, handing the business over to Schott (who was assisted by Edward Sonne of Zurich as Continental manager). However, lest it be imagined that Seebohm was a fair example of the decline of the English industrial spirit, he also brought his scientific bent to bear on the steel business. He was the first to publicize the carbon content of his tool steels—a move that was deeply unpopular amongst those committed to the mystique and secrecy of the crucible—and was one of the first to analyse steel in the laboratory (see below). Though not a steel melter by training, he immersed himself in the technical aspects of crucible steel manufacture: so much so that he became an authority on the subject and one of the crucible's most eloquent spokesmen. Seebohm recognized that, until a better method was found, crucible steel would always hold its place for tool steel manufacture. Confident that this niche in the market was secure, Seebohm, like other firms such as Sanderson Bros., concentrated on the top end of the market by producing mostly the finer grades of tool steel.

The steady growth of Seebohm & Dieckstahl vindicated this stategy. By 1887, new markets, especially in America, had been found and the firm was destined for a surge of expansion as it plundered the demand for crucible steel, which showed no sign of abating. A member of the firm later wrote an informative account of those days when:

crucible steel was used for everything; even the bullets for the first Nordenfeldt gun were made from crucible steel, carefully annealed so that it could be turned in automatics to the correct shape of the bullet. The United States had not begun to make steel for itself, neither had Germany, France, nor Italy. Every Monday morning large orders, running into enormous tonnages, were received from Germany for crucible steel for files. In those days all except the largest and common files . . . were made from crucible steel.

When the Japanese Army was being organised in the early seventies the whole of the steel in the rifles, including the gun barrel, bayonet and breech, was made from crucible steel which had been melted in Sheffield. The largest single order that I remember in those times was one for about 2,000 tons, but orders from the USA for 500 or 600 tons of crucible steel for making tools were not uncommon. In busy years every single melting hole in Sheffield was occupied and working to full capacity, and even then it was not unusual to be six or seven months behind in one's orders in the melting department.[44]

This attracted other Germans anxious to better themselves. Carl Wilhelm Kayser (1841–1906), a scissor-smith, came to England in 1860 'with the simple object of learning and studying the Sheffield manufacture', partly because at that time in his 'neighbourhood at Solingen, there was only one party who kept a carriage and pair'.[45] After a brief return visit to Solingen, Kayser became a traveller with Cocker Bros., the Sheffield wire manufacturers. Naturalized in 1864 (when he became Charles William), Kayser's energy soon brought him to the attention of Wilson, Hawksworth, Ellison, & Co., a steel and cutlery business that had its origins in the 1820s. With its cutlery trade hit by American tariffs, Kayser was recruited in 1869 to develop trade with the Continent and rescue the firm from threatened bankruptcy. On Kayser's initiative and in

---

[44] Lord Riverdale (Arthur Balfour), 'Sheffield Steel: Memories of Fifty Years', *Quality*, 7 (May 1936), 300.

[45] BLPES. Tariff Commission Papers, TC3 1/12. Kayser, 'Evidence', 13.

agreement with the local banks, a major strategic decision was made—to concentrate on steel rather than cutlery—a move which began to turn the business round. Kayser became a partner in the firm in 1872, and when the articles were revised in 1888 it was restyled as Kayser, Ellison, & Co. Ltd. A worthy reports that by 1893 the 'firm eventually came into the sole control of this one-time Prussian boy. Even then he remained traveller, doing prodigious work.' Kayser also recognized the primacy of crucible steel manufacture and his firm became noted for it. Indeed, cast steel was said to be Kayser's 'one great hobby'.[46] According to one of his staff, Kayser was 'one of the few factory directors or owners in Sheffield who really understood steelmaking and the foundations on which the reputation of Sheffield steel had been built'.[47] With his Solingen background, Kayser soon developed steel for hollow ground razors and several other crucible steels that were to give long service to the firm. Rigid quality control in the Sheffield tradition was the watchword.

The most successful of the German immigrants was (Sir) Joseph Jonas (1845–1921). A native of Bingen-on-Rhine (then Grand Duchy of Hesse), Jonas had served an apprenticeship with an iron and hardware firm in Cologne, before working for an iron and steel works in Westphalia. He came to England at the age of 21 in 1867, after refusing to serve in the Prussian army, since as he put it, 'from my early days [I] have always detested the Prussian military spirit'.[48] After two years in London, Jonas arrived in Sheffield and followed the familiar route for an immigrant German—he became a traveller—before launching his own business in 1870, when he opened the Continental Steel Works in Attercliffe. In about 1876 (when he became naturalized), Jonas teamed up with a local land valuer and farmer, Robert Colver (1842–1916). The firm, Jonas & Colver, soon established itself at the forefront of the town's crucible steel trade: in 1870 Jonas had launched the business with only 15 hands, but by 1892, when it was converted into a private limited company, it was capitalized at £125,000 and employed about 700. This success seems to have been a direct consequence of Jonas's emphasis on scientific methods, superior business organization, and marketing skills. The life histories of Jonas, Seebohm and Dieckstahl, and Kayser parallel the careers of other major German immigrants in British industry, such as Lord Hirst, Sir Ernest Cassel, and others.[49]

Sheffield-born entrepreneurs were also active in expanding the town's crucible steelmaking capacity. In 1872 Messrs. Vessey and Friend estab-

---

[46] J. H. Stainton, *The Making of Sheffield 1865–1914* (Sheffield, 1924), 336.
[47] H. Brearley, *Stainless Pioneer* (Sheffield, 1989), 37. See also *Histories of Famous Firms* (1958), 4.
[48] SCL Bound Volume, 'Biographical Notices Relating to Sheffield'.
[49] 'Mr Joseph Jonas of Sheffield', *IMR* 18 (1 Nov. 1892), 16015–6; 'Mr Joseph Jonas of Sheffield', *IMR* 30 (Dec. 1904), 893–4; *Men of the Period* (London, 1896), 71–5.

lished a crucible steel business in Denby Street. By the 1890s Friend had died, leaving John Vessey (d. 1896) to take over the firm with the help of his sons. In 1876 John James Saville (1848–1902) and G. G. Coppel founded the firm of J. J. Saville, later erecting the Triumph Works for tool steel manufacture in Shoreham Street, near the Midland Station.[50] In 1877 Muxlow & Knott founded the Hope Steel Works in Harrow Street: it was made a limited company in 1900.[51] Thomas Swift Levick (1845–1926), who had been a general manager of Cammell's spring department and then a traveller for Seebohm & Dieckstahl, in 1883 began his own steel and file business in Arundel Street. In 1891 he formed Swift Levick & Sons, which operated from the Clarence Steel and File Works in Attercliffe. Harry Fisher (1850–1924), who had earlier worked for Burys & Co., partnered Archibald Buchanan in forming a crucible steel works of the same name at the Kingfisher Works in 1889: he produced steel for tools, and also steel sheets for lagging cylinders and steel beater plates for threshing machines.[52]

The early history of these firms and their owners is often obscure, but their emergence shows the vitality of the crucible steel sector. No detailed sociological or economic analysis of these firms is needed. All were small, family-controlled concerns, usually founded by Sheffielders—or at least, by men with some experience and training in the local industry or by those (such as the Germans) who were willing to absorb the ethic of high quality. They probably started with relatively modest amounts of capital saved by the firm's members, who often built up their wealth as travellers. Each was committed to a high-quality product aimed at a particular niche in the market. Vessey's was devoted to the manufacture of steel for all kinds of cutlery, especially pocket-knives, surgical instruments, razors, edge tools, and machine knives. Saville's concentrated on tool steel for engineering applications and had its own file shops. Swift Levick also made files, but in addition was noted for its drill steels and chisels, punches, taps, and other engineers' tools. Sheffield's version of personal capitalism in steel manufacture, active since before 1800, was still serving it well in the second half of the nineteenth century.

The creation of these new firms stimulated innovation in Sheffield, since the new companies served new segments and tried new approaches that foreign rivals failed to recognize or to which they were too inflexible to respond. The emergence of the steel castings industry, and the establishment of firms such as Hadfield's, Cook's, and Trippett's has already been noted. The crucible also allowed other new markets and fashions to be exploited.

[50] *SDT*, 30 Apr. 1902.
[51] Ibid., 23 Sept. 1939.
[52] *IMR* 15 (1 Feb. 1890), 12687; *IMR* 35 (1 Aug. 1909), 477–8; *IMR* 49 (1 Apr. 1924), 1387–8.

The railways, besides using large quantities of bulk steel, were still major customers for special steels and products. In Sheffield the Turton family (of Sheaf Works fame) in 1860 began operating a crucible furnace in Cross Smithfield. In 1871 the firm of Turton Bros. & Matthews was formed, when the Turton's links through marriage to the Matthews family (one of the town's most prominent industrial dynasties) led to Thomas Bright Matthews joining the partnership. Already established as steel- and filemakers, in the 1880s they began making shear blades and springs. They advertised coil springs by 1876; and in 1879 they transferred their steelmaking activities to Neepsend. In 1882 the firm acquired the web-section railway spring patent of the London engineer I. A. Timmis, and made a great success of producing it in the finest Swedish steel. Meanwhile, George Turton (d. 1907), who had spent twenty-five years as a traveller for the steel- and toolmaking firm of Ibbotson Bros., set up his own business in Savile Street in about 1878 to manufacture his patent railway buffer. In the early 1890s the firm became known as Turton, Platts, & Co. Ltd., when the founder took William Platts (d. 1908) as partner.

The growth of the engineering, transport, and extractive industries was reflected in the growth of Askham Bros. & Wilson Ltd. Founded in 1868 by Philip U. Askham (d. 1905), a former John Brown apprentice, and his brother John, this company's crucible steel output was directed first into the manufacture of tool steel, and then later crucible steel tramway track-points and crossings. It also specialized in stone-breakers, crushing and separating machinery, disintegrators, pulverizers, wrought-iron-cased elevators, patent dust-proof machinery for reducing material to fine powder, and gold-mining machinery.[53]

Several firms began the manufacture of steel wire, steel rope, and rods. Samuel Fox, who began crucible steelmaking in 1860, did not abandon the process when he became a Bessemer licencee. At the end of the 1860s, Fox was still advertising steel wire of 'every description'. John Henry Andrew (1824–84), a self-made Sheffielder 'rising by his own industry from the ranks of labour',[54] worked his way through apprenticeship and partnership to found his own steelmaking business in Malinda Street. In 1870 he opened the Toledo Works in Neepsend Lane, known as J. H. Andrew & Co., and began wire rod production with 120–44 crucible holes. American bridge builders were amongst the firm's major customers. Overseas markets were also tapped by John Shaw Ltd., which had been founded in the 1820s. In the early 1860s John Shaw, the son of the founder, took over the business, and began pioneering the manufacture of steel wire rope.[55]

[53] *The Century's Progress* (London, 1893), 115.
[54] *SDT*, 8 Sept. 1894.
[55] *SDT*, 31 Dec. 1931, 31 Dec. 1935.

The market for cast steel wire was large enough to support another new entrant to the trade in 1874. This was Arthur Lee (1842–1918), who had moved to Sheffield in 1854 from Wakefield (where his family were involved in the worsted business) to become the American representative for Moss & Gamble. In 1874 Lee acquired the controlling interest in the Crown Steel & Wire Mills in Bessemer Road, which had a thriving business in cast steel wire for the ropes drawing ploughs between agricultural steam engines and for hauling coal from the mines. By 1888 this business (soon to be named Arthur Lee & Sons) had expanded to make cold-rolled strip for bicycle frames and wheels, and for the latest spoked-wheel wire. In addition, notes the company's historian: 'A large amount of the daily production of the Crown Works went into articles of fashion. The crinoline was in vogue for ladies at that time and back in 1887 the company had built a cold rolling mill which could produce the steel hoops forming the shape of the gowns. This extra capacity and specialised product knowledge created new opportunities for transatlantic trading.'[56] In 1891 new capacity was purchased at Burton Weir, Brightside, and business was expanding rapidly.

Not suprisingly, the growth in steel capacity demanded new plant for converting, forging, and rolling. In 1872 George Senior & Sons Ltd. was founded at Ponds Forge, a site facing the Midland Station that had been a location for forging activity since 1737. The founder, George Senior (1838–1915), was the son of a Bradfield nailmaster, who had acquired practical steel experience at Parkin's of Middlewood. A traditional family-controlled firm, Senior's specialized in hire-work: but it also entered the sales side by converting iron and producing crucible steel. George Senior concentrated on importing Swedish charcoal iron, especially for the production of medium-temper blister bars for shear steel; and the firm additionally sold Swedish Bessemer steel.[57] Also in 1872, the Sheffield Forge & Rolling Mills Co. Ltd. augmented the town's forging capacity. It was sited in Millsands and occupied the bankrupt works of John and William Charles. Capitalized at £100,000, the Sheffield Forge appears to have had an uneven start, but by 1891 the output was 70 tons a month, with 170 hands.[58]

In 1873 the Hallamshire Steel & File Co. was founded in Neepsend with capital of £60,000 (£45,000 paid up) by William Smith, a man known as the

[56] *Lee Steel 1874–1974* (Sheffield, 1974), 7.

[57] W. T. Pike, *Sheffield at the Opening of the 20th Century* (Brighton, 1901), 79; Eric Stubbs interview, 13 Apr. 1992.

[58] *SDT*, 30 Dec. 1926, 31 Dec. 1929. John and William Charles had taken over Vickers' old site in Millsands and had been one of the foremost crucible steel firms of the day—with 95 crucible holes and five cementation furnaces—but the partnership did not run smoothly and John Charles built the Kelham Works.

'General'. The business, originally known as Earl, Smith, & Co., appears to have been a typical Sheffield hire-worker: a firm which mostly forged and rolled for others, but also made some of its own steel and tools. Initially, the plant consisted of cogging, bar, sheet, and rod mills—one of which was described as the first in the country to be equipped for continuous cogging. There were also 24 crucible holes (which were in use until 1900), and a forge and a file shop, which used outworkers in places such as Grenoside. It sold a wide range of steel—cast, shear, blister, spring, and its own 'Silver' steel—and tools (files and hammers) both at home, on the Continent, and in America, where its trade was said to have been considerable. Meanwhile, the rod mill made everything from nails to needles. Pontefract-born John Hunt (c.1838–1903), who joined the firm in the 1860s, became its able managing director.[59]

Also providing rolling facilities to the district's steel producers, was the business of George Clark (1857–1939), who entered the trade in a modest way in about 1883 and built up a business as a shovel plate manufacturer. In 1893 George Clark (Sheffield) Ltd. was formed, with a rod mill at Penistone Road and a works at Middlewood, named the North British Steel Works. Sheet steel was supplied to the light trades and the re-rollers.[60] Finally, the Wardsend Steel Co. had taken over an ancient water-powered site at Wadsley Bridge and by 1870 was describing itself as a roller, tilter, forger, and shear steelmaker.

The overall picture is one of considerable growth in the special steel trades, with a vigorous development of new firms—this despite the growth of foreign competition and the onset of the Great Depression in the 1870s. Moreover, established firms, such as Huntsman, Sanderson, Butcher, Bedford, and Marsh Bros., also continued to do well. For example, the special steel department at Marsh Bros. grew markedly after 1870: for a time, the melting was given out to Marriott & Atkinson at the Fitzalan Works, but in 1890 the partners at Marsh Bros. purchased a 20-hole melting furnace at Mary Street, where all its melting operations were centralized. Sanderson Bros.' trade also expanded steadily in the 1870s, with advances evenly split between America, Europe, and England; and there were large additions to the firm's crucible melting capacity at the Darnall Works, which by the mid-1870s had 132 coke-melting holes and also gas furnaces equal to the output of a further 60 coke-holes. In 1876, Sandersons reacted to the American tariff on English tool steel by forming its own subsidiary in Syracuse, New York (discussed in Chapter 3). John Bedford & Sons, which had been formed in 1871 when John Bedford (1815–98) brought his sons into the business he had started at the Lion

[59] SCL Hallamshire Steel & File Co. Directors' Minute Books; *SDT*, 24 Mar. 1903; 'The General Saw Years Ahead', *SDT*, 29 Sept. 1949.
[60] *SDT*, 31 Dec. 1925, 31 Dec. 1929, 31 Dec. 1930, 29 Dec. 1993.

Works in Mowbray Street, also successfully captured markets for crucible steel and tools.

The Sheffield crucible steel trade was still evolving and becoming more concentrated. According to one estimate, by the early 1870s there were some 180 crucible steel producers in Sheffield, with a total capacity of some 3,500–4,000 melting holes; and with the five leading firms perhaps responsible for about half the town's crucible steel output.[61] Fortunes could still be made in the crucible steel trade, in the days when a 12-hole crucible furnace, it was said, would run a carriage and pair. As Pollard has highlighted, the Bessemer and Siemens revolution in the 1860s and 1870s, which had turned the bulk steelmakers into giant concerns, 'had not greatly affected the makers of special steel and alloy steels of Sheffield . . . [who] . . . guaranteeing the quality of their own special brands, held their own and even strengthened their position as world trade in cutlery and tools grew, and as new alloys were discovered'.[62]

ALLOY STEELS AND THE BEGINNINGS OF RESEARCH AND DEVELOPMENT

The expanding market for the ordinary varieties of carbon tool steel probably guaranteed Sheffield a steady share of the world's business in this period, given its virtuosity with the crucible, competitive pricing and extensive sales network, and the fact that such a material was the basis for cutlery and tools. But in retrospect, it is apparent that after 1860, with other nations such as Germany and America beginning to catch up with Sheffield by founding their own crucible steel industries, only continued innovation in special steels could retain Sheffield's lead. This was because, having settled many of the problems involved in the *production* of steel, the way was now open for investigators intent on changing the *nature* of steel itself. The next sixty years were to see a period of intensive innovation in the field of special steels, a period as revolutionary in its own way as anything associated with bulk steelmaking (though this has not prevented historians from largely ignoring it). By 1914 most of the major alloy steels had appeared—steels which owed their remarkable properties to elements other than carbon. Integral to this development was the beginnings of scientific steelmaking: in modern parlance, research and development (R&D) became a crucial factor in commercial success.

Before examining Sheffield industry in this regard, two points should be underlined to provide some perspective. Firstly, steelmaking was

[61] J. G. Timmins, 'Concentration and Integration in the Sheffield Crucible Steel Industry', *Business History*, 24 (Mar. 1982), 61–78.
[62] S. Pollard, *Three Centuries of Sheffield Steel* (Sheffield, 1954), 46.

dominated by the rule-of-thumb before the 1860s. In fact, despite the contribution of the chemist to the success of the Siemens and Bessemer processes, even by about 1880 the impact of science upon steelmaking was still very small. By then steelmaking institutions and journals were beginning to play a role in the dissemination of knowledge, but the contents of the early issues of the *Journal of the Iron and Steel Institute*, for example, show that in the 1870s and 1880s there was little discussion of metallurgical problems. Process technology provided the core subject for most of the debates, and reading them it is clear that steelmakers were still searching for a common vocabulary to describe steel. The length of time it took the chemists to solve Bessemer's phosphorus problem highlights the backward state of metallurgical theory. Metallurgy provided neither a training nor a career. The Royal School of Mines in London was beginning to make a contribution in that direction, especially under its distinguished head John Percy; but it was peripheral to events in the manufacturing districts, such as Sheffield. Here the opportunities for a scientific education were limited, since, as one writer put it in 1843, 'the town has little to boast in the cultivation of science'.[63] To the melters in the steel furnaces it made little difference: they continued to judge carbon percentage by fracture with a wondrous accuracy that made chemical tests (ten guineas for a straightforward analysis in the 1870s, when £60 bought a ton of the best tool steel) an expensive luxury. These traditional methods were to survive well into the twentieth century.[64]

Secondly, there had, not surprisingly, been virtually no progress before the 1860s in the development of alloy steels. Michael Faraday had conducted a series of pathbreaking experiments in the early 1820s, with steels containing, *inter alia*, silver, platinum, and rhodium—partly as an attempt to improve their corrosion-resistance. Despite enlisting the help of Sheffield steelmakers such as Sanderson Bros., commercial success eluded Faraday. In Sheffield itself, it was slowly beginning to dawn on steelmakers that the addition of various 'physics' to the crucible during the melt could impart special properties to the steel or prevent undesirable defects. In 1839, for example, Josiah Heath had patented his 'carburet of manganese', which improved the welding quality of crucible steel and allowed the utilization of the cheaper grades of Swedish steel—an idea that seems to have been enthusiastically taken up in Sheffield. But the idea of chemically altering steel so that its characteristics

[63] G. Calvert Holland, *The Vital Statistics of Sheffield* (Sheffield, 1843), 13. Added Holland: 'The town has a philosophical and literary institution-museum, and a society for the study and encouragement of works of art; but these do not receive that liberal support which they deserve.'

[64] G. Tweedale, 'Science, Innovation and the "Rule of Thumb": The Development of British Metallurgy to 1945', in J. Liebenau (ed.), *The Challenge of New Technology* (Aldershot, 1988), 58–82.

were completely transformed was mostly uncharted territory before the 1860s.

Such was the background to the appliance of science in the Sheffield steel industry. How did it perform? On the whole, the town's progress in science-based research has probably been underrated. The most comprehensive account of the Sheffield special steel industry has emphasized the handicraft and art of the crucible steelmaker, rather than the development of scientific knowledge and institutional networks.[65] Other books, if they have mentioned the progress of Sheffield special steels at all, have usually described them as isolated acts of innovation. Yet it remains one of the more remarkable facts of Sheffield steel history—one of those paradoxes in which the city seems to abound—that an industry that had such ancient and conservative roots, was so dependent on the rule-of-thumb, consisted of so many small, family-owned firms and could draw on only a slender scientific tradition, should begin in the late nineteenth century to develop a world-class research effort. Sheffield transformed itself within a few decades into perhaps the most advanced science-based steel centre in the world, with sustained innovation in alloy steels at its heart.

Describing how this occurred—how Sheffield's conservative, tradition-bound steelmakers became revolutionaries—is easier than explaining it. Demand was obviously important (though not always), especially from the growing railway, shipbuilding, and machine-tool industries. Sheffield's position as the leading special steelmaker meant that it felt the need for better materials and cutting tools in engineering quicker than other steel centres. Sheffield's involvement with the quality end of the steel market was also crucial: it was here that the most dramatic breakthroughs in exploring the nature of steel were to be made, whereas many of the advances in bulk steel production tended to be on the production side. Even more important was the depth and spread of the steel industry in Sheffield—the clustering of firms, entrepreneurs, and research facilities—which created a fertile breeding ground for the advance of scientific steelmaking.

Tonnage steel provided the initial impetus. A Bessemer 'blow' was over within thirty minutes (with the steelmakers usually judging the state of the melt by sight alone); but a Siemens' heat took anything from four to twelve hours. This allowed time to analyse and control the composition of the steel, so not surprisingly once this type of melting appeared in Sheffield the first chemical laboratories were established in steelworks. With output now in thousands of tons, it was necessary to check the quality of raw materials, investigate any production problems, and exercise greater quality control in vital engineering components for rails,

---

[65] K.C. Barraclough, *Steelmaking before Bessemer* (London, 1984).

bridges, and buildings. In 1864 Cammell's had appointed a chemist, its directors stating that 'the "rule of thumb" about which so much had been said, had been discarded from their works long ago. They had called in the aid of chemistry and every form of science by which they could ascertain the quality of the iron in which they dealt.'[66] Six years later Vickers were analysing steel in their own laboratory, with J. H. Huxley, a member of the famous Huxley family, as the first full-time chemist. By 1873 Brown, Bayley, & Dixon had installed a chemical laboratory. In 1884, when Siemens melting began at Firth's, a laboratory was set up under Percy Looker. John Brown's Atlas Works was also analysing steel by this time in its own laboratory. Surviving photographs and reminiscences show that these establishments were often quite rudimentary: thus Brown's laboratory had a basic working area, with a balance room, and facilities for drills, mortars, and a still.

But although it would be a mistake to regard these laboratories as having a modern R&D function, they were nevertheless an important advance, especially when scientific steelmaking took a major move forward with the development of alloys. Surprisingly, the first significant step in this direction was achieved not in Sheffield, but in the Forest of Dean, where Robert F. Mushet, the son of the famous Scottish ironmaster David Mushet, was attempting to improve the performance of crucible tool steel. Previously, steel for lathe work had been prepared by heating the tool and then quenching in water—a procedure which hardened the steel, but could also crack the tool. By 1868 Mushet had discovered that the addition to the melt of finely powdered wolfram ore (tungsten) produced a much harder tool steel, which could not only cut twice as fast, but also cooled in the open air. Thus was born 'self-hardening' (or 'air-hardening') tool steel, initially containing about 7 per cent tungsten.[67]

Mushet's attempt to produce tungsten steel commercially ended in failure, almost certainly because he lacked the capital, know-how, and business skills that only the infrastructure of Sheffield could supply. Eventually he licensed the product to Samuel Osborn, who was expanding his Sheffield steel and tool business at this time. After 1870, therefore, 'R. Mushet's Special Steel' (RMS) as it came to be known, was produced at Osborn's Clyde Steel & Iron Works in the Wicker. Its impact in the world of engineering was almost immediate, particularly in railway shops in both Britain and America. Osborn's advertised it as: 'The steel which requires no hardening, turns out at least double work by increased feed and speed, and cuts harder metals and is easier to manipulate than any other tool steel.' It was said that Osborn's held one-half of the

[66] 'Opening of the Armour Plate Mill at Cyclops Works', *SI*, 21 Nov. 1863.
[67] Later it was found that wolfram contained manganese, which was also crucial for the self-hardening quality of Mushet steel.

self-hardening tool steel trade in the world up to the 1890s—a remarkable record for one firm. Certainly the name 'Mushet' and tool steel became virtually synonymous; and Osborn's, after a shaky start, soon established itself amongst the leading tool steel firms.

This success has usually been attributed to the remarkable qualities of Mushet steel, the care lavished on its preparation and production, and the firm's skilful salesmanship. Samuel Osborn himself wasted little time in gaining a foothold in the lucrative American and Canadian markets with numerous transatlantic visits. The intense secrecy that surrounded Mushet steel manufacture may also have played a part. The Mushets' biographer gave a memorable picture of the powdered ore for RMS being made up at Mushet's works in the Forest of Dean and then 'loaded into barrels, then into wagons, and sent from one place to another until its real destination was lost sight of. Only a few men worked at this place and no sound could be heard on the railway near-by. Nothing would induce the men to talk.' Thus although 'other firms tried to imitate RMS...the Mushet method of mixing and melting eluded them'.[68]

This was not entirely accurate. Tungsten tool steel may have been beyond the capabilities of foreign rivals, but in Sheffield domestic rivalry soon overcame the aura of secrecy, helped (rather than hindered) by the fact that Mushet steel was never patented. Seebohm & Dieckstahl, for example, was making 'Wolfram Cast Steel' by 1870. Unfortunately the exact analysis of this is not known—if it was a true Mushet-type tool steel then the firm would rank with (perhaps even surpass) Osborn as a pioneer—but certainly Seebohm & Dieckstahl was manufacturing 10 per cent tungsten self-hardening tool steel by 1875. Perhaps the fact that the two firms stood almost side by side in the Wicker may offer some explanation for this particular transfer of technology! Another Osborn competitor was Sanderson Bros., which in the 1870s and 1880s was producing self-hardening steels not only in Sheffield, but also in America at its Syracuse subsidiary. Many Sanderson tool steels, which had unusually high tungsten contents (up to 22 per cent) and the addition of chromium, were a decided advance on the original Mushet and can be considered forerunners of the more sophisticated high-speed cutting tools that were to appear at the turn of the century. By 1884 Edgar Allen was also advertising a self-hardening tool steel, 'requiring no water'. By the early 1890s Swift Levick was producing 'Clarence Self-Hard'; and Huntsman's was marketing 'Ajax Self-Hard'.

Not coincidentally, these were the very competitors who were most aware of the contribution that science could make to commercial success. 'No one knows better than I do', remarked Seebohm, no doubt thinking of

---

[68] Fred M. Osborn, *The Story of the Mushets* (1952), 80, 96.

the controversy surrounding his idea to attach labels to tool steel to denote carbon content:

the despotic sway of the rule of thumb. I must confess, however, that this rule is a very safe guide until you have found a better. Changes do take place even [in Sheffield] . . . Chemical analysis is by no means unknown . . . [and] . . . for the last ten years no steel has been sold by [my] firm . . . of which we did not know the chemical analysis of all the important ingredients except carbon.[69]

Seebohm spoke truly: Sheffield tool steel firms did rely on analysis, even if they did not always have a laboratory themselves. Instead they could rely on independent chemical analysis, a fact that has until recently been obscured. However, a chance survival of a laboratory notebook of one of the town's leading chemists, William Baker (1830–78), shows clearly the growing dependence on scientific methods. Baker, a former pupil of Dr John Percy, had opened a practice as an 'Analytical and Consulting Chemist' in Sheffield in the late 1860s and until his tragic death (he injured himself fatally when he tried to slide down the stair bannisters at his club) built up a wide range of clients amongst local tool and bulk steel firms. Baker's analyses between 1875 and 1884 are documented in the notebook and show that Sheffield firms—Seebohm & Dieckstahl and Sanderson Bros., for example—had a much greater appreciation of the virtues of scientific investigation than has previously been realized. The notebooks are thus 'a rebuttal to the claim of some writers that Sheffield lagged in steel research whilst overseas competitors advanced'.[70]

Even the Sheffield Literary & Philosophical Society had a contribution to make. This was the type of organization that had fostered so many clergymen and gentry who were interested in making scientific observations and collecting data, while opposing the traditional split between science and the arts. It was the spiritual home of Henry Clifton Sorby (1826–1908), the only child of the owner of John Sorby & Sons, one of the town's most successful edge tool firms. The family had resided in the area for at least three hundred years and its wealth ensured that Sorby was spared the necessity of dirtying his hands in the steel and tool trades. Instead he devoted himself to natural history, particularly geology, a subject he pursued with the aid of a microscope. Yet even so unworldly a character as Sorby could not escape the embrace of the local industry: indeed his work had direct relevance to it when he turned his attention from geological sections to steel. What Sorby viewed through his instrument enabled him to lay the basic foundation for the science of

[69] Seebohm, 'The Use of Steel', *Ironmonger*, 25 (5 Mar. 1881), 290–4, 290.
[70] Callan, *Secrets*, ii.

metallography.[71] Sorby was able to describe the relationship of various well-known properties of iron and steel to certain structural appearances; to identify the pearly constituent of steel and the relevance of this to its hardness under various conditions; to further classify the seven distinct constituents and the physical events producing them; and lastly, to devise efficient techniques for producing metallographic specimens.

The work of Mushet, Baker, and Sorby had given a broad push to the future development of alloy steels. But their efforts were highly specialized, often secret, or awaited full exploitation. Sorby, for example, had made his work known in the 1860s, but it was several decades before it had a widespread practical impact. As regards Mushet, tungsten tool steel found its niche in particularly arduous applications, not in routine machining (firms such as Seebohm & Dieckstahl still doing most of their business in the ordinary carbon tool steel grades), and even after Mushet's experimental work the implications of alloying elements in steel remained largely unexplored. As one steelmaker remarked of Sheffield steelmaking in this period:

very few alloys were used. There was a definite range of carbon crucible steels for different purposes and different types of tools; ferro-tungsten of a crude type, largely produced in Sheffield in crucibles, was used for producing self-hardening steels with high carbon and high manganese, but it varied very much in quality and often caused serious complications in production. A certain amount of ferro-tungsten was used for making magnet steel, and chrome was used in small quantities, chiefly to help the rolling of high carbon razor and file steels.[72]

This situation was revolutionized by the work of (Sir) Robert A. Hadfield (1858–1940), who was arguably the most important genius Sheffield steelmaking ever produced. Uniquely, he became both a renowned metallurgist *and* eventually chairman of one of the country's biggest steel firms. With the possible exception of Sir Henry Bessemer (who actually was not a metallurgist), none of the great names in steel so successfully straddled the commercial and technical spheres. Perhaps this explains Hadfield's striking success, for few careers provide a better case study of the creation of new factor conditions to enlarge Sheffield's competitive advantage.

Hadfield was soaked in the traditions and atmosphere of the steelmaking community in which he was to play so prominent a role. Sheffield born and bred (John Brown was a close relative and he was born within yards of the tomb of Benjamin Huntsman), Hadfield owed his social and

---

[71] Norman Higham, *A Very Scientific Gentleman: The Major Achievements of Henry Clifton Sorby* (1963); Cyril S. Smith, *A History of Metallography* (Chicago, 1960).

[72] Riverdale, 'Memories', 300.

industrial position to his father, Robert Hadfield Sen., whose steel castings business was an established name in Sheffield steel by the time the younger Hadfield decided on his future career. He turned down the chance to go up to Oxford or Cambridge and instead went to Jonas & Colver, to gain early experience, before joining his father at the Hecla Works in the 1880s. Hadfield was a precocious adolescent, already showing the energy, tenacity, ruthless ambition, and obsessive fascination with the mystery of steel which were to make him so successful. In 1882, when he was only 24, he made one of the great breakthroughs in metallurgy—the discovery of manganese steel—the revolutionary nature of which has long been recognized. This steel, containing about 1 per cent carbon and $12\frac{1}{2}$ per cent manganese, is essentially a relatively soft, non-magnetic material: but any attempt to cut or deform the surface makes the alloy intensely hard, so that it cannot be machined by ordinary cutting tools. Recorded Hadfield: 'The extraordinary results obtained from this steel and its examination led the way to entirely new ideas regarding combinations of iron with other elements.'[73]

This discovery was due less to the depth of Hadfield's scientific training—a basic grounding in chemistry from local men such as William Baker and A. H. Allen, combined with the inspiration from a popular science book, John Pepper's *The Playbook of Metals* (1866)—than to Sheffield's distinctive industrial milieu: that blend of experience, practical skills, and business resources that ensured that manganese steel did not remain a laboratory curiosity. This enabled Hadfield to begin melting steel as a teenage pastime in a small furnace his father had installed for him at home; it brought him into contact at the Paris Universal Exhibition of 1878 with French metallurgists, whose work with high-grade ferromanganese was an important stepping-stone to his own investigations; and it took him to America in 1882, where the sight of a rapidly industrializing society that dwarfed anything his own country could offer fired his imagination and led directly to the crucial experiment with manganese steel.

Hadfield was also heir to his father's foundry, which gave him the chance to launch the steel commercially. In contrast to other alloy steel researchers such as Michael Faraday and Robert Mushet (with whom he has sometimes shared the title of 'father' of alloy steels), Hadfield had entrepreneurial ability too. This was important, since manganese steel proved something of an oddity in commercial as well as metallurgical terms: there was simply no demand from engineers for such an alloy. Even Hadfield was unsure what manganese steel's best uses would be—though with the optimism of the young inventor, he was convinced it

---

[73] R. A. Hadfield, *The Work and Position of the Metallurgical Chemist* (Sheffield, 1921), 43.

would have a market. As he explained to his agent: 'in a new material like this and giving such entirely opposite results to ordinary steel, you may be sure that we have to feel our way very slowly, to learn its peculiarities step by step, but I feel confident from the results . . . obtained, that there is a grand future before it'.[74] Backed by the resources of Hadfield's Steel Foundry, he pressed ahead with costly and time-consuming research, whilst energetically attempting to market manganese steel railway wheels in America. By 1884 Hadfield was able to report: 'We know and are sure it can be regularly and successfully made and what is necessary is to get the material into marketable forms and tried in actual work.'[75] Ironically, manganese steel proved unsuitable for railway wheels (because of differential wear), but ideal in tram and railway crossovers, crushing machinery, excavator teeth, burglar-proof safes and numerous other industrial applications where its work-hardening potential could be realized. Hadfield's belief in the alloy had been vindicated and he had the satisfaction of seeing it first introduced on a large scale in 1894 in America, where it was used for tram and railway trackwork.

It was a tremendous achievement. Within little more than a decade Hadfield and his company had firmly established the alloy, so creating a new branch of the steel industry for Sheffield. His tireless efforts also launched the family firm on an upward spiral of growth. He had demonstrated two simple facts: first, that it was impossible to predict the effect of adding elements to steel, other than by experiment; second, research and development could pay rich commercial dividends. Not surprisingly, Hadfield quickly expanded the research activities of the foundry at Newhall Road and after 1882—when he formally established a laboratory with the help of a chemist from John Brown's, Ernest Wheatcroft—he began a period of intensive experimentation into alloy steels (whilst also directing the family business). By remarkable good fortune, Hadfield's notebooks from this period have survived. They await detailed assessment by historians of metallurgy, but it is clear that Hadfield rang the changes on hundreds of different alloy steel combinations, in the search for another 'manganese steel'. His earliest experiments proved to be the most fruitful. By 1886 he had patented another major alloy steel—a low-carbon silicon-iron type—later known simply as silicon steel. Its remarkable electrical and magnetic properties in preventing hysteresis and eddy current losses in electrical transformers resulted in huge energy savings and eventually opened up yet another line of business for Hadfield's Steel Foundry.

Manganese steel was thus a landmark in alloy steel history, signifying that the old empirical methods were at last crumbling before the advance

[74] SCL Hadfield Papers. R. A. Hadfield to J. D. Weeks, 17 Apr. 1884.
[75] Ibid., 4 July 1884.

of science. Sheffield was to retain its dependence on traditional craft skills for some time yet, but from the 1880s a more scientific note is evident. Hadfield's ally in his steel researches was his works laboratory, which he endowed with a special significance—an institution that he clearly regarded as not simply a place to analyse steel, but as the driving force behind the whole company. This was modern research and development and Hadfield became one of its foremost exponents.

A sign of the times was the beginning of a more scientific training for metallurgists in Sheffield. In 1884 Sheffield's Technical School was established, the prototype of Sheffield University's Department of Metallurgy. Supported by Sorby and by one of the town's leading industrialists, the cutlery manufacturer Frederick T. Mappin, the Technical School was founded against the backdrop of national debates about industrial education. Mappin (and other local industrialists) were amongst those who feared that Sheffield might be outdistanced by her foreign rivals. Nevertheless, the Technical School got off to a slow start. The only steel manufacturer to donate to the scheme was Thomas Jessop, suggesting perhaps that 'Sheffield industry did not want a Technical School enough to pay for it.'[76] But by the end of the 1880s subscriptions to the Technical School's courses (especially the Associateship in Metallurgy, which was to become *the* qualification for Sheffield steelmakers in the twentieth century) had risen markedly and government grants had become available to allow the building of new laboratories in 1891–2 and the appointment of a Professor of Metallurgy. This expanding R&D component—coupled with the industry's own technical resources—would make Sheffield a formidable adversary in world steel at the end of the nineteenth century as it set about maintaining its lead in special steels.

---

[76] Arthur W. Chapman. *The Story of a Modern University: A History of the University of Sheffield* (Oxford, 1955), 39.

3

Business Performance and Industrial Structure to 1914

[Sheffield] illustrates further the fact that the tendency to combine for the formation of large business units is by no means an inevitable tendency. On the contrary, we see, side by side with [Sheffield's] huge concerns, large numbers of small flourishing engineering and other businesses engaged in the manufacture of specialities, and we find that such businesses show no tendency to become larger. They do, in fact, usually depend upon the special development of some one branch of manufacture for which there is a more or less limited market, or on some process which does not lend itself to large capital expenditure.

W. Ripper, 'Engineering Industry of the District', *British Association Handbook and Guide to Sheffield* (Sheffield, 1910), 259.

The two decades before the First World War have usually been regarded as a turning point in the development of the British steel industry. As economic historians are fond of telling us, these were the years in which Britain lost its competitive lead to its great rivals, the Americans and Germans; the period when the great British innovatory phase of Huntsman, Bessemer, and Siemens ended and their discoveries were better utilized abroad. The way in which in both the United States and Germany new integrated steelworks appeared is well known. In the 1880s Andrew Carnegie's Edgar Thompson rails works—with its integrated blast furnaces, Bessemer converters, and open-hearth furnaces—was one of the wonders of the industrial world. Sheffielders themselves bore witness to American progress. None other than the young Robert Hadfield, for example, had stood in awe at Carnegie's achievement on a visit to Pittsburgh in 1882, and had pondered its implications for the British steel industry. Soon firms such as Illinois Steel and Jones & Laughlin were building comparable works, fed by the huge domestic demand for rails and structures from a rapidly urbanizing and indus-trializing society. Meanwhile Germany was expanding, too, with firms such as Rheinische Stahlwerke, Hoerder Verein, Krupp, and Dortmunder Union Bergbau rapidly exploiting British innovations (especially the 'basic' process, which allowed them to use readily available low-grade phosphorus ores).

By 1890 America had overtaken Britain as the world's leading steel-producing nation; and three years later Germany had surpassed Britain, too. As Chandler summarizes it: 'As early as 1890 the German and American first movers had already acquired powerful competitive advantages in their national markets, and this, in turn, provided a base for marketing abroad.'[1] By the First World War, American and German steelmakers had taken a lead in all the major markets except the British Empire and Britain itself. From making about 40 per cent of the world's output in 1870, the United Kingdom's proportion of world production had shrunk to about 13 per cent by 1914 (with Sheffield's share of national production at about 12 per cent).

The reasons for this growing American and German superiority have been much mulled over by economic historians, with particular attention focused on the nature of British entrepreneurship. Pollard provides a good summary of this debate, but notes that: 'It is not easy to summarize the multiplicity of data and opinions,'[2] or to provide a general conclusion. Nevertheless, the verdict has been mostly negative: the British were too slow to adopt the 'basic' process (though American and German observers have vigorously denied any error on the part of British entrepreneurs); their works were too small and they were unwilling to join cartels; they were too slow introducing scientifically trained personnel; did not invest enough and were unwilling to scrap old plant; and so on. It has been argued that:

The British iron and steel industry failed to exploit new appliances and production methods as extensively and rapidly as did its overseas competitors in the decades leading up to the First World War. Neither demand constraints, raw material costs, nor the efficiency of inherited practices warranted this neglect of innovations that others employed with profit, and the industry paid the price for its technological conservatism in declining competitiveness and lost custom. Here . . . is clear-cut evidence of a British resistance to technological change.[3]

It will be noted that this debate is conducted entirely in terms of *tonnage*, which says little about product value or technology: consequently none of the commentators on British commercial decline have considered Sheffield or special steels. In this chapter an alternative view of the British steel industry is presented: one that argues that in the crucial area of alloy and special steelmaking Britain did not lag—indeed, quite the reverse. Sheffield maintained its lead, despite growing competitive pressures.

---

[1] A. D. Chandler, *Scale and Scope* (Cambridge, Mass., 1990), 284.

[2] S. Pollard, *Britain's Prime and Britain's Decline* (London, 1989), 30.

[3] M. Dintenfass, *The Decline of Industrial Britain, 1870–1980* (London, 1992), 19.

GROWTH IN SPECIAL STEEL PRODUCTION AND TECHNOLOGY

Commercially, the period from 1893 to 1914 was not one of unbroken advance. There were trade depressions in the early 1890s, particularly in 1894, and in the opening decade of the twentieth century—notably 1902–4 and 1908–9—and manufacturers lamented the end of the good old days. 'Neither masters nor men', it was said, 'do as well as they used to do in years gone by.'[4] Indeed, one unpublished study identifies these decades as a period of 'crisis' in Steel City, caused by the 'declining competitiveness of Sheffield industry'.[5] This surely is an exaggeration. For most Sheffield firms the depressions interrupted progress rather than halted it, and after each contraction the Sheffield steel industry recovered with renewed vigour. The trend in special steels was firmly upward, with Sheffield's new alloys being commercialized.

Arms manufacturers saw their orders rise steadily, especially during the 1890s and in the arms race immediately before 1914. It needs restating that, despite the general aura of desuetude through which historians have viewed these years before the First World War, Britain still had the world's biggest shipbuilding industry and a capability in most sectors of the arms business that was unsurpassed. Only Krupp's in Germany and perhaps Bethlehem Steel in America could compare with the largest Sheffield firms, such as Vickers. As Clive Trebilcock rightly argues: 'Whatever the much paraded superiority of American light engineering—the American System . . . could claim no advantage over the British in the heavier reaches of engineering and shipbuilding, and none, especially, in the high-technology discipline of heavy armaments production.'[6]

In Sheffield the technical battle between armour-plate and projectiles reached new heights between the 1890s and 1914. The introduction of the forged steel shell by Hadfields and Firth's had made the homogeneous all-steel armour-plate of Vickers, Brown, and Cammell vulnerable. One idea to counteract this was introduced in 1891 by a John Brown director, Captain T. J. Tressider, who successfully experimented with hardening compound armour under water sprinklers. Another idea was the Harvey process, introduced in America at about this time, in which compound armour-plates were 'carbonized' on one side by heating them on a bed of wood and charcoal for several days. The Tressider and Harvey processes

---

[4] BLPES, Tariff Commission Papers, TC 3 1/12. C. W. Kayser, Evidence before the Tariff Commission, 5 May 1904, 2.

[5] M. J. Lewis, 'The Growth and Development of Sheffield's Industrial Structure' (Sheffield Hallam University Ph.D., 1989), 62.

[6] C. Trebilcock, *The Vickers Brothers* (London, 1977), 135–6.

(which were combined under the Harvey patents) gave a super-hard surface over an inch deep. In 1892 Vickers became the first firm in Europe to roll a Harveyized armour-plate. In 1895, however, Krupp introduced a nickel-chrome alloy steel for armour-plate, combining it with differential heat-treatment in the final hardening process. This was an outstanding invention and 'Krupp Cemented Plate' became the standard against which all other armour (and projectiles) were judged—indeed, it remained the basis for modern armour right through the twentieth century. Sheffield armour-plate makers had, apparently, no problem in obtaining licences and technical advice and collaboration from Krupp's.

Lest it be thought that this indicated a swing in technical superiority to the Germans, it should be noted that many minor modifications and improvements were made by Sheffield firms to the original Krupp method. Sheffield also tackled one of the drawbacks in armour-plate manufacture: it was impossible to alter the shape of the plate after manufacture, apart from some minor grinding. In 1904 Hadfields introduced 'Era' steel armour for gun shields, which incorporated manganese and other elements, and could be cast in a mould—so allowing complex shapes for turrets and conning towers to be manufactured. This demolished the widespread belief that it was necessary to forge metal to assure qualities of toughness and hardness.

Meanwhile, Sir Robert Hadfield 'never tired of applying his metallurgical brain to the problems involved in the struggle for supremacy between projectiles and armour plate'.[7] His continuing research again gave shells the edge before the First World War. A major innovation at the turn of the century was the soft-cap, which cushioned and lubricated the projectile as it hit hardened all-steel armour. Much attention was devoted to capping shells both by Hadfields and by their main competitor, Firth's. Briefly, the latter appeared to hold a lead, particularly after the introduction of its 'Rendable' shell, the explosive charge of which did its damage after penetrating its target.[8] In 1898, however, Hadfield made an important breakthrough himself: a modification of the shell head with an 'air deflector' (a hollow cap or false nose), which improved aerodynamics and penetration. Later he tackled the problem of shells hitting plate at oblique angles, an increasing occurrence as artillery became more sophisticated and firing ranges increased. A design patented in 1912 included V-shaped recesses in the shell cap, which prevented the shell skidding off the plate on impact and allowed it to function reliably at angles of attack up to 15 degrees. The

---

[7] SCL Hadfield Papers. S. A. Main, 'The Hadfield's of Sheffield: Pioneers in Steel' (unpublished typescript, c.1950), ch. 9, p. 1.

[8] *Modern Projectile Factories of Thomas Firth & Sons Ltd.* (London, 1912). See also *John Brown & Company Ltd.: Atlas Works, Sheffield; Shipyard and Engineering Works, Clydebank* (London, 1903), 61–8.

Admiralty declined to adopt the new design, which gave German gunners a considerable advantage at the Battle of Jutland. Nevertheless, by 1914 Hadfield had made his firm probably *the* world leader in the highly specialized art of armour-piercing shell manufacture. On the eve of the First World War, the leading European arms makers—Schneider-Creusot in armour, Krupp's in artillery, and Holtzer in shells—had largely been surpassed by Sheffield.

Besides armaments, there was also considerable growth in Britain's old-established industries. The country's coal industry, for example, was Europe's biggest producer in 1914 and was still responsible for half of world coal exports. It was a major market for Sheffield castings, alloys, and cutting tools. Such industries were linked with the engineering trades, which were also part of the same development pattern. The United Kingdom, it is true, no longer held the dominant position in engineering that she had some forty years earlier. But as S. B. Saul has emphasized, despite the wonders of the American System of Manufactures, the British engineering industry had many praiseworthy features in the late nineteenth century.[9] 'New' industries were appearing, which were to exert a powerful pull on Sheffield tool steel firms. The arrival of the safety bicycle and pnuematic tyre created a boom in the bicycle industries in Coventry and Nottingham. By 1907 motor-car manufacture was already a sizeable part of the engineering industry and in the next six years output was to expand threefold. Sheffield itself had a small motor-car sector, with two or three promising makers, such as Sheffield Simplex.[10] Naturally, there were corresponding developments in the machine-tool sector, where higher performance machines and more scientific methods were increasingly in evidence. Electrical and civil engineering were involved in this transformation in industry—and all were areas where Sheffield's specialist steel producers could expect a share of the business. This also applied overseas, where Sheffield still held a competitive advantage in special steelmaking, either through direct exports, overseas manufacture, or licences.

Transport was a particularly fast growth sector, each industry—bicycles, motor cars, the railways—calling for a specific steel, which Sheffield, with its specialist knowledge and expertise in manipulating steel, could usually provide. It was a two-way process. Jessop's, which supplied the cycle and motor cycle workshops of the Birmingham Small Arms Co. before the First World War, explained: 'the motor industry

[9] S. B. Saul, 'The Market and the Development of the Mechanical Engineering Industries in Britain, 1860–1914', in Saul (ed.), *Technological Change: The United States and Britain in the Nineteenth Century* (London, 1970), 141–70; Pollard, *Prime*, 19–23.

[10] S. Myers, *Cars from Sheffield: The Rise and Fall of the Sheffield Motor Industry, 1900–1930* (Sheffield, 1986).

has been responsible for rapid development in the steel trade, the experiments, the name of which is legion, which have been essential in the endeavours to meet the demands of the motor engineer for high-duty steels, having resulted in the realisation of greater possibilities in the manufacture of steel'.[11] For example, William T. Flather (d. 1908), the owner of a typical crucible steelmaking business, founded in 1817, did an extensive trade in the steel for bicycle spokes (besides making steel for the 'wortle' plates for wire drawers). In 1890 Flather's introduced the first case-hardened steel for the cycle trade, named 'Ubas' (unbreakable axle steel), which virtually monopolized the trade in this type of steel for several years. Some ten years later, Flather's had developed what was to become the standard method of case-hardening worldwide. According to one report, Flather himself recognized that 'British industry was moving steadily ahead and becoming more and more insistent for steel to finer tolerance than had ever been supplied.'[12] His response was to pioneer the production of bright-drawn steel bar in 1898, expanding the business at a new site in Tinsley. The development of certain sectors of British industry was intimately connected with bright bar, since the round bars were needed for transmission shafts and similar components in the cycle and textile industries.

Arthur Lee's trade in bright-drawn bars and cold-rolled steel strip had benefited greatly from the development of the cycle and car. An important link at the turn of the century was with Hans Renold, the Manchester-based chain-maker. Renold set very high standards, both for his own products and consequently for his suppliers, and 'meeting those very exacting requirements, though difficult, was an experience of great value in the early development of Arthur Lee's own reputation for quality and precision'.[13]

Jonas & Colver, besides doing a good business in armament steels for the British Government, was boosted by the demand from the bicycle industry in the early 1890s, when it took over the firm of W. T. Beesley in Attercliffe for the manufacture of rolled strip and wire. Robert Bunting & Sons, a small crucible steel concern located in Napier Street, expanded with the demand for bicycle wheel spokes. A report on Bunting's activities at about the turn of the century, also noted the production of 7,000 cycle rims a week and an 'unbreakable' steel for bearings in cycles and motor cars.[14] J. J. Habershon in Rotherham also entered the steel strip market at this time, supplying the steel used for cycle-wheel rims, chains, hubs, and mudguards. Kayser, Ellison, & Co. had been supplying steels for bicycle

---

[11] Wm. Jessop & Sons, *Visit to a Steel Works* (Sheffield, 1913), 42.
[12] 'Firm's Founder Saw Dream Come True', *SDT*, 16 Mar. 1950.
[13] Arthur Lee & Sons, *Lee Steel 1874–1974* (Sheffield, 1974), 10.
[14] *Sheffield and Rotherham Up-to-Date* (Sheffield, 1897), 89–92.

wheels since 1879, when sectional steels for solid rubber-tyred wheels were rolled. By 1905 more complex special steels were needed by the motor trade, such as Kayser, Ellison's oil-hardening nickel-chrome molybdenum steels for car gearboxes. The company's close connections with the emerging motor industry are shown by the fact that it not only supplied steel to Herbert Austin, but backed him financially, with Charles Kayser's son, Frank, eventually becoming a director of the Austin Motor Co.[15] Austin, of course, had been managing director of the Wolseley Tool & Motor Co., a subsidiary of Vickers, formed in 1901, which was intended as an outlet for Vicker's forgings and steels. *The Times Engineering Supplement* in 1911 describes many other small-scale manufacturers, now long-forgotten, which were supplying motor-car steel. These included H. & R. Waterfall & Barber and William Oxley & Co., with the latter-named producing a vanadium steel.[16]

Perhaps the firm most profoundly affected by the motor industry was Daniel Doncaster & Sons, the specialists in converting, crucible melting, and forging. In the nineteenth century Doncaster's had ignored the railways and by the early 1900s were mostly involved with tool steel, having installed a 24-hole crucible furnace at Hoyle Street in 1898 and then bought the Penistone Road Forge of John Denton. But henceforth the transport industry was to be a major factor in the firm's growth as Charles M. Doncaster (1879–1948) and later his son, Basil Doncaster (1885–1959), changed the company strategy.[17] In 1907 the die-block business began, followed in 1912 by valve manufacture, and by the 1920s Doncaster's were ready to abandon steel production altogether in favour of the forging business. But Doncaster's links with steelmaking were strengthened in one respect: after 1910 the Sheffield firm became agents for Samuel Fox (with a Doncaster family member on the Fox board). Fox was another company for whom the railways were a lucrative source of business and it proved a relatively easy transition from making steels for crinolines and patent umbrella frames to producing steel axles and coil and laminated springs for rolling stock.

Locomotives and marine engines also offered opportunities for Sheffield steel, especially in steel tubing. The specialists here were Howell & Co., whose interests in mild steel for ship and locomotive boilers had led it in the 1870s into the production of steel tubing. In the late nineteenth century as the demand for seemless steel tubes increased, so Howell began producing those too. In about 1912 it began fabricating the finished article—the superheater elements for locomotive and marine engines. Another specialized job the firm took up was the bending of the steel

[15] Roy Church, *Herbert Austin* (London, 1979), 8–10, 17, 18, 33, 55.
[16] 'Sheffield: The Centre of the Steel Industry', *TES*, 22 Nov. 1911.
[17] Late R. T. Doncaster interview, 23 July 1991.

tubes for the smoke-box of locomotives. Demand from the water, gas, heating, and refrigeration industries kept this firm very busy before the First World War.[18]

In heavier engineering steels (which were also closely linked to transport), after the 1890s the city began reaping some of the rewards for its earlier breakthroughs in alloy steels. The full exploitation of Hadfield's manganese steel occurred in this period, once the production problems of casting and machining such an unusual alloy had been solved and engineers had realized its usefulness. An alloy which actually became tougher the more it was used (one journal advertised its qualities for railway frogs by saying that, 'Flange worn wheels don't make any more impression on it than a shipworm on an armoured cruiser') had many uses. As an example, Hadfield could point to the experience of Sheffield Corporation Tramways in Fitzalan Square: one manganese steel crossings layout installed in 1907 lasted for twelve years—forty-eight times the life of carbon steel crossings. Hadfields was ideally placed to benefit from the tramways boom after the mid-1890s. A Hadfields' trade catalogue of 1905 shows the wide range of manganese steel products and the enormous business this brought to the firm. Not only did the company produce steel, but it incorporated its alloys in products of its own design. These included various kinds of rock crushers and stone elevators, which were impressive engineering accomplishments in their own right. Hadfield's other major alloy, silicon steel, was also entering service in electrical transformers, after Robert Hadfield and the city's electrical engineer had built the world's first silicon steel transformer in 1903. Hadfield's patents were worked extensively on the Continent with Krupp's and Le Creusot as prominent licensees. Hadfield himself had maintained a close American connection, visiting the United States eleven times between 1892 and 1914. He personally introduced manganese steel there through his licensees, the Taylor-Wharton Iron & Steel Co., and also won Hadfields important shell contracts from the United States Army and Navy.

By the 1890s business at Hadfields began to boom and profits began to climb (see Fig. 3.1). Other firms were attracted into this field. Edgar Allen soon found plenty of orders from the locomotive and general engineering trades for the steel foundry he had built at Tinsley. An early success was the production of dynamo magnet steel castings, which replaced those of forged wrought iron. As one trade journal noted in 1894: 'Many things that were formerly forged, either in steel or iron, Messrs Edgar Allen & Co. are now making as castings in their special engineers' quality of steel.'[19] Cranks, gearing, and parts for agricultural machinery and mining

---

[18] C. W. Spalding, 'Tubes of Steel: Being the History of Howell & Co., Sheffield Tube Works, 1865–1971' (c.1971), typescript in SCL.

[19] 'A Visit to the Works of Edgar Allen & Co.', IMR 20 (1 Dec. 1894), 18571–3, 18573.

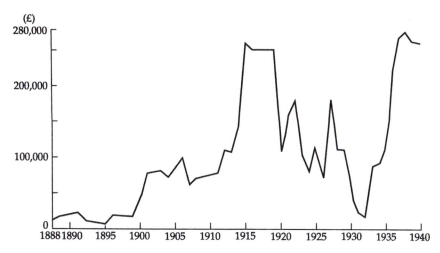

Fig. 3.1. *Hadfields Ltd.: net profits 1888–1940*

equipment were amongst the products; and by the turn of the century Edgar Allen's was producing some of these in manganese steel. In 1903 it absorbed Askham Brothers & Wilson Ltd., the trackwork and crushing machinery specialists, after the firm had become moribund and inefficient (it was said to be still making castings from crucible steel). It seems Edgar Allen mostly acquired the business for its order book, as an outlet for Allen 'Imperial' manganese steel. Allen's soon became especially successful in rolling manganese steel rails, after it had acquired a patent in 1912 for their production. An extensive business from the French railways followed.

Samuel Osborn's foundry at the Rutland Works in Neepsend also increased its steel castings business. By the 1900s its output ranged from motor-car castings of a few ounces to cogging mill rolls and other large pieces of 20 tons. Castings were also made in nickel and chrome steels; and manganese steel castings had been launched in 1906. In 1910 it followed Allen's strategy by acquiring a controlling interest in George Turton Platts & Co., the makers of railway materials, to facilitate the manufacture of Osborn's 'Titan' manganese steel tramways and crossings.

The development of Osborn's shows the wide-ranging products of such firms, since it still manufactured tool steel, files, and tools, besides the heavier work. Similarly, Edgar Allen's manufactured cast steel for planing tools and drills; and cast steel hammers, shovels, and other implements. Although we can pick out a few major themes, such as transport and heavy engineering, some of the products and the new areas of growth defy simple categorization. Magnet steels, pioneered before 1914 by Swift

Levick & Sons, with the help of the industry leaders in magnets in Germany, are an example. Technical developments also occurred in mining tool steels, where the machine drilling of deep holes in rock had encountered problems with chippings and silicosis-inducing dust. In the 1900s, the South African Government banned solid steel mining drills, so Sheffield followed Swedish makers by adopting hollow-drill steels, which allowed high-pressure water or air to be pumped down the drill. In Sheffield John Bedford & Sons took a particular interest in this market, advertising by 1911 hollow-drill steel of 'finest diamond hardness', which had been produced by boring the billet before rolling. Dunford & Elliott, which had been founded in Sheffield in 1898 as an importer of Swedish steels and re-rollers, also acquired in 1907 the Swedish patent rights to make this hollow steel bar.

Enough has been said perhaps to demonstrate the vitality and success of the Sheffield special steel industry: that this was not entirely due to external demand is shown by the fact that behind the scenes an important transformation was continuing in the industry's research capability. As the science of metallurgy began to come of age by 1900, the seeds planted by the foundation of the Research Laboratories & Technical School in the 1880s and 1890s began to bear fruit. Many of the most powerful advocates of science—Edgar Allen, Sir Robert Hadfield, Sir Joseph Jonas—were also in their prime at this time. Both Jonas and Allen regularly donated large sums to Sheffield University, targeting their funding at the development of technical education and improved language teaching. Jonas, who was 'outspoken about the backwardness of English education',[20] did all he could to build up the Technical School of the University and energetically headed a funding drive in 1905. Jonas matched the £5,000 bequest of Edgar Allen in 1915 and the sum was spent on a laboratory, bearing the names of both benefactors. The need for constant research and better education was also a *leitmotif* in the career and voluminous writings of Hadfield. He too made a steady stream of endowments to the University, the gifts culminating in the foundation of the Sir Robert Hadfield Metallurgical Laboratories at Sheffield University in 1938.

Such support allowed J. Oliver Arnold (1858–1930) to exert a powerful influence on the Sheffield steel industry. Born in Peterborough, the son of a railway manager, Arnold took up his first appointment in Sheffield at the age of 20 when he joined the chemical laboratory of Brown, Bayley, & Dixon. After some metallurgical consulting, in 1889 he became the Professor of Metallurgy at the Technical School. Arnold's theoretical ideas were often controversial (a fact not helped by a fiery Irish temper), but his

<hr>

[20] *IMR* 18 (1 Nov. 1892), 16015.

development of phospho-magnetic steels, his Admiralty work on frac-tures, and his investigations on stress testing led to the development of new alloys. After 1899, Arnold found that vanadium greatly improved the tensile strength of steel and thought it might be suitable for automobile parts—a suggestion taken up by Henry Ford.

At the University Arnold presided over one of the most advanced steel research facilities in the world. His laboratory had crucible, Siemens, and Tropenas (side-blown) furnaces and he was one of the first to take an interest in electric melting. His workshops included recalescence (temperature-measuring) devices and his own alternating stress-testing machine. Armed with Zeiss micrographic apparatus he was able to fur-ther the work of his great friend Sorby in metallography. Thus the 'mantle of Sorby descended on Arnold',[21] as he began investigating the consti-tution of all the most important alloy steels. Steelworks, too, began to follow this lead. In 1902 Cammell's were encouraged to set up one of the first metallographic laboratories by their metallurgist Thomas Middleton (*c.*1865–1959), who had been also inspired by Sorby's work. Vickers did the same, also in 1902.

Thus Arnold's prototype industrial research organization—the pure research function of which he was keen to enlarge with 'say, a dozen assistants on the lines of Krupp's laboratory',[22] besides the Jonas and Edgar Allen laboratories—had a great impact on the local steelmaking community. Moreover, as Michael Sanderson's path-breaking study has shown, Arnold's influence extended in other, less publicized ways.[23] His services were available to dozens of local steel firms through the Sheffield Steel Makers Ltd. and the Sheffield High Speed Steel Association—secret organizations that retained Arnold as consultant for an extremely modest fee. Even the smallest crucible steel firms could thus call on Arnold for technical help, in 'special cases for research', and for advice on lawsuits and any other matters for which they would not ordinarily have had the resources. Arnold was also a highly influential teacher, not only providing trained metallurgists for local industry, but also bringing together manu-facturers, scientists, and students, by means of the Metallurgical Society which he founded in 1890. By the 1900s many of his former students had begun careers in Sheffield steelworks where they helped in the establish-ment of research laboratories. J. H. S. Dickenson (1882–1934), who became Vickers' first full-time metallurgist in 1903, claimed to be the first to hold

[21] R. A. Hadfield, T. G. Elliot, and G. B. Willey, 'The Development and Use of the Microscope in Steelworks', repr. from *Journal of the Microscopical Society* (June 1925), 114.

[22] Sheffield University Archives, Arnold Papers, VII/1/27/1. Arnold to R. A. Hadfield, 11 Oct. 1915.

[23] M. Sanderson, 'The Professor as Industrial Consultant: Oliver Arnold and the British Steel Industry, 1900–14', *Economic History Review*, 31, 2nd ser. (Nov. 1978), 585–600.

that post in any British steelworks. In 1904 J. H. G. Monypenny (d. 1949), another of Arnold's students, joined Brown Bayley's as head of research.

Several other Sheffield firms also started their own works laboratories at this time. At Jessop's, Sidney Jessop Robinson (1858–1928), after studying metallurgy, set up what was said to be the first chemical laboratory at a crucible steelworks in the late nineteenth century.[24] In 1902 Kayser, Ellison appointed Harry Brearley, the future discoverer of stainless steel, as their first chemist—an appointment 'forced on them by the fact that alloy steels generally and high-speed [cutting] steels in particular could not be satisfactorily graded by the appearance of the fractured surface of an ingot'.[25] Fox recruited a metallurgist in 1905, besides a chemist, and in 1910 the position was occupied by Percy Longmuir (c.1876–1942), with an assistant named Thomas Swinden (1886–1944). Fox's laboratory employed twenty by 1910, when the workforce was about 2,000.[26] Arms manufacture greatly encouraged the development of analysis. By 1900, John Brown's had fourteen chemists to conduct the 3–4 analyses and 5–6 mechanical tests used to check each armour-plate. In 1908 Brown's and Firth's founded the Brown-Firth Research Laboratory, which soon had Harry Brearley as its head. Private consultancies also catered for the increasing demand for metallurgical analysis: an example was the Sheffield Testing Works, which was active after 1890 from its offices in Blonk Street.

Not surprisingly, both Edgar Allen and Joseph Jonas devoted considerable resources within their firms to research. At Allen's Ernest Herbst appears to have been the first metallurgist, followed in 1898 by Samuel J. Hewitt, when the science of heat-treatment was enlarged. At Jonas & Colver an influential figure was Bartlett Winder (1858–1920), the son of an agent for the Duke of Norfolk's estates, who joined the firm as a boy in 1874. Later a close friend of Arnold and a supporter of the University's Applied Science Department, Winder 'took up the chemical side of the industry, following it with great assiduity at a time when education in this branch was on a very limited scale. He was soon works chemist, and [became] one of the pioneers in the application of chemistry to steel-making. He was one of Sheffield's leading experts in this side of the industry, possessing a very special knowledge of tool steels.'[27] Winder—who became works manager, director, and eventually chairman when Jonas retired in 1918—took charge of Jonas & Colver's laboratories, which were enlarged by 1911, when they were described as 'a typical example of a research department on a large scale'.[28]

[24] *SDT*, 18 Dec. 1928.

[25] H. Brearley, *Stainless Pioneer* (1989), 36.

[26] C. H. Bird-Davis, *Sketches and Illustrations of the Iron, Steel & Allied Trades. Souvenir of the Iron & Steel Institute Meeting, Buxton, September 1910* (London, 1910), 34–48.

[27] *SDT*, 20 Aug. 1920.

[28] *TES*, 22 Nov. 1911.

Hadfield was *the* archetypal research-driven Sheffield steelmaker, the man who more than any other makes nonsense of Carr's and Taplin's assertion that although 'most British steel works employed a chemist by the 1890s . . . his functions were often limited to the analytical testing of samples and the works laboratory was not commonly considered (as it was in Germany) to have the positive task of devising new steels and new methods of making them in addition to its duties of routine inspection'.[29] Hadfield (and many other Sheffield steelmakers) regarded their laboratories in exactly this light.

As Hadfield systematically explored the world of alloy steels, he not only enlisted the support of his own works laboratory, where he was supported by a steady stream of able metallurgists—I. B. Milne, Gifford Elliot, W. J. Dawson, and R. J. Sarjant—but also had assistance from leading scientists such as Sir William Barratt, Sir James Dewar, and on one occasion the resources of the Leyden Cyrogenic Laboratory. The need to test each batch of his silicon steel led in early 1902 to the establishment, as an adjunct of the chemical and mechanical research department, of a physical laboratory at the East Hecla Works, probably the first of its kind anywhere. By 1905 this research laboratory, while it may not have been as large as Krupp's, was no less sophisticated: it included the latest types of weighing balances, stress-testing machines, and metallographic and pyrometric equipment, alongside what was said to be the only dilatometer (for measuring the coefficient of expansion) in existence.[30] Hadfield had also been amongst the first to use the thermo-electric couple in 1894, after corresponding with its French inventor, Henri Le Chatelier. As if to underline Hadfield's standing, the mighty United States Steel Corporation hired him as a consultant at about this time to draft a blueprint for their own belated research effort and to provide general technical help.[31]

The progress in R&D in Sheffield steelworks had been dramatic. Arnold recalled that in the 1870s, even in the big works:

a few small ill-equipped chemical laboratories, having one chemist, and perhaps a single assistant or a laboratory boy, was the extent of the equipment . . . [But by 1911] most firms have fine chemical laboratories with adequate staff, and are provided in addition with appliances for static, shock, and dynamic mechanical testing. The development of pyrometry . . . and of micrographic analysis in works practice has of late years made rapid strides.[32]

---

[29] J. C. Carr and W. Taplin, *A History of the British Steel Industry* (Oxford, 1962), 218.
[30] *JISI* 68/2 (1905), 468–71.
[31] Paul A. Tiffany, 'Industrial Research at the United States Steel Corporation, 1901–1929', unpublished paper presented to 29th annual meeting of the Society for the History of Technology, 25 Oct. 1986, 4–5.
[32] J. O. Arnold, 'The Sheffield Steel Industry: Its Beginnings and Development', *TES*, 22 Nov. 1911.

But science did not make the traditional skills completely redundant. As Arnold himself recognized, the arts of the melter and the forger were as necessary to the production of good steel as was the science of the chemist. According to one manager, when he began work at Firth's in about 1912: 'Instrumentation of Siemens furnaces was practically unknown, and successful operation was entirely dependent upon the skill and judgement of the melters.'[33] Sheffield's unique achievement was to blend science with the more traditional nineteenth-century methods, so that it could have the best of both worlds. Two new developments brought out the advantages of this interplay immediately: one was an innovation in steel melting; the other was a major breakthrough in tool steel.

Advances in electrical engineering towards the end of the nineteenth century led metallurgists to realize that electric melting was likely to be technically and commercially more efficient than the crucible, open-hearth, and Bessemer processes. Arc furnaces were developed in Europe in which an enormous electric current was passed (arced) between two or three carbon conducting rods, generating enough heat to melt a charge of scrap. One of the most successful designs was the work of the Frenchman, Paul Héroult. After melting down the charge in about two and a half hours (this was in, say, a 10-ton furnace), another four were required to refine the metal and obtain the desired composition. The electric furnace was more economical than the crucible, and its extremely good control over the temperature and slag composition made it ideal for many special steels.

Sheffield steelmakers soon recognized the importance of electric steelmaking and watched Continental developments closely. Arnold organized research into electric melting after 1906, the same year that James E. Hutton, the son of a Sheffield silversmith, who was experimenting with electric furnaces at Manchester University, received a sympathetic reception when he lectured on the subject to the Sheffield Society of Engineers and Metallurgists.[34] Also in 1906, Paul Kuehnrich, a German-born Sheffield industrialist (see below), experimented with direct casting using an airtight electric furnace. In 1910 Edgar Allen made the first commercial melts of electric steel in a $3\frac{1}{2}$-ton Héroult arc furnace; Darwin & Milner, a tool steel firm owned by Kuehnrich, also began producing and advertising 'electric steel' in 1910; and within a year or two, Vickers, Jessop's, Firth's, and Kayser, Ellison had firmly launched electric steel technology in the city. Here was yet another new branch of the steel industry, which expanded opportunities. Victor Stobie, who had founded the Sheffield

[33] Article on S. A. Jackson, *British Steelmaker*, 15 (Aug. 1949), 372–3.
[34] G. Tweedale, 'The Beginnings of Electro-Metallurgy in Britain: A Note on the Career of Robert S. Hutton', *JHMS* 25 (1991), 72–7.

Annealing Works in 1910 to market gas-fired furnaces, began melting high-speed steel scale (to recover the tungsten) using the electric furnace, a step along the road to selling such furnaces himself.[35]

Undoubtedly, there was some conservatism in Sheffield in adopting the new process, though not enough to justify one historian's unsupported belief that electric steel technology was given 'insufficient attention'.[36] America, for example, did make more rapid progress than Sheffield in electric melting, though its huge internal market gave manufacturers the profits necessary to persevere until the early technical problems were overcome. Sheffield was more wary of electric steelmaking as a replacement for melting the highest grades of tool steel, especially since the early practitioners of the Héroult furnace had retarded its introduction 'by using rubbish and refining it, rather than by treating the electric furnace as a melting instrument and putting good material into it'. One Sheffield tool steelmaker remembered 'visiting La Praz on the French Italian frontier and seeing Héroult make steel from old mangle scrap and cast teapots'[37]—not a practice likely to endear the technology to Sheffield melters. Initially, the first furnaces in Sheffield (usually no bigger than 8 tons in capacity) were used for melting scrap, or for experimental work, or found their niche in melting the less special of the special steels. Thus Edgar Allen's first Héroult was used, until its dismantlement in 1918, for melting steel for castings: though work by William Henry Everard and Charles K. Everitt with duplexing (melting and dephosphorizing in a small open-hearth furnace before tapping into the electric arc for desulphurizing and finishing) later allowed Allen's to produce hollow-drill steels for the South African gold mines.[38] But mostly, it was to be some time before electric furnaces were in widespread use for high-grade tool steels (though Darwin & Milner had installed their electric furnace in 1910 expressly for this purpose). Nevertheless, the advantages of the electric furnace were to prove overwhelming and the process was firmly established in Sheffield by 1914. The days of the crucible were numbered, though a development in America was to give it a fresh burst of life.

The close-knit nature of Sheffield's steel community, the depth of its research tradition, and its capability for continual innovation were thrown into sharp relief in 1900 by a major breakthrough in tool steel manufacture. Until then, Osborn's Mushet steel and other Sheffield varieties of self-hardening tool steels still held sway in the engineering

---

[35] *JISI* 144/2 (1941), 317.

[36] A. L. Levine, *Industrial Retardation in Britain, 1880–1914* (London, 1967), 40.

[37] Lord Riverdale (Arthur Balfour), 'Sheffield Steel: Memories of 50 Years', *Quality*, 7 (May 1936), 300.

[38] *British Steelmaker*, 26 (Dec. 1960), 409, 430; *JISI* 152/2 (1945), 538.

workshops around the world. Mushet steel, for example, was still considered essential in American machine shops, even though there were indications that Osborn's were having difficulty in meeting the demand. On both sides of the Atlantic engineers appear to have regarded self-hardening steel as a special-purpose tool—useful for tackling a particularly tough job, but not for roughing-out or continuous work. Machine-tool operators, it was said, would keep their favourite piece of Mushet steel in their locker overnight until it was needed on special occasions. These were the days when 'each mechanic was allowed to have his tools forged and ground to his individual taste, with no regard whatever to the earning powers of machine tools'.[39] Thus Rolt, in his well-known study of machine tools, believed that 'the characteristics and potentialities of [Mushet tool steel] as a cutting agent were not fully grasped even by Mushet himself and his invention had no effect on machine tool design'.[40]

This rule-of-thumb era was ended by two Americans: the famous industrial efficiency expert, Frederick W. Taylor, and a metallurgist at the Bethlehem Steel Co., Maunsel White. Taylor had begun analysing the performance of machine tools, particularly with reference to contemporary tool steels, in about 1880 at the Midvale Steel Co. in Philadelphia. By 1890 he had moved to Bethlehem Steel and with that company's financial backing and the help of White he was able to bring to fruition his lengthy practical experiments in cutting tools. (Taylor claimed that the cost of his project was $200,000 over twenty-six years.) At Bethlehem, Taylor and White began producing some remarkable results: firstly, by varying the chromium and tungsten levels of Mushet tool steel (something Sheffield makers had been doing for some years, though less systematically); and secondly, by devising new heat treatments. Their most remarkable finding was that by heating tool steels close to melting point prior to use—a temperature above the level at which many authorities believed the temper of the tool would be ruined—machine-cutting performance was dramatically improved. They patented their heat-treatment (for use with a tool steel containing about 8 per cent tungsten, 1.85 per cent carbon, 0.3 per cent manganese, and 3.8 per cent chromium) in 1899 and in the following year demonstrated it at the Bethlehem Steel Co. exhibit at the Exposition Universelle in Paris. The sight of their tool steel machining other metals even when it became red hot (an unheard-of event) caused a sensation in the engineering world.

The demonstration of this new 'high-speed steel', which was three times more efficient than ordinary hardened tool steel, sent shock waves

---

[39] *British Association Handbook and Guide to Sheffield* (Sheffield, 1910), 225.
[40] L. T. C. Rolt, *Tools for the Job* (London, 1965), 196.

through the Sheffield tool steel industry. Later the city's steelmakers were to argue that the Americans had no priority and that their work had been anticipated in Sheffield—though as one of them pointed out, the fact that the discovery had been made in America and not in Sheffield was:

one instance among many, such as the introduction of cast steel by a clock-maker, and the discovery of the basic process of steel-making by a Civil Servant, which surprise the reader of metallurgical history. The unbiased student is impressed by the importance of Taylor and White's work. After the publication and demonstration of their results, it was easy for steel manufacturers to claim prior knowledge of their disclosures; but it must be concluded that those who claimed to know before the event either did not know what they knew, or were singularly lacking in commercial aptitude.[41]

As it happens, some of the contemporary notes and letters written by Osborn directors at Paris have survived.[42] They show clearly that the results of the Taylor–White demonstration did come as a surprise. 'Tremendous'; 'red hot'; 'attempts to get information useless'; 'sounds like a fairy tale'—are some of the comments as the Osborn directors tried to come to terms with the new discovery. The initial reaction was that RMS was 'done for', presumably along with much of Sheffield's tool steel trade.

Yet within a few years, Sheffield tool steelmakers had completely turned the tables on the Americans. No sooner had news of the Taylor–White work begun to seep back to Sheffield from their directors and agents in America (Bethlehem, even before the Paris Exhibition, had allowed free access to their workshops, even encouraged it) than firms began immediately producing their own versions of high-speed steel. Seebohm & Dieckstahl were apparently the first Sheffield firm to produce a high-speed steel in 1901. Most of the city's leading crucible steelmakers—such as Firth, Jessop, Sanderson Bros. & Newbould, Edgar Allen, Jonas & Colver, and Osborn—were not far behind. Even the smaller crucible steel firms entered the trade. Saville's were one of the earliest to recognize the possibilities of high-speed steel, later helped by their director Walter Carter (c.1874–1932), whose experience at Armstrong Whitworth's plant at Openshaw and in demonstrating tool steels in America enabled him to become 'one of the outstanding figures in the application and treatment of alloy steels of all kinds, and particularly in regard to high-speed steels'.[43] Beardshaw's rapidly developed a high-speed steel and in 1905 the directors referred to the fact that: 'A considerable sum has been expended out of revenue in the perfection of the

[41] H. Brearley, *Steel-Makers* (London, 1933), 119–20. See generally, Robert Kanigel, *One Best Way: Frederick Winslow Taylor and the Making of the 20th Century* (forthcoming).

[42] SCL Osborn Papers, 103.

[43] *SDT*, 21 Nov. 1932.

manufacture of high-speed steel in which speciality the Company has gained an excellent reputation.'[44] Even the cutlers and toolmakers who melted their own steel—notably W. A. Tyzack and Thomas Turner—had turned their hand to high-speed steel by 1910. New firms were also attracted into high-speed steel manufacture. The Andrews family, well known as the owners of Wortley Ironworks and amongst whose number was the renowned metallurgist Thomas Andrews, opened a Sheffield steel plant in 1901 expressly to market one of the first high-speed steels.

Once these firms found that high-speed steel's remarkable qualities were due to heat-treating versions of Sheffield tungsten tool steel, rather than any revolutionary new alloy, they soon took the Taylor–White work a stage further, by reducing the carbon content to produce a more uniform, reliable, and easily heat-treated tool. Seebohm & Dieckstahl concentrated on producing a steel which only required a simple manipulation to enable it to cut at a higher speed than the American patents. Thomas Andrews' 'Wortley Special' high-speed steel was similar, practically requiring 'no special treatment, and any good tool smith can work the steel straight away'.[45] Thus within three years of the United States challenge Sheffield manufacturers had risen 'to the occasion and produced a steel far superior to American steel', and were said to be 'supplying to the United States more high-class crucible steel than at any previous time'.[46]

Sheffield varieties of high-speed steel contained 10–20 per cent tungsten and 2–6 per cent chromium, with much less carbon and hardened from about 1,300 °C. By 1908, further research, particularly by Arnold at Sheffield University, had demonstrated the usefulness of adding vanadium to high-speed steel. Osborn's were pioneers in producing vanadium high-speed steel commercially, experiments having been started by Frank Hurst, who had joined the company as an office boy and later became a director. Thus was born the famous 18–4–1 (18 per cent tungsten, 4 per cent chromium, and 1 per cent vanadium, with under 1 per cent carbon) high-speed steel—the most typical twentieth-century mix for the alloy. With this alloy, Sheffield firms recaptured, even extended, their world trade. Jonas & Colver emerged as a market leader, with its 'Novo' tool steel described in 1904 as 'the best known high-speed turning tool steel at present on the market'.[47] At this point, tool steel technology began to outpace machine-tool design, so that Sheffield firms had the opportunity to produce slightly less efficient cutting steels, while machine-tool designers caught up. Thus Osborn's 'Clyde' brand, 'while not strictly a

[44] SCL MD 7081. Beardshaw Directors' Minute Book, 20 Nov. 1905.
[45] SCL MD 7063. Letterbook, 1901–2. Letter 22 Feb. 1902.
[46] *IMR* 30 (1 Dec. 1904), 894.
[47] *IMR* 30 (1 Dec. 1904), 894.

high-speed steel', was said to give 'a higher output than ordinary cast steel . . . [with] . . . a better finishing surface than high-speed steel'.[48]

The Americans were powerless against this onslaught and large United States sales of Sheffield high-speed steel added insult to injury. Eventually, Bethlehem (who had acquired the Taylor–White process from the patentees in 1900) took an American tool steel user, the Niles Bement Pond Co., to court in a landmark legal case in 1909. The court case was long and involved, with Sheffield makers assisting the American defendants. Despite the undoubted novelty of the Taylor–White work, Bethlehem's case proved vulnerable: technically, the patents were limited in scope; Bethlehem was trying to patent a simple heat treatment—never an easy job; and some of the most advanced Sheffield tool steels (notably those produced by Sanderson Bros., Syracuse, New York, in the 1890s) were very close to the patented composition. Not surprisingly, Sheffield firms such as Osborn's maintained that Taylor and White had merely discovered a heat treatment applied to tungsten steels and that the principle underlying their treatment had been anticipated in Sheffield. Henry Mushet (the son of Robert) and Fred M. Osborn, a director of the firm, travelled to the United States to provide evidence that the tungsten content of Mushet steel had been raised to 14 per cent before 1900 and the heat treatment, together with changes in the alloy contents, had been in use since 1890. Partly as a result, Bethlehem lost the case and Sheffield and American firms had unrestricted access to high-speed steel technology. The high-speed steel wrangle was to remain a sore point in Sheffield for years,[49] but commercially the American threat to Sheffield had been thwarted.

This was rough justice to Taylor and White—though they have always been credited by historians with the discovery of high-speed steel, whilst Sheffield's contribution, apart from Mushet, has been forgotten.[50] But it was a remarkable demonstration of the advantages of a closely clustered industrial community. When the Bethlehem lawyers travelled to Sheffield before the court case, naïvely expecting to gather legal evidence from a highly fragmented crucible steel industry, they were shocked to find a tightly knit business community that was perfectly able to defend itself

---

[48] *IMR* 32 (1906), 563–4.

[49] In the 1950s, an article in a British trade journal, crediting Taylor with the discovery of high-speed steel, elicited an angry rebuff from Osborn chairman Frank Hurst, who argued that high-speed steel 'was not discovered by Taylor. He tried to make a steel to oust Mushet and others but failed; what he did was to demonstrate a higher heat treatment. But even in this he had been anticipated in the [Osborn] Sheffield works.' See letter by Hurst to *British Steelmaker*, 23 (Nov. 1957), 349; and T. A. Seed, *Pioneers for a Century, 1852–1952: The Growth and Achievement of Samuel Osborn & Co. Ltd.* (Sheffield, 1952), 35–6.

[50] Perhaps the best example of this is Rolt, *Tools*, 197–200, who treats high-speed steel as entirely an American development and makes no mention of the Niles Bement Pond case.

against much bigger rivals. The crucible steel industry's secret arrangements with the University through Arnold gave it a technical strength that was not always apparent to outsiders. The wealth and power of one of America's largest business corporations mattered not a jot in the world of tool steel, where Sheffield still held first place.

Even while the court case was being decided, another revolution was under way. Wrote one trade journal: 'The introduction of high-speed steel has been remarkable no less for the revolution it has brought about in machine-tool design than for the improvements it has rendered possible in workshop practice. Lathes and drilling machines have been completely remodelled.'[51] New tools were now in demand and Sheffield began producing those, too. Previously tool steel firms had not busied themselves much with the manufacture of twist drills, a trade monopolized by the Americans and Germans. The fact that Sheffield was for a time the sole producer of high-speed steel, and the fact that many engineering firms were reluctant to use the new steel (partly because they had stocks of the old self-hardening tools) gave Sheffield firms an opportunity to begin 'own-house' use of their steel. Twist drill manufacture led, in turn, to the production of circular milling cutters, hobs, reamers, and slitting saws.

The first firm to begin twist drill manufacture was apparently Leadbeater & Scott, a small tool steel firm that had been in existence since about 1846, and was located in Penistone Road.[52] The lead was soon followed by Firth's, who began using high-speed steel in their own tool department in 1901 and soon afterwards for drills and cutters. This was the start of the company's Engineers' Tool Department, which was repeatedly extended and reorganized, and finally rehoused some thirty years later in an entirely separate factory. Seebohm & Dieckstahl also began manufacturing high-speed tools; and J. J. Saville were making twist drills by 1905. At Osborn's, a trade journalist reported that they had:

taken up the production on an extensive scale of high-speed twist drills and milling cutters. At the Clyde Works they have erected a complete plant, composed of the most modern and efficient tools for drill making, and they have put on the market drills which will bear favourable comparison with the best that the tool manufacturers of America or any other country can show.[53]

This statement may have contained a touch of hyperbole, but the expansion at Osborn's was real enough and involved the partial demolition of a Sheffield landmark—the Tower Grinding Wheel—as the firm reorganized the Wicker factory. Beardshaw's had a twist drill patent by 1910 and were actively seeking to develop the business on 'thoroughly scientific lines' by

[51] 'Samuel Osborn & Co. Ltd.', *IMR* 32 (1 Sept. 1906), 561–9, 561.
[52] *Quality* (March 1957), 69.
[53] *IMR* 32 (1 Sept. 1906), 563–4.

an alliance with a suitable firm.[54] G. & J. Hall, established for nearly half a century by 1911, made cast steel and high-speed steel twist drills. Marsh Bros. began making twist drills in 1912, launching a business which was eventually to supplant its older lines in steel and cutlery. Richard W. Carr & Co., a crucible steelmaker founded in 1902, also joined the ranks of the twist drill makers in 1914. By then the development of specialist firms such as the Sheffield Twist Drill & Steel Co.—founded in 1913 by two engineers C. W. Claxton and H. A. Dormer—underlined the growing importance to the city of this new business.

Closely related to these cutting steels was another group of alloys introduced at about this time: these were high-carbon, high-chromium tool steels, which had their origin in the 'wortle plate' compositions used for many years in Sheffield in the cold-drawing of wire. They were used for operations involving the shaping of cold metal where the tools do not become heated in use. Their pioneer was a naturalized German immigrant, Paul Richard Kuehnrich (1871–1932).

Kuehnrich's name does not immediately spring to mind when discussing Sheffield steel. Yet when he died in tragic circumstances in 1932, it was said that 'for twenty years or so he undoubtedly has been one of the most-talked-of men in the [Sheffield] steel industry, and certainly one of the most criticised, partly because he is not a British-born subject and partly because of his drives for business in many branches of the steel trade'.[55] Since then he has been completely forgotten in his adopted city, and even his work as a metallurgist has gone unrecorded.

Born in Saxony, Kuehnrich came to Sheffield at the age of 17, having acquired experience in his uncle's steel business in Germany. In 1889 he got a job at Marsh Bros. as a confidential clerk and manager of the firm's foreign department. He succeeded brilliantly as a salesman, but after falling out with the Marsh management, in 1906 he founded his own business by buying up a moribund Sheffield die-making firm, Darwin & Milner. Using this firm as his 'shell', Kuehnrich ambitiously began building a business empire that by the early 1920s included a Rhineland factory for hacksaws; a successful American agency in Cleveland, Ohio; and a sales office in Brussels. Kuehnrich's Sheffield headquarters was in Carlisle Street in the East End, where he had bought Sybry, Searls, & Co.'s Cannon Steel Works. This gave him a pedigree in crucible steel manufacture (he liked to say that it had been founded in 1774), and an entree into the flourishing tool steel business in Sheffield.

Darwin & Milner Ltd. established Kuehnrich's fortune and reputation. A striking, bearded figure, he became well known for driving to work in

[54] SCL MD 7081: Directors' Minutes, 1914.

[55] J. T. Higgins, 'Mr Paul Kuehnrich', *SI*, 28 Apr. 1932. See also G. Tweedale, 'The Razor Blade King of Sheffield: The Forgotten Career of Paul Kuehnrich', *THAS* 16 (1991), 39–51.

one of the finest carriages and pairs in the city. The firm gave him a base for his intensive research, not only into electric furnaces, but also into tool steel manufacture. His experiments into tool steel were apparently extensive: in fact, he was once referred to as having carried out more tool steel alloying experiments than anyone alive. In 1911 he took out his first tool steel patent for an alloy containing $2-3\frac{1}{2}$ per cent carbon and 13–17 per cent chromium, with titanium, tungsten, and vanadium added as desired. In 1915 he took out a patent for a cutting steel (containing chromium, silicon, and aluminium) which did not require heat treatment after casting to shape; and he was also one of the first metallurgists to experiment with cobalt and molybdenum tool and high-speed steels.

This work resulted in important new commercial alloys, belonging to the high-carbon, high-chromium range of tool steels. First Kuehnrich introduced 'Neor' brand—a high-carbon (2 per cent), high-chromium (12–14 per cent) steel—which despite its high chromium was not a heat-resisting or stainless steel, but did have great resistance to abrasion. 'Neor' was found to wear from 25–50 per cent better than high-speed steel and from five to eight times as long as carbon tool steel, when used for cold-forming. This made it ideal for press tools and forming dies of every description, lathe centres, hobbing tools, rolls, spinning tools, gauges, and punches. It was to be improved further by Kuehnrich during the First World War (in fact, 'Neor' was to remain a firm favourite in English and Continental workshops until the 1960s).

High-speed steels and die-steels were vital to the engineering industry, yet they meant little to the general public. Most of the steel they encountered, such as in table cutlery, razors, and gardening tools, was of the plain carbon variety. These steels could take a good cutting edge, but even the most expensive varieties soon became tarnished and, at worst, rusty. Indeed, before the First World War the rusting of steel was regarded as an inevitable fact of life, and even learned metallurgists saw this as immutable. One authority remarked in 1914 that: 'the prospect of producing a cheap form of iron and steel which shall be practically incorrodible is extremely remote'.[56] Even as this remark was made, a Sheffield metallurgist had discovered the world's most famous alloy steel—the alloy that has become the most widely used of all—stainless steel.

Apart from an article by an American metallurgist, published in a steel trade journal in the 1940s, historians of technology had paid little attention to the development of stainless steel. That has changed over the last decade or so, with the work of R. D. Gray, John Trueman, and others,

---

[56] Walter Rosenhain, quoted in W. H. Hatfield, 'Stainless Steels', Paper read before the Institution of Production Engineers, Sheffield Section, 7 Oct. 1935, 5. Rosenhain, a pioneer in aluminium, was an internationally renowned metallurgist.

which has unravelled the complex story of this remarkable alloy.[57] It is clear that numerous metallurgists had made trials with chromium (the crucial ingredient in stainless steel), both in America and in European countries such as Germany. In Sheffield, Henry Seebohm (in secret) and Sir Robert Hadfield had experimented with chromium, but like other researchers had failed to recognize its ability to make steel rustless. Apparently, Thomas Middleton, at Cammell's, had produced a stainless knife in 1903—work 'which would have become widely known and recognised . . . but for the air of secrecy with which manufacturers surrounded developments in his day, and for his own retiring nature'.[58] But chromium was increasingly finding its way into alloy steels before 1914 and clearly the formula for stainless steel was, to use Alfred Marshall's term, 'in the air'—just as the idea and formula for high-speed steel was emerging prior to the Taylor–White work—awaiting a metallurgist with the imagination to recognize its potential.

That man was Harry Brearley (1871–1948) at the Brown-Firth Research Laboratory. One of the most interesting characters in Sheffield steel, Brearley had been born in a local slum and was largely self-taught. A socialist, as happy reading Thoreau and Carpenter as a scientific text, and a brilliant writer (his *Knotted String* is a classic industrial autobiography), Brearley was a maverick technologist. In 1912, while researching steel for small arms, he made trials with low-carbon steels containing about 12 per cent chromium. These steels had the happy ability (due to the formation of a chromium oxide film on the steel's surface) of resisting corrosion, a fact recognized by Brearley almost immediately. He also saw the commercial potential of his discovery and alerted Firth's.

Such are the bare bones of the story. Perhaps the most interesting question is why stainless steel was discovered in Sheffield and not elsewhere. This is a particularly intriguing question, since Brearley's chromium formula had been pre-empted in America by Elwood Haynes; while in Germany, Eduard Maurer and Benno Strauss at Krupp's had patented in 1912–13 a chromium-nickel alloy that was to have even more potential as a stainless steel than Brearley's composition. Part of the answer undoubtedly lies in the industry's growing research strength. Brearley himself and others have been inclined to view the discovery of stainless steel as a classic example of individual genius and innovation, but clearly the alloy was one of the first results of Sheffield's commitment to R&D that had been several years in the making. But that is not the

---

[57] R. D. Gray, *Alloys and Automobiles: The Life of Elwood Haynes* (Indianapolis, 1979); John Trueman, 'The Initiation and Growth of High Alloy (Stainless) Steel Production', *JHMS* 19 (1985), 116–25; G. Tweedale, *Sheffield Steel and America* (Cambridge, 1987), 75–83.

[58] *Quality*, 6 (May 1959), 36.

whole story. Equally crucial was the unique richness of Sheffield's industrial environment, which allowed Brearley to immediately link his discovery with the scores of little mester workshops he had seen as a boy.
These led him to suggest that the steel might be useful for cutlery; and
they also provided him with the expertise necessary to make the product
a commercial success. Eventually, he found a Sheffield cutlery manager—
Ernest Stuart of R. F. Mosley's—who was willing to help. Recorded
Brearley: 'I knew nothing of knife-making, and had not previously seen a
single table-blade of any kind made. But I knew the temperature at which
this particular steel could be most easily worked and most efficiently
hardened, and in the course of an afternoon we made a dozen or more
blades.'[59] This collaboration was crucial with stainless steel, since its hardening properties made it far more difficult to work and grind than the old
carbon steel and far less easy to soften and temper correctly. The result
was that within a few months of the beginning of the First World War
stainless steel production had begun in Sheffield and its future success
was assured.

ENTREPRENEURSHIP, STRATEGY, AND STRUCTURE

In view of this intense activity, it is hardly surprising that this era saw a
steady, even spectacular, advance for the established firms and offered
new opportunities for others.

Perhaps the best example of how a local cluster of industries became
the basis for national and then global competitive advantage was in
Sheffield's arms-related companies. It is no coincidence that the top
five Sheffield steel producers in 1914—Vickers, Brown's, Cammell's,
Hadfields, and Firth's—were heavily involved in arms manufacture. Each
had grown massively in the decades before the First World War in both
capitalization, profitability, workforce, products, and subsidiaries (see
Table 3.1). In 1850 these firms (judged by a national yardstick) had been
prosperous, but medium-sized, crucible steel- and toolmakers; by 1914
their ambitions had become national, even international, in scope. The big
three—Vickers, Brown, and Cammell—pursued a programme of vertical
integration and diversification that spread their operations well outside
Sheffield (shown in Fig. 3.2). So far-reaching were these changes that by
1914 it is scarcely accurate to describe some of these firms any longer
as primarily steelmakers; or indeed, perhaps, even as Sheffield-based.
Vickers, for example, ranked amongst the top ten industrial firms in
Britain in capital and amongst the top fifteen in workforce; while John

---

[59] H. Brearley, *Knotted String* (London, 1941), 128.

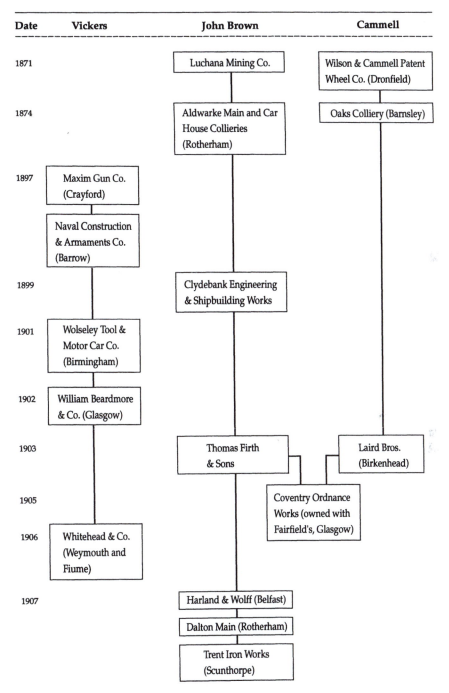

Date	Vickers	John Brown	Cammell
1871		Luchana Mining Co.	Wilson & Cammell Patent Wheel Co. (Dronfield)
1874		Aldwarke Main and Car House Collieries (Rotherham)	Oaks Colliery (Barnsley)
1897	Maxim Gun Co. (Crayford)		
	Naval Construction & Armaments Co. (Barrow)		
1899		Clydebank Engineering & Shipbuilding Works	
1901	Wolseley Tool & Motor Car Co. (Birmingham)		
1902	William Beardmore & Co. (Glasgow)		
1903		Thomas Firth & Sons	Laird Bros. (Birkenhead)
1905		Coventry Ordnance Works (owned with Fairfield's, Glasgow)	
1906	Whitehead & Co. (Weymouth and Fiume)		
1907		Harland & Wolff (Belfast)	
		Dalton Main (Rotherham)	
		Trent Iron Works (Scunthorpe)	

Fig. 3.2. *Vertical integration and diversification in the leading Sheffield firms*

Table 3.1. *Net profit and ordinary dividends of Vickers, Brown, Cammell-Laird, and Hadfields, 1890–1918*

Year	Vickers		Brown		Cammell-Laird		Hadfields	
	Profit (£)	Dividend (%)	Profit (£)	Dividend (%)	Profit (£)	Dividend (%)	Profit (£)	Dividend (%)
1890	95,372	$7\frac{1}{2}$	115,971	$7\frac{1}{2}$	187,527	$12\frac{1}{2}$	20,534	$7\frac{1}{2}$
1891	85,292	$6\frac{1}{2}$	174,914	10	175,712	$12\frac{1}{2}$	26,067	$7\frac{1}{2}$
1892	87,235	$6\frac{1}{2}$	180,518	10	161,342	10	12,102	$7\frac{1}{2}$
1893	55,126	4	94,113	$7\frac{1}{2}$	56,142	$7\frac{1}{2}$	9,637	$6\frac{1}{2}$
1894	102,868	$7\frac{1}{2}$	63,383	5	71,210	$7\frac{1}{2}$	7,792	$5\frac{1}{2}$
1895	244,013	10	61,033	5	141,238	10	7,845	5
1896	285,369	10	122,368	$7\frac{1}{2}$	197,498	$12\frac{1}{2}$	19,008	$6\frac{1}{2}$
1897	216,371	15	113,588	$7\frac{1}{2}$	152,122	$12\frac{1}{2}$	19,377	7
1898	347,470	15	61,127	$6\frac{2}{3}$	193,647	15	18,080	8
1899	404,653	20	129,514	10	244,689	$17\frac{1}{2}$	17,368	9
1900	542,891	20	273,528	15	260,015	$17\frac{1}{2}$	39,500	20
1901	646,332	15	440,393	20	201,403	15	82,818	25
1902	541,434	$12\frac{1}{2}$	232,789	15	144,725	10	86,121	25
1903	556,121	10	185,750	10	144,670	$7\frac{1}{2}$	84,051	35

1904	686,895	12½	159,109	8⅓	185,730	7½	76,866	30
1905	787,778	15	198,936	8⅓	231,806	10	86,733	30
1906	879,905	15	223,881	10	273,780	10	101,497	35
1907	768,525	15	234,237	10	1,617 loss	2½	66,170	17½
1908	416,846	10	218,405	10	152,134 loss	Nil	72,554	17½
1909	288,044	10	204,896	7½	50,715	Nil	68,234	17½
1910	510,668	10	202,017	7½	218,836	7½	69,955	17½
1911	641,686	10	212,523	7½	120,962	7½	79,477	17½
1912	872,033	10	227,109	7½	144,908	10	116,297	20
1913	911,996	12½	271,901	7½	174,126	2½	109,512	20
1914	1,019,035	12½	377,498	10	237,829	7½	139,301	22½
1915	1,099,678	12½	521,007	12½	303,841	10	265,403	25
1916	⎱	12½	485,120	12½	321,372	10	252,126	30
1917	4,493,726	12½	494,029	12½	308,122	10	257,509	30
1918	⎰	12½	453,317	12½	282,064	10	202,895	30
1919								

Sources: J. D. Scott, *Vickers: A History* (London, 1962), 389–91; John Brown & Co., Annual Reports, London; Cammell-Laird Directors' Minute Books, Birkenhead; Hadfields Ltd. Directors' Minute Books, SCL; *Stock Exchange Yearbook*. The 1894 profit for Brown's includes £63,317 from reserve. The figures for Firth's are not available.

Brown was another top-twenty United Kingdom company. In highly specialized arms manufacture, Sheffield had companies to vie with the largest German and American makers.

Vickers' move towards the arms sector was under way by 1884, when Albert Vickers became chairman of the newly formed Maxim Gun Co., set up to manufacture the machine guns of the extrovert American, Hiram Maxim. But although Vickers were substantial shareholders in the Maxim Co., they were by no means in the majority. Nor did Vickers find that being steelmakers with one foot in the armaments sector was very rewarding or profitable (declared dividends between 1883 and 1897 averaged a modest 8 per cent, compared with 13 per cent between 1897 and 1916). Only when it became clear to the Vickers' board that such a half-way-house arrangement was unsatisfactory did the company make a major move into arms manufacture. In 1897 the Maxim Gun Co. was acquired for £1.3 million; and in the same year the Naval Construction & Armaments Co. was bought at the bargain price of £425,000. Four years later, Vickers absorbed Wolseley Cars, partly with an eye on military vehicles. In 1902 Vickers extended their empire again to include a half-share in William Beardmore & Co., the armour-plate and warship makers of Glasgow, and in 1906, a similar-sized holding in Whitehead & Co., the torpedo makers of Weymouth and Fiume. After 1900 Vickers also developed an interest in submarine and aircraft manufacture and began creating foreign subsidiaries or holding companies in Spain, Italy, Japan, Russia, and Turkey (see below). Vickers, Sons & Maxim, as it became known, was then in the unique position of being able not only to build a battleship, but also to equip her with engines, fit her with armour, provide the necessary guns and shells, and, in fact, launch her from Barrow ready for immediate service. 'All this we can do without outside help,' stated its chairman, Tom Vickers.[60] Significantly, by this time the firm's head office had shifted to London.

In 1899, John Brown's, after integrating backwards to secure supplies of iron ore and coal, also acquired a shipyard—in this case, the Clydebank Engineering & Shipbuilding Co., which had been founded as J. & G. Thomson in 1846 and with which Brown's had long had links. This provided a convenient outlet for a new steel-forging plant and was intended to broaden the base of the firm's operations (at the annual meeting in 1907 the chairman of Brown's, Sir Charles McLaren, remarked that when he joined the company in 1884, it was entirely dependent for its profits on armour-plate and coal). Meanwhile, in 1902—in the first merger amongst the large Sheffield firms—Brown's took a controlling interest in their smaller neighbours, Firth's. After an exchange of shares and directors, it

---

[60] *SDT*, 20 Oct. 1915.

Table 3.2. *Sheffield's arms producers, 1890–1914*

Name	Paid-up Capital (£)		Workforce	
	1890	1914	1890	1914
Vickers	1,500,000	7,050,000	?	22,000
John Brown	910,120	3,573,000	6,000	20,000
Cammell Laird	1,050,000	2,372,895	?	15,000
Firth	308,000	520,000	2,000	3,100
Hadfields	90,750	700,000	500	5,690

Sources: Company papers and *Stock Exchange Yearbook*.

was agreed that 'each place should be at the disposal of the other, and that the arrangement should be quite reciprocal. Both firms would then have an equal advantage by an interchange of knowledge, and by the benefit of each other's experience.'[61] Brown's also shared an interest in the Coventry Ordnance Co., linking it with another Sheffield neighbour, Cammell's (and also with Fairfield's shipyard in Glasgow). Coventry Ordnance's speciality was field guns, and Brown's hoped to develop new lines in naval guns and mountings. Finally, Brown's extended its shipbuilding interests by acquiring the controlling share of Harland & Wolff, Belfast.

Cammell's provides a similar story: backwards integration to secure supplies of coal and iron and then, shortly after the turn of the century, the major purchase of Laird Bros., the Birkenhead shipyard. A horizontal linkage—already referred to—was then developed with Brown's in the Coventry Ordnance Co.

The momentum generated by these firms between the passing of the Naval Defence Act in 1890 and the outbreak of the First World War can be seen in their capital and profit records in Tables 3.1 and 3.2. Vickers' profits were relatively steady during the early 1890s, when the dividend hovered around 6 per cent. But in 1895 profits jumped to over £240,000 for the first time—with dividends hitting the 10 per cent mark with bonuses—a harbinger of the massive lift to profits that occurred in the early 1900s. In 1900 profits were over £0.5 million (with the dividend now reaching about 15 per cent). Beneath these figures lay unprecedented works expansions, which were financed by the raising of the issued capital from £2.5 million to £5 million between 1899 and 1902. According to Vickers' historian: 'Naval expansion at home and foreign armament

[61] SCL Firth Minute Book, 20 Mar. 1903. The details were as follows: 560 ordinary shares of £500 each in Firth's were handed to Brown's; Firth's received 2,400 5% cumulative preference shares of £10 each and 90,000 ordinary shares of £1 each. Bernard Firth, Mark Firth's fourth son, became chairman of Firth's and also sat on the Brown board.

orders had, between them, with some help from merchant shipbuilding at Barrow and from general engineering, doubled the company's capital in three years.'[62] Naturally, the arms business was highly volatile and this period was not one long orgy of arms spending. After relatively moderate prosperity for the arms firms in the 1890s, there was a severe recession after the ending of the Boer War in 1902 and another severe lull between 1907 and 1910—when Vickers, like the other arms makers, suffered from the effects of falling Government orders. But from 1910 to 1914 the War Office supplied Vickers with £55,000 annually in orders; the Admiralty in the same period ordered £3 million a year. By 1913 profits at Vickers were again climbing—towards £1 million by 1913—and share capital was £7 million. Average annual profits since 1897 had been £589,391, and the average dividend paid to ordinary shareholders had been 13.3 per cent tax-free.

Brown's dividends averaged about 10 per cent between 1890 and 1904, when $8\frac{1}{3}$ per cent merited an apology, then about 9 per cent to 1914. At Cammell's profits also followed the vagaries of the arms cycle. A profit of £56,142 in 1893, when the annual report stated that 'the manufacture of armour plates was almost at a stand', had leapt to £260,000 by 1900, when dividends were over 15 per cent. After a dip at the end of the Boer War, profits had recovered to £273,780 by 1906. Like Vickers, over the same period, Cammell-Laird had more than doubled its issued capital: from about £1.33 million to about £3 million—though it was the only Sheffield arms manufacturer not to maintain this record. A catastrophic drop in profits occurred in 1906, when the firm was struck off the Admiralty list for alleged irregularities in pricing at the Grimesthorpe Works.

Firth's and Hadfields were in a slightly lower division compared with the 'big three': remaining mostly Sheffield-based, they eschewed vertical and horizontal integration and concentrated on the more specialized alloy steels, which precluded too massive an expansion. Firth's were the less dynamic, but still expanded in the years before the First World War. Firth's workforce rose from about 2,000 in the 1890s to over 3,000 by 1914; while scattered data in the company's files shows sales increasing from £597,692 in 1910 to over £1 million by 1913. Hadfields' performance in this period was particularly interesting. Between 1900 and 1914, Hadfield's dedication, his many patents, his heavy expenditure on research, and his assiduous cultivation of both commercial and military business in alloy steels began reaping rich dividends. Dividends averaged a remarkable 25 per cent each year between 1900 and 1914. Hadfields was supplying the Government with half its requirement for armour-piercing projectiles, with military orders now accounting for about 18 per cent of turnover.

---

[62] J. D. Scott, *Vickers* (London, 1962), 80.

Abroad the performance was no less impressive: manganese steel trackwork was sold as far afield as Australia; projectile orders were received from Japan; mining equipment was in heavy demand in South Africa; and Hadfield's patents were worked extensively on the Continent and in America. Profits began to rise steeply after the late 1890s (see Fig. 3.1). As its capital and workforce burgeoned, the original Hecla Works was now no longer adequate and in 1897 commercial work was transferred to a major new factory, the East Hecla Works, built on a green-field site at nearby Tinsley. These Works were soon described as the largest foundry in the world for steel castings. From almost nowhere, Hadfields by 1914 had become the fourth biggest Sheffield company in capital and second only to Vickers in workforce. This was a remarkable achievement, since Hadfields' competitors had an earlier start, were all vertically integrated concerns, and derived strength from alliances and large teams of managers.

What of the other firms? These also were doing well, increasing their capital, workers, and products with internally generated growth. The picture can only be drawn impressionistically, but a few random examples illustrate the flourishing state of Sheffield steel. Jessop's had retained a prime position both for specialist steel castings and for its tool steel. Its workforce grew from 1,300 in 1903 to 2,000 by 1914. J. J. Saville, who used Jessop's for its hire-work, was also expanding at the turn of the century with its high-speed steels and through the takeover of another crucible steelmaker, Joseph Ashworth. After 1905, Saville's and Jessop's decided (like Brown and Firth) to loosely fuse their interests into what was claimed to be the world's largest crucible steelmaking capacity. Jonas & Colver was another rapidly expanding tool steel firm: it doubled its workforce from 700 in the early 1890s to 1,500 by 1909, while capital was increased from £125,000 in 1892 to £432,000 in 1914. Besides its steel plant and its Beesley's subsidiary for steel strip, by 1905 Jonas & Colver operated the Pilot Works in Corporation Street for tools.

Osborn's business empire was becoming even more comprehensive than this, embracing works for tool steel, steel sheets, castings, and tools. It employed about 700 men in 1896, a number that had increased to over 1,000 in 1910, when it acquired George Turton, Platts for manganese steel production. In 1915 Osborn's added another 700 or 800 workers to its staff by absorbing Bury & Co.—a specialist in Bessemer and crucible steels and agricultural tools—for its forging and rolling capacity.[63] With its new foundry at Tinsley, in the 1890s Edgar Allen's began enjoying a rapid spurt of growth that was to raise it from relative obscurity to one of Sheffield's leading medium-size producers. By 1897 it was a public com-

---

[63] *IMR* 34 (1 Dec. 1908), 965–6. Bury's had been founded in the 1840s and made miners' picks, steel beater plates, files, and crucible steel castings.

pany capitalized at £350,000 with about 400 workers; by 1908 capital had been raised to £450,000.

At this point many of the smaller special steelmakers start to disappear from our view—at least statistically—but there is no reason to expect that their fortunes were any different. For example, Sanderson Bros. steadily enlarged its business in high-grade steel. In 1900 it absorbed a neighbouring tool firm of Samuel Newbould, which had been established since about 1735 and was well known for its edge tools and machine knives. The fusion of steel and tools allowed Sanderson Bros. & Newbould to market new products, such as the high-speed steel hacksaws they introduced in 1915. Seebohm & Dieckstahl in 1899 took over the adjacent works of C. Meadows & Co. Ltd. for its forge and rolling mills, making it a fully integrated steel and tool producer. John Bedford & Sons, which had expanded steadily to employ 300–400 hands by 1897, appears to have been a hive of activity. By 1905 it was producing 'Grand Vitesse' high-speed steel, mining steels, 2,000 dozen files a week, and 10,000 tools per month.[64] At Marsh Bros., steelmaking capacity was extended in the 1890s with the purchase of new furnaces at Mary Street and the Effingham Steel Works & Rolling Mills were acquired in 1896. Henceforth Marsh Bros. moved out of direct cutlery production (apart from razors), so that they could plunder the rising demand for special steels.

Eyewitness accounts show a Steel City seething with vitality. The visit of the Iron and Steel Institute to Sheffield in 1905 presents a useful opportunity to review developments. It brought the city into the full, and not entirely welcome, glare of publicity. From the Institute's viewpoint, the visit was long overdue, since some twenty years before Sheffield had refused to consider the idea—an unprecedented snub. Now that Robert A. Hadfield was the Institute's president, the city bowed to the inevitable. During the visit, Sheffield steelmakers made their excuses—Bernard Firth disingenuously claiming that the Institute's visit 'had been delayed, partly because he had always taken the view that Sheffield was in a state of continual improvement, and he always hoped to be able to show them something better than they had at any particular time'[65]—and then got on with the job of giving the visitors a tour of the steel arts that was without equal—a tour that can still be savoured vicariously in contemporary publications.[66]

[64] *Souvenir of the Master Cutlership of Henry Hall Bedford JP, 1907–1908* (Sheffield, 1907).

[65] *JISI* 68/2 (1905), 477.

[66] See the description of Sheffield works in the *JISI* 68/2 (1905), 460–504. The illustrated volume, *Industries of Sheffield and District* (Sheffield, 1905), is particularly useful on individual firms. At a slightly later date, *TES*, 22 Nov. 1911, is devoted to Sheffield. The following also provide a detailed, if uncritical, view: *The Century's Progress* (London, 1893); *Men of the Period* (London, 1896); *Sheffield and Rotherham Up-To-Date* (Sheffield, 1897).

One thing was clear: foreign countries might have caught up with, even surpassed, Sheffield as regards output and productivity, but the city's industry remained in many ways unique. Here was both the old and the new. At Huntsman's works could be seen the original crucible process practised by the inventor's direct descendants. At Firth's 36-ton ingots were being forged under a 3,000-ton hydraulic press; while at Brown's Atlas works across the road the visitors saw something of the 43 furnaces which consumed 500 tons of coke and coal daily. They witnessed the traditional skills of file-cutting and cutlery manufacture; whilst at Hadfields the laboratory was filled with the latest microscopes, pyrometers, and apparatus for testing special alloys.

Nor did this exhaust the possibilities: amongst the firms open to visitors were the numerous silver plate, refractories, coal, bronze, iron founding, wire, and general engineering enterprises. Particularly striking at this time was the clustering of related Sheffield industries in engineering, which orbited around its steelmaking nucleus. These industries have rarely been emphasized—or even much noticed before—yet their development offers an excellent illustration of Porter's view that 'one internationally competitive industry also creates new related industries, through providing ready access to transferable skills, through related entry by already established firms, or by stimulating entry indirectly through spin-offs'.[67] This close relationship could hardly be otherwise, given the extremely close linkage of steelmaker and engineer. Advances in Sheffield steel, made in response to engineering demands, created another largely self-reinforcing system, which produced global competitors.

It is difficult to do justice to the wide range of such industries active in Sheffield in the early twentieth century: the subject demands treatment in its own right. But even a general survey (summarized in Table 3.3) demonstrates their variety.

It must not be forgotten that the steel industry leaders—Vickers, Brown, Cammell, and Hadfields—were not only major engineering firms themselves, but also created a demand for special steelmaking plant necessary to convert the masses of steel into armour-plate, heavy forgings, and castings. Giant presses, massive steam boilers, huge rolling mills, and furnaces were needed in unprecedented size, making Sheffield firms important 'first movers' in this branch of the steel industry, too. Davy Bros. was such a company. After David Davy was killed in 1865 by the bursting of a blower-fan shaft, the firm began concentrating on steelworks plant, including rolling mills and large forging presses. For example, it installed

---

[67] Michael Porter, *The Competitive Advantage of Nations* (London, 1990), 151.

Table 3.3. *Sheffield engineering firms, 1914*

Name	Established	Products
Aurora Steel & Iron Gearing Co.	*c.*1900	Gears
Baker Blower Engineering Co.	*c.*1890	Engineers
Brightside Foundry & Engineering Co.	*c.*1864	Steel plant/iron founding
William Buckley & Co.	1866	Pistons
Cravens Ltd.	1862	Railway wagons
Davy Bros.	1830	Steel plant
John Dewhurst & Son	1873	Consultant engineers/colliery and mill furnishings
Durham, Churchill, & Co.	*c.*1888	General engineers
Hattersley & Davidson	*c.*1890	Mechanical engineers
Hawksley, Wild, & Co.	1860	Boilers
J. & P. Hill	*c.*1900	Machine tools
W. S. Laycock	1880	Railway furnishings
Lockwood & Carlisle	1876	Pistons
Pattinson Bros.	*c.*1864	Engineers
Princeps & Co.	*c.*1900	Engineers
Newton, Chambers, & Co.	1793	Steel plant/iron castings
Ambrose Shardlow	*c.*1869	File and saw machines/crankshafts
Sheffield Simplex Motor Works	1906	Motor cars
Tasker's Engineering Co.	1839	Roll grinding machinery
S. A. Ward & Co.	*c.*1910	Piston rings
Thos. W. Ward	1878	Scrap/general engineering

Sources: There is no history of engineering in Sheffield, but scattered information on some of these firms was gleaned from: *British Association Handbook & Guide to Sheffield and District* (1910), 258–81; information from Davy McKee, Sheffield; P. H. Grinyer and J.-C. Spender, *Turnaround: The Fall and Rise of the Newton Chambers Group* (London, 1979); *Industries of Sheffield and District* (1905); Joan Jones and Mel Jones, 'A Most Enterprising Thing' (Chapeltown, 1993); 'Laycock's is Birthplace of Everyday Things', *SDT*, 16 Feb. 1950; *Laycock Centenary 1880–1980* (1980); John Merrill, *A Hundred Years of History: Lockwood & Carlisle Ltd. 1876–1976* (Sheffield, 1976); Stephen Myers, *Cars from Sheffield* (Sheffield, 1986); 'Ambrose Shardlow & Co. Ltd.' (typescript, n.d., in SCL); *SDT*, 12 Jan. 1923 (Brightside Foundry & Engineering); Eric N. Simons, *Lockwood & Carlisle Ltd. of Sheffield: A Chapter of Marine History* (Sheffield, 1962); Thos. W. Ward Ltd., *Outline of Progress: Commemorating 75 Years Industrial Service* (Sheffield, 1953).

the 4,000-ton press at Cammell's in 1885–7. By the early twentieth century it was an international competitor, supplying plant as far afield as Japan. It employed over 500 by 1914, its expansion reflecting the general upward trend in the British (and world) steel industry. The Brightside Foundry &

Engineering Co., founded by Ambrose Firth (1845–1923), also concentrated on the same market, building giant steel rail mills, and later using this experience to expand into brickmaking machinery, ventilation engineering, and iron founding. Steel plant (and gasworks equipment) was also produced by Newton Chambers & Co., which had been started as an ironfounding business at Thorncliffe, near Sheffield, in 1793. This was the basis for a wide-ranging business organization, which, *inter alia*, marketed 'Izal' toilet paper as a spin-off from its coking activities. Other firms developed equally complex and widespread activities interlocking with steel. Thos. W. Ward Ltd., founded by Thomas W. Ward (1853–1926), grew rapidly before the First World War, providing the Sheffield steel mills with their lifeblood—steel scrap. By 1914 it was capitalized at £350,000 and had a workforce of 1,235—almost as large as the top ten steel firms. After the War, its expertise in such activities as shipbreaking led to a large, if sprawling, conglomerate that eventually took in road materials, cement works, wagons, ironfounding, and machinery.

The fact that Sheffield produced such high-quality steel led naturally into some steel firms becoming engineers, too, blurring the line between the two industries. The way in which Howell & Co. began manufacturing the steel tubes for fireboxes and boilers, and then finally the complete article, has already been noted. Meanwhile, some toolmakers became engineers. The Hardy Patent Pick Co., for example, which had made its fortune in mining picks, in the early twentieth century began manufacturing pneumatic machinery for drilling rock and coal, besides washing and screening installations. Sheffield also had an embryonic car industry before 1914, with Sheffield Simplex as its most noted producer. Though this industry soon declined, other engineering products linked to cars— such as crankshafts and gear manufacture—did take root. Here firms such as Ambrose Shardlow, the crankshaft makers, which had been successful in the manufacture of file-cutting machines, and the Aurora Gearing Co., were prominent. Carriage building and wagon manufacture also remained in the city. W. S. Laycock (1842–1916), for example, built up a successful business providing the fittings and furnishings for railway carriages, before moving into the automotive trades. The history of these firms and their relationship with the steel industry await further exploration.

The rankings of Sheffield steel firms are shown in Table 3.4. Readily apparent from these figures and those in Table 3.2 is the dominance of the giant firms—Vickers, Brown, and Cammell-Laird—with only Hadfields running them close in their impact on the national and local scene. Beneath these companies were not much more than half a dozen steelmaking firms employing from 1,000 to 3,000—large in Sheffield terms, if only medium-sized undertakings nationally—and then a number of

Table 3.4. *Largest steel firms in Sheffield and district, 1914*

Name	Established	Employees	Major Products
Vickers	1820s	6,000	Armour-plate/guns/ forgings/alloys
Hadfields	1872	5,690	Alloys/castings/shells
Cammell Laird	1837	4,894	Armour-plate/guns/ forgings/alloys
John Brown	1837	3,200	Armour-plate/guns/ forgings/alloys
Firth	1842	3,100	Forgings/shells/tool steel
Jessop	1793	2,000	Alloys/castings/tool steel
Fox (Stocksbridge)	1842	2,000	Railway materials/alloys/ wire/strip
Steel, Peech, & Tozer (Rotherham)	1871	1,800	Railway materials/forgings
Jonas & Colver	1873	1,500	Tool steel/tools
Park Gate Iron & Steel (Rotherham)	1823	1,500	Pig iron/bulk steel
Samuel Osborn	1851	1,000	Tool steel/tools/castings
Sanderson Bros. & Newbould	1776	1,000	Tool steel/tools
Howell & Co.	1850s	700+	Steel/tubes
Brown Bayleys	1873	800+	Railway materials/alloys
Burys	1840	800+	Steel/agricultural tools
Edgar Allen	1868	500+	Castings/tool steel/tools
John Bedford	1792	300+	Tool steel/tools
Seebohm & Dieckstahl	1865	300	Tool steel/tools
George Senior	1872	200–300	Steel/forging
J. H. Andrew	1860	200–300	Tool steel/wire rods
Kayser, Ellison	1825	200–300	Tool steel

Note: Vickers, Brown, and Cammell totals refer to the works in Sheffield and district only: most of their activities by this time took place outside Sheffield.

Sources: The best available information on employment is presented from company papers, business histories, and various contemporary and industrial publications. Other measures could have been chosen—capital, tonnage, rateable value—but each has drawbacks, not least the difficulty of finding accurate data. These figures, too, are occasionally only approximations, since no official figures exist.

companies with workrolls of a few hundred. What is not apparent from this listing, however, is that numerically these twenty or so companies were in a minority. They employed about 20,000 in 1914 in Sheffield itself, but at least as many were employed by the remaining Sheffield steel producers. Estimating the number of these other steel firms is difficult. Sheffield trade directories list nearly 200 steel firms, not all of which would have melted steel: some were factors, re-rollers, and stockholders, who operated in the shadowy world of hire-work. Nevertheless, the total number of steel producers in Sheffield was certainly over 150 in 1914. The *typical* Sheffield steel firm was therefore not the giant multinational company, or even the firm with over a thousand workers, but the small-scale manufacturer, employing perhaps less than 150, often less than 50. These were still companies with a worldwide reputation and included such luminaries as Huntsman, Beardshaw, Flather, Marsh Bros., Doncaster, and Turton Bros. Sheffield's steelmaking heart still lay as much in the backstreets around the town centre as it did in the huge Brightside works.

Sheffield provides a fascinating case-study for the business historian. On the one hand are the large-scale, multi-plant, hierarchical organizations that historians such as Alfred Chandler and others have seen as models for twentieth-century corporate success. On the other, are the scores of small, family-owned enterprises more typical of nineteenth-century British industry. But despite the fact that general trends in the United Kingdom economy favoured concentration and integration, the number of these small companies in Sheffield showed no sign of decreasing in the late nineteenth and early twentieth century. In fact, quite the opposite appears to have been the case. Mervyn Lewis has conducted a painstaking analysis of Sheffield firms at this time, using rateable values as a proxy for firm size. His data show that 'small' firms made up about a half of Sheffield industrial undertakings in the metal trades in 1880; by 1911 they made up nearly 65 per cent of the total; and by 1921 the number of small firms was approaching nearly 70 per cent.[68] This at a time of considerable growth and merger activity amongst the leading steel firms.

Explaining this increase in small firm activity presents a problem, especially since Lewis expects 'a high failure rate of small firms given the growing competitive pressures and periods of severe depression which affected the industry prior to 1914'.[69] But as the foregoing discussion has shown, between 1890 and 1914 special steel demand burgeoned, spawning new products and entirely new industries in Sheffield. Moreover, until the electric furnace made its impact during the First World War, the unit of production in the special steel trades was the 60-lb crucible—a fact that ensured that for some firms steelmaking could remain a small-scale activity. We can also point to Sheffield's capture of the high-speed steel and twist drill markets as favouring the fortunes of the small firm and leading to new start-ups. As we shall see, in the First World War, in both the steel industry and the light trades, several economic developments ensured the persistence—even increase—of the small firm. Although it

[68] Lewis, 'Sheffield's Industrial Structure'.   [69] Ibid. 62.

may buck the national trend, therefore, the persistence of the small firm in Sheffield may not be that surprising.

Crucible steelmaking could still provide an entrée for the small-scale manufacturer. A good example was James Neill & Co., which began as a small crucible steelmaking business in Bailey Street. The founder was James Neill (1858–1930), the son of a wealthy and successful Rotherham industrialist, George Neill (1831–99). Son succeeded father on the board of Tinsley Rolling Mills in 1899, and in that year James Neill launched his own steel business. At first only about ten hands were employed, but Neill successfully found his niche—the production of 'composite' steel (a combination of iron and crucible steel, which produced a cutting edge with a weight of iron behind it)—and the business slowly prospered, moving to larger premises outside the city centre at the Composite Works in Napier Street in 1904. Neill's attempts to sell hacksaws in America failed, though this led him after 1911 to begin hacksaw manufacture himself under the 'Eclipse' brand-name—another niche that laid the basis of the firm's fortunes after the war.[70] The founding in 1902 of another crucible steelmaker, Richard W. Carr & Co., has already been mentioned. The founder, Richard W. Carr (d. 1936), established the business with Sidney J. Walker in a small factory in Bailey Lane, off West Street. The son of a chemist and dental surgeon, Carr's early experience was as the Russian traveller for J. J. Saville.[71] Also in 1902, Dunford & Elliott (Sheffield) Ltd. was incorporated as an importer of Swedish steel. By the First World War, besides hollow-drill steel production, the firm had an interest in motorcycle manufacture at a factory in Birmingham. Hall & Pickles, a Manchester iron and steel stockholders founded in 1812, shifted their centre of operations to Sheffield in 1914, when the firm began crucible steelmaking at a small premises in Arundel Street. The firm was to become an important tool producer after the war, with a factory at Ecclesfield.[72]

The management, entrepreneurship, and business organization of this environment is not surprisingly highly complex. The most profound changes were in the big three—Vickers, Brown, Cammell-Laird—where some evidence can be seen of the development of professional managerial hierarchies. Vickers' management has been analysed in detail by Clive Trebilcock, who has shown how the autocracy of Tom and Albert Vickers—who maintained the firm's family ethos by sharing the chairmanship between 1873 and 1918—was blended with a flexible and

---

[70] *Men of the Period*; W. T. Pike, *Sheffield at the Opening of the Twentieth Century* (Brighton, 1901); Frazer Wright, *James Neill: A Century of Quality and Service 1889–1989* (Sheffield, 1989).

[71] Gordon Harrison interview, 5 Nov. 1991; *SDT*, 23 Mar. 1936.

[72] 'Hall & Pickles 1812–1987', anniversary supplement, *South Yorkshire Topic* (May/June 1987).

broadly-based cabinet style of central management.[73] Several family members later joined the business, such as Tom's son, Douglas, who became a director in 1897, but others were chosen for their commercial and professional qualifications. These included the shadowy arms agent Basil Zaharoff; Lieutenant Trevor Dawson, a naval officer and technologist, who emerged as one of the company's most powerful and effective directors during the last years of Albert's life; and Vincent Caillard, who after 1906 applied his financial expertise to Vickers' expanding armaments business. According to one observer, visiting the London head office was 'more like a visit to a great Government department than to a private firm. The directorate is drawn from whatever genius can anywhere be found . . . [and] . . . are all bound by one rule; they are all full-time directors. You find them at their desks as early and assiduously as their clerks or their secretaries; their work is departmentalised.'[74] According to Trebilcock, much of Vickers' success was due to Tom and Albert—one a technologist, the other a salesman and strategist—and their synergy with the talents of their personally chosen 'cabinet'. Certainly, Vickers were the most conspicuously successful of the big Sheffield firms, though how much was due to its brilliant management style is debatable. Kenneth Warren has questioned the superb quality of the Vickers' team by emphasizing its mismanagement of Beardmore's before 1914.[75] Vickers also suffered from the vice of other Sheffield firms in becoming over-committed to the precarious and unpredictable business of armaments; and its organizational failings in the 1920s (which Trebilcock does not discuss, but which nevertheless had their roots in the Victorian and Edwardian eras), lead one to suspect that any portrait of Vickers as a model of superior management may be overdrawn.

A detailed examination of Vickers' Sheffield competitors—Brown's and Cammell-Laird—is more difficult, since only the directors' minute books have survived. As Brown's business expanded after 1900, it brought with it the need for 'special organisations' and various sub-committees, to provide 'assistance to the directors of the Company, who naturally cannot have the same intimate knowledge of the particular difficulties or needs of the various branches of the company's activities'.[76] But how effective these organizations were is unclear. Brown's takeover of Firth's in 1903 was only a loose amalgamation, not a far-reaching reorganization. There were plans to merge the foundry and crucible departments—the Brown business in both being small—but mostly the deal was only a gesture towards

[73] Trebilcock, *Vickers Brothers*.
[74] T. P. O'Connor, *Daily Telegraph*, 16 July 1919.
[75] K. Warren, *Armstrongs of Elswick* (London, 1989), 102–8.
[76] *John Brown & Co. Ltd., 1864–1924* (Sheffield, 1924), 17. See also J. Brown & Co., *Report of 43rd Annual Meeting* (28 June 1907). Copy at J. Brown PLC.

the rationalization of arms competition, with perhaps the chance for some price fixing on the side. The two firms retained their separate identities, apart from exchanging directors.

At Cammell-Laird the merger of two large companies seems to have been less than smooth. After the company fell foul of the Admiralty and War Office in 1907 over a pricing scandal at the Grimesthorpe works, the chairman, John Macgregor Laird, and two managing directors, Albert Longden, and F. C. Fairholme, resigned. How damaging this was to the company can be seen in Table 3.1. After profits rose from £144,670 in 1903 (the year of the merger) to £273,780 in 1906, the company incurred losses of over £150,000 between 1907 and 1908. Dividends evaporated, exacerbated by Cammell-Laird's problems with a Russian subsidiary and overseas mining interests. It looked as if the company might not survive, or would have to contract severely. The situation was saved in 1910 when the board made the inspired appointment of Lionel Hichens (1874–1940) as chairman. A colonial administrator without industrial experience, Hichens nevertheless returned the company to profitability before 1914. In the Cammell-Laird Archive in Birkenhead are the volumes of data on the firm's internal workings, compiled for Hichens' personal attention and with his initials on the spine. They enabled him to keep a hawk-like eye on the firm's shaky finances. Nothing like them are extant before he took over, leading one to suspect—though it would need better evidence to make it a firm conclusion—that the old Laird family and Cammell directors were poor managers.

The degree of survival of a 'family'-business culture in a firm like Cammell-Laird is an interesting, if unanswerable, question. But below this level there can be little doubt that family control and the small firm permeated the Sheffield steel industry before 1914.

For many of the backstreet crucible steel firms, the partnership remained the basic unit, and retained profits or the personal wealth of the owners were the major sources of new finance. As one of the most capital-intensive industries, however, it was not long before the leading firms needed external capital. As Table 3.5 shows, by 1900 nearly all the top twenty Sheffield steel firms had embraced limited liability, beginning with Cammell and Vickers in 1864. This distanced owners, to a certain extent, from their business, but generally it did not signify that these firms became any less 'private'.[77] As Tom Vickers told a Royal Commission in

---

[77] Interestingly, Charles Kayser stated in 1904 that limited liability had 'interfered very largely with the trade in this country, particularly so in the town of Sheffield . . . [because] . . . in limited liability companies the directors or managing director do not want to be bothered with engaging apprentices, and do not want to look after them either. This leads to the workmen not being up to the standard of what they were in former days.' Kayser, Evidence, 4.

Table 3.5. *Limited company formation in Sheffield steel*

Name	Date	Capital (£)	
		Authorized	Issued
John Brown	1864	1,000,000	750,000
Cammell	1864	1,000,000	800,000
Park Gate Iron & Steel (Rotherham)	1864	300,000	195,000
Vickers	1867	155,000	155,000
Sanderson Bros. & Newbould	1869	150,000	?
	1901 re-reg.	224,960	206,610
Fox (Stocksbridge)	1871	300,000	240,000
Brown Bayleys	1873	100,000	100,000
	1888 re-reg.	160,000	150,000
Steel, Peech, & Tozer (Rotherham)	1875	70,000	?
Burys	c.1880	?	?
Firth	1881	308,000	308,000
Jessop	1885	384,350	230,610
Hadfields	1888	110,000	90,750
Edgar Allen	1890	100,000	?
	1900 re-reg.	350,000	?
Howell & Co.	c.1890	?	?
Jonas & Colver	1892	125,000	?
	1907 re-reg.	500,000	423,009
Kayser, Ellison	1895	230,000	205,000
John Bedford	1897	50,000	?
J. H. Andrew	1898	230,000	205,000
George Senior	c.1898	?	?
Seebohm & Dieckstahl	1899	150,000	118,500
Samuel Osborn	1905	200,000	155,000

Sources: Company papers, trade press, *Stock Exchange Yearbook*.

1886: 'it has been an advantage to my company to be a Limited Liability Company—because I have always had as much power as a director of this company as I had as a partner and the resources of the company are greater than the resources of the old partnership'.[78] Until the turn of the century and beyond, most of the original family owners or their descendants continued in control.

At Firth's, for example, when it became a limited company in 1881, all the 616 £500 paid-up ordinary shares—the vital voting component of the stock—were taken up by the Firths (Edward, Charles Henry, Thomas,

[78] Quoted in Peter Payne, *British Entrepreneurship in the Nineteenth Century* (London, 2nd edn., 1988), 17.

John Bradley, Lewis John, and John Loxley). They continued to conduct business in the boardroom of the Norfolk Works, in much the same way as they had before incorporation. This family element of control was virtually dictatorial. When Hadfields embraced limited liability in 1888, the young Robert Hadfield used it to expand the firm's capital base, not to delegate responsibility. He told his foundry manager: 'I am therefore investing much more of my own money than intended, principally for the purpose of being able to have matters so that you and I with my father's interest can control affairs and not be interfered with by anyone.'[79] After 1888 Hadfield became both chairman and managing director, exercising, until his death, absolute control over the company through a large personal shareholding and his voting powers at board level, which meant he could never be removed or outvoted.[80]

Again, when Jonas & Colver became a limited company in 1892, a trade journal noted that 'no shares were offered on the market, as they are all held by Mr Jonas, Mr Colver, Mr Beesley, and Mr Jonas's two oldest employees, Mr Hahn and Mr Winder'.[81] When J. Beardshaw & Son became a limited company in 1893, the £22,008 in ordinary shares were taken up by the Beardshaw clan, who directed its steady growth before 1914. Although details for the other firms are lacking, similar arrangements certainly operated. Even companies which marketed their shares before 1914, such as Edgar Allen and Kayser, Ellison, did not disperse them widely. When Kayser, Ellison registered as a public limited company in 1895, the owners took a third of the £105,000 ordinary shares; the rest were subscribed privately. Thus, as Peter Payne remarks, there was 'little movement towards the differentiation of management from ownership, towards the elongation of organisational hierarchies'.[82]

Obviously much depended on the talents of the individual family members. Since this could be highly variable, this is an area that has often been identified as a weakness in family-controlled firms. How did Sheffield firms perform before 1914?

Of the medium-size crucible steelmakers, Sanderson Bros. & Newbould was losing some ground to its competitors between 1904 and 1914, when it struggled to pay a dividend on the ordinary shares. J. H. Andrew & Co., lacking heirs amongst the Andrew family, was also a relatively poor

---

[79] SCL Hadfield Papers. Hadfield to John Mallaband, 7 Apr. 1888.

[80] The directors' minute books reveal that in 1888 when the foundry became a limited company, Hadfield took up all 3,300 £10 fully paid ordinary shares; and 4,100 of the 7,700 £7 10s. ordinary shares. No one else had more than 200 of the latter. By 1931 Hadfield held 240,000 of 1,844,784 £1 ordinary shares, with no other director holding more than 30,000. While he held 30,000 shares or more Hadfield was automatically managing director and chairman and could neither be rotated nor retired. He also had the right to utilize his patents for his own benefit.

[81] *IMR* 18 (1 Nov. 1892), 16015.   [82] Payne, *Entrepreneurship*, 17.

performer in this period, even thought it averaged dividends of about 7 per cent. The business 'failure' of these firms, if it can be termed such, was unusual in Sheffield; but nothing is known of their management. Of the leading six Sheffield firms, only two companies—Firth's and Jessop's—seem to have lacked dynamism, and even they were broadly successful. The Firth family board seems to have been competent rather than inspired. Bernard Firth (1866–1929), the third son of Mark Firth, became chairman after 1903. An old-style conservative Sheffield industrialist, he directed a mixed bag of family members. Most hardly emerge from the printed and manuscript sources and at least one board member, Edward Firth (c.1829–1907), preferred country life to business, retiring from the running of the company in about 1880. Only one director was outstanding. This was Lewis J. Firth, who successfully managed the fortunes of the company's Pittsburgh subsidiary after 1893. To some extent, Firth's relied on outsiders: notably, James Hoyle (1856–1926), a talented Manchester-born engineer, who became a director on Lewis Firth's departure for America.

At Jessop's, the chairman of the company after 1887 was William Jessop (1856–1905), a classic example of third generation gentrification. Commented an obituarist: 'Possessed of ample means and inheriting considerable landed estates, it was his chief delight to follow a country life. He was keenly interested in agriculture, and an ardent sportsman, who loved to handle the rod and gun himself, and to hospitably entertain sporting friends.'[83] Responsibility devolved on to (Sir) Albert Hobson, the cutlery magnate, who became a director of Jessop's in 1891 and eventually assumed the chairmanship. Sydney Jessop Robinson (1858–1928), the son of a Jessop managing director, managed the Brightside Works and the overseas operations.

These few lacklustre examples, however, can easily be outweighed by the performance of others—the Jonases, Hadfields, Vickers, Allens—who were rarely absentee owners, did not depend on professional managers (at least for the central direction of company strategy), and commanded respect for their commitment to business. They were often trained in the crucible furnaces themselves, or had an expert appreciation of the technology through daily contact with the shop floor. They were men like Thomas Jessop, Mark Firth, or Samuel Wardlow (1808–85), who was 'one of the old school of Sheffield manufacturers, who by hard work and practical skill laid the foundations of a profitable business in steel-making'.[84] Tom Vickers cut his teeth in the rough world of the steel castings foundry, where he had a reputation as a man who did not know when he was beaten. Sir Robert Hadfield's breakthroughs in alloys were

---

[83] *SDT*, 5 July 1905.   [84] *SDT*, 12 Oct. 1885.

the result of long hours of personal, and often frustrating, work in the foundry.

Some steelmakers were scientists and innovators. Hadfield, with his string of metallurgical honours, was perhaps the best example. But there were plenty of others. There was Thomas Brown (b. 1831), the managing director of Bury's, who was 'always displaying a talent for mechanics' and was decribed as the 'original patentee of Patent Horseshoe Steel';[85] there was George Turton (d. 1907), who founded George Turton, Platts, & Co. to market his patent railway buffer; while Paul Kuehnrich, William T. Flather, and Charles W. Kayser all provided direct technological inputs into their companies. Kayser, for example, 'built up his business and conducted it out of his own head. What others knew by hearsay, he knew by observations and by cautious deduction. [He] could walk into the forge and tell with his eyes shut whether the men were forging English or Swedish Bessemer steel.'[86] The deep knowledge of such men made up for a lack of scientific training, which has been so bemoaned by business historians.

Most of these steel owners were natural autocrats, feared and respected rather than loved, with the small-scale crucible steelworks as their kingdom. A few, such as Thomas Jessop—with his reputation as a jovial beer drinker—appear to have kept a trace of their humble origins, but at most firms the gulf between master and artisan was wide (despite the fact that this class difference was said to have been less in Sheffield than in other English industrial cities). Most steelmasters presented a traditional Victorian persona, in the manner of Edward S. Tozer (1857–1907), the director of Steel, Peech, & Tozer. A strict disciplinarian, whose chief interest was drilling the Volunteers, Tozer was said to be a 'typical Sheffielder. The look of him suggested the stern stuff that [had] built up the commercial prosperity of Sheffield.'[87] Charles Kayser 'stood as straight as a drill sergeant, and amongst the work people he was apt to behave like a drill sergeant'.[88] James Neill had a similar demeanour: he rarely let his staff leave work before his own dinner at 7.30 p.m., and his workers 'never saw him smile, although he was said to do so outside work'.[89] Sir Robert Hadfield, with his stand-up, white collars and rather hard and stiff manner, presented a similarly chilly exterior, which did not brook familiarity. Hadfield's dominance was apparent at the company's annual shareholders' meetings, which became 'legendary for their long-windedness' as Hadfield held forth for hours on the firm's latest glories.[90] Others demonstrated their authority in a different way. When Tom Vickers was chair-

[85] *Men of the Period*, 75.   [86] Brearley, *Stainless Pioneer*, 36.
[87] *SDT*, 9 Dec. 1907.   [88] Brearley, *Stainless Pioneer*, 35–6.
[89] Wright, *James Neill*, 18.
[90] L. Daniells, 'Metropolis of Steel', ch. 4, p. 11. Typescript in SCL.

man, the shareholders: 'soon came to realise that curiosity was a folly which could not be indulged in pleasantly while this man of iron occupied the chair. In time the enquiring shareholder became as extinct as the Dodo, and the annual meeting of Messrs Vickers was . . . compressed within four or five minutes.'[91]

With this autocracy, however, went a high degree of paternalism. Labour relations at most of these firms were good, even enlightened. In 1894 Hadfields became the first firm in the steel industry (and perhaps the first in the country) to introduce a 48-hour week. It was also a stable environment, in which even at the smallest steelworks son would often succeed father, and many workers could point to a family line in the business that went back several generations.

The keynote of Sheffield's business philosophy remained quality, which was enforced by a close, even obsessional, control of company affairs. Frank Huntsman (1852–1910), a direct descendant of the famous Benjamin, exercised a 'close supervision of the business' over thirty years;[92] Tom Vickers was so involved with the art of steelmaking that he often slept at the River Don Works; while it was said of W. F. Beardshaw (1857–1936) that it was 'quite in the ordinary course of things that he should reside at the works, where he had a room for fifteen years'.[93] J. D. Ellis, at John Brown's, was reputed to take only two days' holiday a year. Others shunned public life in favour of business, so that relatively few steelmen (John Brown, Joseph Gamble, Samuel Osborn, Joseph Jonas, and H. P. Marsh) became aldermen or mayors. Although several steelmakers served on the local council, for most business was occupation enough. Edgar Allen's activities were mostly confined to steelmaking: outside that sphere he was a shadowy, almost secretive, figure. Tom Vickers' hobbies were playing chess and drilling the Hallamshire Volunteers, and he took little interest in political or social life. Of his brother Albert it was said that 'he did not allow his energies to be frittered or his spirits to be disturbed by other pursuits: there were only two things in the world that interested him—his business and shooting'.[94] Manufacturers with a similar outlook included: Joseph B. Ellison (c.1859–1913), who had a 'reserved disposition';[95] W. F. Osborn, 'who was not fond of the limelight, and was seldom seen on a public platform';[96] and Samuel Wardlow, 'who took no part in municipal or political life, devoting his working hours to business'.[97]

The dedication of two Sheffield steelmakers was notable, even by the standards just described. Sir Robert Hadfield's energy was phenomenal. Immensely ambitious and vain, he regularly worked a sixteen-hour day

---

[91] *SDT*, 20 Oct. 1915.   [92] *SDT*, 28 Jan. 1910.   [93] *Quality* (May 1957), 40.
[94] *Daily Telegraph*, 16 July 1919.   [95] *SDT*, 24 Jan. 1913.
[96] *SDT*, 17 June 1936.   [97] *SDT*, 12 Oct. 1885.

and was described as the 'hardest working man under the sun. He worked in his home, in his office, at the works, in the train, in the drawing room, at the club, in his car.'[98] He had a staff of at least six male secretaries, one of whom was constantly at hand, even at night. Naturally, Hadfield was invariably present at important or prestigious occasions. Only once did he miss an annual company meeting; that was in 1909 when the pressures of such an intense work-load resulted in such a serious nervous breakdown that it took a world cruise to restore his health.

Hadfield's efforts were matched by those of Arthur Balfour (1873–1957), who arrived in Sheffield from London in 1882, the illegitimate son of a woman who later married Robert Schott, the head of Seebohm & Dieckstahl. Balfour's early business career was in America, where his first job was as a moulder in the Buffalo Works of the New York Car Wheel Co. Within a few years, his energy and talents had made him manager and in 1896 he was recalled by Schott to assume the same responsibility at Seebohm & Dieckstahl. By 1914, Balfour had taken control of the firm, replacing the German 'family' members. 'Even as a young man', recalled his son, '[Arthur Balfour] was a workaholic. Considering his beginnings, it was, perhaps, not entirely surprising. But this passion for business took its toll.' In about 1906–7, Balfour had a breakdown, though it hardly altered his attitude: 'all his interests were in the same field, related to business'.[99] By the war, Balfour was not only helping to build up the business of Seebohm & Dieckstahl by some prodigious feats of travelling, but was also beginning to combine it with a wide-ranging commitment to public service. The careers of men such as Balfour show that the customary criticism of family-controlled firms, that they are only interested in short-term profit and not long-term strategy and investment, has little substance when applied to Sheffield at this time.

Balfour was one of the few Sheffield men to become active on the national industrial scene and it is significant that Sheffield had no steelmaking MP or peer before 1914, and very few knights (the first was John Brown; the only others, Robert A. Hadfield and Joseph Jonas).[100] The stamping-ground of these men was not the national scene, but their own locality, where they could pursue their personal values and maintain their old-established networks. They were happy to share their power on the shop floor with the melting managers and workers on whom they de-

---

[98] *Engineer*, 170 (11 Oct. 1940), 235.

[99] 'Lord Riverdale Remembers', *Quality* (Sept./Oct. 1984), 32, 33.

[100] Robert Armitage, the chairman of Brown Bayley's after 1895, was, however, mayor of Leeds, 1904–5, and MP for the Central Division of Leeds, 1906–22. Douglas Vickers (1861–1937) became the first Sheffield steel MP (Coalition-Unionist) in 1918, though he was one of the most silent. *Hansard* records no speeches or oral questions by him. His obituary, *SDT*, 23 Nov. 1937, remarked that it was 'a curious anomaly that Sheffield had never sent one of its captains of industry to represent it in Parliament'.

pended for the high quality of their products. But in politics and religion Sheffield steelmasters represented tradition and the continuance of older, simpler values.[101] They were overwhelmingly Conservative (with some occasional exceptions, such as Robert A. Hadfield and Joseph Jonas, who were Liberals) in an increasingly Liberal city that was to become a Labour stronghold after the First World War. The Andrews, Beardshaws, Bedfords, Firths, Flathers, Huntsmans, Jessops, Marshs, Matthews, Vickers—were all Conservative. Most of them were also Churchmen, though here Sheffield's reputation for independence and Nonconformity surfaces, particularly in regard to several prominent Methodist manufacturing families. These included the Osborns, the Firths, the Wardlows, and the Woods (of the Wardsend Steel Co.).[102] Meanwhile, the Doncasters were amongst the town's best-known Quakers during the nineteenth century.[103] Many were also freemasons and the brotherhood seems to have been particularly entrenched in some of the small crucible steelmakers—the Bedfords, Huntsmans, Lees, Wardlows, and Vesseys. William J. Bedford, Sydney B. Halcomb (Sanderson Bros. & Newbould), John Hunt (Hallamshire Steel & File), Arthur Lee, Arthur S. Lee, Edgar Muxlow (Muxlow & Knott), Arnold Spencer (W. Spencer & Co.), and Edward S. Tozer are all described as 'prominent' freemasons in the local press; while David Flather was a leader in the movement and an authority on its history and traditions.

Sheffield's cluster of steel firms therefore nurtured a close-knit community of shared values. The fact that few of these men ran totally integrated mills intensified an industrial network of complex linkages. These linkages were of course reflected socially, by intermarriage and a complex networking of families—too complicated to describe here—that often extended into the banking and financial scene in the city. The spiritual home of these men was the Company of Cutlers (and, to a lesser extent, the Sheffield Club), a largely honorific body that nevertheless gave them a public platform and allowed that characteristic intermingling of business interests, Conservatism, and freemasonry for the select few.[104]

There would be nothing notable about Sheffield's special steelmakers, of course, if only their political and social values were taken into

[101] Utilizing Peter Harvey's 'Sheffield Obituary' (in SCL), I traced the obituaries of Sheffield's steelmakers, combining this with other published and unpublished data, when available. This method has obvious shortcomings, though it gives the best broad analysis of the political, religious, and other affiliations of Sheffield's steelmaking community.

[102] The Methodist steelmaking group also included: Frank Hurst (Osborn), John K. Baker (John Baker & Sons Ltd., crucible steelmakers), Richard W. Carr, George Cowen (Turton, Platts, & Co.), Benjamin Freeborough (Hadfields), and Hugh K. Peace (W. K. & C. Peace Ltd.).

[103] Other Nonconformists were Harry Fisher of the Kingfisher Works and Walter Spencer.

[104] Alan P. White, 'Formation and Development of Middle-Class Urban Culture and Politics: Sheffield 1825–1880' (Leeds Ph.D., 1990).

consideration; but their remarkable innovations in manufacturing alter the picture. Once again Sheffield can be seen to turn on their heads some familiar precepts about small-scale British business at this time. For many business historians, the small family firm after the late nineteenth century has a low standing: unable to adapt to the pressures of competition and change, it was both a cause and a symptom of Britain's wider industrial malaise and decline. Worse, in Sheffield at this time steelmakers were conservative, maintained traditional social values, and refused to merge or to grow spectacularly. And yet—in complete contrast to Chandlerian tenets—these firms were globally competitive.

The reason for this apparent paradox is that making special steels was not a large-scale activity, nor could it be. It depended on a limited market and the development of specialities. Sheffield steelmakers' recognition of this fact meant that (like the small Pittsburgh steel producers and the Philadelphia textile families) they conducted their affairs with energy and success.[105] In doing so, they were conservative revolutionaries.

OVERSEAS STRATEGY AND PERFORMANCE

Sheffield's national competitive superiority enabled it to become a major exporter of products, capital, and manpower in special steels technology before the First World War. This fact has largely escaped notice, since most of the standard accounts of the steel industry fail even to mention the subject. The dominance of the American steel industry in the late nineteenth century, especially in export markets, has been accepted more or less unquestioningly, despite the fact that this was where Sheffield firms were most influential.

This section reviews Sheffield's overseas performance and also discusses aspects of marketing—an area which has recently begun to attract interest amongst economic historians, despite the problems of data and interpretation. It should be stated at the outset that the evidence for Sheffield's overseas trade has to be stitched together from a patchwork of sources: there are few good caches of business records that deal with the Sheffield export trade; there is no run of official (or unofficial) export data for special steels; and comparisons with overseas rivals are hindered by the fact that (for the same reasons) their firms and industries also remain shadowy and mostly unknown. However, some general trends can be identified and some tentative conclusions drawn.

---

[105] J. Ingham, *Making Iron and Steel: Independent Mills in Pittsburgh, 1820–1920* (Columbus, Ohio, 1991); P. Scanton, *Figured Tapestry: Production, Markets, and Power in Philadelphia Textiles, 1885–1941* (New York, 1989).

The central fact of Sheffield's foreign trade before 1850 was the dominant American trade; the chief problem thereafter was how to replace it with another market that was equally profitable. The United States trade began to deteriorate during the American Civil War, when the disruptions to certain branches of it caused many Sheffield manufacturers to begin looking further afield—to China, India, and South America. An increasingly stringent American tariff policy, beginning with the Morill Act in 1861, reinforced this trend, as did the growth of the American crucible steel industry. As Sheffield crucible steelmakers began examining their commitment to this market, three strategies emerged: some makers abandoned the American market for good; others decided to continue trading, for even a much-diminished American market was far too lucrative to give up without a struggle; others switched their business across the Atlantic and began manufacturing there themselves.

These transatlantic firms—Sanderson Bros., Firth's, Jessop's, Edgar Allen—can be seen in Table 3.6. A detailed account of their performance has appeared elsewhere and here only some general conclusions will be made in the context of United Kingdom multinational activity.[106] Like most British multinationals in this period, the dominant motive for these firms opening overseas operations was defensive: it was a response to the American steel tariff and the emergence of America's own special steel industry. It was also, secondarily, an attempt to transfer high-grade crucible steel technology—where Sheffield still retained a marked advantage— and make it work on foreign soil. Also worth highlighting is the fact that these Sheffield subsidiaries support the view that 'size was not a necessary precondition of multinational growth',[107] since most were (by United Kingdom standards) only medium-sized, family-owned concerns. Nevertheless, Sanderson's, Firth's, Jessop's, and Edgar Allen's established viable concerns that survived into the twentieth century—some in rather modified form up to the present day. The Sanderson and Firth factories, especially, became important centres of special steel technology in America, conduits through which Sheffield imparted vital know-how to the American industry in stainless and tool steels.

Commercially, the results of Sheffield's American operations were more mixed: in 1900 Sanderson's sold its Syracuse plant to the Crucible Steel Co. of America, the newly formed combination of crucible steelmakers, and used the proceeds to buy the Newbould tool subsidiary in Sheffield; Jessop's sold its Pittsburgh plant in about 1920, as did Edgar

[106] G. Tweedale, *Sheffield Steel and America* (Cambridge, 1987); Tweedale, 'Transatlantic Specialty Steels: Sheffield High-Grade Steel Firms and the USA, 1860–1940', in Geoffrey Jones (ed.), *British Multinationals* (Aldershot, 1986), 75–95.

[107] Jones, *Multinationals*, 6.

Table 3.6. *Overseas subsidiaries of Sheffield firms*

Sheffield Firm	Overseas Company, Location	Dates
Fox	William Fox & Co., Amiens, France	1859–1914
Sanderson Bros.	Sanderson Bros. Steel Co., Syracuse, New York	1876–1900
Jonas & Colver	Black Forest, Germany	c.1892–?
Firth	Firth-Sterling Steel Co., Pittsburgh	1896–1949
	Salamander Works, Riga, Russia	1904–15
Vickers	Placencia de las Armas, Spain	1897–1935
	Canadian-Vickers Ltd., Montreal	1911–27
Jessop	Jessop Steel Co., Pittsburgh	1901–20
Cammell	Russia Cammell File Co., Odessa	1901–5
Saville	Libau, Russia	1901–c.1917
Edgar Allen	Edgar Allen Manganese Steel Co., Chicago Heights, Illinois	1910–20

Note: With regard to Vickers, only those overseas firms in which the company had the majority shareholding are listed. Vickers' overseas holdings were much more extensive than this and are described in R. P. T. Davenport-Hines, 'Vickers as a Multinational', in Geoffrey Jones (ed.), *British Multinationals* (1986), 43–74.

Allen. Only Firth-Sterling fulfilled Sheffield expectations by earning high profits from its inception and it was still earning good dividends for its Sheffield parent after 1918. Part of Sheffield's performance reflected poor management structures and the problems these family-based firms had in operating over long distances at that time. On the other hand, exogenous factors also played a significant part: the impact of the First World War, changes in crucible steel technology, sluggish demand for tool steels (Firth's luckily timed the opening of their works to coincide with an upsurge in tool steel demand at the end of the 1890s), and the merger movement in the American steel industry. Labelling the overseas strategies of these companies as either 'successes' or 'failures' is therefore difficult.

Whatever the fate of these transatlantic subsidiaries, it was inevitable that Sheffield's overseas trade would become much more diversified after the 1860s and 1870s (and this even applied to the American traders who tried to retain the United States market). As Samuel Osborn stated in 1886, 'during the last twenty years we have developed new markets for Sheffield steel, which, to a certain extent, have made up for the diminution of the American trade'.[108] After the 1870s Sheffield began to develop what it would refer to, with some justice, as a 'worldwide' trade. Marsh Bros.,

---

[108] *RC Appointed to Inquire into the Depression of Trade and Industry* (1886). C. 4621, 105.

Table 3.7. *Sales of J. Bedford & Sons (£)*

Country, etc.	1867	1887
Sheffield	26,779	842
Rest of England	9,310	7,969
France	8,380	8,283
Italy	1,040	9,555
Switzerland	402	1,439
Germany	2,844	3,498
Spain	3,867	15,616
Portugal	911	2,390
TOTAL	53,533	49,592

Source: British Industry and Commerce (1967), 22.

for example, although only a relatively small steel and tool firm, was supplying an 'astonishing variety of foreign markets' by 1914.[109] The company records describe transactions in the Argentine, Brazil, Uruguay, and Paraguay; in Lille, Saint-Étienne, and Paris; in Berlin, Breslau, Aachen, and Baden; in Montreal, Cairo, and Riga; in Italy, Spain, Holland, Belgium, Japan, Manchuria, Formosa, and Korea.

The Continent was not surprisingly an early focus of attention for Sheffield. Ever since Huntsman's steel had been so enthusiastically received in France in the late eighteenth century, the French market proved a good customer for Sheffield steel. John Bedford, who was educated on the Continent, shifted the centre of his operations to Paris in the early 1860s, where he amassed the fortune he used to establish John Bedford & Sons in 1864. This was the launching pad for a wide export trade, as Bedford's broadened its customer base in the 1870s and 1880s. Table 3.7 reproduces the figures recorded in a now apparently lost Bedford company ledger, which give a good idea of its widespread markets. In 1867 turnover was mainly local; twenty years later almost 85 per cent of sales went to Western Europe.

Also active in France was Samuel Fox, who opened a small subsidiary in Amiens in 1859 for the fabrication of umbrella frames. Only moderately successful, it was closed on the outbreak of the First World War. Edgar Allen, who had been educated in Paris, was another French trader. His firm did a particularly good trade there before 1914 in manganese steel trackwork. Allen's familiarity with French engineers was evident in his connections with Alexandre Tropenas, whose side-blown Bessemer-type

---

[109] S. Pollard, *Three Centuries of Sheffield Steel* (Sheffield, 1954).

converter Allen used for castings, and with Paul Héroult, who helped Allen install the first arc furnace in Sheffield.

Southern Europe, particularly Spain, also offered good prospects. Spain was Marsh Bros.' best customer in the late nineteenth century. Correspondence for this period in the Marsh company papers shows the immense variety of goods that the company sold: steel, tools, wire, vices, and cutlery and razors. Vickers also targeted Spain as part of its aggressive policy of overseas expansion at this time: its Placencia subsidiary was opened in 1897 to supply armaments, but proved a persistent loss-maker to its parent.

Further afield, newly developing countries, especially those with extractive industries, such as South Africa and Australia, proved a happy hunting-ground for Sheffield firms with drill steels, mining equipment, and railway materials to sell. Until about 1912, all South Africa's solid-drill steel came from Sheffield, though later there was much competition in hollow-drill steels from America and Sweden. Hadfield's manganese steel and the South African diamond mines were made for each other. Although most of the company's early orders for steel castings came from United Kingdom engineering firms, by the end of the century South African orders for stone-breakers and patent gyrator crushers were keeping Hadfields very busy. As ever, Edgar Allen shadowed Hadfields' moves. By 1897 Edgar Allen's had eleven representatives, seven at home and on the Continent, and four travelling in Australia and South Africa. The company had opened a Johannesburg branch in 1894, after William Crosby, a home representative of the firm, was sent out to South Africa and successfully opened up the trade, particularly in mining steels. In 1905 the firm opened another branch office in Japan.

However, two major Sheffield markets emerge from the rather sparse documentation. The first was Germany. This might appear surprising. Many Sheffielders disliked the Germans intensely, especially since they were becoming increasingly competitive in Sheffield's cutlery and tool trades. Germany's alleged 'dumping' of cheap cutlery and its fraudulent use of Sheffield trade marks were hardly calculated to inspire a fondness for Germans. Yet many Sheffield steelmasters were sent to Germany to complete their education. H. P. Marsh, Frederick Neill, H. K. Peace, Ronald Matthews, and Tom and Albert Vickers all finished their schooling with a spell in Germany. And several firms did a good trade with Germany in steel and tools, despite the fact that, as the Sheffield steelmen well knew, the end result might often be increasing imports of German cutlery made from Sheffield steel.

Not surprisingly, the Sheffield firms most active in that market were those with German origins or links: notably, Seebohm & Dieckstahl, Kayser, Ellison, Jonas & Colver, and Marsh Bros. Germany was an important component in Seebohm & Dieckstahl's thriving Continental business: the firm's day books for the 1860s show regular shipments via Hull and Grimsby to Dortmund, Stuttgart, and Remscheid—besides Paris, Liège, and St Petersburg. Although no business records have survived for Kayser, Ellison, it seems likely that Charles W. Kayser would have used his intimate knowledge of the Solingen cutlery trades to further the expansion of his firm's highly regarded razor steel. Jonas & Colver had financial interests in Germany, one trade journal in 1892 describing Joseph Jonas as a 'chief partner in a concern in the Black Forest, Germany, where they work up cold-rolled steel, supplied by his firm in Sheffield, into clock springs, electric bells, etc, and where several hundred hands are engaged'.[110] Germany was also Marsh Bros.' most important overseas market before 1914, largely due to the energetic salesmanship of Paul Kuehnrich. They too catered for the demand from Black Forest clock-makers for fine clock-spring steel, which was behind Marsh Bros.' decision in 1896 to acquire the Effingham Steel Works & Rolling Mills, so that the firm could produce its own cold-rolled strip.

Sheffield's Russian trade appears to have been equally important and three firms—Cammell, Saville, and Firth—established factories there. Cammell's first important links came in 1869, when they entered an agreement with the Yorkshire Engine Co. and the Gloucester Wagon Co. to buy a plot of land for development on the banks of the River Neva in St Petersburg. Besides armour-plate, Cammell's wished to exploit the trade in rails, locomotive and carriage wheels and axles, and other railway materials. By the end of the century Russian protectionism ensured that Cammell's needed to approach that market more directly and in 1900 the company decided to erect a file factory in southern Russia at Odessa. The Russia Cammell File Co. was capitalized at £30,000, with Cammell's investing about £20,000. Four years later the Cammell-Laird directors reported that it had 'rapidly extended its business', but that it had yet to earn a profit. In 1904 the business was shut and Cammell's withdrew from Russia.[111]

J. J. Saville's Russian factory was established in 1901 in Libau, near Riga, by workmen sent out from Sheffield. Almost nothing is known of its history, though an engraving shows it to have been, as one would expect, a small Sheffield-style works, with a single converting furnace. It appears to have operated until the First World War. More is known about Firth's involvement in Russia.[112] In 1901 the firm established a small file-making facility in Riga, then two years later bought a newly built steelworks nearby. This was the Salamander Works, a grandiose scheme conceived

---

[110] *IMR* 18 (1 Nov. 1892), 16016.
[111] Cammell-Laird Papers, Birkenhead. Directors' Minute Books.
[112] SCL Firth Directors' Minute Books, Nos. 4–5.

by Austrian and Russian interests that had rapidly gone bankrupt. Using gas-fired crucible furnaces and a small basic Siemens furnace, Firth's hoped to repeat their great American success with Firth-Sterling by manufacturing tool steel and projectiles. But they were to be disappointed. Although Russia's war with Japan appeared to promise large shell orders, the Revolution of 1905 immediately brought complications. A manager at the file factory accidentally shot himself, a foreman was murdered, and the life of the managing director, John G. Crookston, was threatened and military protection was needed. The Salamander Works was also badly managed. Harry Brearley, who was sent to Riga until 1907 to provide technical support, recorded that blooms for projectiles were to be imported from Sheffield and then forged and machined—'simple and straightforward operations, when carried out by experienced men in a well-equipped factory; but the Riga factory was not well equipped, and [there were] no experienced men'.[113] Local men were soon trained, but once they had learned their jobs they struck for higher wages.

Firth's evidently believed that the appointment of a suitable managing director at a high salary—Crookston was earning about £4,000 a year—would allow the Riga works to function with occasional visits from the Sheffield board. Although that policy had worked well in Pittsburgh, under someone as able as Lewis J. Firth, it proved a mistake in Riga, where Crookston was 'not an ideal manager'. By 1907 Firth's had invested £185,000 at the Salamander site, but no large shell orders had materialized, and the venture was beginning to strain the resources of the Sheffield company. One director stated that the Riga Works would never be properly run until a board of directors was appointed and made systematic visits. Lewis J. Firth, recognizing a disaster when he saw one, refused to visit Russia, arguing that he had enough on his hands in Pittsburgh and that the trips already made to Riga by five directors of Brown and Firth's, three managers of Sheffield departments, and Firth's works engineers 'ought to be sufficient'. By about 1910 the Riga Works had edged into profit, but Firth's capital outlay had reached over £380,000. The company were paying £20,000 a year interest on the Riga debt alone and the Russian Government also owed the firm money. In 1912 the first large shell order had at last arrived from the Government, but by then Firth's had decided that no more capital should be provided and were planning to sell the works. However, it remained in production until 1915, when the war caused its evacuation. After the subsequent political upheavals in Russia, Firth's, like many other foreign firms, never recovered its assets.

Besides these firms, there were a number of others who traded largely with Russia. Joseph Dixon (c.1841–1890), one of the partners in Brown,

---

[113] Brearley, *Knotted String*, 72.

Bayley, & Dixon, brought the firm into close touch with the Russian market: he had worked in St Petersburg as a foreign traveller for John Brown. Kayser, Ellison built up a large Russian business before 1914. So, too, did Seebohm & Dieckstahl. Edgar Allen's had a Russian branch until 1916. Richard W. Carr was founded expressly to exploit the Russian crucible steel trade, where the partners had extensive experience, and a warehouse was opened outside Moscow, with depots elsewhere in Russia. The First World War and the Russian Revolution ended this Sheffield involvement abruptly, causing losses of both assets and outstanding debts. It was an experience that was common to many foreign ventures in Russia, most of which rarely realized their directors' expectations.

Although the history of these subsidiaries enables a few generalizations to be made, it is almost impossible at this distance to assess Sheffield's overall entrepreneurship and performance in overseas markets. Certainly, the town's exploitation of the American market before about 1870 was one of the great success stories of British nineteenth-century industrialization. It was done with some prodigious feats of travelling: J. H. Andrew with his 60 American trips; Joseph B. Ellison, with 70 or more journeys; Arthur Balfour with 73 transatlantic sea crossings. It was difficult to better this performance in the late nineteenth century, especially since overseas markets now contained few easy pickings. There was growing competition in steel from Germany, France, and America, where indigenous industries had been helped by a large internal market hedged in by protective duties. These were an increasing problem for Sheffield's exporters after the 1870s, when France, Switzerland, Belgium, the Zollverein, Italy, Spain, and America had introduced tariffs on steel.[114] In the United States these tariffs had a devastating effect on the Sheffield tool steel trade. Above all other factors, this was the one identified by Sheffield steelmasters as the reason for the relative decline of the city's export markets in the late nineteenth century. Moreover, some foreign countries had policies that favoured domestic productions. In 1904 Charles Kayser, in evidence before the Tariff Commission, highlighted the

general disposition of the buyers abroad to favour home productions. This is particularly the case in Germany, France, and Russia to a very large extent. If you go to Germany they will openly tell you that if they can buy from their home producers they will not buy anything from England. You will have the same reply made in France, and the Russians have gone so far that their Government has forbidden such works which are under Government control, and the railways, to use foreign materials at all.[115]

---

[114] Frederick Brittain, *Address . . . Before Council of the Sheffield Chamber of Commerce, 4 November 1875, on the Results of Foreign Tariffs, especially with Reference to Sheffield* (Sheffield, 1875); id., *British Trade and Foreign Competition* (London, 1877).

[115] Kayser, *Evidence*, 2.

In these circumstances, Sheffield's claim as a worldwide exporter became more difficult to sustain. There were also weaknesses in marketing, as there were in other English manufacturing towns. It was surely no coincidence that many of the best performers in the export trade, such as Edgar Allen, were linguists and salesman who had a keen appreciation of the need for making a special effort abroad. Allen's advertisements in directories by 1870 show him catering for the Continental market by offering orders 'executed in metrical or any other foreign measures or weights, and of shapes or forms suited to foreign markets'. Few Sheffield firms followed his example. Again, in 1892 Joseph Jonas was said by one trade journal to have

travelled most extensively not only over the whole Continent, but also over America, Canada, Turkey, and other countries. It is to his intimate knowledge of them, together with his familiarity with their peoples—their manners and customs and languages—that he attributes much of his success in winning business for his firm. When, at the meetings of the Chamber of Commerce, Mr Jonas has, in excellent idiomatic English, expressed his views on important questions of trade and commerce, the question has arisen—how many of the Englishmen he was addressing could interest and instruct in an equal degree a gathering of Germans in their mother tongue?[116]

In truth, few Sheffielders had much expertise in foreign languages: apart from Edgar Allen and the German-born Sheffield steelmen, only John Bedford, Arthur Balfour, John Rollin of Vessey & Sons, and James R. Hoyle of Firth's seem to have had linguistic skills out of the ordinary.

In this context, the experience of Paul Kuehnrich at Marsh Bros. is instructive. When he became the firm's foreign traveller he earned £100 a year in the beginning, but his commissions steadily mounted as he pushed up the firm's turnover. In 1894 he earned £800; by 1896 over £1,000; and the following year his earnings had topped £2,000. According to Kuehnrich, Marsh Bros.' turnover increased from £6,000 when he joined to £130,000 in 1897. Though Marsh Bros. contested Kuehnrich's figures, arguing instead that they were £17,000 and £120,000 respectively, it was nevertheless a remarkable performance. It appears to have been entirely due to Kuehnrich's selling efforts and shows that there was definitely room for improvement in Marsh Bros.' salesmanship. One wonders how many other traditional Sheffield family firms might have benefited from a similar injection of sales skills. Sheffield's overseas trading effort before 1914 appears to have been creditable, but Kuehnrich raises the question as to whether it might have been even better.

[116] *IMR* 18 (1 Nov. 1892), 16016.

4

Sustaining a Lead in
Cutlery and Tools

Sheffield cutlery has taken the lead, and kept it, not by any development of the factory system, or wholesale introduction of machinery,
but by the simple means of putting the best workmanship on the
best materials. Nowhere perhaps in the kingdom are the ideas of
masters and workpeople more conservative than they are here. The
old methods are universally regarded as the best, and no new-fangled
notions are supposed to have any chance against special knowledge
and skill of hand and eye.

As regards foreign competition, the mind of the typical Sheffield
artisan is strongly imbued and fortified with the notion that it can
never touch him seriously. He admits that the low-priced labour of
France, Belgium, and Germany will enable those countries to under-
sell him in the very commonest wares, but he cares little for that; he
contends that the business of a cutting instrument is to cut, and if that
is what is wanted people must come to *him*. It takes a great deal to
disturb his equanimity on the subject.

Charles Hibbs in *Great Industries of Great Britain* (London, 1886), iii.
190, 225.

The contrast between Sheffield's pleasant leafy suburbs to the south-west
of the town and the grimy manufacturing districts along the River Don
has always been marked. But in a city intersected by so many hills and
streams, the character of Sheffield's inner residential suburbs can also
offer some surprising contrasts. To the south of the city centre lies an area
known as Sharrow. To reach it, a visitor approaching from Sheffield town
centre will probably pass through the old tool and steel manufacturing
area known as Little Sheffield, and its associated residences. However,
only a mile or two distant from the city, the character of these suburbs
changes abruptly. Wide tree-lined roads, flanked by large, attractive grey-
stone houses, suddenly replace the narrow residential streets. The roads
converge at the stone-arched entrance to an impressive landscaped estate,
built on one of the gently sloping valley sides overlooking the River Sheaf.
Here, nestling in the trees is the largest mansion of all—Kenwood
House—the former home of cutlery manufacturer, George Wostenholm.
Built by Wostenholm on the profits of the American trade (and, it was

said, designed by him as an homage to the urban landscapes he had admired in America), Kenwood was a conscious advertisement to the town of his success and status. Even today, there is no better way of appreciating the unparalleled wealth and prestige of the Sheffield cutlery industry in the nineteenth century than a walk around the leafy roads of Kenwood.[1]

When George Wostenholm was transforming Sharrow in the 1850s and 1860s, the Sheffield cutlery and tool industry was unrivalled. The light trades were still a dominant part of Sheffield's cluster of steel-producing industries—a potent emblem of the town's unique craftsmanship. In the two decades after 1850, the determinants of Sheffield's prosperity in cutlery and tool manufacture—the craft skills of its workforce, the extreme subdivision of labour, the interconnections of its myriad trades, the reputation of its leading firms, and the prestige of the Sheffield mark—all continued to extend Sheffield's pre-eminence over both domestic and foreign centres of production.

At the fountainhead of the international supply of crucible steel, Sheffield steadily tightened its grip on cutlery production in the United Kingdom. Sheffield employed about 60 per cent of the country's cutlery workers in 1841; but after 1881 it appears that Sheffielders never accounted for less than 80 per cent of United Kingdom cutlers, and the figure may have approached 100 per cent by the end of the century, when the number of cutlers (narrowly defined) was about 13,000.[2] Sheffield's victory over the old English centres of cutlery—Salisbury, London, and Birmingham—was almost complete. Sheffield also had a major share in the manufacture of other steel tools. In file manufacture, for example, its employment share rose from about 55 per cent in 1841 to about 65 per cent in 1901. Its grip on other sectors of the steel tool trade was less pronounced; nevertheless, Sheffield's share of the national workforce in cutlery and various classes of tools never slipped below 50 per cent in the late nineteenth century.

Internationally, Sheffield overshadowed its foreign rivals before 1870. Neither the old cutlery centres in Germany and France—Thiers and Solingen—nor the new competitors in New England could match Sheffield in either quality or output. British exports of hardware and cutlery (a rough measure of Sheffield's performance) hit £4 million in 1857 and surpassed that amount for several years in the mid-1860s. The trade fell away slightly in the years up to 1870, but then the upward trend

---

[1] Nether Edge Neighbourhood Group, *They Lived in Sharrow and Nether Edge* (Sheffield, 1988).

[2] G. I. H. Lloyd, *The Cutlery Trades* (London, 1913), 434–42; S. Taylor, 'The Industrial Structure of the Cutlery Trades, 1870–1914', in C. Binfield *et al.* (eds.), *The History of the City of Sheffield* (Sheffield, 1993), ii. 194–210, 194; S. Pollard, 'Labour', in Binfield, *History*, 260–78, 262.

was resumed: exports reached a peak in 1872 when they registered £5 million.[3] The export trade to the United States was particularly good, since American industry was still finding its feet and tariffs were at an extremely low level. Sheffield trade directories show that the American trade still dominated the output of the town's cutlery manufactories before 1860. The Bowie knife trade was still a good source of income for the industry leaders, Wostenholm and Rodgers, as the Mexican War and the California Gold Rush stimulated demand. Other makers also cleverly exploited new fashions and demand across the Atlantic. Henry Barge specialized in three- and four-blade Congress knives; John Hinchcliffe advertised 'fancy spring, lock, sneck, dagger, and American Indian Knives'; and Unwin & Rodgers manufactured their patented pistol-knife.

The industry leaders reflected this expansion. Joseph Rodgers was at the height of its dominance: its workforce had grown from the 500 of the 1840s to about 1,200 by the early 1870s. Its Sycamore Street site in the city centre had steadily swallowed adjacent properties, so that by the 1860s the firm owned the whole block of buildings skirting Norfolk Street, Milk Street, Sycamore Street, and Flat Street. The result was the 'most compact and complete' cutlery factory in the world.[4] The Norfolk Street showrooms, which had been refurbished in 1860, were still the world's biggest shop window and advertisement for top-quality cutlery. Wrote one contemporary, in 1862: 'It is impossible for the visitor to get a better idea of what is accomplished in the finish and elaboration of cutlery and other Sheffield manufactures, than by inspection of these show-rooms; and nothing can furnish a more striking example of the industry and skill of man, acting upon the raw products of nature.'[5] Rodgers had extended its product-line to include silver- and electroplated goods; it had also acquired a London office, besides those in New York, Montreal, Toronto, and New Orleans, and India had become an important market.

George Wostenholm & Son, after a later start, had expanded particularly rapidly, especially during the heyday of the American trade. Its workforce had mushroomed to about 650 in 1855, and though this was not maintained, in 1871 Wostenholm's still employed 525 men, women, and children. Though its markets were not as widespread as Rodgers'—even after the American Civil War, George Wostenholm's main customer was the United States—he had succeeded in making the I*XL mark internationally renowned and had made the Washington Works the second largest cutlery factory in the town. Not far behind these firms was Mappin

---

[3] Lloyd, *Cutlery Trades*, 481.

[4] 'Messrs. Joseph Rodgers & Sons, Cutlery Manufacturers, Sheffield', *Ironmonger*, 13 (31 Jan. 1871), 5–6.

[5] *Pawson and Brailsford's Illustrated Guide to Sheffield and Neighbourhood* (Sheffield, 1862), 138–9.

Bros.' Queen's Cutlery Works, with about 300 to 400 workers in the 1860s. At that time these were the largest cutlery factories in the world.

Sheffield's craftsmanship in cutlery was also reaching a peak at this time. The town's unmatched technical virtuosity was apparent at virtually every trade exhibition, where Sheffield manufacturers grew accustomed to carrying away the prize medals. At the Great Exhibition in 1851, the town's newspapers expressed 'a conviction that Sheffield bears away the palm from all competitors'.[6] At the Crystal Palace the most dazzling expression of Sheffield's artistry was the showcase of Joseph Rodgers & Sons, containing its Norfolk Knife. A giant sportsman's knife—measuring nearly three feet when opened—with 75 blades and tools, carved pearl scales, and superbly worked and acid-etched blades, the Norfolk Knife still stands today (in Cutlers' Hall in Sheffield) as arguably the finest example of cutlery craftsmanship ever made. Wostenholm's also produced its share of exhibition pieces, which are now bought at fancy prices at antique fairs (at an American auction in 1992 a large I*XL exhibition Bowie knife changed hands for $120,000!). The firm's pattern books at about this time, with their carefully hand-drawn ornate folding knives, confirm that this was a golden age of Sheffield cutlery—a period when the handicraft of the little mester was perfectly attuned to the demand for premium hunting, pocket, and trade knives.[7]

The tool trades were part of this expansion up to the early 1870s, though these have been far less studied by historians than has cutlery.[8] Table 4.1 shows that this sector was also typified by the increasing diversity and number of trades and firms. Naturally, there was considerable overlap amongst the firms enumerated—a leading manufacturer might appear in several of the categories—so that these figures should not simply be totalled as an estimation of the size of the Sheffield tool industry. Nevertheless, the number of firms must have been well over 250. Many were small-scale manufacturers—little mesters, employing only a few hands—but several of these firms had become fairly large, employing anything between 200 and 400 men. In tracing their history, we are hindered by a lack of business records, but information culled from the trade press and other sources shows them keeping pace with the cutlery firms. This should not be surprising, since many of the largest tool companies were integrated businesses, melting their own crucible steel and performing many of the finishing processes themselves. As crucible steelmakers in their own right, they could share in the rising demand both for tools and for steel.

[6] *SI*, 10 May 1851.

[7] SCL Wostenholm Records (hereinafter Wos) 536. Pattern books, especially the volume for 1861–70.

[8] Ruskin Gallery, *The Cutting Edge* (Sheffield, 1992).

Table 4.1. *The Sheffield tool trades, 1871*

Trade	Number of Firms
Anvils and vices	19
Augers and gimlets	24
Awl blades, steel tacks, and sack needles	20
Bookbinders' tools	10
Braces and bits	10
Edge tools	78
Engineers' tools	49
Engravers', carvers', and turners' tools	7
Files	171
Garden shears	11
Garden tools	11
Hammers	39
Hay and manure forks	42
Joiners' tools	56
Mill chisels	2
Plasterers' tools	3
Rules (box and ivory)	5
Saws	104
Scythe and sickle	27
Sheep shears	20
Silversmiths', coppersmiths', and tinners' tools	6
Spade and shovel	11
Strickles	3
Weavers' shears and nippers	6

Source: White's General and Commercial Directory of Sheffield (Sheffield, 1871).

The file business was of enormous importance to Sheffield and so great was the number of firms involved that it is impossible to describe them all in detail. One of the most ancient was W. K. & C. Peace, which was amongst the oldest crucible steelmakers in the town. Having occupied premises in Neepsend, in about 1854 they moved to Mowbray Street, where the business began expanding steadily. A key component in this expansion were American orders, cultivated by one of the firm's partners, Charles Peace (1823–94), who took up residence there from 1853 to 1875.[9] Other important makers included Thomas Jowitt & Son at the Scotia Works and J. R. Spencer & Son at the Albion Works, both of which had

[9] 'The Story of W. K. & C. Peace: Sheffield Firm's Bi-Centenary', *IMR* 36 (1 May 1910), 71–2. This firm should not be confused with Peace, Ward & Co.'s Agenoria Works, which was also a major manufacturer of steel and files and was said to have employed over 500 hands in the early 1860s. See *Ironmonger*, 5 (31 Aug. 1863), 212–15.

built up a reputation for hand-cut files. Describing the activities of Thomas Jowitt, one trade journal, using a somewhat tortured fishing metaphor, had remarked that he had 'sedulously and profusely baited' the manufacturing fishing ground of America and Canada, so that 'the harvest puts his successors beyond the necessity of seeking new fields'.[10] When his son, Albert Jowitt, became a partner in 1862, he continued the policy, making the pilgrimage across the Atlantic every summer. Larger premises were soon needed for the business at the Royd Works, Attercliffe. Another leading maker of files was the firm of William & Samuel Butcher. The two brothers' steel- and toolmaking business, which embraced a steelworks in Neepsend and large multi-storey factory on Arundel Street, reached its peak in the 1860s with about a thousand workers, producing files, razors, chisels, and planes.

Other makers were closely identified with saws. Spear & Jackson was probably the most prominent, now firmly established in the Aetna Works on Savile Street, where it employed over 600 workers by 1880, producing saws and files, edge tools, and machine knives from its own steel.[11] Taylor Bros., founded in about 1835 and based at the Adelaide Works, also had a reputation for its saws and tools. A trade journal noted that the Taylors' name on saws was a household word and that the partners had steadily pushed the business forward—'as one market has been closed to them, opening out another'—and extended 'their premises from time to time to meet the ever-increasing demand for their goods'.[12]

In scythe manufacture, Tyzack's gradually emerged from the pack. After acquiring in 1847 the water-powered Abbeydale Works, with its crucible steelmaking capacity, the firm (which became W. Tyzack, Sons & Turner, after a son-in-law, Benjamin Turner, was taken into partnership in 1870) pioneered several new branches of the trade. Besides continuing with the production of its 'Crown' (forged) and 'Patent' scythes, they were credited as the first company to manufacture reaper and mowing machine sections. By 1876 Tyzack's had outgrown their Rockingham Street premises and had purchased a new site at Heeley, alongside the Little London Dam, from which the new works took its name. Later, further rolling mill, steel-, and scythe-making capacity was added, so that the firm could eventually produce

not only various descriptions of single and double shear, blister, and other steels, but the manufacture of all kinds of knives for reaping and mowing machines,

[10] 'The New Master Cutler of Sheffield [Albert A. Jowitt]', *Ironmonger*, 28 (2 Sept. 1882), 326.

[11] 'Messrs Spear & Jackson's Etna Works, Sheffield', *IMR* 5 (3 Jan. 1880), 2694–5.

[12] 'Messrs Taylor Brothers' Adelaide Works, Sheffield', *IMR* 7 (3 Oct. 1881), 3886–8.

knives for chaff and turnip cutters, knives for paper mills and tobacco works, all sorts of irons for planing, tonguing and carving for wood-working machinery, saws, scythes, forks, files and other similar goods.[13]

In 1868 relatives of the owners founded William A. Tyzack & Co. at the Stella Works in Hereford Street, a separate business for the manufacture of scythes and steel. In about 1872 this firm introduced steam-powered hammers for forging scythes, besides using machinery to 'fly' out its agricultural knives from sheet steel.[14]

One area with particularly fast growth potential before the 1870s was the production of sheep-shears. Sheffield makers had long supplied the domestic (and foreign) markets with shears, but the American Civil War, by disrupting the supply of cotton, stimulated the trade by encouraging sheep-breeding in South America, South Africa, and, especially, Australia and New Zealand. By 1875 it was calculated that in Australasia alone there were some 64 million sheep. One of the most successful new entrants to the shear trade in Sheffield was David Ward (d. 1889), owner of the edge tool business of Ward & Payne. Ward had initially expanded the company after the 1860s by buying the London carving tool business of S. J. Addis: though this prospered, it was soon overshadowed by Ward's success in the sheep-shear trade. By 1877, when the firm's workforce was approaching 400, Ward & Payne's trade to Australasia and the Cape was said to be larger than all the other Sheffield sheep-shear houses put together.[15] Another innovative newcomer to the trade was Burgon & Ball, a partnership launched in 1866 between Charles Burgon, a cutlery manufacturer, and James Ball, a scythe-maker. The business was formed to exploit Ball's sheep-shear patent, which covered the manufacture of shears blanked from sheet steel, so obviating forging and the complicated joining of shanks and blades. In 1873 Burgon & Ball opened the La Plata Works at Malin Bridge, on the banks of the River Loxley to the north-west of Sheffield, where machinery was installed to turn out 300–400 dozen patent shears weekly.[16]

Other firms and trades also illustrate this overall expansion and Sheffield's success in niche marketing. In the making of joiners' tools, William Marples & Sons had built its success on their metallic frame

---

[13] 'Messrs W. Tyzack, Sons & Turner's Works, Sheffield', *IMR* 13 (1 Dec. 1887), 10083–4. See also 'W. Tyzack, Sons & Turner Ltd. Centenary of Noted Sheffield Firm. Little London Works', *IMR* 38 (1 Aug. 1912), 497–8. See also R. M. Ledbetter, 'Sheffield's Industrial History from about 1700, with Special Reference to the Abbeydale Works' (Sheffield University MA, 1971); J. Peatman, 'The Abbeydale Industrial Hamlet: History and Restoration', *Industrial Archaeology Review*, 11 (Spring 1989), 141–54.

[14] 'William A. Tyzack & Co., Stella Works, Sheffield', *IMR* 5 (1 June 1879), 2266–7.

[15] 'David Ward Esq.', *IMR* 3 (3 Oct. 1877), 1189–90.

[16] 'Important Movement in the Sheep Shear Trade', *IMR* 5 (1 June 1878), 1595.

brace.[17] Based in Westfield Terrace, their premises had expanded by the 1870s almost back into Rockingham Street. Marples, aware of the way in which growing technical education was stirring an interest in popular mechanics and woodworking (in what was perhaps the first manifestation of 'Do-It-Yourself'), marketed their 'Amateur's Tool Chest', which was soon said to be accounting for half or more of the profits of the business. The firm of James Chesterman also manufactured braces and other hand tools, but it increasingly specialized in measuring tapes and equipment. By the mid-1860s, shortly before the founder's death, Chesterman's had expanded into a new site along the Ecclesall Road.[18] The output of other firms was equally specialist: George Barnsley & Sons manufactured an extensive range of shoemakers' tools;[19] while the output of Charles Skelton's Sheafbank Works, opened in 1870, was devoted to shovels and garden tools.[20]

Rodgers, Wostenholm, Spear & Jackson, Tyzack—these were the most visible signs of Sheffield's pre-eminence in cutlery and tools. However, cutlery factories employing over 500 and tool firms with more than 250 or so were still very much the exception. The expansion of the light trades up to 1870 had not altered this sector's traditional structure: the large firms were at the top of a squat pyramid. Even in the biggest factories, inworkers were not always in the direct control of the firm, and instead rented a bench and power from the bosses. They continued to pay for their own tools and materials and sold their products to any manufacturer. In slack times, factory owners were more than happy to allow these men to take on work from outside. Thus the whole industry functioned through a huge army of outworkers (making, of course, any employment rolls for the big firms highly approximate). The Norfolk Works and the Washington Works, despite their size (which was often exaggerated in contemporary reports and engravings), were really no more than large tenements. Dixon's huge Cornish Place Works at Neepsend and William Butcher's Arundel Street factory still stand as prime examples. Anyone inspecting their crumbling brickwork and grimy workshops in the 1990s, will recognize the truth of a Wostenholm cutler's portrait of the Washington Works (which has now been demolished) in the 1860s. It was 'not very elevating, everything was so crude and sordid: makeshift buildings, shops and closets, while hygienic conditions were never considered or even thought of. Washington Works . . . was generally lacking in

---

[17] 'William Marples & Sons, Hibernia Works, Sheffield', *IMR* 8 (2 Jan. 1883), 4821–22. See also Reg Eaton, *The Ultimate Brace: A Unique Product of Victorian Sheffield* (Hunstanton, 1989).

[18] Douglas J. Hallam, *The First 200 Years: A Short History of Rabone Chesterman Ltd.* (Birmingham, 1984).

[19] R. A. Salaman, *Dictionary of Leather-Working Tools c.1700–1950* (London, 1986).

[20] C.T. Skelton & Co., *Announcing One Hundred Years of Progress, 1855–1955* (Sheffield, 1955).

"tone". The dirty shops, the disregard of sanitary demands, and the arbitrary way the workmen were treated, all tended to low ideals of life.'[21]

The workers remained highly individualistic, resistant to change, and heavily unionized. The unions had helped produce a working class that was well fed and well housed in comparison with other working towns; but also one that had enough power, when it wished, to terrorize workers and masters when they failed to pay union dues, tried to cut wages, took on too many apprentices, or tried to introduce machinery which threatened handicrafts.[22] One writer commented in 1849 that 'the spirit of unionism seems to pervade the very atmosphere of the town: it is a habit of mind of which the inhabitants cannot get rid'.[23]

On the other hand, the Sheffield worker could still be described as the best in the world (in the traditional craft sense), with an unmatched commitment to quality and skill. One observer, noting that Sheffield knife blades were still ground with 'all the laborious application of an artist adding a few delicate touches to his work', added: 'It is doubtful whether any other trade of the same magnitude has derived so little advantage from mechanical agency in essential requirements, and to this happy chance may be ascribed the survival in the Sheffield cutler of that hearty interest and wholesome pride in his work which are seldom found in workmen whose intelligence has been discounted by a precise mechanism.'[24]

The adherence to craft skills and quality wares was also apparent at the top, amongst the owners of the larger factories. These men had certain similarities to their counterparts in the crucible steel trades: they were usually devoted to business, avoiding outside commitments, were often politically conservative, and ran their concerns as personal fiefdoms. Most of the large cutlery firms remained private partnerships: by the 1880s only Rodgers and Wostenholm had followed the steel firms in adopting limited liability (in 1870 and 1875, respectively), and even these retained their private character. At Rodgers' the family element was maintained by Robert Newbould and Joseph Rodgers, both related to the founders, becoming chairman and vice-chairman.[25] George Wostenholm had sold the business shortly before his death in 1876, but all the shares in the newly registered company were held by the board and associates within the concern. The main shareholders were William Nixon, the secretary and managing director, and James C. Wing, the co-managing director.

[21] Henry Coward, *Reminiscences* (London, 1919), 15.

[22] S. Pollard (ed.), *The Sheffield Outrages* (Bath, 1971).

[23] *Sheffield Times*, 30 June 1859.

[24] Henry J. Palmer, 'Cutlery and Cutlers at Sheffield', *The English Illustrated Magazine* (Aug. 1884), 659–69, 665.

[25] Joseph Rodgers & Sons, *Under Five Sovereigns* (Sheffield, 1911).

Bernard Wake, the chairman, and the firm's American agents, Asline Ward and Joseph Fisher, held the remaining shares. These men were from Sheffield's prosperous manufacturing class, either successful in other branches of the town's life—Wake was a partner in a well-known local solicitor's firm—or long-serving members of the company—Wing had joined Wostenholm's aged 11. Revealingly, they described themselves in the company minute book as 'gentlemen', and not until James Paine became a director in 1887 did one of the firm describe himself as a 'manufacturer'.[26]

But the cutlery business leaders differed in important respects from their cousins in the steel trades. In the same way that the craft unions in cutlery and steel were quite distinct—the latter were more distanced from their employers than the inbred, small-scale, craft-based unions in the light trades—so too were the cutlery and steel entrepreneurs. The different scale of operations and culture meant that, apart from exceptions such as Frederick Mappin and Albert Hobson,[27] who bridged the divide, the steelmakers and cutlers inhabited different spheres. Cutlery and tool manufacture was probably a more 'closed' world than steel by the 1870s, both socially and technologically. There was obviously nothing to compare in the light trades with the enormous revolution in scale and techniques that occurred in steelmaking after 1856, which brought new capital, labour, and ideas into the region. Whereas this habituated steel managers to continual change—so that their conservative political views were not unduly extended into the business world—cutlery manufacture remained largely indigenous, mostly immune to disturbing crosscurrents, and lacking the cosmopolitanism of steel. For example, the occasional foreign entrepreneur chanced his hand in the town's cutlery and tool trades before about 1880, but there was nothing to compare with the major entrepreneurial input that the Germans supplied in crucible steel.[28] The town's well-known dislike of the Germans was perhaps influential in ensuring that the industry was almost entirely run by Sheffielders.

[26] G. Tweedale, 'Strategies for Decline: George Wostenholm & Son and the Sheffield Cutlery Industry', *THAS* 17 (1993), 43–56.

[27] Sir Frederick Mappin (1821–1910), who had directed one of the leading cutlery firms until 1859, moved into steel in the 1860s after buying Turton's and then became involved in the town's railway, gas, and water interests. See A. C. Howe, 'Sir Frederick Thorpe Mappin', in D. J. Jeremy (ed.), *Dictionary of Business Biography* (London, 1984–6), iv. 115–20; *SDT*, 19 Mar. 1910. Sir Albert Hobson (1861–1923) owned one of the largest cutlery firms in Sheffield at the turn of the century—Thomas Turner's—and also became chairman of the steelmakers, Jessop's. See 'Sheffield's First Citizen: Remarkable Career of Mr A. J. Hobson: Business Lord Mayor', *IMR* 37 (1 Dec. 1911), 1006–7; *SDT*, 21 Apr. 1923.

[28] Continental immigrants did not make a decisive impact on the cutlery industry until the Richartz arrived in the city in the 1930s (see Ch. 8). In my searches of the obituaries of 19th-c. cutlers, the only significant foreign-born cutler was Ernest Reuss, head of the Mazeppa Works on West Street, who arrived in Sheffield from Alsace in about 1868. See *SDT*, 3 Feb. 1898.

In the light trades, Sheffield business leaders and their workers were determined to defend the status quo, confident in the belief that quality would win the argument over quantity. There was something in this, as we have shown: hand-forged and hand-ground cutlery made from shear and crucible steel is in some respects better than can be had in the 1990s. But this belief led Sheffield to discount foreign competition and the need for innovation and the upgrading of factors of production. In 1867 a revealing report appeared, written by John Wilson, the official Sheffield artisans' reporter for the French Exhibition of 1867. Although he admitted that Continental productions showed generally a great advance after the trade exhibitions of 1851 and 1862, he had an explanation: 'If the progress made by other countries seems greater than our own, it is because in the manufacture of cutlery we are much nearer perfection; and therefore it is impossible that our progress should be as marked as those emerging from a rude state of manufacturing.'[29]

This was remarkably complacent; nor was it very accurate, since even the light trades could not avoid change. First, the steel industry was about to overtake cutlery as a major source of the town's wealth, allowing steelmakers the chance to make fortunes that would dwarf even those of John Rodgers and George Wostenholm. In the second half of the nineteenth century, the arrival in Sheffield of the Bessemer and Siemens processes, and the continued expansion of the crucible steel trades, transformed the overall structure of the town's industry. Before 1850, Sheffield was regarded as essentially 'one great workshop for the production of cutlery and edge-tools',[30] with steelmaking subservient. By 1900, the city was distinguished by its heavy steel trades, with cutlery and tool manufacture relegated to second place. The transformation was reflected in the changing structure of employment. In the mid-nineteenth century about 21,350 workers could be counted in the light trades, as against only about a quarter of that figure in steel. By 1891, however, steel was beginning to catch up: the figures being 32,100 and 21,384, respectively. By 1911, according to the census, employment in Sheffield itself in the heavy trades was nearly 40,000, with the light trades in second place with about 35,000 workers.[31]

Secondly, by the 1860s the Sheffield light trades were facing severe competition in overseas markets, particularly in America and Europe. In the United States, that foundation of many of the fortunes in Sheffield

---

[29] Quoted in *Great Industries of Great Britain* (London, 1886), iii. 225. Wilson's report is contained in *Reports of Artisans Selected by a Committee Appointed by the Council of the Society of Arts to Visit the Paris Universal Exhibition 1867* (London, 1867), 52–63. The volume also includes reports on saws and tools by William Bramhall, 37–51.

[30] *Penny Magazine* (1844), 161.

[31] Pollard, *History of Labour*, 331–4; Pollard, 'Labour', 269–70.

cutlery, the town's manufacturers found themselves squeezed between the rapidly developing home industry in Massachusetts and Connecticut and the influx of cutlery from Germany. The Americans had first made their mark in the 1840s in the production of woodworking tools, such as axes and saws, then followed this up by making a success of the production of cutlery. The reasons for the achievements of the Americans in hardware manufacture are by now well known: they had the advantages of a rapidly expanding domestic customer base, increasingly protected by the highest tariff barriers in the world; vast natural resources (the almost limitless acreages of forest were an especially great stimulus to the tool trades); shortages of skilled labour, which encouraged the use of machinery; a workforce largely free of union restrictions, which allowed technological innovation and new workplace practices to flourish; and the input of skilled Sheffield immigrant cutlers. The number of Sheffield cutlers involved in the birth of the American cutlery industry was particularly marked.

Yet although these men brought important technical skills and knowledge with them, those that stayed (and many soon returned) never succeeded in nurturing—except in isolated pockets—the clustered, handicraft cutlery industry they had left behind. According to one British hardware correspondent:

Most of the [Sheffield] immigrants who have rated as highly skilled mechanics at home get the conceit taken out of them before they have been long in [America], not by encountering the competition of men more highly skilled than themselves, but by the, to them, unequalled competition with the intelligence which adapts machinery to mechanical ends, and so enables unskilled labour to produce results which, by mere handicraft, are unattainable.[32]

American manufacturers used what know-how they needed from Sheffield cutlers, but high labour costs and the demand for low-quality, standardized patterns in very large quantities dictated a move to mechanization. Soon United States cutlery firms were stamping out their blades and parts from steel sheets (dispensing with forging) and grinding them by machine. While the Sheffielders were preening themselves at the trade exhibitions on the beauty and complexity of their wares and believed that other nations could never overtake them, the American manufacturers simply moved the goalposts, concentrating on simple, mass-produced items that would sell in huge quantities to the country's mainly agricultural (but rapidly urbanizing) population. The Germans had followed the same route towards mass production, which allowed them to increase their share of the American market at the expense of

[32] 'Sheffield v. American Cutlery', *Ironomonger*, 34 (25 July 1885), 171–2. See generally G. Tweedale, *Sheffield Steel and America* (Cambridge, 1987), 130–4.

Sheffield. By the mid-nineteenth century, for example, Germany had already captured the American scissor trade.

Consequently, Sheffield's exports of tools to America were already in decline by the 1840s; and exports of cutlery soon showed worrying signs of contraction. This at a time when the town's crucible steel trade was booming (ironically, supplying the raw material for American, and sometimes German, advances). The anxiety is reflected in the Sheffield press in the late 1840s, when there was an extended debate over the industry's failings—not dissimilar to the ruminations of 1970s' and 1980s' critics over the roots of the 'British disease'. One Sheffielder summarized the view from across the Atlantic and believed that the decline in the town's American trade was due to:

First, an habitual slowness in the early history of the town to *anticipate* or *even meet* the varied deviations from ordinary patterns of goods exported to different customers desired by their customers; Second, a gradual growth of vigorous, active manufacturers [in the United States] fostered by a rigorous system of protection against Sheffield; Thirdly, an equally determined and formidable competition with the products of German manufactories, which draw their advantage from Sheffield, not from any fiscal protection in their favour, but from the extremely low standard of living to which her simple people have been accustomed, and the consequent cheap rates at which labour can be had; and Fourthly, the very uncertain and impracticable state in which prices have for years been, owing to the constant disputes between masters and men.[33]

To this catalogue, we might in retrospect add others:

1. As the age of mass-produced cutlery began to appear across the Atlantic and in Germany, Sheffield industry, despite the quality of its products, was still in many respects antediluvian: workshops were still located in nooks and crannies, the tools primitive, working conditions poor, and wages often low. By the 1880s the industry was looking dated.

2. Supply, although highly flexible in meeting a variegated demand, was constrained by the limit set by hand methods. A failure to meet overseas orders was already apparent before the 1880s, when one manufacturer had admitted that his steel and files could not be 'produced in sufficient quantities to avert complications'.[34] The days when a handicraft industry based in one relatively isolated locality could supply the industrialized world were, not surprisingly, passing after the 1870s.

3. Though there was considerable growth potential in the Colonies and elsewhere for Sheffield products, many American and European countries were becoming increasingly urbanized, demanding cutlery that was better finished, packaged, and distributed than was customary in Sheffield. Tastes in tools were also becoming more sophisticated. As one reporter

---

[33] *Sheffield Times*, 30 June 1849.   [34] 'New Master Cutler', 326.

remarked in 1883, it was once the case that 'the appearance of the tool was not valued in the slightest degree; no matter how clumsy or ugly it was, satisfaction was felt if it would only do its work. Now, tools that are made for the mechanic must be "eyeable", otherwise they will not sell; and the more artistically they are got up and the more beautifully they are finished the more highly are they valued and appreciated.'[35]

4. Competition was intensifying, especially at the low-priced end of the market, which was not Sheffield's forte. This posed a difficult question for Sheffield manufacturers. Should they follow the German and American lead in mechanizing production to produce cheap products, so forsaking Sheffield's reputation; or should they restrict themselves to their traditional better-quality goods, and accept a smaller market?

In short, the Sheffield cutlery industry needed to find answers to a wide range of problems, if it wished to retain its competitive advantage. How did it respond?

When Godfrey Lloyd, in his study published in 1913, considered the question of the transition to machine methods in Sheffield in the late nineteenth century, he drew a portrait of an industry steadily relinquishing its craft heritage. He emphasized particularly the increasing use of steam-power after the 1850s, which favoured industrial concentration and the move to large-scale production: though he also noted that the reliance on manual skill was still characteristic of the industry, especially in the pocket-knife trade.[36] Subsequent research has not greatly altered this picture, though considerably more detail is available, which emphasizes— perhaps more than Lloyd allows—the pervasive resistance to new technology.

The sawmaking trades, being amongst the most physically arduous in the light trades, were the first to be mechanized. In the 1850s machines designed in America, a country which was on the brink of assuming world leadership in saw manufacture, were installed in Sheffield for circular-saw grinding. The pioneer was Spear & Jackson in 1851, though the firm had to tread very gingerly in introducing its first machine. Noted a trade journal: 'with respect to it, the men employed upon the premises pursued a somewhat singular policy. They offered no objection, but they rendered no assistance.'[37] Spear & Jackson were, however, more fortunate than John Wheatman, a small-scale sawmaker who had returned from America with the latest ideas on machine-grinding. When he introduced a machine for grinding long-saws there was an attempt to blow up his factory, instigated by William Broadhead of the infamous Saw Grinders' Union, and the machine was removed. The episode was a chapter in Sheffield's famous 'outrages'.

---

[35] 'William Marples & Sons', 4821–2.   [36] Lloyd, *Cutlery Trades*, 178–91.
[37] 'Messrs Spear & Jackson's Etna Works', 2694.

In edge tool manufacture, Burgon & Ball in the late 1860s also encountered problems in their attempt to introduce their patented sheep-shears. 'The sheep-shear grinders were members of a union, and they looked with grave suspicion upon any change that was made in their trade. Machine-made shears were given to them to grind, and not only did they refuse to do the work, but some of the shears have never been returned to this day,' reported a trade journal in 1878.[38] In scythe-making, the Tyzacks of Abbeydale fame had long been familiar with the risks of upsetting the unions: in 1842 a grinding hull at Abbeydale was blown up with gunpowder and twenty years later Joshua Tyzack, then joint manager of the works, was shot at several times on his way to work. In 1874 William A. Tyzack & Co. had put down steam-powered machinery for forging scythes, but the response was predictable: 'their men persistently refused to use the hammer, and threw every possible obstacle in the way'.[39]

Delay in introducing best-practice in the tool trades was unfortunate, since the window of opportunity in these matters is invariably narrow. Already by the 1860s, American tools were on sale in Sheffield—often better finished and more thoughtfully adapted to the requirements of the customer than Sheffield makes. According to one tool collector, the augers of the Russell Jennings Co., Connecticut, were the first United States product offered for sale by a Sheffield merchant in 1864. Within a decade or two, Disston saws, Stanley planes, and Millers' braces were amongst the United States products sold by British dealers. William Marples stocked a full range of such tools by 1880,[40] besides selling a range of their own American 'novelties'. Underlining the North American influence was the Hardy Patent Pick Co., founded in Sheffield in about 1875 by Charles Hardy and Edward Saynor, which made a speciality of mining picks with interchangeable heads. The owners were American and Canadian, respectively.[41]

This did little to stem Sheffield's industrial Luddism, perhaps the best example of which was in file manufacture. This had proved one of the most difficult processes to mechanize, since not until after the 1860s were machines available that could match the unique blend of delicacy and physical force of the craftsman. Besides allowing for minute variations in the steel, it was said that with each deft hammer-blow the hand-cutter could impart a peculiar twist to the chisel, giving the teeth of the file a

[38] 'Important Movement in Sheep Shear Trade', 1595, which noted that Ward & Payne were in dispute in 1878 with their grinders for exactly the same reason. Another dispute in the sheep-shear trade led to the founding of a new company. See 'New Works of the Co-operative Sheffield Sheep Shear Society Ltd.', *IMR* 32 (3 July 1906), 314–16.

[39] 'William A. Tyzack & Co., Stella Works', 2266.

[40] Kenneth Roberts' introduction to William Marples Ltd., *Price List of American Tools and Hardware* (1909, repr. 1980).

[41] 'The Hardy Patent Pick Co.', *IMR* 3 (1 Mar. 1878), 1439–40; *IMR* 11 (1 Oct. 1885), 7603–4.

greater sharpness than could be obtained with the 'dead' strokes of the machine. However, it seems clear that by the 1880s—when there were well-publicized trials between machine-made and hand-made files—most of the technical difficulties in machining files had been solved, and only specialist files needed hand-cutting.[42] File-cutting machines were rapidly adopted in America, where manual methods had died out by the 1890s. One would have imagined that file-cutting machines, which freed workers from one of the most unpleasant and tedious jobs in the light trades, would also have been welcomed in Sheffield, even if there was some initial opposition. Far from it. Even after the unions had lost a bitter dispute in 1865 over the introduction of machines for grinding files, hostility to machine-cutting continued. Although some of the leading firms had laid down machines—by 1910 W. K. & C. Peace had 30 to 40 machine file-cutters—there were still some 2,300 hand-cutters at work in Sheffield (even Peace's had a hand-cutting shop on the premises). After the Second World War, there was at least one hand-cutting file workshop in Sheffield, at Hillsborough.

It should be emphasized that this conservatism was not confined entirely to the workforce. Factory owners were often opposed to the new technology, mainly because of machinery's impact on the quality of the products and the mystique of the trade. For example, one of the leading filemakers, J. R. Spencer & Son, stood out against machine-cutting. In 1878, it was said that, having built up its reputation with hand-cut files, the firm was not 'in any degree prejudiced against machinery as such; only that, not yet, in their opinion, has the machinery been produced that will do the work equally well with the human hand and human eye'.[43] By then, such an attitude was probably unwarranted, but it was shared by others such as the owners of George Fisher & Co., who in the early 1890s, 'steadfastly set [their] face against file-cutting machines'.[44] Even in 1913, makers such as William Spencer & Son advertised in local directories that their files were 'guaranteed entirely hand-cut'.

In cutlery manufacture a similar reluctance to disturb the tried and trusted ways is also evident. Mechanization appears to have first arrived in the town in 1861, when James Drabble & Co. began manufacturing

---

[42] For an account of traditional filemaking, see Walter White, *A Month in Yorkshire* (London, 5th edn., 1879), 256–62. For modern methods, see Eric N. Simons, *Steel Files* (London, 1947). This book, written by a man who had the benefit of being intimately acquainted with both hand- and machine-cutters in Sheffield, provides the following verdict on which was best (p. 31). 'The machine-cut file is unquestionably superior because (a) it is made of better quality material; (b) the teeth are consistently uniform; (c) it is made by a process capable of more scientific control.'

[43] 'J. R. Spencer & Son, File Manufacturers, Albion Steel Works, Sheffield', *IMR* 4 (2 Oct. 1878), 1829–30.

[44] *The Century's Progress* (London, 1893), 114.

machine-made table knives, so that it 'could compete with American and German manufacturers, the former having set [Sheffield] an example twenty years ago of applying machines to the purposes of manufacturing table cutlery, etc; and the latter by cheap labour'.[45] A handful of other makers were similarly inspired by the Americans: Nixon & Winterbottom in an 1876 Sheffield trade directory announced 'Cutlery by Machinery! The Interchangeable System!' above an engraving of the company's table and carving knives. In 1884 Samuel Staniforth introduced steam-powered forging of table and butcher blades at his factory in Carver Street—apparently successfully.[46] However, these developments were not widespread and they occurred in the more mass-produced items, such as table knives. In the more labour-intensive branches, such as pocket-knives, mechanical methods made much slower headway. Joseph Rodgers had mechanized some of its processes, such as polishing, by the 1870s, and some of its blades were 'goffed' (power-forged) for its medium and cheaper wares. But for top-quality work, especially folding, hunting, and trade knives, traditional hand-forging held sway, since Rodgers believed that 'for many processes in the manufacture of cutlery the human hand cannot be superseded by the most dexterous mechanical arrangements'.[47]

Wostenholm's were equally conservative. The firm's directors were perfectly aware of developments across the Atlantic. One of them visited a factory at Bridgeport, Connecticut, and noted that instead of the laborious Sheffield hand-forging:

Their blades are punched out of sheet and ground by machinery. They say they leave the steel, as far as possible, to the steelmaker, and ask him to supply a grade that does not require forging to make it fit for use, thus they avoid any risk of burning by the forger. Their blades, they say, cost more to grind, but they save the cost of forging, squaring, straightening, etc, and have no wasters.[48]

But in Sheffield craftsmanship reigned supreme, the firm reporting proudly in about 1897: 'The manufacture of first-class Spring Knives does not admit the use of much machinery, and in these works hand-labour—except for grinding and polishing—is almost exclusively employed, even Table Knives and Carvers being forged in the old way.'[49] They were withering in their scorn of mass-produced blades. One director, James Paine, stated: 'Goffed blades are no good. All those I saw when in the States, even those of Rodgers' make, are good for nothing. If anyone wants

---

[45] 'Machine-Made Table Knives', *SI*, 29 May 1862.
[46] *SDT*, 5 Oct. 1910.
[47] *Pawson and Brailsford's Illustrated Guide* (Sheffield, 1879 edn.), 164.
[48] SCL Wos. Letter from Colver's first US trip, 7 Nov. 1913.
[49] Ibid. Secretary's copybook No. 5, press release, n.d. Spring knives are pocket-knives: i.e. knives with blades which open and close on a spring.

a good Table Knife, there is nothing for it but Hand-Forged Double Shear, and the time will come when people will realise that fact.'[50]

While American makers were turning out 'their knives as regular in appearance as are a dozen of Colt's pistols of one pattern',[51] Sheffield was moving in the other direction towards the high-quality end of the market—a move partly dictated by the structure of the industry, and partly by the conviction that the old standards should not be compromised. Some firms restated the quality ethos with even greater emphasis. Brookes & Crookes, for example, a cutlery firm founded in 1858 by John Brookes and Thomas Crookes, established a reputation for particularly fine folding- and gadget-knives. In 1882, it was said that: 'Their policy has been to make themselves acquainted with what persons under special circumstances and in following special pursuits required in the shape of tools, and then [combine] practical utility with the highest art and most perfect workmanship.' The result was some superb pieces of Victoriana, 'in a great variety of patterns, with "scales" of pearl, ivory, shell, stag and buffalo. Some of them are elaborately carved, the blades and instruments are of the best steel, and the backs of some of them are most skilfully worked.'[52] The manuscript pattern books of Christopher Johnson & Co., another high-class maker of sportsman's knives, show the enormous care that was lavished on these products. One knife is described as follows:

$5\frac{1}{2}$-inch diamond-cut black buffalo sporting knife, + beards and washer, five springs, long clip blade, buttonhook, turnscrew and file combined at end, leather punch, saw and disgorger combined, sacking needle and pen blade at head, scissors and picker on pile side, tweezers and ten-inch rule in mark side, full sunk, the inside metal scales milled, centre spring polished, the springs on either side milled, outside spring lapt, lock at head, [oval] shield in centre, the inside of centre springs fluted, large [?] shackle, corkscrew and gimlet corn blade and nail file on back.[53]

Such knives, almost entirely hand-made, sold for anything from 40s. to 74s. each in the early 1900s—a considerable investment for a pocket-knife.

The commitment of the King of Cutlers, Joseph Rodgers, to its craft heritage was not surprisingly undimmed. In 1887, to ensure greater quality control, it began the manufacture of shear steel at a site at Wadsley Bridge; then in 1894 it began producing its own crucible steel at its River Lane Works in Sheffield. The manufacture of a large array of pocket-knives, complicated sports knives and ornate daggers and hunting knives was still this firm's forte. No matter that this could sometimes be a restricted market: in Sheffield this was seen as a virtue. Of the table cutlery

---

[50] Ibid. Copybook No. 4, Paine to F. B. Gurney, 8 Aug. 1896.
[51] 'Sheffield and Its Manufactures', *Ironmonger*, 37 (15 Jan. 1887), 89.
[52] 'Messrs Brookes & Crookes, Atlantic Works', *IMR* 8 (1 July 1882), 425–6.
[53] SCL Wos. Christopher Johnson Pattern Book, n.d., but probably late 19th c.

manufacturer Richard Elliott (*c*.1805–92), it was said that 'his motto was "quality". He preferred to be content earning a livelihood by doing the best possible work, even if it had to be sold at an inadequate price.'[54]

It was unusual for foreign entrepreneurs to join this rarified craft industry. Interestingly, one of the few that did—the American, Andrew Jordan (*c*.1846–1929), a St Louis merchant—was attracted by the opportunity to make goods of only the highest quality. He refused to deal in machine-made articles and when he opened his East India Works in Sheffield in about 1870 he specialized in kitchen and butcher knives, many of which he shipped to his homeland. In his catalogues, Jordan called these kitchen and butcher knives the 'Best on Earth'. Writes one antique cutlery dealer: 'Although his was an era of grossly exaggerated advertising claims, this claim, as far as I can tell, was true.'[55] Jordan used a special formula of double shear steel for the blades, a steel renowned for its cutting properties, along with seasoned Persian boxwood handles, a wood that wears almost like iron.

A feature of the move into the luxury goods market was the growth of the silver, electroplate, Britannia metal, and nickel-silver business. Sheffield firms benefited from the Victorian passion for gadgets and ornate tableware, including dinner services, asparagus dishes, soup tureens, egg-boilers, wine coolers, decanters, sugar crushers, flasks, besides a wide variety of cutlery items—silver fruit knives, fish slicers, and spoons.[56] Sheffield was able to compete with Birmingham by supplying the demand for top quality (the Midlands city producing lighter and cheaper wares)—a market which, although it appears to have peaked by 1904, was to offer further openings in the Colonies. Walker & Hall were the leaders in the electroplate market, the company reaching its maximum extent in the decade or two before 1914; and James Dixon's Cornish Place Works were not far behind. Several cutlery firms also entered the market. For example, by the late 1890s Needham, Veall, & Tyzack and Wheatley Bros. extended their product ranges to include the manufacture of electroplate and other luxury goods. So too did Rodgers, whose showrooms sold silver cigarette cases and flasks, dressing cases of toilet requisites, travelling sets, fancy needlework kits, and cutlery in presentation cases. Mappin & Webb—formed in the 1860s by Frederick Mappin's younger brother, John—took this policy to its logical conclusion: before the First World War they began abandoning the mass cutlery market entirely in favour of silverplated wares, then jewellery (absorbing Mappin

---

[54] *SDT*, 18 June 1892.

[55] B. Levine, *Levine's Guide to Knives and Their Values* (Northbrook, Ill., 2nd edn., 1993), 485.

[56] Gill Booth, *Diamonds in Brown Paper* (Sheffield, 1988); Frederick Bradbury, *History of Old Sheffield Plate* (Sheffield, 1912).

Bros. in 1902). (The result is apparent in the 1990s, since Mappin & Webb are no longer identified as Sheffield cutlers, but London luxury-goods dealers.) After 1880 even second-ranking firms, such as George Butler's and Christopher Johnson, began offering plated ware and a range of dessert spoons and fish carvers.

To ensure that these high-quality products remained competitive, there was an enormous emotional and practical commitment to the defence of Sheffield trade marks. No one who examines the history of the Victorian and Edwardian Sheffield cutlery industry can fail to note the amount of attention and resources that firms poured into defending both their illustrious 'Sheffield' name and their own marks. The subject dominates trade discussions in the local press, the work of the Cutlers' Company, the minute books of the Sheffield Chamber of Commerce, and the evidence of the city's industrialists to government committees. In 1911 'honest trading' was described in Sheffield as the 'foundation-stone of the commercial edifice' and the trade mark issue as a 'burning topic at Sheffield at the present time'.[57] The subject is indeed of considerable interest: whatever one may think of the wisdom of Sheffield's fascination with the subject, no trading centre—as the city was fond of pointing out—suffered so much from counterfeit marking. As a consequence, no other manufacturing centre was as influential in formulating and contributing to trade mark theory and legislation.

Wostenholm's I*XL and Rodgers' Star and Maltese Cross were the most copied marks of all. In 1908 Rodgers had noted with satisfaction that in Persia, India, and Ceyon, they had been paid the ultimate compliment of having their name enter the language as an adjective for superlative quality. But the company minute books show that the firm also spent much time attempting to deal with fraudulent marking. In 1911 Rodgers noted that 'every year a considerable amount of money is spent in defending either the name or trademark'.[58] Wostenholm's reputation was sufficient for both firm and product to be known simply as 'I*XL'. Many rivals, even in Sheffield, attempted to include some of these famous letters in their mark: Joseph Allen, for example, called its cutlery NON-XLL; while Parkin & Marshall favoured XL ALL. It was the Germans, however, who were the biggest offenders. Their copying of Sheffield marks on low-priced cutlery, which had begun in America before 1850, even if it was not quite as prevalent and damaging as Sheffield firms proclaimed, was certainly a worrying feature for the United Kingdom hardware trade by the late nineteenth century.

---

[57] *TES*, 22 Nov. 1911. G. Tweedale and D. Higgins, 'Asset or Liability? Trade Marks in the Sheffield Cutlery and Tool Trades', *Business History* (forthcoming).

[58] Rodgers, *Five Sovereigns*, 13. On the prestige of Rodgers' name, see John Keane, *Six Months in Mecca* (London, 1881), 148; and SCL Rodgers' Minute Book No. 4, 29 May 1908, letter from J. C. Willis, Ceylon, re *Rojas* meaning 'very good'.

Pressure from Sheffield manufacturers had been instrumental in the passing of the Trade Marks Act (1875): that and subsequent Acts (1883, 1887, and 1888) aimed to solve the problem of duplication by making marks the exclusive property of the owner, who could sue for infringement both in the United Kingdom and abroad (where reciprocal arrangements were soon in force). But establishing legal rights was one thing, enforcing them was another, especially abroad. For decades Sheffield's leading cutlery firms attempted to come to grips with fraudulent marking: though they were occasionally successful, the problem refused to go away. The experience of Wostenholm's was typical. In 1906 they began proceedings against a 'Jew firm of merchants' in New York, Kastor Bros., which had purchased the business and name of a small razor-maker in Sheffield, Joseph Wostenholm. Naturally, they intended using the illustrious name. In this instance, legal threats forced Kastor's to retreat, but this was time-consuming and expensive (Wostenholm's had once lost £1,200 in an Australian case on a technicality), and also on some occasions practically useless. No sooner had one heresy been stamped upon than another would appear. Kastor soon responded by registering a mark which included the letters XLNT, also paid Allen's a royalty on its look-alike mark, and then, to Wostenholm's fury, 'the aliens' had the temerity during the First World War to buy up the old Sheffield cutlery firm, W. & S. Butcher.[59]

Sheffield firms were not helped by the fact that the legislation only covered individual, not regional, marks. Significantly, the words 'Made in Sheffield' were not protected, a weak spot readily exploited by the Germans. From the late nineteenth century, Sheffield manufacturers began a campaign to have this mark too legally protected, but this did not happen until the 1920s (see Chapter 8). It may not have mattered. The economics of trademarking is complex, and some historians have seen the trade mark as a vital asset in the rise of the modern corporation:[60] but in Sheffield's case, trade marks seem to have been a mixed blessing, rather than an intangible asset. The anger of firms such as Rodgers and Wostenholm is understandable, but there is no doubt that by the First World War trade mark litigation was becoming a case of diminishing returns: it blinded Sheffielders to the fact that German success was not so much due to their unscrupulous techniques as to more efficient production and marketing. As one observer warned: 'In an open market all questions of spurious marks, common goods etc. will in time regulate themselves. Sheffield has not lost her position in the market by dishonest

---

[59] SCL Wos. Copybook No. 6, Paine to William Gay, 3 June 1906; No. 8, Paine to J. Watson & Sons, 28 Jan. 1916, Paine to Hobson, 22 Jan. 1917. There are many such examples of counterfeiting in the Wostenholm letterbooks.

[60] Mira Wilkins, 'The Neglected Intangible Asset: The Influence of the Trade Mark on the Rise of the Modern Corporation', *Business History*, 34 (Jan. 1992), 66–95.

trading, as some seem to think; and all the "corporate marks" in the world, if the patterns and the prices of the goods are not right, will never regain that position for her.'[61] In Sheffield, trade mark protection was a defensive measure, a sign of a conservative industry increasingly feeling the impact of foreign competition. Trade marks were worth defending up to a point, but generally the city's efforts would probably have been better spent in modernization.

After the brief boom of the early 1870s, competition became much tougher for Sheffield in the world hardware markets. United Kingdom exports of hardware held up reasonably well until the early 1880s (briefly surpassing £4 million in 1882), but thereafter there was a decline: by the end of the 1880s average annual exports were below £3 million, and by the late 1890s the figure had fallen to below £2 million. Cutlery exports, which were enumerated after 1898, were relatively static in the early 1900s, and though there was a boom between 1910 and 1913 (when declared exports were over £800,000), there were disturbing signs of growing import penetration (running at about £170,000 per annum before the war).[62]

Unfortunately, evidence on the overseas performance of Sheffield cutlery and tool firms is sparse. As with steel, the most seismic event was the loss of the American market after the 1870s, the result of the growth of the United States cutlery industry and a swingeing tariff. This hit the industry leaders, such as Wostenholm, most of all, as the company's surviving business records indicate. Wostenholm's was not entirely typical within the Sheffield industry—its dependence on the American market was greater than most, and it had a more restricted product range (heavily centred on pocket-knives and razors)—nevertheless, it can be regarded as an exemplar of the trauma inflicted on Sheffield by the winding down of the great American trade.

The days when Sheffield dominated the United States market were over, even before George Wostenholm died in 1876. Armed with his revolver and rifle, the American frontiersman no longer needed his I*XL Bowie knife. The Gold Rush was over, the buffalo had been decimated, and the Indians had been sent to the reservations. But for the first decade or so after 1876, Wostenholm's profits—like those of Rodgers—held up well and steady dividends were returned (see Table 4.2). Despite the rising American tariff, Wostenholm goods were not yet excluded. Thus in 1884, although the tariff had its expected effect, the directors were able to report that, although there had been some decline in business, the results were 'satisfactory'. The American market remained the main focus and the company secretary's letter-press copybook is thick with missives to New York. The company employed about 700 in 1890—a peak.

---

[61] *Sheffield Times*, 30 June 1849.   [62] Lloyd, *Cutlery Trades*, 481.

Wostenholm's reputation and ability to supply the highest class of goods served it well. In fact, it was amongst a small number of Sheffield firms— Brookes & Crookes, Harrison Bros. & Howson, and John Clarke, for example—which still targeted America for its premium knives and 'novelties'. As trade catalogues and artefacts show, American cutlers— despite the influx of Sheffield craftsmen—never achieved Sheffield's pre-eminence for the most expensive grades of cutlery, such as sportsman's knives; and mostly these were still imported before 1900.

But the Americans were about to break the back of Wostenholm's trade on the anvil of protectionism. In 1890 the McKinley Tariff raised duties on cutlery to an unprecedented level. The rates became even higher in 1901 and 1909. By then Wostenholm's knives—which cost less at the factory gate than United States ones—cost the American retailer and customer over twice as much as the domestic product. With some justice, Wing complained that they were 'victims of a Tariff framed with consummate

Table 4.2. *George Wostenholm & Son: financial data, 1876–1913*

	Sales £	Net profit £	Profit £		Dividend %	
			knives	razors		
1876	36,460	7,939 (23,653)	5,253	1,065	5	(17½)
1877	28,215	9,482 (24,482)	2,721		10	(17½)
1878	38,390	10,951 (23,076)	4,951	774	10	(17½)
1879	37,711	8,426 (22,924)	1,657	1,156	10	(17½)
1880	63,085	14,218 (23,087)	10,947	1,818	10.	(17½)
1881	77,756	18,432 (25,128)	14,776	2,745	10	(17½)
1882	83,769	19,692 (24,372)	15,924	3,544	10	(17½)
1883	87,904	20,258 (17,821)	15,924	2,949	15	(16)
1884	71,031	18,910 (18,136)	15,191	1,727	49	(14½)
1885	43,331	10,849 (16,031)	6,683	999	15	(12)
1886	64,197	15,946 (15,354)	13,033	1,937	15	(12)
1887	56,545	14,213	10,868	2,237	15	
1888	59,685	15,127	11,271	2,346	15	
1889	71,671	17,944	13,968	2,352	15	
1890	65,186	15,813	11,368	2,500	27½	
1891	42,941	10,242	5,106	1,246	12½	
1892	40,666	8,525	3,829	1,308	10	
1893	39,088	8,535	3,346	932	10	
1894	23,892	5,433	275	40	7½	
1895	61,016	10,664	8,831	739	10	
1896	49,711	10,749	7,669	833	10	
1897	52,606	10,545	7,831	921	7½	
1898	30,818	3,836	1,560	187 (loss)	0	

Table 4.2. *(Cont.)*

	Sales £	Net profit £	Profit £ knives	razors	Dividend %
1899	36,153	10,051	2,885	312	0
1900	45,209	6,028	4,236	676	0
1901	43,341	5,532	3,698	524	0
1902	42,096	6,897	4,100	459	$2\frac{1}{2}$
1903	46,730	9,256 (20,963)	5,699	611	5 $(12\frac{1}{2})$
1904	49,031	10,217 (21,376)	5,092	505	5 $(7\frac{1}{2})$
1905	50,706	11,416 (20,698)	4,793	967	5 $(7\frac{1}{2})$
1906	51,926	16,932 (21,421)	5,497	1,454	5 $(12\frac{1}{2})$
1907	57,443	15,962 (22,028)	7,792	1,777	$7\frac{1}{2}$ $(12\frac{1}{2})$
1908	57,324	11,257 (19,316)	5,892	1,007	$7\frac{1}{2}$ $(12\frac{1}{2})$
1909	51,679	11,958 (22,527)	6,498	715	$7\frac{1}{2}$ $(12\frac{1}{2})$
1910	56,398	14,644 (22,874)	9,100	1,038	$7\frac{1}{2}$ $(12\frac{1}{2})$
1911	72,203	17,193 (23,690)	10,344	1,047	10 $(12\frac{1}{2})$
1912	66,116	11,348 (24,139)	9,410	698	10 $(12\frac{1}{2})$
1913	64,601	11,452 (20,581)	8,474	745	10 $(12\frac{1}{2})$

Note: Paid-up capital: 1876: £33,600 ordinary shares; 1877: £43,400 ord. shares; 1883: £43,400 ord. shares; £26,600 6% preference shares; 1885: £56,000 ord. shares; £26,000 6% pref. shares; 1890: £56,000 ord. shares; £26,000 6% pref. shares; £7,000 5% pref. shares.

Sources: SCL Wostenholm records: Minute Books; 'Summaries 1876' volume. No data available for some years. Figures in brackets are for Joseph Rodgers & Sons, from SCL Rodgers' Minute Book No. 1, 1871–87, No. 4, 1903–20; and board papers amongst Wostenholm records.

ingenuity to stop our trade or kill our profits'.[63] He wrote to Ward in 1895: 'Our prospects are none too bright, we have hardly anything to do, orders come in slowly, and when we do get the results of 1894–5 they will be far from making up for the four lean years of McKinleyism, while the almost certain advent of the protectionists to power in the next elections is a threat to our prosperity we dare not lose sight of.'[64] In the 1890s, compared with the previous decade, Wostenholm's sales fell by over a third; its net profits by over a half (Table 4.2 and Fig. 8.1). Wing stated in 1897: 'We are entering upon a terribly dull time, and we do not know the extent to which our resources may be tried, but we do know that it is a crisis which will show whether the Company has a backbone or not. I am now engaged in remorselessly pulling down our prices and hope the result will be that we shall keep the [American] trade until happier days.'[65] The firm's

[63] SCL Wos. Copybook No. 5, Wing to Ward, 29 Mar. 1899.
[64] Ibid. Copybook No. 4, Wing to Ward, 26 June 1895.
[65] Ibid. Copybook No. 5, 19 Aug. 1897. See also Wing's letters to the Secretary of the Spring Knife Cutlers' Union, 6 Aug. 1897, reducing prices and wages, refusing any promises to keep men on, or allowing them to work for other makers.

New York agent, Edward Beckett (appointed in 1891), was involved in bitter disputes with the Custom's appraisers, who consistently rejected Wostenholm's valuations and refused to countenance its attempt to import knives with slightly substandard pearl handles to reduce the dutiable cost. 'You cannot do anything to avoid this tyranny,' Wing told Beckett, which he believed was inspired by the personal animus of the Customs officers.[66]

Not surprisingly, Sheffield firms soon began switching to colonial and other markets. The trade press between 1880 and 1914 records this in broad outline.[67] Tyzack, Sons, & Turner traded with the Colonies, especially with Australasia; the Hardy Patent Pick Co. did the same, concentrating on, for example, 'the better class of shovels for the Australian market, most of them being polished to the highest degree of perfection'; Spear & Jackson compensated for the loss of the American market by selling in Canada, India, China, and Japan; the sheep-shear makers, such as Burgon & Ball, Ward & Payne, and the Co-operative Sheffield Sheep Shear Society, continued to target the sheep-breeding areas of the Colonies; W. K. & C. Peace after 1875 switched their attention to Far Eastern markets, especially India and Japan, and also South America. Other toolmaking firms, such as John Kenyon and Samuel Newbould, found a market for their saws in Russia.[68] By 1910 the British dominions took about five-eighths of United Kingdom cutlery exports. Low tariff barriers, weak home competition, and developing agricultural economies, perhaps led Sheffield to believe it could repeat its earlier American success. If some firms did regard these as 'soft' markets, however, they were to be disappointed. Sheffield fared badly against American competition, especially in saws, axes, and other agricultural tools. By 1900 Sheffield's trade in saws in Australia had all but been wiped out by the American firms, Disston and Atkins, with their better designed, packaged, and marketed (though not cheaper) products.

In cutlery, Frederick Rawson (1843–1909), of the Globe Cutlery Works (established in 1870), was said to have been the first Sheffield maker to have opened up a trade with India and the Far East, which he visited in 1885.[69] Both Rodgers and Wostenholm followed this shift towards the Far East and Australasia. Rodgers soon adapted its products to suit Far Eastern buyers and also had an Australian agent, who was performing satisfactorily in the 1880s, in what was to become briefly the best market for Sheffield cutlery. One of the Rodgers family directors set out on a business trip there in 1887. By about 1910 Rodgers had agencies in Bombay and

---

[66] Ibid. Copybook No. 4, Wing to Beckett, 10 Oct. 1896.
[67] The journals are already cited in the preceding footnotes.
[68] John Kenyon & Co., *Bi-Centenary Celebration, 1710–1910* (Sheffield, 1910); B. Callan, *400 Years of Iron and Steel* (Sheffield, 1971).
[69] William Pike, *Sheffield at the Opening of the Twentieth Century* (Brighton, 1901), 92.

Calcutta, Cape Town, Melbourne, Christchurch (NZ), Montreal, and New York. Wostenholm's, too, recognized the 'supreme importance' of Australia. The directors were confident, even complacent: 'goods of the quality and style such as we produce, could and would make their way very rapidly, and hold it firmly, in any market where they were introduced with ability and energy. Such has never failed to be the invariable rule of the past.'[70] In March 1879 Wostenholm's appointed an agent in Sydney named King; began exhibiting at trade exhibitions in Sydney and Melbourne (winning prize medals); and by 1883 had sent over stock valued at £6,578. Within four years, however, Wostenholm's were complaining bitterly about King, especially since in selling only half the stock he had incurred expenses of nearly twenty per cent. They were unhappy with, 'the meagre business being accounted for by letters, arriving at more or less lengthy intervals, and containing merely vague general regrets and expectations. We are as completely in the dark as to whether Mr King places our patterns before buyers or not.'

They added: 'We ought to be laying firm hold on the Australian market as an outlet for our productions; instead of which, to our deep dismay and annoyance, golden opportunities ... are being let slip, while other traders are busily occupying ground which should and could be ours, and from which it will be most difficult to dislodge them in the future.' No doubt, Wostenholm's had in mind Christopher Johnson & Co., which in the 1880s was busy opening up a large Australian and New Zealand business with the help of its energetic agent, J. W. Bunby.[71]

Wostenholm's soon transferred the agency to George Christie & Co., but that proved no better. In 1888 a Wostenholm representative was sent to investigate its affairs, since according to Wostenholm's: 'Mr C[hristie] spends very little time at the office, apparently being occupied with accountant's affairs. The man in charge and who sends the foolish stock orders we receive is Wm Christie who is described as almost imbecile.'[72] Yet another agent was appointed, but by then Wostenholm's, as it had feared, had lost ground to the competition. By the end of the century, the Australian agency had never made a profit. As Wing admitted, in 1898: 'This did not matter much when we were making good profits elsewhere, and there was a prospect of obtaining a stable footing in the colonies, but in the present state of affairs ... we are compelled to economise on every hand.' Bad management was obviously to blame; so too was the fact that, as a Wostenholm agent remarked: 'our difficulty is that our goods are rather above the requirements of the

[70] SCL Wos. Copybook No. 1, Nixon and Wing to Wake, 19 Dec. 1883. Subsequent quotes are from same source.
[71] SCL MD 2374–5, 1883–1905. C. Johnson & Co., Australian letters.
[72] SCL Wos. Copybook No. 2, Wing to Barber, 3 May 1898.

market'.[73] Here Wostenholm's were especially vulnerable. Concentration on America meant that they not only had no experience or marketing network in other countries, not even in England (where they could not match Rodgers' Sheffield showroom, London office, and Royal Warrant), but also that sales were heavily dependent on a few high-quality lines. Its output was dominated by knives (mainly pocket-cutlery) and razors, which accounted for well over 90 per cent of the profits. Wostenholm's eschewed general lines, such as table cutlery, and the cheap end of the market. Firms such as Christopher Johnson and Thomas Turner—though they too had a commitment to quality—had more to offer colonial markets: they spread their risks with steel, files, and tools, besides a wider range of cutlery.

Nevertheless, Wostenholm's pressed ahead with opening foreign agencies. By 1888 it was able to state that its business was no longer primarily American: agents had been appointed in Canada and South America and goods were being sent through merchants in the West Indies and on the Continent.[74] The success of these operations was, however, another matter. Wostenholm's South American agent, who had convinced the firm that rich pickings were to be had there and in the West Indies (and had thus persuaded Wostenholm's to appoint him), was personally blamed by the firm in 1897 for the small sales and profits.[75]

Wostenholm's clung to the American market far too long and their move into other markets was slow and half-hearted. Moreover, the directors expected the trade in new territories such as Australia to behave exactly as it had in America, where the demand was for high-quality goods, sold from a central office as in New York, where 'an agent could sit on his office seat and smilingly receive orders to obtain which he had made little or no effort'.[76] Wostenholm's relied far too much on distant agents in countries which they hardly ever visited themselves. Wostenholm's foreign offices were expected to operate almost independently—a risky policy, especially in view of the firm's almost complete inability to select good agents. When one of the firm's more competent salesmen, Asline Ward, criticized Wostenholm's 'poor choice of men', Wing had to admit that what he said was 'most true'.[77] In contrast to that indefatigable transatlantic traveller, George Wostenholm, his successors strayed abroad only occasionally. Comfortably ensconced in the leafy suburbs of Ecclesall and Kenwood, the life of a salesman appears to have had little attraction for them while the firm turned in reasonable

---

[73] Ibid. Copybook No. 6, George Quirk to Paine, 29 May 1907.
[74] Ibid. Copybook No. 1, Wostenholm's to John Watson & Sons, London.
[75] Ibid. Copybook No. 4, Wing to D. S. B. Batchelor, 4 May 1897.
[76] Ibid. Nixon to Colver, 27 Oct. 1925.
[77] Ibid. Wing to Ward, 29 Mar. 1899.

dividends (which it did for some twenty years). This was a highly damaging weakness in a firm that relied so heavily on exports, especially since other Sheffield firms had men of sufficient energy and calibre to capture Wostenholm's trade.

This was not a very impressive record by one of the largest firms. How typical was it? Apart from Lloyd's work, we now have the benefit of a magisterial survey by Sally Taylor of the cutlery trades between 1870 and 1914. Using many little-known manuscript and printed sources, this study reaches a generally favourable verdict on the strategies and structure of the industry. It argues that most manufacturers appear to have benefited from the system as it then operated, particularly in respect to outwork, which reduced entrepreneurial risks, costs, and management responsibilities. In short, given the constraints of its craft heritage, the Sheffield cutlery industry was reasonably efficient and well-adapted.[78] There is something to be said for this view. Certainly the limited data for the leading firms, such as Rodgers and Wostenholm, shows them turning in respectable dividends in some years before 1914. Unfortunately, such a view begs as many questions as it answers: if the Sheffield cutlery industry was so well adapted, why was steady decline evident after the early 1870s?; and even if one grants that Sheffield held its own up to 1914, when *did* business failure set in? My view is that the Sheffield cutlery industry was far from well-adapted in this era and that the entrepreneurial failure (and labour shortcomings) that characterized it were crucial to its poor performance after 1914. A few of the leadings firms may have performed adequately—largely feeding off 'soft', developing markets in the Far East and Australasia—but their strength will be shown to have been illusory.

Sheffield was still a considerable force on the eve of the First World War: its leading firms (listed in Table 1.2), though they had passed their peak, were still amongst the largest such factories in the world. The city's best craftsmen could still surpass the efforts of lesser mortals in Germany and America. However, this was not a measure of the industry's economic performance, which had several deficiencies. If we recall the shortcomings listed earlier in this chapter, we can get some measure of how well Sheffield was adapting to new trends.

The first weakness was the break-up of the old crafts before the First World War, even at the best firms. The declining demand for many of Sheffield's traditional patterns, the rising costs of labour and materials, the introduction of machines, and the weakening of the apprentice system were responsible. Commented one reporter in 1906: 'The coming of the large and highly organised firm has left little room for the working master

---

[78] S. Taylor, 'Tradition and Change: The Sheffield Cutlery Trades 1870–1914' (Sheffield University Ph.D., 1988). See also Taylor, 'Industrial Structure'.

man. Gradually he has had to disappear before the centralising tendency of the times. Owing to the fierce competition the "little mester" is a vanishing quantity.'[79] This verdict was somewhat premature—the little mester proved to be a remarkably enduring 'quantity'—but the general point was accurate. In the same year, a Wostenholm director had difficulty in supplying a particular pattern:

These are all ground by one man (Clack) and as they are done considerably under usual rates, no union man will touch them. The present shortage has been caused partly by Clack having influenza and doing nothing for a fortnight, but principally by Kanner and others ordering largely patterns made by this particular grinder. Clack has set on two more men this week, and we hope to get more blades through now. Givens has been very independent and awkward to get on with for some time. Cadman finds him as much work as he cares to do. He picks his work and at present time is doing more work for Cadmans than for us. We are doing everything possible to get more blades.[80]

By 1914 Wostenholm's was sending all its best razor grinding to Hamburg, where 'they had to pay for it at a price never dreamt of in Sheffield'.[81] This raises the question as to whether, even if Wostenholm's had found a demand for quality cutlery, it could have supplied it by 1900. In busy times, Sheffield was being found wanting: thus Christopher Johnson's believed that in 1901 Australian orders for pocket-knives and scissors were 'far beyond the power of Sheffield to supply'.[82] Shear steel was becoming an expensive luxury that would soon become very difficult to obtain; and there were also problems with crucible steel. Rodgers' decision to begin making its own steel may have been an attempt to avoid the kind of supply and quality problems that were beginning to afflict its smaller rivals. In 1904 Paine wrote to Wostenholm's usual supplier, Thomas Firth & Sons, after a consignment of steel was found to have cracks: 'We still have a preference for your steel. From our experience of steel makers, they all get [it] wrong at times. Your ancestors did, but as soon as the fault was pointed out, they were able to remedy it in the future and paid our claims for waste. They never were (what you appear to be) hopelessly beaten and unable to overcome the difficulty.'[83] The days when

[79] *SDT*, 28 Dec. 1906.
[80] SCL Wos. Copybook No. 6, Alexander Brown to Paine, 14 Nov. 1906. Johnson's were also experiencing similar labour problems. They wrote to their Australian agent that they were months behind with orders: 'the consequence will be that some orders will have to be incomplete, and worst of all, workmen are getting very independent and wages are stiffening in the lower grades of goods'. In the pocket-knife and scissor trades 'workmen continue as scarce as ever'. SCL MD 2375: Letters to Bunby, 23 Aug. 1901, 6 Sept. 1901.
[81] SCL Wos. Copybook No. 8, Paine to C. P. Spencer Smith, Sylvester Works, 29 Jan. 1914. Paine noted that the Sheffield firm, Butcher's, were using machine-grinding and that 'the men who finished [the processes] after the machine were earning handsome wages'.
[82] SCL MD: letter to Bunby, 25 Jan. 1902.
[83] SCL Wos. Copybook No. 6, 13 Jan. 1904.

Sheffield's crucible steel firms could devote their attention to a relatively small customer were obviously fading: Wostenholm's had to look elsewhere, to smaller local steel producers such as Vessey's.

This inability to supply rising demand stemmed from the lack of mechanization in Sheffield. The situation had not changed markedly since the 1880s and 1890s; nor had the attitude of the workers. In one celebrated instance in 1910, George Schrade, a German-born cutlery entrepreneur and inventor resident in America, was invited to Thomas Turner's works to install a machine he had invented for routing out the shield (nameplate) holes in knife handles (a process laboriously done in Sheffield with a fiddle-drill, known as a 'parser'). Turner had a contract to supply rubber-handled knives to the British Army. Despite the fact that Schrade's machine was introduced secretly, as soon as the men saw the machine-made holes, aprons were off and they refused to resume work until the offending machine had been removed.[84] However, the factory owners themselves were far from brimming with new ideas and Turner's initiative appears to have been rare. Wostenholm's, for example, well knew that the trade unions made the introduction of machinery very difficult. On the other hand, no serious attempt was made to introduce up-to-date methods at the Works, except in one instance. In 1896 Wostenholm's contacted H. Boker & Co. at Remscheid, Solingen, concerning German razor-grinding machines. After a delay—due to the fact that Wostenholm's were unable to read German and had to ask Boker's to write again in English—they recruited the services of a German mechanic-cum-inventor, Ferdinand Grah. Wostenholm's sent him £250 to come to Sheffield to install a new razor process. Another £125 inducement was needed before the appearance of Grah, who returned to Germany after remaining only half his allotted time, and then demanded full payment (£600) before venturing abroad again. He did eventually return to Sheffield, but his continued absence would have been no great loss: his razor process, which aimed magically to reduce razors by an electric current in a bath, was a complete failure.[85]

It was hardly suprising that Sheffield failed to exploit the real revolution in the razor trade—a revolution that involved the demise of the cut-throat razor, one of Sheffield's staple industries. Hand-forged from crucible steel, often hollow-ground for extra sharpness, and produced in an enormous range of sizes and handle materials to suit every chin and

---

[84] B. Voyles, 'The Decline and Fall of the Sheffield Empire', in Ken Warner (ed.), *Knives '86* (Northbrook, Ill., 1985), 7–11, 10. Schrade found a better reception in Solingen and also America. After the First World War, Sheffield firms had to import Schrade's machines from the US, where they were worked successfully.

[85] SCL Wos. Copybook No. 4, Wing to Boker, 1896; Wing to Grah, 9 Apr. 1897; No. 5, Wing letter, 12 June 1897.

pocket, the Sheffield razor was as much a work of art as the act of shaving itself. A product of incredible skill (and even more incredible mortality for the men who ground them in such dusty conditions), the razor seemed to sum up the town's industrial ethos. Almost every nineteenth-century cutlery firm worth its salt sold straight razors and they had a world-wide sale: it must have seemed to Sheffielders that the town was forever destined to manufacture them.

They were wrong. In 1904 an American inventor-cum-entrepreneur, King C. Gillette (1855–1932), launched the safety razor from his factory in Boston. Gillette turned upside-down all the old Sheffield precepts about shaving: his blades were wafer thin and held in a protective holder and, above all, they were meant to be thrown way after a few shaves. By 1914, it was clear that Gillette's disposable blade—which, until the introduction of stainless steel after the First World War, was the greatest single up-heaval in cutlery history—was sweeping the market.

Why was the safety razor invented in America and not in Sheffield? It was hardly due to America's greater inventive genius. Sheffield was al-ready familiar with the idea in the early nineteenth century. The cutlers Thomas Champion & Son advertised in the *Sheffield Directory and Guide* (1828) one of the earliest designs—a 'Frame Bladed Razor'. Later in the nineteenth century, similar ideas were patented in Sheffield and attempts were made to launch the business. Hunter's Talbot Works in Sheffield produced a safety razor in the late 1880s known as the 'Chaflin'. John Watts of Sheffield patented a safety razor in 1896. These usually consisted of a hollow-ground carbon steel wedge-blade, clamped in a crude holder.[86] Even then the Americans had their eyes on the trade and towards the end of the century A. J. Jordan became an agent for the American Kampfe Brothers' 'Star' safety razor.

The greater resources available to Gillette may have been important, especially in overcoming the early technical difficulties. He was also helped by the receptiveness of the American market to standardized goods. In Sheffield the key obstacle seems to have been the industry's lack of a mass-production tradition. At Wostenholm's, for example, we know that in 1904 there was an attempt to manufacture wedge-type carbon steel blades for an early version of the safety razor. It failed, since as Wostenholm's admitted, it was 'practically impossible to keep within [the] margin for variation . . . with our tools'.[87] Culturally, too, the whole idea of a *disposable* blade was alien to Sheffield, where items were made to last as long as possible, preferably a lifetime. This explains the paradox that despite a cutlery industry that was hundreds of years old, which had

---

[86] See Phillip L. Krumholz, *A History of Shaving and Razors* (Bartonville, Ill., 1987).
[87] SCL Wos. Copybook No. 6, Paine to Firth's, 13 June 1904.

abundant skill in working steel, and, above all, the raw material itself—high-grade steel—Sheffield lagged behind.

While Gillette concentrated on turning out every blade the same, Sheffield prided itself on the vast number of its patterns. At Turner's, a centenary publication titled significantly, *Handicrafts that Survive* (1902), stated: 'To the varieties of [pocket-knives] now made there is practically no end. It is calculated that at different times no fewer than 10,000 different patterns have been produced at the Suffolk Works alone, and the average number kept there in stock or "to order" will be from 2,000 to 3,000.'[88] A Rodgers catalogue, distributed at about the same time, lists a similar number of patterns. It had over sixty pages of pocket-knives alone, each page illustrating a dozen or more different styles.

Working conditions had not altered much, either. After 1900, Sheffield slowly began noticing the new cutlery methods and organization abroad. The picture that emerged from the reports of the representatives of commercial and labour bodies was consistent: America and Germany were far ahead in working conditions, education, and wages. In America, Robert Holmshaw, of the Sheffield Cutlery Council, found that: 'Factory management is far better in America than in Sheffield. Every attention is given to the comfort and convenience of the men, with the result that the great waste of time so common in our town is there unknown.'[89] More disturbing, because it was—superficially at least—so much like Sheffield, was the situation in Solingen and Remscheid. There the transformation from domestic to factory organization had progressed rapidly—though interestingly, most of the labour force were outworkers. The forging and finishing processes were usually highly mechanized factory processes; grinding, though it was still done on an outwork basis, was powered by electricity and subject to stringent working and safety regulations. Sheffielders noted that in Solingen, 'advantage is taken of every facility, no matter how slight, and of every labour-saving device, no matter how small or insignificant it may appear, if it will help [the cutler's] work or increase his output'.[90] Unlike Sheffielders, German owners took great trouble in advertising and displaying their wares. The workers were better educated, with an elaborately equipped *Fachschule*, and compulsory apprenticeship. Sheffield visitors saw another striking difference: the introduction of machinery by the employers had occurred alongside the development of a vigorous labour movement. As Sheffield trade-

---

[88] Turner & Wingfield Rowbotham, *Handicrafts that Survive: Centenary Souvenir 1802–1902* (Sheffield, 1902).

[89] *Mosely Industrial Commission to the United States of America* (Manchester, 1903), 103.

[90] SCL MD 3466. Spring Knife Workers' Amalgamation, Table & Butcher Blade Grinders, *Report of Deputation Visiting Solingen* (May 1914), 5. This report is amongst the papers collected by Lloyd on his trip to Solingen in 1908. The series also contains a similar file by Dr Scurfield, Medical Officer of Health.

unionists noted: 'The German workman is up-to-date because he has organised, paid and fought to be so.'[91] To Godfrey Lloyd, who also visited Solingen in 1908 when collecting material for his book, this development of a factory system concurrently with the creation of a labour organization proved that the older crafts could prosper in the changed conditions of the twentieth century.

The result was that with a cutlery workforce not much different in size from Sheffield's—about 12,000 or more before 1914—Solingen's output soon dwarfed its rival. By 1900 Solingen's cutlery exports topped those of England, France, and the United States of America *combined*. The export figures for 1911 were Germany £1.4 million, the United Kingdom, £851,000, and the United States £229,000. German quality was also getting better. In 1914 Wostenholm's Canadian agent sent to Sheffield samples of Boker's cutlery. Noted Wostenholm's: 'the style of these patterns was foreign, but their manufacture showed the great advance which was being made in regard to quality'.[92]

Belatedly, Sheffield manufacturers reacted. According to documents in the Wostenholm records, in 1913—in what must be one of those rare instances of an economic history publication having a contemporary impact—Lloyd's descriptions of the efficiency and output of German cutlers galvanized some of Sheffield's manufacturers into touring Solingen themselves. (That Sheffield businessmen needed to rely on such a source for basic information offers its own comment on the state of statistical intelligence in the industry.) They returned convinced of the need for mechanization, unaware that the outbreak of war was about to make ever greater demands on their manufacturing capabilities.

[91] SCL MD 3466. *Report*, 8.
[92] SCL Wos. R. 168. Review of Circumstances Surrounding Resignation of Paine, July 1922. Bound typescript.

5

Arsenal of the World

[Sheffield] is at the present moment the greatest Armoury the world
has ever seen.
British Association Handbook and Guide to Sheffield (Sheffield, 1910), 217.

Life in the trenches is paradise compared with the cutlery trade at the
present time.
SCL Wostenholm Records. James Paine to William Nixon, 13 March
1915.

Steel was the primary instrument in the carnage of the First World War. In
the words of one Sheffield metallurgist, writing in the 1920s and expressing misgivings that would have been out of place in Sheffield before 1914:
'metallurgical advances in themselves made possible the form and magnitude of warfare typical of the [First] World War. The modern battleship,
destroyer, submarine, airplane and the armored tank, together with their
armaments, were impossible but for the collaboration of the engineer and
the metallurgist.'[1] He might also have added that many of these advances
were made in Sheffield. In almost every area of war material—from the
soldier's manganese steel helmet to the armour-plate of a Dreadnought,
from the rifle bullet to the largest naval projectile, from the army razor to
the bayonet—Sheffield steel was on the front line on both land and sea.
Not surprisingly, the city was more profoundly affected than almost any
other English manufacturing centre by events between 1914 and 1918,
when the arms trade revealed its full potential for destruction and, of
course, for profits.

In this period, when the arms trade was taken to its logical conclusion,
when the weapons which the Germans, British, and French had been
selling round the world were turned against each other, Sheffield will-
ingly embraced its destiny as the armoury of the nation. With armaments
already accounting for much of their business and with hatred of the
Germans rife, Sheffield workers and industrialists had few qualms about
producing weapons. As the city announced proudly:

At no time in the history of Sheffield were so many firms engaged in the manufacture of materials for the purpose of carrying on war, and the output of material of
that kind was never so large. It is fortunate that the requirements of the British

[1] W. H. Hatfield, *The Application of Science to the Steel Industry* (Cleveland, Ohio, 1928), 66.

Government and the Powers for which Sheffield firms work have increased in peace times to such an extent that the resources for the production of guns, armour, gun-shields, shells and other munitions of war were never so large as they are today.[2]

In these circumstances, armaments became central to the culture in Sheffield. Yet describing Sheffield's role in the War and its impact on the city presents problems. The subject has never been adequately covered, even in the most detailed accounts of Sheffield industries, due to the limited source material. Company and public records are scarce, often non-existent, and since many developments were secret the published sources are often mute. The bald statistics on wartime production are often available, especially in company publications, but the total picture is still lacking. The War brought an immense increase in output and labour; led to massive investment in new plant; often completely altered the normal run of business; quickened the pace of technological change; diverted output into a single market; and introduced far greater Government control. It also intensified the clustering of steel and its related industries around Sheffield.

STEEL AND ARMAMENTS

The overall picture, as one would expect, was of massive expansion. Commented one newspaper: 'Enormous new shops, tens of thousands of pounds' worth of new machinery, and thousands of extra workers have been provided and fully employed since war broke out. Further extensions are still to be carried out on a scale which would have made the directors of old stand aghast.'[3] This was accomplished mostly under the initiative and direction of the steel companies themselves, though after 1915—when the Ministry of Munitions responded to shell and other shortages by setting up 'controlled' establishments—a measure of government direction was introduced, mostly related to the control of prices and profits.

By 1915, 25,000 tons of steel a week were leaving Sheffield for Allied use. The great demand for shells was felt early and soon became 'so great that nearly every firm with the capacity to melt shell steel is employed on that work, and even the crucible steel furnaces are being utilised for that purpose'.[4]

The demand for labour rocketed. One newspaper stated in 1915: 'Wages are high, overtime is general in the East End, and no skilled worker worth

---

[2] *SI*, 19 Dec. 1914. It was calculated that about three-fourths of the industries of Sheffield were engaged in arms manufacture. See *SI*, 14 Nov. 1914.

[3] *SI*, 12 June 1915.

[4] *SI*, 14 Nov. 1914. See also 'The World's Greatest Naval Armoury', *SI*, 6 Aug. 1915.

his salt is out of employment. After five months of war, the number of unemployed in the city is only a thousand out of a population of about half a million, and of that number the major part are unskilled or unemployable, while there is the usual seasonal unemployment of painters.'[5] Almost immediately there was a shortage of skilled men, especially in the engineering branches. This was met by men drawn in from the light trades in the city, attracted by high wages. Others arrived from abroad, such as Dutch and Belgian refugees and Canadians. Some were said to be 'of fine physique', a useful quality since teemers and pullers-out were in demand, though there were also said to be 'some strangely-composed' gangs of labourers, which included, 'bookmakers, racing touts, music-hall vocalists, acrobats and others'.[6] Women were recruited in increasing numbers after 1915, especially in the shell shops, such as at Firth's Templeborough Works (where 5,000 women were employed) and at Hadfields (where female labour accounted for 500 by 1918).

The number of workers pouring into the factories was a reflection of the massive increase in capital, output, and plant. The three biggest firms based in the city—Vickers, Brown, Cammell-Laird—spearheaded the armaments drive. At their head was Vickers, now in a class by itself, and becoming even less a Sheffield firm. (Although steel was at the heart of the Vickers empire, it would be more accurate to describe it as a London-based multinational, with a Sheffield subsidiary.) Its growth during the War, when its products—battleships, naval guns, machine-guns, torpedoes, aircraft, and submarines—could be found in every theatre of war, continued unchecked. By the end of 1916 nearly 11,000 workers were on the River Don site. By 1919, the company's £20 million issued capital meant that only Coats, Lever Bros., and Imperial Tobacco surpassed it in capital-size as a United Kingdom industrial firm—though this expansion was not entirely welcome to the old family members. Albert Vickers, who was coming towards the end of his life, felt misgivings that the company was no longer under such close personal control. So rapid was the company's expansion that accounting procedures collapsed under the strain and in 1919 the profits for four years had to be lumped together by the Vickers' accountants: the total was about £4.5 million. The profits for the period 1914 to 1919 were over £6 million; and the average annual dividend on the ordinary shares was $12\frac{1}{2}$ per cent tax free for each year up to 1918, and $11\frac{1}{4}$ for 1919 (see Table 3.1). As Vickers' historian puts it: even if the shareholders had done well out of the war, 'they had not done extravagantly well'.[7]

As Table 5.1 shows, no other Sheffield firm could match Vickers' expansion in capital, though some firms were relatively more profitable for their

---

[5] *SI*, 9 Jan. 1915.   [6] *SI*, 12 June, 11 Dec. 1915.
[7] J. D. Scott, *Vickers: A History* (London, 1962), 133.

Table 5.1. *Issued capital of leading Sheffield firms, 1914 and 1919 (£)*

	1914	1919
Vickers	7,015,000	20,663,237
John Brown	3,573,000	4,187,500
Cammell-Laird	2,372,895	4,018,416
Hadfields	700,000	1,900,000
Firth	520,000	1,600,000

Sources: Company records and *Stock Exchange Yearbook*.

shareholders. Brown's ordinary dividends averaged 12½ per cent between 1914 and 1919. Its Sheffield workforce was considerably less than any of the other Sheffield arms firms—only 3,500 at the end of 1916—but there were several extensions in plant: a new power station, extension of the East Forge, and a new rolling mill in 1915, electric arc furnaces in 1916, new hammer shops in 1917, and a new forging press and tempering shops in 1918.

At Cammell-Laird in the years immediately preceding the war, the chairman, Lionel Hichens, was still grappling with the problems created by his predecessors. These included the poor financial position at the Birkenhead shipyards, which was draining funds from the more success-ful Sheffield steelmaking activities; difficulties at the Coventry Ordnance Works; losses caused by labour troubles; the hangover from being struck off the Admiralty list; and the problems of funding expansion at a company weighted with heavy debenture charges. The War provided a respite. Armour-plate and warship orders had lifted profits before the conflict—arms orders probably accounting for about half the firm's busi-ness at that time—and the upward trend continued during the war (see Tables 5.2 and 5.3). Besides an expansion in steel and shipping out-put, Cammell-Laird undertook the building and running of one of Sheffield's three National Projectile Factories at Nottingham (the others were built by Firth's and Hadfields). With Ministry of Munitions backing, they also spent over £0.5 million in erecting six Siemens' furnaces and a cogging mill at the Penistone works. Hichens, one of the few armaments chairmen who were sensitive to the charges of war profiteering, argued that the rise in profit and turnover would have occurred to a large extent anyway;[8] nevertheless the rise in arms orders obviously did the company no harm.

At Firth's sales increased from £1.2 million to £4.9 million, with the production of over 4 million shells, over 9,000 tons of gun forgings, 750

[8] *SI*, 1 Apr. 1915.

Table 5.2. *Employment at Cammell-Laird's Sheffield works, 1914–1918*

	1914	1915	1916	1917	1918
Cyclops	1,407	1,468	1,303	1,418	1,450
Grimesthorpe	2,726	3,184	3,700	3,670	3,663
Penistone	761	841	883	899	954
TOTAL	4,894	5,493	5,886	5,987	6,067

Note: These figures do not include the company's projectile factory at Nottingham, which was also under Sheffield supervision. Employment there was 340 in 1916; 1,225 in 1917; and 1,189 in 1918.

Source: Cammell-Laird Papers, Birkenhead.

Table 5.3. *Sales at Cammell-Laird, 1914–1918* (£)

	1914	1915	1916	1917	1918
Cyclops	865,931	906,422	841,577	966,834	1,065,732
Grimesthorpe	625,471	1,107,284	1,971,472	1,934,379	2,080,441
Penistone	374,423	465,191	930,561	901,906	756,267
Birkenhead (completed contracts)	1,504,057	2,811,407	3,882,839	3,641,575	4,022,795
TOTAL	3,369,882	5,290,304	7,626,449	7,444,694	7,925,235

Note: Figures allow for returns, but not the deduction of discounts.

Source: Cammell-Laird Papers, Birkenhead.

tons of air vessel ends and parts for torpedoes; and 10,000 tons of marine shafts and turbine forgings. In 1916 extensions costing £610,000 were authorized by the Government. A new Siemens plant was installed in 1918, containing one 60-ton, two 40-ton, and one 25-ton tilting furnaces; a 4,000-ton press was erected at the Gun Works; and there were extensions to the Engineers' Tool Department and the Research Laboratories. In 1915 Firth's was also entrusted with the erection and management of a National Projectile Factory at Templeborough. Firth's labour force rose from 3,100 (including 100 women) in 1914 to 6,868 (1,984 women) in 1918.

The First World War saw Hadfields and its chairman at full stretch. The firm supplied the Government with everything from guns and projectiles, to armour-plate and tank treads. Warlike uses were even found for manganese steel in the soldier's 'tin hat'. As usual, the development of Hadfields cannot be understood without reference to the personality of its chairman. Hadfield's rantings against the Germans reached new heights during the War, as he continually lambasted them in the press for their militarism (oblivious to the irony of this from a Sheffield arms manufacturer) and contrasted the 'Teuton's' scientific achievements unfavourably with Sheffield's. No other Sheffield steelmaker dominated the local newspapers at this time as did Hadfield.[9] This Germanophobia, coupled with Hadfield's personal obsession with armaments—a close colleague said that nothing gave him greater excitement than the sight of shells hitting armour—and his manic energy were a potent combination.

Unable to resist government demands for increased armaments capacity, Hadfield extended the works dramatically. By 1917 he believed that no other works in the country involved in such special lines had expanded so much.[10] Hadfields organized a completely new government shell factory within the works; greatly increased its electric steelmaking capacity; began the production of new lines such as howitzers and trench mortars; while Hadfield himself became a member of nearly a hundred councils, committees, and subcommittees. His directors were also 'working day and night seven days a week [which] imposed upon them a physical and mental strain almost beyond endurance'.[11] The firm's workforce more than doubled from 5,690 in 1914 to over 13,000 in 1918; while the value of its output soared from £1.7 million a year to nearly £10 million. By the end the War, Hadfields was probably the biggest employer in Sheffield itself. It was also extraordinarily profitable. Between 1914 and 1918, its net profits exceeded £1 million (see Fig. 3.1), on a capital at the start of the War of £700,000, and with ordinary dividends averaging over 20 per cent a year. Little wonder that Hadfield later remarked: 'We have never drawn breath from the moment the War started until the Armistice came.'[12]

Although the Sheffield armaments industry inevitably conjures up images of Dreadnoughts and heavy guns, even the smallest firms were miniature arsenals, since with a little imagination almost any steel product could be used for weaponry. At Osborn's:

Practically the whole output was used directly or indirectly for war purposes, although this was not obvious, as the standard lines—tool steels, twist drills, milling cutters, springs, files, steel sheets and steel castings were manufactured as usual.

At the beginning of the war the company held the War Office and Admiralty contracts for tool steels and their requirements doubled immediately, and after the

[9] For a characteristic outburst, see 'English and German Methods Contrasted', *SI*, 4 Mar. 1915.
[10] 'Miles of Shells: Hadfields' Stupendous War Output', *SI*, 27 Mar. 1917.
[11] SCL Hadfield Papers. Hadfield to Ministry of Munitions, 25 Oct. 1918.
[12] Public Record Office, Reco 1/730. Hadfield to Minister, 2 Jan. 1919. Reference courtesy Richard Davenport-Hines.

National Shell Factories were opened, the demand was terrific. The number of workpeople was increased. The drill-making plant was extended, and for the first time, women were employed in making drills. A very large quantity of sheet steel was rolled and thousands of springs for motor vehicles were made. Tools for the making of shells, cartridge-making tools, special cutters, alloy steels for aeroplane parts, and tons of steel for balls and ball bearings for aeroplanes and tanks were among the direct contributions to the war effort.

Files were supplied to many Government departments and factories as well as to engineering firms employed directly in the making of guns, rifles, tanks and other implements of war. But it was in the steel foundry and sheet mills where output could be most directly related to war work.

In the foundry such castings as cylinders for shell-making plants, wheels for axles for the army light railways in France, castings for sea-mines, depth charge throwers, boom defences of our naval bases, and for the paravanes, were supplied in large quantities. Possibly the most important contribution was the castings supplied for the first experimental land ships, or tanks as they were afterwards called, and others of later design. Aerial bomb cases up to a quarter of a ton in weight were made in thousands.[13]

By the end of the War, Osborn's workforce had expanded from about a thousand in 1914 to well over 1,500 by 1918; and profits of about £35,000 per annum had reached nearly £100,000 in the same period.

For the other tool steel and alloy firms, it was very much the same story of high profits (despite excess profits duty) and plant extensions. Edgar Allen continued its expansion into the War years, acquiring the Park View Steel Works in 1915 so that the firm could control its own forging capacity. Between 1914 and 1919 dividends on its ordinary shares averaged about 18 per cent; while the firm's issued capital grew from £490,000 to £604,000. Jonas & Colver remained the biggest high-speed steel producer during the War; and it was also one of the most important suppliers of aircraft steels. By 1918, its workforce had doubled to 3,000; and after £200,000 in extensions had been made its issued capital had climbed from £423,009 in 1914 to £634,514 in 1919.

Kayser, Ellison, which was involved in the same sector of the special steel trade, had a particularly profitable war: dividends on the ordinary shares averaged 18 per cent between 1914 and 1918, with a 100 per cent bonus paid from reserve in 1918. Its issued capital rose from £205,000 in 1918 to £350,000 in 1918. Samuel Fox's profit record was also striking: annual profits averaged £39,000 between 1909 and 1914; between 1915 and 1919 they averaged £268,000. The Beardshaws—typical of the smaller tool steelmakers—also enjoyed bonus dividends as the firm's net sales climbed from about £80,000 a year before the War to a record £263,235 in 1918. Any firm that was paying less than a 10 per cent annual dividend on

---

[13] T. A. Seed, *Pioneers for a Century* (Sheffield, 1952), 44.

its ordinary shares during the War—J. H. Andrew appears to be one of the few documented examples—was an exception and doing very badly.

The tool steel trade was one of the busiest sectors of the Sheffield steel industry, with demand mirroring the rapid growth of the engineering industry. More lathes, projectiles, and aero-engines simply meant a greater call for cutting steels, especially for high-speed steel. Crucible steel production reached a yearly peak of about 110,000 tons in the War, while the pre-war annual high-speed steel output of about 6,000 tons tripled. By April 1915 a Sheffield newspaper noted that: 'The demand for high-speed steel is enormous,'[14] adding a few months later that its supply was:

causing considerable anxiety because the output is already inadequate, and there is great activity in extending plants for shell turning. This work cannot be done without the above-named steel, and the war requirements are certain to be largely increased in the near future. So far as can be seen at present there are no means of increasing the output. Steps are being taken to check the export of such steel, but France, Italy and Russia are clamouring for it for their munition work and Canada needs a good deal for the same purpose.[15]

Two problems in supplying the demand for high-speed steel (and ordinary tungsten tool steel) were soon apparent: one was the shortage of skilled melters; the other was a shortage of metallic ingredients for alloy steels, especially tungsten powder. Until the outbreak of war this had been imported from Germany, which monopolized the processing of tungsten ore (a situation that arose, as one trade journal put it, 'from the inferior commercial power of British individualism when opposed to German collectivism').[16] About the former, Sheffield tool steelmakers could do little in the short-term (though the development of the electric furnace offered a partial solution towards the end of the War); about the latter, they had no alternative but to begin manufacturing tungsten themselves.

At the end of 1914 a consortium of about thirty of the leading Sheffield tool steelmakers (who were responsible for about 80 per cent of the output), along with Armstrong Whitworth Ltd., had registered High Speed Steel Alloys Ltd. with a subscribed capital of £50,000. A. J. Hobson, the chairman of Jessop's, and Arthur Balfour, of Seebohm & Dieckstahl, were leading lights in the venture, which immediately began the building of a factory for processing tungsten powder at Widnes under the supervision of Julius Vogel (d. 1943).[17] By 1916 Sheffield was assured of its own supplies of tungsten and the company had secured two mines in Burma

---

[14] *SI*, 17 Apr. 1915.   [15] *SI*, 3 July 1915.   [16] *Engineering*, 102 (1916), 509.
[17] 'High Speed Steel Alloys', ibid. 509–10; 'Tungsten Manufacturing at Widnes', ibid. 104 (1917), 432–4; 'Some Metals and Alloys Used in Steelmaking', *Metallurgia*, 14 (July 1936), 63–6.

for the raw material. Like the making of scientific instruments, ball bearings, chemical and laboratory glassware, and certain chemicals such as benzol—tungsten manufacture was an example of a British industry that scarcely existed before the War and had to be established because of the ending of imports from Germany. By 1918 $4\frac{1}{2}$ million pounds of tungsten powder had been produced by the company and it was ready to begin the manufacture of other alloying elements. High Speed Steel Alloys was to supply the Sheffield tool steel industry until about 1960.

Though this ended the shortage of tungsten, the tool steel firms still had difficulty in keeping pace with the demand. Many were said to be a year or more behind in their orders, press reports which are confirmed by the few business records available. Seebohm & Dieckstahl reported in 1915 that 'at the present rate of production we have one year and six months melting ahead. It was therefore decided that we should accept no more large orders, or orders from merchants nor open any new accounts.'[18] The firm had nearly 3,000 tons of tool steel on their books for the Japanese Arsenal alone. Its high-speed steel output had increased dramatically from about 500 tons a year in 1914 to over 1,500 tons in 1917.

Most of the orders for tool steel were taken up by the existing capacity of firms such as Seebohm & Dieckstahl, though there was one new entrant to the crucible steel trade during the War. T. W. Pearson Ltd., which began as a file manufacturer in about 1893, started melting crucible steel at this time in Matilda Lane, close to the Midland Station.[19]

This steel directly fed another big growth area—high-speed steel twist drill manufacture. Carbon twist drills were less in demand, because they did not prove efficient enough for the fine diameter holes in fuses and aeroplane parts. 'There is an enormous demand for the best classes of twist drill', observed one reporter, 'Some five or six firms put down expensive plants for the manufacture of these goods during the last few years, but their resources are far from meeting the situation.'[20] Balfour's had large toolworks extensions on hand at their Broughton Lane Works by 1916, helped by a £1,000 government grant for research. Marsh Bros. continued to make rapid progress in twist drill manufacture during the War: by 1918 30,000 of these tools per week were turned out by the firm, which had absorbed the twist drill business of Johann Judex.[21]

The development of the high-carbon, high-chromium die steels, developed by Paul Kuehnrich, also continued uninterrupted during the War. Following up his original experiments on these alloys, Kuehnrich reduced the carbon in them to $1\frac{1}{2}$ per cent and added a small amount of

[18] SCL BDR 78, Director's Minute Book 1913–21: 17 Dec. 1915, 20 Dec. 1916.
[19] Information from Roger Hague, 28 Jan. 1992.
[20] *SI*, 3 July 1915.
[21] S. Pollard, *Three Centuries of Sheffield Steel* (Sheffield, 1954), 55.

molybdenum and cobalt, making a strongly air-hardening steel (thus reducing the risk of cracking during treatment) possessing negligible distortion characteristics. This he called 'PRK-135'. Its virtues—it was said to harden with the minimum distortion of any tool steel—were vigorously publicized by Kuehnrich in the Sheffield newspapers in 1917. Full-page advertisements announced Kuehnrich's 'NEW STEEL', which he described as an air-hardening tungstenless high-speed steel and branded as 'Cobaltcrom'. Readers were informed that the steel was especially suitable for milling cutters, twist drills, reamers, taps, automatic forming tools, screw-cutting, and finishing tools in general. Such adventurous marketing (running such a press campaign was unique at that time for a Sheffield tool steelmaker) of an alloy that was a major development proved highly successful. Kuehnrich emerged from the War with his commercial standing and wealth greatly enhanced, ready to exploit 'Cobaltcrom' in the cutlery industry.

Though the general trend in steel demand was to raise the profile of the city's steel industry, the experience of individual firms did vary markedly according to their strategies and the prevailing circumstances. One problem faced by some of the Sheffield tool steel firms was anti-German hysteria.[22] In 1915 Seebohm & Dieckstahl announced it was to change its name to Arthur Balfour & Co., a recognition of the fact that Balfour himself was now the principal shareholder. But the need for a new company title—a move not to be undertaken lightly by any long-established Sheffield firm which relied on its name for its reputation—was mostly due to the prejudice against German names.[23] Some of the smaller firms soon fell victim to this hostility: the Poldi Steel Works in Napier Street was temporarily wound up as an 'alien business'; and Bohler Bros., an Austro-German high-speed steel firm with a Sheffield depot, also attracted attention at this time because of its 'enemy alien' origins and did not survive the War.

It was Sheffield's German-born steelmakers, such as Charles W. Kayser Jun., Paul Kuehnrich, and Sir Joseph Jonas, who were the most vulnerable. These men were still outsiders, to a certain extent, in Sheffield (it is noticeable, for example, that none of them, not even Jonas, were made Master Cutler by that Establishment body, the Cutlers' Company). All somehow escaped internment. The Kaysers, despite their somewhat unfortunate name, appear to have been sufficiently long-established to escape hostility. Kayser, Ellison were amongst the biggest flag-wavers of the Sheffield firms at the start of the War, with a well-publicized appeal for their staff to join the armed forces.[24] Kuehnrich, however, was not so lucky

---

[22] See generally P. Panayi, 'Germans in Sheffield 1914–1918: A National Story on a Local Scale', in C. Binfield *et al.*, *The History of the City of Sheffield* (Sheffield, 1993), iii. 250–9.

[23] *SI*, 4 Dec. 1915.   [24] *SI*, 8 Aug. 1914.

and was hounded throughout the War by the authorities. Questions were asked in Parliament about his work in Sheffield; there were rumours that he was a friend of the Kaiser; that he drilled a secret army at his residence, Holly Court, in Ecclesall; and that he had stockpiled arms and ammunition. In a letter to the *Sheffield Independent*, 30 April 1915, Kuehnrich denounced the 'unscrupulous jesters' and rumourmongers, and offered to allow the police to tour Holly Court. He continued to be harassed, however, and in the following year he was fined twice: once for showing a powerful light in the evening at Holly Court; and once for possessing 69 pounds of bacon (though a lesser charge of hoarding Bovril was dismissed!). In 1918 certain German patents relating to cobalt tool steel in which Darwin & Milner had an interest were also successfully challenged in the courts by Balfour's.

More serious were the charges brought against Sir Joseph Jonas in 1918 when he was arrested for allegedly passing information on armaments to the enemy. Jonas's supposed crime was the communicating of commercial information about a Vickers rifle works to a correspondent in Berlin, something which appears considerably less incriminating once it is realized that it took place in 1913. Such was the absurdity of the charges that Jonas was eventually acquitted of conspiracy, but he was nevertheless found guilty of 'misdemeanour', fined and censured. By the end of the War he had retired from his business, having suffered the disgrace of having his knighthood revoked—something which would have been particularly hurtful to Jonas, who took great pride in the honour, even to the extent of naming his firm Sir Joseph Jonas & Colver Ltd.

In the works themselves the War brought other problems. These ranged from the trivial—one firm responded to the shortage of horses for haulage by harnessing an elephant![25]—to the major. The influx of outside workers led to 'dilution' in the skilled engineering trades, which in turn caused labour unrest. Militancy erupted between 1916 and 1917, when Sheffield, under J. T. Murphy, became a leader in the shop stewards' movement, which was committed to the revolutionary goal of workers' control.[26] Organizing plant extensions in many Sheffield steel firms, even in the large-scale producers in the Don Valley, also proved difficult. As one correspondent noted: 'The difficulty in Sheffield is that industries have grown far beyond the dreams of the pioneers of the Sheffield steel trade, and there is a lamentable lack of space for the necessary new shops.'[27] Hence Cammell-Laird's decision to build its shell works in Nottingham. The lack of space and the consequent *ad hoc* nature of many of the extensions in this period were to leave many Sheffield manufactur-

[25] *SI*, 29 Jan. 1916.
[26] James Hinton, *The First Shop Steward's Movement* (London, 1973), 162–77.
[27] *SI*, 21 Aug. 1915.

ers with a legacy that was to dog them through the inter-war years and beyond.

The War also allowed little opportunity to make the most of commercial opportunities, especially overseas. Orders, especially for products once supplied by the Germans, continued to arrive, but:

A large proportion of these have to be hawked among the various manufacturers before anyone is found who can take on any additional business. The majority are so short-handed that the orders already on their books will occupy months in execution. Practically speaking, all the organisation for winning business is suspended simply because without any effort on the part of manufacturers more comes forward than can be dealt with. Travellers are at a discount except in trades which canvass the London and provincial distributors.[28]

'The steel trade traveller', noted another reporter, 'is like a fish out of water . . . deprived of the joy of "telling the tale" or figuring out an elaborate bill of expenses. He longs for peace on the Continent and freedom at home.'[29] Part of the problem was the disruption of two of Sheffield's favourite hunting grounds for business: Russia and Germany.

Technologically the war proved a forcing house. Sheffield rapidly needed to become self-sufficient in many products previously imported from Germany. Tungsten manufacture has already been mentioned; the development of magnets is another example. Although Swift Levick had pioneered magnet production in Sheffield, German magnets were still widely regarded as the best. The sudden demand for home-produced magnetos for aircraft and vehicle engines, however, soon stimulated the development of an indigenous permanent magnet industry. Besides Swift Levick, Neill's were amongst those firms whose expertise in cast steel allowed Sheffield to become independent of Germany during the War.[30]

No major new alloys or breakthroughs in production processes were made during the War, but the available technology was rapidly explored and extended. The development of electric melting provides a good example. The arc furnace provided a solution to the problem of the large quantities of waste turnings from the machine shops; it was also the ideal melting instrument for the new alloys, such as stainless steel. Wartime installations of arc furnaces therefore rapidly accelerated. Unfortunately, no official figures are available on electric furnace plant in Sheffield, so that the information has to be collected piecemeal. One newspaper in 1917 referred to 30 such melting units in the city, with the number expected to rise to 50, and virtually all the leading Sheffield high-grade steelmakers

[28] *SI*, 10 July 1915. See also 'Resources Monopolised for War Material', *SI*, 18 Sept. 1915.
[29] *SI*, 1 Apr. 1916.
[30] Frazer Wright, *James Neill: A Century of Quality and Service, 1889–1989* (1989), 11–12.

had installed electric arc furnaces by 1918.[31] Hadfields had 10 arc furnaces by 1917, producing about 1,000 tons a week—probably the largest concentration of electric steel-melting capacity in the world; Firth's had 8; Vickers 4; and Osborn 3. Even the smaller tool steelmakers and tool works installed electric furnaces at this time. These included firms such as Balfour; Kayser, Ellison (which had installed 4 furnaces between 1913 and 1917); Beardshaw; J. H. Andrew; Spear & Jackson; even Thomas Andrews. There was no indication here that small firms were conservative in the face of new technology.

The largest of these arc furnaces were between about 10 and 15 tons capacity. For most firms, electric melting was used for the less special of the special steels—such as the alloys used in aircraft and motor cars—and not for high-grade tool steels. But towards the end of the War, such was the demand for high-speed steel that even here Sheffield steelmakers had begun to use the arc. For example, by 1917 high-speed steel melting was well under way at Spear & Jackson, which had also acquired a Rotherham firm, Sheffield Alloys Ltd., to augment its electric steel capacity. Only in the manufacture of high-grade steel for turning tools did the arc prove unsuitable: here the crucible still reigned supreme in Sheffield.

Inevitably, the growth of electric furnace production triggered new Sheffield industries. Firms were established to supply not only the carbon electrodes which constantly needed replacement, but also the furnaces themselves. Many of the early arc installations had been of Continental design or manufacture, but during the War Sheffield began to produce its own. The Greaves-Etchells furnace, designed and built by T. H. Watson & Co., was the most successful. By 1917 over 6 of these furnaces were at work and Greaves-Etchells' furnaces were also being sold abroad.

With the electric furnace, Sheffield was able to exploit the rapidly growing demand for new engineering steels. As Oliver Arnold pointed out, the war imposed new demands on engineers and metallurgists, with submarines and aviation requiring new materials and engines of unusual design.[32] During the War, Brown Bayleys became one of the principal producers of all types of high-tensile alloy steels for aircraft, with the firm making, it was said, about half the steel used for aero-crankshafts. Jonas & Colver were the other major government suppliers of these crankshafts. Meanwhile, Kayser, Ellison led the way in the development of aircraft steels, particularly for poppet-valves. Vickers, Cammell, Hadfields, and Jessop soon recognized the potential of this market: all took a prominent part in Goverment-sponsored research into the physical properties of the new steels. Research programmes in Sheffield steelworks were therefore intensified. For example, Brown Bayleys production of aircraft steels led

---

[31] *SI*, 14 Feb. 1917.   [32] 'Science in Steel', *SI*, 19 Jan. 1915.

to the building up of a system of metallurgical control at the company after the War.

The development of Sheffield's new stainless steel—which, we may recall, had been discovered during corrosion tests on rifle barrels—went ahead rapidly during the First World War. Harry Brearley later complained that his employers, Firth's, had dragged their feet over the introduction of the alloy. But they did not do so for long, Brearley himself admitting that soon the new steel was 'an absorbing topic of conversation among cutlers and steel-makers and the subject of newspaper comments'[33]—a fact easily confirmed by a search of the contemporary press. For example, the *Sheffield Independent*, 17 April 1915, commented that 'rapid development is being made in the non-rust steel for cutlery. Severe tests have proved that the steel fully comes up to expectations. It is anticipated that the uses of the steel will be extended to other articles of domestic use.' Sheffield soon had a clear lead over its international rivals.

Remarkably, Brearley never patented stainless steel in Britain (one source later explaining that this was because the discovery had spread so rapidly in Sheffield, that patenting was thought scarcely worthwhile), so any manufacturer could make it. However, Brearley and Firth's soon tied up the rights on stainless steel in the United States, Canada, Italy, France, and Japan, so that any Sheffield firm wishing to export to these countries needed a licence from the Firth-Brearley Stainless Steel Syndicate (established in 1917)—a very profitable arrangement for Firth's, who naturally were also manufacturing the alloy themselves. In America, Elwood Haynes had to be accommodated in any arrangements. He had nothing like the close-knit local expertise available to launch his own discovery of a rustless alloy, though his prior claims enabled him to reach an agreement with Firth's and Brearley so that he could rightfully share in the commercial rewards in America. It was Sheffield steelmakers, though, who provided much of the technical expertise when stainless steel was first melted in Pittsburgh in 1915—appropriately at Firth's subsidiary in the city.

In Sheffield, the first stainless manufacturers were Brown Bayley's, John Brown's, Sanderson Bros. & Newbould, Hadfields, Osborn, Howell's, and Firth's. For example, Samuel E. Howell (1847–1928), the son and successor of the tube maker, J. B. Howell, was 'an early convert to stainless steel': he began using it for boilers and advocated its use in cutlery.[34] Stainless steel helped revitalize some firms. At Brown Bayley's, where the retirement of the able managing director, J. H. Barber (*c.*1837–1911), had led to falling profits and labour troubles, Robert Armitage attempted a strategic

[33] H. Brearley, *Knotted String* (London, 1941), 129.   [34] *SDT*, 16 Apr. 1928.

redirection of the company. This involved a switch from carbon into alloy steels, especially stainless steel. Armitage recruited Harry Brearley from Firth's in 1915, modernized the research and chemical laboratories and installed electric furnaces to melt the new steel.

Besides cutlery, an industrial use was immediately found for stainless steel in aero-engine valves. Indeed, more or less at the same time as Brearley was conducting his pioneering work with cutlery, Firth's had developed a derivative known as 'Firth's Aeroplane Steel', the valuable features of which included resistance to weather corrosion and great strength. Towards the end of the War, a slight improvement was made in the analysis of steel for exhaust valves by lowering the chromium from 12 to 8 per cent and increasing the carbon and silicon. The material was stonger at temperatures of 700 °C and highly resistant to scaling.

CUTLERS AT WAR

The cutlery industry had seized on stainless steel with alacrity. Despite their innate conservatism, Sheffield cutlers immediately recognized the alloy for what it was—a major breakthrough, that 'may revolutionise the whole cutlery trade'.[35] By early 1915 about six firms had taken up stainless steel (or, as it was known at the time, non-rust or rustless steel), and were beginning to apply themselves to the problem of how to keep a good cutting edge on knives made from it.[36] By the end of 1915 stainless table cutlery was said to be growing in popularity week by week.[37] But as demand for the alloy for knives began to outstrip supply and there were also shortages of ferro-chromium, in 1917 the Government restricted stainless steel's use to the production of aero-engines.[38] A rapidly developing sector of the cutlery industry immediately went into abeyance, until the prohibition was lifted at the end of the War.

As this experience shows, wartime expansion and high profits were not a foregone conclusion, especially in the cutlery trades. Here the impact of war was uneven. Generally, wartime demand had a levelling tendency, hitting the luxury end of the market, but boosting the trade of medium- and cheap-priced makers. Almost immediately, it threw some of the deficiencies of the Sheffield light trades into sharp focus.

With the War naturally directing output into weapons, the cutlery and tool firms that concentrated on bayonets and army knives, or could adapt production to military contracts (for cooking utensils, for example), did best. By December 1914 there was already a brisk demand for cutlery and

[35] *Arsenal of the World* (Sheffield, 1918), 18.   [36] *SI*, 13 Feb., 3 July 1915.
[37] *SI*, 27 Nov. 1915.   [38] *SI*, 22 Sept. 1917.

razors for the Army and Navy. The sword industry (previously often catered for by Germany) had also returned to the city, now that weapons with a good cutting edge were required, rather than ceremonial objects. There was a demand for products as diverse as knitting needles, surgical instruments, and sharpened steel darts, which French aviators showered on the hapless German infantry. Millions of entrenching tools were also required: Spear & Jackson made 150,000 of them during the War, a new line for the firm.

On the other hand, toolmakers with a large Continental trade with Germany and Russia were faced with a falling demand and anxiety over their accounts. And although orders for electroplate and nickel-silver spoons kept the firms producing such goods busy for a time, it was soon clear that this sector would be hit by a fall in the demand for high-quality work. 'The silver trades are very depressed, the demand for luxurious articles having fallen to vanishing point,' noted one report.[39] Another stated that: 'If it were not for the fact that Sheffield houses many factories where articles of luxury are made in the shape of silver- and electro-plate goods, there would be very little unemployment to record.'[40] Soon workers from the silverplate firms would be finding employment within the growing arms industry, where they could earn more. The slump in the luxury market was reflected in the fortunes of Mappin & Webb: it had paid moderate dividends to its shareholders before the War, but in the early years of the conflict it could only meet debenture charges.

Falling demand for high-quality cutlery also hit the leaders in the cutlery industry, such as Wostenholm and Rodgers. Rodgers' profits dropped by nearly half during the War, from about £20,000 a year to £12,000. Wostenholm's profits fell to about the same level (see Table 8.1). About 75 per cent of Wostenholm's output was devoted to war work, but this was not a line which fitted easily with the company's culture. Wrote Wostenholm director, James Paine:

People see in the newspapers statements respecting pressure of work in the cutlery trade, and the wonderful wages the men are earning. All this is quite correct, [but] the trade is [also] very shorthanded, and the output greatly below that of normal times; also that with a business like ours, whose trade is chiefly in better class goods, there is practically no demand . . .

This terrible war is making havoc with the cutlery trade. The shortage of labour and urgent demands for various sorts of cutlery for the Armies and the scarcity of materials have put prices sky high. The workmen, what are left of them, are earning such wages as were never known. We get scarcely any commercial work made. The rate of wages being higher and as this cannot be turned out quickly enough, we must do War work or let our men go where they can have it. Our trade

[39] *SI*, 14 Nov. 1914.   [40] *SI*, 24 Oct. 1914.

is practically held up and we can sell in spring knives only such as we still have stock of.[41]

The Wostenholm workforce fell from about 400 in 1914 to about 200 during the War (most of whom worked in the spring-knife department); and thirty-six never returned from the colours. Rodgers had also lost fifty-five men in the War. So critical did the skilled labour supply become, that by the end of the War firms such as Rodgers were appealing against the call-up of their men: it was felt that the enlistment of skilled men in the trade had gone too far. The permanent loss of their best grinders and cutlers was to hit these quality-makers particularly hard after the War.

The movement of skilled men into the heavy trades, the shortages of materials, and the increasing demands for standardized army lines, produced with high output—all these factors were dictating a move towards mass production. Moreover, high-volume orders were underlining a fact that had become apparent by 1914: the cutlery industry needed to mechanize more if it was to cope effectively with demand. Soon the cutlery firms were said to be six months behind with their orders. A call by the War Office and Admiralty in 1914 for a million-and-a-half razors had caused problems in an industry where the annual output was normally only a million items. Unable to increase the production of straight razors, the industry, through the Company of Cutlers, was forced to launch a public appeal in 1915 to collect enough razors for the troops.[42]

A small, but significant exhibition at Cutlers' Hall in 1915, drove the point home. Hatred of Germany and German *kultur* was as prevalent amongst the cutlery manufacturers as amongst the steelmakers, perhaps more so. Early in the War, there was an attempt to induce makers to abandon the term 'German silver'—the name always used for the 'nickel silver' metal used for knife parts; and there was the usual witch-hunt against any German influences in the trade.[43] Nevertheless, the Company of Cutlers went ahead in March 1915 with an exhibition of German cutlery. Its impact is recorded in the Sheffield press:

A lot of business is being offered in the lighter trades, which German manufacturers used to do, and those who have the business to place are willing to pay 20 percent above the German price, but in many cases this does not bring the Sheffield price anywhere near the German. Samples of cutlery of German manufacture, which will be on exhibition in Sheffield next week, reveal an excellence in

    [41] SCL Wostenholm Records. Secretary's copybook No. 8, Paine to John Weetson & Sons, 28 Jan. 1916; and Paine to T. F. Curley, 1 Sept. 1916.
    [42] *SI*, 6 Mar. 1915.
    [43] In 1915, for example, Charles Ern, the German-born managing director of Sheffield 'Blanks' Ltd., was prosecuted by his own firm for importing German scissor blanks—probably a common and innocent practice before 1914, when Sheffield had difficulty supplying scissors in sufficient quantity. *SI*, 27 Feb. 1915.

finish and a cheapness in price which is a revelation to the Sheffield cutlery manufacturer. It is conceded that a revolution in methods of manufacture will be necessary before Sheffield firms are able to compete successfully with German manufacturers. Resources of production in Sheffield of cutlery and razors are quite inadequate, and within the last few days the British Government has been compelled to place an order with two American firms for pocket-knives for the Army to the extent of over two million knives. The price is about a shilling lower per dozen than the Sheffield price. American firms are also supplying a large quantity of razors for the Army, Sheffield resources being unequal to the requirements.[44]

Germany's dominance had been achieved by 'the application of machinery, by the use of a complete system of standardisation, by cutting down the number of patterns, which was the curse of the Sheffield cutlery trade'.[45] But a recognition of Sheffield's weaknesses was one thing, applying the remedy was another. This was especially so, since the same forces that dictated mechanization—the depletion of the skilled labour force, the weakening of the bigger firms that relied on the luxury market, even the pressure to increase output itself—also hindered it.

Some firms did try. One mechanized industry that did make its appearance during the War was the manufacture of safety razors. This was accomplished by a handful of small firms, which included Edgar Pease Burrell, Edley & Hill, Robert S. Mitchell, and, shortly after the War, the American-based firm of Durham-Duplex, which later acquired another Sheffield safety-razor maker, W. & S. Butcher. It was a small-scale industry, which was unable to satisfy the demand from the Army (which, in any case, required cut-throats as regulation issue). There were also isolated reports of certain branches of the trade installing machinery, such as in that preserve of German makers, scissor blank production. Some Sheffield unions who had visited Solingen before 1914 also agreed on the need for modern machinery, together with the introduction of women to prepare handle materials in the trade.[46]

There were also a few progressive manufacturers. Walter Tyzack (1857–1925), head of Needham, Veall, & Tyzack, watched German developments closely and was one of the few Sheffield cutlery makers to comprehend fully the achievement of the Solingen industry, compared with the 'lamentable amount of indifference' he saw in Sheffield.[47] It was Tyzack who had played the lead in collecting German cutlery for the Cutlers' Hall exhibition. In 1915, he hired Herbert Senior, a Sheffielder

---

[44] *SI*, 6 Feb. 1915. This exhibition is not mentioned in any histories of the Cutlers' Co.
[45] Remarks of Col. Herbert Hughes, *SI*, 26 Feb. 1915.
[46] *SI*, 27 Nov. 1916.
[47] Tyzack's speech before Sheffield Society of Applied Metallurgy, re German cutlery exhibition and competition, *SI*, 17 Apr. 1915.

working in America, to install German pocket-knife machinery and modernize Needham, Veall, & Tyzack's Pond Street Works. By 1918, although Tyzack was handicapped by his old workshops, he was regarded as 'ahead of anyone in Sheffield' in mechanization. The company was tooled up to manufacture a single pattern of pocket-knife (a two-piece Army knife), with blades and springs 'flyed' out of sheet steel and spread under drop hammers, the scales pierced by foot-press, and assembly done by girls and even by the blind. The result was an Army knife that was better than any of the Sheffield competition.[48]

But apart from these examples, there were few signs that the Sheffield cutlery manufacturers were in the mood for change in the war years. A more typical reaction to mechanization can be found at Wostenholm's. There, too, some of the directors recognized the need for change. Nixon told Wing: 'I believe that a drastic reform of manufacturing processes in the cutlery industry is being forced upon us, and that this period [1914–18] when our chief Continental rivals are temporarily paralysed is the best possible one in which to begin a thoroughly practical effort to effect reform.'[49] Frank Colver, their new, young, and energetic director, was chosen to spearhead the drive to modernize the old company. He began a wide-ranging review of the firm, highlighting and attempting to deal with the Washington Works' antiquated administration. A revision of old methods of pricing stock, for example, transformed a loss for one year into a small profit. He planned to make an extensive tour of American cutlery factories in 1918, with a view to purchasing a range of pocket-knife machines to inaugurate Wostenholm's launch into machine-production.

Unfortunately for Wostenholm's, the autocratic and conservative managing director, James Paine, was less happy about forsaking Wostenholm's craftsmanship. A power struggle developed within the company during the War, so that the new technology arrived only after an agonizing catharsis. Paine opposed Colver's activities at every turn, quarrelled bitterly with his directors, and effectively blocked the mechanization programme for the duration of the War.

For Wostenholm's and other firms, this meant lost trade. While the steelmakers made an effort to cater for Germany's former customers in America, Australia, New Zealand, and South America, the cutlery firms reacted more conservatively. Some Sheffield makers were suspicious of orders which suggested that 'the desire to do business with Sheffield is prompted by the necessity to place orders somewhere until the German manufacturer can again supply, and in such cases where the installation of new plant would be necessary, the Sheffield manufacturer is not follow-

---

[48] SCL Wostenholm Records. Wing correspondence, letter from Colver (?), 16 Dec. 1918.
[49] Ibid. Nixon to Wing, 4 Mar. 1915.

ing up the inquiry'.[50] Wostenholm's were in a similar situation: they were unable to expand business, because the firm lacked the means. Nixon lamented in 1918: 'We have lost golden months and years ... while our resources are dwindling, and our markets are being taken from us because we cannot meet their demands.'[51]

Generally, it proved too much to ask that the Sheffield cutlery and tool trades, that had been set in their ways for over a century, could transform themselves within two or three years into an industry on the German model. 'Business as usual' was the motto in Sheffield cutlery during the War, with the trades maintaining their traditional appearance and practices. In 1915 a newspaper article by an old Sheffield cutlery craftsman contrasted the city's industry unfavourably with its German and American competitors. It is worth quoting at length:

When you consider the conditions under which the Sheffield cutlers are working, with tools handed down from one generation to another, it is only by their wonderful skill that they have been able to maintain their reputation. Today it should be one of the best paid trades instead of the worst.

The [Sheffield] trade is far more unhealthy and dangerous now, since the introduction of power into small and confined rooms. The majority of the shops are insanitary, badly lighted and 'pinched' for side or bench room, which the cutler pays dearly for. His tools are antiquated. Some of them were made in his grandfather's day ... All outworkers must find all tools and material and pay shop rent, and that goes on whether they have work or not or when the power is down. Much time is lost going to the warehouse, waiting for a job, and then having to go to different parts of the city to collect material ...

Compare it with the German and American system. It will be seen it is not the fault of the Sheffield workmen that Germany and America have been so successful in competing with the Sheffield manufacturers. There, the place selected for the works is easy of access for either rail or water transport. The shops are specially built ... well-lighted and ventilated; there is ample side or bench room for each workman and plenty of drawers and racks of files, etc. All tools and working material are provided. Cupboards are provided for the workmen's clothes and there are wash-bowls and towels, the men paying a small amount for soap and towels washing. This is the only thing the workmen pay out of their pocket.

Each storey is connected with a lift. Material is sent up to the workmen right to their benches in basket lorries, and finished work is fetched to the warehouse with the least labour or loss of time. There are special rooms for 'mousing' [glazing down of bone] or emery glazing and good fans to take away the dust, etc., keeping the other rooms quite free. Buffs, glazers, dollys, etc., are made on the premises. All small machines for drilling, squaring, flying, etc., are made by mechanics employed for the purpose.

[50] *SI*, 10 Oct. 1914.
[51] SCL Wostenholm Records. Paine resignation letters. Nixon to Wing, 10 Jan. 1918.

The grinding hulls have plenty of room and light, with hot and cold water for every trough ... The blade forgers' shops, machine shops, etc., or sheds, are separate from the other buildings and can be thrown wide open in the summer and partially closed in the winter. All their blades are forged under small trip hammers, and there are various machines for various purposes, such as plating, bolstering ...

Everything in each branch or department is well thought out for the reduction of cost and labour in the continuous passage of material from one process to another until it becomes the finished article in the warehouse.[52]

These words echo precisely those of Robert Holmshaw after his tour of American cutlery factories in 1902 and show how little the industry had progressed. With its scores of factories and hundreds of individual cutlers (the cutlery section of the city's trade directory in 1919 filled twenty tightly packed columns), it was an industry which was still highly fragmented and individualistic.

THE IMPACT OF WAR

Armour-plate production had already peaked by 1915, and two years later came the first signs that wartime pressure on the steel mills was easing. The call for high-speed steel, that barometer of activity, began to lessen. Sheffield began to look ahead at how best to utilize what was undoubtedly the greatest production centre for high-quality steel and its related products in the world. By 1916, commented the *Sheffield Independent*:

Manufacturers in all sections of local industry are giving serious consideration to the problems of trade after the war, and preparations are being quietly made with the object of finding outlets for their enlarged outputs and new commodities ... The news as to the economic future of Sheffield is generally optimistic and not many authorities look for a prolonged slump on the declaration of peace. This opinion is being based upon the complete world exhaustion of stocks of steel goods.[53]

As part of the preparation for post-war trade, plans were said to be in hand at the end of 1916 for the 'perfection of organisation for after-war trade', since 'certain sections of industry are very powerfully organised, with a definite understanding between the various manufacturers, which in some cases amounts to a working agreement, if not amalgamation'.[54] The War had undoubtedly fostered co-operation in certain sectors of the trade. Sometimes this was of a mainly technical nature. For example, the

[52] Article on 'Sheffield Cutlery Trades', by 'Trenchante', *SI*, 1, 2 Oct. 1915.
[53] *SI*, 24 June 1916.   [54] *SI*, 11 Nov. 1916.

government-inspired Alloy Steel Production Committee, composed entirely of Sheffield makers, continued independently after the War as a trade body named the Alloy Steelmakers' Association. The War also encouraged commercial alliances in both the heavy and the light trades. The most notable example, which had occurred by the end of the War, was the merger of the leading Rotherham and Stocksbridge firms into the United Steel Companies (considered in detail in Chapter 7). But smaller firms also saw advantages in this route. At Marsh Bros., for example, the pressure of war work had fostered an alliance with Brittain's, a local tool and cast steelmakers. In August 1918 amalgamation of the two businesses took place, with the capital of Marsh Bros. being raised to £50,000. Meanwhile, at Balfour's in May 1918 the chairman informed the board of the United Steel amalgamation, which:

had caused some of the larger crucible steel manufacturers to enquire whether they would be compelled to amalgamate also, in order to effect savings not only in manufacture but in the stocking and selling of their goods, especially abroad, so as to be able to compete successfully against these large combines. Wm Jessop & Sons Ltd, Edgar Allen & Co Ltd, Samuel Osborn & Co Ltd and ourselves were considering the matter but nothing of a definite nature had yet been formulated. It was considered by the Board that the inclusion of the following firms would strengthen such an amalgamation: Brown Bayleys Steel Works Ltd, W. T. Flather Ltd and Kirkstall Forge [Leeds].[55]

Merger and co-operation were also in the air in the tool industry, where in 1917 Spear & Jackson considered an amalgamation of its edge tool business with four other firms.[56] Even the cutlery industry was not immune from these trends. In 1917 Wostenholm's and Needham, Veall & Tyzack broached the subject of merger, one Wostenholm director stating that: 'As a principle I am in favour of amalgamation and have always deplored the want of union in our trade.'[57] These were encouraging signs in businesses that had traditionally jealously guarded their independence.

Sheffield's own optimism about the future was based on this new-found unity and on the unprecedented expansion of its steel industry. Before the War the iron and steel industries in Sheffield had employed about 50,000; by 1916 nearly this number alone worked at the leading arms makers (Vickers, Hadfields, Cammell-Laird, Brown's, and Firth). No official totals are available on employment in the Sheffield steel industry at the end of the War, but by 1918 total employment was probably

[55] SCL BDR 78–9, Directors' Minute Book, 8 May 1918.
[56] R. Lloyd-Jones and M. J. Lewis, 'Business Structure and Political Economy in Sheffield: The Metal Trades 1880–1920s', in C. Binfield *et al.*, *The History of the City of Sheffield* (Sheffield, 1993), ii. 227.
[57] SCL Wostenholm Records. Wing to Colver, 24 July 1917.

approaching 100,000 (though many were temporary staff). In Sheffield *and* Rotherham it may have reached 120,000.[58]

Equally impressive was Steel City's hinterland, where a vast engineering industry produced forging presses; boilers and tubes; electric steel furnaces and electrodes; grinding, crushing, pulverizing, and separating machinery for coal, quarry, and cement plant; milling and drilling machines; heating and ventilating plant; tool cutting and grinding machines for saws and files; and gas and oil engines.[59] The War had given as big a push to the engineering trade as it had to steel, and in this sector, too, companies had had a 'good war'. For example, Davy Bros.' expansion during the War, when it supplied plant to the shell- and armour-makers, was such that by 1921 it had opened a new factory in Darnall.[60] Thos. W. Ward, whose authorized capital rose from £450,000 in 1914 to £700,000 in 1919, found its expertise in shipbreaking, supplying steel plant and railway materials, and recycling metals more in demand than ever. The company supplied on average 1,000 tons of scrap per day to the country's steelworks.

This chain of steel spread far beyond Sheffield, linking the city with gas- and oil-engine makers in Keighley; collieries around Barnsley and Doncaster; coal-cutting machinery makers in Wakefield; tube, gas pump, and colliery-gear firms in Chesterfield; locomotive, textile machinery, and hydraulic machinery makers in Leeds; aero-engine manufacturers in Derby; tank and agricultural machinery makers in Lincoln; the bicycle and motor-car industries of the West Midlands—to say nothing of the larger consumers of Sheffield steel in the shipyards of Birkenhead, the Clyde, and Belfast. The net impact of the War had been to intensify the clustering of industries both in and around Sheffield. Steel City was now at full tide: but could this momentum be maintained in the inter-war years?

---

[58] *Arsenal of the World*, 24–5, estimates the peak total of wage earners in the city at 200,000, a quarter of whom were women. Unfortunately, it does not quantify the numbers in the steel trades.

[59] *Industrial Sheffield and Rotherham: The Official Handbook of the Sheffield and Rotherham Chambers of Commerce* (1919).

[60] *The Record of Davy Bros. Ltd. in the World War, 1914–1918* (Sheffield, 1918).

2. THE CORNISH PLACE WORKS OF JAMES DIXON & SONS

James Dixon & Sons' Cornish Place Works on the River Don at Neepsend. In the nineteenth century, it was one of the largest silver- and electro-plate factories in Sheffield, employing at its peak over 1,000 workers. In 1993, it stands — like many of the old cutlery and steel factories in the district — largely deserted. (Photo by the author)

3. CRUCIBLE MELTING SHOP
AT ABBEYDALE INDUSTRIAL
HAMLET.

Situated on the outskirts of Sheffield, this is the only extant crucible
steel furnace in the world. It shows
the simplicity of the layout and tools
involved: the coke-hole and its
cover, a funnel for 'charging' the
crucible with blister steel, tongs for
pulling out the pot and pouring the
steel, and crucibles ready for use on
the shelves. The key to the success of
this technology lay in the empirical
skills of its practitioners, rather than
the sophistication of the furnace
plant. (Photo by the author)

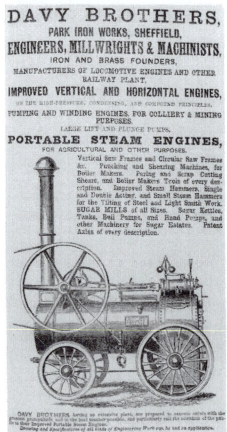

DAVY BROTHERS,
PARK IRON WORKS, SHEFFIELD,
ENGINEERS, MILLWRIGHTS & MACHINISTS,
IRON AND BRASS FOUNDERS,
MANUFACTURERS OF LOCOMOTIVE ENGINES AND OTHER
RAILWAY PLANT,
IMPROVED VERTICAL AND HORIZONTAL ENGINES,
ON THE HIGH-PRESSURE, CONDENSING, AND COMPOUND PRINCIPLES.
PUMPING AND WINDING ENGINES. FOR COLLIERY & MINING
PURPOSES.
LARGE LIFT AND PLUNGE PUMPS.
PORTABLE STEAM ENGINES,
FOR AGRICULTURAL AND OTHER PURPOSES.

Vertical Saw Frames and Circular Saw Frames
&c. Punching and Shearing Machines, for
Boiler Makers. Paring and Scrap Cutting
Shears, and Boiler Makers Tools of every description. Improved Steam Hammers, Single
and Double Acting, and Small Steam Hammers
for the Tilting of Steel and Light Smith Work.
SUGAR MILLS of all Sizes. Sugar Kettles,
Tanks, Bull Pumps, and Hand Pumps, and
other Machinery for Sugar Estates. Patent
Axles of every description.

DAVY BROTHERS having an extensive plant, are prepared to execute orders with the
greatest promptitude and at the most moderate terms possible, and particularly call the attention of the public to their Improved Portable Steam Engines.
Drawing and Specifications of all kinds of Engineering Work can be had on application.

4. ADVERTISEMENT FOR THE
ENGINES AND MACHINERY OF
DAVY BROS.

Sheffield steel manufacture from the
beginning was intertwined with the
development of engineering, as
companies began supplying the
demand for engines and heavy tools.
One of the most important was Davy
Bros., founded in the 1830s, which
later became a world leader in the
manufacture and installation of steel
production plant. (Courtesy Sheffield City Library)

5. THE AGENORIA WORKS OF PEACE, WARD & CO., IN ABOUT 1860.

Note the conical cementation furnaces (on the left) for producing blister steel for the crucible furnaces. Both in layout, size, and product range (it used its steel to manufacture its own files and edge tools) the company can be considered as a fairly typical medium-sized Sheffield steel firm. Like its competitors, though, it would not have been entirely self-contained. Few Sheffield firms had all the production processes within their works and nearly all relied, to a greater or lesser extent, on having work such as forging and rolling done by other specialists. This was known in the trade as 'hire-work'. (Courtesy Sheffield City Library)

6. A BESSEMER CONVERTER IN ACTION

Whereas the crucible melted steel in pounds per hour, Sir Henry Bessemer's invention transformed the scale of steelmaking operations by melting *tons* in *minutes*. Bessemer (and later Siemens' open-hearth) technology, however, complemented rather than superseded the crucible, since the tonnage processes were unable to melt the highest grades of cast steel. They, in fact, greatly boosted the demand for tool steel. This engraving, from *Great Industries of Great Britain* (1886), may show Bessemer's own works in Sheffield, which he founded in 1858. (Photo by author)

7. SIR ROBERT A. HADFIELD (1858–1940)

Sir Robert A. Hadfield was arguably the most influential and successful figure in Sheffield steelmaking. Uniquely, he was both a metallurgist *and* steel manufacturer, who grasped early the potential for developments in alloy steels. His discovery of manganese steel in 1882, when he was only 24, was a landmark event in alloy technology. Vain, autocratic, and immensely hard-working, he dominated his company's business in alloys, castings, and armaments until almost the end of his life. (Courtesy Sheffield City Library)

8. SIR JOSEPH JONAS (1845–1921)

Sir Joseph Jonas was one of a number of German-born entrepreneurs, who made their fortunes in the Sheffield tool steel trade after the 1870s. His company, Jonas & Colver Ltd., was one of Sheffield's fastest-growing crucible steel firms in the late nineteenth century. Its success was based on Jonas's typically Germanic emphasis on scientific methods, superior business organization, and marketing skills. (Courtesy Sheffield City Library)

9. EAST HECLA WORKS OF HADFIELDS LTD. IN ABOUT 1905

The largest Sheffield firms were approaching their peak in the years before 1914, fed by the demand from the engineering industry and the huge growth of the world arms trade. Hadfields Ltd., whose East Hecla Works is depicted here in about 1905, was one of a triumverate of firms (Vickers and Cammell-Laird were the others) whose workforce in the city was approaching 5,000 or so on the eve of the Great War. The difference in the scale of steelmaking operations of the big three, compared with the older crucible steel works (in pl.5), will be apparent. (Courtesy Sheffield City Library)

10. HIGH-SPEED STEEL TWIST DRILLS

Small-scale enterprise still flourished in Sheffield before 1914, despite the apparent dominance of the large arms firms. Niche producers, like Leadbeater & Scott, were world leaders in high-speed steel manufacture. The firm, based in Penistone Road, was said to have pioneered in Sheffield the manufacture of high-speed steel twist drills. (Courtesy Sheffield City Library)

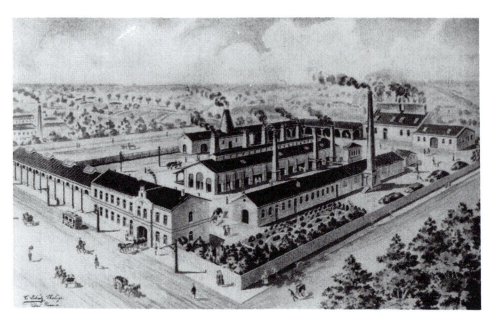

11. J. J. SAVILLE'S LIBAU WORKS

Sheffield's competitive advantage in special steelmaking was demonstrated by the foundation of several overseas subsidiaries before the First World War. America and Russia were the favoured locations. This illustration shows the Libau Works of J. J. Saville, near Riga, founded in 1901. The cementation furnace (centre) shows Saville's intended to follow the traditional Sheffield methods of crucible steel manufacture. (Courtesy Sheffield City Library)

12. HAND-FORGING TABLE-KNIFE BLADES IN SHEFFIELD IN ABOUT 1900

The skill of the forger improved the quality and cutting performance of crucible steel by compressing the grain structure, but had obvious limitations for mass production. In the late nineteenth century, American and German manufacturers soon abandoned such laborious methods and began blanking blades directly from steel sheet. In Sheffield, however, the structure of the industry and the adherence to the old skills meant that hand-forging was only slowly superseded by machines. A hand-forger was still at work in Sheffield in 1980. (Courtesy Sheffield City Library)

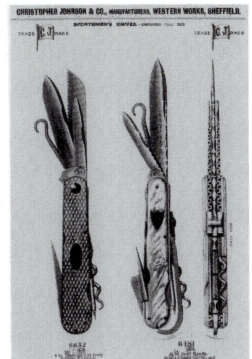

13. TOP-QUALITY SPORTSMAN'S KNIVES, MANUFACTURED BY CHRISTOPHER JOHNSON & CO. IN ABOUT 1900

Almost entirely hand-made from the best materials and sold at a premium price, such knives were unsurpassed by any foreign competitors. Note the extensive file-work (chasing) on the blade backs and springs. Unfortunately, the demand for this type of knife had already peaked before 1914 and was to decline swiftly after the War. (Courtesy Sheffield City Library)

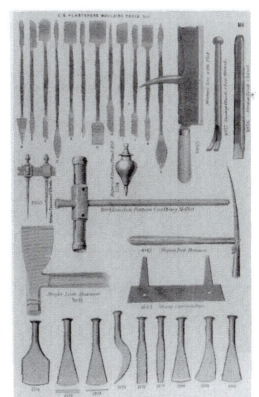

14. ILLUSTRATION FROM *THE SHEFFIELD LIST* (1882)

Sheffield's reputation as the world's foremost steel workshop was based not only on its steel and cutlery, but also on its huge range of tools. This illustration from the town's hardware trade catalogue, *The Sheffield List* (1882 edition), shows a selection of plasterers' and slaters' tools. (Courtesy Sheffield City Library)

15. VICKERS' HEAVY GUN SHOP

The term 'Arsenal of the World' was coined, apparently, by an Australian ambassador to describe Sheffield's dominance of the world arms industry. The massive growth and development of the leading Sheffield firms — Vickers, Hadfields, Cammell-Laird, and John Brown — between the 1890s and 1918, was largely due to the arms trade. This is a view of Vickers' Heavy Gun Shop in about 1898. (Courtesy Sheffield City Library)

16. FIRTH'S SHELL SHOP

Besides armour-plate and guns, a leading Sheffield speciality was projectile manufacture. Firms such as Hadfields and Thos. Firth were leaders in the field and were especially noted for their armour-piercing shells. The photograph shows Firth's shell shop before the First World War. (Courtesy Sheffield City Library)

17. HIGH-FREQUENCY INDUCTION MELTING OF TOOL STEEL AT EDGAR ALLEN & CO. IN THE EARLY 1930s

Essentially an electric version of the crucible process, induction melting began superseding the traditional Huntsman technology in the interwar period. Electric melting was more economic and produced 'cleaner' steel than its competitor, but it was still a skilled activity. (Photo by the author from *The Iron & Steel Institute, Sheffield, 1933*)

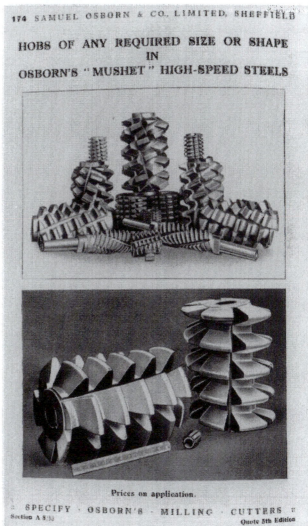

174 SAMUEL OSBORN & CO., LIMITED, SHEFFIELD

HOBS OF ANY REQUIRED SIZE OR SHAPE IN OSBORN'S "MUSHET" HIGH-SPEED STEELS

Prices on application.

SPECIFY · OSBORN'S · MILLING · CUTTERS
Section A 3/35
Quote 5th Edition

18. ADVERTISEMENT FROM SAMUEL OSBORN & CO.'S *COMPLETE CATALOGUE*

Tool steel firms such as Samuel Osborn & Co. survived the depression on the strength of their wide product range of special steels and the continued demand for engineering products. This is a page from Osborn's *Complete Catalogue* (1935), advertising its high-speed steel milling cutters. (Courtesy Sheffield City Library)

19. THE BROWN-FIRTH RESEARCH LABORATORIES, ESTABLISHED IN 1908

The Brown-Firth Research Laboratories was the largest such facility in Sheffield. Its first director, Harry Brearly (1871–1948), had discovered cutlery stainless steel there before the First World War. In the inter-war period, W. H. Hatfield (1882–1943) led the work at the Laboratories, which included the further development of rust-, acid-, and heat-resisting steels. (Courtesy Sheffield City Library)

20. STAINLESS CUTLERY

The world's first stainless cutlery was produced in Sheffield at the beginning of the First World War. Supplies of the revolutionary new alloy were then commandeered for aero-engines, and it was not until after 1918 that stainless cutlery production got into full swing. Nevertheless, by the 1920s the 'Firth Stainless' mark was spreading around the world, as firms such as Harrison Fisher & Co. made the most of Sheffield's early lead. Stainless steel was the most important innovation in cutlery manufacture since the introduction of crucible steel. (Photo by author)

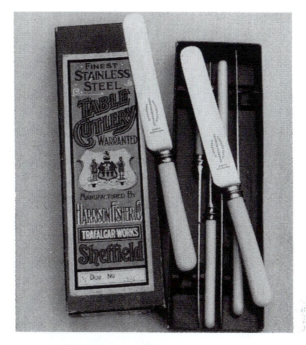

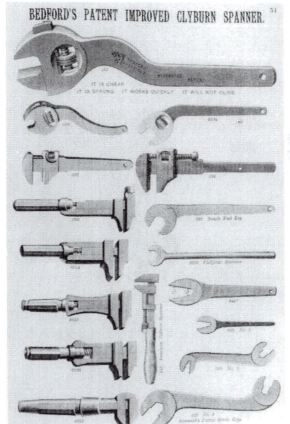

21. SHEFFIELD TOOLS IN THE INTER-WAR YEARS

The Sheffield tool industry proved commercially more resilient in the inter-war period than that of cutlery. The tool firms (many of which were leading steelmakers, too) were perhaps less conservative and more innovative than the cutlers; they were also able to tap the demand from industries such as automobiles, which continued to grow through the depression. The illustration is from a John Bedford & Sons' trade catalogue of the 1920s. (Courtesy Sheffield City Library)

22. 'TALL BOY' AND 'GRAND SLAM' BOMBS

Sheffield reverted to its role as the country's leading arsenal during the Second World War. Amongst the weapons were these 12,000 pound 'Tall Boy' and 22,000 'Grand Slam' bombs, produced at the English Steel Corporation. (Courtesy Sheffield Newspapers Ltd.)

23. GIANT HOLLOW BOILER-DRUM FORGINGS

A major source of business to the leading Sheffield steel firms in the 1950s and 1960s was the manufacture of giant hollow boiler-drum forgings for power stations. Many weighed over 200 tons. Forging such drums (like the one shown here under the 8,300-tonne press at the English Steel Corporation's River Don Works) was a highly skilled activity, but after 1960 welding techniques made giant hollow forgings obsolete by allowing drum fabrication in separate parts. (Photo by Alan Faulkner Taylor, ESC)

24. TAPPING ONE OF THE TWO 100-TONNE ELECTRIC ARC FURNACES AT THE TINSLEY PARK WORKS OF THE ENGLISH STEEL CORPORATION

Completed by 1963, and costing about £26 million, Tinsley Park was a typically expansionist investment in the Sheffield steel industry after the boom of the 1950s. The Works, which soon included a degassing unit (though not continuous casting), was aimed at satisfying the projected demand from the expansion of United Kingdom industry, especially automobiles. When this demand failed to appear, this and other Sheffield developments ran into problems. The ESC was nationalized in 1967 and the Tinsley Park Works closed in the mid-1980s. (Photo by Alan Faulkner Taylor, ESC)

25. VACUUM-INDUCTION MELTING AT FIRTH-BROWN IN THE 1970S

In the 1970s, 'precision steelmaking' techniques for making even purer special steels made their impact. One of the new techniques — vacuum-induction melting — is shown here at Firth-Brown, the leader in the field in Sheffield by the late 1970s. In the foreground can be seen the tilting controls and furnace viewing windows; while the main panels house power controls and recording instruments. This process revolution took steelmaking out of the hands of the old furnace operators — a transformation with profound implications for Sheffield, which had relied upon its traditional skills for its competitive advantage. The nature of this revolution can be seen by comparing this photo with the frontispiece photo of the craft skills of crucible steelmaking. (Courtesy Sheffield City Library)

26. A LARGE TURBINE SHAFT AT THE RIVER DON WORKS OF SHEFFIELD FORGEMASTERS

In 1993, the Sheffield steel industry is a shadow of its former self. Yet the River Don Works of Sheffield Forgemasters — the company formed from the English Steel Corporation and Firth-Brown in 1982 — still makes some of the most advanced steel products in the world. Giant forgings, such as this large turbine shaft, show the traditional Sheffield concern with high-quality, state-of-the-art, value-added manufactures. (Courtesy Sheffield Forgemasters)

27. ANDREW COOK, CHIEF EXECUTIVE OF WILLIAM COOK'S

In the 1960s and 1970s, the United Kingdom steel castings industry — much of it located in Sheffield — was highly fragmented and cursed by over-capacity. Yet the leading firms were strong enough to resist rationalization. In the severe contraction of the 1980s and early 1990s, however, Andrew Cook, the chief executive of Sheffield-based William Cook's, was able to streamline the steel castings industry and make his company the largest steel caster in Europe. (Courtesy William Cook PLC)

28. DESMOND MAWSON, CHAIRMAN OF ROSS & CATHERALL

After the Second World War, Sheffield dominated the manufacture of advanced aero-engine steels, with firms such as Jessop's amongst the market leaders. Desmond Mawson, who had worked for Jessop's, built on this experience to make Ross & Catherall — a high-technology metals and materials producer based at Killamarsh — a leading supplier of superalloys to the aerospace industry in the 1970s and 1980s. Mawson is pictured with an engine by Rolls Royce — one of Ross & Catherall's major customers. (Courtesy Desmond Mawson)

29. A NEW PRECISION MILL, COMMISSIONED BY BARWORTH FLOCKTON LTD.

Tool steel manufacture, for so long the preserve of Sheffield's craft skills, succumbed to technological advances after the 1950s. There was still a place for Sheffield's independent family-owned firms, but only those — such as Barworth Flockton Ltd. — which were prepared to invest heavily in the latest tool steel technologies. In 1994 Barworth Flockton commissioned a new precision mill from the Austrian manufacturer GFM. The new mill, the result of a £4.5 million investment programme, rolls flat and square sections with sharp corners previously unattainable. (Courtesy W. N. Edwards)

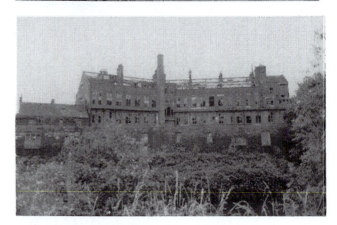

30. THE RUINS OF THE BRIGHTSIDE WORKS OF WILLIAM JESSOP & SONS

In the mid-nineteenth century Jessop's had been among the leading crucible steel firms in the world and a major exporter of tool steel to America. By the 1990s the ruins of its head office epitomized the decline of Sheffield steel in the Don Valley. Shortly after this photo was taken, the building was demolished. (Photo by author)

PART II

MEETING THE CHALLENGE
OF COMPETITION
IN THE 1920s AND 1930s

neurial failure' in the nineteenth-century British steel industry, continues with the same theme into the 1920s, agreeing with Duncan Burn that this was the 'black decade'. He concludes that in this period, British steelmakers 'were paying the price for the earlier failure to make an investment large enough and to recruit a management organization large and effective enough to exploit fully the new technology of mass-producing steel'.[2] Chandler's account draws heavily on the study of inter-war British steel by Steven Tolliday, who also emphasizes the stagnation of the industry, the result of the unchanging structures of individual firms. Tolliday's contribution has been to highlight the failures of the banks and Government (themselves riddled with antiquated ideas and traditions) to effect reform.[3]

However, these studies are not comprehensive. Concerned as they are with the bulk steel sectors of the industry, none have examined the experience of special steels in the difficult inter-war years. The foregoing discussion and Chapter 7 aim to make good this omission. The analysis is split in two: this chapter examines the development of the smaller tool steel and alloy firms; the next investigates the heavier side of Sheffield special steelmaking and the fortunes of its large-scale businesses. Generally, the small steelmakers were privately-run, often family-operated businesses—the Huntsman's, Balfour's, Osborn's, and Beardshaw's—employing less than a thousand (often less than 400), and involved in tool steel, high-grade alloys and castings, and perhaps engineers' tools. The bigger firms—such as Vickers, Firth-Brown, Cammell-Laird, United Steel, and Hadfields—were usually publicly quoted companies, employing thousands rather than hundreds, and concerned with heavy forgings and castings, armaments, and the mass production of alloys for engineering. This division is somewhat arbitrary and the exact line between the small- and large-scale manufacturer in Sheffield must remain somewhat blurred. Some of the large firms, such as Hadfields, demonstrate many characteristics of small-scale family business and vice versa; and all were at the high-quality end of the market. But such a division best serves our purpose for this analysis.

At the end of the War, still the most striking feature of the Sheffield tool steel industry was the huge number of firms involved in the trade and the enormous variety of products. The industry was at full tide. *White's Sheffield and District Directory* lists some 220 steel firms in 1920. Not all would have manufactured steel, since at least some operated as merchants, re-rollers, and stockholders buying in steel made by other firms, but a figure approaching 200 would not seem unreasonable. The direc-

    [2] A. D. Chandler, *Scale and Scope* (Cambridge, Mass., 1990), 321–32, 330.
    [3] S. Tolliday, *Business, Banking and Politics: The Case of British Steel, 1918–1939* (Cambridge, Mass., 1987).

tories also give some idea of Sheffield's vast product-range. Not only did these firms melt steel in a wide variety of analyses and sections, but the ingots soon found their way into all kinds of forgings and stampings, especially for axles and crankshafts, railway materials such as wheels and buffers, marine castings, mining tools and steels, punches and dies, reamers, magnets, ball-bearings, cutlery and electroplate, edge tools, files, saws, garden tools, machine knives, and gauges.

There were few steel products Sheffield did not produce, at least somewhere, and if it did not make a product it was often willing to do so as a custom-made item. 'In Sheffield at that time', recalled one tool steel manufacturer, 'it was possible to get anything made without too much trouble.'[4] Moreover, enormous varieties of steel and tools were made *within* each firm, even the smallest. Arthur Balfour & Co., for example, were not only expert crucible steelmakers, but with a workforce of less than 500 between the Wars, also manufactured (or could supply) files, saws, shear blades, screwing tackle, steel strip, die blocks, hammers, chisels, magnets, bandsaws, stainless steel cutlery blanks, drill chucks, tungsten-carbide, and various mining and railway specialities.

The business philosophy was unchanged: a commitment to high quality and added value. Tool steel was also still an intensely individualistic industry. In the inter-war period each firm still jealously guarded its trade marks and secrets, regarded other Sheffield companies as rivals—so much so that a melting manager could be dismissed if he was seen talking to his opposite number in another works—and rarely considered working together, even in foreign markets. Trade associations, such as the High Speed Steel Association, existed, but often these were merely cosy clubs for setting prices or for dealing with emergencies, such as impending foreign tariffs. The First World War had given some of these firms a taste of actively working together, but it was soon forgotten. Balfour's and those other firms which considered amalgamating in early 1918 had soon abandoned the idea, the Balfour's directors' minute book simply stating in 1918 that the idea had 'fallen through'.[5] Their independent outlook would not allow it, once the pressure of war work lessened.

The crucible and tool steel industry in Sheffield remained highly localized. With the exception of Peter Stubs's crucible steelmaking facility at Rotherham and Armstrong-Whitworth's Openshaw Works (which was soon destined to become a Sheffield satellite), virtually all the United Kingdom's tool steel was melted in Sheffield. With such a large number of firms in the industry, it is impossible to analyse in detail the ownership of each company. But most of the available evidence points in one direction: the industry stayed mostly in the hands of the city's industrialists and

---

[4] Lord Riverdale interview, 26 Apr. 1991.   [5] SCL BDR 78–9, Directors' Minute Book.

many of the firms were still family-controlled or private limited companies. Arthur Balfour, for example, was the principal shareholder in his company in the inter-war period, bringing his son, Robin, into the business in 1918. The latter remembers going through the business— treading the clay, pulling the pots, and teeming—much in the same way as earlier generations of steelmasters' sons had done. 'It gave [him] the kind of all-round knowledge that was essential and became impossible to acquire later.'[6] At John Bedford & Son, a steady stream of able family chairmen and managers took the firm into the fourth and fifth generation of family control. At W. T. Flather's, the wife of the founder had steered the business through the War, before David Flather (1864–1948)—W. T. Flather's son—took over as chairman between 1918 and 1941. Flather's became a limited company in 1919 with a capital of £106,142, but it remained a family concern, enjoying a period of 'quiet consolidation' between the Wars.[7] This enduring family component could be found in many other Sheffield steel firms. A good example is Arthur Lee & Sons, the steel-, wire-, and strip-makers. The founder, Arthur Lee, had died in 1918, but by then his three sons—Arthur, Percy, and Alfred—were in the business. The management team of Arthur Samuel Lee (1873–1941) and Percy Wilton Lee (1874–1949) proved very successful in the inter-war period. Percy Lee, who headed the company from 1904 to 1939—when he handed over to his son (Sir) Wilton Lee (1904–86)—took the crucial deci- sion in 1932 to expand production in the depth of the depression by investing in a hot rolling mill, so freeing Lee's from dependence on hot strip from Sweden and Germany.

Even the few tool steel firms that had marketed their shares, such as Osborn's (which went public in 1920 with share capital of £600,000), still retained significant family control. As the *Sheffield Daily Telegraph* ob- served, 30 December 1926: 'It is rather striking to learn that, even after such a long career and in these days of limited companies, [Osborn's] still retains its family character. True, it has been formed into a limited company, but the leading parts in its management are played by descend- ants of the founder.' The chairmen in the inter-war years were succes- sively William F. Osborn (1861–1936) and (Sir) Samuel Osborn (1864–1952), both sons of Samuel Osborn. Another son of the founder, Fred M. Osborn (1874–1950) was also on the board; so too was a third- generation member, Samuel Eric Osborn (1891–1951), son of W. F. Osborn. Only Edgar Allen failed to found a dynasty: he parted from his wife in 1892 and had no children. When he died in 1915, non-family member Robert Woodward took over as chairman until 1929, when tech- nically trained managers, such as Charles K. Everitt (c.1867–1945), began running the company.

---

[6] Riverdale interview.
[7] 'Firm's Founder Saw Dreams Come True', *SDT*, 16 Mar. 1950.

There were hints, though, that the old order was changing. In 1919 Jessop's was bought by one of its major customers, the Birmingham Small Arms Co., for £1.2 million (Jessop's share capital was £404,480). This was part of BSA's peacetime diversification programme, which linked Jessop's through its new parent with other companies, such as the West Midlands toolmakers Burton Griffiths.[8] Why Jessop's sold out to BSA is not entirely clear. It had paid steady 15 per cent ordinary dividends during the War; on the other hand, its American trade and Pittsburgh subsidiary were increasingly less profitable; and Saville's works in Russia would have been another source of losses. BSA intended that within the group each company should maintain its own separate identity, so that Jessop's status was unchanged and soon it was functioning almost as a completely autonomous unit within BSA.[9] On one level, the takeover had formalized a link that had long been close and hardly destroyed Steel City's local focus. Nevertheless, it was the first time that an outside firm had bought its way into Sheffield. This was to be repeated in 1930 when Howell & Co. became part of Tube Investments.

There were also signs that the expansion of the Sheffield tool steel industry had ended. Demand for high-speed steel, for example, had collapsed after the War to about 50 per cent of the maximum wartime level of about 19,000 tons, due partly to the large government stocks of tool steel. Thereafter there was a recovery, helped by orders from the automobile and some export markets. But the level of tool steel demand (allied to the increasing costs of establishing a business) no longer encouraged a large number of new entrants into the trade.

Of the new arrivals, three—F. M. Parkin, C. G. Carlisle, and Barworth Flockton—started in a small way and survived as an enduring presence. The first-named was established in 1922 by Frederick M. Parkin (d. 1953), who by 1928 was operating crucible steel furnaces in Arundel Street. In 1936 the business became a limited company and in the following year moved to a site on Aizlewood Road, south of the city centre.[10] Carlisle's was established in 1923 and was unusual in that from the outset the firm used a 10-cwt. arc furnace combined with a small machine for dressing ingots. The principal shareholder, Charles G. Carlisle (c.1879–1946), had been a metallurgist at Firth-Brown (he was also the son of C. L. Carlisle, who had helped Beardshaw's set up its arc furnace in 1916).[11] The firm probably intended to exploit the demand for stainless steels. Equally modest were the origins of the Barworth Steelworks (later known as Barworth Flockton): launched by Harry Worthington and another

[8] University of Warwick, Modern Records Centre. BSA Papers.
[9] W. H. Bailey interview, 8 Oct. 1991.
[10] 'Parkin's Progress', *Quality*, 5 (Jan. 1958), 23–4; *British Steelmaker*, 25 (1959), 314.
[11] *JISI* 154/2 (1946), 474; *British Industry and Commerce* (1967).

businessman named Barron in 1925 in Trent Street, it began life with five hands working a 12-hole crucible furnace. Carbon tool steel and high-speed steel were sold to reputable makers, who then resold it to engineers.[12]

These firms were aimed at a particular niche in the market and grew modestly. But in the 1920s a more ambitious newcomer, the Neepsend Steel & Tool Corporation, appeared—the brainchild of (Sir) Stuart Goodwin (1886–1969). Born in Upperthorpe, Sheffield, Goodwin had begun his career by joining the family's steel merchanting firm, Goodwin & Co., at the age of 11. In 1920 he began organizing the Neepsend Corporation as an integrated steel and tool business, which initially consisted of Goodwin & Co., Neepsend Rolling Mills, Slack, Sellars & Co., Premier Steel Co., and the Loxley Steel Works. For a time, the company's and Goodwin's future seemed to be in doubt, when he was stricken by diabetes and was expected to die. But in 1923 Goodwin became one of the first diabetics to be treated with insulin and, after his miracle cure, Neepsend began expanding again.[13] In the depressed steel market, Goodwin thrived by spotting bargains and the potential in unworked assets. His most important acquisition was in 1929, when he bought a bankrupt Jonas & Colver from the Midland Bank for £33,000.

Jonas & Colver was perhaps the most spectacular casualty of the interwar period in Sheffield. Joseph Jonas had retired in 1918 after his conspiracy trial, and died three years later. According to his obituaries, he was a broken man, though at 76 he may have simply died from old age. Bartlett Winder had succeeded him as chairman, but predeceased Jonas in 1920. The end of this exceptionally successful management team, combined perhaps with the decline of the firm's lucrative American trade, may have been a fatal combination in the 1920s. According to Stanley Speight, a future Neepsend chairman, the occasion of Jonas & Colver's demise as an independent company was its subsidiary Beesley's disastrous experience trying to make safety-razor steel for Gillette.[14] The General Strike had not helped either.

The purchase of Jonas & Colver proved an excellent bargain for Goodwin. He brought in James G. Widdowson, a former melting manager at Osborn's, as managing director. Widdowson later told Speight that 'there was more value in the high-speed steel he found lying on the floor, than Goodwin had paid for the company'. When trade recovered, Goodwin was able to complete his empire by buying Hobson, Houghton, the sheet rollers. Neepsend's dividend record in the 1930s was easily the most outstanding amongst the tool steel firms (see Table 6.1). He had

[12] W. N. Edwards interviews, 2 May, 22 Oct. 1991.
[13] 'Sir Stuart Goodwin: An Appreciation', Quality, 16 (June 1969), 26–7.
[14] S. Speight interview, 5 July 1991.

Table 6.1. *Dividend record (% paid on ordinary shares) of Sheffield tool steel firms, 1918–1938*

	1918	1919	1920	1921	1922	1923	1924	1925	1926	1927
Edgar Allen	$17\frac{1}{2}$	$17\frac{1}{2}+33\frac{1}{3}$	15	10	5	5	$2\frac{1}{2}$	$2\frac{1}{2}$	5	$3\frac{3}{4}$
Andrews Toledo	$7\frac{1}{2}$	5	5	0	0	0	0	0	0	0
Balfour	12	16	—	—	—	—	5	10	10	—
Bedford	—	15	10	5	$2\frac{1}{2}$	$2\frac{1}{2}$	$2\frac{1}{2}$	$2\frac{1}{2}$	5	5
Brown Bayley	$7\frac{1}{2}$	$7\frac{1}{2}$	—	$7\frac{1}{2}$	0	0	0	0	0	0
Darwin	—	—	—	—	—	—	—	—	—	—
Huntsman	—	—	10	—	5	5	$7\frac{1}{2}$	10	10	10
Kayser, Ellison	$12\frac{1}{2}+7\frac{1}{2}+100$	9	8	5	0	0	0	5	5	5
Neepsend	—	—	—	—	—	—	—	—	—	3
Osborn	—	—	—	—	—	—	—	—	—	5
Sanderson	10+5	10+5+50	6	0	0	0	3	3	0	$2\frac{1}{2}$

	1928	1929	1930	1931	1932	1933	1934	1935	1936	1937	1938
Edgar Allen	$2\frac{1}{2}$	$2\frac{1}{2}$	$2\frac{1}{2}$	0	0	0	0	0	5	$7\frac{1}{2}$	10
Andrews Toledo	0	0	0	0	0	0	0	0	0	0	0
Balfour	$7\frac{1}{2}$	8	8	—	—	—	—	6	—	—	—
Bedford	5	$7\frac{1}{2}$	5	5	5	5	5	$2\frac{1}{2}$	$2\frac{1}{2}$	$7\frac{1}{2}$	—
Brown Bayley	0	0	0	0	0	0	0	0	0	10	15
Darwin	0	0	0	0	0	0	0	0	0	0	0
Huntsman	5	4	$2\frac{1}{2}$	0	0	0	0	0	5	5	5
Kayser, Ellison	5	6	6	0	0	1	5	$7\frac{1}{2}$	$12\frac{1}{2}$	$17\frac{1}{2}$	$17\frac{1}{2}$
Neepsend	6	9+9	10+5	9	5	$7\frac{1}{2}$	$12\frac{1}{2}$	20	20+15	20+15+50	20+20
Osborn	$5\frac{1}{2}$	7	7	0	0	$2\frac{1}{2}$	4	7	$12\frac{1}{2}$	15	15
Sanderson	$2\frac{1}{2}$	0	0	0	0	0	—	—	—	—	—

Sources: *Stock Exchange Yearbook* and company records. No data available for some years.

found the depressed inter-war period a far from uncongenial business climate.

These appear to have been the only new entrants into steel melting in Sheffield in the inter-war years. However, there was evidently some scope on the processing side. In 1933 Tinsley Wire (Sheffield) Ltd. was founded, with a capital of £100,000. It had its origins in the United Kingdom agency of the Belgian wiremakers, Tréfileries Léon Bekaert, which like many Belgian steel firms had exploited the large (and unprotected) British market in the 1920s. When the Government reversed this situation with the tariff and went off the Gold Standard, Léon A. Bekaert decided to begin manufacture in Sheffield by joining with British Ropes Ltd. and the United Steel Companies in the building of a wire and wire products company at Tinsley. Under a skilled sales team, led by its old, long-established agent, E. H. Farris, Tinsley Wire's sales increased from 3,000 to 20,000 tons between 1933 and 1939.[15]

One reason for the slowdown in new start-ups was that the traditional route into Sheffield steel that had served the industry so well—a back-street works, with a few crucible holes, and a small gang of teemers and labourers—was becoming a thing of the past. Although Sheffielders are fond of pointing out that crucible steelmaking survived into the 1950s and 1960s (Marsh Bros., for example, did not shut down its crucible holes until 1953), the old process declined as a commercial force in the inter-war period. The introduction of the electric arc furnace first weakened its hold during the First World War, then in 1927 came the crucible's death blow. In that year, Edgar Allen's introduced a high-frequency induction furnace specially designed for tool steel—which the company claimed as a world 'first'.[16] The designer was an American engineer, Edwin F. Northrup, though it was to be another year before the first United States firm installed this type of furnace.

Induction melting was described at the time as the 'radio' method: the steel to be melted was placed in a crucible (somewhat larger than the old clay pot) and then heated up by eddy currents induced in the metal, by the alternating current in a surrounding copper coil. It was a kind of electric crucible, with several advantages over its erstwhile competitor. It combined the economy and versatility of the arc (which had never been wholeheartedly embraced by Sheffield tool steelmakers because the carbon electrodes contaminated the steel) with the close control of the old crucible. There was no fear of external contamination, the furnace could be switched on and off at will, it did not need the sweat, skill, and labour

---

[15] *TWIL: Fifty Years On* (Sheffield, 1983).
[16] Vickers had installed an induction furnace in 1907, but its low-frequency current meant that part of the charge had to be left in the furnace to melt the next batch—a severe hindrance when making successive charges to different specifications.

of physical teeming, and it could run twenty-four hours a day, seven days a week, if necessary. It could make dozens of different steels in the same week, and this was to make it very popular where small quantities of special steels were required—such as for automobile valves, ball bearings, tools, and die steels. Along with the arc furnace, it was soon to provide the bulk of stainless steel.

Some firms retained the crucible, even if they had electric melting: there was still some emotional commitment to the old process and for small quantities it still served the purpose. Jessop's was one firm which did so, one of the firm's directors remembering that when he joined the company in 1939, 'a young boy was still being sent out daily to the pub to collect draught beer in jugs and even white enamelled buckets—to quench the insatiable thirst of the [crucible] melters working in such horrendous conditions'.[17] But generally there was no sign of conservatism when faced with this new technology.

The most important tool steelmakers had all installed high-frequency furnaces by the late 1930s, abandoning the crucible. As with the arc, there are no official statistics for induction furnace installations in Sheffield at this time. But scattered information in company files and published sources shows that the following firms had induction furnaces (with installation dates in brackets): Edgar Allen (1927); Arthur Balfour (1928); Vickers (1928); Fox (1930); Firth-Brown (1930); Osborn (1931); Kayser Ellison (1931); Darwins (1932); Andrews Toledo (1935); Swift Levick (1935); English Steel Corporation (1935); Senior (1938); Turton Bros. & Matthews (1938); Neill's (1940).[18] Hadfields, which had a full range of all kinds of furnaces, and Sanderson Bros. & Newbould, are also known to have had high-frequency furnaces. The end result was soon apparent: before the First World War there were probably about 150 firms selling crucible steel; by the mid-1930s the number was about 50. Meanwhile the electric arc furnace continued to make inroads for the less special of the special steels. For larger tonnages, some firms supplemented this with the output from Bessemer and especially open-hearth furnaces.

The adoption of electric induction melting helped Sheffield maintain its lead in special steel technology in the inter-war years, though (paradoxically) by heralding the demise of the crucible it also had the long-term effect of reducing Sheffield's technological pre-eminence. In other respects, too, that position was being slowly eroded. For nearly two centuries, Sheffield had maintained its competitive edge over other nations by continually pulling new discoveries out of the hat. In the 1920s this was accepted as part of the natural order. As the *Sheffield Daily Telegraph* stated

---

[17] W. H. Bailey, letter to author, 11 Oct. 1991.

[18] This list is probably not exhaustive, nor does it take account of firms uprating their induction furnaces as the technology improved.

in 1927: 'When in the course of the year any of [the city's discoveries] became common property, Sheffield was usually beaten in the matter of price, and the makers have had to invent or discover something else which was unknown to the world. Sheffield possesses the finest metallurgical minds in the world, and they show no sign of exhaustion.'[19] But unfortunately, the era of major discoveries in special steel production—which for argument's sake, we can say ran from about the 1860s to the First World War—was virtually over. After the 1920s it becomes increasingly difficult to put names to advances in metallurgy: the technology was becoming more diffuse, more complex and costly, more often spread between several inventors and countries, and breakthroughs harder to achieve. Significantly, the composition of manganese, tool, and stainless steels has remained basically unchanged since the 1920s. This was realized at the time. As one Sheffield director explained in 1930: 'The greater part of the progress is being made by steady work directed to improving the properties and reliability of steels intended for specific types of service, by studying and modifying various factors in manufacturing processes which affect the quality of materials, and by the systematic evolution, as the result of research work, of new variations in alloy steels.'[20]

Tool steel is an example. According to one Sheffield metallurgist, writing in 1950, 'since the initiation of high-speed steels, the development of this branch of special steels has consisted very much of variations on a theme, with tungsten as the predominant element'.[21] Paul Kuehnrich's die steels, which had appeared on the market during the First World War, were perhaps the last major Sheffield breakthrough. In 1920, uranium looked as though it might be a valuable alloying element in high-speed steel, but proved useless. Tantalum was also unsatisfactory. Though the city remained an expert in tool steel manufacture, and its metallurgists were continually making improvements, the recipe for such steels had settled with the '18–4–1' combination and these have been produced worldwide until the present day. Meanwhile, overseas competitors were able to explore other additions to tool steel better suited to their resources. Thus the Americans, spurred on by tungsten shortages during the War, in the late 1920s made advances in molybdenum high-speed steels, which allowed them to utilize their own extensive molybdenum ore deposits. Though the properties of these 'substitute' high-speed steels were often no better than Sheffield's tungsten varieties, they were more economical (with the result that the former are now the most widely used) and

---

[19] SDT, 30 Dec. 1927.
[20] SCL ESC Papers. A. Williamson, 'General Report on Prospects', 23 Apr. 1930.
[21] D. A. Oliver, 'Twenty-One Years of Progress in Special Steels', Metallurgia, 42 (Nov. 1950), 279–82, 280.

allowed America to close the technological and commercial gap with Sheffield.[22]

Meanwhile, Krupp's in 1927 introduced an entirely new material—cemented carbide—a sintered alloy of tungsten-carbide and cobalt that was twice as hard as the hardest steel (hence its other name, hardmetal). Cutting tools made from this material were launched under the name 'Widia' ('wie diamant'), and by 1931 Krupp's had a United Kingdom subsidiary, the Tool Manufacturing Co. Ltd. in Coventry. Although the production of cemented carbide was small during the 1930s and its introduction was slow, it was gradually realized that this was the tool material of the future where maximum performance was needed. Sheffield firms soon began manufacturing tungsten-carbide tools, but had to acquire a licence. Firth-Brown Tools appear to have been the first to do so in 1935. Apart from a brief moment when Vickers had paid for the Taylor–White patents, this was the first time any of the city's firms had to pay for foreign cutting materials technology. Worse, powder metallurgy was not a business such as crucible steel that Sheffield could monopolize. Sintered products could be made in other localities, where firms were willing to invest.[23]

This weakening of Sheffield's competitive superiority was naturally translated into difficulties in trading overseas, where again the legacy of the war was not very positive. The conflict had totally disrupted many of Sheffield's favourite foreign markets, and by the time conditions improved demand had often evaporated. This was the case in three pillars of Sheffield's pre-1914 tool steel trade, Germany, Russia, and France. Germany became a cartelized and restricted market from the 1920s, greatly reducing Sheffield's import trade. Before the War, for example, Germany had taken over a third of Huntsman's crucible steel; by 1939 this had fallen to 11 per cent.[24] Meanwhile, Sheffield tool steel firms active in Russia lost their trade and, in some cases, their assets after the Revolution. Nothing more was heard of Saville's and Carr's Russian involvement, and Kayser, Ellison had closed its Petrograd account in 1918, terminating that firm's merchanting business. The depreciation of the French currency, tariffs, and the development of France's own tool steel industry also forced the closure of many of Sheffield's French depots during the 1920s. As one newspaper noted: 'The quality of [France's] product may be infe-

[22] See L. K. Everitt, 'Modern Tool Steels', *Metallurgia*, 19 (July 1939), 114, 118; A. Linley, 'The Development and Characteristics of "Substitute 66" High-Speed Steels', ibid. 25 (Apr. 1942), 179–82.

[23] Jack Sandford, 'Hardmetal: The History to 1950', *JHMS* 19 (1985), 85–9; 'The Development of Carbide Tipped Tools', *Metallurgia*, 27 (Mar. 1943), 201–2. There is also a useful chapter on cemented carbides and hard metals in Sandvik AB, *Transformation: Sandvik 1862–1987* (1987), 120–7.

[24] SCL Huntsman Directors' Minute Book, 1918–54.

rior to that of the best Sheffield brands, but it is cheaper without allowing for differences of exchange and duties and freight which force up
the Sheffield rates.'[25] Edgar Allen's continued its manganese steel trackwork business with France, reaching an agreement with a firm at Hirson
for manganese steel production in 1925, but development was slow.
Huntsman's wound down its French depot in the 1920s and closed it
in 1932, by which time the trade had almost vanished: yet before 1914
France had accounted for 12 per cent of Huntsman's total sales. Only
Marsh Bros. seem to have still cultivated the French market with any great
success: it was the firm's most important overseas market during the
1920s.

In America, easily the world's biggest market for tool steel before 1914,
Sheffield's trade may have declined anyway with the development of the
United States tool steel industry. But it was not helped by yet another
tariff—the Fordney McCumber Act of 1921—which virtually ex-
tinguished Sheffield tool steel exports to America. The trade, even before
the tariff was passed, was a shadow of its former extent, but Sheffielders
still thought it worth defending. Arthur Balfour and leading representatives of the high-speed steel trade travelled to Washington to protest,
Balfour himself testifying before the United States Senate in 1921. This
swansong of Sheffield's once mighty American trade was unavailing.
Some firms—Jessop's, Edgar Allen's, Balfour's, and J. H. Andrew
amongst them—attempted to hold on to the remnants of the trade.
Jessop's, for example, still did a profitable business in tool steels through
its New York agency under Fred Lantsberry.[26] But most firms had abandoned America by 1940, their steels no longer competitive enough to
breach its protected market. Behind the tariff, Sheffield's own American
tool steel subsidiaries were also in decline. Jessop's relinquished its Pittsburgh base in the early 1920s; and Firth's links with that city had also
become moribund by 1940.

With the loss or declining importance of these markets, Sheffield firms
turned their attention elsewhere. Territories that assumed greater significance included South America, China, and Japan. In particular, there was
a marked desire to exploit the preferential tariffs in Commonwealth
countries, especially Australia and Canada. Some Sheffield industrialists
saw Sheffield's 'salvation in the development of Empire Trade' in the
1930s.[27] Sir Robert Hadfield, in particular, favoured the Commonwealth
market, which he hoped to cultivate with an Empire Development Board.
Many Sheffield firms were active in colonial markets. Sanderson Bros. &
Newbould, for example, established an Australian branch—the Saben

[25] SDT, 30 Dec. 1927.

[26] SCL Jessop's Steel Co., New York, Directors' and Shareholders' Minute Book, 1910–47.

[27] Remarks of Master Cutler and Spear & Jackson director, A. K. Wilson, SDT, 31 Dec.
1929. See also C. W. Kayser's comments in SDT, 30 Dec. 1927.

Steel Co.—in 1935, for selling its steel and tools. In Canada, agents and branches of most of the leading Sheffield tool steel firms, such as Sanderson & Newbould, Edgar Allen, and Balfour, could be found in Montreal and Toronto. South Africa still provided good orders for mining and other steels. Brown Bayleys established a branch there in 1931; Sanderson & Newbould in 1940.

For some firms, overseas trading was still crucial. For these companies—for example, Marsh Bros., Sanderson Bros. & Newbould, Edgar Allen, Samuel Osborn—it was still the case that 'the catalogue of the countries visited by representatives before 1939 would read like a lesson in geography'.[28] Arthur Balfour & Co. was such a firm. Its surviving business records enable us to chart in detail its foreign activities in Table 6.2. The importance of certain markets, such as Australia, is apparent; so too is the emergence of new trade with China and Japan; and the expansion of business with South America. This counterbalanced the decline of the United States trade. Also notable is the contribution foreign orders made to total sales. For over a decade after 1924, overseas orders were never less than 30 per cent and were often over 40 per cent.

However, Sheffield was undergoing an important change in the relationship between its domestic and foreign business—a reflection of general trends in British steel exports during the inter-war period. Before the war some 40 per cent of British steel production was exported each year, aside from its use in ships and engineering products sent overseas; but by the late 1930s this had fallen to about 12 per cent. Despite the worldwide trade of firms such as Balfour's, Sheffield's attention was also inevitably switching to the home market. The sea-change is clearly signalled in the business records of Benjamin Huntsman. Before 1914, the United Kingdom accounted for 42 per cent of this firm's total sales, most of the firm's steel heading for the Continent; by 1939 the United Kingdom figure was 83 per cent.[29] The same trend can be seen at John Bedford's, where the firm's nineteenth-century strategy of expansion in export markets was revised in the inter-war period, when the directors decided to make a push for the United Kingdom market by extending the home sales force. At Carr's, the dominant Russian business was forgotten, and it too decided to concentrate on the domestic market. Even firms with large foreign order books did not neglect opportunities at home. Marsh Bros., for example, overhauled its sales office in London in 1928, and a separate office in Birmingham was also established.

This movement was encouraged by the tariff. Calls for the Safeguarding of steel (as well as cutlery, which was protected from 1925) were growing in Sheffield in the late 1920s, as they were in other sectors of the United Kingdom steel industry. In 1932 import duties on steel of $33\frac{1}{3}$ per cent

[28] S. Pollard, *Three Centuries of Sheffield Steel* (Sheffield, 1954), 58.
[29] SCL Huntsman Directors' Minute Book, 1918–54.

Table 6.2. *Overseas steel sales of Arthur Balfour & Co., 1920–1936 (£)*

	1920	1921	1922	1923	1924	1925
Australia	78,531	70,640	28,758	—	53,824	64,649
Canada	43,113	13,229	8,798	—	21,513	—
China	—	—	—	—	46,468	39,102
India	26,149	11,956	—	—	7,527	11,151
Japan	—	—	—	—	10,099	10,231
S. Africa	7,608	4,686	2,001	5,495	3,312	—
S. America	13,987*	33,747	20,639	25,209	28,819	31,404
USA	42,444	787	2,006	—	6,052	8,085
TOTAL	211,832	135,045	62,256	30,704	117,614	164,622
	(24)	(28)	(21)	(8)	(41)	(38)

	1926	1927	1928	1929	1930	1931
Australia	54,634	67,480	52,661	52,559	53,574	22,840
Canada	23,313	16,916	7,538	31,231	18,155	3,895
China	—	—	49,960	31,156	36,260	37,669
India	—	—	13,042	9,777	11,019	7,083
Japan	19,002	17,698	—	21,876	14,431	14,520
S. Africa	3,338	2,763	4,168	3,837	2,734	2,164
S. America	23,539	34,245	34,445	43,120	28,465	20,173
USA	6,163	4,466	810	1,779	637	472
TOTAL	129,989	143,568	162,624	195,425	165,275	108,816
	(32)	(33)	(37)	(43)	(44)	(40)

	1932	1933	1934	1935	1936	
Australia	34,415	—	53,711	71,737	35,198	
Canada	9,181	—	15,927	19,101	23,887	
China	23,548	—	35,812	29,721	28,923	
India	6,632	—	15,384	14,327	11,539	
Japan	23,371	—	31,042	28,042	29,214	
S. Africa	2,048	—	5,609	7,248	6,583	
S. America	24,476	—	39,696	36,668	34,104	
USA	—	—	—	—	—	
TOTAL	123,671		197,181	206,844	169,448	
	(40)		(41)	(30)	(31)	

* Oct.–Dec.

Note: Figures in parentheses under running totals are foreign sales as a percentage of total sales. For some years, evidently there was no data to record; or the data is incomplete.

Sources: Calculated from SCL BDR 96/1–5. Analysis Books.

were finally instituted, which pleased Sheffield makers anxious that the United Kingdom's tariff policy should be brought into line with other countries. As Steve Tolliday has pointed out, these duties on steel 'were not associated with any strategy for reorganization' of the industry, but it was hoped by the Government generally that 'reorganization would be eased by protection'.[30] In Sheffield this appears to have been a secondary consideration to the question of keeping out 'cheap' imports from the Continent and America. Sheffield tool steelmakers were unanimous in their condemnation of 'unfair' competition from Europe, but the question of reorganization definitely took second place. The chairman of Huntsman's stated in 1929 that: 'The strong individual effort animating the majority of the [Sheffield] makers still survives, and this same spirit does not desire to fly to rationalisation as a passing remedy, but prefers to boldly ask for fair conditions at home and abroad.'[31] Only Sir Arthur Balfour pointedly observed that, although Safeguarding might be justified, it should not be used to bolster inefficient industries.[32]

One aspect of this inefficiency was the widespread number of trade associations and pricing agreements within Sheffield industry—all later ruled illegal. The city's firms may have hated the idea of losing their independence by merging their interests and brand names, but they happily colluded in setting prices, distributing work and exchanging certain technical information. Almost every Sheffield industry had its trade association. A confidential report in 1935 amongst one firm's papers lists nearly fifty organizations, most of them centred in Sheffield, covering products as diverse as armour-plate, railway springs, tram tyres, crucible steel, files, and twist drills.[33] A tool steelmaker was likely to be a member of High Speed Steel Alloys (controlling the flow of tungsten from Widnes), the High Speed Steel Association (setting prices), the Crucible Steel Makers' Association (governing the interchange of technical information), and probably several others if it was involved in forging or tool manufacture. Any discussion of Sheffield individualism in steel should remember this hidden web of collusion, which was fostered by the fact that a deal could be struck by simply walking a few streets to a neighbouring works.

Thus, although many Sheffield steelmasters in the 1920s had believed that the revival of world trade was crucial to the city's recovery, that came more to depend on the growth of the domestic economy and import substitution. This was especially true after the mid-1930s, when the stimulus applied by the rearmament programme would also increase the

[30] Tolliday, *Business, Banking, Politics*, 299.
[31] Comments of William Patrickson, *SDT*, 31 Dec. 1929.
[32] *SDT*, 31 Dec. 1928.
[33] SCL. List of Agreements of the ESC, 20 May 1935. Copy courtesy of Kenneth Lewis.

attractions of the home market. Henceforth, Sheffield did not forsake overseas trade, but its steel industry was now more closely linked to home demand.

It was in the United Kingdom that some of the best opportunities lay for special steels, especially with the development of the aircraft and motor-car industries. The rise of these 'new' industries was linked to another important shift in steel production towards rolled plate and sheet products that were aimed more towards the consumer rather than the producer sector. This was a great opening for a city that had launched the ultimate flat product—stainless steel (the development of which is considered more fully in Chapter 7). The growing strength of the home market as the industry emerged from depression was noted by Sheffield business leaders by 1934, when W. F. Osborn stated: 'The improvement in business has come both from the home and foreign markets, but that from the home market has been far the more pronounced. Whilst the demand for standard lines, such as high-speed steels, twist drills, milling cutters, castings, etc., has been maintained at a high level, the most marked increase in demand has been for stainless and heat resisting and special steels.'[34]

Much of this demand came from the motor-car, motor-cycle, and aircraft industries, which made enormous gains during the inter-war period despite the depression. Annual private car sales in the United Kingdom were under 50,000 at the start of the 1920s, but were climbing towards 400,000 by the end of the 1930s. The number of aircraft produced in the United Kingdom rose from about 500 in 1924 to about 1,800 in 1935; whilst the output of aero-engines increased from about 900 to over 3,000.[35] This was not enough to exert anything like the pull on the steel industry that the same industries did in America, but the fact that by the late 1930s the United Kingdom had the second biggest car industry in the world was of great significance to Sheffield. Commented the *Sheffield Daily Telegraph* in 1925:

The growth of the motor-car industry has been simply a godsend to Sheffield in making good the loss of trade in other directions. The building of a motor vehicle lays several branches of industry under tribute, and the maintenance of those in use has created a new and permanent addition to the outlets for tools and accessories which Sheffield is admirably situated to supply. A good deal of Sheffield steel of one kind and another goes into the construction of a motor-dray or a pleasure car, and the workshops in which they are made consume tool steel, files and engineers' tools. The garage tool chests and repair kits carried by the owners

[34] *SDT*, 31 Dec. 1934.
[35] See articles by M. Miller and Roy Church (cars) and Peter Fearon (aircraft), in Buxton and Aldcroft, *British Industry*.

of motors represent huge quantities of tools, and Sheffield enjoys a fair share of the supplies of these and various accessories.[36]

The large-scale producers of special steel felt this demand the most (see Chapter 7), but the smaller Sheffield firms were also heavily involved in supplying motor-car and aircraft steels.

In 1923 Brown Bayley's was one of the first firms to be approved as steelmakers by the Aeronautical Inspection Directorate. In 1929 horizontal forging machines were laid down at the company to produce half-shafts for motor vehicles, and other similar shapes in special steels. In 1931 began the hot and cold rolling of stainless steel sheet and strip and in addition to the mills, many items of ancillary equipment—descaling plant, annealing furnaces, flattening and polishing machines, slitters and shears—were installed. Also during the 1930s large extensions were made to the machine shop and centreless grinding machines were provided for the production of bright bars.[37]

Beardshaw's noted the beneficial impact of an upturn in demand for motor-car steels in 1924: it was an important factor in keeping bar and sheet mills occupied in bad years.[38] Kayser Ellison built on its wartime experience with engine valve steels and in 1923 introduced a major austenitic heat-resisting steel—KE965. This was a special valve steel with a wide range of useful properties: it retained its strength and toughness at high and low temperatures; did not air harden at any temperature, nor harden in water or oil; and could be easily machined.[39]

W. T. Flather Ltd. were mostly engaged in the production of bright-drawn steel bars, which were principally used in the motor vehicle trades where rapid repetition work in engines and gears was required. Despite American competition, by 1925 demand from this sector was said to be bringing the works close to full capacity after wartime expansion.[40] Another producer of bright-drawn bars (and cold rolled strip) for the motor-car and cycle trades was Arthur Lee & Sons. It also had a special department in the 1920s for the wires and tie rods for aeroplane rigging.[41]

Sheffield's cutting steels and die steels—for example, the milling cutters and hobs for cutting car gears, made by firms such as Osborn's—assumed an increasing importance in the 1920s. Naturally, the development of engines and other engineering products greatly increased the business of

---

[36] 'What the Motor Car Has Done for Sheffield' *SDT*, 31 Dec. 1925.

[37] *Brown Bayleys: A Story of Development* (n.d). See also 'Messrs. Brown Bayleys' Steel Works', *Engineering*, 120 (1925), in several parts, *passim*, 192–794.

[38] *SDT*, 31 Dec. 1924.   [39] *Histories of Famous Firms* (1958), 5; *SDT*, 31 Dec. 1925.

[40] 'Special Steels for the Motor Trade', interview with David Flather, *SDT*, 31 Dec. 1925.

[41] 'Wire and Strip: Work for Motor and Aeroplane Trades', *SDT*, 30 Dec. 1926; *Lee Steel 1874–1974* (Sheffield, 1974), 12.

Sheffield's twist drill makers. Another growth area was the magnet trade, where several manufacturers—Darwin & Milner, Edgar Allen, Swift Levick, Turton Bros. & Matthews, and Neill's—were active. Although the introduction of the loudspeaker, telephone, and household electricity meters required large quantities of magnets, so too did the magneto in motor cars. Such orders helped resuscitate Swift Levick after the mid-1920s. This company's fortunes were further improved in 1932, when on the advice of G. D. L. Horsburgh—a loudspeaker magnet pioneer—high-frequency melting was introduced to improve the quality of its magnet steels.[42] Magnet production was one area where Sheffield could claim to have taken advantage of the war and established an industry that could compete successfully with the German market leaders.

As orders from the car (and aircraft) industry spread through the steel industry and into the city's tool sector, the involvement of some steel firms with tool production intensified. Certainly, several companies—Bedford's, Marsh Bros., Neill's, Darwin & Milner, Sanderson's, and Turton Bros. & Matthews—began relying almost as much on tool production as on steel itself. (For a fuller discussion, see Chapter 8.) Many Sheffield firms began resembling steel and tool factories for the motor trades. Sanderson Bros. & Newbould, for example, produced a wide variety of both carbon and high-speed steels for general engineering; drills and cutters for machining; clutch plates for motor vehicles; motor shafts; and machine parts in stainless steel. Some of the steel firms (like some of the cutlery and tool firms) became light engineers. Sanderson Bros. & Newbould, for example, in the 1930s began marketing a heliocentric (speed-reducing) gear for use in industrial plant (such as in conveyor belts used in glass, pottery, and steel manufacture).

So far we have examined the general economic environment for Sheffield tool steel firms between 1918 and the mid-1930s—a period marked by increasing competition in special steels. This was caused by continued international competition; changes in tool steel technology; the weakening of overseas demand for Sheffield products; and a rising domestic demand for alloy steels, especially from the car and aircraft industries. We have also looked generally at how Sheffield firms reacted to this environment. But how did specific firms perform? Any answer to this question must necessarily be selective, in view of the large number of firms and the fact that their documentation is often sparse. But a useful picture can be built up.

One failure—Jonas & Colver—has already been highlighted. Another well-known firm that found the going tough was J. H. Andrew, which had been in steady decline since the departure of the founding dynasty at the

---

[42] *British Industry and Commerce* (1967), 20–1.

turn of the century. By the 1920s its reputation for wire, rods, and mining steel had been largely dissipated. This was due to a failure by its lacklustre management (about whom little is known) to invest. It had ceased innovating in drill steels, allowing Swedish and other competitors to usurp its trade; neglected to keep abreast of high-frequency melting and other production technologies; and avoided expenditure on plant for the finishing processes and manipulative work. One observer wrote in 1930 that, 'this fine old business has simply stood still, literally "dying on its feet". Handsome profits have given place to continuous losses, and every one of its principal lines of production have been cut by competitors—mostly foreign, until nothing short of a drastic re-organisation can impart fresh vitality into it.'[43] By 1928 the company was virtually bankrupt with debts of £220,000.

In 1929 the London bankers, Dawnay, Day, & Co. bought the firm for £300,000 and renamed it Andrews Toledo. A new management team was recruited and an attempt was made, against the backdrop of the world depression, to repair a decade or more of bad management. A high-frequency furnace was installed in 1935 and new lines were launched in aircraft steels. By then the company had moved back into profitability—but only just—and it did not prove enough. In 1938 Andrews Toledo was taken over by another Sheffield firm with an equally chequered history—Darwins Ltd.[44]

Darwins had been formed in 1926 by Paul Kuehnrich, and was composed of the constituent parts of his Darwin & Milner steel business. Darwins also included as its headquarters the Fitzwilliam Works of the moribund Sheffield Simplex Motor Works, which Kuehnrich had bought in 1924 as a site for a major project—the launch of the safety-razor industry in Sheffield. Kuehnrich's venture—described in more detail in Chapter 8—with its highly geared capitalization (£50,000 ordinary shares and £300,000 preference shares) needed fast growth. Instead, Darwins failed spectacularly and by 1927 it was in receivership, with Kuehnrich's dream of making Sheffield the razor capital of the world in tatters. Two years later, Darwins, too, was taken over by a London banking consortium and Kuehnrich lost control of the firm (though he was retained for a time as a technical consultant until his death in 1932).

Darwins' new management, under the chairmanship of Sir James Calder, rescued the business by returning it to its core steel business.[45] Safety-razor manufacture was gradually phased out in the 1930s, in

---

[43] Bank of England: Securities Management Trust. SMT4/16, SMT 6/6. Andrews Toledo, confidential report, 13 Jan. 1930.

[44] SCL Aurora 56, 57, 60. Accounts and Directors' Minute Books of Andrews Toledo.

[45] Sir James Calder (1869–1932) was head of the Edinburgh and London timber firm Calders Ltd.

favour of more profitable specialities. Although Kuehnrich's safety-razor scheme was unsuccessful, his emphasis on science-based research was a more enduring legacy and allowed the company to re-establish itself with its renowned tool steels, magnets, and hacksaws. Magnet manufacture proved to be a crucial growth area for the firm; by 1935 the managing director noted the large increase in magnet orders, especially for telephones. An Ajax-Northrup high-frequency furnace installed in 1934 at a cost of £8,875 replaced the crucibles at Carlisle Street and allowed Darwins to begin manufacturing stainless and heat-resisting steels. On the other hand, the atrocious works management at Darwins continued into the 1930s, when contracts for products as diverse as safety razors and audio turntables were taken at unremunerative prices 'simply in an attempt to increase turnover at all costs'.[46] Darwins barely made a profit between 1930 and 1937, when £157,000 had to be written off the paid-up share capital.[47] Eventually, another management upheaval followed: Calder resigned as chairman in 1937 and was replaced by Harold L. Armstrong, who immediately recommended the takeover of Andrews Toledo.[48]

New management and technical skills were also needed by other tool steel firms by the 1930s. Static or falling demand, the reluctance to introduce new melting technologies, the continued dominance of old family members and the loss of former markets—all contributed to a lack of dynamism. A classic example was Benjamin Huntsman Ltd., a firm approaching its 200th anniversary. The Huntsman board steadfastly clung to their 'old and valued connections' and congratulated themselves on the fact that 'the principal shareholders in the company are members of the Huntsman family and direct descendants of the inventor'.[49] The crucible process was sacred at the company, despite the fact that by 1934 the firm admitted to:

a very serious difficulty in obtaining suitable raw material or cementation bar steel, owing to the changed conditions of steel melting brought about by the advent of the high-frequency electric furnace. About eight cementation furnaces are in use in Sheffield today whereas many years ago the number was over 200. This shortage of material in suitable tempers for our business is likely to remain a considerable source of anxiety in the future.

[46] SCL Aurora 1. Darwin Directors' Minute Book. Report of J. D. Stevens, 27 June 1935.

[47] Darwins' issued capital in 1933 was £530,000 (£30,000 ordinary shares and £500,000 preference shares).

[48] H. L. Armstrong was the son of the H. E. Armstrong FRS, the chemist, and had held management posts at Port Sunlight, in the oil industry, and at British Mannesmann Tube Co. Ltd.

[49] This and subsequent quotes are from SCL B. Huntsman Ltd. Directors' Minute Book, 1918–54.

But instead of adopting high-frequency melting, now an established part of the Sheffield scene, Huntsman's began stockpiling blister steel and took a financial interest in R. S. Holland & Co., an importer of Swedish bar iron. Despite the dismal trade in the early 1930s—Huntsman paid no dividends between 1930 and 1935—the chairman, William Patrickson, managed to find comfort in the fact that 'the number of high-grade crucible steel makers and melters of best material has never been less than it is today. This fact does hold out considerable hope for the future business of the firm.' Such conservative and complacent management did not bode well for the future.[50]

Similar managerial sclerosis can be seen at J. Beardshaw & Son, where William F. Beardshaw clung to power as long as possible. When the 72-year-old chairman became ill in 1929, he told the board that he 'still possessed all his mental faculties and hoped soon to be in a position to resume his usual activity'. As good as his word, Beardshaw was soon back at the helm and quickly took the precaution of passing a special resolution, which meant that he could never be retired provided he was 'physically and mentally capable'. He remained chairman until his death in 1936, by which time the firm badly needed new investment in electric sheet mills.[51] The reluctance to modernize may have accounted for the fact that it was slower than some of the other tool steel firms to benefit from the economic upturn after 1935.

In the performance of Andrew's, Darwins, Huntsman, and Beardshaw, there is plenty of evidence of entrepreneurial shortcomings. On the other hand, many firms did rise to new challenges. Edgar Allen's, for example, continued to make progress in the difficult inter-war years. No major strategic redirection took place at Allen's (though file manufacture, one of the early bases of its fortunes, was abandoned in 1931), but the company steadily exploited the potential of its wide product line: tool steels, steel castings, tools, circular and stone saws, magnets, trackwork, and various types of crushing and grinding machinery. The trade in steel castings grew steadily: allied with the firm's engineering departments, it helped offset slack demand for steel. The large number of orders for cement plant and crushing machinery, needed for world reconstruction after the First World War, augured well for this branch of the business. In the early 1930s, agreements with the American Allis Chalmers Manufacturing Co. and Buell Combustion Ltd., London, extended Allen's range of industrial plant and pulverizing machinery. Magnet manufacture was another growth area in the depression: production had reached 10,000 permanent

[50] For more blinkered comments by Patrickson, see 'Crucible Steel: Handicaps of a Historic Industry', *SDT*, 31 Dec. 1929.
[51] SCL MD 7081. Beardshaw Directors' Minute Book.

magnets per week by 1933. Allen's main focus, though, was in cutting steels, in almost every aspect of which it was in the vanguard. Despite the firm's commercial difficulties in the depression—its £1 ordinary shares were written down to 13s. 4d. in 1935, amidst a boardroom battle—it maintained an enviable record of innovation. The highlights are recorded in the pages of the company's *Edgar Allen News*, one of the best British house journals of the time. Allen's major contribution was its installation of the first high-frequency induction furnace for tool steel in 1927. This was not simply a more economic and efficient way of melting tool steel: it also produced a purer and more uniform steel, because the electrical stirring action did not allow the heavy alloying elements to settle on the bottom of the furnace, but diffused them throughout the molten mass. This paved the way for Edgar Allen's introduction of the first of the so-called 'super' high-speed steels, which contained about 12 per cent cobalt (alongside about 21 per cent tungsten). Marketed as 'Stag Major', it was the most effective tool steel available at that time for especially difficult cuts: for example, for the first time manganese steel could be machined.[52] Allen's also adopted improved methods of making hollow-drill steels in 1929. Another advance was the introduction by Allen's (and by Osborn's) of butt-welded cutting tools, in which a cutting portion of high-speed steel was electrically welded to a high-grade steel shank (dispensing with the costly solid high-speed steel shank). This process enabled the user to obtain the benefit of the superior cutting properties of high-cobalt super steels at a lower cost; reduced the chance of wastage due to faulty treatment; and allowed the marketing of a range of tools that reached the customer ready for use. By 1936 Allen's had also begun the manufacture of tungsten-carbide cutting tools, which were recognized as being even more effective for certain classes of work than super high-speed steels.

Samuel Osborn also made steady progress. It had about 1,500 employees in 1922 and although this fell to around 1,290 during the depression, by 1937 the workforce had surpassed the old levels at around 1,700. Osborn's maintained its profitability and dividends—except in bad years, such as 1931 and 1932—and continued to market new products. In fact, like Edgar Allen's, its very wide range of tool steels, castings, forgings, sheets, and tools allowed the firm to exploit new opportunities as they arose. An Osborn trade catalogue, published in 1935, gives some idea of the extent of its product range. Like many British trade catalogues from this era, the *Osborn Complete Catalogue*, with over 400 pages, is a document of extraordinary variety. In its pages are myriad crucible and high-speed

---

[52] E. N. Simons, 'A Century of Tool Steel Development', *British Steelmaker*, 18 (Apr. 1952), 191. See also Simons' history of Edgar Allen, 'The Story of a Great Steel Firm', *Edgar Allen News* (Dec. 1953–Oct. 1958).

steels; manganese steels; stainless and heat-resisting steels; twist drills and reamers; files; springs; steel sheets; steel castings for mines, collieries, and light railways in the shape of steel wheels, manganese dredge buckets, and crushers; steel forgings; circular saws; hammers; chisels; shovels; and woodworking tools. Osborn's was still a world leader in tool steel technology and in 1928 it marketed its own cobalt super high-speed, the so-called 'SOBV' cutting alloy. Its introduction of butt-welded high-speed steel tools (under the brandname 'Solidend') was claimed as a first by the company in 1930. Early in the following year, Osborn's made the crucial decision to install a 5-cwt. Metrovick high-frequency induction furnace (to supplement its five Héroult arc furnaces) and this allowed Osborn's to meet the rising demand for stainless and heat-resisting steels, when it appeared in 1933.[53] Recognizing the potential for such steels, by 1935 two larger high-frequency furnaces (one $\frac{1}{2}$-ton and one $\frac{1}{4}$-ton capacity) were melting steel at the Wicker Works.

Arthur Balfour & Sons responded to the severe drop in sales in the early 1920s with a variety of initiatives. Some of these were successful—electric melting, hacksaw production—some not—such as stainless cutlery blanks and tungsten carbide tool bits. But the company broadly maintained its place as one of the leading producers of high-quality steel and tools. As we have seen in Table 6.1, overseas markets remained crucial to the firm, despite the disappointments caused by the loss of the American trade. Balfour's reacted to the increasing self-sufficiency of the United States, Germany, France, Italy, and Russia by opening new accounts in China, Japan, India, and South America and the firm's business in the important Australian market was further extended. The reliance on overseas markets enabled Balfour's to survive the worst effects of the slump, though even for Balfour's the early 1930s slump was a close-run thing. Its losses between 1930 and 1932 totalled nearly £50,000 and the company was heavily overdrawn at the bank.

The recovery of the export position at Balfour's represented a considerable achievement for such a family firm, and the indefatigable travels and salesmanship of Sir Arthur Balfour played a large part. According to his son, Balfour was:

at the height of his powers . . . After a journey he would return, work two secretaries, at once and then in relays, aided by messengers and a red-hot telephone. Starting at the top of an enormous pile of mail he would go down to the bottom, never putting on one side, never selecting, always making a decision on the spot, unless he sent it to another for action. In some incredible way the impossible was done.[54]

---

[53] 'Samuel Osborn & Co. Ltd.: Increased Demands by Home Trades', *SDT*, 29 Dec. 1933.
[54] Arthur Balfour & Co., *A Centenary: 1865–1965* (Nottingham, 1967), 37.

However, Balfour's achievements rested on other family members—his brother Bertram (and Bertram's son, Gerald), and his own sons, Francis and Robin. This family management team was evidently sound enough for Balfour himself to spend an increasing amount of time between the Wars not only organizing the local industry (along with Sir Robert Hadfield, he was Sheffield steel's leading spokesman at this time), but also on advisory work for the Government, especially in international trade matters. His most important appointment was as chairman of the Committee on Industry and Trade between 1924 and 1928. The final report, which appeared in 1929, contained a searching examination of the country's industrial competitiveness and made recommendations concerning the United Kingdom's future ability to compete in overseas markets. It was to be one of the ironies of Balfour's career that his own company (and other Sheffield tool steel firms, some of which were called to give evidence) epitomized many of the problems that the Committee had so extensively documented—particularly its small-scale structure, wide product range, and lack of selling organization overseas.[55] On the other hand, Balfour's achievements were real enough and he showed that the family-owned crucible steel firm could survive in a difficult environment.

Evidence for the business performance of some of the other tool steel firms is more patchy. But the general impression, as a Marsh Bros. director stated:

is of the extraordinary resilience and adaptability of [the] small private firm . . . When demands for one particular product for some reason or other disappeared, those in charge for the moment always seemed capable of striking out on a new line—or where a market faded out they had the initiative and the energy to explore the possibilities of another part of the world; nearly always, it would appear, with favourable results.[56]

Marsh Bros. themselves had only three bad years—1927, 1928, and 1931—and persevered in the face of rising tariff barriers to export steel and tools worldwide. Its tool business, in particular, expanded in these years. John Bedford & Sons continued its innovations in hollow-drill mining steels, where Sheffield had faced severe competition from Swedish and American makers. The pre-war production method of boring a billet before rolling had often produced an irregular hole and consequent risk of fracture. This was countered by rolling billets on a powdered core,

---

[55] Board of Trade, Committee on Industry and Trade (Balfour Committee), *Minutes of Evidence; Survey of the Metal Industries* (London, 1927–8).

[56] W. Lockwood Marsh, in Foreword to Pollard, *Three Centuries.* Quoted R. Lloyd-Jones and M. J. Lewis, 'Business Structure and Political Economy in Sheffield: The Metal Trades 1880–1920s', in C. Binfield *et al., The History of the City of Sheffield 1843–1993* (Sheffield, 1993), ii. 215.

which was then removed by compressed air: but this, too, was not ideal, since the packing material also produced a rough bore prone to fracture. After much experimentation, one of the firm's directors (and later chairman), Reginald A. Bedford (c.1888–1948), patented in 1928 the first hollow-drill steel bar, produced on a metal (copper) core. By inserting a stainless tube in addition to the copper bar, a stainless lining was produced when the copper was withdrawn. This was 'an improvement which miners had been looking for for years' and the Bedford Patent Copper Core Process became standard for most hollow drill steel produced in the world until the 1960s.[57]

Whatever the vicissitudes in the commercial world, little weakening of R&D is evident in Sheffield. For example, Kayser, Ellison's new motor-car and aircraft steels derived from one of the best-equipped research laboratories in the industry. There was also an unusually strong research effort at Jessop's, where in the late 1930s there were about forty to fifty research staff in a company employing about 2,000–2,500. The director of research was Donald Oliver (c.1906–90), who had joined Jessop's in 1934 from the GEC Research Laboratories. Go-ahead and energetic, Oliver 'recruited successive generations of bright young men', as he expanded Jessop's research department.[58] These included Geoffrey Harris (1917–91), who became Oliver's collaborator after 1938.[59] Oliver's first main field of interest had been in magnets, but prior to the War a more promising line of development suggested itself in high-temperature materials. The implications of Oliver's and Harris's work were to become apparent during the War, with the appearance of the jet engine.

At Brown Bayley's the influence of Harry Brearley, as works manager, and J. H. G. Monypenny, as head of research, ensured that the company was amongst the leaders in alloy production. Its research effort was directed particularly at the new stainless and heat-resisting steels. Monypenny produced one of the standard textbooks on this subject.[60] The firm claimed to be the first to produce a 'stainless iron' (a low-carbon stainless steel) in 1920; and four years later the first molybdenum austenitic stainless steel.

How are we to summarize this highly complex picture for the smaller tool steel and alloy firms? The optimum strategy for Sheffield tool steel firms in the inter-war period was perhaps one in which they switched as soon as possible from crucible to high-frequency melting, using the new technology to improve further their tool steels; developed alloys for the aircraft and motor-car industries, particularly in the new stainless and

[57] 'The Lion of Sheffield', *British Industry and Commerce* (1967), 22.
[58] *Metals and Materials*, 6 (July 1990), 461.
[59] Ibid. 7 (Apr. 1991), 249.
[60] J. H. G. Monypenny, *Stainless Steel: and Iron* (2nd edn., 1931).

heat-resisting steels; concentrated on the technology for flat-rolled consumer products; extended their expertise in tools and general engineering
products; and adjusted their marketing orientation to make the most of
United Kingdom demand.

On the whole, Sheffield firms seem to have done exactly that—though
with varying degrees of success—and only in a handful of cases was clear
entrepreneurial failure evident. There were weaknesses. The industry
remained highly fragmented, with little movement towards rationalization. In 1935 the Crucible Steel Makers' Association in Sheffield had some
fifty-four member-firms, some of which had also joined the High-Speed
Steel Association (which listed a further eighteen tool steel firms, not
involved with crucible steel). No attempt was made to co-ordinate overseas selling, which was probably the industry's weakest link. From the
high tide of overseas expansion before 1914, Sheffield was in retreat,
increasingly forced back onto its own markets. Often its response to
foreign competition was defensive: in its trade mark policy, calls for
protection, and the proliferation of local pricing agreements and cartels.
On the other hand, most of the Sheffield firms could claim that in a
difficult, sometimes horrendous, business climate they had held their
ground, even if they had not made much profit. The survival of a large
number of family firms still made Sheffield a highly competitive environment; and the city still held first place for high-quality steels, though now
by a very narrow margin from the Americans and Germans. Its adherence
to a wide product range and individualist ethos may have had its drawbacks and hindered rationalization, but it may also have been Sheffield's
salvation. Experience abroad, such as in America—where the formation of
the Crucible Steel Co. of America had led in the inter-war period to a
bloated, inefficient loss-maker—showed that merger was not a panacea.[61]
In Sheffield it was left to the larger steel firms to try this route.

---

[61] Crucible Steel Co. of America was an attempt to establish a universal provider of tool
steel comprising over a dozen firms. After making a fortune during the First World War, an
autocratic (and often corrupt) management failed to integrate production and sales, so that
its inter-war performance was extremely mediocre. See 'Crucible Steel', *Fortune*, 20 (1939),
74–9; G. Tweedale, 'Crucible Steel Company of America', in Bruce Seely (ed.), *Encyclopedia of
American Business History and Biography: Iron and Steel in the Twentieth Century* (Columbia, SC,
1994), 106–7, 207–8.

7

Mergers, Diversification, and Large-Scale Special Steelmaking

> there are too many works in existence now and . . . even when trade
> revives it will be impossible to operate most or any of them profitably,
> and therefore it behoves those concerned to get together to do some-
> thing, and not merely to sit still and starve to death.
>
> SCL Firth-Brown Records. James B. Neilson (English Steel
> Corporation) quoted by a Firth-Brown director, 14 July 1931.

> True rationalisation in the common steel trade, where the products are
> largely standardised, is clearly feasible. In our own trade, where
> specialised products are the essential source of profit, our opinion is
> that successful rationalisation is necessarily somewhat handicapped
> until the industries, which consume our products, rationalise, or, at
> any rate, show more signs of standardising the form and character of
> the materials they take from us.
>
> SCL Firth-Brown Records. Directors' report on proposed ESC
> merger, 18 March 1931.

At the beginning of this study, attention was drawn to an important
division in steel manufacture between the bulk producers, largely located
in areas such as the north-east and South Wales, and the special
steelmakers, mostly centred in Sheffield. It will be readily apparent by
now that there was a further split in Sheffield special steelmaking itself.
This was between, on the one hand, small-scale businesses involved in the
manufacture of such products as high-speed steel and engineers' tools
(branches that had their origins in the Huntsman crucible); and, on the
other, giant Sheffield concerns producing bulk (but still specialist) steels
and forgings for armour-plate, engineering plant, and the leading consumer goods industries. The roots of this type of special steel manufacture
lay in Bessemer and Siemens steelmaking and the emergence of the arms
trade in the 1870s. In this sector were numbered Vickers, Cammell-Laird,
John Brown, Thos. Firth, Hadfields, and the satellite firms in Stocksbridge
and Rotherham (Samuel Fox, Steel, Peech, & Tozer, and Parkgate).

Like the tool steel firms, in the 1920s these companies found themselves
in a very different world from that of pre-1914 days. Sheffield's lead in
alloys, forgings, steel castings, and specialist engineering fabrications had
lessened appreciably: patents had expired, American and Continental

competitors had copied Sheffield methods, and the war had over-expanded capacity. For the armament firms the hangover from the First World War was greatest. As one director of Vickers lamented: 'before 1914' armament companies 'made a great deal of money', but 'for their ultimate welfare the money was perhaps too easily made'.[1] Wartime expansion itself involved often ruinous expense and then saddled these firms with useless plant. Sir Robert Hadfield complained to the Minister of Munitions that 'we have entirely destroyed our capacity for commercial developments, that we have absolutely not a square foot of land left in our site of over one hundred acres, that is unless we pull down at great expense the various important buildings erected at large cost and start over again'.[2] The War had left Sheffield industry with a legacy of surplus labour and armament plant that in the 1920s was to lie unused. 'Sheffield contains acres of forging shops filled with huge machines which have been idle since the Armistice', stated the *Sheffield Daily Telegraph* in 1927: 'The explanation is that the material produced in them is not now wanted. Among other things they were employed for manipulating armour-plate, great guns, and steel parts for warships. That trade has almost gone.'[3] Even the modernization of plant achieved during the War now counted against Sheffield, since orders could be dispatched in half the time.[4]

Initially, the post-war outlook had been optimistic as steel orders flowed in the rush of reconstruction. 'Competition was non-existent. Business poured in from all directions, a large proportion of it being refused or even ignored, with a nonchalance never before observed,' stated a local newspaper.[5] But the early euphoria evaporated. The boom gave way to slump in 1920; unemployment appeared as the number of workers in the heavy trades in Sheffield fell to about 66,000 in 1921 (ten years later the figure was 47,000); and for the first time there was talk of rationalization and diversification. By the end of the inter-war period, of the top nine firms in Table 3.4, only Hadfields still stood alone.

The mergers and diversifications, then, were essentially a defensive response to reduced orders, increased competition, and the inevitable need to switch from war- to peacetime work. However, there were more positive aspects to the trend. The 1920s may have been a 'black decade' for much of the British steel industry, but the slump in trade was not spread

---

[1] Sir Noel Birch, quoted in R. P. T. Davenport-Hines, 'The British Marketing of Armaments, 1885–1914', in Davenport-Hines (ed.), *Markets and Bagmen: Studies in the History of Marketing and British Industrial Performance, 1830–1939* (Aldershot, 1986), 146–91, 154.

[2] Public Records Office, Reco 1/730. Hadfield to Minister of Munitions, 2 Jan. 1919. Reference courtesy Richard Davenport-Hines.

[3] 'Sheffield Trade Review', *SDT*, 30 Dec. 1927.

[4] 'Sheffield's Case: Still Carrying Heavy Burdens', *SDT*, 31 Dec. 1925.

[5] *SDT*, 31 Dec. 1920.

evenly amongst products and regions. As Sheffield steelmakers well knew, there were several promising lines of business that were less susceptible to the depression. The big Sheffield firms may have been linked to the switchback of armament orders, but they were also intimately linked with the development of new and growing industries in the British economy. One of the most important was electrical engineering, where the development of giant power stations for a national 'grid'—besides resulting in orders for new generating plant—also spurred the introduction of a vast array of consumer durables such as radios, cookers, refrigerators, and washing machines. Hardly less important were the motor-car and the aircraft industries, already discussed in Chapter 6, as a source of business for the smaller Sheffield tool steel firms. Although only about half a million cars were on British roads by 1923 (compared with about 10 million in America) and the aircraft industry was in its infancy, Sheffield steelmakers correctly forecast the inevitability of rising orders from these sectors, despite depressed trade. The chemical, soap, and oil industries, increasingly dominated in this period by large firms such as ICI, Courtaulds, and Unilever, also continued to make rapid strides: the introduction of man-made fibres, and the building of large-scale plants for fixing nitrogen and catalytic cracking occurred at this time. Oil refining, for example, was to greatly boost a Sheffield speciality in the 1920s—the production of giant hollow-drum forgings.

Since all these industries contined to grow, despite the depression of the early 1930s, and all offered an outlet for special and alloy steels, this added up to a large business for Sheffield steelmakers. The more demanding steel consumers became, the better, since it was at this crucial interface between various branches of engineering and steel, where growing industries were 'constantly calling upon the [steel] makers for higher and higher performances',[6] that Sheffield continued to excel.

Consequently, in the inter-war years advances in alloy steels and their range of applications continued apace. Developments included the wider application of alloy steels for constructional and engineering purposes, the production of heat-resisting steels and alloys, and the super-hardening of steel and its application to general engineering. What did this translate into? There were better- (and safer-) performance steel forgings in crankshafts, camshafts, connecting rods, and valves, which often had greatly increased strength-to-weight ratio. High-pressure boilers for locomotives and generating plant were developed able to withstand temperatures up to 1,000 °F and pressures up to 1,500 lb. per square inch. Exhaust turbine rotors in chromium, nickel, and molybdenum were available

---

[6] Sir Robert Hadfield, 'Development of the Motor Trade: Its Importance to the Iron and Steel Industry', *SDT*, 29 Dec. 1923.

which boosted the supply of air to aircraft engines at high altitudes. Perhaps the biggest advance at this time was the introduction of stainless steel for large-scale fabrications, an area in which in the early 1920s Sheffield undoubtedly led the world.[7]

The production and marketing of these alloys demanded exactly the same kind of metallurgical and business skills that had been needed when Sheffield had launched the crucible process: they were high value-added materials, in which price was often (though not always) a secondary consideration; in which liaison was often needed between steelmaker and customer; and in which there was a good deal of tailoring the product to suit individual needs. Nevertheless, most of these alloys—especially stainless steel—needed large-scale production to be economic. Sheffield's future success would depend upon its ability to adapt its powerful forging presses and rolling mills in the Don Valley to such work; and to alter its nineteenth-century individualist ethos in favour of more mass-production business methods and organization for making special steel. How did it perform?

The first large combine, the United Steel Companies, had emerged by early 1918. It was a combination of heavy steelmaking and rolling capacity, based on an assured supply of raw materials, whose main impetus came from Henry ('Harry') Steel (1863–1920), the chairman of Steel, Peech, & Tozer. This company had become one of the most successful in the Rotherham (and Sheffield) area, specializing in acid and basic steels, produced mostly by the open-hearth process, which it fabricated into railway materials and also marketed as billets. Its interest in special steels and alloys was also growing. Harry Steel, the son of the founder of the business, is a rather shadowy figure who hardly emerges from contemporary sources and business records. What is known suggests a wealthy, ambitious, commercially-minded man who was an astute fixer. The First World War provided a congenial climate for Steel and, with government support, he embarked upon the building of a massive new melting shop at Templeborough which would be the largest in the country. This was to be followed by a continuous mill for making standard billets and slabs; and then a continuous strip and bar mill. Harry Steel was thinking ahead and thinking big, with the confidence of a man whose company profits had surged forward from under £100,000 a year before the War to over £700,000 in 1918. He was fired by the vision of a post-war situation in which civilian outlets for steel were restored and British manufacturers could exploit a Continental steel industry dislocated by war. He embarked upon a classic piece of vertical integration, by combin-

---

[7] J. W. Donaldson, 'Alloy Steels—Their Development and Application', *Metallurgia*, 7 (Feb. 1933), 127–9; 'The British Industries Fair; Some Outstanding Features', ibid. 15 (Feb. 1937), 113–27.

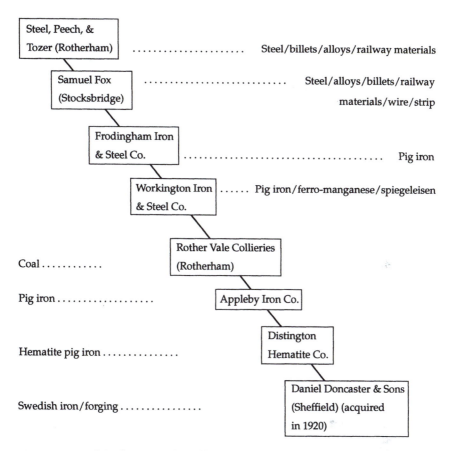

Fig. 7.1. *United Steel merger, 1917–18*

ing with Samuel Fox and then adding further steel and pig-iron interests in Scunthorpe and Workington and also the Rother Vale collieries (see Fig. 7.1).

The history of the United Steel Companies has already been told by Philip Andrews and Elizabeth Brunner in their book, *Capital Development in Steel*; and this has been supplemented by Jonathan Boswell's illuminating comparative study of United Steel and its competitors Dorman Long and Stewarts & Lloyds.[8] It is therefore proposed to omit much of the detail

---

[8] P. W. S. Andrews and E. Brunner, *Capital Development in Steel* (Oxford, 1951); J. Boswell, *Business Policies in the Making* (London, 1983). S. Tolliday, *Business, Banking and Politics* (Cambridge, Mass., 1987), also contains material on United Steel's relationships with the banks. There is no study of the Rotherham steel industry, though *A Lifetime in Steel: A Pictorial History of Iron and Steelmaking in Rotherham* (Rotherham Borough Council, 1987) provides some basic information.

concerning the development of this company and confine ourselves to a brief outline, except in a couple of instances.

With its issued capital of over £8 million, United Steel was one of the largest combines in the country, but it performed poorly in the depressed 1920s. This was owing less to its structure—which was logical and reasonably complementary—or even to the fact that the merger aimed at security and economy of supplies rather than true rationalization. What crippled United Steel was its indebtedness—a hangover from the optimism of the immediate post-war era, when United Steel had saddled itself with over £3.5 million in debentures and other charges. The company had to find about £330,000 each year for debenture interest and preference dividends alone! After initial profits of £1 million in 1919 the group soon began making losses. These were thus, writes Jonathan Boswell, 'anxious years for United Steel, loaded as it was with heavy indebtedness, bold expansions which had turned sour in the depression and a long tail of commercially declining operations, its leadership dogged rather than inspired'.[9]

The fate of United Steel is important to Sheffield steel history for two reasons. First, it underscored the growth of the 'heavy' side of special steelmaking, which had been a part of the industry since the time of Bessemer and Siemens. Second, it emphasized the growing importance of Rotherham and Stocksbridge—areas then administratively outside Sheffield, yet destined to wield an increasing influence on the city. Thus United Steel represented the beginning of a subtle shift in economic advantage away from a purely Sheffield-city focus. Despite its tribulations, United Steel had started on a trajectory that would eventually lead it in the 1960s and 1970s to become the dominant voice in the Sheffield region and an important influence on Britain's steel industry.

Before this could happen, drastic restructuring of United Steel was necessary in 1928, when (with the financier Clarence Hatry acting as a catalyst) its capital was halved and professional managers replaced the older family interests. Many key decisions occurred surprisingly quickly between 1928 and 1929, largely the work of the chairman, (Sir) Walter Benton Jones, and his managing director, (Sir) Robert Stuart Hilton. The head office was made independent and more streamlined, with a symbolic new location in Sheffield itself. From there, Jones and Hilton swiftly tightened control over investment, sales, and group finance; and particular attention was paid to public relations and personnel policies. New blood was introduced by over a dozen managerial appointments, with the emphasis on the sales side. Centralized purchasing and costings systems,

    [9] J. Boswell, 'Sir Walter Benton Jones', in D. J. Jeremy (ed.), *Dictionary of Business Biography* (London, 1984–6), iii. 539–43, 539.

time studies, and an efficiency drive were instituted. And there were important strategic decisions involving the scrapping and sale of redundant plant and the rationalizing of output.

Some decisions had a major significance for steelworks that were either in Sheffield or nearby. Daniel Doncaster & Sons, which had earlier switched from its main business of blister steel production to that of drop forgings for the motor-car trade, was absorbed by United Steel in 1920. The combine wanted an outlet at the high-quality end of the alloy steel market and Doncaster's, which were also linked with the Birmingham special steel merchanting business of Martino Steel & Metal, provided it. According to one of the Doncaster family, United Steel 'got tired of putting in money' and also 'did not have the know-how to run Doncasters'. So Ronald Steel (a son of Harry Steel) organized its breakaway from the United Steel group and its return to family control in 1936. Ronald Steel became Doncaster's managing director and under his direction the old Quaker firm launched a programme of modernization and expansion. It began forging valves by extrusion after linking with Thompson Products in Cleveland, Ohio.[10]

The United Steel board, however, did have a role for Samuel Fox & Co. Roughly coinciding with the appointment of Gerald Steel (1895–1957)—another son of Harry's—as general manager in 1932, Fox was deprived of many of its traditional products and asked to develop instead its expertise in the rapidly expanding manufacture of alloy and stainless steels. Until the end of the 1920s Fox was concerned mostly with the production of standard alloy steels: however, it was already building up its lines in special steels for the automobile and aircraft industries. United Steel decided to invest at both ends of the production process for these steels. In 1931 a Steckel mill was installed, which combined the old method of rolling by pressure with a new principle of reduction by tension to improve the surface quality of steel. A major investment was also made in the new high-frequency method of electric melting. Andrews and Brunner describe in detail the thinking behind this decision, arguing that besides United Steel's awareness of the intrinsic merits of the high-frequency furnace, this also appealed because it was something new and untried and would enhance the firm's prestige.[11] Frank Bagnall, the son of a works manager at Fox, supervised the move into high-frequency melting, having gained experience with electric furnaces in Canada. A 20-lb. induction furnace was in use by 1930 for research. So successful was it that by 1933 two larger furnaces were in operation (one of 12 cwt.), and

[10] Late Richard T. Doncaster interview, 23 July 1991. See also R. T. Doncaster, 'Daniel Doncaster & Sons and the Poppet Valve Trade', *The Cutting Edge: Magazine of the Sheffield Trades Historical Society*, 7 (1991), 14–18.

[11] Andrews and Brunner, *Capital Development*, 214–22.

these in turn were replaced within a year by two others, including a furnace of 5 tons capacity. This was described as the 'largest and most modern high-frequency steel-making plant in the world'.[12] Fox could now enter the market for stainless steel for both strip and sheet; and in 1936, in what Andrews and Brunner describe as 'an act of faith',[13] the company sanctioned a large plant for rolling stainless sheet. Stainless steel was also behind two other developments in 1936—the installation of German cold-rolling strip mills to deal with the expanding trade in razor, stainless, and alloy strip; and the extension of the wire department. By 1936 a new spring-making plant was also in operation, and there was a growing involvement in springs for road vehicles. (According to one journal, by 1937 the firm was supplying 60 per cent of the springs for British commercial vehicles.) These investments did not bring about a magical transformation of Fox's business immediately—it was the least profitable part of United Steel in the 1930s—but they were to bear fruit in the future.

The same could be said of the decision, taken in about 1930, to build a Central Research Department at Stocksbridge at a cost of £28,500. Quite distinct from the works laboratories, the new Department, which was opened in 1934, was to concern itself with matters which would bring economy to the production of the firm's steel and also undertake 'long-range' investigations into advanced steels. Its first director was Thomas Swinden, a Sheffield-born metallurgist very much in the Brearley–Hadfield mould. After graduating in metallurgy from Sheffield University in 1905, Swinden embarked upon a glittering research career (he was the first Sheffielder to win the Carnegie gold medal), before joining Fox's in 1909 as their chief chemist. Immensely hard-working and dedicated to a wide view of research in the industry (he was an enthusiastic proponent of industry- and government-sponsored research and standardization), Swinden 'not only built up one of the most efficient research organisations in the industry but acquired an exceptional influence on all the technical activities of the largest company in the British steel industry'.[14]

It was to be exactly a decade after the United Steel merger, before the next big rationalization plan in Sheffield. This involved the creation of the English Steel Corporation (ESC). It was the armament producers which had suffered most in the 1920s: Vickers, Cammell-Laird, and Brown's all faced major strategy decisions when arms orders virtually vanished, which led to attempts to diversify into other industries. In the depressed state of trade, the results were unhappy. Vickers and Cammell-Laird, for

[12] 'Progress in the Production of Special Steel', Metallurgia, 11 (Dec. 1934), 43–4, 43.
[13] Andrews and Brunner, Capital Development, 219.
[14] British Steelmaker, 10 (Nov. 1944), 480–4, 484. See also K. J. Irvine, 'Swinden Laboratories: 50 Years of Steel Research' (Rotherham, privately published, 1984), 6–7.

example, both made disastrous diversifications into rolling stock and electro-technology. In 1928, however, a merger between Vickers and Armstrong's provided the chance for the rationalization of these firms' steel interests at the River Don Works, Openshaw and Elswick—an opportunity that was soon extended when Cammell-Laird's Sheffield steel capacity (at the Penistone, Grimesthorpe, and Cyclops Works) was added. The ESC was capitalized at £8.2 million (with Vickers' shares predominant), with a workforce approaching 7,000 in the early 1930s. The combine was soon extended by acquiring the ordinary share capital of Taylor Bros. & Co., producing tyres, wheels, and axles at Manchester. The combine thus brought together:

Vickers Armstrong Ltd.	*Cammell-Laird Ltd.*
River Don Works, Sheffield	Grimesthorpe Works, Sheffield
Holme Lane Works, Sheffield	Cyclops Works, Sheffield
Whitworth Street Works, Manchester	Penistone Works, Penistone
North Street Works, Openshaw, Manchester	
Taylor Bros. & Co. Ltd., Trafford Park, Manchester	

While this went ahead, the ESC was making a far-reaching appraisal of its layout and performance and attempting to impose some kind of order on its empire. Rationalization was inevitable given that the steel capacity of the ESC's plant in 1927 was 680,000 tons, but actual output was only 344,492—only 55 per cent of capacity. And this was aside from the extensive duplication in products and melting and forging facilities (shown in Table 7.1). Desire for rationalization was sharpened by the awareness of the foreign situation. One commissioned ESC report concluded that, although German steelmakers, such as Krupp's at Essen, had lower wages, the uncompetitiveness of United Kingdom forging companies was due to the fact that they 'are out of date in almost every important feature. In plant, layout, service and transport facilities, size of units, process materials, and frequently in organisation, they are behind the best modern practice.'[15]

The ESC directors were also greatly impressed by the Continental trend towards large-scale concentration, of the kind that had resulted in the formation of the Vereinigte Stahlwerke AG in Germany in 1926.[16] Their inferiority complex was further heightened by a tour of America's awe-

[15] SCL ESC Papers. H. A. Humphrey, Report to Directors, July 1928.

[16] Ibid. G. R. T. Taylor and Alex Williamson, 'Report on a Visit to Steel Works Plants, Engineering Establishments and Research Laboratories, in Germany and Czechoslovakia', Sept. 1928. See also A. D. Chandler, *Scale and Scope* (Cambridge, Mass., 1990), 550–63.

Table 7.1. *English Steel Corporation: steel tonnage, 1927*

	River Don Works	Openshaw	Taylor's Trafford Park	Cyclops	Grimesthorpe	Penistone	TOTAL	GRAND TOTAL
Open-hearth ingots	86,886	14,655	70,080		42,528	130,133	344,492	368,671
Electric furnace ingots	7,877	850					8,627	
Crucible	713			351			1,064	
Castings	2,344	285			6,292		8,921	
Iron castings		1,988			1,149		3,137	
Armour-plate	401	271		727	1,031		2,430	
Hydraulic press forgings	10,329	3,780			4,479			18,588
Hammered forgings	13,220	1,126		4,753	1,600	545	21,344	41,529
Light forgings		1,260			1,245		2,505	
Axle forgings			8,859	8,831			17,680	
Cogging mill	37,810	2,739				78,011	118,560	129,018
Rails						10,458	10,458	
Bar mill	8,005	3,011				10,513	21,529	24,680
Rod mill	1,884						1,884	
Guide mill	1,267						1,267	
Sheet mill	800							800
Tyres	5,923		26,888			12,546		45,357
Stampings and forgings	9,150							9,150
Springs								
Coiled	246				1,335			1,581
Volute	57							57
Laminated rail	1,712				2,937			4,649
Laminated road	1,327							1,327
Buffers					161			161
Motor frames	1,150							1,150
Files	277				380			657
Wheel centres			21,132					21,132

Source: SCL ESC Papers. G. R. T. Taylor, Report to Directors, Sept. 1928.

some integrated steelworks. They were astounded by the Illinois Steel Co. in Gary, one of the largest works in the world, which they found 'difficult to speak of . . . without using superlatives'. Illinois Steel was producing as much steel every month or so as the Sheffield firm produced in a year! The output was not directly comparable (the Americans concentrating on carbon steel qualities, not alloys), and Sheffield was judged better at producing the superlative grades of steel, but what impressed the Sheffielders was the 'extraordinary cleanliness and order of steel-making plant, which in Sheffield is always associated with grime, dirt and disorder'.[17] Bill Pugh, who later became a deputy chairman of the ESC, worked at Illinois Steel in the late 1920s and also found Illinois Steel 'an extraordinary place'. Though Pugh found that the amount of scrap the firm produced was 'frightening', its laboratory was first-class: it housed about 250 staff, who had a 30-ton furnace 'just to play with'.[18]

At the River Don Works, in contrast, the melting furnaces were judged obsolete, the casting pits cramped and overmanned, and the slow melting rate prevented the production of clean steel. Although parts of the Cammell sites were slightly better, all the ESC's works needed extensive modernization and capital expenditure. On the forging side, the picture was equally depressing. Through its connection with the Wolseley Car Co., Vickers had become predominant in the highly profitable drop-forging trade for the car industry before 1914. During the War, however, competitors gained experience rapidly, while Vickers was forced to expand its plant with little thought to layout and economy, and the shortage of capital goods meant that unsuitable drop hammers were installed. As technical requirements rose during the War and after, Vickers suddenly found its drop-forging works were obsolete, wasteful in fuel, and technically deficient. A report noted that in 1931 much of the departmental transport was by hand-barrows! By the inter-war period, it seems that Vickers and Cammell had even fallen behind in an area in which Sheffield had traditionally excelled—research. Bill Pugh believes that the ESC was not spending enough on research at this time, a view supported by a contemporary review of expenditure by the director of the ESC Laboratories at the River Don Works, Harry Dickenson: he found that spending on research was initially a mere $4\frac{1}{2}$ pence per ton. Modernization was needed to introduce routine metallographic analysis and to increase the funding for speculative research.[19]

Against this troubled backdrop, the ESC, backed by the findings and views from a small army of accountants, directors, management consult-

[17] SCL ESC Papers. 'Report on a Visit to Steel Works . . . in the United States', Apr. and May 1928.   [18] W. D. Pugh interview, 29 June 1992.
[19] SCL ESC Papers. J. H. S. Dickenson, 'Report on Metallurgical and Research Department, Vickers Works, Estimated Expenditure for 1930', 28 May 1930.

ants, and bankers, attempted to formulate a coherent strategy. The first idea, popular in the early days of the merger, was for a completely new green-field site (probably near the coast) at a projected cost of some £2 million. This was the plan favoured by the Bank of England, whose chairman and experts had a peripheral influence in ESC matters through their financial links with Vickers.[20] Firth-Brown was also brought into the negotiations for the creation of a super steel and forging plant. But in Sheffield this plan soon fell by the wayside. Discussions with Firth-Brown lasted a year or two, but never looked likely to succeed. The ESC was worried about Firth-Brown's indebtedness to the banks. Firth-Brown, in turn, was reluctant to become involved with the ESC's sprawl of companies, having just implemented its own more tightly-focused rationalization and having a different outlook and product mix, centred around its eminent research laboratories.

The depressed steel business—in 1929 none of the ESC works were making a profit—also bred caution rather than boldness, and there was no stomach for the huge cost involved. As one Firth-Brown director argued:

if the maximum efficiency is to be obtained, not only should steel melting furnaces, forging presses, treatment plants and machine shops be erected, but blast furnaces and coke ovens should also be available so as to obtain the utmost thermal efficiency from getting the ore to the production of the finished article. Such a scheme would run into many millions. Thus it appears that the wiser course would be to make improvements in the best of the existing plants . . . until such time as the new company can be shown to be capable of earning profits, when a still further concentration of plants might be gradually undertaken.[21]

The ESC agreed. A plan for a new site was rejected and the combine decided to try and achieve results 'reasonably approximating to those which a complete rebuilding would give, with a minimum of capital expenditure'.[22] This meant utilizing the existing set-up along revised lines, as follows:

1. Forging was concentrated at the River Don Works after the forging plant at Grimesthorpe was closed and the forge at Whitworth Street was dismantled. The massive 7,000-ton Grimesthorpe press (installed in 1914 for the manufacture of gear wheels and hardly ever run continuously) was reconditioned and transferred to the River Don Works.

2. Steel casting production was concentrated at Grimesthorpe.

3. Spring production was located at Grimesthorpe.

4. Tyre, wheel, and axle production was concentrated at Taylor Bros., the plant at Penistone being dismantled.

[20] Tolliday, *Business, Banking and Politics*, 195–7.
[21] SCL Firth-Brown Records. A. J. Grant to Lord Aberconway, 18 Dec. 1928.
[22] SCL ESC Papers. Viscount Falmouth, 'Report on Reconstruction' (Nov. 1931), 1.

5. Armour-plate production was concentrated at River Don, the plant at Manchester being dismantled and the sites at Grimesthorpe and Cyclops being retained in reserve.

6. Production of basic steel billets at Penistone was abandoned and the whole of the plant was dismantled and the buildings and site sold.

7. The Whitworth Street Works was sold to the Admiralty in 1939, who erected new buildings and installed plant for gun and gun-mounting production, which was operated by Vickers Armstrong Ltd. during the War.

8. The East Cyclops Works was cleared of plant and the buildings and site sold to Thos. W. Ward Ltd., which later passed them to Firth-Brown. File manufacture was transferred to Holme Lane and tool steel production to North Street, Manchester.

9. At the North Street Works all buildings and plant other than those used in the manufacture of tool steels and engineers' tools were dismantled.

By 1932, the ESC had also absorbed a neighbouring open-hearth steelmaker, Industrial Steels Ltd., which had been founded in 1921 to supply steels for cars, aircraft, the railways, and textile machines. It also decided to buy Darlington Forge for about £0.5 million and concentrate its forging capacity there, so realizing at least part of the plan for a first-rate forge plant on the north-east coast. However, the original scheme for a green-field site outside Sheffield became a fading memory.

Was the ESC's strategy correct? It was certainly logical, especially the decision to retain Sheffield as a centre. Local skill in alloys and forgings was crucial, ensuring that the idea of moving the whole Brightside operations of Vickers and Cammell was never realistic. The ESC recognized that the tradition of skill and craftsmanship at Vickers and Cammell was 'still an important factor in the trade'.[23] This was especially so in view of the ESC's wide product range. As one director noted in 1930:

we are already making over 120 different types of steel. These range in composition from simple carbon steels to highly alloyed steels containing large percentages of nickel, cobalt, tungsten, chromium and other elements. In size the articles manufactured from these steels range from hacksaws weighing an ounce or so, through small tools, motor car parts, railway forgings and ships shafting, to the largest gun forgings and reaction chambers made anywhere in the world. As regards form, we produce tubes, castings, forgings, drop-forgings, bars, billets, and a very great variety of finished steel articles, permanent magnets, railway springs, road springs, finished motor car and railway cranks. We do not make structural steel sections, rails, ship and boiler plate, or cheap dead mild steels, and are entirely engaged on steels which may be classed as either good quality

[23] Ibid. 17.

engineering steels or forgings and special steels, but as regards these it covers a range of type which is not exceeded by any firm in the world and probably equalled only by Krupps in Germany and the Bethlehem Steel Co in America, the latter being a little doubtful.[24]

Sheffield as a site, though at a slight disadvantage for certain products, was in no sense inferior to any other location when this diversity of products was taken into consideration, especially since many completed products were destined for Yorkshire, Lancashire, the Midlands, and the South. The massive cost of a new works could also have been disastrous in the early 1930s: as it was, such was the severity of the depression, that the ESC's issued capital had to be written down in 1931 from £7,884,447 to £2,511,669, when the Corporation ran at a loss.[25] Industrial Steels was liquidated as a separate company in 1934 and was later known as the Stevenson Road Works. Darlington Forge was mothballed between 1932 and 1936 and its capital reconstructed. On the other hand, the Bank of England and some of ESC's own directors, such as Lionel Hichens, were probably right in pressing for a more rational layout based upon an entirely new site.[26] By patching-in, the ESC found a workable solution to a very complicated problem, but the River Don site was left with a legacy of poor layout and congestion, which influenced its development until the late 1950s, when an attempt was made to make a clean break with its nineteenth-century legacy.

Nevertheless, there was nothing wrong with the ESC's execution of its more limited rationalization plan. The chairman, (Sir) Charles Craven, with his 'irresistible energy [and] his back-to-the-wall toughness',[27] forced through during the 1930s a massive expenditure programme of over £1.5 million. The heaviest investments were at the River Don Works in an array of three 60-ton open-hearth furnaces and new electric furnaces (including two 10-ton arcs). The forge was also reconstructed and the 7,000-ton press installed.[28] By 1938 ESC could cast open-hearth ingots up to 250 tons; and forgings could be made up to 230 tons with the big press.

---

[24] SCL ESC Papers. Alex Williamson, 'General Report on Prospects', 23 Apr. 1930.

[25] After 1931, Vickers held 65% of the ordinary share capital and 81% of the preference shares; Cammell-Laird the rest. An issue of 848,340 ordinary shares of £1 each was made in 1936 for cash, the shares being taken by Vickers and Cammell-Laird pro rata.

[26] Hichens, in particular, was critical of the ESC's changes in policy after 1929. He told the ESC chairman, Charles Craven, that after Darlington Forge was acquired 'our satisfaction was short-lived for the scene changed once more with astonishing rapidity. Before the ink of the agreement was dry the rats of doubt began to gnaw at our vitals; more experts were called in who proceeded to contradict everything that anyone had ever said and left us—if not in the dark, at any rate in Sheffield and there we are to this day.' SCL ESC Papers. Hichens to Craven, 20 July 1932.

[27] J. D. Scott, *Vickers: A History* (London, 1962), 193–4.

[28] 'New Siemens Melting Plant', *Metallurgia*, 8 (Sept. 1933), 135–8; 'A New Heavy Forge', ibid. 11 (Mar. 1935), 141–2.

There was also a new drop forge and improvements in forging, rolling, and heat-treatment plant.

On the research side, Harry Dickenson succeeded in reinvigorating the ESC's research facility.[29] Although this did not match the Brown-Firth Research Laboratories, Dickenson and his staff of about 80 launched a major research effort into stainless and heat-resisting steels, since the chemical industries were 'almost clamorous for a steel which will resist sulphuric and sulphurous acids'.[30] He also investigated the influence of nickel on high-chromium steels and the effect of mass and 'ageing' on cobalt magnet steels; and began researching the internal structure or 'heterogeneity' of steel ingots. Dickenson became a specialist in the movement and failure of metals subjected to stress at high temperatures, a phenomenon known as 'creep'. In 1930 he reported that the installation of six greatly improved tensile creep-testing units and one new torsional creep-testing unit had almost been completed, and that he was about to commence creep tests on various special steels for boiler drums, superheater tubes, and valves at elevated temperatures. As he stated: 'Steam and other engineers are anxiously awaiting new alloy steels capable of reasonably cheap production, but giving greater strength at high temperatures than is at present attainable.'[31] Although he died prematurely before the significance of his work was properly appreciated, Dickenson laid the modern foundation for creep tests.

Trading conditions improved slightly in 1933 and in the following year the ESC swung back into the black. In 1935 a profit of £539,337 enabled the payment of a first dividend of 20 per cent on the ordinary shares; and after that profits increased substantially. The ESC board could be criticized for piecemeal expansion and making do with existing plant, rather than starting afresh, but nevertheless the ESC remains one of the most successful merger schemes in this period.

The same factors that had brought together United Steel and the English Steel Corporation also strengthened the links between Thomas Firth & Sons and John Brown's. Although Brown's still held the majority shareholding in Firth's, the latter still functioned very much as a separate company. In 1922 a directorate had been set up 'to promote a more thorough system of co-operative working and to suggest how best the interests of the two firms could be served in future by partial or complete amalgamation if found desirable'.[32] But little was done. For the moment, Firth's remained a curious mixture of the old-fashioned and the new. It

[29] 'Research Laboratories at ESC', ibid. 5 (Jan. 1932), 73–6.
[30] SCL ESC Papers. J. H. S. Dickenson, 'Metallurgical and Research Department Report, 1931', 3 Mar. 1932.
[31] Ibid. Dickenson, 'Metallurgical Research Programme for 1931', 18 Dec. 1930.
[32] SCL Firth-Brown Records. Firth's Directors' Minute Book, meeting 30 Mar. 1922.

was one of the most dynastic of the major Sheffield steel firms. Bernard Firth (1866–1929) was chairman of Firth's until his death, when an obituary described him as a 'Conservative of the old school . . . [for whom] . . . it was a matter of regret that owing to the growing volume of business . . . it was impossible for him to be personally acquainted with all the workmen employed by the firm.'[33] Firth's, however, also had professional managers and some brilliant technologists, such as W. H. Hatfield (1882–1943), who had succeeded Harry Brearley as head of the Brown-Firth Research Laboratory.

Firth's strengths and weaknesses were reflected in its business performance in the 1920s, which was uneven. Its Riga subsidiary had disappeared during the War and the Pittsburgh steelworks became steadily less profitable. In response, Firth's decided to enter the expanding market for motor car forgings; took a minority shareholding in Huntsman's crucible steelworks; tried to expand in Australia; and pondered the possibilities of linking with the Coventry Ordnance Works and Rolls-Royce. This scattergun approach produced one notable success—the establishment of Firth-Derihon Stampings Ltd. in 1919 for high-quality forged components. This venture was based upon the pioneering work of a Belgian refugee, J. Julien, who had brought to Sheffield his expertise in the control of grain flow in drop-forged aero-engine valves. This involved an extensive use of hand-forging prior to the use of the closed drop-hammer die. With an initial capital of £120,000 (split at first between Firth's and Julien, though later the company became a wholly-owned Firth subsidiary), Firth–Derihon Stampings began business in the old National Shell Factory in Tinsley. The company rapidly made a name for itself in the drop-stamping trade by paying particular attention to quality and to liaison with its main customers in the car and aircraft industries.[34]

Aside from this initiative, Firth's was most successful in basic research and development through the Brown-Firth Laboratories. Its star material was stainless steel, launched successfully during the First World War and licensed by the Firth-Brearley Stainless Steel Syndicate.[35] Firth's also became in the early 1920s the leading stainless steel producer in the world, pioneering both its manufacture and marketing. Already the market Firth's was targeting was huge. As yet, though, the trade was confined to cutlery-type (martensitic) stainless steel, which was mostly supplied in bar, or as forgings or castings. This was because Brearley's original 13 per cent chromium steel had one great drawback: its hardness made it difficult to roll into sheets, making it unsuitable for mass production. How-

---

[33] *SDT*, 19 Feb. 1929.
[34] Allan Grant, *Steel and Ships* (London, 1950), 75–6; 'Forging Steel Components', *Metallurgia*, 14 (May 1936), 1–4.
[35] SCL Firth-Brown Records. Firth-Brearley Stainless Steel Syndicate Files.

ever, the two Krupp pioneers of stainless steel, Eduard Maurer and Benno Strauss, had already found a solution to this problem: their version of the alloy (austenitic stainless steel) had an addition of nickel, which allowed its rolling into sheet.

In 1923 Firth's did a straight swop with the Germans: they exchanged their martensitic expertise for Krupp's austenitic breakthrough, plus a royalty of 3 per cent; while both firms agreed to keep out of each other's country, with the neutral markets of the world being divided between them in competition with others. A key figure at this time was W. H. Hatfield. Sheffield-born (his father was a manager at the cutlers, Joseph Rodgers) and another protégé of Oliver Arnold, Hatfield emerged during the inter-war period as one of Sheffield's finest research metallurgists.[36] In the popular mind, he made no famous breakthrough to compare with his predecessor's stainless alloy, but he excelled Brearley in other ways: hard-working and ambitious, he was more commercially minded than Brearley and proved superb at product development, especially in his chosen field of rust-, acid-, and heat-resisting steels. Once the Krupp agreement was reached, he launched a major investigation of the austenitic corrosion-resistant steels and produced a better version than Krupp's. This was Firth's famous 18/8 (18 per cent chromium with 8 per cent nickel) steel, which was to become the world's most widely used type of stainless steel.

The 18/8 alloy—marketed by Firth's as 'Staybrite'—opened a huge market to Firth's and other Sheffield firms, since the uses of a steel with good formability and corrosion-resistance appeared almost limitless.[37] Martensitic stainless still held its place for products that needed a good cutting edge, such as cutlery. But in other products, the true mass market in stainless steel—everything from the kitchen sink to the shop front—had arrived. For polishing its stainless sheets, in 1926 Firth's acquired a Blackheath works, Padley & Price. Noted one Sheffield newspaper in 1926:

The last four years have been a time of steady but continuous progress in the adaptation of this new and wonderful alloy to industrial purposes, and the pace had been accelerated by the development of . . . 'Staybrite' . . . which being more

---

[36] George B. Waterhouse, 'The Services to Metallurgy of the late W. H. Hatfield FRS', *JISI* 153/1 (1946), 369–75. See also Hatfield, 'Developments and Applications of Acid and Heat-Resisting Steels', *Metallurgia*, 17 (Dec. 1937), 53–5; id., 'Corrosion and Heat Resisting Steel', ibid. 19 (Dec. 1938), 59–61.

[37] See John Trueman, 'The Initiation and Growth of High Alloy (Stainless) Steel Production', *JHMS* 19 (1985), 116–25; and G. Tweedale, *Sheffield Steel and America* (Cambridge, 1987), 75–83. K. C. Barraclough offers an overview in 'Sheffield and the Development of Stainless Steel', *Ironmaking and Steelmaking*, 16 (1989), 253–65, a paper described as the result of research sponsored by British Steel Stainless. But it appears to owe much to Trueman's pathbreaking account and to my own work, though curiously neither is credited.

malleable and offering greater resistance to corrosion than the earlier compositions, [has] widened the possibilities of application, not only in the industrial but even in the domestic field, as [it will] make excellent spoons and forks and hollow-ware vessels.[38]

The chemical industry, to give only one example, was a major application for 18/8 stainless steel. One of the early milestones was the erection of the first stainless steel plant in the world at the ICI Works at Billingham in 1929. Across the Atlantic, American-manufactured 18/8 was given its most prominent advertisement in New York when it was used for the facing of the Chrysler Building and in the pilasters of the Empire State Building. The metals are still as brilliant at the end of the twentieth century as they were when they were constructed in the late 1920s. In the United Kingdom 'Staybrite' was superbly marketed by Firth's as they took on the task of educating the consumer in its usage. 'Staybrite City' at the *Daily Mail* Ideal Homes Exhibition in 1934 was a typically imaginative marketing coup.[39]

It was soon found that other materials—molybdenum, tungsten, copper, and silicon—could be added to the 18/8 types, either singly or in combination, to improve their corrosion resistance. Again, this knowledge spread rapidly through the Don Valley. 'Anka' (Brown Bayley's), 'Maxilvry' (Edgar Allen), 'CR3' (Hadfields), 'KE 965' (Kayser Ellison), and 'HR Crown' (Firth's), rapidly appeared in the late 1920s as examples of modified 18/8 steels. By raising the nickel in this class of steels to 20–40 per cent, corrosion resistance at high temperatures was improved. Hadfields' 'ATV' and Brown Bayley's 'Hotspur' alloys were variants.[40]

Technical advances in these steels were soon occurring across a broad front, with Sheffield for the moment keeping ahead of any foreign competition. It is not always possible to attribute priority in stainless steel advances, but not surprisingly Hatfield and Firth's retained their prime position in research and manufacture. Many problems needed to be overcome. Hatfield's solution of the problem of corrosion in welded joints of stainless steel ('weld-decay'), by adding elements such as titanium, was one highlight from amongst many.

This outstanding record of research and development undoubtedly helped Firth's through the difficult 1920s; but it was hardly enough by itself to ensure prosperity in an industry dogged by overcapacity and

[38] *SDT*, 30 Dec. 1926.
[39] Firth-Brown Ltd., *The Staybrite Book* (Sheffield, 1934). See also British Steel Stainless, *75 Years of Stainless Steel, 1913–1988* (Sheffield, 1988), 20–2.
[40] The following little-known accounts offer perhaps the best contemporary view of these events: R. Wadell, 'The Properties and Engineering Uses of Stainless Steel', *Brown Bayley's Journal* (30 Aug. 1927), 57–73; J. H. G. Monypenny, 'Corrosion-Resisting Steels and Their Applications' ibid. (23 July 1930), 109–51; id., 'Corrosion-Resisting Steels for Chemical Plant', ibid. (10 Aug. 1931).

inefficiency. Between 1923 and 1926, Firth's paid no ordinary share dividend; and though net profits lifted from below £100,000 in 1925 to nearly £160,000 in 1928 (enabling the payment of a $6\frac{1}{2}$ per cent dividend in 1929), a closer link with Brown's was becoming inevitable. Brown's had pushed ahead with its own technical developments, particularly in case-hardening. A 'Nitralloy' class of steels was developed, which could be hardened to an unprecedented degree by a simple low-temperature treatment in ammonia gas. In another sphere, the use of high-pressure superheated steam for turbines led to the intensive analysis of the properties of carbon steel at elevated temperatures, which in turn was the basis for the manufacture of huge, forged, seamless steel boiler drums. These became a speciality of Brown's at the end of the 1920s and by 1929 about 130 of them had been turned out by the Atlas Works.[41] These were the bright spots in a company crippled by the fall in armour-plate and shipbuilding orders and the disruptions in the coal trade.

In 1930 a proper merger of the steelmaking interests of Brown's and Firth's was agreed. Thomas Firth & John Brown Ltd. was formed, with the transfer of Firth's Atlas and Scunthorpe works to Brown's, with the latter acquiring a further large shareholding in that company. The authorized capital was set at £5 million (£1,562,500 issued), with Brown's owning almost all the ordinary shares. The fit between Brown's heavy steel trade in forgings and Firth's in special steels and tools allowed the pooling of electric melting capacity at Firth's; the closure of the old crucible shop, with the installation of new furnaces; while at Brown's the Siemens' plant was remodelled to permit the production of ingots over 200 tons. All foundry work was transferred to Scunthorpe and in 1934 Firth-Brown opened a new Engineers' Tool Factory on Carlisle Street for its 'Insto' saws, 'Millenicut' files, and 'Speedicut' high-speed tools.

There was much talk of 'economies' and 'rationalization' from the John Brown chairman, Lord Aberconway, and the new organization certainly centralized different types of melting operations. In some respects, it was an impressive set-up: its 30-ton electric arc furnace was then the largest in Europe and it was complemented by new high-frequency capacity; its expertise in hollow-drum forging and hardened steel roll production was state of the art; and it was a European leader in stainless steel, only perhaps conceding a little to the Americans here in terms of tonnage. But it was all much tidier than Aberconway made it appear, since both the Atlas Works and the Norfolk Works were badly broken up by roads and railways into, in effect, nine separate units—a legacy from the nineteenth century. Aside from this, Firth-Brown had two works at Tinsley (for forgings and stainless steel), a foundry at Scunthorpe, and a factory at

---

[41] 'John Brown & Co.: Progress in Hollow Forged Drums', *SDT*, 31 Dec. 1929.

Table 7.2. *Firth-Brown output, 1930*

Product	Tonnage	Value (£)
Armaments	1,200	195,404
Forged boiler drums	2,206	150,197
Forgings	6,459	302,923
Tyres and axles	8,284	187,163
Carbon and alloy steels	8,692	259,432
Stainless	3,280	434,389
Crucible steels	699	105,587
Hardened steel rolls	82	9,670
Springs	2,477	109,122
Nitralloy	237	13,259
Engineers' tools	536	181,120
Foundries	4,289	175,355
Drop stampings	2,010	120,509
Stainless foundries	127	25,231
Cold-rolled stainless strip	86	24,949
TOTAL	40,644	2,294,310

Sources: SCL Firth-Brown Records. Directors' Reports.

Blackheath. Though Firth-Brown's spread of products was very wide, giving it strength in the manufacture of specialities (see Table 7.2), the whole organization was not a recipe for the most efficient manufacture.

In the four years between 1930 and 1933, Firth-Brown's net profits totalled a mere £157,541 and no ordinary dividends were paid. But the limits of Firth-Brown's merger and rationalizing sentiments had been reached. When the ESC proposed to extend their merger scheme in 1930 to include Beardmore's and Firth-Brown, it had little support from the latter. Firth-Brown directors were far less impressed than the ESC by the wonders of American large-scale producers, such as US Steel, pointing out that despite the Americans' huge domestic market and tariffs their profits margins were thin and their export performance, compared with the United Kingdom, was weak. Nor did they like the product-mix at the ESC, which was less 'special': in 1931 the ESC sold steel that was typically about £30 per ton, while Firth-Brown's ranged from £60 to £88. They objected to the 'psychological' effects of such a merger, since Firth-Brown's products were so dependent 'upon delicate personal friendship and relationships which can be marred by unknowledgeable handling'.[42] Naturally, a merger with the ESC had no support from W. H. Hatfield,

---

[42] SCL Firth-Brown Records, Report upon Firth-Brown and ESC, 18 Mar. 1931; and attached correspondence.

who saw it as a direct threat to the powerful research effort he had built up at the Laboratories. Instead, he argued for 'benevolent' commercial under-standings—in other words, trade associations—since it appeared to him and other directors at Firth-Brown:

that no advantage can be anticipated from attempts at rationalisation of dissimilar manufactures, even though they may all be branches of the same trade, for their only common ground is the production of the raw steel . . . [though] . . . any prac-ticable scheme that could be evolved for the complete rationalisation of similar products would have our hearty support. That is, separate rationalisation of the whole of the heavy forging trade of the country, of the steel foundry trade, of the railway tyre, axle and spring business, etc . . . But from the nature of things, owing to the large number of firms of all sorts dealing with almost each class of manufac-ture, this appears to be impracticable of voluntary achievement.[43]

There was one area, however, where the chances of a merger with the ESC were more promising—stainless steel. Even in the depression this was Firth-Brown's most profitable product, since the firm had about 80 per cent of the home market and substantial overseas sales. Even in the depression demand soared and by 1933 Firth-Brown's stainless orders had topped £0.5 million. However, supplying the burgeoning demand was already becoming a problem. It was becoming clear that this was an area that would require continuous heavy investment in plant and mar-keting organization; far greater resources, in fact, than could be provided by Firth-Brown, which had a £650,000 overdraft in the early 1930s. When the ESC's Charles Craven, anxious for his firm to gain a foothold in a major market, suggested a deal, Firth-Brown readily agreed. In October 1934 the ESC agreed to pay Firth-Brown £307,500 for its stainless steel interests and also to pay £390,000 for shares in a new company—Firth Vickers Stainless Steels Ltd.—with the ESC taking half the shares offered to Firth-Brown. Production was centred on Firth's Tinsley Works in Weedon Street, with Firth-Brown also occupying the empty Cyclops Works in Savile Street, where new rolling mills and heat-treatment plant were erected. The firm made a steady start and when capital was in-creased to £1.1 million in 1936 turnover was well over £1 million. It was a shrewd deal for Firth-Brown, since it improved its cash flow and pre-served a large measure of control, something that was to cause resentment from the ESC almost from the beginning (see Chapter 9).

Merger was not the chosen route for every firm and for some diversifi-cation was far more congenial. As ever, the position of Hadfields was singular. As we have noted, Sir Robert Hadfield had made this company into the biggest and most profitable arms machine in the city by 1918. As Hadfield well knew, once arms orders vanished, the firm would have to

[43] Ibid., F. C. Fairholme to G. R. T. Taylor, 30 Apr. 1931.

pay the price for its expansion. Naturally, he had no intention that Hadfields should lose its powerful position. Immediately after the War, while he hounded government ministries for subsidies and orders to prevent the closure of its armour-piercing shell plant and also glorified the firm's war work, he began a major reorganization. With characteristic energy, he tore down most of the old shell shops, mothballed much of the Hecla plant, and concentrated production at the East Hecla site where he installed a new electrically-driven rolling mill. In the immediate post-war euphoria, Hadfield was optimistic. 'What we all want to do', he urged, 'is to put our shoulders to the wheel and produce, produce, produce.'[44] But as the short boom melted away and the firm was hit by rising wages, higher raw materials costs, and shortages of skilled moulders, the impact of the War on Hadfields became all too apparent. The conflict had seen a formidable rise in overheads, particularly establishment charges.[45] Accounting procedures had become lax under the pressure of the War, leading Hadfield on one occasion to complain about the 'succession of weird figures [on output and profit], which to my mind simply mean nothing of value'.[46] Comparing the situation in 1913 and 1923, Hadfield found that despite a quadrupling of the issued capital, turnover had increased from £1.5 million to only £1.9 million; a drop in turnover in terms of real value, which Hadfield stated 'almost seems incredible'.[47]

Some disturbing trends underlay these figures. Hadfields' technical lead was much thinner now that the chairman's alloy steel patents had expired and fresh discoveries were becoming harder to find. The demand for castings had also begun to stagnate, as growth in the industry switched to rolled products and the newer heat-resisting and stainless steels for cars and aircraft. National labour problems in the 1920s had also ended the stable labour relations at Hadfields and for the first time in its history the company had disputes with its workforce, beginning with a three-month moulders' strike in 1919, which cut an estimated output of 29,000 tons of steel castings by a quarter. Hadfield himself was growing old. He had turned 60 in 1918 and three years later a major operation for a fistula meant that, henceforth, Hadfield needed the regular ministrations of a male nurse. This at a time when major strategy decisions were needed, if Hadfields was to maintain is position.

Before 1914 Hadfields had no major involvement with any other firm, apart from the chairman's extensive overseas licences and the firm's oc-

---

[44] Letter on the steel industry, *The Times*, 11 Nov. 1920.
[45] SCL Hadfield Papers. 'Report by Mr. Brown and Major Clerke in conformity with the request embodied in the chairman's memo L. 7856. Dated Aug. 18, 1920'. At the East Hecla Works the numbers of supervisory and research staff had risen from 411 to 563, with a corresponding rise in the wages bill from £1,025 to £2,886.
[46] Ibid. Hadfield to board, 22 May 1920.   [47] Ibid. Hadfield to board, 31 Jan. 1924.

casional linkages with other arms producers and companies supplying raw materials. Hadfield's liking for personal control combined with the enormous demands that the firm's Sheffield activities made on the management, meant that little thought could be spared for outside operations. After 1918 the need for new lines of business meant that this position was reversed as Hadfields began investing in other companies and acquiring subsidiaries.

This radical change in strategy was undertaken by a management that remained virtually unchanged throughout the inter-war period. Such stability was undoubtedly important in the highly specialized world of steel casting and armour-piercing shell manufacture, and Hadfield and his long-serving team ensured that the company avoided the tortuous boardroom intrigues that afflicted other armaments giants, such as Vickers. In Sheffield at this time, Hadfields' works management was under the joint directorship of (Sir) Peter B. Brown (1866–1948) and Major Augustus B. H. Clerke (1871–1949). Brown, alongside his chairman, was one of the longest-serving members of the firm, having joined as assistant manager and draughtsman in 1888. Described as a man 'of great tact and ability, which was demonstrated by advancement from one position of responsibility to another',[48] he was made deputy chairman in 1930 and succeeded to the chairmanship ten years later. Clerke had become a Hadfield director in 1913, having acquired his early experience as an inspector at the Royal Arsenal. Other important board members included John B. Thomas, the financial director; William B. Pickering, the commercial director; and William E. Parker, the local director.

Even before the outbreak of the First World War, Hadfield had begun to delegate the everyday running of the works to these men. He moved to fashionable Carlton House Terrace in London, so that he could become more involved in the scientific milieu of the technical societies, which he relished so much, and—more importantly—be on the doorstep of the supply ministries for armament orders. Regular winter spells at his villa in the South of France also meant that Hadfield had less time to devote to Sheffield affairs. Nevertheless, he was still a frequent visitor to the works in the 1920s, driving up from the capital to his mansion, Parkhead House, in his Rolls-Royce (which was driven at a speed at which he could dictate to his male secretaries). One secretary recalled how: 'Things would start to liven up after the London message had been passed that "the old man's coming up for a few days"; his big first floor office [at Hecla Works] was always ready.'[49] All policy decisions were referred to him and, through a constant stream of hundreds of cables and telephone messages, he kept a

[48] Ibid. William Francis Kett typescript notes, n.d., 162.
[49] Late Marjorie Sheard, letter to author, 16 Aug. 1991.

strong hand over his directors, who rarely appeared to have questioned his decisions. The distinctive red-lined memoranda that have survived amongst the company files show the immense energy that Hadfield poured into the running of the firm. His large personal shareholding, his formidable reputation in metallurgy, and his capacity to inspire loyalty in the board, ensured that he retained his hold over the company and its compliant shareholders until almost the end of his life.

His business strategy was still characterized by its independence. He declined to ally the firm with any of its rivals (as Firth's and Brown's had done), and instead devised his own schemes. Since United Kingdom arms orders were so scarce, he looked across the Atlantic for a way of exploiting Hadfields' lead in armour-piercing shell manufacture. In 1919 Hadfields went into partnership with an Ohio maker of brick and cement machinery, forming the Hadfield-Penfield Co.[50] It was a realization of Hadfield's long-standing dream to begin production in America—the world's biggest market for alloy steels. Hadfield intended to use this partnership to exploit American Goverment orders for projectiles (a feat already accomplished by Firth's subsidiary in Pittsburgh), with the added attraction that it might also provide an entrée into the United States manganese steel and commercial castings market. Meanwhile, at home Hadfields acquired an interest in Bean Cars, a West Midlands-based firm, which the Sheffielders hoped would both provide an outlet for surplus alloy steel and give the firm a route into an entirely new industry.[51] The move into the car market, which was strengthened in 1926 when Hadfield took complete control of Bean Cars, was a popular one amongst the steel and engineering firms: BSA, Vickers, Armstrong-Whitworth, and Beardmores were all attracted, for better or worse, into car production.

Hadfield also tried to maintain the company's technological edge. The trend towards stainless and heat-resisting steels in the inter-war period was one to which the firm could relatively easily adapt and Hadfield poured resources into this area in an attempt to carve his own niche. Building on wartime experience with aero-engine steels, Hadfield concentrated on exploiting stainless steel's special advantages at elevated temperatures. The result was 'ATV' steel, with 20–40 per cent nickel, which could withstand high temperatures and corrosion attack and so provide a superior alternative to bronze in turbine blades. Hadfields collaborated on these alloys with the French firm Commentry-Fourchambault et Decazeville, of Imphy. Hadfield also exploited his knowledge of projectile technology to launch another new line: the special hardened steel rolls,

---

[50] Tweedale, *Sheffield Steel*, 121–7.

[51] G. Tweedale, 'Business and Investment Strategies in the Inter-War British Steel Industry: A Case Study of Hadfields Ltd. and Bean Cars, *Business History*, 29 (Jan. 1987), 47–72.

used in many types of rolling plant such as in the production of sheet metals. In a further effort to find new technologies Hadfield succeeded in attracting to Sheffield the American inventor and businessman William Millspaugh (1868–1959), famous for centrifugal bronze castings and his patented suction rolls and papermaking machinery. In 1933 Hadfield leased Millspaugh a site in the East Hecla Works—a factory within a factory—so that he could establish a centrifugal foundry and continue his castings in bronze and steel, as well as develop his suction rolls.

These ventures performed disappointingly. Hadfield-Penfield proved a complete miscalculation: the projectile orders from the American Government never materialized and the firm was unable to establish itself in the United States steel castings market, where there was a good deal of over-capacity in the 1920s. Through no fault of Hadfield, the venture was probably twenty years too late; though the Sheffield firm should bear some of the responsibility for the technological and managerial fiasco that ensued in Ohio. The Hadfield management proved incapable of organizing a business that was several thousand miles distant, despite their regular transatlantic trips. Closer to home, Bean Cars did no better. Unable to find a satisfactory general manager, and without adequate engineering and marketing skills themselves, the Hadfield board was soon out of its depth. By 1931 Bean Cars was bankrupt, having never made a profit. Hadfields' attempts to find a winning commercial formula with its new corrosion and heat-resisting alloys also brought poor returns, since the product was expensive to develop and the market relatively limited. An exasperated Hadfield castigated his fellow directors for their lack of effort and highlighted Firth's success with its new stainless steels, He appears to have blamed everyone but himself. On one of those rare occasions when his views were contested, Peter B. Brown replied:

Firths since the war, as you know, linked up with [Krupps] and got all the advantage of their experience which, of course, gave them a good start. We started much later, and, mainly due to the attitude you personally took up, confined our attention over a very long period to practically ATV steel. We now have a department for pushing these steels, but this takes time. We are all anxious to do the best we can in this direction, but it does not help us much simply to draw attention to what Firths are doing ... Of course, we could make a splash if you would like to give instructions to that effect, and spend £50,000 or £100,000, but that would not end the expenditure. I believe in walking before we start running.[52]

Millspaugh was successfully established at the East Hecla Works, forming the basis for the Millspaugh Group at Hadfields, which manufactured suction rolls and eventually a wide range of paper and pulp machinery. But commercially it hardly offset the firm's major blunders, which proved

---

[52] SCL Hadfield Papers. P. B. Brown to Hadfield, 6 Dec. 1927.

costly. Profits began to dip (see Fig. 3.1), and during the early 1930s the unthinkable happened—Hadfields passed the share dividend for four consecutive years and then wrote down its capital. For the first time shareholders—usually kept completely in the dark about the fine points of the Hadfield balance sheet—began asking awkward questions at the annual meetings: answers to which Hadfield, with his stiff manner and carefully rehearsed speeches, was ill-equipped to provide.

The main problem was the difficult trading conditions of the inter-war period. But Hadfield himself must also carry some of the responsibility, as must his fellow directors. They attempted to transfer a nineteenth-century style of management into the twentieth, with little attempt at modernization. Hadfield's numerous caustic memoranda concerning Bean Cars and his tireless attempts to find world markets for Sheffield steel show that he was far from losing his grip on business events in the 1920s. But undoubtedly the attempt to direct affairs from London or France had its limitations and was far from efficient. At the centre of events in the 1920s Hadfields often endured a degree of incompetence that the absent chairman would never have tolerated; whilst on the periphery, Hadfield often became exasperated with his lack of personal control, complaining to his directors at one point: 'over and over again I am led from pillar to post, constantly misled, first one thing then another, until I do not know what to believe'.[53]

His co-directors, who by the Second World War had a record of over 200 years' service with the company, were broadly Hadfield's contemporaries (significantly, the two most important board members, Brown and Clerke, did not survive the decade of their chairman's death, whilst another, W. E. Parker, died in the same year), and their activities in the past had centred on Hadfield's successful lines in projectiles and engineering steels. None of them had any extensive experience in mechanical engineering of the kind needed to run a car company, or in operating overseas. Consequently, the task of running Hadfields' disparate subsidiaries proved beyond them. The firm became particularly streched during the early 1920s, when it was attempting to run both Bean Cars and the Hadfield-Penfield Co. Remarked Hadfield: 'This rushing over of our reps. [to the United States] won't do at such a critical time. They leave and no one remains . . . It's a pretty kettle of fish.'[54] The management problem appears to have been recognized, but it was impossible to contemplate an overhaul while Hadfield was chairman. He had no intention of retiring. Like many powerful businessmen—the tool steelmaker Arthur Balfour (Lord Riverdale) is another example—Hadfield continued working far too long and completely neglected making any arrangements for a successor.

[53] SCL Hadfield Papers. Hadfield to Brown and Clerke, 17 Mar. 1928.
[54] Ibid. Hadfield memo, 30 Apr. 1923.

Hadfields needed new blood in the 1930s: instead it lived on past glories. Hadfield became an increasingly irritable old man, obsessed by fame and honours. Those who knew him well at this time found that 'his chief interest appeared to be his abiding fame (already assured by his achievements)'.[55] In late 1937 Hadfield had a complete mental and physical breakdown, one of his staff recording that 'the interests which had hitherto held him became burdensome. It was with repugnance that any matter requiring mental effort . . . was brought to his attention, and there was a particular aversion against putting pen to paper . . . the spirit that had sustained him after his serious illness in 1921 was no longer there. The upright military figure had become stooped.'[56] Hadfield died in 1940, aged 81, alone and without an heir, completely burned out after a lifetime's unremitting toil. All told, it had been a magnificent industrial career (whatever one may think of Hadfield's less attractive personal characteristics), which had brilliantly combined science and business. But Hadfields was also a classic case of British industrial decline through 'family' capitalism—the firm aging alongside its great chairman. Certainly, Hadfield's refusal to step down, or groom an heir-apparent, or merge with other firms (such as Firth's, Edgar Allen, or Osborn) probably damaged the firm's long-term prospects—though it was to be some time before this became apparent.

How are we to summarize the development of the Sheffield steel firms in the period from 1918 to the mid-1930s? We may recall that the consensus view amongst historians is that not only did the British steel industry do badly, but its performance was far worse than it might have been: it had too many firms, its plant was out-dated and poorly-located and its productivity low. Overall, writes Kenneth Warren: 'Despite the achievements, the most distinctive legacy of the inter-war years in steel was in problems unsolved and possible solutions compromised.'[57] Particular criticism has been levelled at the industry for its failure to rationalize sufficiently fast, and many historians have been as appalled by the fragmented and Victorian outlook of the industry as were some contemporary critics. Warren cites the remarks of one iron and steel man, who in 1917 stated that what was needed for British steel was, 'nothing short of a complete replacement of the great majority of existing plants by very much larger and more efficient units'[58]—a view with which most historians appear to have agreed.

---

[55] K. Headlam-Morley (Secretary of the Iron and Steel Institute), *British Steelmaker*, 6 (Nov. 1940), 12.

[56] SCL Hadfield Papers. S. A. Main, 'The Hadfields of Sheffield Pioneers in Steel', n.d., ch. 13, p. 2.

[57] K. Warren, 'Iron and Steel', in N. K. Buxton and D. H. Aldcroft, *British Industry Between the Wars* (London, 1979), 103–28, 125.

[58] Ibid. 105.

Leaving aside the question of whether these criticisms are justified overall—and not every steel historian has accepted this verdict[59]—we may note that, again, the argument has been entirely confined to the tonnage side of the industry. Sheffield and its special steels have rarely been considered. In that city, the situation we have described was highly complex, making simple conclusions hazardous. The most advanced steel technologies—electric melting and new research laboratories—operated alongside centuries-old hand-processes, such as the crucible. Similarly, large corporate empires—the ESC, Firth-Brown, United Steel—were surrounded by scores of small steelmaking enterprises that in business organization and marketing techniques were as old as the crucible process itself.

Sheffield certainly had many weaknesses: too many firms, selling too many similar products, in a world where standardization was increasing. But this can be balanced by the considerable achievements of Sheffield manufacturers in retaining a large share of foreign trade despite increasingly self-sufficient markets; and by the attempts of the major firms to diversify and rationalize. There was also the city's outstanding research record. It can be safely stated that in the large-scale production of alloy steels, Sheffield still had a pervading influence in world steel, even if it was increasingly sharing this position with Germany and America. The 1920s was far from a 'black decade' for special steels. It saw the introduction of stainless and heat-resisting steels, the development of high-frequency electric melting, and the mastering of the techniques of producing hollow steel drums and 200-ton forgings. Certainly in the first of these, and probably in the second, Sheffield was a world leader in the 1920s; and it was up with the American and Continental producers in forging expertise. It was also a world-class producer of hardened steel rolls, magnets, and high-quality tool steels and tools. If its research institutions gave something away to some American and German firms in size, they conceded little in terms of quality. In the field of alloy steel research, the Brown-Firth Research Laboratory under Hatfield had emerged in the 1920s as second to none. Mention should also be made of Sheffield University's steadily expanding department of metallurgy (and engineering) under first Professor C. H. Desch and then his successor J. H. Andrew. The University's links were still exceptionally close with local industrialists, who continued making a steady stream of donations. It was in their interests to do so: the steelworks benefited from its courses—especially the Associateship in Metallurgy—which gave them a supply of well-trained staff, through courses which were effectively subsidized.[60]

---

[59] See Andrews and Brunner, *Capital Development*, 347–67.

[60] The University's industrial work was regularly featured in the New Year Industrial Supplements of the *SDT*. See e.g. 'Sheffield University's Close Link With Industry',

In retrospect, one is struck by the constraining influences, especially the massive inertia created by the historical structure of firms and their highly fragmented layout. This had been exacerbated by the First World War. It was also partly a reflection of the specialized and varied nature of much of the United Kingdom demand for steel from the engineering and consumer goods industries. The rationalization schemes that had resulted in United Steel, the ESC, and Firth-Brown were on the whole a well-balanced response to this situation. Historians might lament that these firms did not scrap the legacy of the past and start afresh—but this was never a serious option in the depressed 1920s and in a city that was so dependent upon skilled labour and its cluster of related trades. Instead, Sheffield industrialists chose business organizations that freed them as much as possible from the dead weight of the past, while preserving traditional strengths that stemmed from individualism and ancient skills in manipulating steel. And in the depths of the depression of the early 1930s, they, like everyone else, simply hoped for the best.

ibid., 31 Dec. 1931. Professor W. B. Pickering stressed to me the steel industry's reliance on the A. Met., an evening course, for which it never paid the full cost. Interview with author, 12 Nov. 1991.

8

Individualism in the Era of Mass-Produced Cutlery and Tools

The reputation of certain Sheffield cutlery is world-wide and the competition of cheapness and mass production can accordingly be withstood—within limits. But, while Sheffield skill counts for a great deal in this trade, as in every other of the city's industries, the old order is being appreciably undermined. In the old days, the illiterate Indian sought the sign of Sheffield reputation on his knives. Now, the more literate Indian has new and more nicely commercial standards; he balances price against price, and may in the end buy Japanese.

'Sheffield Steel and Cutlery', *The Economist*, 130 (26 March 1938), 688.

The 1920s and 1930s were also black decades for the Sheffield cutlery and tool trades. However, as was the case with special steels, negative trends for the industry—such as growing international competition, trade depressions, the erosion of craft skills, and changing consumer demand—were offset by other developments which offered new opportunities. The inter-war period was, in fact, one of the most significant eras in the history of cutlery. Above all, it marked the arrival of the modern knife—stainless, machine-produced, and reaching the customer through the channels of mass distribution and advertising. This chapter explores Sheffield's response to these trends.

As we have shown, the First World War provided Sheffield cutlers with unexpected opportunities to meet the challenge of overseas competition. It did so in three ways. It made Sheffield industrialists more aware of the advantages of co-operation in the task of reforming the industry. Secondly, it forced the city's producers to provide many of the products—such as razors, scissors, and swords—that had previously come from abroad, And thirdly, it kept German cutlery producers out of international markets for almost half a decade and gave Sheffield the opportunity to catch up with, perhaps even usurp, its old rival. Technologically, Sheffield steelmakers had also supplied the industry with a trump card—stainless steel—which was to revolutionize cutlery in the 1920s. Leading Sheffield industrialists were keenly aware of these opportunities. Many would have agreed with the *Sheffield Independent* when it stated that 'the war has brought the country up to date. We have caught up more pushful rivals in those departments where England had been steadily losing ground.'[1]

Unfortunately, as our analysis of the War has highlighted, translating these opportunities into competitive advantage was not easy. Although German competition had vanished overnight in 1914, its spectre continued to haunt the Sheffield cutlery industry during the War. The sudden rise in demand for razors and scissors, for example, merely highlighted how much there was to be done in attuning the industry to the twentieth century. The pressure of wartime orders meant that there was little time to alter deep-seated, centuries-old rigidities. Ironically, the War had weakened the largest firms, perhaps the very ones which should have led any modernization, and had actually fostered even more individualism. While money could be earned on war contracts by muddling along with the old ways, it was hardly surprising that calls for reform fell on deaf ears. Thus at the War's end, it was said that:

The problem of turning out the cheapest classes of cutlery, such as Germany had been making, and in bulk quantities, has not been solved. There was some expectation that a number of cutlery houses would unite their forces in order to carry out on a heroic scale, schemes for producing cutlery cheaply in vast quantities, and also for organising the marketing of the goods all over the world. Nothing, however, appears to have been done in this direction. The strong spirit of individualism which runs right through the cutlery trade has not been much shaken by the war and seems to be an effective barrier against those merged schemes which are so common in other industries.[2]

There was one promising development—Sheffield Steel Products—a company established in 1918 to mass-produce cutlery (its development is considered below). On the other hand, Wostenholm's plans to merge with Needham, Veall, & Tyzack were soon forgotten once the war ended. Frank Colver told his fellow directors that he admired Walter Tyzack, the architect of the mechanized pocket-knife shop, but did not trust his motives.[3] Other plans for a combination of the larger firms were also quietly shelved by 1920, as they were in the crucible steel trade, and did not resurface for another decade. Whatever happened in the industry in the inter-war period, Sheffield firms were determined to deal with problems in their own way.

Sheffield steel might have helped defeat the Germans, but the old enemy still set the agenda for the city's cutlery industry. No sooner had the War ended than some of Sheffield's more progressive cutlers were travelling to Germany for another look at the Solingen industry. Their tour of some seventy cutlery establishments in 1919 merely confirmed

[1] *SDT*, 30 Dec. 1918.   [2] *SDT*, 30 Dec. 1918.
[3] SCL Wostenholm Papers (hereinafter Wos) 519, Colver to Wing, 25 July 1917.

what they had seen before the War. Despite some irritating evidence of
the usual German skullduggery—false-marking, dumping, and the use of
inferior steel marked 'Sheffield-made'—the Sheffielders were impressed
again by the high output and better working conditions. With a cutlery
workforce of about 12,000—not much bigger than Sheffield's—the German output was about three times Sheffield's in value. In certain classes of
cutlery, the Germans had established a commanding lead: some 80 per
cent of the world's scissor trade, for example, was in German hands.
Remarkably, this was achieved with an industrial structure that still
closely resembled Sheffield's, especially in the prevalence of outwork. A
large Solingen cutlery works might employ about 800, while the number
actually working for that firm would be about 2,400. Nearly all the grinding and cutlery work was done by outworkers, while forging and
finishing were done in the factory; but hundreds of 'little mesters'
finished, wrapped, and labelled the article. Conditions were markedly
superior in the 700 grinding wheels in Solingen, nearly all of which were
powered by electricity. Also notable was the greater attention German
producers paid to pattern, embellishment, and finish. The Sheffield cutlery mission concluded that: 'There will no doubt be a very large demand
for cutlery in the future, but we fear Germany is very much better organised at present to supply that demand than Sheffield is.'[4]

It must be emphasized, though, that the firms that sent members
to Solingen, who returned doubtless hoping to spread the gospel of
mechanization, were a minority. The War had made little difference to the
profile of the Sheffield industry, with its predominance of small manufacturers. These makers were not so well disposed to mass production. In
1920 the local press noted attempts to belittle the cutlery reform movement and castigated:

the apparent inability of so many members to grasp the vast possibilities of foreign
trade, although the knowledge now possessed of what Germany did before the
war ought to have opened their eyes sufficiently. Unfortunately, so many of them
are apt to think in dozens or even half-dozens, whereas their minds ought to be
occupied with visions of hundreds of thousands of grosses. It is this big view of
trade which explains Germany's pre-war position in the world. As the result of all
this *laissez-faire* and lack of imagination, cutlery is being made in much the old
way . . . and . . . of the necessary scrapping of ancient methods, little is heard.[5]

Unknown to Sheffield cutlers, the Solingen industry had passed its peak
and in the more difficult inter-war years the German town proved unable

---

[4] SCL NVT 22. Sheffield Cutlery Manufacturing Association, 'Report of the Sheffield
Cutlery Mission to Solingen' (July 1919), 3. Firms which sent representatives were:
Needham, Veall, & Tyzack; Harrison Bros. & Howson; Wostenholm; Southern &
Richardson; Thomas Turner; Kitchin; and Petty. See also reports and photographs on the
Mission, *SDT*, 31 Dec. 1919; 31 Dec. 1920.

[5] *SDT*, 31 Dec. 1920.

to recover its pre-1914 position. However, the international cutlery industry did not stand still: mechanization continued apace and social trends began to affect the nature of demand throughout the world.

Stainless steel, as Sheffield cutlers predicted, began to transform the industry in the inter-war years. It became, not surprisingly, one of the few growth areas in the trade and by 1921 was described as the 'salvation of the cutlery trade'.[6] Sheffield's achievement in producing the world's first stainless cutlery should be emphasized. Firth's calculated that by 1934 some 60–70 million knives marked 'Firth-Stainless' were in circulation. Many of these old Sheffield stainless table knives survive in kitchen drawers around the country, still providing good service after more than fifty years. Stainless steel also brought with it new products. By 1927 hypodermic needles in vast quantities were being made in Sheffield and exported around the world and the surgical instrument trade expanded.[7] Some of these products, ironically, gave further scope to the little mester, who with his low overheads could still thrive as mechanization and stainless steel drove prices downwards. But generally stainless steel was fatal to Sheffield's craft-based industry. It encouraged the use of machine-grinding by firms, who installed in-house plant to render themselves independent of the traditional public 'wheels'. It also brought with it cutlery of remarkable cheapness: cheese and dessert knives, for example, that cost only 6*d.* each instead of about 2*s.* 6*d.*[8] This immediately threatened Sheffield's luxury market by cutting margins and posed the uncomfortable question for the old firms of whether they could afford to ignore this new mass market. Not surprisingly, ruthless cost-cutting developed even in the absence of foreign competition.[9]

In this situation, new competitors were drawn into an industry which no longer relied on traditional skills and an ancient 'name'. As one manufacturer stated in 1925: 'It is very easy to become a cutlery manufacturer nowadays.'[10] Cheap, stainless, ground blades could be bought from one firm and the handles from another, while a third company could fit them together. Manufacture could even be undertaken by firms in other sectors of the steel industry. For example, in 1933 George Clark's North British Steel Works began the production of a mass-produced stainless knife in a variety of patterns named the 'Voluto'. It was made entirely from a single piece of stainless steel, with a volute twist in the middle to divide the handle from the blade.[11] These knives did not need hand-forging as did those made from Sheffield's old and cherished blister and crucible steels: they could be blanked out of the stainless steel sheets, relying on machining to provide enough quality.

[6] *SDT*, 30 Dec. 1921.   [7] *SDT*, 30 Dec. 1927.   [8] *SDT*, 30 Dec. 1926.
[9] *SDT*, 30 Dec. 1927.
[10] McClory's managing director, Milton Street, quoted, *SDT*, 31 Dec. 1925.
[11] *SDT*, 29 Dec. 1933; 31 Dec. 1934; 31 Dec. 1935.

Stainless steel did not lend itself to the old hand-methods. It was air-hardening—a type of tool steel, in fact—which was hard work to forge and grind manually. The more exacting heat-treatment required for stainless steel, and the need to have it ground and polished to high standards in large volumes, were also incompatible with the old empirical techniques. That was why its introduction into the Sheffield cutlery workshops was initially delayed: it slowed the men up and threatened their piece-rates. There was a celebrated debate, too, as to whether stainless could take and hold a hard cutting edge. This is of little importance to modern consumers, now that the quality of hand-forged steel has been forgotten and we no longer expect knives to have a good cutting edge, but it was a crucial consideration to the industry in the 1920s. None of these technical problems held up the development of stainless steel or long delayed its domination of the cutlery industry. By the Second World War, though carbon steel continued to be used for some pocket-knives and tools, cutlery was almost universally produced from cold-rolled stainless sheet and strip, and traditional forging and grinding were condemned to wither away.

The crafts in Sheffield were also being hit by the decline in the number of traditional apprentices. The long training, irregular hours, poor working conditions, low wages, and under-employment meant that the cutlery trades had little success in attracting new recruits. In the depressed 1920s and 1930s few firms were willing to suffer the expense of training cutlers for many years; those that did found that it was impossible to recruit them. George Ibberson & Co. complained in 1929 that they had difficulty in finding new apprentices and that 'craftsmanship [was] being neglected'.[12] Government legislation was also closing down many of the old tenement workshops and factories.

Meanwhile, further sectors of the industry were being mechanized. In America, cutlery firms were to prove that even the pocket-knife was not immune to the 'American System' of mass production. In the 1920s machinery for this class of cutlery was almost universally adopted by leading makers such as Imperial, Schrade, Ulster, Simmons, and Winchester. The entrance of arms manufacturers looking for new business, such as Remington, highlighted the trends. Having grown fat on war contracts, Remington invested heavily in cutlery machinery and interchangeable parts, and launched its brands with aggressive advertising. In the early 1920s Wostenholm director Frank Colver observed:

The Remington people have shown what can be done. In three years they have worked up to an output of 5,000 dozen knives a week. They have certainly decoyed workmen from other factories, but most of their hands are new to the

---

[12] *SDT*, 31 Dec. 1929.

cutlery trade. Their quality is quite good and is continually improving. I have a knife in my pocket that they gave me, a three-blade lobster, that is a very creditable piece of work.[13]

By 1931 Remington's production was 10,000 knives per day, a massive 2.8 million a year. This output, aimed at a huge internal market protected by the Fordney McCumber Tariff of 1922, was far beyond the capability of any Sheffield manufacturer.

Mass production was aimed at a society that was becoming more urban, in which the demand for cutlery was far more focused and cost-conscious. Many cutlery items were becoming obsolescent or were no longer needed in such great quantities. These included Bowie knives, dirks, and daggers; cut-throat razors; eraser and quill knives; fleams (for bleeding animals); multi-blade horseman's knives, with hoof picks; buttonhooks and dress pocket-knives. The demand for a large variety of trade and agricultural knives was also significantly less. These were the very markets Sheffield was geared to supply. One of Wostenholm's Canadian agents summarized the bad news in 1928:

The introduction of safety razors has killed the razor trade. The introduction of Eversharp pencils and pencil sharpeners and small manicure pieces has reduced the demand for good-quality pocket-knives almost to nothing. Who wants a four-blade pearl knife nowadays? Then the introduction of motor cars and the disappearance of horses has reduced the demand for jack-knives, especially those with trace borers in them, that used to sell so well. Then the much advertised Community plate, that is silver knives with silver-plated handles and forks and spoons to match has, in this country [Canada], reduced the demand for good-quality white handle table knives. As the demand for cutlery has been so reduced, dealers are less interested in it, which makes matters worse. The only cutlery that is being sold in any quantity is of the cheapest quality, much from Germany and France.[14]

Wostenholm's found that:

price appears to be the only things buyers look at nowadays, and it is very difficult to make them realise differences in quality, and when you do get them to admit that our goods are better they only say something to the effect that the man in the street wouldn't see any difference. A very regrettable change appears to have come over the buying public. When they find they have anything to buy [in cutlery] they often go to Woolworth's and see what is to be had there.[15]

Fundamental question were being asked of the Sheffield cutlery manufacturers at this time—ones that had been asked before, but had never been clearly answered. What was to happen to Sheffield's traditional

[13] SCL Wos. Colver to A. S. Keeton, 20 June 1923.
[14] Ibid. Colver to Wostenholm from Canada, 22 Feb. 1928.
[15] Ibid. Colver to Wostenholm, 29 Feb. 1928.

reputation for quality? Should the industry embrace the mass market with a range of cheap products, or should it concentrate its energies on the luxury market? Sheffield's preferences were undoubtedly with the latter, one director in the 1920s expressing the 'conviction that the future cutlery trade of Sheffield will more consist of the better than the inferior class of goods. We can win on the former. We should lose on the latter by reason of cheap foreign competition.'[16] This was perfectly astute, even prophetic, but would mean that Sheffield restricted itself to a relatively small segment of the market. And even if this course was followed, it still left unsettled the question as to how to deal with the decline in craft skills and how far mechanization was to proceed.

Inevitably perhaps, given the depressed state of the industry in the inter-war years, Sheffield cutlers never formulated a coherent strategy: instead, a number of compromises and half-measures emerged. The initial reaction was defensive, many in the cutlery trade arguing that the city should abandon its old *laissez-faire* attitudes and plead for protection for the industry, especially against the renewed threat of German competition. This was much reduced, but in 1924 Germany still accounted for one half of the quantity and one-eleventh of the value of cutlery imports. In 1925 Sheffield's application for 'safeguarding' duties was granted, and a $33\frac{1}{3}$ per cent duty was imposed on foreign cutlery; however, the government hearings noted that Sheffield had made very little attempt to cater for the very cheap trade.[17] Most manufacturers supported Safeguarding unreservedly, though as with steel, it was a case of tariffs first, reorganization later. In 1932 the cutlery duties were increased to 50 per cent *ad valorem*, but the initial results proved disappointing. The growth of the scissor and safety-razor trade was said by some to be the direct result of protection, but significantly these were machine trades: the tariff appeared to have done little to revive the prospects of the larger handicraft section of the trade, which was closer to the hearts of Sheffield manufacturers and perhaps the main object of their protectionist instincts.[18]

Another defensive manœuvre was in trademarking. Many of the leading Sheffield cutlery firms still spent an inordinate amount of time worrying about the infringement of their illustrious marks and names. Instead of fading away in the era of machine-made, cheap goods, Sheffield's obsession with the subject was undimmed. The city's cutlers tried a new tactic: instead of trying to defend the marks of individual firms, in 1924 the Cutlers' Company succeeded in registering 'Made in Sheffield' as a

---

[16] SCL Wos. Nixon to Wing, 27 Oct. 1925.

[17] *SDT*, 31 Dec. 1925; Board of Trade, Safeguarding of Industries, *Report* (1925). Cmd. 2540.

[18] 'Safeguarding: Great Help to Cutlery Trade', *SDT*, 31 Dec. 1930; 'Better Outlook for the Cutlery Trade: Effects of Tariff Changes', *SDT*, 30 Dec. 1932.

trade mark, so that the whole industry could be protected and so that the Company 'could re-group its forces and go foward to a fresh campaign' of trade mark defence.[19] The details of this campaign—the long-drawn-out saga of the Sheffield cutlery industry's attempts to protect its virtue—are told in portentous length in L. Du Garde Peach's history of the Cutlers' Company. Since the policy was expensive, entirely defensive, and the Company never instituted any minimum quality standards, in the long-run it proved largely a waste of time and money, even its adherents admitting that 'no sooner is one adversary down than another appears'.[20]

On those rare occasions when it concerned itself with the debate over mechanization, the Cutlers' Company (which reflected the industry itself) was characteristically conservative. When the Company investigated machine-grinding in 1924, the Master Cutler (William W. Wood) was distinctly unimpressed and reached the astonishing conclusion that there was little point in the cheapening of articles, which he believed the householder bought once in a lifetime.[21] The Company was therefore unable to provide a lead in the controversy over cheap products and mechanization. In this debate Sheffield manufacturers found themselves facing in two directions at once: logic dictated the introduction of machine methods; emotion lay with the old craft skills and traditional quality. The result was that most manufacturers remained devoted to quality, though they made some attempt to introduce machines. Thus Rodgers stated that, 'while the company were effecting economies by the introduction of modern methods and machining they were jealously maintaining their high standard of quality'.[22] This resulted in the firm introducing machine-forging of its knives before 1914; but it had still not adopted machine-grinding by the early 1920s, because the firm did not find that it reached their high standards of finish.[23] Needham, Veall, & Tyzack's installation of machinery during the War had not altered its belief in high-class articles. In 1926, a new managing director, W. C. Veall, identified a supposed slackening of consumer demand for cut-price goods and a greater desire for articles which would last and prove cheap in the end. He regretted that ironmongers 'were not wise enough to stop selling inferior articles'.[24] When J. W. Ibberson, the owner of George Ibberson & Co., a typical small, family-owned Sheffield cutlery firm, was interviewed by a reporter in 1928, 'almost the first word [he] said was "quality"'. The firm's stainless steel table cutlery was machine-forged, then ground by machine *and* hand. 'We find', said Ibberson, 'that machine grinding for table blades is very good

---

[19] L. Du Garde Peach, *The Company of Cutlers in Hallamshire in the County of York, 1906–1956* (Sheffield, 1960), 78.
[20] Ibid. 75.   [21] Ibid. 76.
[22] SCL Rodgers' Minute Book No. 5, 1920–32: Annual Meeting, 15 Mar. 1929.
[23] *SDT*, 29 Dec. 1922.   [24] *SDT*, 30 Dec. 1926.

indeed, but we always finish them by hand.'[25] Significantly, these views were stated in an issue of the *Sheffield Daily Telegraph* industrial supplement, which stressed 'the craze for low-priced goods', both at home and abroad—a result of the growth of the bazaar trade, the Colonies' obsession with 'motor cars, dress and amusement' (which left them with little to spend on Sheffield goods), and the growth of the café habit (which meant people needed less domestic cutlery and plated ware).

The commitment to hand-forged steel remained unshaken. In 1927 the crucible steelmaker David Flather recognized the impact of the stainless revolution, but still believed there would be a large field for high-grade, hand-forged cutlery, which Sheffield would be able to cultivate. At this time, Joseph Rodgers were still producing shear steel cutlery; and so too were Needham, Veall, & Tyzack.[26] The blades of Ibberson's pocket-knives were hand-forged and hand-ground to maintain high standards. When Billy Ibberson, the son of the owner, toured the North American market in 1930, armed with a film of the old Sheffield ways, he stressed the importance of hand-forging and Sheffield craftsmanship.[27] For leaders in the time-honoured traditions of the trade, such as Rodgers, switching to cheaper steels—which were invariably needed if machine production was to be a success—was almost too painful to contemplate. Anyone who has handled razor-sharp hand-forged Rodgers' pocket-cutlery will know why; yet this understandable conservatism created problems in mass production. It was impossible to have the best of both worlds, since, as Rodgers noted in 1922, the use of high-grade steel was not always compatible with machine-forging and grinding. Unless the machines were 'humoured' with such steel, the dies and cutters were soon ruined.[28] Even after 1930, there was still much commitment to the hand-forged article and in 1935 the Cutlers' Company and other cutlery trade associations still thought the subject important enough to issue a definition of the term 'hand-forged'.[29]

Wostenholm's experience in the 1920s demonstrates in detail the conundrum faced by Sheffield cutlery manufacturers. By 1922 the 73-year-old managing director, James Paine, had been forced out after a long power-struggle within the company. Such was the trauma to the company of his protracted resignation that the evidence and correspondence relating to the matter was collected and bound by Wostenholm's—a testimony to the agony of a Sheffield firm facing the era of mass production. Paine's place was taken by Frank Colver, who by now had succeeded in installing a range of imported American pocket-knife machines in the Washington Works. They were intended to manufacture jack-knives (simple folding

---

[25] *SDT*, 31 Dec. 1928. See also issue, 31, Dec. 1935.   [26] *SDT*, 30 Dec. 1927.
[27] *SDT*, 31 Dec. 1930.   [28] *SDT*, 29 Dec. 1922.   [29] *SDT*, 31 Dec. 1935.

knives). The first results from the workshop were encouraging, though characteristically the sight of a Wostenholm machine-made pocket-knife caused much soul-searching amongst the older directors. Having spent years indoctrinating Colver with the ethos of quality, there was still unease at letting him off the leash. Nixon wrote to Wing: 'But please turn over in your mind the question of the use of our name upon any production save such as it has become synonymous for. Is this wise? Or would it not tend to affect injuriously what we so jealously guard, our general reputation?'[30] As it happened, the new pocket-knife machine performed to expectations, but the pride in the finished product was fast disappearing. Wing grudgingly told Colver that the new machined pocket-knife was satisfactory, but added: 'Of course, it is rough and shouts *machine.*'[31]

Wostenholm's nervousness was perhaps understandable in the parlous state of the industry in the 1920s. For over a decade from 1922 Wostenholm's paid no dividends (see Fig. 8.1 and Table 8.1). Rodgers' profits had also evaporated in the early 1920s and by 1925 the firm was incurring significant losses. At Wostenholm's something akin to panic was appearing amongst the directors, desperate for 'tonnage' to reduce overheads, which had mushroomed to 25 per cent of turnover. Wing told Colver:

The value of the 'Goodwill' of the old firms has suffered enormous depreciation lately, besides the quality can't be kept up. Our policy is to keep as near to I*XL standard as possible and sell cheap 'tho at a profit. Certainly the overheads are awful. We never realised how awful. They are enough to swamp any business ... The ship must be lightened and everything not imperatively wanted thrown overboard, whether persons or things.

He added:

The market now is competitive and to make goods above the ordinary means a very small trade because of the price and the difficulties to persuade a shopkeeper to speculate ... My present feeling is to select a few patterns, which if price will give a chance will sell largely—make them in masses, push them by travellers, sample dozens and so forth and so give our men a sporting chance. So long as we meander peacefully along the valleys of our empty warehouses and silent shops, waiting for the heavens to shower down orders for our incomparable I*XL goods, we shall deservedly drop down the nick and be done with ... the I*XL quality at slopshop price will have to be attained.[32]

But Wostenholm's were unable to tap the new and expanding markets for cutlery products in the inter-war period. The pocket-knife machine

[30] SCL Wos. Paine resignation letters. Nixon to Wing, 22 Oct. 1919.
[31] Ibid. Wing to Colver, 13 Apr. 1925.
[32] Ibid. Wing to Colver, 8 June 1925; 28 June 1925.

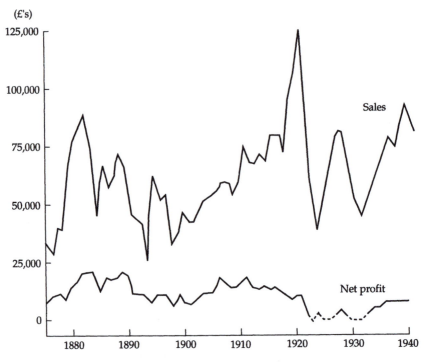

Fig. 8.1. *Sales and net profits of George Wostenholm & Son, 1876–1940*

shop appears to have had little impact on the firm's outlook, judging by a trade catalogue published in 1930, with its range of blades 'forged by hand in exactly the same way in which they have been forged in Sheffield for probably a thousand years', and its long-serving workmen, one of whom had been at the Washington Works for seventy years. The company had broadened its product range and by the mid-1920s sales of table cutlery (which had been introduced as a major line in about 1904) surpassed those of pocket-knives. A German scissor-making plant was also purchased and installed in 1930. But Wostenholm's failed, as did other leading Sheffield firms, to exploit fully other lucrative markets after the War.

What of the overseas trade? Wostenholm's performance abroad was as dismal as ever. The directors recognized that the American trade had virtually gone, but were still reluctant to abandon it. Colver was appalled by the laziness and inefficiency of the New York office. One American distributor told Colver to go and see German competitor Henckel's office, which was in the same building: 'there you will see everything in first class shape and everything in good order. They are clearly out for business. Go upstairs and call on [Wostenholm], and note the difference

Table 8.1. *George Wostenholm & Son: financial data, 1914–1940*

	Sales £	Net profit £		Profit £		Dividend %
				knives	razors	
1914	67,877	12,583	(10,899)	10,644	678	10 (7½)
1915	64,456	11,669	(12,127)	8,085	1,973	9 (7½)
1916	78,364	12,090	(12,952)	7,740	2,194	10 (7½)
1917	76,776	10,778	(15,734)	12,599	3,722	10 (7½)
1918	68,169	8,121	(20,947)	11,798	3,719	10 (10)
1919	90,810	6,976		11,692	4,286	10
1920	100,706	8,253	(16,535)	17,880	6,685	11 (10)
1921	122,029	8,782	(5,765)	27,700	4,370	10 (5)
1922	90,506	1,078 (loss)		15,084	659	0
1923	52,409	1,974 (loss)	(9,132 loss)	19,021	254	0 (0)
1924	34,996	1,213	(6,818 loss)	7,847	776	0 (0)
1925	47,540	739 (loss)	(14,902 loss)	8,662	955	0 (0)
1926	56,075	248 (loss)		10,845	1,189	0
1927	67,257	1,287		13,111	1,019	0
1928	77,503	2,251		16,663	1,097	0
1929	77,842	1,702		17,180	898	0
1930	61,650	2,606 (loss)		12,035	669	0
1931	48,115	3,575 (loss)		9,857	269	0
1932	41,877	3,262 (loss)		6,887	377	0
1933	48,939	256		8,114	347	0
1934	56,097	2,910		11,733	205	4
1935	61,344	3,071		11,289	493	5
1936	70,034	5,595		13,709	394	6
1937	75,679	5,461		14,749	435	7½
1938	70,946	4,530	(1,635)	16,016	429	7½
1939	80,328	6,324	(2,604 loss)	17,113	816	10
1940	91,065	6,224	(3,263)	18,144	1,266	10

Source: See Table 4.2. Bracketed figures are for Joseph Rodgers & Sons.

... the place is a dump.'[33] Colver agreed, but his subsequent reorganization did little to stem the losses and the New York office was closed in 1933. Its sales had never covered expenses since before the First World War.

By then, the firm's international trade had become more dispersed, as Table 8.2 shows. The home trade had now replaced America as the main market, while abroad Canada was easily the best buyer of Wostenholm cutlery. Here Colver's numerous North American trips in the 1920s and

---

[33] SCL Wos. Paine resignation letters. Colver to Nixon, 8 June 1923.

Table 8.2. *George Wostenholm & Son: sales by country, 1927–1937 (£)*

	1927	1928	1929	1930	1931	1932	1933	1934	1935	1936	1937
UK	15,356	22,456	27,244	28,210	27,115	23,078	26,369	28,212	31,643	33,867	36,560
Canada	14,606	15,706	13,004	6,600	4,358	3,553	6,114	8,909	9,889	12,705	11,364
S. Africa	2,822	3,691	4,505	2,369	1,987	1,996	2,738	3,465	4,258	4,360	5,171
N. Zealand	5,635	6,517	7,019	6,673	3,958	3,373	3,704	4,117	5,142	6,015	7,422
India	9,481	8,677	9,192	8,046	4,607	4,681	4,539	5,850	3,972	5,590	6,012
W. Indies	2,608	3,195	4,004	3,491	2,741	1,865	1,928	1,139	1,460	2,114	3,161
S. America	172	189	207	66	32	33	7	—	—	—	—
Gen. Foreign	1,698	2,322	1,532	1,111	1,345	971	909	1,038	964	1,189	968
USA	6,090	6,184	5,614	1,889	1,155	690	762	1,355	1,279	1,561	1,784
Australia	8,789	8,566	5,536	3,160	817	1,637	1,824	2,012	2,719	2,633	2,967
TOTAL	67,257	77,503	77,842	61,615	48,115	41,877	48,939	56,097	61,344	70,034	75,679

Source: SCL Wostenholm Records: Directors' Minute Books, 1928–37, 1937–51.

1930s and the reasonably efficient activities of Wostenholm's agents, such as Archie MacFarlane, ensured a steady trade. Colver did what he could to get Wostenholm's into new lines, such as bread knives, telling Wostenholm's in 1928: 'I do not think I have been seen very often in the streets of either Montreal, Toronto or London, without a loaf of bread under my arm.'[34]

This was counterbalanced, however, by the firm's continued ineptitude elsewhere. In 1924 the directors reviewed a decade of Australian trade and found that they had never enjoyed more than about 5 per cent of total Sheffield exports to that country—far less than firms such as Christopher Johnson (which enjoyed the luxury of holding no stock in Australia, yet had a year's advance orders). Worse, in 1923 Wostenholm's had discovered that their Sydney agency, Reslaw Green—which in the usual fashion had been completely unsupervised by Sheffield over the years—had quietly embezzled about £7,000. A Sheffield steelmaker, asked by Wostenholm's to visit the agency, found an office largely devoid of staff, and 'although they had . . . something like a shop window, only crockery was displayed there. After he had been there some time, he asked where the cutlery was, and was shown a small back room where [Wostenholm] goods were on display. Altogether he thought the space devoted to the stock of crockery must be twenty times that given to cutlery.'[35] Eventually, Green's relatives paid the debt to avoid a scandal, but Wostenholm's still lost over £1,000 in the affair, aside from its damaging impact on the firm's trade. The Australian trade never recovered.

In South America Wostenholm's trade had foundered in the depression of the 1930s, while in South Africa the company never succeeded in establishing itself in one of Sheffield's best markets. In 1921 the firm's South African agent wrote disparagingly:

You have all your heads in the sand, I fear. One firm have placed their business with Taylor's for butcher's knives, saying they have so much difficulty with you, and their prices are more favourable. As far as I can judge, the trade I worked up for you is slipping away to others, as the firms think you are too independent, old-fashioned and out-of-date in your methods—no catalogues, no prices, and general indifference to whether you have the trade or not.[36]

As ever, the directors expected the trade in new territories such as Australia to behave exactly as it had in America, where the demand was for luxury goods. Until Colver appeared, few of the directors had any taste for foreign sales trips in the style of George Wostenholm. The firm's Canadian agent in 1924 stressed the importance of someone at the firm

---

[34] SCL Wos. Paine resignation letters. Colver to Wostenholm, 22 Feb. 1928.
[35] Ibid. Nixon to Colver, 27 Aug. 1924.
[36] Ibid. Comments amongst Paine resignation papers, 1922.

making a round-the-world trip to open up a connection for I*XL: he believed that had that been done 'twenty years ago, we should have had a world-wide trade'.[37]

It is difficult to assess how typical Wostenholm's overseas performance was compared with other Sheffield cutlery firms. After all, the firm's most striking blunder—the extent to which the firm clung to the American market, long after any reasonable hope had passed that trade would revive—was probably peculiar to Wostenholm. Other failings, though, may have been more typical in an industry which had yet to establish a large-scale mechanized cutlery factory and an integrated overseas sales network.

Sheffield Steel Products was perhaps the industry's only attempt to cater fully for the mass market in the inter-war period. This company was the creation of a consortium of ten firms—among them W. K. & Peace, Boswell Hatfield, and Moses Eadon—which in 1918 took over Firth's National Projectile Factory at Templeborough.[38] The intention was to mass-produce cutlery and tools, something which was viewed with predictable contempt in Sheffield. One toolmaker later said: 'This firm was quite big and produced in quantities for the lower end of the cutlery market. In other words, rubbish.'[39]

The development of Sheffield Steel Products is obscured by the lack of any surviving business records or information. However, it appears to have been a typical post-war boom flotation, its capital rising from £1 million to £2.4 million in only two years. It expanded by acquiring Oxley Bros.' foundry in Mowbray Street and also launched a stores division to supervise the opening of a multiple-shop chain around the country. By 1924 17 firms were involved, some outside Sheffield. But in that year the stores scheme collapsed: a reorganization was needed with the aid of a government grant, and the company extended its product-range by manufacturing two-wheeled trailers. By 1929 (when its paid-up capital had plummeted to £53,000) the output was even more diverse and included automatic scales, bacon slicers, vending machines, and safety razors. In the early 1930s, when the depression hit its standard lines of cutlery, files, and other tools, the company began manufacturing magnets, forgings, and stampings for the motor trade. By 1935 it was reported to be working at full capacity, with subsidiary factories as far afield as Kidderminster and Warrington, and continuing in its attempts to mass-produce cutlery and reduce the number of patterns. Quantifying the success of Sheffield Steel Products in the inter-war period is difficult, but clearly it never lived up to its founders' expectations of giving Sheffield its

---

[37] SCL Wos. A. MacFarlane to Nixon, 24 June 1924.
[38] *Stock Exchange Yearbook*, 1920+.
[39] Ashley Iles, *Memories of a Sheffield Tool Maker* (Mendham, NJ, 1993), 19.

first big mechanized factory. It was no longer listed on the Stock Exchange by 1940.[40]

More illumination can be shed, though, on Sheffield's attempts in the inter-war period to meet the challenge of competition in safety razors. The social and economic revolution in shaving launched by Gillette in the early 1900s had accelerated during the First World War. By 1917 his firm had sold over a million razors and the 'name of Gillette had become almost a generic word for safety razor'.[41] The trade was worth some $20 million a year by 1920, with the Americans accounting for a major share of the output. By the mid-1920s Gillette had added insult to injury by establishing a factory at Slough, near London, so that he could get a bigger slice of the United Kingdom market, and Sheffield at that stage did not even supply the strip steel (which came mostly from America and the Continent). Although some purchasers still preferred Sheffield's old-style cut-throat, it was rapidly becoming an antique. Commented one newspaper correspondent:

A new branch of the cutlery industry [the safety razor] has recently sprung up, unfortunately not in Sheffield, and without the advantage of Sheffield marks, [which] has already outstripped its older rival . . . Here is an article entirely produced by machinery, and the machine-produced edge of the safety razor has been pronounced by several cutlery experts to be the finest ever produced. That is the product of a machine![42]

The safety razor was the archetypal mass-market cutlery item. Gillette's blades were machine-produced by the million every day, wrapped and packaged automatically, and then sucked into a distribution network that was itself increasingly dominated by mechanization. Sheffield's reaction to it can be used as a litmus test of its attitude to new technology.

Even the most traditional Sheffield firms could not ignore this threat. The city's first safety-razor firms had appeared during the War, but mostly these had not included the old-established cutlery names. In the 1920s, however, several of the larger firms tooled up for safety-razor production: Joseph Rodgers in 1924; George Butler a year later; and Needham, Veall, & Tyzack. There were also a number of smaller cutlery firms, which either introduced safety razors alongside their other lines (such as Ibberson's) or made a speciality of the new product (such as George Lawrence and Swann-Morton).[43] There were also a few small firms, such the Dominion Steel Corporation's Fleet Works, which made

[40] Sheffield Steel Products was regularly featured in the annual business supplements of the *SDT*. See e.g. 29 Dec. 1933; 31 Dec. 1935. The company was still in business after the Second World War, but, like many Sheffield cutlery firms, it faded away in about the 1960s.

[41] Russell B. Adams, *King C. Gillette: The Man and His Wonderful Shaving Device* (Boston, 1978), 92.

[42] *SDT*, 30 Dec. 1921.   [43] Swann-Morton, *The First Fifty Years* (Sheffield, 1982).

privately branded razors. A product that broke down barriers to entry inevitably attracted firms from outside the traditional cutlery sector. James Neill, the steel- and hacksaw-maker, for example, began safety-razor production in 1926 because, it was said, the owner could not buy a good blade. J. Stead & Co., a pioneer textile pin-maker founded in the outlying Derbyshire village of Hathersage in 1901, moved to Sheffield thirty years later as a safety-razor (and gramophone-needle) manufacturer.[44] Thos. W. Ward, which had become involved in selling mass-produced cutlery and plated ware to department stores and shipping companies, also saw an opening and launched its 'Wardonia' brand in the 1920s. After 1926—when the War Office abolished the issue of the cut-throat—Ward's regularly landed the Army contracts for safety razors.

The most ambitious bid for the safety-razor market, though, was launched by Paul Kuehnrich in the mid-1920s. Ever the entrepreneur, Kuehnrich was looking for ways of further expanding Darwin & Milner by using his 'Cobaltcrom' alloy for razors and cutlery. He planned to make razor blades that would last three times longer than Gillette's, 'of a new design, stainless and rustless, which do not need wiping down and drying as ordinary safety razors do after they have been used'.[45] Having purchased the Fitzwilliam Works in Tinsley in 1924, he announced that he intended to make the factory (and his renamed company, Darwins) the largest safety-razor blade maker in the country. As a local newspaper remarked, Kuehnrich's plan was that: 'Sheffield was to "shave the world" and this was to be done by big-scale mass production that feared neither American nor Continental competition. His ambition also was to develop big scale production of cutlery as opportunity offered.'[46]

Darwin's assault on the razor market was much publicized in Sheffield, where it was a welcome sign in a city scarred by unemployment. A big, emotional man, much given to grand gestures and with a bushy white beard (all the more unusual in a manufacturer of razors!), Kuehnrich had all the eccentricity expected of a German immigrant and had little difficulty in generating publicity.[47] With a workforce of about 1,400 (mostly girls), he planned to manufacture initially half-a-million blades a day (Gillette's production was said to be two million a day) to be sold at 5 pence each throughout the world. One-and-a-half million circulars, alongside press advertisements, were also issued in the United States, where

---

[44] J. Stead & Co., *Steady Progress for Half a Century, 1901–1951* (Sheffield, 1951).

[45] 'Safety Blades for the World', *SI*, 14 Nov. 1924. See also 'Big Works Deal: Hope for Many Unemployed', *SI*, 5 Apr. 1926.

[46] *SI*, 28 Apr. 1932.

[47] G. Tweedale, 'The Razor Blade King of Sheffield: The Forgotten Career of Paul Kuehnrich', *THAS* 16 (1991), 39–51.

the Darwin Safety Razor Blade Co. Inc. was established in Cleveland, Ohio, to co-ordinate sales.

By the mid-1920s, therefore, Sheffield's response to Gillette was fully under way. How did these safety-razor firms perform subsequently? Assessing this before 1939 is difficult, especially since all (including Gillette) were to pass through the depression of the early 1930s. Some firms did not stay in the business long. Rodgers had raised their output to a puny 9,000 dozen blades per week by 1928, when it was decided to reorganize razor production; but by 1930 the Rodgers' company minute books record that the machinery had been sold off and razors discontinued. Darwins soon ran into trouble during the General Strike and was bankrupt by 1927, mired in a host of technical and marketing problems. Kuehnrich's cobalt high-speed steel blades proved unsuitable for safety razors (or at least the company was unable to solve the problems involved in producing them by the million); plans to market the firm's 'Miracol' razors in America proved far too ambitious and expensive; and the firm only succeeded in arousing the ire of Gillette, who soon countered with his usual threats of patent litigation. For Kuehnrich, the safety-razor débâcle had tragic consequences. No longer in control of the company he had founded, after another abortive cutlery venture bankrupted him again in 1932, he shot himself.

Other firms' experiences were not quite so disastrous. Stead's safety razors (at a penny each) kept the firm busy, even through the depression, and its workforce grew from two employees in 1901 to 300 some thirty years later. In the early 1930s George H. Lawrence's production of its 'Laurel' blades had surpassed a million per week. Ibberson's also expanded its production, taking over the machinery of Brookes, Haywood, & Co., and concentrating the department in premises in West Street, which had belonged to William Hutton, the silverplaters.[48] By 1932 Sheffield safety-razor production was regarded as a bright spot in a depressed industry. Over a dozen firms were said to be in production and exports of safety razors and blades exceeded the combined totals of all other classes of cutlery. Ward's 'Wardonia' range, selling in about thirty different styles, grew in popularity during the 1930s, and by 1939 the firm was probably the largest safety-razor maker in the city. Sheffield was then said to be 'gradually getting the lion's share of the world [razor] trade'.[49]

This was certainly an exaggeration. It was too much to expect that Sheffield cutlery firms, with their far more limited capital base for production, research, and advertising, would ever make up the lost ground on Gillette, especially between the Wars. Their performance was creditable— and Sheffield certainly did, as one writer has put it, 'cream some of the

[48] *SDT*, 30 Dec. 1932.   [49] *SDT*, 30 Dec. 1938.

British market away from [American producers]'.[50] But despite its closely allied steel industry and its centuries of experience in metalworking, the city never captured first place, even in the United Kingdom. The industry declined in Sheffield after 1940. Neill's, though successful in hacksaw and steel production, found the safety-razor business unprofitable in the 1920s. It was discontinued during the Second World War, though Neill blades still appeared on the market for a few years—manufactured by Gillette! Swann-Morton continued razor production until the Second World War, when the firm switched to scalpel manufacture. Ibberson's had abandoned the trade by 1940, though, like Neill's, it continued to buy blades from other makers. When the British safety-razor industry did take off in the 1960s, it was not in Steel City but close to London, where Wilkinson Sword successfully challenged the Americans.

The safety-razor story highlights the conservatism of the Sheffield cutlery industry; its commitment to quality; and its weakness in mass-production engineering. In a city where most cutlery products were still hand-made, many makers were unable to accept this revolution in shaving and some still believed that there was life in the old Sheffield razor. In 1926, a year when the safety razor was worth some £120,000 in exports and there were some 700 unemployed straight razor makers in Sheffield, some firms were said to be confident of the survival of the old razor: after all, it was said, barbers all over the world, who knew most about shaving, preferred cut-throats.[51] In the following year, the manager of Needham, Veall, & Tyzack looked forward to an increasing trade in its old hollow-ground razors, which were such a good investment over the years and gave a cleaner shave.[52] This view was echoed by Butler's, who also believed that the ordinary razor would reassert itself, since 'people get tired of continually purchasing new blades for safety razors, whereas the old-fashioned razor lasts a generation or two, and only requires doing up very occasionally'.[53] Thus Butler's and most of the old firms continued to produce straight razors—the old and the new methods of shaving often appearing together in advertisements. A Wostenholm catalogue of 1930 advertised the firm's 'I*XL' safety blades, but these were tucked away in the corner of a page dominated by its old 'Pipe'-brand straight razors.

Other makers were unable to accept fully the Gillette idea of a cheap, disposable product. One of Needham, Veall, & Tyzack's specialities was a safety razor with 'a hollow-ground blade, single-edged, which is calculated to have a very long life'.[54] Characteristically, James Neill was also unable to resist making quality the keynote. The Neill 'Eclipse' razor (marketed under the stolid slogan that recommended it 'for stiff beards

---

[50] Frazer Wright, *James Neill: A Century of Quality and Service, 1889–1989* (Sheffield, 1989), 16.   [51] *SDT*, 30 Dec. 1926.
[52] *SDT*, 30 Dec. 1927.   [53] *SDT*, 31 Dec. 1928.   [54] *SDT*, 30 Dec. 1926.

and tender chins') was beautifully turned from solid brass and con-structed with precision and care, offering automatic blade-centring, 'mi-crometer'-style adjustment of cutting edges, and a built-in magnet so that blades could be picked up without cut fingers. With this policy, it was perhaps not surprising that Neill's made no money from razors and that the product became nothing more than 'an expensive hobby of the founder'.[55]

Sheffield's unfamiliarity with mechanized processes compounded these mistakes. Its heavy engineering branches may have been the equal of any in the world, but mass-production technology in the light trades had a short history in Sheffield and, significantly, the city's first safety-razor machines were imported from Germany. The business records of Darwins are revealing on this point. After Kuehnrich's death, a new general manager was appointed and his first report in 1935 provides some explanation for the company's poor showing. He found:

the shops are not as tidy as they ought to be . . . the arrangement of machinery is to a great extent haphazard and in the Razor Department, for example, there is no continuity of operations, so that a good deal of wasted energy occurs and costs based on the present system, or want of it, are really worthless . . . There is no one here who I have yet met with any accurate knowledge of production, by which I mean the most economical layout and sequence of operations for making a definite article.[56]

Kuehnrich's attempt to manufacture a stainless razor compounded his problems. Even Gillette found the task of mass-producing a disposable stainless steel blade beyond his technical and financial resources. In fact, the stainless blade did not arrive until the early 1960s when Wilkinson Sword introduced the 'Super Sword Edge' coated razor.

Finally, Sheffield had little experience in the type of intensive and ruthless advertising campaigns that were Gillette's speciality. Many cus-tomers vouched for the durability of Sheffield blades, but they also emphasized that the industry needed to do much more to compete with Gillette's low prices, free samples, and widespread advertising. Sheffielders such as Kuehnrich recognized some of these problems, but nevertheless they found themselves completely out of their depth.

The brief flurry of safety-razor activity in Sheffield failed to alleviate the general stagnation of the cutlery trades. Employment, which was under 10,000 in 1920, was still at the same level in 1930, and had only increased to 10,699 by 1935. Britain's share of the world cutlery market and of the home trade rose only slowly in the 1930s. The market for Sheffield luxury goods was hit badly by the depression, and though the vagaries of

[55] Wright, *James Neill*, 17.
[56] SCL Aurora 1, report of J. D. Steven, 26 Feb. 1935.

the exchange rate, and the effect of war, and Safeguarding had blunted German competition (allowing Sheffield into the scissor and razor trade, for example), a new threat had arisen from Japan. In that country the industry began in Tsubame in the 1920s with the adoption of Western methods, so that cutlery was one of the first Japanese light industries to be mechanized.[57] The *Sheffield Daily Telegraph*, 31 December 1934, reported that Japanese competition had first made its appearance in secateurs and pruning shears.

When demand began to pick up in the mid-1930s—cutlery production rising from £2.2 million to £3.2 million between 1930 and 1935—few firms were positioned to take advantage of the upturn. Few new factories or extensions appear to have been opened at this time, though, according to the local press, Frank Cobb & Co., a business founded in West Street in 1903, and Viners, one of the largest firms in the plate and cutlery trades, were doing better than most.[58]

Two new arrivals in the cutlery industry in the 1930s should be mentioned, however. These were B. & J. Sippel and Richards Brothers & Sons. Two things were striking about these firms: they were founded by Germans; and their factories were designed for bulk production. The Sippels came to London in 1931 to assist English manufacturers mechanize plated spoon and fork production and two years later opened their own works in Arundel Street, Sheffield. By 1939 the business had relocated in Cadman Street, where the Sipelia Works was said to be the largest press plant for forks and spoons in the country. The workforce had grown from about 75 in 1933 to 400 by 1939.[59] Richards began in 1932 in Broomhall Street as a small factory, founded by the Richartz brothers (Stephan and Paul), who before their arrival in Sheffield had run a family cutlery business in Solingen. This appears to have been the first time that German entrepreneurs had tried their hand in the Sheffield cutlery industry—some fifty years or more since German immigrants began making their presence felt in crucible steel. The Richartz brothers, with the help of a German colleague and engineer, Wilhelm Muller, were to be as influential. Their factory at Solingen had produced pocket-knives and straight razors, with the emphasis on quantity not quality. The formula was repeated in Sheffield and was evidently soon successful. In 1934 Richards had only 134 employees, but this had increased to 400 by 1938 (when the trio of owners decided to become naturalized). The company was poised

[57] Roger Hayter and Jerry Patchell, 'Different Trajectories in the Social Divisions of Labour: The Cutlery Industry in Sheffield, England, and Tsubame, Japan', *Urban Studies*, 30 (1993), 1427–45.

[58] SCL Frank Cobb Group of Companies Records. Cobb's featured in the *SDT* Dec. Industrial Supplement 1927, 1932–5; Viners in 1931, 1932, 1934.

[59] *SDT*, 28 Dec. 1939; *SDT*, 20 Nov. 1946 (B. Sippel obit.).

to become one of the city's most successful cutlery firms after the Second World War.[60]

Generally, however, large-scale reorganization was deferred and the industry maintained its traditional structure. The *Sheffield Daily Telegraph* described cutlery manufacture in 1927 'as largely an assembling trade. Only a small proportion of the manufacturers are self-contained or approximately so.'[61] Ten years later the situation had not changed. Even the depression of the early 1930s had not succeeded in bringing the cutlery makers together. Rodgers and Wostenholm considered amalgamating in 1932, but nothing came of the idea. Rodgers stumbled on alone, enduring a shareholders' revolt in 1937, when the Rodgers' management came under intense criticism. Only one significant takeover occurred—that of Thomas Turner by Viners in 1932—but this appears to have stemmed more from the depression than from any new-found desire for rationalization. In 1938 there were 900 separate manufacturing operations in the Sheffield cutlery industry: about 300 firms proper and 600 establishments doing work for larger firms and employing no more, and often fewer, than ten men each.[62]

The tool trades in the city had a similar mixture of small-scale, family-run enterprise, operating across a wide product range with scores of operating units. Since they were not homogeneous—the Sheffield tool trades produced everything from hacksaws and drills to slide rules and planes—they defy categorization and easy generalization. Few historical studies exist, even of specific trades.[63] The tool industry employed about double the number involved in cutlery (about 20,000 compared with about 10,000), a differential that had widened as the city began to recover from the depression in the mid-1930s. In 1935 employment in the tool trades had increased to about 24,000, about one-and-a-half times the number in cutlery. The value of Sheffield tool production was about £7.8 million in 1935, more than double the figure for cutlery.

An impressionistic examination of the leading firms confirms that the outlook was slightly better for tools than for cutlery. The steady demand for engineering tools was sustained in the inter-war years, with Sheffield continuing to extend its product base in those lines in which the Americans and Germans had been so successful before 1914. By 1930, not only was the hacksaw trade firmly established, but sawmaking was much improved, and new products such as the metallic plane and micrometer had been introduced in Sheffield.[64] In 1934 Firth-Brown extended its

---

[60] Jim Taylor, *Edges* (Oct./Nov. 1987), 20–1, 29; Paul P. Richartz obit., *SDT*, 15 Aug. 1961. Whether the Richartz's (and the Sippels') arrival was due to the business prospects offered in Sheffield or to the political climate in Germany is unknown.

[61] *SDT*, 30 Dec. 1927.   [62] *The Economist*, 130 (26 Mar. 1938), 688.

[63] Ruskin Gallery, *The Cutting Edge* (Sheffield, 1992).   [64] *SDT*, 31 Dec. 1930.

toolmaking operations by opening a new factory. In the inter-war years, Marsh Bros. made continual extensions to its twist drill plant and gradually approached its ideal of making all its tools in-house. Turton Bros. & Matthews also moved into twist drill manufacture in 1922, when it acquired the Century Drill Works, as an outlet for high-speed steel. The Sheffield Twist Drill & Steel Co. was also growing. In 1933 a new three-storeyed building was opened on Napier and Solferino Street to the south-west of the city centre.[65] The Napier Street area was also the base for another increasingly successful company, James Neill. Having begun as primarily a tool steel manufacturer, during the 1930s its business in tools grew to such an extent that by the Second World War this was the firm's main business (though it continued to melt its own crucible and 'composite' steel). Besides its well-known 'Eclipse' hacksaws, in 1934 it introduced a permanent magnet chuck, which proved to be a company landmark and placed Neill's substantially ahead of its rivals. By the 1930s Neill's employed about 400. John Bedford & Sons also started a new tool line in the 1920s: they were the first United Kingdom producers of nail-files and followed this up with the manufacture of so-called 'Swiss files', that is a range of precision files which were originally mainly required by watchmakers, but became essential to the tool, die-making, and precision industries generally.

Spear & Jackson also succeeded in its strategy of running an integrated operation that made both steel and tools. The firm used the impetus provided by the War to reorganize its plant and extend its overseas markets. Having expanded its steelmaking output with the takeover of a Rotherham works, by the early 1920s it had absorbed the sawmakers Drabble & Sanderson, and the toolmaking concern of E. & W. Lucas in Dronfield. Although the company records reveal that its production technology and output were still easily surpassed by the big American sawmaking firms, Spear & Jackson still managed to open up new markets in the Far East, especially in Japan and South America. It also established successful overseas subsidiaries, first in Vancouver in 1924, and then in Tacoma, Washington, in 1935.[66]

Sanderson Bros. & Newbould were also very active in tool manufacture in the 1920s, with a bigger steel output than Spear & Jackson and probably a larger saw department, too. There were at least two new products in the 1920s: the 'saw-plane' for cutting wood with an exceptionally fine finish, and a high-speed steel inserted-tooth saw for heavy-duty metal-cutting. The bayonet department was converted for hacksaw production after the War, and a new line in tungsten steel hacksaw blades was introduced

---

[65] *Histories of Famous Firms*, 18 (1957), 20–1; *SDT*, 29 Dec. 1933, 31 Dec. 1937.
[66] SCL Spear & Jackson Records; G. Tweedale, *Sheffield Steel and America* (1987), 153–7.

alongside the existing high-speed steel blades. Unlike Neill's, Sanderson's made no attempt at general hardware trade distribution, but confined their marketing to industrial users and engineers' tool merchants, in addition to government departments, the railways, and GPO telephones. Abroad, although the directors travelled overseas, the company relied heavily on agents in the colonies, North America, and Eastern countries. Perhaps the most active salesman in the inter-war years was Joe Baumber, who roamed the Far East. A visitor wrote of Sanderson's in 1922:

> To me, the steel warehouse, I think, presented the most interesting feature . . . for it is here that one realises, almost fantastically, the universal appeal which the products of old-established Sheffield firms like Sandersons make: port marks of countries where one would hardly believe steel was in demand at all; indications of mining activity where the layman knows none; steel for Shanghai; for the beautiful port of Sydney; for up-country ports in the Empire of India, for Rio, Chicago, Christiania and Cairo.[67]

Other Sheffield tool firms enjoying reasonable prosperity in the late 1930s included James Chesterman & Co., which maintained its output of high-quality measuring tapes and gauges; and the Footprint Works, which had made engineers' hand tools at Hollis Croft since 1899, under T. R. Ellin.[68] Significantly, overseas manufacturers saw potential in Sheffield tools. In 1936 James A. Chapman—a small Sheffield brace- and plane-making firm employing about 70—was bought by the Stanley Plane Co. of New Britain, Connecticut, as a spearhead for Stanley's drive into European and Empire markets.[69]

Why this relative prosperity in tool manufacture? Perhaps United Kingdom tariffs were responsible. Sheffielders pointed out that some of the most marked rises in exports of Sheffield goods (with a correspondingly large drop in foreign imports) were in those classes of goods, such as safety razors, which had secured a special protective duty. But the percentage rise in exports of engineers' tools between 1931 and 1936 was almost as big as that of safety razors (about 85 per cent compared with 88 per cent), despite the fact that the duty on tools was lower. So tariff rates can hardly have been responsible for the resilience of the tool sector.

Probably more important was the pull exerted by the main tool-using sectors of the economy—the engineering trades, housebuilding, the 'new' industries of aircraft and cars—many of which began feeling the effects of rearmament after the mid-1930s. The impact of the new industries can be

---

[67] *House of Saben*, 1 (Apr. 1922), 17–18. Information and reference courtesy of Bernard Callan.

[68] Douglas J. Hallam, *The First 200 Years: Rabone Chesterman 1784–1984* (1984); *SDT*, 31 Dec. 1925.

[69] Frazer Wright, *Stanley 1936–1986* (Sheffield, 1986).

seen with the development of Tyzack, Turner, & Sons. Famous for its cutlery and tools—saws, scythes, and agricultural machine knives—after 1918 it found its saw steel much in demand for the friction plates in car clutches. This led Tyzack's to develop a big trade in the actual production of these plates. A light engineering department was formed, which then took over the manufacture of circular knives, shear blades, guillotine knives, and similar products. The firm had taken an important step to becoming general engineers.[70]

In contrast to a rapidly cheapening product like cutlery, there was also still scope in the tool trades for exploiting Sheffield's traditional strength—its ability to provide quality. Many of these trades, such as the making of measuring instruments, planes, and specialist engineers' tools, had not yet been fully mechanized. Spear & Jackson advised in 1925 that:

something which has the outward semblance of a saw or cutter can be made very cheaply and can possibly do a fair work for a time, with frequent sharpening, but it is quite impossible to make a first-rate blade either of cheap material or with anything but the most highly skilled workmanship. It is this class of tool we are out to uphold.[71]

Even in the depression, it was said that customers still wanted quality tools, not least because they offered a good long-term investment.

To a certain extent, the tool trades confirmed Sheffield's belief that 'the scope for metal goods is such that a decline in one branch may be offset by the growth of others'.[72] But this did not mean that the traditional structure of the industry was crumbling. In file manufacture, for example, one observer was shocked to discover that in the inter-war period there were more than 300 file manufacturers in the United Kingdom, most of them in Sheffield. The industry was marked by 'its tame surrender to foreign competition'; the lack of a selling policy; the tendency of the British maker to carve 'his industry into tiny gobbets . . . while his American competitor thinks big, makes big, sells big'; and, above all, the parochialism of the Sheffield family firm. Unless reform was introduced, it was predicted that 'apart from a few, dark, grisly dungeons producing with sweated labour a few locally needed files, [the industry] will be swept aside and replaced by the scientifically organized workshops of a competing country, be it America, Germany or the Soviet Union'.[73]

Even in the late 1930s, Sheffield still had dozens (often scores) of firms involved in the different branches of manufacture: saws, hammers, files, edge-tools, and joiners', masons', mining, and engineers' tools. This hive

[70] British Industry & Commerce (1967), 24–5.
[71] Sawmill Magazine, 1 (May/June 1925), 4.
[72] The Economist, 130 (26 March 1938), 688.
[73] Eric N. Simons, Steel Files (London, 1947). 122–5.

of industry is better described by Sheffield toolmakers themselves, than by dry statistics:

the whole picture had all the ingredients of a tropical forest: a cacophony of sounds, an almost impenetrable jungle of workshops and narrow streets, with an abundance of colourful species in the one vast melting pot. Whole sections of the city were vast rabbit warrens of outworks ... Imagine going through a dark archway from the pavement of a narrow street into a tenement block of workshops. Through a door and up one, two and even three flights of almost vertical wooden stairs, your lungs assailed by a pungent mixture of a century of dust, rancid mutton fat, powdered emery, and the soot from potbellied stoves. Sometimes your journey would take you onto an outside wooden platform, or a bridge in mid-air reminiscent of the rope bridges crossing Tibetan ravines. At the end you would be greeted by a world-famous manufacturer in a leather apron ... There were hundreds of them, all in similar circumstances.[74]

In outlook and organization the tool industry, like that of cutlery, was still essentially Victorian in the inter-war period.

[74] Iles, *Memories*, 60.

PART III

FROM BOOM TIMES TO THE LOSS OF COMPETITIVE ADVANTAGE: THE LATE 1930s TO THE 1980s

9

Sheffield Steel in War and Peace to 1960

> In retrospect, it has been work and war, war and work.
>
> W. H. Hatfield, *Sheffield Burns* (Sheffield, 1943), 13.

> Sheffield [in the 1950s] is now a city crowded with works of all sizes, where the tradition of the small private company has largely been retained. Within its boundaries, some 130 separate companies are engaged in steel-making and processing and a great many of these have engineering departments ... In addition, a host of purely engineering firms are engaged in converting forgings, castings, and rolled sections into a range of products which are bewildering in their complexity.
>
> David Linton (ed.), *Sheffield and Its Region* (Sheffield, 1956), 279–80.

The world steel industry had been hit particularly hard in the great depression because of its dependence on the capital goods sector. At the end of 1931 the *Sheffield Daily Telegraph* stated that: 'The year now at an end has been unquestionably the most disastrous in the history of Sheffield's staple industries. ... The reports of the limited companies large and small, have been an almost unbroken record of operating at a loss and the passing of dividends.'[1] As production fell, a large part of the industry's capital had to be written off. 'No industrial centre suffered more', it was said, as Sheffield firms, 'losing money week after week made desperate efforts to keep their heads above water, and just as the struggle appeared to have reached breaking point there came signs of a change for the better.'[2] By 1933 a recovery was under way, assisted by the tariff of 1932 and the formation in 1934 of the British Iron and Steel Federation (BISF), which was to co-ordinate the industry and promote rationalization. By 1934 the output of the Sheffield district had reached 1.25 million tons, surpassing the 1929 level, and the trend was firmly upward. By 1936 output was over 1.6 million tons, with Sheffield's share of United Kingdom production at about 13 per cent (though its proportion of value was, of course, much higher). Local newspapers noted approvingly that the city's skyline was once more becoming obscured by the haze from its smoky chimneys.

After the mid-1930s, Sheffield's recovery not only reflected the general turnaround in British steel (the country's share of the world's output rose

---

[1] *SDT*, 31 Dec. 1931.   [2] Ibid. 29 Dec. 1933.

from 7.6 per cent in 1931 to 9.7 per cent in 1937, as United Kingdom steel output more than doubled), but also the increasing impact of the rearmament programme. Assessing the precise influence of increasing arms orders is difficult. Sheffield was benefiting from a world upturn as industry came out of the depression, and it was also sheltered by the tariff. But the orders for rearmament were certainly of the greatest significance for the city, especially for the old arms firms—the English Steel Corporation (ESC), Firth-Brown, and Hadfields. Most of these companies had retained their research and productive capacity for arms.

Sir Robert Hadfield, for example, in contrast to most of the other specialist private armourers of 1914, who had largely left the sector within twenty years, had been reluctant to move entirely out of armaments. Although domestic orders in the 1920s had been scarce—the only large foreign order came from Japan—Hadfield reported in 1931 that, although with the curtailment in Naval requirements, 'the orders nowadays are terribly small', nevertheless, 'work of special nature which is going, is coming our way, which is some satisfaction in these parlous times'.[3] Hadfields' turnover from armaments remained at a relatively high level in the early 1930s (it averaged about 17 per cent of total turnover between 1930 and 1935). Over roughly the same period, Hadfield employees involved in arms manufacture averaged 566, with 3,391 as the corresponding figure for commercial work. The company continued ploughing resources into projectile research and in the early 1930s Hadfield and Clerke developed an advanced type of long-range armour-piercing shell, which impacted at high obliquity. Similarly, the ESC did all it could to keep its armour-plate capacity working—its arms turnover averaged over 20 per cent in the early 1930s (workforce figures for commercial and military business were 5,050 and 860, respectively).[4] This was a significant commitment in an era of relative peace and disarmament.

The decision to stay with armaments had positive and negative aspects. On the one hand, it was to pull these large Sheffield firms (and many of the smaller ones) out of the doldrums and provided the weaponry for the country to fight a hideous ideology. On the other, it masked many of the industry's underlying problems, whose solution could be conveniently ignored and postponed.

Even firms with a relatively low military involvement found themselves back on the arms switchback in the late 1930s. This can best be charted by looking at the record of one of the few firms for which we have detailed documentation—Firth-Brown. Its arms order at the beginning of

---

[3] Hadfields Ltd., *AGM* (1931), 6.
[4] *Royal Commission on the Private Manufacture of and Trading in Arms. Cmd. 5292. Minutes of Evidence* (London, 1935–6).

Table 9.1. *Firth-Brown: value of deliveries, 1935–1944* (£)

	1935	1938	1941	1944
Armour-plate	263,842	652,466	254,456	426,235
Armour castings	2,359	207	—	—
Tank	—	—	528,474	1,100,247
Bullet-proof plates	51	—	—	—
Armour-piercing shells	127,212	387,879	894,281⎫	948,376
Gun forgings/air vessels	37,104	222,078	1,178,505⎭	
Hollow-rolled drums	1,913	21,903	25,664	51,830
Forged high-pressure boiler drums	191,940	253,684	195,701	110,849
General forgings	453,604	685,370	944,052	1,086,731
Dredger forgings	8,319	21,274	384	—
Hardened steel rolls	8,405	6,261	36,201	43,082
Staybrite & other special castings	49,013	113,500	85,480	50,618
Tyres and crank axles	195,814	252,088	258,089	302,173
Buffer coil springs	8,389	6,222	—	—
Springs: laminated, railway and road	30,092	28,761	50,566	66,272
Rolled heavy bars/billets	98,906	203,070	455,600⎫	371,598
Rolled light bars/billets	252,235	400,191	820,478⎭	
Hot- and cold-rolled sheets	6,480	24,659	5,929	3,617
Hacksaw sheets	23,034	33,294	45,390	70,534
Tube billets—stainless and Staybrite	—	—	225,302	243,903
Tool steel	81,210	137,468	199,834	132,590
Springs: laminated special	21,223	5,730	—	110,273
NB Treatment	—	—	—	688,272
Twist drills/cutters	166,050	374,961	1,282,922	1,305,671
Carbide tools	—	11,248	575,708	262,193
Circular saws/hacksaws	35,278	57,295	92,280	123,925
Files and rasps	50,075	61,043	100,579	97,191
Nitralloy and nitriding processes	31,375	51,145	194,845	190,721
Foundry—Scunthorpe	104,041	177,313	300,850	262,822
Dredger castings	23,823	27,940	6,283	1,048
Light alloys	—	—	50,577	215,146
Workmanship	7,460	14,921	46,493	74,018
Workmanship (shell)	—	—	34,144	19,566
Merchandise	55,714	99,813	67,445	49,384
Miscellaneous	6,212	15,190	90,911	54,566
TOTAL	2,335,583	4,346,974	9,047,423	8,463,431

Note: The figures do not include deliveries for Firth-Vickers Stainless Steels.

Source: SCL Firth-Brown Records. Board Papers.

the decade amounted to only about 10 per cent of its turnover: but by 1935 armour-plate and shell orders alone accounted for 18 per cent of the value of its deliveries, a figure that had jumped to 29 per cent by 1938, and 43 per cent by 1939 (see Table 9.1). Moreover, these are conservative estimates, since much of the other Firth-Brown output (such as tool steel, files, and forgings) was destined for weapons. The firm could see what was coming in early 1935, the directors stating that 'the demand for our products appears to be unabated . . . [and] . . . it is quite easy to see that with the proposed extension in the Air Force . . . we have not really touched the figures to which we are likely to arrive in the course of a few months' time if the government programme is carried out, and this renders the consideration of the necessity for acceleration of the electric steel melting plant and the new heat-treatment plant, of very great urgency'.[5]

Orders for armour-piercing shells once more launched Hadfields on a hectic upward course, as the productive capacity for shells was filled and then soon outstripped. Orders for the national defence programme began in June 1935 and by 1938 Hadfields' arms output had increased five times. In the same year, new capital expenditure was sanctioned for the installation of two electric arc furnaces. By the outbreak of the Second World War, net profits had surpassed the levels reached between 1914 and 1918 (see Fig. 3.1), and the firm had largely restored the losses incurred during the inter-war period. The fiascos of Bean Cars and the Ohio subsidiary must have seemed like a nightmarish interlude, before the resumption of the business the firm knew best.

Orders for armour-plate were also substantial, with the Admiralty programme in 1936 demanding some 168,000 tons of finished armour within four years (at a time when the annual plate capacity of the United Kingdom industry was only 40,000 tons). The orders were split between a 'pool' of three armour-plate makers—Beardmore, the ESC, and Firth-Brown—with the latter two taking 50 per cent and 25 per cent of orders, respectively. The ESC's massive investment programme in the early 1930s—mostly financed by the company—had been fortuitously timed. But the battleship programme demanded armour-plate far in excess of the ESC's capacity and so the Admiralty financed £1 million of works extensions in the Hawke Street machine shop; in re-equipping the Cyclops' West Works; in installing a 30-ton electric arc furnace; and in additional heat-treatment furnaces at River Don. The Ministry of Supply also equipped the West Machine Shop for the machining of tank armour. All the ESC's plant now became fully occupied: Darlington Forge was re-opened in 1937 and much of the plant scheduled for scrapping in the 1931 reorganization was brought back into production. By 1939 the ESC's la-

---

[5] SCL Firth-Brown Records. Directors' report, June 1935.

bour force had increased from 7,000 to about 9,000, including some 900 employed at Darlington.

At Firth-Brown, the first large order in early 1936 was for the side-armour of HMS Prince of Wales: completed by the end of 1937, it was one of the largest batches of armour in the firm's history. By 1939 1,000 tons of armour was being made every month and liquid steel production by the firm had hit a record 145,000 tons (compared with 79,000 tons in 1934).

The increase in the demand for alloy steels for aircraft engines was also particularly marked. By 1938 Rolls-Royce began looking to Samuel Fox as a new and major supplier of aero-engine steels, which led Fox to install a 10-ton electric arc furnace. The demand for stainless, valve, and magnet steels was also heavy. By the following year, as the relationship with Rolls-Royce strengthened, two new heat-treatment plants were needed, though the Fox directors still thought that 'difficulty will be experienced in maintaining all the trade we have secured'.[6]

Firth-Brown also benefited from the increasing demand from the Air Arm Extension Programme, especially on the drop-forging side of the business, where it was able to reap the benefit of its commitment to high-quality forgings and excellent customer advisory services (especially through its subsidiary Firth-Derihon Stampings Ltd.). New qualities of nitriding steels were also introduced and soon generated considerable interest from the aircraft industry. Behind these new steels lay the talents of Hatfield and the finest works laboratory in the city—the Brown-Firth Research Laboratories—which had again been extended in 1936. The ESC had also developed its own range of special steels for aircraft parts, including nitrided 'Hykro' steels for crankshafts and the cylinders of air-cooled engines. Both the ESC and Firth-Brown were also setting records for the production of their speciality forgings at the other end of the spectrum—the huge hollow-drum and heavy forgings for use in heavy industry (such as power stations and chemical plant). By 1938 the ESC was producing heavy forgings in alloy steel up to 230 tons.

Inevitably, expansion in engineering increased the demand for tools. By 1936 Firth-Brown's orders in the Engineers' Tool Department were already outstripping capacity, while in files the firm was 'swamped with orders'. On the eve of the War, the government departments and Shadow factories were calling for enormous numbers of cutters and twist drills. The firm recognized the 'almost unlimited market' for carbide tools and, with its policy of 'keeping in the van of all new inventions', planned to expand production fivefold to about £80,000 a year.[7] The smaller Sheffield tool firms were also responding to the same pressures: the workforce of

[6] SCL Samuel Fox, Board Minutes No. 9 (1931–40), 9 Aug. 1938, 10 Oct. 1938, 31 Jan. 1939.
[7] SCL Firth-Brown Records. Directors' reports, 30 May 1938, 27 June 1938.

Table 9.2. *Steel and alloy production during the Second World War* ('000 tons)

	1940	1941	1942	1943	1944	1945
UK steel	12,975	12,312	12,941	13,031	12,142	11,824
Alloy steel*	825	1,052	1,592	1,595	1,126	706
Sheffield alloy steel*	606	727	897	821	643	461
High-speed steel	—	23	29	21	11	13
Corrosion & heat-resisting steel	—	—	53	61	54	44

* Excluding high-speed steel, but including corrosion- and heat-resisting steel.

Source: British Iron & Steel Federation, *Statistics of the Iron and Steel Industries*.

the Sheffield Twist Drill & Steel Co. had grown from a handful in 1920 to about 600 by 1939. Small tool manufacture was becoming more complex, increasing the demand for skilled men, who were in short supply by the late 1930s. Unemployment in the city—certainly in the steel trades—was rapidly becoming a fading memory.

By 1939, on the outbreak of war, Sheffield was again ready to become the major arsenal of the country. Its expertise in heavy armaments allowed its mills to produce armour-plate and armour-piercing shells; its high-quality forgings for crankshafts and other engine parts powered the ships, tanks, and aircraft; it had a virtual monopoly in the advanced heat-resisting and other alloys used in turbine engines; and its tool steels in cutters, drills, and files were indispensable in the manufacture of almost every item of war.

The Government again took over the national direction of the steel industry on behalf of the war effort. But there was to be no drastic expansion of steelworks capacity as in the First World War: until Munich, a relatively limited war was envisaged, which would make relatively light demands on steel. Once the War began it was national policy not to permit the construction of new plant, which would have taken two or three years to come into production and would have drained scarce labour and resources. The aim was rather to secure the maximum output from existing plant, with any shortages met by imports. Thus in the general history of Sheffield steel, the impact of the Second World War was much less dramatic than that of the First. As Table 9.2 shows, during the War national steel output was fairly flat at about 12–13 million tons per year, with existing plants (many of them already worn out in 1939) run as hard as possible.[8] However, the aggregate figures mask important differences between sectors of the steel industry. The output of alloy steels was

[8] Duncan Burn, *The Steel Industry, 1939–1959: A Study in Competition and Planning* (Cambridge, 1961), 3–50.

greatly expanded: in fact, it virtually doubled in only two years between 1940 and 1942, when its share of total crude steel output rose from 6 to 12 per cent. This was underpinned by a rapid development in electric steel output, which tripled between 1939 and 1943 (from about 300,000 tons to 1 million tons). It seems curious, then, that Table 9.2 seems to indicate that the increase in the production of Sheffield alloy steel was not quite so rapid. However, one must remember that almost all the new Sheffield electric steel plant sanctioned and funded by the Government was dispersed to other locations to avoid any strategically dangerous concentration in the city (which at the start of the War produced about 90 per cent of the country's electric steel).

Perhaps the largest and best-equipped new electric melting shop was organized by United Steel at Distington, near Workington. Here, within eighteen months of the plant being sanctioned in February 1941, five (and later six) 20-ton electric arc furnaces were installed.[9] When fully manned (with 1,700 workers) and in full production, it was the largest electric steel plant in the country. But it had no facilities for finishing alloy steels (ingots had to be sent to Sheffield or Scotland) and no local scrap, and after the War it was dismantled. Of the big new plants, only the one built at Openshaw by the ESC flourished commercially after the war. It had new mills and drop forges.

In and around Sheffield there was some new electric steel capacity. Samuel Fox developed its trade in spring steel during the War, quadrupled its output of stainless steel and also took over the management of a government factory at Keighley for coiled springs for Bofors guns. It installed another 10-ton electric arc furnace in 1940 and also, at the expense of the Government, a 2-ton high-frequency furnace, which the company acquired after the War. Firth-Brown needed a new 20-ton arc for armour and aircraft steels in 1942 (the £80,000 cost being met by the Government); and the ESC also had another 30-ton arc installed at about the same time. In Sheffield itself, it is interesting to note that such was the demand for tool steel that some defunct crucible furnace holes at Tyzack's Abbeydale Works and at Kayser, Ellison's Darnall Works were worked again. The teemers donned their 'rags' and sweat-towels, the coke-holes were relit, and the Huntsman process enjoyed something of a swansong.

As war production intensified, one is struck, as ever, by the enormous diversity of steel products. Firth-Brown provides a good example. Despite weekend working, this firm stated that by spring 1940, 'the pressure upon us for Government orders is becoming increasingly severe and the difficulty of satisfying the various demands is almost insuperable'.[10] Besides

---

[9] P. W. S. Andrews and E. Brunner, *Capital Development in Steel* (Oxford, 1951), 241.

[10] SCL Firth-Brown Records. Directors' reports, 29 Apr. 1940.

gun forgings and naval and tank armour, the most urgent demands were from the aircraft firms and the two aero-engine builders, Rolls-Royce and Bristol Aeroplane. After an initiative by Lord Beaverbrook, Firth-Brown had joined other leading Sheffield forging and alloy steelmakers for daily meetings to co-ordinate supplies of steel. Each day a search was made in the various steelworks in the city to find where material of the requisite specification could be produced. W. H. Hatfield (along with other metal-lurgists, such as Thomas Swinden at United Steel) was active behind the scenes, organizing meetings between Sheffield firms and the Air Ministry, so that Air Board specifications could be slightly relaxed. This allowed a large quantity of steel to be released and enabled Firth-Brown in May 1941 to produce the remarkable output of 10,000 bars of steel in one day. Besides producing centri-spun castings for aero-engine sleeves, the firm also began experimenting with them for use in other aircraft parts, 'as this process will undoubtedly develop largely in the future, and we want to keep the matter as much as possible in our own hands'.[11] On this and other matters, the Laboratories were very active, doubling their staff to about a hundred or more and generating an enormous body of research into tool steels and carbides, light alloys, aluminium (another of Hatfield's initiat-ives), heat-treatment, tank armour, high-manganese and boron steels, and analysis of German alloys. Meanwhile, the firm did what it could to make the most of increased tool demand and was also involved in moving what production it could outside Sheffield. By the middle of 1942, the firm had a new heat-treatment plant for plate at Monk-Bretton, near Barnsley, and a steel-melting plant at Sprotborough, near Doncaster. It was also super-vising factories—mostly for tool production—at Brymbo, Halifax, and Nottingham.

The ESC was the largest producer of alloy steels, gun forgings, and tank armour. For a long period, the drop forge was the sole producer of crankshafts for Rolls-Royce 'Merlin' aircraft engines and the principal supplier of cranks for Bristol engines. Recalls ESC director Bill Pugh: 'Every Spitfire had a River Don crankshaft forging and each one was quite a job.'[12] Many extensions were made at government expense: at North Street, Manchester, new facilities for aero-engine parts, high-speed steel, and tank armour; at Sheffield, for gun forging equipment; and at Darlington Forge and Taylor Bros., open-hearth furnaces and finishing plant for gun forgings. The foundry produced many cast steel turrets for tanks and was also responsible for the development and production of castings for the large bombs ('Tall Boys'), designed by Barnes Wallis.

---

[11] Directors' reports, 30 July 1941. In centrifugal casting (for casting pipes and other similar shapes), a mould without a core is spun at speed, so that the molten metal is flung to the face of the mould, producing a dense, uniform, hollow cylinder.

[12] Bill Pugh interview, 29 June 1992.

The impact of the War on the smaller firms can be gauged from the experiences of Samuel Osborn & Co. During the conflict Osborn's was a major producer of high-speed steel and cartridge die steels; it set up new factories for Mushet tools in both Sheffield and Doncaster; it increased its output of twist drills by five times (according to the firm's historian, this was not surprising once it is realized that in the manufacture of a Lancaster bomber half a million drill holes are needed); it boosted sheet steel output at the Regent Works by five times; became the largest supplier of light armour-plate for Bren gun carriers; produced large quantities of bullet-proof castings and track links for tanks; and devoted the output of its manganese steel department to spares for the crushing machinery used for building landing strips, fortifications, and roads.[13]

Despite the boost in production, however, the War seriously affected the modernization and expansion schemes of Sheffield steel firms. Though they suffered little from enemy attack (Brown Bayley's appear to have been the only steelworks seriously damaged, when a land-mine hit the billet and bar mills), expenditures and outlays were heavy, despite government support. Eliminating glare from the furnaces (a Bessemer blow could be seen for miles in the skies on a clear night) and the slag heaps was a major problem and expense. Pressure for output from operatives under worsened conditions meant improved welfare amenities. Thus works 'maintenance' costs soared. For many firms, net trading profits after tax diminished compared with before the War, and dividends were often reduced. There was to be no massive lift to dividends, as had occurred at some firms during the First World War.

On the other hand, the War led to important developments in the technology of special steels. As in 1914, supplies of important raw materials were completely curtailed or interrupted during the conflict. The increase in alloy and tool steel output led to scarcities in alloying elements, such as ferro-chromium, tungsten, and vanadium. Over 80 per cent of the ferro-alloys used had to be imported. The special steel firms moved quickly to counter shortages by stockpiling, by devising new steels with less alloy content and by recovering more alloying elements from scrap. Particularly important as a conservation aid were the so-called 'En schedules', issued by the Ministry of Supply in consultation with the steelmakers, which aimed to reduce some 1,500 alloy steel specifications to a hundred or so permitted grades. These schedules led to substantial advances in processing, design, and fabrication technique, particularly in low alloy and high-tensile steels.[14]

Shortages of tungsten forced Sheffield makers to take a more serious look at the molybdenum 'substitute' tool steels, pioneered in the United

[13] T. A. Seed, *Pioneers for a Century* (Sheffield, 1952), 57–62.
[14] J. W. Donaldson, 'Alloy Steels in War and Peace', *Metallurgia*, 33 (Dec. 1945), 79–81.

States between the Wars. In 1940 the Americans offered the technology to Joseph Gillott & Sons, which became the first Sheffield firm to produce a 6–6 high-speed steel (6 per cent tungsten, 6 per cent molybdenum). Bob Young, the manager of Gillott's, remembers that there was initially much resistance to the new steel in Sheffield, but it was cheaper and eventually the Ministry of Supply forced the issue by rationing tungsten.[15] Firth-Brown, Edgar Allen's, and Wardlow's (at Abbeydale) were also experimenting with these 'substitute' steels, which were a step towards the establishment of a variety known as M2 (6 per cent tungsten, 5 per cent molybdenum, and 2 per cent vanadium) as the leading high-speed steel. This released tungsten for another new development—the use of tungsten-carbide in the noses of armour-piercing projectiles. Carbide technology also advanced in the War, especially at Firth-Brown, where there was much development work on its 'Mitia' hard metals. The company was one of about six in the United Kingdom, which raised carbide production by 1942 up to ten times what it had been three years earlier. Carbide tools could dramatically improve production. In the difficult machining of alloy spar-booms for Lancaster bombers, for example, special tipped cutters reduced the timing of one operation from 150 to 20 minutes.[16]

Disruptions in the supplies of Swedish iron led to a search for methods of producing similar grades in England. Huntsman's took the precaution of obtaining supplies of other varieties of Swedish iron, though they were found to be inferior to the older grades. The Low Moor Alloy Steelworks in Bradford, founded in 1938 and in which Senior's had a controlling interest, led the search for alternative irons.

The most spectacular developments in alloys, however, were in the field of heat-resisting steels as a response to the wartime development of the jet-engine. The early development of the gas turbine was based largely on materials then available, especially 'Stayblade', an 18/8 derivative produced by Firth-Vickers Stainless Steels. This material was superior to any other up to about 550 °C, but future developments in these engines were clearly going to be at even higher temperatures, where alloys were susceptible to 'creep'—the slow stretching of a material over many months or years that could cause fractures. Fortunately, in 1941 Hatfield completed a major investigation into a complicated alloy known as 'Rex 78', which may perhaps be considered the first of what became known as the 'super-alloys'. Rex 78 was found to have exceptional creep-resistance and was used for the inlet nozzle and rotor blades in (Sir) Frank Whittle's

---

[15] Robert G. Young, interview, 25 Feb. 1992.
[16] Jack Sandford, 'Hardmetal: The History to 1950', *JHMS* 19:1 (1985), 85–9; 'The Development of Carbide-Tipped Tools', *Metallurgia*, 27 (Mar. 1943), 201–2; H. Burden, 'Modern Uses of Hard Metals', ibid. 38 (May 1948), 27–33.

prototype.[17] In 1941 Whittle had written to Hatfield: 'The contribution which you and your firm have made to the development on which we are engaged has been very important, and indeed, without the special steels which you have developed, it would not have been a practical proposition.'[18] Along with the 'Nimonic' alloys of the nickel-chromium type (developed by the Mond Nickel Co. in 1942), Rex 78 was intensively researched and used. All these alloys had the disadvantage of being machinable only with great difficulty, though this was partly side-stepped by making the inlet nozzle blades for gas turbines as precision castings by the 'lost-wax' process (the essential feature of which, as developed largely in America, was an expendable pattern in wax, which was melted before the mould was filled with steel). Blades so manufactured needed only a minumum of grinding.

But this was only the start, as higher operating temperatures inevitably demanded even better materials. At Jessop's, the research director Donald Oliver set out to improve matters. According to a colleague, Oliver and Geoff Harris 'took the best exhaust valve steel at Jessop's and tried to improve it. We increased creep tests and were making experimental melts to get an improving trend.'[19] The result in 1943 was the development of the complex austenitic alloy steel, G18B. Virtually the first of the gas-turbine disc materials, G18B was an immediate success and was almost universally adopted after the War.[20]

Improvements had also continued in the machinability of steels, leading to the widespread use of 'free-cutting' steels. Additions of lead and other materials had greatly eased the machining of screws and other machine parts, giving a high degree of surface finish without grinding. In work that was to become important later, research into hairline cracks in alloy steels had shown that steel impregnated with hydrogen was more susceptible to cracking and had a lower ductility than steel free from hydrogen.[21]

By May 1943 the demand from the Ministry of Supply for special steels began to lessen. In the following year Firth-Brown noted 'a considerable falling off in the products of its engineers' tool department, the electric melting furnaces and the heavy forgings department'.[22] It planned to shut down one and possibly two electric furnaces. Fox had begun to plan for

[17] L. Rotherham, 'Some Aspects in the Development of Alloy Steels', ibid. 35 (Dec. 1946), 75–7.

[18] F. Whittle, *Jet: the Story of a Pioneer* (London, 1953), 178.

[19] Bill Bailey interview, 8 Oct. 1991.

[20] D. A. Oliver, 'Twenty-One Years of Progress in Special Steels', *Metallurgia*, 42 (Nov. 1950), 279–82. See also G. Lucas and J. F. Pollock, *Gas Turbine Materials* (London, 1957), 1–25.

[21] Charles Sykes, 'Developments in Alloy and Special Steels', *Metallurgia*, 37 (Dec. 1947), 75–9.

[22] SCL Firth-Brown Records. Directors' reports, 29 Mar. 1944.

the end of the War as early as September 1943, debating, for example, as to whether its expertise in hot-coil tank springs might prove useful for railway vehicles. The familiar problem of the switchover from arms to commercial production began raising its head.

The steel firms began counting the cost. That steel plant was 'flogged to death', is a common comment by businessmen who lived through the War—a term that applied literally to some individuals. Both Hatfield and Swinden collapsed and died during the War, both men severely over-worked. Arthur Balfour, who had taken control of the family's tool steel firm during the War while the other family members were away, had a serious breakdown (he was into his seventies) and was never the same again. According to his son, Balfour and his team were 'out on their feet [and with] no replacements behind them . . . the structure was weak at the very moment when intense effort was necessary to rebuild exports and turnover'.[23] There was a general air of being played out and the old order changing in other firms, too. At Hadfields, the company was faced, as it was in 1918, with the collapse of the company's order books as ordnance contracts evaporated. In 1945 the board felt 'disquietude for the future prospects of the Company', in the face of overmanning, poor deliveries, and the inefficient utilization of plant. 'What we really require is "mass produced" lines,' stated the Hadfield directors, '[though] the steps we may be called upon to take may be revolutionary, so far as this company is concerned.'[24]

Other firms faced similar problems, especially the ESC, which had relied almost entirely on armaments both before and during the War and had neglected overseas markets. It did not return to its normal rhythm until 1948. At Firth-Brown, the directors stated in 1946 that: 'Armament work is ceasing to have any major importance,'[25] and the production of shells, guns, and bombs soon ceased. The electric arc and high-frequency furnaces were in good shape, but a drastic overhaul of the accounting system was needed, besides much product-development. Production facilities for alloy bars were departmentalized and scattered, involving excessive transport and paperwork—the whole needing to be incorporated into a continuous layout.[26] But removal to a new green-field site was thought to be too risky and expensive. Firth-Brown remained, like many Sheffield firms, a mixture of the obsolete and the modern—one new director finding that horse-drawn transport was still used, the choice based erroneously on the low operating cost, without relating this to tons moved!

[23] Arthur Balfour & Co., *A Centenary* (Sheffield, 1957), 46–7.
[24] SCL Hadfield Papers. Report (1945), Directors' Minute Book.
[25] SCL Firth-Brown Records. Directors' reports, 30 Jan. 1946.
[26] Eric Mensforth, *Family Engineers* (London, 1981), 86.

Nationally, plans for the post-war reconstruction of the steel industry were laid as they were for other industries. The effectiveness of government direction was seen by some as strengthening the case for nationalization. The steel industry opposed this idea and itself prepared a reorganization scheme for the Government, subsequently issued as a White Paper in 1946, which planned to implement modernization plans shelved during the war, to enlarge steelmaking facilities, and to concentrate production into more efficient units. However, the Labour Government, somewhat reluctantly, pushed ahead with the nationalization of the steel industry in 1949. The Iron & Steel Corporation of Great Britain was established to control companies with the largest capacity (over 100,000 tons or more per annum), bringing firms such as the ESC, United Steel, Park Gate, Firth-Brown, Brown Bayleys, and Hadfields into the net.

Nationalization was bitterly opposed by the Sheffield steel firms, as it was in the rest of the industry. Wilton Lee of Arthur Lee & Sons expressed the industry's gut reaction: 'We saw the distinct possibility of having our birthright taken from us, something that three generations had struggled to develop was going to be stolen from us, and I wasn't going to have it.'[27] Sir John Green of Firth-Brown was regarded as nothing less than a traitor for agreeing to serve as the only 'steelman' on the Iron & Steel Corporation board and was later ostracized by the old guard in Sheffield industry.

Other criticisms were more measured. In particular, industry leaders were concerned because of Sheffield's unique position as both steel producer and consumer. Its firms were not 'steel companies' in the sense of the Government's nationalization plans: steel production was closely bound up with engineering, even *within* firms, to say nothing of its wider relationship with other centres. Sheffield's cluster made nationalization complex, as can be seen at the ESC and Firth-Brown. At the ESC, the chairman told shareholders that the company was 'essentially an engineering works', and nationalization—which the directors were unable to prevent—was an amputation, seriously disrupting its close technical collaboration with other parts of the Vickers group. The Weybridge aircraft division, for example, relied on its intimate daily association with the River Don to solve various technical problems far more quickly than if the ESC had been an outside firm. The Vickers' board estimated that the Government was going to nationalize the ESC to get—at most—one-fifth of it.[28]

[27] *Lee Steel 1874–1974* (Sheffield, 1974), 15.
[28] J. D. Scott, *Vickers: A History* (London, 1962), 329–36. According to Scott, nationalization was a disconcerting episode to Vickers, which had seen its huge assets nationalized 'as it were, by accident, because they were engineering plant which happened to be administratively tied up with steel trading'.

At Firth-Brown, in the immediate post-war years the company had acquired a Canadian distribution facility (Firth-Brown Steels), made its tools division into a separate company (Firth-Brown Tools Ltd.), bought the Coventry machine tool firm of Wickman (which had introduced Krupp's carbides into the United Kingdom), and established a separate engineering division around the production of mechanical presses and rolling mill parts. Some of these subsidiaries were split off to lessen the danger of nationalization to the Brown group as a whole. But Firth-Brown were still worried, as were the ESC, because of the interlocking ('jobbing') layout of much of the firm and the intimate linkages of steel with the rest of the business. If steel was taken away by the Government, they believed that the rest of the businesses would become unprofitable, especially if an 'average of industry' base was used, because of the inherently high cost of the firm's products. As it was, in 1951 Brown's were able to negotiate, at a price, for the retention of Firth-Brown Tools and Firth-Brown Steels; but the whole episode had 'disrupted profitable activities and resulted in uncertainties as to the amounts, manner and timing of the monetary compensation, and how, if at all, the lost fields of management endeavour and sources of income should be replaced'.[29] The 1951 nationalization had therefore raised many of the problems that were to surface in more acute form nearly twenty years later.

In the event, company structures and managements were left untouched by nationalization and plans to rationalize the industry made little headway. As one ESC director put it: 'In the early 1950s we didn't know we were nationalised. We just carried on as normal.'[30] In 1953 a Conservative Government denationalized steel and firms were gradually returned to the private sector,[31] though the industry remained under close Government scrutiny and an Iron & Steel Board was established to supervise the industry at a national level. United Steel, the ESC, Brown Bayleys, Hadfields, and Firth-Brown were then sold off by the Government's Iron & Steel Realization Agency by 1955. Only John Brown & Co. declined to buy back their steelmaking interests and Firth-Brown was sold back to private interests at a price of £6.8 million, including a £3 million debenture. Firth-Brown then proceeded to purchase from the Agency the Glasgow firm, Beardmore's, for its additional forging capacity.

Ideological debates soon gave way to an overwhelming demand for steel of any kind, however inefficient the plant. The steel industry in Britain was about to enter a boom which was to last until the end of the 1950s. These were years of strong economic expansion. At the world level Britain and other European countries were shedding their imperial links;

---

[29] Mensforth, *Family Engineers*, 80; SCL Firth-Brown Records. 'Confidential Memo—Factors Affecting the Segregation of Certain Portions of the Works'.
[30] Bill Pugh interview.   [31] K. Burk, *The First Privatisation* (London, 1988).

on the other hand, Continental trading areas were being created, such as the European Economic Community in 1957 and the European Free Trade Area in 1960, which encouraged economic expansion and compensated for the loss of the old colonial markets. In addition, major steel-consuming industries, especially automobile and aircraft manufacture, were expanding. British steel production surged forward from over 13 million tons in 1939 to over 24 million tons in 1960 (world steel production itself more than doubled between 1947 and 1957 to reach 288 million tons). Alloy steel production did not increase at quite such a rapid rate as crude steel, but alloy steel output in Sheffield roughly doubled between the late 1940s and 1960, and there was marked growth in tool and stainless steels (see Figs. 10.1–6). In short, these were halcyon days for British steel in which the Sheffield special steel industry fully shared.

The late 1940s and 1950s were a time of intense activity in Sheffield, not easily summarized. However, reference to our earlier determinants of Sheffield's steelmaking successes—factor conditions, demand, related and supporting industries, and company structure and strategy—will enable us to pick our way through the main developments.

Throughout this book, Steel City's ability to maintain (and constantly upgrade) certain factor conditions—especially its stock of scientific and technical knowledge to counteract any geographical and physical disadvantages—has been identified as the mainspring of its success. In the 1950s, although Sheffield was not without some advantages in terms of location (it remained ideally placed for its main customers in the industrial Midlands and north-west) and resources (such as refractories), it was its human and knowledge base that still gave it the competitive edge.

Sheffield remained a major centre for steel research in the 1950s. At the Brown-Firth Research Laboratories, (Sir) Charles Sykes (1905–82) continued the highly successful metallurgical tradition of W. H. Hatfield. During the War Sykes had supervised work on armour-piercing shells at the National Physical Laboratory, before becoming director of the Brown-Firth Research Laboratories in 1944. An affable, widely respected figure, with a formidable reputation as a metallurgist, Sykes laid the foundation for Firth-Brown's success in gas-turbine components, alternator rotor forgings, and hardened steel rolls. He soon moved into the higher echelons of the company's management (eventually becoming chairman between 1964 and 1967), being replaced at the Laboratories by H. W. Kirkby.

Meanwhile at United Steel, the managing director, Gerald Steel, in 1945 initiated a major expansion of the company's research facilities, despite post-war shortages of capital and materials. This resulted by 1952 in a new Research & Development Department, named Swinden Laboratories, which was situated in Rotherham. Under a new director, Frank Saniter, the Department set out to take 'a wider view of research and apply it to cover every element of [United Steel's] operations'.[32] In the fields of fuel technology, refractories, and production processes, especially continuous casting, United Steel made outstanding contributions to metallurgy. Jack Chesters, for example, became one of the pioneers in refractories. 'We spent a [£] million a year on [fire] bricks and the approach to the technology was amateur,' he recalled: 'But after the war I began to think about the fundamentals of gas flow. Open-hearth furnaces turned out to be like aeroplanes—they needed streamlining.' Chesters established refractories technology on scientific principles, work which had enormous practical benefits. 'Steel, Peech & Tozer told us we were saving them thousands of pounds. We went on to save millions.'[33]

In the finishing processes, a major new development that appeared in the 1950s was continuous casting. The concept of casting molten steel into billets and slabs directly from the furnace, without prior cooling into ingots, had long been a steelmaker's dream (Bessemer for one had considered the idea), because of the huge savings in energy costs and greatly improved yields.[34] Today continuous casting—in which the molten steel descending from the furnace is ingeniously solidified by a water-cooled mould—is a *tour de force* of the steelmaker's art. But in the beginning the technical problems were immense. The important pioneering work began in the 1930s in Germany and, after contributions in the immediate post-war period from America as well as Europe, the idea was taken up by British firms in the late 1940s and early 1950s. Sheffield's involvement began at about this time when the Low Moor Alloy Steel Works installed an experimental continuous casting plant in 1946, work that was continued with the help of Osborn's when they took the works over in 1954. In the previous year a consortium of eleven Sheffield steelmakers had also set up a continuous casting plant in the melting shop at Jessop's, amid hopes that the technique could be used for tool and high-speed steels.[35] It was United Steel, however, which made a decisive contribution to continuous casting technology with its experimental work under Iain

[32] K. J. Irvine, *Swinden Laboratories: 50 Years of Steel Research* (Rotherham, 1984), 8.

[33] J. H. Chesters interview, 9 Dec. 1991.

[34] Manfred M. Wolf, 'History of Continuous Casting', in *Steelmaking in the 20th Century: From Black Magic to Technology* (Warrendale, Penn., Iron & Steel Society, 1992), 47–101. Wolf credits an American steelmaker, Benjamin Atha, as the pioneer in 1886. Interestingly, his works—the Benjamin Atha & Illingworth Steel Co. of Harrison, New York—was one of the pioneering crucible steel works in the United States and established with steelmakers from the Sheffield area. The Illingworth partners were from Stocksbridge. I am grateful to Derek Stapley for bringing this to my attention.

[35] J. S. Morton, 'Continuous Casting of Steel', *British Steelmaker*, 21 (May 1955), 152–7; B. H. C. Waters *et al.*, 'Continuous Casting of High Speed Steel', *JISI* 190 (1958), 233–48. As it happened, continuous casting did not prove appropriate for tool steel and high-speed steel, and today the process is only economic for bulk steel production.

Halliday at Barrow in 1952. This work established the concept of strand bending as the steel descended from the mould, which was used world-wide. Such experiments successfully established continuous casting and thereafter the process grew rapidly.

By the end of the 1950s, the Swinden and Brown-Firth Research Laboratories were as impressive as any steel research organizations in the world. But they were not the only firms supporting such facilities. Jessop-Saville, although not the largest firm in the city (with about 3,200 employees in 1958), employed nearly 200 physicists, metallurgists, and engineers in its research department under the director Geoffrey Harris. Besides the Brightside laboratories, a new research department was opened at Whiston Grange, near Rotherham.[36] Sheffield was also home to national efforts in steel research, the most notable of which was the Hoyle Street laboratories of the British Iron & Steel Research Association. BISRA had organized the consortium that began experimenting with continuous casting at Jessop's.[37] In fact, there was a wide range of small research bodies—among them the Spring Manufacturers' Research Association, the Drop Forging Research Association, and the British Steel Castings Research Association. These organizations, which enjoyed a heyday in the 1950s, were of particular help to the smaller companies who were unable to afford major investments in R&D. Meanwhile, the University continued to be a prolific source of qualified personnel for the industry.

Sheffield's laboratories did not make any sensational discoveries, such as the Hadfield manganese and Brearley stainless alloys, but then nor did anyone else. The research effort was as strong as ever. Tests for steel used under critical conditions could now sometimes take thousands of hours. Notwithstanding, substantial progress continued to be made in improving properties and making new modifications to steels, pushed forward by the relentless demands from the automobile, aircraft, chemical, petroleum, and atomic energy industries. Reviews of the technical literature at this time report interesting developments in constructional steels, corrosion-resisting steels, and high-temperature materials.[38] Considerable attention, for example, was devoted to improving the creep-resistance of ferritic stainless steels for use in high-temperature gas turbines. One Jessop's metallurgist recalled that: 'In 1939 I would guess there were no more than a dozen creep test points in Sheffield; by 1950 there were hundreds, mainly at Firth-Brown and Jessop's. We alone had over a hundred.'[39]

[36] 'William Jessop & Sons Ltd.: Research and Technical Development', *British Steelmaker*, 24 (Feb. 1958), 46–9.

[37] 'BISRA's New Sheffield Laboratories', *Metallurgia*, 48 (Dec. 1953), 265–72.

[38] G. T. Harris and E. Johnson, 'Recent Progress in Alloy and Special Steels', ibid. 51 (Jan. 1955), 17–23.

[39] Bill Bailey interview.

The virtuoso skill in hand and eye that had made Sheffield a centre for steelmaking in the nineteenth century was still an important factor in the 1950s, though the scene was beginning to change rapidly. In tool steel manufacture the high-frequency induction furnace was now the standard method for melting and the crucible and converting processes were virtually extinct. Doncaster's made (and filmed) the last cementation heat in its Hoyle Street furnaces in 1951; and though some firms—Huntsman, Doncaster, Pearson, and Mawhood Bros.—continued to make crucible steel into the 1960s, its commercial status was negligible at this time.[40] Some of the older firms, such as Huntsman—absorbed by Dunford & Elliott in 1951—saw their influence wane along with the crucible. The surviving firms, even the smallest, now needed to invest as tool steel technology became more intensive. Other countries had now caught up with Sheffield in tool and high-speed steel manufacture. One manufacturer noted in 1947 that 'to meet foreign competition the standard quality of the company's high-speed steel, which is probably typical of British practice, will have to be improved'.[41] Better surface and longer bar-lengths were needed to match the substantial improvements being made in America and Europe. This meant a steady stream of expenditure in new arc and high-frequency furnaces, improved rolling mills, better heat-treatment facilities, and more sophisticated laboratory methods.

The bulk special steel plants, where the main source for high-quality engineering steels continued to be the basic electric arc furnace, still relied on traditions of local skill first nurtured by the crucible. According to a manager of one arc melt shop: 'it was 1960 before you could really say that the steel was taken out of the hands of the operators'. Until then, 'it was all rule of thumb. We did play around with devices such as thermocouples, but they were so unreliable, we tended not to use them.'[42] Forces for change were the increasing capacity of these furnaces and the growing complexity of alloy steels. In 1954 Fox's installed Europe's largest electric arc furnace for alloy steel manufacture: this 70-ton furnace led to a greater realization of the merits of large arc furnaces and influenced the decision to embark upon even larger developments. It was also realized that the production of large forging ingots sufficiently low in hydrogen would be a problem, so United Steel became interested in a German technique—vacuum degassing—that offered a solution. A pilot plant was commissioned by the Research & Development Department in 1959.

[40] Richard Doncaster, shortly before he died, told me that he was 'probably the last man who worked on a cementation furnace'. Interview 23 July 1991. The last commercial crucible melting furnace continued to operate in Matilda Street until 1972. See Bob Hawkins, 'The Distribution of Crucible Steel Furnaces in Sheffield' (SCL Information Sheet, 2nd edn., 1973).

[41] Firth-Brown Records. Directors' report, 26 Feb. 1947.

[42] Bernard Connolly interview, 29 June 1992.

At the other end of the spectrum, where even more specialist steels were demanded for applications such as jet engines, new technology was developing. Typically, the initial ideas (which had often been around some time) were European or American in origin: nevertheless, Sheffield helped perfect the processes. The most important to emerge at the end of the 1950s was the technique of remelting steel in a vacuum, which produced an extremely clean product. In Sheffield the pioneers were Jessop's, which in 1957 installed a consumable vacuum arc furnace for titanium. The technique proved especially useful for melting the increasingly exotic alloys demanded by the aircraft designer, and also gave Jessop's the chance to utilize the furnace to become the first British firm to remelt steel in a vacuum in production quantities.[43]

Supporting, indeed triggering, this development in research and production technology, was a demand for special steels that was both extensive and sophisticated. Underlying this was the expansion of the British (and European) economy in the 1950s, with a rate of economic growth that was perhaps greater than at any previous time. British industrial output, according to one estimate, grew by 3.7 per cent a year between 1948 and 1960, compared with 3.1 per cent in the inter-war period, and 1.6 per cent between 1877 and 1913.[44] This was the performance of a highly successful industrial economy, which (although it had some shortcomings by international standards) provided several lucrative markets for the special steelmaker.

The demand for armaments was not greatly significant over the decade as a whole. However, the impact of the Korean War in the early 1950s, which sucked in over half the national alloy and stainless steel output in 1952, was an important event. At Hadfields some directors believed arms orders for Korea greatly delayed the move into commercial products, something which may have happened to other Sheffield firms. When normal business resumed, the big money at the top end of the commercial special steel market was in the giant forgings needed for turbo-generating equipment, nuclear pressure vessels, forged pipemoulds, huge crankshafts, downhole drilling equipment and offshore structures. This was the glamorous sector of heavy industry, where firms such as the ESC and Firth-Brown led a highly select field. The ESC's River Don Works, with one of the largest forging presses in the world (the 7,000-ton Openshaw press), was producing by far the largest forgings of anyone in the country.

---

[43] 'Vacuum Melted Metals: Steel, Titanium and Zirconium in Production', *Metallurgia*, 57 (Mar. 1958), 139–42. In aircraft quality ingots, air melted steels had impurities equivalent to about thirty parts per million; while ordinary commercial grades contained 300 parts per million or higher. In vacuum melted steel inclusions could be as low as five parts per million.

[44] S. Pollard, *The Development of the British Economy, 1914–1990* (London, 4th edn., 1992), 229.

The biggest forgings—so-called monoblocs—were for boiler drums for power generation plants. As generating capacity increased—by 1950 there were plans for power stations up to 150–200 megawatts; by 1960, 200–330 megawatts—so the size of monoblocs increased. They were sold at a premium price, as one of the selling points was that they were made in one piece. No welds were used, even at the drum ends, which were bent over. Making each one was a task requiring the greatest expertise. As one ESC man put it: 'Even the cranemen were highly skilled.'[45]

The drive towards greater generating efficiencies, higher steam temperatures, pressure, and set sizes also involved the development of improved high-temperature boiler plant steels, together with higher strength 12 per cent chromium steels to meet the higher working stresses developed in the longer turbine blades. Progress in this area benefited greatly from concurrent work for military and civil aircraft. In the 1950s the development of nuclear weapons and then the nuclear energy industry also demanded new alloys and unprecedented standards in metallurgical control. Jessop's and Hadfields were amongst those firms that developed alloys for nuclear reactors.

At the heavy end of British industry, Sheffield also satisfied the demand for hydraulic presses and power systems, hot and cold rolling mills, and associated auxiliary equipment for the steel and non-ferrous metal industries. Firth-Brown, for example, in 1946 reached agreements to build large mechanical presses for E. W. Bliss and heavy steel and metal working plant for the Loewy Engineering Co. 'The demand for forgings can only be described as staggering,' stated the Firth-Brown directors in 1947.[46] One particularly good trade was in hardened steel rolls. In the 1950s, recalled Firth-Brown's marketing manager, the company 'could not make rolls fast enough'.[47] Hadfields also had a very profitable share of the rolls business, a technology that had developed from armaments. Its Millspaugh subsidiary (which had been hived off when Hadfields was nationalized, but which had been repurchased) was also part of this heavy engineering sector. It continued to make suction rolls for the paper industry.

Less exotic, but of huge commercial significance to the Sheffield steel industry, was the demand from the transport industries. In shipbuilding, the United Kingdom lost her world lead in the 1950s, but still relied on Sheffield for a steady supply of forgings. Railway material—wheels, axles, springs, manganese steel crossings, and locomotive parts—though no longer as significant to Sheffield as it was in the nineteenth century, was

[45] Bill Pugh interview.

[46] Firth-Brown Records. Directors' report, 2 May 1947. See also 'Capital Equipment for Metal Working', *Metallurgia*, 41 (Nov. 1949), 11–14.

[47] Geoffrey Lucas interview, 14 May 1991.

still made in considerable tonnages. But it was the car industry that was centre stage in the 1950s. At the start of the decade, Britain was the world's greatest car exporter, sending three times as many cars abroad as the Americans, and was second to the United States in overall production. In the United Kingdom car production grew from 219,000 in 1946 to 1,353,000 in 1960. The car industry's orders for crankshafts, half-shafts, springs, bars, and strip and stainless steel made it Steel City's biggest customer by the 1950s. And by the following decade, one Sheffield steel expert estimated that at least 65 per cent of the steel produced in the region was destined either directly or indirectly for the car industry, dominantly to home producers.[48]

Technically, the aircraft industry made even more severe demands on Sheffield steelmakers. In particular, the principal components of the jet engine—the compressor, the combustion chambers, the stator blades (or nozzle guide vanes), the rotor blades, and the rotor disc—all demanded increasingly specialized properties at elevated temperatures. In the late 1940s and early 1950s, firms such as Jessop's, Firth-Vickers, and Fox's laid the foundations for a large business in such alloy steels, which had the required high strength and creep-resisting properties. G18B had placed Jessop's in the forefront of the turbine disc suppliers. They claimed to supply over 90 per cent of the discs used in the United Kingdom and this, at its peak, amounted to over 1,000 discs per month, since there were then many domestic engine-builders—Rolls-Royce, Armstrong-Siddeley, Bristol, Napier, and de Havilland. Later, with the introduction of H46 in 1948, Jessop's also led the field in ferritic disc materials, though by then other firms, such as Firth-Brown (with its Rex 448), were competing hard. It was the demand from the aircraft industry that led Jessop's into the new titanium alloys and vacuum melting.

Daniel Doncaster & Son, while it made ready to shut down its old cementation technology, entered the new era immediately after the War by developing a relationship with Rolls-Royce for nickel ('Nimonic') stampings for gas-turbine aero-engines. In 1951 Doncaster's purchased Monk Bridge Iron & Steel Co. in Leeds to make forgings for the blades for jet engines and then established Doncasters Moorside Ltd. in Oldham in 1956 for machining these components. It was a marked change in location for the firm (though it still had its head office and forging division in Sheffield) and also in outlook, since the change from steel alloys to nickel and titanium 'was too much for the conservative Sheffield workforce'.[49] Osborn's also went into this market: its Low Moor works in Bradford specialized in extrusions for the aircraft and aero-engine industries. The aircraft industry was also a factor in one of the few new start-ups in the

[48] K. Lewis, Master Cutlers' Address, Cutlers' Hall, 2 Oct. 1973.
[49] Richard T. Doncaster interview.

1950s—G. L. Willan Ltd.—founded in 1952 as Roblan Steels. The originator was Geoffrey Willan, the local director of a London-based electric furnace company, who with £10,000 capital, eight staff, and a high-frequency furnace, began melting alloy steels for bar stock and castings for aircraft from premises in Furnival Steet. It too moved into vacuum melting and ferro-alloys (notably ferro-titanium), buying Marsh Bros.' steelmaking activities in 1959 (which brought the workforce up to about 250).[50]

Other segments of demand are less easily summarized. As the economy expanded, there was a great expansion in consumer durables, almost all of which offered a market for stainless steels. The demand for stainless, most of which was melted in Sheffield, has never stopped growing since 1945. As ever, few industries could function without good-quality tool steel—still virtually a Sheffield monopoly in the 1950s—for punching, drawing, cutting, and stamping. Richard Carr's specialized in cold-die and hot-die steels and expanded rapidly in the 1950s, with GKN as its major customer. Besides high-speed steel and the tungsten-carbides, there was still a big market for the ordinary qualities of tool steel. Sanderson Bros., for example, built up a market in ground flat stock, especially in oil-hardening tool steel. 'It was almost like a retailing trade,' recalls one member of the firm, 'pieces were wrapped up, with the heat-treatment instructions on each packet and the customer got a tool steel that was easy to use and manipulate. We could not make enough of it.'[51]

As in the nineteenth century, Sheffield's national superiority was the basis for international competitive advantage. The demand for special steels in the 1950s began exceeding Sheffield's ability to supply it (at least, not without a long wait by customers), and part of the problem was the pressure from overseas. In 1947, Firth-Brown, for example, noting the orders from Luxembourg and Switzerland, commented that the prospective demand for hardened steel rolls was very great, and would tax the resources of the company. The firm's rolls business was 75 per cent export and accounted for some 20 per cent of the firm's turnover. During the 1950s the company got hold of most of the Canadian market in steel rolls, and also held a dominant position in Belgium and Australia. Competition from other European makers, such as Germany, hardly mattered yet, since they lacked Sheffield's level of expertise. In its overall export trade, by 1951 Europe was Firth-Brown's main market, taking about 40 per cent of sales, followed by Australasia with about 20 per cent. Fox meanwhile exported large tonnages of stainless steel sheet to Australia; and the company was also probably the leading supplier of safety-razor carbon-strip

---

[50] *British Steelmaker*, 25 (Aug. 1959), 298–9; *Quality*, 4 (Oct. 1957), 24–6; *Quality*, 22 (July/ Aug. 1975), 20–1.
[51] Bernard Callan interview, 29 Mar. 1994.

steel in the world. The industry's disasters with this type of steel in the 1920s were well behind it: in fact, Gillette in America was Fox's best customer!

Jessop's found that its turbine disc technology was much in demand abroad, with Switzerland as a particularly receptive market. After the War, the Swiss immediately began developing gas-turbine technology for power generation, with Sulzer, Brown Boveri, Escher Wyss, and Oerlikon ordering Jessop materials. The Sheffield tool steel and tool firms were sometimes less overseas-oriented and often relied almost exclusively on the United Kingdom market (Carr's export trade, for example, never amounted to more than about 10 per cent). Nevertheless, some—such as Balfour's, Sanderson Bros. & Newbould, and Marsh Bros.—still had widely-based overseas selling agencies, which had been in existence from the inter-war period and before. Sanderson Bros. & Newbould had stockholding agencies and subsidiaries in Australia, Canada, and South Africa; so too did Marsh Bros. and Osborn's. This ensured that these firms were not simply steel producers, but worldwide groups engaged in marketing engineering products.

Sheffield could still draw great strength from its related and supporting industries. The unique cluster of metal-working and engineering industries, though it had some weaknesses, was still in vigorous health in the 1950s. The production within a dozen miles of Sheffield of nearly 70 per cent of the country's alloy steels, with a similarly high percentage in castings, forgings, rolled sections, and strip, had ensured the continued development of mechanical and electrical engineering in the area. This was a larger employer than the steel industry itself. Sheffield was home for some world-ranking companies. Davy's, for example (renamed Davy & United Engineering), employed about 3,000 in 1960 with a machinery division fully established on the Darnall site and a 500-strong factory and drawing office in Glasgow. It was a major supplier and installer of steelworks plant. The contract to build the Durgapur steelworks in India, taken in 1957, generated large profits and converted the company from a mechanical mill builder into a turnkey contractor.[52] Ward's meanwhile had become one of the largest and most comprehensive contractors' plant departments in the country. Its Sheffield workforce topped 3,000 in the 1950s (with nearly 12,000 in the group) and from offices in Sheffield and London operated nearly fifty branches.

Around Sheffield, Doncaster remained a centre of railway and mining engineering, and had also developed the production of agricultural machinery, such as tractors, and electrical equipment. Chesterfield had a similar range of interests, with industrial furnaces and tube manufacture

---

[52] E. C. Hewitt, 'Organisational Developments at Darnall', typescript, Nov. 1990. Courtesy Davy McKee.

being important. A blast furnace at Sheepbridge, near the northern edge of the town, was linked with a large iron foundry and engineering works. Rotherham's industries to a certain extent mimicked Sheffield's, but a large industry had developed to fabricate steel into such products as refrigerators and domestic boilers.

Within Sheffield itself, the tool industry was still an important consumer of steel and was, of course, an area with which many of the steel firms had the closest links.[53] Both the major and smaller steelworks benefited from the growth in the demand for tools in the 1950s. Almost all the tool steel firms involved in tool production either expanded their product lines or absorbed other companies at this time. Bedford's began the production of chrome-vanadium plated spanners and tungsten-carbide drill rods; Edgar Allen built a new engineers' tool department at Shepcote Lane, bought a magnetic chuck subsidiary in Oldham, and by 1961 had also acquired the Sheffield Hollow Drill Co.; Osborn's opened a Mushet Tool Works on Penistone Road in 1943 to expand production of twist drills and small engineers' tools; and Marsh Bros.' trade in twist drills and reamers became the firm's main business. Firth-Brown Tools Ltd., founded in 1946, besides its segmented saws and files, developed tools for the watchmaking and instrument industries, including twist drills down to 0.005-inch diameter. In 1950 it also introduced 'Surform', one of the few innovations in tool design in recent times, which was pioneered by its works manager, a naval commander named Booth. A cross between a rasp and a plane, Surform tools could be used for the quick smoothing of wood and soft metals. Neill's had also steadily expanded in the 1950s, acquiring Hallamshire Steel & File along the way, so that by 1960 the company employed over 1,000. In 1958 Neill's was described by the *Sunday Times* as the largest family firm in the country.

Of the more specialist tool producers, Sheffield Twist Drill enjoyed its most dramatic growth in the 1950s, when it bought subsidiaries in Birmingham amd Hednesford, built a factory at Worksop, and greatly expanded its premises in Sheffield. By the late 1950s its employees numbered over 1,300. Hall & Pickles, manufacturing its 'Hydra' tools at Ecclesfield, employed over 4,000 by the end of the 1950s. Tyzack, Sons, & Turner expanded its Little London Works with the rising demand for agricultural machine parts, and the company also made automobile components and still produced saws and scythes. At Stanley Tools, the 1950s were a time of vigorous expansion, with the firm developing its own United Kingdom marketing force for the sale of Stanley planes, the

---

[53] *Histories of Famous Firms* (1957); Douglas Hallam, *The First 200 Years: Rabone Chesterman, 1784–1984* (Birmingham, 1984); F. Wright, *James Neill: A Century of Quality and Service, 1889–1989* (Sheffield, 1989); Ruskin Gallery, *The Cutting Edge* (Sheffield, 1992); F. Wright, *Stanley 1936–1986* (Sheffield, 1986).

popular 'Yankee' spiral-ratchet screwdriver, and the Stanley knife. Like other tool firms, such as James Chesterman, it benefited greatly from the upsurge in 'Do-it-Yourself' as consumer affluence and housebuilding increased. The structure of the industry was still mostly small-scale in Sheffield, but the smaller companies were now being absorbed. Competition was growing, especially from overseas, whose countries did not fail to spot opportunities in a country rebuilding its infrastructure.

The cutlery and plated trades were now a far less significant part of the cluster, relative to their dominant position before 1900. The small-scale nature of the industry had hardly changed. In 1954 only about a dozen cutlery firms had more than 200 workers, and well over 100 firms had less than fifty. About 450 manufacturing entities, employing some 2,000 workers from a total Sheffield workforce of about 10,000, had less than ten workers. The industry was neither progressive in its technology, nor in its pay or labour relations.[54]

However, the few business records that are available for this period show the cutlery firms evidently sharing in the general boom for consumer goods in the 1950s. At Wostenholm's, for example, company profits hit record levels as the demand for steel and cutlery at any price surged: sales more than quadrupled from about £60,000 in 1945 to nearly £220,000 by 1960. The emphasis was on production rather than selling and the era was typified by an indifference to customer requirements and slow deliveries. In Canada, still Wostenholm's best overseas market, the firm's managing director, Sidney Fowler, was greeted with the words: 'Your goods are OK, but your delivery is B. awful.' Fowler stressed: 'Should an order be obtained, delivery must be quick. We might think delivery has not been too bad—but the point is, it has not been good enough for this customer.'[55] Closer to home problems arose with deliveries of kitchen cutlery to leading London department stores: in 1961 Wostenholm's were unable to guarantee a delivery date for one customer. Partly, this reflected production problems. In 1958 pocket-knife manufacture was plagued by 'operational bottlenecks', while 'Monte Carlo' kitchen sets were troubled by 'the finish which was not quite right after repeated trials ... which have caused us to be behind in deliveries, and Lewis's [the department store's] order has been postponed in delivery.'[56]

The Sheffield cutlery industry was clearly ill-at-ease in the era of mass production, but its older high-quality markets were being further eroded after 1945. Stainless steel and the dawn of the modern era of air travel sounded the death knell of the Sheffield silver- and electroplate trade (it

[54] Harry Townsend, 'The Structure and Problems of the Sheffield Cutlery Trade', *District Bank Review* (1954), 19–24.

[55] SCL Wostenholm Records, Fowler to Wostenholm, 12 June 1959.

[56] Ibid. Wostenholm to S. Fowler, 29 Apr., 6 May 1958.

was calculated that after a voyage an ocean liner might need a 25 per cent refit of silverware due to pilfering by souvenir hunters—a steady business for Sheffield).[57] Any changeover to stainless steel required expensive capital investment in retooling—no easy matter for the smaller businesses—and so by the end of the 1950s this sector was in trouble. Only at the cheap end of the cutlery market were openings to be found, and only one cutlery firm seems to have had an impact here.

Significantly, this was Richards Bros., founded by the German Richartz brothers and their partner, Muller. In 1945 they built a new factory (under the name Richards) near the city centre, installed the latest die-casting machines and began producing a product range similar to Rodgers' and Wostenholm's—pocket-knives, kitchen cutlery, and scissors. In the 1950s the business took off: with a workforce of 750, Richards soon became the largest cutlery factory in Sheffield, which enjoyed about 60 per cent of the United Kingdom's pocket-knife production and 30–40 per cent of the home output for scissors. The firm became noted for its inexpensive, celluloid-handled pocket-knives, which sold in large quantities—exactly the type of knife the old Sheffield cutlers despised.

Not only in cutlery had the old nineteenth-century structure and strategies survived. In the steel industry, by the mid-1950s some 130 firms were involved in steelmaking and processing, employing over 41,000 workers. As of old, Sheffield accommodated some of the largest steel firms in the country and some of the smallest. In Sheffield itself, the ESC was the major employer, with a workforce of well over 10,000 in the mid-1950s (the ESC group employing over 15,000). Firth-Brown was the next largest with some 6,000 workers (the majority of whom were Sheffield-based), closely followed by a number of other steelmakers, such as Hadfields, Jessop's, Osborn's, and Brown Bayleys, with work rolls from 3,000 to 5,000. Nearby was the dominating presence of United Steel, with some 35,000 employees in 1955 (making it one of the largest British firms), about 7,000 of whom worked at Samuel Fox and over 8,000 at Steel, Peech, & Tozer.

Beneath these giants, the small tool steel firms plied their trade, employing scores or hundreds rather than thousands, with their traditions of small, private enterprise largely intact. The survival of nearly all the prominent nineteenth-century crucible and high-speed steelmakers into the 1950s is striking. There were nearly a hundred constituent firms of the Crucible and High-Speed Steel Associations and, allowing for some adjustment due to the fact that a few did not melt steel, some eighty or more manufactured tool and high-speed steel, about a dozen of them relatively large. These included all the well-known names, such as Balfour,

[57] Gill Booth, *Diamonds in Brown Paper* (Sheffield, 1988), 9.

Beardshaw, Bedford, Huntsman, Ibbotson, Jessop, Jonas & Colver, Kayser Ellison, Sanderson Bros. & Newbould, Vessey, and Wardlow.

The gap between these firms and the industry giants was wide. United Steel and the ESC, and to a lesser extent, firms such as Firth-Brown and Hadfields, were following a route which had been marked out for them since the 1860s: the large-scale manufacture of steel, albeit at the special end of the market. They were public companies, employing millions in capital, with widely dispersed shareholdings (a trend reinforced by the brief nationalization), and boards of professionally and technically trained managers. The big firms had long ceased to be 'independent' in the old sense and the 'dynastic' element had mostly faded, though not entirely. The burden of the past lay perhaps the most heavily on Hadfields. The old team under Sir Peter Brown had steered the company through the War, but when Brown retired in 1945 no successors presented themselves. An outsider, Lord Dudley Gordon (1883–1972), had to be appointed. An Harrovian, he brought with him *gravitas*, but little direct knowledge of the industry, having gained his early experience with a London refrigeration engineers. There were still directors at the company, such as Richard Lamb, who had worked under Sir Robert Hadfield.

United Steel was recognized as the best-managed of the steel firms. Sir Walter Benton Jones remained as chairman until 1962, with Gerald Steel (1895–1957) as general managing director. Steel, a grandson of one of the founders of Steel, Peech, & Tozer, was especially interested in personnel and industrial training, reflecting his company's professional approach to such matters. It had introduced formal management training schemes during the 1930s. At the ESC, the chairman in the late 1950s was (Sir) Frederick Pickworth (1890–1959), the son of a Sheffield stonemason, whose early training was in accountancy at Cammell-Laird. At Firth-Brown, the board of managing directors after the war was filled with engineers—men such as Sir Allan Grant, Sir Arthur Matthews, (Sir) Eric Mensforth, and (Sir) Charles Sykes FRS—who reflected the strong techno-logical bias of the company.

The profitability of these companies dwarfed that of the smaller con-cerns. At United Steel profits hit record levels in the period from 1954 to 1960, rising from £9 million to £23 million. Its subsidiary Fox's found its special steels particularly lucrative: net profits, from a low point in 1947 of £122,263, climbed to over £2 million in 1957 and had surpassed £4 million in 1960. In the late 1950s, the ESC customarily returned profits of £4–5 million; while Firth-Brown's trading profits increased from £586,173 in 1949 to £2.2 million in 1960.

On the other hand, steel plant was becoming larger to achieve the required economies of scale. Investment in stainless steels, for example, demanded bulk production in order to be economic. Until after the war,

Table 9.3. *Stainless steel ingot production, 1950–1959* ('000 tonnes)

	1950	1951	1952	1953	1954	1955	1956	1957	1958	1959
France	28	35	50	43	49	70	81	94	92	125
Germany	38	62	72	53	99	131	129	125	136	188
Italy	4	6	8	11	14	17	26	24	33	42
Sweden	53	57	62	65	70	84	95	103	109	142
UK	91	90	100	101	109	137	143	168	151	171
Other Europe	10	15	15	17	15	18	21	23	23	35
TOTAL (Europe)	224	265	307	290	356	457	495	537	544	703
USA	755	847	844	952	769	1,105	1,132	947	810	1,024
Japan	4	8	8	16	24	40	67	76	80	136
Other	25	33	30	32	30	35	34	31	36	54
TOTAL	1,008	1,153	1,189	1,290	1,179	1,637	1,728	1,591	1,470	1,917

Source: Market Research Inco Europe Ltd., *Stainless Steel Statistics: Post-war Historical Series* (London, 1977).

hand-mills had been used at Fox's and Firth-Vickers Stainless Steels for making sheets. A Firth-Brown metallurgist recalls watching the men hand-rolling stainless steel at Firth-Vickers' Weedon Street Works: 'Cogging formed what was known as a "mould" and this was then passed through a two-high mill cornerways to get the right shape. It was highly skilled and very strenuous.'[58] But such laborious methods had been made obsolete in America with the Sendzimir mill and other machinery for the continuous rolling and finishing of sheets. Simultaneously, therefore, both Firth-Vickers and Fox ordered a Sendzimir mill from the United States after the War, though in a period of post-war austerity the Government would only sanction expenditure on one. This led in 1948 to United Steel (Fox's) and Firth-Vickers commissioning jointly Shepcote Lane Rolling Mills in Tinsley for bulk stainless steel finishing, with United Steel taking a one-third share in the venture. It was initially costed at over £2 million, though this had risen to nearly £3½ million by 1955.[59]

It was not until about 1952 that the Sendzimir mill was installed, and even longer before the unavoidable early teething problems in mass-producing stainless steel had been solved. This may have accounted for the fact that United Kingdom stainless production rose somewhat sluggishly in the early 1950s, as shown in Table 9.3. In fact, although Britain was the second largest manufacturer of stainless steel in the world, after the United States, for most of the 1950s, by 1959 it had been overtaken by

[58] John Trueman interview, 22 July 1991.
[59] 'FVSS Ltd. with Samuel Fox & Co. Ltd.', *Iron & Coal Trades Review* (30 Sept. 1949), 66–9; 'Recent Progress in the Production and Fabrication of Stainless Steels', *Metallurgia*, 42 (Dec. 1950), 367–71; 'At Shepcote Lane', *Quality*, 5 (May 1958), 24–8.

Germany and Japan. The reason for this loss of leadership in a product in which Sheffield had led the world in the 1920s may lie in the much larger markets for stainless products in those countries; or it may reflect the much greater capital input from post-war reconstruction programmes in Germany and Japan. Some Sheffield industrialists have also said, both in print and to the present writer, that the split management of Firth-Vickers, with the chairmen from the ESC and Firth-Brown alternating every two years, did not help either. It resulted in 'cautious policies and . . . it was a possible factor in delaying the large-scale production of stainless steel in the UK for forty years.'[60] After the War, it has been said, no one had the ability to force through a larger vision of United Kingdom stainless production.

Certainly, the original agreement between Firth-Brown and the ESC was less than ideal, at least from the latter's viewpoint. The agreement (which no doubt reflected Hatfield's influence) ensured that Firth-Vickers' research was to be done at the Brown-Firth Research Laboratories, which only supplied the ESC with the minimum of technical information on stainless steels. This was a source of irritation to the ESC, which was compounded by the fact that although stainless sheet and castings could be ordered by customers direct from Firth-Vickers, orders for stainless forgings (for which Weedon Street did not have the capacity) had to be doled out between the ESC and Firth-Brown. But Firth-Vickers vetted the orders and this caused friction. According to one director: 'Sir Charles Craven [the ESC chairman] was a tough nut, but he slipped up on the stainless steel set up. ESC got to know about forging orders secondhand, which was galling because the orders gave an entrée to other things.'[61] If this did contribute to stainless steel's slow growth in these years, then it is a good example of the industry being bound to a certain extent by its older nineteenth-century structures and outlook.

Shepcote Lane was not the only large-scale capital development (though it was perhaps the only significant joint project in Sheffield in these years). United Steel followed a policy of updating and expansion with the Brinsworth Strip Mill in 1955–8 and by the end of the decade was ready to replace Steel, Peech, & Tozer's open-hearth capacity with an array of electric arc furnaces in a project known as SPEAR (Steel Peech Electric Arc Reorganization). Fox's, unable to meet the demand for special steels, were discussing plans to extend its melting capacity and rolling mills by the end of the 1950s. The Park Gate Iron & Steel Co. com-

[60] Mensforth, *Family Engineers*, 34.
[61] Pugh interview. See also SCL Firth-Brown Records. Directors' report, 26 June 1946. According to John Trueman, interview, FVSS got so fed up with the problems this created that in the 1960s they told both companies they should compete properly and customers were asked to approach each for a quote.

missioned an 11-inch continuous bar mill in 1953 at Roundwood and, by the end of the decade (having been bought by the engineering group Tube Investments in 1956), had plans for redeveloping its Aldwarke site.

Meanwhile, Vickers and its partners Cammell-Laird, in a bullish mood after reacquiring the company after nationalization, sanctioned a plan for expansion on a disused colliery site of 500 acres at Tinsley Park at a projected cost of £15 million. This was the brainchild of Fred Pickworth, who conceived it after the War as a way of at last rationalizing the complicated and congested layout of the ESC's River Don operations. It involved a new open-hearth melting shop and forge, with the future seen largely in terms of giant monoblocs of 250 tons and over (in fact, it was thought at one time that the demand might extend to 500 tons!). The Tinsley furnaces would produce an ingot of 400 tons, which would be reduced to 200 tons and then moved down to the River Don Works. By the late 1950s, work had still not started at Tinsley and after Pickworth retired the scheme was suddenly revised on the advice of newly appointed engineer, Ken Chatterton. Appalled by the monobloc idea because of the dangers of idle steel capacity (apparently, Chatterton's first question after seeing Pickworth's plans was: 'What are you going to do with all the steel?'), he persuaded the board to accept a new scheme in which the open-hearth furnaces would be replaced initially by two 100-tonne electric arcs, alongside a plant for billet and bars. This was a recognition that the company and its subsidiaries were 'very much bound up with the prosperity of the car industry'.[62] By the end of the decade, after a perhaps crucial delay, the ESC were ready to move forward rapidly on this plan.

The small tool steel firms also prospered in the 1950s. The boom period was typified by the Neepsend group, which by 1960 had been built up by Sir Stuart Goodwin into a conglomerate of over twenty small firms. On issued capital of about £1 million, Neepsend turned in average dividends of over 40 per cent a year in the 1950s, making Goodwin a multi-million-aire and allowing him to become the city's most famous philanthropist. Like Neepsend, many other Sheffield firms still had a significant degree of family control, a fact celebrated in a 1957 issue of the journal of the Sheffield Chamber of Commerce, which ran a feature on hundred-year-old firms.[63] At Bedford's the fifth-generation head of the company had died in 1954, but the business was still partly under family control. Leadbeater & Scott was still family-owned; the chairman of Huntsman's was descended from the founder; Marsh Bros. still had a Marsh in the business; and W. T. Flather's shares were still held by that family, two of whom from the fifth generation were still active. In the 1950s Gillott's described itself as 'the last of the family businesses of Sheffield, with no

[62] K. Chatterton, 'The Reason Why', *British Steelmaker*, 29 (Nov. 1963), 386–7.
[63] 'A Roll of Honour', *Quality*, 4 (Mar./Apr./May, 1957).

outside shareholder and no board of directors'.[64] Changes in personal taxation were undoubtedly loosening the grip of family owners in the 1950s (for example, Sam Gillott sold his firm to Cardinal Steels in 1953, and Balfour's went public in 1950 with £0.5 million capital for that reason), yet even when family managements had become diluted or had ended, the firms were notable for the long-service records of employees: workers who had been with a firm forty, fifty, and even sixty years were common. Osborn's was typical: of its 2,860 workers, 14 per cent had been there for twenty-five years or more. Osborn's contained the great-grandsons of the founder, while the board was chaired in the 1950s by the crusty figure of Frank Hurst (c.1884–1967), who had been there since the 1890s. A teetotal, non-smoking Methodist, who refused to fly and was to celebrate his eightieth birthday by starting work as usual at 8.30 a.m., Hurst was said to 'belong to the tradition of Victorian and Edwardian steelmen . . . Solid, assured, increasingly paternal, the firm he ran mirrored his stability, and the workers over whom he presided looked to him as a father figure.'[65]

The private nature of many of these companies makes it difficult to generalize about them with any certainty, or to describe their company performance or management in detail—so how widespread this air of desuetude was is difficult to say. One criticism levelled at some of these small tool steelmakers is that in the 1950s they rode the boom, but failed to replace largely depreciated plant. This criticism probably has a good deal of truth, even if it is difficult to prove quantitatively at the present. Goodwin, for example, may have acquired a personal fortune, but his reputation amongst some of the steel fraternity was of a buyer of clapped-out old companies, which he worked hard to maximize output in a flourishing market, but failed to rationalize or modernize. On the other hand, some family firms were successful and well managed after the War. Arthur Lee's enjoyed steady expansion in the 1950s, under the latest generation of the family. After purchasing a Sendzimir mill in 1948, it moved into the stainless steel strip market and then in 1960 bought a wire rope firm in Worksop. By 1962, Lee's employed 2,700 and its capital had increased from £400,000 in 1943 (when it went public) to £4 million in 1960. According to one of the Lee chairmen, this success had been achieved by always taking the best financial advice and by 'balance' in its strategy—the firm being neither too conservative nor too adventurous.[66] Richard W. Carr's, still totally owned and controlled by the family under Denys Carr, made the most of the growth of United Kingdom engineering in the 1950s. With only about forty workers in 1953 and only a modest

---

[64] *The Gillotts of Sheffield* (Sheffield, 1951).   [65] *SDT*, 14 Apr. 1967.
[66] Peter Lee interview, 8 Apr. 1991.

plant at Wadsley Bridge (though it melted its own steel in a high-frequency furnace and rolled as much as it could, it relied for the forging of larger pieces on Doncaster's and Jessop), it established a highly successful stockholding system centred on a Birmingham warehouse. By the mid-1970s this firm sold a third of the tool steel in the United Kingdom and employed about 400 at the firm's peak.[67]

Nor did firms in which ownership was more widely dispersed necessarily do any better. Perhaps the best example is Darwins, which in the 1950s passed through a management crisis which was bizarre even for a company that had survived the Kuehnrich era. Darwins had already forced its chairman, Harold Armstrong, to resign in 1939 because of the number of his outside appointments, but worse was to follow in 1946 when the company was acquired by the Nawab of Bhopal. Behind the deal was an Indian confidence man, Narayna Das Chopra, who had persuaded the Nawab to buy 90 per cent of Darwins' ordinary shares for £235,000 (plus a £200,000 loan).[68] Chopra promised to place at Darwins' disposal certain 'secret' metallurgical processes and to help the company get into the business of installing steel plant in India, favours for which he extracted the chairmanship and a £5,000 salary package. This soon proved inadequate and in 1948 Chopra voted himself a personal consultancy fee of £7,000 (for which he later did only one experiment, which was a failure) and began running up a £16,000 bill by high living at various Sheffield and London hotels. By the end of 1949 the company was almost bankrupt and labour relations were chaotic. A London stockbroker, Frank Thompson-Schwab (1891–1961), was called in, Chopra was removed (and in 1951 jailed), and in 1953 the firm was back in British ownership. In the 1950s Thompson-Schwab brought the company back into profitability, since its underlying metallurgical expertise was sound.

One unique feature from Sheffield's industrial past still lingered after the War—hire-work. The firms involved in forging and melting for others still thrived in the 1950s because the economics still made sense, even if some of the practices did not. One director of Gillott's, when customers asked to see his plant, would take them to Senior's Pond Forge (which did much of Gillott's work). 'Since everyone at Senior's knew [him] and they came and went by the back door, the visitors were none the wiser.'[69] However, hire-work perpetuated the fragmentation of the industry. In the 1950s, Jessop's rolled stainless steel for Spartan Steel & Alloys, a firm which melted its steel in Birmingham. In Sheffield itself hire-work allowed the survival of the pseudo-manufacturers, such as C. R. Denton Ltd. Stan Speight, later chairman of Neepsend, who has stressed

[67] Gordon Harrison interview, 13 Dec. 1991.
[68] SCL Aurora 1, 2. Darwins' Minute Books; John Monks interview, 30 June 1992.
[69] Bob Young interview, 25 Feb. 1992.

that Sheffield was the only place in the world where hire-work was conducted, remembers one of Sheffield's leading tool steel firms even changing rolls in the mill, purely for the convenience of one of these pseudo-firms.[70]

What of company strategy in this era? That too remained the same, with a wide product range, a commitment to quality and customer liaison, all operating in a highly competitive environment. At the ESC the spread of products covered almost every high-quality steel item from hollow-drum forgings of over 100 tons, down to engineers' cutting tools weighing only a few pounds. Similarly, Fox's Stocksbridge Works made large forgings and springs for the transport industries alongside umbrella frames (though by 1961 Fox was admitting that this department had outlived its usefulness). At Osborn's the old lines in tool steel, castings, sheet, and cutting tools had been made even more extensive by interests in aero-engine valves and steels. Sheffield's competitive edge still lay in its ability to supply specialist sizes and qualities of steel. Firth-Brown illustrated this in 1947, when it described the 'growing use of large pieces for pressure casting moulds. These moulds require extensive workmanship, and the quality of the steel is more important than the price. [For one order] the value of the steel for each mould is about £220, but the mould when complete is worth over £3,000. This is a growing market for high-quality material.'[71] Again, in hardened steel rolls: 'Price is not in these trades the prime consideration, what matters is the effective output from the roll, and the ease with which it is kept in condition.'[72] In many products, especially those which were custom-made (such as the presses and power systems made by Firth-Brown for Loewy Engineering), Sheffield firms were able to supply advanced customer liaison.

The Sheffield scene remained highly competitive, but the seller's market that emerged in the 1950s had not been without its impact on company strategy. In the 1950s the emphasis was on producing steel rather than selling it: in fact, selling the product had never been easier, as steelworks 'allocated' steel rather than sold it. 'There was a constant need to improve production, to get more out, with no emphasis on sales,' recalls one Sheffield special steels director.[73] Prices were set by the Iron & Steel Board, with competition regulated in Europe through agencies such as the Continental Fine Steel Producers' Club, and in Sheffield through numerous trade associations. One Brown Bayleys' director describes it thus:

---

[70] Stan Speight interview, 5 July 1991. Denton's was founded in 1936 by Charles Ramsden Denton in Gilbert Street. By the 1950s, under Edgar Denton it sold a wide range of tool steels and tools, besides having interests in a steel firm, Inca. See *Quality*, 5 (Feb. 1958), 35–7.
[71] Firth-Brown Records. Directors' report, 2 May 1947.
[72] Ibid. Directors' report, 28 Mar. 1949.   [73] Bernard Cotton interview, 8 July 1991.

Sheffield was very parochial in the 1950s. Order books could be four years long. When [the boss] at Brown Bayleys got unsolicited orders, he used to go through them and pick out the ones he wanted—usually only ten percent. With the Iron & Steel Board setting prices . . . selling was a gentleman's existence, with Sheffield operating as a big cartel. Orders were reported first to the respective trade association and committee and at the end of the day they would tell you what prices to quote. The price-fixing was incredible. There was no import threat . . . and there was a lot of complacency.[74]

Most of the directors interviewed for this book had anecdotes about this period and it is difficult to resist repeating some of them. A Jessop director recalled in the early 1950s:

having visited Rover and Austin with the Jessop Birmingham sales manager. Both companies were working on gas turbine cars and their technical people had requested a discussion on test materials. However, after these meetings were over, the Birmingham area manager begged me to accompany him to Austin's chief buyer and explain to him, from head office as it were, why he could not have any more valve steel. Those were the days![75]

Abroad, Sheffield needed to demonstrate little expertise in dealing with foreign customers: prices were still quoted in sterling and English weights and measures, while customers could also wait many months, sometimes years, for deliveries. One Sheffield sales director remembered visiting a Swiss firm: 'I told them, you can have your order next week. They didn't know what I was talking about. Their order was one year overdue from a two-year delivery date. They'd completely forgotten about it.'[76]

But Sheffield's dominance in the special steel industry in this sellers' market led to a failure (as it did in America in bulk steels) to appreciate the uniqueness of this situation.[77] Because they sold all the tool steel they could make, many Sheffield steelmakers assumed they would always sell it. And because they confronted few competitors at home or in many overseas countries, they assumed that that situation, too, was permanent. Finally, because it had such a long tradition of innovation in special steels and had some of the most advanced research facilities in the world, many Sheffielders assumed that only they could make good alloy steels. In other words, Sheffield steelmakers, like the bulk producers in the United States, were supremely confident of their position.

[74] Gordon Polson interview, 21 Nov. 1991.   [75] W. H. Bailey interview.

[76] George Holst interview, 9 July 1991.

[77] John P. Hoerr, *And the Wolf Finally Came: The Decline of the American Steel Industry* (Pittsburgh, 1988); Mark Reutter, *Sparrows Point: Making Steel—The Rise and Ruin of American Industrial Might* (New York, 1988); Paul Tiffany, *The Decline of American Steel: How Management, Labor and the Government Went Wrong* (New York, 1988).

10

Rationalization and Nationalization

The Victorian era in Sheffield steel did not end until the 1960s.

Bernard Cotton (Osborn chairman), interview with author, 8 July 1991.

Let there be no smugness in [Sheffield] about full order books, lower unemployment ratios, or relative absence of disruptive labour disputes—all admirable factors in their own way—as long as it is true, for example, that the UK motor manufacturers' share of the total European market is declining.

Kenneth Lewis (Master Cutler), Cutlers' Hall, 20 Oct. 1973.

In 1964 the members of the Iron and Steel Institute made one of their periodic pilgrimages to Steel City.[1] Sheffield was still the most famous name in steel and when the Institute toured the city they found an industry that still bore the hallmarks of its nineteenth-century heyday. In structure and products, in location and ownership, Sheffied was still recognizably the place that the Institute had first visited in 1905. It certainly remained the city that the Institute had seen in 1933, since apart from some merging of interests the names and ranking of the leading firms (shown in Table 10.1) had remained very much the same.

The Sheffield special steels industry had entered the decade on a confident note: order books were buoyant and production was at record levels after the advances of the 1950s. Sheffield made about 3 million tons of ingots and castings in 1960 (a year when every area enjoyed very full employment in steelmaking capacity). This was only a small part of the national total of over 24 million tons, but Sheffield's continued pre-eminence was demonstrated in its dominance of alloy steel production (over a million tons out of a national total of 1.6 million in 1960). The Iron and Steel Institute's visit was well timed, as in 1964 steel production in Sheffield (especially from its electric furnaces) was expected to take a big leap forward as the development plans of the late 1950s came to fruition.

About £150 million had been spent on the post-war modernization of Sheffield steel, with United Steel and the ESC amongst the largest individual spenders. United Steel's SPEAR project at Steel Peech, & Tozer,

[1] *British Steelmaker*, 30 (Aug. 1964), devoted a whole issue to the Iron & Steel Institute's visit to the city.

Table 10.1. *Leading steel firms in Sheffield and district, 1964*

Company	Employees
English Steel Corporation	14,140
Steel, Peech & Tozer	9,315
Samuel Fox	7,679
Firth-Brown	7,500
Park Gate	6,200
Hadfields	4,000
Balfour Darwin	3,500*
Brown Bayleys	3,500*
Osborn	3,000
Arthur Lee	2,700
Jessop-Saville	2,550
Edgar Allen	2,000
Sanderson Kayser	1,900

Note: Steel, Peech, & Tozer and Samuel Fox were part of United Steel, which had a total workforce of 41,735, including 447 at Swinden Laboratories and 466 at McCall & Co. (Sheffield). The Firth-Brown total includes workers at Beardmore's; and the ESC figure includes about 2,000 staff at Darlington and Manchester.

*Approximate figures.

Sources: Contemporary trade press and company records.

which replaced its old and now uneconomic open-hearth furnaces with electric arcs, was a typically expansionist move of the time. Operation SPEAR moved ahead in 1960 and was finished on schedule by 1963 at a cost of £11.5 million, slightly below the original estimate. It was a considerable technical achievement, since the new installations had to be phased in without interrupting normal production. The new Templeborough Electric Melting Shop replaced twenty-one open-hearth furnaces (fourteen of which had been housed in the quarter-mile-long old Templeborough shop—the longest open-hearth shop in Europe) and destroyed one of the landmarks in the district—fourteen huge chimneys along the Sheffield Road. In their place went the world's largest electric steelmaking unit of six 110-ton electric arc furnaces. Capable of an annual capacity of over 1.25 million tons, Templeborough was designed to meet a forecast annual demand (accurate enough, in the beginning) of 1.2 million tons or more and had a profit capability of £1 million every month. The profile of steels produced was much the same—a wide range of carbon and low-alloy steels for general engineering, especially for automotive applications. Replacement of open-hearth capacity was also planned at Fox, where by 1964 plans were on the drawing board for the £6 million 'Sapphire' project, which began the installation of four electric arc furnaces in the following year.

Meanwhile, closer to Sheffield, by 1963 the ESC had opened its new £26 million Tinsley Park works, where two 100-tonne electric arc furnaces had a theoretical output of up to 300,000 (later rising to 500,000) ingot tonnes a year for bloom and billet rolling. After the delays of the 1950s, under Ken Chatterton's direction the company moved quickly into the project and it was completed within twenty-seven months, half a year ahead of schedule. The plant included a pioneer vacuum degassing unit licensed from Germany, which removed hydrogen and oxygen from molten steel and greatly improved the quality of big ingots (besides obviating the need for soaking and rolling down to billet).

Over £30 million was also invested at Tube Investments' Park Gate Works in new electric arc and oxygen steelmaking equipment. This boosted the total ingot capacity of the company from 450,000 to 850,000 tonnes a year. In the 1950s Park Gate had moved away from its traditional market of iron and steel plate for the shipbuilding and other heavy industries, to the production of billets, bars, and sections. The increase in steel capacity was designed primarily to meet Tube Investments' needs for hot-rolled billets for its seamless tubes. Again, it was very much aimed at the automobile industry.

These developments were based on expectations of ever-expanding steel demand. The ESC, for example, when planning Tinsley Park, had 'gone along to the motor car makers, who all said they were getting bigger. Everyone thought things would go on growing.'[2] In 1960 a rising trend for world steel in the industrialized nations was accepted unquestioningly. As one tool steelmaker put it: 'We were worried in the 1950s about the state of steel. But later everyone believed that industry was going to expand with a huge demand for world steel. We couldn't have been more wrong.' But at the time, the appearance of new markets in the developing nations was assumed to be part of the natural order of things. Somehow no one had foreseen that these countries might one day begin making steel, even alloys, for themselves. Nor was it imagined that while their home markets were developing, they would start exporting overseas. 'Sheffield did not realise that a few very aware metallurgists with instruments and computers could produce steel as well as the craftsmen,' remarked one Sheffield metallurgist. A Jessop's technical director recalls becoming aware of competition from Germany and America in the early 1960s, but what really stuck him was:

[2] The quotes in this chapter are from interviews I conducted between 1991 and 1993 with the individuals cited in the sources.

the increase in Japanese technical ability, which grew at an alarming rate. In the late 1950s the Japanese asked to visit Jessop's and when they came over we had a little giggle to ourselves after they had gone: their questions were naïve and totally ill-informed. But by 1970 I was writing to them to ask for access to *their* works. We were delighted to be able to visit them—an incredible turnaround.

A worrying feature for the leading producers was that the background of strong, post-war economic expansion began to waver in the 1960s, so that by the mid-1970s the steady upward growth of world steel production and demand first slackened and then levelled off. Average world growth in steel production was about 6 per cent in the 1960s, not too different from the previous decade and equalling previous record growth between 1900 and 1910. But this plummeted to 2 per cent in the 1970s and less than $\frac{1}{2}$ per cent in the 1980s.[3] Even worse, the proportion of that constant production shared by the large traditional producers (such as America, Europe, and Japan) had declined from about 60 per cent to 40 per cent, while the newcomers in developing countries had increased their share from 5 per cent to 13 per cent.

In the 1960s, as competition became apparent, and just after the United Kingdom joined the European Economic Community, the first oil crisis broke. 'Since then', it has been said, 'the experience of manufacturing business, and of steel even more acutely, has ranged between uncertainty at best and severe recession at worst.'[4] United Kingdom crude steel production reached a peak of about 28 million tonnes in 1970 and then went into decline, output falling by nearly two-thirds by 1980. Similar trends can be seen in both national and Sheffield alloy steels (see Figs. 10.1–6).

As world steel production stagnated and overcapacity became a problem, so individual companies restructured and moved into higher-quality steels. This process was not confined to advanced economies, since some newly industrialized countries such as Brazil and Spain also began to increase their special steel output. When British alloy steel production began to slump towards the end of the 1970s (despite some growth in stainless steel output), the unthinkable happened: Sheffield was overtaken by countries as diverse as Brazil, Italy, Spain, and Sweden.[5]

Sheffield's special steel cluster was also highly dependent on the expansion and structure of the economy. After the 1970s, the keynote of British

---

[3] Bernard Keeling, *World Steel: A New Assessment of Trends and Prospects* (London, Economist Intelligence Unit Special Report No. 1124, 1988).

[4] R. Scholey, 'European Steel: What Future?', *Ironmaking and Steelmaking*, 14 (1987), 257–65, 258.

[5] Sheffield City Council, *Sheffield and Rotherham Steel Industry Study* (Sheffield, 1980); id., *Steel in Crisis: Alternatives to Government Policy and the Decline in South Yorkshire's Steel Industry* (Sheffield, 1984); R. Hudson and D. Sadler, *The Uncertain Future of Special Steels: Trends in the Sheffield, United Kingdom and European Special Steels Industries* (Sheffield, 1987).

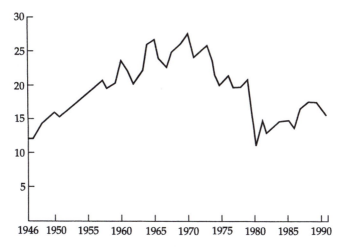

Fig. 10.1. *UK crude steel production (million tons tonnes)*

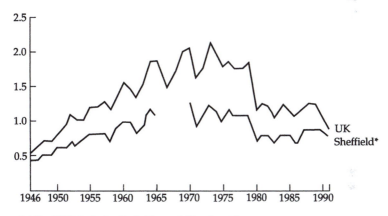

* After 1970, includes Yorkshire and Humberside

Fig. 10.2. *UK and Sheffield alloy steel production (million tons tonnes)*

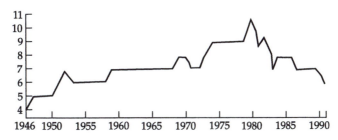

Fig. 10.3. *UK alloy steel production as a percentage of UK total crude steel*

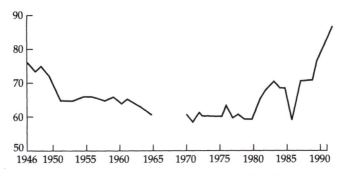

Fig. 10.4. *Sheffield alloy steel production as a percentage of UK alloy steel*

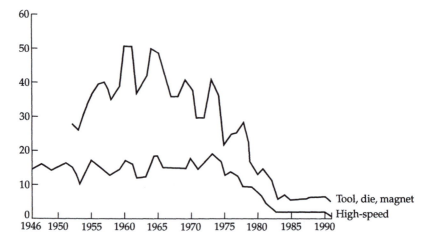

Fig. 10.5. *UK alloy tool, die, magnet, and high-speed steel production ('000 tons tonnes)*

economic history was a slowing down of industrial growth and a fall (at first slow and then rapid) in manufacturing employment. Other features were an increasing divergence between old and new industries, a marked shift towards the service sector, and rising import penetration (combined with a poor British export performance abroad).

The share of manufacturing output in total GDP, measured at constant prices, increased steadily between 1948 and 1974—rising from about 26 per cent to over 30 per cent. However, since that date United Kingdom manufacturing output has been fairly flat: indeed in the 1970s there was no growth at all—an unprecedented event—and in the early 1980s manufacturing output actually fell. Meanwhile, the output of services continued to grow, so making the early 1970s an important benchmark. Thus, the marked differential in manufacturing-services output growth

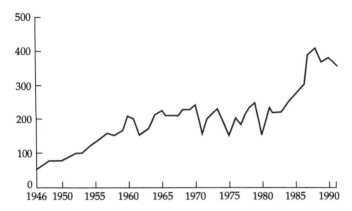

Fig. 10.6. *UK stainless steel production ('000 tons/tonnes).* Source for all figures above: Annual Statistics, *published initially by the Iron & Steel Board and the BISF, then by the BSC and the Iron & Steel Statistics Bureau, and finally by the Iron & Steel Statistics Bureau. Data not available for some years.* Tons up to and including 1970; tonnes thereafter. One tonne = 0.9842 ton.

rates—with services surging ahead of manufacturing—is a phenomenon which really dates from 1973–74, since when the output structure of the UK economy has undergone a shift of truly enormous proportions.'[6] A major sign of that shift was a fall in manufacturing employment from a peak in 1966 of 8.5 million workers to about 5 million in 1990, contrasting with a rise in service sector employment from about 12 million to over 15 million over the same period.

After the 1970s, the overseas trading performance of United Kingdom manufacturing industry weakened, part of a long-term trend. In 1950 the United Kingdom share of world trade in manufactures was about 25 per cent, but this had slipped to 17.7 per cent in 1959 and 11.2 per cent ten years later. By 1979 Britain's share had fallen to about 9 per cent. The trade balance in manufacturing was also deteriorating. In 1983, for the first time in British history manufactured imports began exceeding manufactured exports. Britain, for example, had briefly become a net importer of crude steel in the mid-1970s (see Table 10.2).

Not surprisingly, British economists and academics began asking whether the country had 'too few producers' and to talk of 'de-industrialization' as a serious economic problem—a view endorsed in 1985 by a Select Committee of the House of Lords, which agreed that the economy was in deep crisis: a crisis, moreover, that, if not corrected, would become

[6] John Wells, 'Uneven Development and Deindustrialisation in the UK since 1979', in Francis Green (ed.), *The Restructuring of the United Kingdom Economy* (Hemel Hempstead, 1989), 25–64, 32.

Table 10.2. *Crude and alloy steel imports and exports, 1975–1991*

	1975	1976	1977	1978	1979	1980	1981	1982	1983	1984	1985	1986	1987	1988	1989	1990	1991
Crude steel (million tonnes)																	
Imports	3.7	4.1	3.7	3.7	3.8	4.6	3.3	3.8	3.3	3.5	3.7	4.1	4.2	5.0	5.2	5.1	5.3
Exports	3.0	3.5	4.2	4.2	4.3	2.6	3.7	3.3	3.9	3.9	4.6	5.0	6.2	6.4	6.4	6.7	7.6
Alloys ('000 tonnes)																	
Imports	128	172	184	177	218	274	242	292	310	395	423	438	464	580	629	635	623
Exports	242	274	307	325	359	236	298	274	279	385	481	471	552	680	740	629	656

Note: Due to amendments in the statistical classification of alloy steels, the pre-1980 figures are slightly understated in comparison with post-1980.
Source: United Kingdom Iron & Steel Statistics Bureau, *Annual Statistics*.

Table 10.3. *Deliveries of finished alloy steel to consuming industries ('000 tonnes)*

	1960	1965	1970	1975	1980	1985	1991
Drop forgings	294.3	362.7	392.4	324.5	212.5	196.7	120.7
Motor vehicles	153.6	120.8	121.2	80.1	49.0	35.2	20.3
Aircraft	18.9	14.0	9.6	11.5	6.8	no data	no data
Implements—tools, cutlery, etc.	13.5	18.5	19.7	18.8	10.6	6.9	5.6
Shipbuilding	10.6	10.2	9.0	8.3	6.8	4.2	no data

Source: United Kingdom Iron & Steel Statistics Bureau, *Annual Reports*.

'a grave threat to the standard of living, and to the economic and political stability of the nation'.[7] It was feared that the United Kingdom economy had lost the competitive position of the post-war years, and was fast becoming a producer of relatively labour-intensive, low value-added goods.

What this meant for alloy steels can be seen in Table 10.3. Almost invariably after 1960, the picture in key industries—shipbuilding, aircraft, automobiles, and engineering—was one of declining sales volumes, leading to a diminishing consumption of alloys. The supply of the United Kingdom drop forgings to British industry—a rough measure of the state of the country's manufacturing industry—fell by nearly a third in the thirty years since 1960. The steep fall in deliveries to the motor vehicle makers offers its own comment on the demise of Britain's indigenous car industry. Since 1960, demand from the shipbuilding and aircraft industries has steadily declined.

To be sure, this is not entirely due to problems in the consumer industries. Steel was less in demand, too, because cost considerations reduced the amount of steel used in certain products. For example, the proportion of steel found in jet aircraft has declined steadily since the 1970s. By the end of the century, the proportion of steel found in a civil jet engine is expected to make up only 13 per cent of the total weight—compared with 40 per cent in the 1970s.[8] A similar trend is observable in cars, in the face of competition from non-ferrous metals, plastics, and ceramics. Changes

[7] House of Lords, 1985, quoted in David Coates, *The Question of United Kingdom Decline: The Economy, State and Society* (Hemel Hempstead, 1994), 15. The literature on UK decline is large, but the following are a useful introduction: R. Bacon and W. A. Eltis, *Britain's Economic Problem: Too Few Producers* (London, 1976); F. T. Blackaby (ed.), *De-industrialization* (London, 1978); Sidney Pollard, *The Development of the British Economy 1914–1990* (London, 4th edn., 1992), 229 ff. See also my article in R. Coopey and N. Woodward (eds.), *The Troubled Economy* (London, 1995).

[8] Hugh Everson, 'Aerospace Steels Challenged but not Grounded', *Metal Bulletin Monthly*, 259 (July 1992), 13, 15.

in weapon technologies and defence strategies meant that Sheffield no longer had a role to play as an armaments centre. Big naval guns, shells, and huge armour-plated dreadnoughts were almost obsolete in an era of nuclear missiles and push-button destruction.

Even special steels were becoming simply another product, best produced in large quantities, wherever energy and labour costs were cheapest, where there was the economic or political will to invest in the latest special steels technologies, and where the product could be aggressively marketed in high volume. Production technology now became paramount (whereas for much of Sheffield's history the discovery of new steels was the area where revolutionary developments were sought): Sendzimir rolling mills, automatic forging machines (GFMs), and computers for statistical process-control made their impact after the 1970s. So too did so-called 'precision steelmaking' techniques of producing purer steel. In Sheffield electric arc steelmaking was still the favoured method for special steels (though furnace size as ever was increasing), but new secondary refining techniques (described below) boosted the quality of special steels. Environmental regulations following the Clean Air Act of 1956 further increased the costs of steel production, especially since the primary costs fell on the steel producers (unlike in Japan, where these were met by the Government).

Events in the 1960s and 1970s, therefore, administered a sharp shock to the easy attitudes of previous decades, as merger and rationalization were suddenly forced on a sales-led and often fragmented Sheffield industry. So too was another, mostly unwelcome, development: the renationalization of steel in 1967, introduced by a Labour Government convinced that the private steel companies were not doing enough to restructure the industry. Political change was now added to economic imperatives to produce some of the most complex and eventful years in the history of Sheffield steel. Ironically, towards the end of this period, privatization once more became the fashion and the steel industry was denationalized yet again.

For convenience and clarity, events will be considered in four parts: the impact of nationalization on Sheffield; developments in private-sector forgings, castings, and general-purpose steels; attempts to rationalize the privately owned tool steel companies; and the transfer of the nationalized industry once more to public ownership.

The instrument of the government's nationalization programme was the British Steel Corporation, created in July 1967. A merger of fourteen major companies and their 200 or so subsidiaries, the BSC was the second largest steel company in the non-Communist world. Its chairman, Lord Melchett (1925–73), assumed control of a combine which had a total capital of £1,400 million and a labour force of 270,000. Though in some ways hardly a logical choice for the job—a scion of the Mond family of ICI fame, he was a banker with no experience of steel—Melchett worked hard to master the details of the industry and his tact and enthusiasm soon won over many of his colleagues, especially when he persuaded the Government to back an expansionist strategy based on the Japanese model: large-scale, integrated steelworks, producing tonnage steels that were marketed in sufficient volume to secure economies of scale.[9] By 1972 an ambitious £3,000 million development plan had been formulated—the largest capital investment programme in British history—which aimed to boost the BSC's annual output to 36–8 million tonnes by 1983, with investment concentrated at major sites around the country—Port Talbot, Llanwern, Scunthorpe, Lackenby, Ravenscraig, and Teesside.

As world steel demand collapsed in the 1970s in the wake of successive oil crises, this was to prove one of the most ill-timed blunders in British industrial history. A measure of the miscalculation can be gauged by the fact that total United Kingdom crude steel production from the public *and* private sector was never to reach 30 million tonnes. The BSC's position was also not helped by the United Kingdom joining the European Community, where excess steel capacity was at the highest level in the world and where the BSC could no longer rely on an 8 per cent tariff to keep out imports. From Sheffield's viewpoint, nationalization was also unfortunate in other ways. A simple yardstick had been chosen to divide the public and private sectors: only firms producing 475,000 tonnes a year were to be included in the BSC. This crude benchmark was politically and administratively expedient, but in ignoring output *value* it lacked industrial logic, as was soon apparent in Sheffield. The BSC took over some 90 per cent of crude steel production, but as Table 10.4 shows, it left in the private sector (besides the balance of crude steel output) a significant proportion of the forging, rolling, and special steels industry, much of it located in Sheffield.[10] To take just one instance—about 85 per cent of the bright bars, which were cold-drawn from top-quality steel for precision engineering, were to be made by the private sector. The actual turnover figure for the companies left outside the BSC was about a third of the total at £1,200 million. The result was that of the companies with works in or near

---

[9] G. F. Dudley and J. J. Richardson, *Politics and Steel in Britain, 1967–1988* (Aldershot, 1990); Keith Ovenden, *The Politics of Steel* (London, 1978).

[10] Interestingly, the industry's own analysis of its problems, contained in its Benson Report, also left Sheffield special steels alone. It commented: 'In the case of the "special" steel sector . . . Its structure is complex; the steelmaking operations are closely interlocked with user operations; and the typically small scale of operations in the trades utilising special steels exerts a limiting effect on movements towards larger-scale units in the special steel-producing trade. The Committee has, therefore, left the possible rationalisation of the special steel sector on one side in preparing the Report.' See *The Steel Industry: The Stage I Report of the Development Co-ordinating Committee of the British Iron and Steel Federation* (London: BISF, 1966).

Table 10.4. *Private sector steel production, 1968 ('000 tons)*

	Private Sector	%	National
Non-alloy			
Raw steel	1,611.9	7	23,989.4
Billets, blooms, and slabs	393.8	6	6,501.5
Plates	276.8	9	3,181.5
Other heavy products	398.9	14	2,900.1
Wire, rods, and bars in coils	788.1	42	1,844.6
Light sections and hot-rolled bars	1,248.3	54	2,293.5
Bright steel bars	466.7	93	501.1
Hot-rolled strip	303.1	17	1,793.4
Cold-rolled strip	365.7	66	557.0
Sheets	1.2	—	4,276.3
Tinplate	—	—	1,252.6
Tubes, pipes	336.7	25	1,318.9
Tyres, wheels, axles	7.0	9	74.8
Forgings and castings	225.5	92	245.8
Tool and magnet	6.4	94	6.8
Alloy			
Raw steel	677.5	36	1,872.8
Billets, blooms, and slabs+	212.1	29	735.1
Plates	15.2	20	74.4
Wire, rods, and other rods in coil	28.4	43	65.4
Sections and hot-rolled bars	231.0	58	398.0
Bright steel bars	52.4	78	67.6
Hot-/cold-rolled strip+	29.4	72	40.6
Sheets	27.4	48	57.4
Tubes, pipes	87.2	71	123.2
Tyres, wheels, axles	3.6	71	5.1
Forgings and castings	132.3	81	163.4
High-speed steel and tool and magnet	28.2	93	30.4

Source: BISPA, *Annual Report* (1969).

Sheffield, only three—the ESC, Park Gate, and United Steel—were nationalized, and the rest, about fifty, were left in private ownership. But, as we shall see, the split was not as clear cut as that, leaving in Sheffield 'a peculiar left-over situation'.[11]

The impact of nationalization on Sheffield is therefore difficult to evaluate. Its defenders argue that from the broadest perspective the BSC

[11] 'Sheffield Special Steels', *Investors' Guardian* (29 Oct. 1971), 1058. See also Montague, Loebl, Stanley, & Co., *Special Steels* (Apr. 1976). Copy in SCL Local Studies.

through its Special Steels Division was able to provide the massive investment necessary to compete in world steel in mass-produced products
such as stainless steel. They also highlight the poor performance of the
steel companies both nationally and in Sheffield. One analysis of the
companies taken over by the BSC showed that in the year before
nationalization they made a collective profit of £9 million after tax. As one
financial journalist pointed out, 'this was a miserable return for a group of
major steel companies, which the Government itself values for compensation purposes at between £500m and £600m'.[12] In Sheffield, Dunford &
Elliott, Neepsend Steel, Daniel Doncaster, and Sanderson Kayser had
been getting a good return on capital ranging from 20 to 35 per cent. But
the record of others was poor—in the two years before 1967, for example,
Edgar Allen had returned 4.1 and 5 per cent and Hadfields had been
fluctuating between 5 and 8 per cent. It was difficult to escape the view
that the industry had not invested enough in the 1950s and that it would
have problems surviving.

More significantly, aside from parts of United Steel (Fox's return on
capital averaged 13 per cent in the four years between 1964 and 1967), the
prospects for the big steel firms around Sheffield did not look good in
1967. Park Gate and the ESC had not made the expected profits from their
massive investments. The ESC, for example, was not making money when
it was nationalized. The expected growth markets in car steels, pressure
vessels, and diesel crankshafts for railway engines were not materializing.
The new layout had another failing. 'The sad thing about Tinsley', recalled
one director, 'was that it was designed as an orthodox plant, but what we
wanted was continuous casting.' It had been considered, but at the time
this commercially unproven technology was thought too risky. 'Tinsley
was also completed a little too fast—a little later and continuous casting
would have been installed.' The failure to anticipate the process, however,
made Tinsley dated almost before it was launched. It would obviously
soon need rescuing.[13]

As one director in the new private Sheffield steel sector admitted: 'The
reality of the situation in 1967 was that only United Steel was going to
survive.' But some remained sceptical of the Sheffield industry's ability to
achieve the inevitable rationalization on its own. As one former ESC man
put it, when discussing the forgings industry shortly after the BSC was
formed: 'It was already obvious that there wasn't room for River Don,

---

[12] Royden Hodson, 'Forging Ahead with Private Steel', *The Times Business News*, 26 Apr.
1967.
[13] See Harold Evans, *Vickers: Against the Odds 1956–1977* (London, 1978), 131–6. For criticisms of the structure and technology of the steel industry at this time, see David W. Heal,
The Steel Industry in Postwar Britain (Newton Abbot, 1974).

Hadfields, Firth-Brown and Summers [Shotton] to invest in this area. There was a great unwillingness to talk, though, so that the chances of any rationalisation happening voluntarily were zero.'

Many of the private steelmakers dispute this view, arguing that even without nationalization the big firms would have modernized and so would the small makers, if they had been left alone. They also add other criticisms: that the uncertainty in the years before nationalization prevented firms from investing and then triggered an untimely and unprecedented rush to modernize; that the BSC itself was a bloated bureaucracy, 'over-administered, with too many layers of non-essential managers';[14] and that a 'big brother' run by the United Steel 'Mafia' had been created—one that was backed by Government and supported by public funds, which could behave uncommercially if it wished. The political and economic muscle of the BSC caused particular resentment, especially because of the complex and intricate relationship between the BSC and the city's private firms, stemming from the fact that the two sides were suppliers, customers, and increasingly competitors. With the BSC producing about 90 per cent of the country's crude steel, it was easily the private sector's largest supplier. Inevitably, there were areas of overlap, products where the BSC and private firms competed directly, and instances of Sheffield private firms buying their steel from the BSC. When conflict arose over major causes of complaint—such as the BSC's pricing structure—the private firms and their trade organization BISPA (British Independent Steel Producers' Association) felt themselves disadvantaged and much bitterness ensued.[15] The private firms believed that Governments—either Labour or Tory—were unsympathetic to the BISPA case, especially the demand for investment help for their own sector. (As one director stated, to the present writer, when discussing the activities of Sir Ian MacGregor—'any fool can rationalize, if they are given the money'.) In short, critics in Sheffield felt that the creation of a closely juxtaposed private and public sector in one city—a situation found nowhere else to the same degree—was a recipe for commercial chaos. Commented one private steel director: 'Wherever there was an area of contact, it created difficulties, especially when business was bad. But whatever the argument the BSC came out on top.'

Whatever the merits of these views, it is difficult to deny that nationalization acted as a catalyst, knocking heads together and forcing companies to confront the deep-seated structural problems in the industry. Not surprisingly, these problems were at their most acute in those great relics of

---

[14] See also the comments by Peter Thompson, *Sharing Success: The Story of NFC* (London, 1990), 38–9.

[15] Heidrun Abromeit, *British Steel: An Industry Between the State and Private Sector* (Leamington, 1986), 218–53.

Victorian industrial might—the big Brightside works of Firth-Brown and particularly the ESC. An immediate conundrum was created by the BSC's takeover of the ESC, which brought with it a half-interest in Firth-Vickers Stainless Steels and a share in the stainless steel rolling plant at Shepcote Lane. Superficially, this was a headache that Melchett and the BSC could have done without; on the other hand, it offered an opportunity. Almost by accident, the chance appeared for a rationalization of stainless steel production, since the BSC also controlled the stainless ingot capacity of Fox's Stocksbridge Works. It seemed an area ideal for the full BSC treatment: it was a mass market with a huge potential, but, as we have seen, Britain's consumption and production had begun to lag behind the general trend during the 1950s and henceforth the United Kingdom was overtaken by a string of countries, such as France, Germany, Sweden, and Japan. Partly this reflected the peculiarities of the split management at Shepcote Lane, which was becoming increasingly cumbersome. In 1964 Fox's directors were worried about the plant's future: 'Difficulties included the quality of the Shepcote Lane product, the limit of 40 feet on maximum width and the restriction on growth imposed by the one-third/two-thirds relationship. There was serious doubt whether long-term aims in the stainless field could be realised under these conditions.'[16] By the early 1970s one-third of all stainless flat products consumed in Britain came from abroad; and by the late 1970s the United Kingdom was supplying only 35–40 per cent of its home market. Shepcote Lane had hardly begun to explore the commercial market for stainless steel.

Technological advances were also occurring in stainless steel production. A major advance after the 1960s was the Argon-Oxygen-Decarburization (AOD) technique, in which a low-pressure mixture of argon and oxygen is used to facilitate the removal of carbon. The process also enabled the use of cheaper, high-carbon ferro-chromium. The high-powered electric arc furnace could now be used simply as a melting unit, with the refining of the liquid steel conducted in a separate AOD vessel. This gave faster bulk production opportunities and furnace size rose to about 120 tonnes.[17]

Faced with these developments, the question for the BSC was a simple one: should it quit or compete? It decided to leapfrog back into the race, after first resolving the complicated ownership of stainless steel facilities with Firth-Brown, the other joint-owners of Firth-Vickers Stainless Steels.

[16] SCL. Fox Directors' Minute Book, 4 Nov. 1964.
[17] For a discussion of the AOD process, see J. C. C. Leach, 'Secondary Refining for Electric Steelmaking', *Ironmaking and Steelmaking*, 4 (1977), 58–65. This article was part of a set of proceedings, published ibid. 3–4 (1976–7), of a Sheffield conference, which contains much of interest on the introduction of new precision steelmaking technologies in the city in the 1960s and 1970s.

Firth-Brown, keen to neutralize ESC competition in forgings (as one of its directors has remarked, what they feared especially was a nationalized River Don Forge), bargained hard. Eventually, in 1972 an agreement was negotiated: the BSC River Don Works was to abandon one of its main markets (namely, special melted steels and alloy steel open-die forgings up to 75 tonnes), in return for the controlling interest in Firth-Vickers Stainless Steels and Shepcote Lane. As Firth-Brown's managing director admitted: 'For River Don it was a terrible deal. The tonnage restriction took out a huge slab of the market.' Nor were the former ESC River Don managers happy with an agreement that helped Firth-Brown cherry-pick the best parts of the business. For Melchett, however, keen to get hold of the mass market in stainless, the solution was an attractive one—especially since he was simultaneously grappling with the rationalization of the former ESC River Don Works, Tinsley, and the various Rotherham and Stocksbridge works. A crucial problem was what to do with the massive old forging presses at the River Don site. Firth-Brown had retreated from the big forging market and had decided to concentrate on ingots below 80 tonnes even before the BSC deal, leaving River Don to market the giant forgings of 200 tonnes and over—a market that was increasingly plagued by overcapacity and intense competition. (United Kingdom annual sales of open-die forgings fell from £200,000 a year to below £130,000 between 1960 and 1974.) The BSC decision to move rolling from River Don to Tinsley Park had lessened the load on the furnaces at River Don even more. According to one BSC director, who was involved with the negotiations: 'Melchett found the Firth-Brown deal attractive: it reduced the size of the River Don problem and it gave him stainless steel. He was a humane man, but he felt it was a price that had to be paid. He said that the deal must go through, even if the River Don site was closed down.'

Ironically, Melchett and his successor (Sir Monty Finniston) proved no more capable of closing down the River Don Works than the private sector would have been. The threat of closure and the possible loss of 4,500 jobs provoked industrial militancy on a scale unknown in Sheffield—a sure sign that the era of good labour relations that had lasted almost from the birth of the industry was over—and the BSC was forced to retreat. The upshot was a renewed look at the markets and a decision that River Don was viable after all. The management worked hard on the turbo-generator market to find orders, and tried to find openings for crankshafts for diesel-electric locomotives, though neither proved good markets when the economy turned down. They also introduced vacuum ladle techniques, developed in Chicago by Chuck Finkl, which involved the use of 'holding' techniques in the production of large ingots. Steel could be tapped and held in a ladle, while another charge was melted, as a way of reducing the number of furnaces. This was intended to solve a classical problem facing forgemasters—the necessity of having enough melting capacity on hand, while avoiding installing plant that did not have enough throughput when big ingots were not needed. This gave great flexibility in making 200-ton ingots and on one occasion a 500-ton casting was completed using four ladles around the Finkl unit. Some even bigger ingots were contemplated, but without airships (which were once discussed) it was impossible to get them out of Sheffield. Here the city lost out to better sited German plants. And although the Finkl technique was successful, the closure of furnace capacity made operators redundant. It was a bleak scenario, but the River Don site struggled on as a loss-maker in the mid-1970s, subsidized by the BSC.

But however patched the solution was to the River Don problem, it paved the way for stainless steel. In 1976 BSC Stainless was created as a separate profit centre and work began transforming the Shepcote Lane site into the biggest purpose-built stainless steel plant in Europe, with the aim of more than doubling output from 100,000 to 220,000 tonnes. This decision reflected the influence of men such as (Sir) Robert Scholey and Derek Bray, who were committed to recapturing the major share of the United Kingdom stainless market (they believed they could get 4 per cent growth a year) and to increasing the share of overseas trade. It took two years to formulate the plan and three to four years to commission and build the plant, partly due to the problems of dismantling the complex structure of the old stainless interests (at Firth-Brown and Fox), and partly due to the fact that Sheffield had now fallen behind in stainless mass-production technologies. Though BSC Stainless could draw upon United Steel's expertise in continuous casting, the technology was now handled by multinational consortia sharing patent rights and licensing arrangements. Sheffield had to learn from the new masters of the trade—the Germans, North Americans, and Japanese—when it installed continuous casting. As with most developments of that nature in Sheffield, the new equipment had to be phased in while the older operations—especially the finishing departments at Shepcote—were still in production. As the head of the stainless division emphasized: 'All this was happening while we were trying to build a market image. We were doing all the wrong things from a business point of view, which of course affected our image in the market place.'[18] But the development, which came on-line in the late 1970s and employed about 6,000, represented a considerable achievement. The cost was also considerable, rising from a projected £130 million to nearly £200 million, in what was virtually the last great milestone in the Tinsley

---

[18] Bray had worked his way up from apprentice at Steel, Peech, & Tozer, studying metallurgy part-time at Sheffield University. He became head of British Steel Alloy & Stainless in 1971. See 'Stainless: An Inside BSC Special', *Quality*, 25 (July/Aug. 1978), 35–43.

area of Sheffield.[19] But it allowed British Steel Stainless to enjoy a large share of the dramatic growth of the country's stainless steel consumption in the late 1980s, which in some years averaged over 12 per cent—even though some felt that the development was a decade too late. It used continuous slab casting with some success, but the slabs still had to be sent to Ravenscraig in Scotland for primary rolling before being returned to Sheffield for finish-rolling at Shepcote Lane.

Elsewhere the interface between the public and private sectors was even more complex, leading to what was described at the time as 'untidiness'. This was partly resolved by the formation of Sheffield Rolling Mills Ltd., which in 1969 enjoyed the distinction of being the only denationalized part of British Steel—the latter owning 47 per cent and Balfour-Darwins and James Neill the rest. Ultimately the private interest was sold to BSC. Another venture was Lee Bright Bars, formed by a merger of the plants of the BSC at Warrington and Govan and the bright drawing facilities of Arthur Lee & Sons at Meadowhall. This created a highly versatile company, 55 per cent owned by Arthur Lee and 45 per cent by the BSC, with a wide range of the highest quality bright bars. The partnership lasted until 1982.

In Rotherham the sharp downturn in demand in the early 1970s, coupled with changes in technology and the BSC's rationalization programme, soon had its effect. The massive expansion of electric arc steelmaking in the area in the early 1960s now appeared to have been mistaken. The Park Gate blast furnaces were scheduled for closure in 1974; so too was the company's Swedish Kaldo refining process, which was a failure both mechanically and metallurgically (maintenance of the Kaldo revolving vessel proved difficult and the molten iron picked up non-metallic inclusions from the lining). The progress of Steel, Peech, & Tozer's vaunted battery of electric arc furnaces was halted by scrap shortages and was also overtaken by the new basic oxygen furnaces, which were appearing in Scunthorpe, Teesside, and South Wales.[20] These new furnaces—some producing 300 tonnes of steel in 30 minutes—also needed a sizeable share of scrap. As a response, the Templeborough operations were run down and the electric furnaces transferred to the BSC's Aldwarke melting shop, which, in conjunction with the rolling mills at

---

[19] 'BSC's Stainless Steel Challenge', Steel Times, 203 (Nov. 1975), 893–908; 'Stainless Steel at Shepcote 2', ibid. 205 (July 1977), 594–605; 'BSC's Stainless Sheffield Works', ibid. 206 (July 1978), 538–73; British Steel Stainless, 75 Years of Stainless Steel, 1913–1988 (Sheffield, 1988).

[20] The development of oxygen steelmaking after the 1960s was a great leap forward in the industry, making the Bessemer and open-hearth processes obsolete. In its original form the process, as it was developed in Austria, involved the blowing of a high-pressure, supersonic jet of almost pure oxygen onto the surface of molten steel. Along with the electric arc, it now produces the bulk of the world's steel, except for specialist alloys melted by the induction furnace and secondary steelmaking processes.

Roundwood and Thrybergh, became the new centrepiece for the Corporation's Special Steels Division.

In a further reduction of steelmaking capacity, the ESC's showpiece Tinsley Park works was also closed by the mid-1980s. There had been little doubt about its ultimate fate after nationalization, when the ESC directors had lost the argument within BSC to have two special steels groups (one centred around Tinsley, the other around Fox). The closure reflected the influence within the BSC of the United Steel 'Mafia', notably Robert Scholey, who had argued that any nationalization of steel must include the ESC (thus bringing it within the BSC's power).[21] Once this was accomplished, Scholey had the chance to rationalize Park Gate, Tinsley, and Stocksbridge. Since the former Fox works had more steelmaking capacity than Tinsley, the latter was shut, and continuous casting when it came was installed at Stocksbridge.

What was happening in the private sector? Here too rationalization continued apace in steel castings, forgings, and alloy steels, producing bedfellows that would have been unthinkable in the nineteenth century. Hadfields was one company which had found the going increasingly tough in the 1950s and early 1960s. By 1962 control of the company had passed to Sir Peter Roberts (1912–85), a local Conservative industrialist, who was chairman of a consortium know as the Steel Trust. He recruited Norman Hanlon, an engineer from Dorman Long, as managing director to rebuild and rationalize Hadfields. Hanlon found a company with aging plant (it still adhered to Sir Robert Hadfield's practice of using Bessemer converters for ordinary manganese castings), much weighed down by the past. The Millspaugh subsidiary was absorbing large amounts of working capital. In particular, the foundry—once the biggest in Europe—was losing money, as overcapacity in the steel castings industry became a problem. The foundry at Osborn's was facing a similar situation and so in 1967 they and Hadfields merged their steel castings interests into a separate production centre in the latter's East Hecla Works. The sudden attempt to mix the production and management of the two concerns was a disaster, compounded by bad management. It proved difficult to isolate the production departments at Hadfields' works, because steel casting was a continuous process, financial controls were initially poor, and a 'them' and 'us' situation developed amongst Hadfield and Osborn personnel.

Meanwhile, Hadfields' steelmaking activities were losing £250,000 a year. As a way out, Hanlon tried to buy Dunford & Elliott, the re-rolling firm, because of its fit with Hadfields' remaining business and because he

---

[21] Ironically, Scholey was the son of an ESC director, though his own experience had been in Rotherham. He had joined Steel, Peech, & Tozer in 1947 as an engineer and by 1967 was a director and works manager there. See D. J. Jeremy and G. Tweedale (eds.), *Dictionary of 20th Century Business Leaders* (London, 1994), 183.

wished to develop the trade in car steels with Fords. To Hanlon's chagrin, Dunford & Elliott—though it was far smaller than Hadfields, with only 400 workers—succeeded in mounting a reverse bid of £4.8 million in 1968 (Hadfields' net assets were £9.7 million). The bid was masterminded by the Irish merchant bankers, William Brandt's, and their managing director, Frank Welsh. The latter—following the vogue amongst merchant bankers at that time—was on the lookout for businesses to restructure and he wanted a situation where the bank could do this not just by financial control, but through active participation in management.

Brandt's installed Welsh as chairman and brought in a new managing director, Peter Edwards.[22] This team soon sold the Osborn-Hadfield foundry to the Weir Group, and Millspaugh to the Swiss firm, Escher Wyss. Briefly, after a management and capital restructuring programme that took three years to complete, prospects looked better for the group and in 1971 Welsh took Brandt's out of the business, along with about £1 million profit from the share sale, while he stayed on as executive chairman. This was a shrewd move for Brandt's, since although Dunford & Elliott's profits had risen from £0.2 million in 1969 to £2.2 million (pre-tax) in 1973, it was in a difficult position: it needed to expand steelmaking capacity to maintain its independence and its share of the alloy steel market, but this was perilous with so much overcapacity in the industry.

After failing in an audacious £26 million reverse bid for Firth-Brown, in 1973 (when it had a staff of around 2,300 and a turnover of about £15 million) Dunford & Elliott instead bought Brown Bayleys Steels. In 1969, this firm had been acquired by the Industrial Reorganization Corporation when it looked as if the Government was to sponsor the modernization of the Sheffield special steel industry. The IRC had asked Tom Kilpatrick, and ex-United Steel and BSC man, to be chairman of the firm, which still employed about 2,800. He found an 'early twentieth-century establishment', which although it had spent about £6 million from its own resources in new equipment, still had archaic management and needed further modernization. Backed by the IRC, Kilpatrick began a massive expansion, funded by heavy borrowing. No sooner had this begun, however, than a new government scrapped the IRC and Brown Bayleys was offered to Dunford & Elliott—not a move that was designed to create happiness, since the two firms were bitter rivals. The price was £5.5 million and it created a firm with 5,600 employees and an annual turnover of £40 million. The takeover was not well timed. In early 1974 a series of events—strikes, the Arab–Israeli War, rises in the oil price, and high interest rates—dogged the merger and Dunford & Elliott had to borrow heavily. Delays in commissioning new furnaces at Brown Bayleys meant

---

[22] 'How Peter Edwards Kept His Eye on "The Constant Horizon"', *The Director* (Sept. 1973), 388–91.

that the combine missed the marked four-year cycle in the forging industry. The two concerns were never an ideal fit anyway—Brown Bayleys' product was higher-value; Hadfields had five main customers (all in the automobile trade), Brown Bayleys about 800—and the rationalization soon stalled. For Hadfields, so long the epitome of the independent company, it had been an eventful seven years.

During these years, a depressing pattern of mergers, plant closures, strikes, and redundancies unfolded as these firms attempted the risky strategy of expensive and long-needed modernizations in an era of recession, overcapacity, and high interest rates. There was a high personal cost, both for the steelworkers who lost their jobs, and for many of the business leaders who saw the traditional network of personal relationships in the industry sundered. Ever since the 1740s, Sheffield steel had been remarkably self-contained, drawing its talents and investments mostly from the locality. The industry generated almost a 'club' atmosphere in such institutions as the Company of Cutlers. Now the old structure was breaking up. Although the Special Steels Division of the BSC was at first largely staffed by men who had been trained and had worked locally—Scholey, Ken Lewis (an ex-ESC forge director), H. P. Forder (ex-Samuel Fox), John Pennington (ex-United Steel)—the formation of the BSC had marked a political shift. Decisions could now be made at BSC headquarters in London, rather than in Sheffield—and even if they were made locally, often Rotherham and Stocksbridge interests were paramount. Meanwhile, the private sector began attracting the 'predators', the outsiders with no background in steel, who saw the industry through the eyes of cost accountants rather than metallurgists. They brought a new entrepreneurial ruthlessness with them, which clashed with the more gentlemanly ways of Steel City, and their arrival and influence in the city created much bitterness amongst Sheffield's close-knit steel community in the 1970s.

Frank Welsh was an example of the new breed. Another was Oliver Jessel, who joined Firth-Brown. In the late 1960s, this company had reached the height of its powers, still concentrating on highly specialist steels at the Atlas Works and through its various subsidiaries and investments—Beardmore, Firth-Derihon, Firth-Vickers, and Alloy Steel Rods—with *the* works laboratory in the country. Boasted one managing director: 'There was no better company in the world at the time for special, special steels.' In 1967 it bought the steel interests of Jessop-Saville for £3.3 million (the latter's titanium interests being sold separately to another buyer, Imperial Metal Industries). Some, however, felt that the company was over-developed technically and perhaps too committed to buyers such as Rolls-Royce—'the management was top heavy with technologists', was one view, while others believed it was too unionized. But the fame of its laboratories and long research tradition counted for less in an era of major changes in the structure of the industry. The demand for large open-die forgings began falling after the 1960s, as changes in engineering design had their impact. With developments in welding technology and non-destructive testing (such as cobalt radiography), it was found perfectly acceptable to make the huge hollow-drum forgings in sections, then simply weld them together. By the mid-1970s, with the decline of large capital projects in power stations and chemical plant, orders for very big forgings had almost gone. The result was under-utilization of the expensive and sophisticated steelmaking and refining plant that had been installed at the firm's Atlas works.[23] The Laboratories had stopped recruiting by about 1968 and there was a general rundown; while the tool steel interests of Jessop-Saville did not fit well with the company's other lines and, in any case, faced severe overseas competition.

Firth-Brown's trading profit dipped from £2 million in 1970 to £1.5 million in 1972. In the following year, after resisting the bid from Dunford & Elliott, the company accepted an offer from Richard Johnson & Nephew. This old Manchester wiremaking firm had become the vehicle for the ambitions of Oliver Jessel, who had built his fortune as a wheeler-dealer on the London Stock Exchange in the 1960s and through his City group, Jessel Securities, had acquired control of Johnson & Nephew in 1970.[24] His arrival in Steel City created a stir. 'Sheffield had not seen anything like it,' remarked one Firth-Brown director: 'The entrepreneur was unknown in Sheffield. He was refreshing in his approach and, though he had no masterplan, he had vision.' However, Jessel's flamboyance—he was remembered, particularly, for flying around the city in a helicopter—was regarded with contempt by others in the industry. Nor did they like his cadre of young, business-school trained executives, who had no experience in the industry and who, they felt, Jessel had elevated to positions of authority far too soon. In the event, Jessel proved no better at reversing the fortunes of his acquisition (named Johnson & Firth Brown) than his predecessors. The collapse of the stock market in 1975 hit Jessel Securities, and its chairman, denied a rescue by City bankers, began selling his assets. His 34 per cent share in Johnson & Firth Brown was sold off piecemeal in the City and the company became truly independent. Attempts to restructure Firth-Brown and stem its losses continued, but by the early 1980s the dramatic decline of the forging industry, in which the BSC's River Don Works shared, was unabated: in 1973 some 13,000 had been employed at these two sites, but by 1983 the number had fallen to 5,000.

---

[23] For an extensive discussion of Firth-Brown and its plant, see A. Barker and E. Pinder, 'Precision Steelmaking—Then and Now', *Ironmaking and Steelmaking*, 3 (1976), 195–204.

[24] Michael Seth-Smith, *200 Years of Richard Johnson & Nephew* (Manchester, 1973), 272–81.

In tool steel manufacture, the start of a new order was evident in 1960 when Sanderson Bros. & Newbould merged with Kayser, Ellison.[25] Within walking distance of each other in Attercliffe, the two firms had long had close links in the production of such specialities as silver steel. The match between the two companies was satisfactory: Kayser, Ellison, although it was somewhat 'cosy and comatose', as one Sanderson man described it, had a good range of specialities in bright bars and forgings (such as its selenium stainless steel for automatic screw-cutting lathes), an 800-ton forging press, and a number of United Kingdom warehouses—all of which complemented Sanderson's Newhall Road products and overseas marketing operations. The merger was amicable and there were no redundancies. In the following year Balfour's and Darwins also merged names and company. The heads of both favoured the move—ThompsonSchwab because he wanted to run a bigger group; Arthur Balfour's son, Robin (the second Lord Riverdale), because he felt the firm should diversify and because of personal reasons (he had no wish to work himself to death, as had his father). The move did not bring any dramatic benefits and although Thompson-Schwab died almost as soon as Balfour & Darwins was organized (as did Darwins' sales director Pat Wilde), giving Balfour's a freer hand, rationalization proceeded slowly with both firms still regarding themselves as separate. Like the Sanderson Kayser merger, it had not produced a single integrated site.

Rationalization was becoming imperative, since the tool steel industry in Sheffield was about to undergo a decade of rapid change, as developments in the world industry caught up with it. The fact that such a large number of the old firms had survived into the 1950s was not necessarily a sign of strength—many were seriously exposed. According to one Sheffield tool steel manufacturer: 'by the early 1960s the industry was working in a multitude of small Victorian works, crammed with machinery which was virtually worn out through long years of high usage without any significant capital replacement'.[26] Practices unique to Sheffield, such as hire-rolling, continued unchanged. Like the other steel industries discussed so far, world tool steel production was on the verge of great changes in the 1960s. In the United Kingdom the Restrictive Trade Practices Act in 1964 took away the price-fixing activities of the Sheffield tool steel firms (as it did in other branches of the industry), thus intensifying competition. The greater use of steel stockholders and increasing standardization in the 1960s helped erode the value of the old Sheffield names and trade marks.

---

[25] G. B. Callan (ed.), 'Two Hundred Years of Special Steel', *The Sanderson Kayser Magazine*, 2 (1976).

[26] 'The Ecclesfield Project Manual' (1973), internal Osborn report kindly made available to me by Bernard Cotton.

Beneath this standardization were new production techniques. Electroslag refining, which was first installed in Sheffield by Firth-Brown in 1964, was one example.[27] Automatic rolling mills and forging machines were making the old hand-techniques redundant and tool steelworks abroad were taking the opportunity to make even high-speed steel a more mass-produced commodity. High-speed steel for drills and similar items could now be produced in coil, which could either be used directly for manufacture or cut into the required length. There was also competition from tungsten-carbides, ceramics, and powder metallurgy and spray-deposition techniques. Both Sanderson Kayser and Alloy Steel Rods Ltd. (jointly-owned by Arthur Lee, Firth-Brown, and the ESC) had invested in automated rolling mills in the 1960s.[28] But generally, Sheffield had fallen behind technically and in many of the smaller firms it remained 'an article of faith that tool and high-speed steels should be produced in small quantities and be able to answer specialist needs'.

One firm did make an attempt to break away from these old ideas. Samuel Osborn, whose famous Mushet tool steel had helped launch the modern tool steel industry almost exactly a century before, epitomized many of the problems of the industry. By the 1960s, still recognizably the firm assembed by the founder, it was feeling the dead hand of its Victorian heritage. The company had melting and rolling at Low Moor Alloy Steel Co., Bradford, producing valve and stainless steel; the Regent Works in Sheffield for sheet; the old Wicker works for melting and rolling high-speed steel; Parkhouse works in Sheffield for finishing steel; the Holbrook Works in Sheffield for the high-frequency melting of steel; and also its Sheffield Mushet tools plant (which had been expanded by the acquisition of Marsh Bros. Tools in 1976). It was a management nightmare, with control of the scattered plants difficult, with each tending to operate in isolation as an autonomous unit, and with the problems compounded by anachronisms such as hire-rolling. It was not unusual for Low Moor to sell ingots to people who often sent them into the Osborn Wicker Works for rolling into billets and bars.

It cried out for rationalization and in the mid-1960s the challenge was taken on by Bernard Cotton. Trained in metallurgy at Sheffield University, Cotton had worked for a time at the Round Oak Steel Works in Worcestershire, before joining Osborn's in 1957. His experience as sales manager in the North American market had given him a wide appreci-

---

[27] In this method, remelting is carried out through the intermediary of a very fluid slag, which tends to absorb or dissolve non-metallic particles, producing a steel with only very small widely dispersed inclusions. The quality of the steel is very similar to that obtained by vacuum remelting, but since the equipment required is basically cheaper the cost of electroslag steel is lower.

[28] 'Advanced Rod Mill Rolls Top-Quality Alloy Steels', *British Steelmaker*, 32 (July 1966), 42–50.

ation of the changing world market in alloy steels and made him, in his own words, a 'confirmed European' in outlook. After a boardroom coup finally forced the 80-year-old Frank Hurst and the Osborn family interests to withdraw, Cotton assumed the central direction of Osborn's and took on the task of pulling it into the modern era. While grappling with the foundry merger with Hadfields (already described), he began by buying the steelmaking interests of Hall & Pickles at Ecclesfield and the business of C. R. Denton. The purchase of Hall & Pickles brought with it a 33-acre site at Ecclesfield and the chance to rationalize Osborn's activities, which by 1968 were being carried out at thirteen separate works. Cotton, helped by a £1.75 million grant from the IRC, launched the Ecclesfield project in 1969. This aimed at concentrating production at three main sites, much of it at a custom-built factory at Ecclesfield.[29]

In the words of Osborn Steel's managing director, the Ecclesfield project was

a big jump forward in almost every part of the process route—melting, electroflux refining, billet heating, atmosphere controlled annealing, non-destructive on-line testing, excellent plant layout, computer controlled production, first-rate quality control—but there remained the weak link of dependence on small hand-mills with their limited productivity.

The timing was also unfortunate. After reaching a peak in the early 1960s, demand for tool and high-speed steels began to fall and there was to be a particularly severe drop in the world recession of the mid-1970s (see Fig. 10.5). The tool steel industry also faced intense competition at this time from overseas. European markets were larger (in Germany, for instance, the market was five times that of Britain; in France three times as large), so allowing home producers the chance to achieve economies of scale. These producers targeted the British market, where they established marketing operations, cut prices, and attracted customers with excellent quality and back-up services. Some of these producers, such as the Austrians and Swedes, were backed by government subsidies, or were part of large, often diversified groups. The Sheffield tool steel producers, however, felt that their protests to the Government about the activities of these firms fell on deaf ears. One tool steel director believed that:

The problem was accentuated by nationalisation. No one believed that Sheffield steel was of strategic importance any longer. The nationalised Austrian industry running enormous losses was dumping steel with impunity in the UK market. But no amount of pressure or proof would shake the obduracy of the government in their refusal to act. The Community countries decided they would join the rout and Germany and France made hay. Most extraordinary was the refusal of the government to insist that the measures adopted by the Community under the

[29] 'Osborn Steels Today', *Steel Times*, 200 (Dec. 1972), 869–85.

Davignon declaration to apply quotas and restraints on price-cutting, should apply to all steels. In short, they accepted the pleas of the big German companies that they would only accept the quotas and restraints if they were free to run amok in the area of high alloy steels. This they did with relish.

Perhaps the Ecclesfield project was already ten years too late; perhaps the tool steel industry (as one Sheffield director has suggested) could have only survived by being nationalized itself, so that it could invest sufficiently in new technologies. What is certain is that, as foreign imports soared to 80 per cent, Osborn's Ecclesfield plan ran into trouble and in 1978 the company fell to a Sheffield engineering combine, Aurora Holdings Ltd.

Aurora's star was rising rapidly at this time, under its chairman (Sir) Robert Atkinson. Like Welsh and Jessel, Atkinson was an 'outsider' in the industry and came to Steel City after a varied military and industrial career. Born into a Tynemouth seafaring family, he trained as an engineer, then became a decorated naval commander during the War. He later began a promising career as a manager in various engineering firms before joining the merchant bankers Kayser Ullman, with responsibility for their industrial interests. In 1972 he was recruited to restore the fortunes of Aurora, the obscure Sheffield gear manufacturers, and rapidly turned the company round.

From almost nowhere, by 1978 Aurora had become the fifth largest engineering group in Sheffield (between 1972 and 1977 profits had climbed from £220,000 to £2.5 million), and Atkinson had turned his attention to the ailing tool steel industry.[30] Increasingly, Atkinson's ambitions were to effect the awaited transformation in this sector. Osborn's difficulties provided a great opportunity; the means were provided by the fact that Oliver Jessel had bought a 30 per cent shareholding in Osborn before he left Johnson & Firth-Brown. Atkinson persuaded JFB to sell the shares to Aurora (much to the annoyance of the Osborn directors, who had expected the shares to be offered to them), which enabled him to launch a successful bid for Osborn and purchase it for £11 million. Atkinson in 1979 then paid £14 million for Edgar Allen Balfour,[31] making Aurora the biggest British special alloy steel producer, with a workforce of 4,000.

The company revolved around the personality of Atkinson, who was energetic, audacious, and a clever publicist. Under his direction the steelworks got cleaner, flagpoles sprouted around the company grounds (so much so, that someone once said that it was difficult to know whether it was a petrol station or a military establishment), and company reports

---

[30] 'Robert Atkinson: The Ace in Aurora's Pack', *Quality*, 25 (May/June 1978), 20–1.
[31] Edgar Allen and Balfour & Darwins merged in 1975. The BSC had meanwhile sold its tool and high-speed steel plant at Openshaw (formerly owned by the ESC) to Edgar Allen.

became glossier. But Atkinson's sometimes abrasive style did not always prove popular; nor did his business strategy. Critics accuse him of bringing little to the industry except a burden of debt (when he took over Osborn's he offered double the previous market price of the shares) that hastened the collapse of Aurora Steels almost as soon as it had been launched. Weighted with interest charges on loans, which absorbed the £1 million profit Osborn Steels was making, Ecclesfield was closed in 1981 with a loss of 230 jobs; and in 1983 all Aurora's steelmaking ceased when Openshaw shut with another 200 jobs lost. The Group had run up a deficit of over £17 million, with total debts of nearly £40 million.[32] Since Aurora accounted for over 60 per cent of national tool steel production, it was a landmark event and a bitter disappointment to those (not only within the company) who had hoped that it would help restore the city's position.

The remaining tool steel firms—Barworth Flockton, Carlisle's, Carr's, Johnson & Firth Brown, Neepsend, and Sanderson Kayser—were left to pick up the pieces. The industry was now much reduced, even compared with the situation in 1970. United Kingdom tool, die, and magnet steel production had fallen by about a third between 1970 and 1980 (from 38,000 to 13,000 tonnes); high-speed steel output was down by more than half from 19,000 to 8,000 tonnes. It was clear that the small size of the industry—which now employed under 5,000—would not attract large-scale Government support either in subsidies or in action on 'dumping'. Nevertheless, in 1980 the Bank of England and the Department of Industry, in consultation with the firms and BISPA, sponsored a study to assess the industry's future. The resulting Warner Report recommended support, but only if the remaining firms agreed to rationalize and reorganize into a single high-speed steel and tool steel producer. Characteristically, the solution was met with, as one insider put it, 'a typical Sheffield reaction. Rejection. The company owners just couldn't face up to it.' Over a hundred years of Sheffield individualism in tool steel was not so easily abolished.[33]

By the start of the 1980s both the BSC and the private firms were in serious difficulties. Between 1970 and 1980, the BSC had incurred losses of £2,836 million and, while its production had fallen from 24.2 million to 14.1 million tonnes, the workforce had declined from 252,400 to 166,400. The United Kingdom private sector had fared better than the nationalized industry during the 1970s and its share of the domestic market (about 25 per cent) remained fairly steady over these years, mainly a reflection of the fact that the high-quality steels in which it specialized had been less

---

[32] By then Atkinson was chairman of British Shipbuilders, a post he held from 1980 to 1984, and for which he was knighted.

[33] Sir Frederick Warner, 'An Enquiry into the Special Steels Industry' (July 1981).

susceptible to the slump in demand. However, it too was in trouble by 1980 as a recession hit public and private sectors alike.

In the 1980s, a new pattern emerged in the British steel industry: joint ventures between the BSC and the private sector, which were code-named 'Phoenix' to symbolize an industry rising from the ashes. Describing the development of these joint-schemes and their history is often complicated: however, essentially, they boiled down to one thing—a reduction in capacity and in jobs, that went ahead under the euphemism of 'rationalization', with the Government picking up the bill (albeit discreetly) for the social and economic costs of closure.

The first Phoenix to stir—one that did not involve South Yorkshire—was Allied Steel & Wire, formed in 1981. This brought together, after nearly two years of negotiations, the wire-rod and bar manufacturing interests of the BSC and the engineering company GKN. Phoenix II, which was a more ambitious project and was first discussed in 1980, also involved GKN and the BSC. This time the engineering steels sector of BSC was at the centre of the proposals and this involved the steelmaking capacity at Templeborough, Aldwarke, and Stocksbridge.

Phoenix II negotiations were not completed until 1986, a delay caused by the complex business of reducing capacity in the United Kingdom engineering steels sector. This could only be achieved by a substantial rationalization amongst the private firms. First the Duport Works in Llanelli closed in 1981 after heavy losses. In 1982 Round Oak Steel Works (formerly owned jointly by the BSC and Tube Investments) was closed along with the re-rolling mills at Tipton in the West Midlands, sold by Duport to the BSC in 1981. Shortly afterwards, it was the turn of Dunford Hadfields. In the difficult aftermath of the Brown Bayleys takeover, this firm was bought in 1977 for £14 million by Lonrho, since Tiny Rowlands was keen to boost the United Kingdom earnings of his group by buying engineering firms. In debt to the banks to the tune of £21 million, Dunford Hadfields was hit by a recession and various union disputes in the automotive industry. In 1980 it had also been drawn into the national steel dispute, when BSC strikers picketed the East Hecla Works in some of the more unpleasant and most-publicized scenes in the dispute. Soon afterwards, Lonrho formed a company with the BSC and GKN known as Hadfields Holdings Ltd., which in 1982 closed the Leeds Road operations (in other words, the old works of Brown Bayleys) and the East Hecla Works a year later. Not much more than a century after it had started, Hadfields was no more, and the huge factory—once one of the biggest and most famous steel foundries in the world—was promptly demolished.

However, with the recession having cleared the ground for Phoenix II (sometimes quite literally), the negotiations dragged along slowly. GKN were first suspicious that the plan would involve the closure of its Brymbo Works in North Wales (it had not gone unnoticed that the Government's policies invariably seemed to end with closures in the private sector) and were hoping for demand to improve. The Government, meanwhile, were reluctant to give their approval to the Phoenix II plans, since they seemed likely to need substantial amounts of funding. Eventually, the Government did agree to sink £55 million into a new company, which began operating in April 1986 under the name of United Engineering Steels (UES). The company's joint assets amounted to £400 million, 58 per cent contributed by the BSC, but with ownership split fifty/fifty. To bring GKN's contribution up to the half-share mark, its various forgings businesses were added to the group; while BSC contributed the melting and finishing facilities at Aldwarke, Templeborough, and Stocksbridge (Tinsley Park, which had been part of the original discussions, had by this time been shut). UES's workforce was 10,500. One of the first acts was to begin a £60 million modernization programme of the Aldwarke plant at Rotherham, with a new continuous bloom caster by 1988 along with secondary steelmaking facilities and a bloom reheating furnace. It was vaunted as the largest producer of 'engineering steels' in Europe, competing with European giants Thyssen and Krupp (West Germany), Deltasider (Italy), and Ascometal (France).

Phoenix III took place much more rapidly in November 1982 when Johnson & Firth-Brown merged its steelmaking interests with the BSC's River Don Works to form a new company—Sheffield Forgemasters. The merger also included the JFB subsidiary River Don Stampings and JFB's cast roll companies, Midland Rollmakers of Crewe and R. B. Tennent and Miller & Co., both based in Scotland. Originally announced in August 1982, the merger was held up by difficulties in raising the required £1 million to complete the financial structure. The BSC had just invested in a £14 million 10,000-tonne forge at River Don; while JFB had spent £12 million on a precision forge. But JFB had mustered profits of only £10 million (on a total turnover of £470 million) over the previous six years. In the 18 months prior to the merger, JFB suffered losses to the tune of £15 million, while BSC River Don had lost around £33 million in the last five years and had made no profits for at least a decade.

From this dismal backdrop, Sheffield Forgemasters was supposed to create a stronger base for forgings and special steels, with JFB and the BSC each having a 50 per cent stake. Inevitably, rationalization soon began with 1,000 of the 5,000 jobs inherited by the company being shed. The first victim of the merger was JFB's Beardmore foundry in Glasgow, where just under 400 redundancies were caused by the closure of the plant.[34]

---

[34] John R. Hume and Michael Moss, *Beardmore: The History of a Scottish Industrial Giant* (London, 1979), 293.

Forgings that had previously been done at Beardmore's were now switched to Sheffield.

By the mid-1980s, therefore, Steel City had acquired a new, much more simplified look. Excluding stainless steel, the picture in the bulk special steels was as follows: steel melting and continuous casting at Stocksbridge and Templeborough; steel melting, primary and finished rolling at Rotherham (taking in Roundwood, Thrybergh, and Aldwarke); with GKN providing downstream customers with its string of forging subsidiaries. But could these drastically restructured companies survive in the recession-hit 1980s?

11

Survivors and New Agendas

> The days when Sheffield and Rotherham were the epitome of steel cities are long gone. In Sheffield, the socialist local authority now employs three times the numbers working in steel; only Sheffield Forgemasters in the private sector employs more than Bassetts, the liquorice allsorts sweets maker.
>
> *Metal Monthly Bulletin* (Oct. 1985), 87.

In the 1970s, despite the steady erosion of Sheffield's share of world steel which had been going on throughout the century, the local economy still prospered. Until 1981—when Sheffield had the third highest employment-dependence of any urban area on the mining, iron and steel, and other metals sector of the economy—the city's unemployment level was continuously below the national average. In 1979, however, Sheffield's manufacturing base began shrinking drastically. In only three years, between 1980 and 1983, the steel and engineering sector lost about 20,000 jobs. The result was that after 1981 the city's unemployment rate remained higher than the national average. 'The transformation has been astonishing—indeed, frightening', stated the journal of the Sheffield Chamber of Commerce.[1] It was a change that was to cause a radical revision of outlook, in both local government and industry.

The transformed relationship between local government and industry is outlined in the Epilogue. In this chapter, the response of companies and businessmen to this period of decline (which many have described as collapse) is examined in the different sectors of Steel City's industry—forgings, castings, special steels, and cutlery and tools. What new strategies and changes of attitude (if any) can be discerned in the 1980s and early 1990s?

The River Don site, the inheritor of so much of Sheffield's traditional skill in steelmaking and engineering (see Fig. 11.1), as usual faced the biggest problems. After its formation in 1982, Sheffield Forgemasters had the characteristic difficulty of Steel City companies attempting to restructure: how to bring together numerous disparate firms and activities at a time when the business outlook was bleak.[2] Sheffield Forgemasters itself

---

[1] *Quality*, 29 (Sept./Oct. 1982), 50.

[2] The following account is based on my interview with Forgemasters' directors; annual reports and other literature supplied by the company; the trade press, especially *Steel Times*; and Anita van de Vliet, 'Out of the Furnace', *Management Today* (Dec. 1990), 51–3.

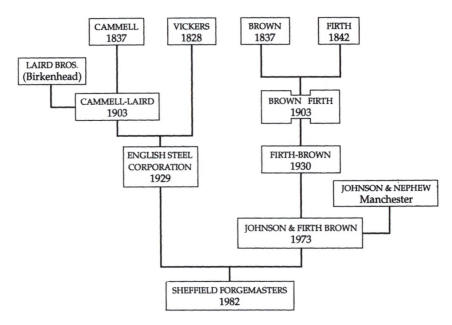

Fig. 11.1. *Sheffield Forgemasters*

was a holding company, which attempted to bring together seven entirely different business philosophies and traditions. The two major constituents, Firth-Brown and River Don, had been in competition with each other and had particularly marked differences in style (or as economists and business historians have become fond of calling it, rather inappropriately, 'culture'). River Don had been sheltered within the BSC and had occupied a curious position, never quite fitting in with the Corporation's other strategies, yet never having to worry about making a profit. Firth-Brown, on the other hand, had had to compete for business in the real world: consequently, its financial controls were much tighter. Also, there were several other differences of the kind that occurred whenever organizations merged. Pay differentials varied in each company; and Firth-Brown and River Don staff were in a better pension fund than Forgemasters could devise.

Overriding all these problems, however, was the collapse in the market for forgings, caused mainly by the high exchange rate and the demise of other British industries, such as shipbuilding. The combined turnover of the companies in Forgemasters in 1981 was £135 million; in its first year of operations this had fallen to £92 million. Forgemasters lost £60 million in the first three years (much of it in writing-off fixed assets that were simply closed down). The finance director of the company, Malcolm Brand, was appalled to recall that Forgemasters had spent £10 million before it started

(£8 million of which was spent by River Don) in losses and working capital. Closures soon followed. British Steel investments, such as the 10,000-tonne press, set the agenda for many of these cutbacks, which tended to be on the Firth-Brown side. Beardmore and the presses in the Atlas Works were the main casualties. But as the decline spread, over-capacity caused closures in the other works too. Forgemasters had planned to retain both melting shops—the one at River Don, which had been uprated in 1970; and the one at the Atlas site, built in 1973—since they believed there would be enough sales for both. But eventually the Atlas shop became surplus and was closed in 1983, an action triggered by a breakout-of-metal fire that was settled by a large insurance claim. A £3 million scheme was then approved to uprate the River Don shop for what was seen as a likely future capacity—a sound decision which, in fact, provided enough steel into the 1990s.

By 1984 it was apparent that Forgemasters was close to receivership. Recalled one director:

Cash was haemorrhaging away with the losses and need for rationalisation was increasing. Despite redundancies [which reduced the workforce from 7,200 to 3,900 in three years], senior management had been untouched and the two com-panies had simply shared out double the number of jobs. We were losing money on redundancy, closures, rationalisation and the overhead structure was too big. Labour relations were poor and there were a lot of strikes. It was obvious that the company structure was daft, with branches as far away as Edinburgh.

Forgemasters started a divisional structure, while it drew up a new busi-ness plan for a grant from the Department of Trade.[3] British Steel gave a £5 million trading facility and the banks also offered support, providing the Department of Trade backed it (which they did) and providing there was a management shake-up. Frank Fitzgerald and Martin Llowarch from British Steel were put on the board, while the bankers Lazard's had recruited Tom Kenny, a company doctor and chairman of GEI (a metals and packaging-machinery conglomerate that by now owned Sanderson Kayser), to become chairman in January 1985. Kenny, and his right-hand man Ed Thompson, brought in a new forcefulness. On 26 February 1985, he addressed Forgemasters' senior management in the idiosyncratic and plain-spoken style for which he was noted. He began by describing GEI as 'a public and very profitable concern embracing sixteen subsidiary com-panies. It is comparable in size to Sheffield Forgemasters. It has ten people in head office—you have over four hundred.' As regards Forgemasters, he believed it was undoubtedly 'a substantial and viable business with many attractive elements and big names as customers. [But] it seems to have gone off its direction since incorporation. The reasons are various ...

[3] 'Sheffield Forgemasters Completes Restructuring', *Steel Times*, 212 (Aug. 1984), 371–3.

[but] ... there seems to have been a lack of distinction between board meetings and management meetings: the two got fused.' Kenny stated he was going to abolish the divisional structure and establish subsidiary companies. He also demanded a change in attitude towards more customer-oriented strategies: the whole selling and marketing approach was to be reviewed at weekend conferences:

You may not welcome [the] idea of a conference straddling a weekend and if you choose to be absent, without good cause, then you may remain in that situation for the following years. At the moment, our costs of sales matches the income from our sales so that the overheads represent our losses. The logical deduction from this is that we are either selling too cheaply or producing too expensively or have too many overheads. The question has to be answered and quickly.

Kenny also planned a job review—'I hazard a guess that you will be surprised at how many people are not doing a constructive job or who should not be on the pay roll'—and promised to make Forgemasters profitable in two years.

Kenny created a system of profit centres in the form of limited trading companies, though this did little immediately to stop the rot. He had also decided, in the spirit of the times, that union power needed curbing, at least when it tried operating on a company-wide basis. This was a direct contrast with the old Firth-Brown management under Donald Hardwick, where an effort had been made to involve the unions on key decisions and where there was a hierarchy of shop stewards' committees. In the summer of 1985 the unions were told that central pay bargaining was abolished and that each company within the group would negotiate separately. Two convenors at Forgemasters were also told they would no longer be required. Interpreted as a blatant attempt to divide and rule, this immediately resulted in October 1985 in an acrimonious strike, in which the Firth-Brown workers came out first, and were soon followed in sympathy by River Don. Despite pressure from the banks, British Steel, and Johnson & Firth Brown the management at Forgemasters refused to compromise. The lay-off was not entirely damaging for the company, since while the workers were out, cash was being generated. In fact, working capital was reduced by the strike.

Meanwhile, Kenny decided on further management changes, appointing Philip Wright as a new managing director in 1985. (Kenny and Thompson were to retire in 1989.) Wright, a metallurgist and MBA-trained management consultant, had a reputation for company rescues in Sheffield (notably at Edgar Allen Balfour). He was not impressed by Forgemasters, where there were 'hundreds of acres of blackened, broken-backed buildings, sprouting buddleia and breeding inefficiency. The place was filthy, there was junk all over the place. There was no discipline.

Table 11.1. *Sheffield Forgemasters: profit and turnover, 1986–1993 (£000)*

	1986	1987	1988 (9 months)	1989	1990	1991	1992	1993
Turnover	97,274	95,619	77,713	115,873	137,218	142,670	130,495	122,637
Pre-tax profit (loss)	(2,387)	571	2,004	9,118	17,374	17,585	16,734	8,625

Source: Sheffield Forgemasters, *Annual Reports.*

Quality was poor, some orders were three years late. Equipment was standing idle. Vast quantities of stock lay strewn across the floor.'[4] Some 30,000 tonnes were to be picked off the floor, recouping £5 million in three months.

Wright continued the decentralization and the attempt to instil in the workforce a new commercialism. Within a fortnight, however, the banks threatened to withdraw, convinced that the situation at Forgemasters was irretrievable: the company was losing nearly £2 million a month on a 1985 turnover of £102 million. At a crucial meeting, Kenny literally swore at the institutional shareholders and said he would bring the company round and break even in a year. The banks eventually agreed and he and Wright were given a second chance.

The decentralization continued. Firth Vickers Stainless Steels (the old Weedon Street site, which had not become part of British Steel) and River Don Stampings were hived off first—their plants had not been devastated in the rationalization, they had their own management styles and could be split off rapidly. Wright then persuaded the senior managers of the new limited companies to 'find' 500 redundancies. Special Melted Products, Tennents and Miller (Scotland), and Forged Rolls were then disengaged from the main group and the other companies were scheduled for flotation. In February 1986 the 16-week strike was settled on Forgemasters terms, with pay and productivity bargaining decentralized to a divisional level and with no full-time union officials on site. Since then Forgemasters has never lost money at the operating stage. Kenny had succeeded, not only in breaking even, but also in making a profit (see Table 11.1).

As Forgemasters began improving in health, it presented an attractive opportunity for a management buy-out: in fact, that may have been the reason why Wright and Kenny took on the challenge. The original shareholders agreement had said that if British Steel was privatized, then it had to dispose of its interest in Forgemasters. Johnson & Firth Brown, although it wanted to keep its profitable forging interests centred around Firth-Derihon, was also keen to sell its shareholding. Wright and Brand

---

[4] van de Vliet, 'Out of the Furnace', 52.

set up the buy-out throughout 1987, but there were varying conflicts of interest and various offers were rejected. Doug Morton, a director from Aurora, was on the board of Forgemasters and Aurora (now a general engineering and steel stockholding company) expressed an interest in March 1988 with an offer with 'due diligence'. The shareholders told the Forgemasters' team that the Aurora bid had to be settled first.

The venture capital groups Schroder Ventures and Causeway Capital aided Wright and his men, who were working all day with the accountants of Aurora, then using the evenings for work on their own buy-out scheme. Aurora eventually did not confirm its bid, due partly to antagonism from the Forgemasters' management and partly to their own projections, which showed that massive capital expenditure was needed. Aurora decided it could not take the risk. The venture capitalists backed the Forgemasters' team and the deal was completed by October 1988 (after a slight delay due to an American writ for $25 million damages served on Forgemasters and others concerning the failure of an oil-rig crane hook), with the price set at £26.2 million. After a redemption of loan stock, the BSC and Johnson & Firth Brown shared just over £11.5 million. The BSC had lost assets worth £41 million, including £17 million in cash, proving that, in this case at least, privatization did not work miracles.

Wright's new structure was based around ten (later eleven) companies, which were grouped in three divisions—aerospace, engineering, and rolls. He made many management changes. By 1993, from the ten subsidiaries, only three of the managing directors had been there since 1982. The changes were symbolized by the new head office—a secluded old rectory in Whiston, on the outskirts of Rotherham, where Wright, Brand, and about a dozen others directed affairs. In 1985 the headquarters had been an imposing block employing about 500, with 1,300 reporting to it. In the new leaner organization cash was controlled daily at the centre; and the financial system was completely overhauled, so that every month each company submitted a simple statement of profit, loss, and other accounting indicators, alongside a brief managing director's report, with various projections under different sub-headings. This devolution allowed each company manager to concentrate on his own business, while knowing little about the others. There was a greater emphasis on results, rather than on the old 'jobs for life' syndrome, when companies had reported proudly that workers grew grey in their service. Language abilities were now demanded for overseas sales jobs and, in another contrast to the time-honoured ways, where jobs depended upon family or local contacts in steel, an attempt was made to recruit from other industries such as oil and chemicals (though in certain parts of the business, such as castings, the firm still preferred local recruits).

Forgemasters has, though, attempted to reinforce one traditional Sheffield virtue—quality—and also attempted to improve another—customer service. One company in the group, River Don Castings, headed by managing-director Bryan Cookson, has been particularly successful. Cookson had moved to Sheffield from Liverpool and found Steel City complacent and conservative, having benefited commercially from two world wars. In 1976 he remembered 'talking to a purchasing manager of a large company, who in the 1960s had come up to River Don for a large casting and drove back feeling pleased with a two-and-a-half year delivery! This went on into the 1970s.' One of Cookson's first jobs was, as he put it, 'persuading people to go back to castings—they'd got out of the habit'. Now situated in the old Siemens River Don melting shop (to where it was moved from Grimesthorpe), River Don Castings has used its advantages—the availability of high-quality steel from Forgemasters—to market, for example, a wide range of products in the offshore oil industry (where in 1992 it took 90 per cent of all offshore castings orders worldwide). The firm is recognized as the world leader in the design and production of structural steel cast nodes and heavy-lift equipment. Its link with its parent—uniquely it does not have any steelmaking capacity of its own, but gets its steel literally from over the road from Forgemasters' electric arc furnaces—means that it could make a 300-tonne casting if required, using vacuum arc degassing and vacuum oxygen decarburizing ladle steelmaking techniques. Since 1981 the company has supplied 90 per cent of United Kingdom steel castings, with only Finland and Austria as real competitors.

Sheffield Forgemasters did not win admirers everywhere, especially in a city with such strong Labour sentiments. Wright's showdown with the unions did not prove popular with the socialist Sheffield council, whose sympathies lay with the strikers, even to the extent of sending them Christmas hampers—a gesture which infuriated the Forgemasters' management. Also controversial was Forgemasters' involvement in 1989 in the 'Supergun' affair, when the company was accused of contravening export regulations to Iraq by supplying Saddam Hussein's dictatorship with a giant alloy steel gun barrel. The company were later exonerated by the Government (not perhaps surprisingly, since they had given the go-ahead on the project), though the duplicity and secrecy surrounding much of the ensuing 'Arms-for-Iraq' scandal did little to soften Forgemasters' image. Nevertheless, the commercial future looked better for the company by the end of the 1980s. According to Malcolm Brand: 'Our role at first appeared to be to effect as painless as possible a withdrawal from steel and engineering—that seemed to be what we were involved in. But since 1985 I like to think we have reversed that.'

Another Sheffield company, which has reversed the decline (at least in its own fortunes), is William Cook in the steel castings industry. After its founding in the 1880s in Glasgow and Sheffield, Cook's had developed as a typically small, if rather undynamic, family steel casting firm. In the inter-war period it employed about fifty, but after induction melting was introduced in 1947, the firm began growing. It expanded on its original Attercliffe site and was floated as a public company in 1956. With capital of about £200,000, Cook's was making good profits from a turnover of about £600,000, benefiting from the rise in orders from a mechanizing coal-mining industry and from commercial vehicle production. By the mid-1960s, when Cook's had about 300 workers and turnover was approaching £1 million a year, new works were acquired at Parkway on the old Nunnery Colliery site, near Attercliffe. These were opened in 1968, though it was to be another six years before the foundry came up from Washford Road.

In 1973 Andrew Cook, the 23-year-old great-great-grandson of the founder, joined the firm.[5] Trained as a barrister, Cook first helped install the new foundry, which completed the move from Attercliffe by 1974. No growth followed, but steady profits were earned through the decade, until 1980 when the slump arrived. The United Kingdom steel castings industry had been in decline since 1975, when domestic deliveries were 239,343 tonnes; by 1980 these were only 143,440 tonnes and in the following year the total had dropped to 119,193 (and meanwhile imports of castings were growing). Andrew Cook vividly remembered how 'the phones stopped ringing and the order book fell through the floor', as a 100-tonnes output a week suddenly dropped to 60 tonnes. At this point Cook became managing director, when his father retired. This marked a crisis in the company, with Andrew Cook identifying bad management as one of the root problems both within the United Kingdom steel castings industry and within Cook's itself. The older generation of Cook's had shown little interest in modernizing the business and pursuing growth. As Andrew Cook expressed it: 'they had a sneaking regard for the non-manufacturer, but I was committed to the steel industry'. The result was a family disagreement, after which Cook removed some of the older management, brought in his own men and introduced his own more entrepreneurial style. Like the old Victorian steelmasters (Sir Robert Hadfield is perhaps the man he most closely resembles), Cook was an autocrat, who slept on a camp bed at the works if the occasion demanded it. His strategy was

---

[5] The following information on Cook's is derived from my interview with Andrew Cook, 9 Mar. 1993, and the following publications: 'The Lawyer Who Broke the Mould', *Engineer* (15 Sept. 1988), 28–9; 'Cook's Recipe for the Steel Industry', *Director* (21 Mar. 1990); Andrew Cook, 'The Facts of Life', *Foundry Trade Journal* (23 Mar. 1990); William Pitt, 'A Test of Metal', *Director* (Apr. 1992), 35–8. Philip Hansen is currently writing a history of the Cook group.

simple: first, to survive; and then become a leader in quality. A policy of acquisitions followed.

In 1982 Andrew Cook became chairman and he immediately cut the workforce from 300 to 150, and then began his investment and modernization programme. When Cook became managing director the company could not make high-alloy castings because of low productivity, quality-control problems, and overmanning. Cook overcame all this by installing modern equipment (though he shrewdly bought secondhand when he could). One major project was the construction of a heavy foundry, where castings could be made from 100 kg. up to 100 tonnes. Production was soon up to 100 tonnes per week and a heavy fettling shop was added. By March 1986 sales exceeded £10 million and profits topped £1 million—both records for the company. Four years earlier, sales had been under £4 million and profits only £100,000. The capital came from within the company, though the Department of Trade had helped with grants for modernization.

Cook's next main move was in November 1986, when he bought the Weir group of foundries. According to Cook himself, this strategy was dictated by the fact that 'organic growth for the company was no longer possible, because of severe competition and contraction of the UK engineering industry—the top market. The creation of new capacity was no longer viable. Cook's needed to grow because the castings business was self-destructive.' There were still over sixty steel foundries in the United Kingdom, many in Sheffield where the industry had been established since the 1850s, though now the trade had spread to other localities. Partly through historical accident, but mostly because the customer base was so wide and because castings could vary so much in type and price (castings could range from a hundred tonnes or more for oil rigs, down to a few grammes for aerospace), the industry was highly fragmented and competitive, and profit margins lean or non-existent.

Andrew Cook assumed the role of the classic rationalizer: buying up companies as cheaply as possible, then either closing them or bringing them into a more coherent whole. Cook reckoned that after loss-making companies closed, prices would rise. Meanwhile, because profits in the industry were low, investment on research and development were low. The Government had tried to remedy this already, by supporting a scheme put forward between 1975 and 1981 by the merchant bank, Lazard's. It had mixed success and it was left to Cook to achieve singlehandedly many of Lazard's objectives. Weir, which cost £12.9 million (financed by a rights issue of £2 a share) brought the ownership of Catton's, Jopling's, Holbrook, OH Hi Tec, and Weir Fabrications. Cook closed Jopling (Sunderland), and transferred some work to Catton's

(Leeds). He then succeeded in finding a new home for OH Hi Tech by purchasing David Brown Foundries in Penistone (renaming it Hi Tec Integrity Castings); invested in Catton's and Holbrook (at Eckington, near Sheffield); and sold Weir Fabrications.

Castings up to 35 tonnes could be made at Hi Tec; while precision castings as small as a few grammes could be manufactured at Holbrook. The bigger commercial castings could be undertaken at the main foundry in Sheffield and at Catton's. But Cook still felt he was 'a long way from home base, because all the group needed an overhaul'. The company was competing for the first time in higher technology areas such as defence products and valves. Further acquisitions were deemed necessary, and in 1986 Robert Hyde (Chesterfield) was purchased, which gave Cook's a strong position in castings for the coal mining industry. This was run for a time, but was later closed and merged with the Sheffield parent. Cook then bought George Blair (near Newcastle) for its market position in the track business for tanks. This was on four sites, of which two were closed and two modernized. Other additions were Blackett Hutton—a pure job-bing foundry in Guisborough—and Lake & Elliott in Braintree for the order book, which Cook closed.

At the beginning of 1990 he bought Lloyds of Burton on Trent, which was the only steel caster in valves that was not part of the Cook group. By now Cook's market share of the United Kingdom steel castings industry was beginning to arouse the interest of the Monopolies and Mergers Commission.[6] But this only temporarily interrupted Cook's efforts and after 1990 there were further rationalizations. Not every venture was a success. In an interesting example of history repeating itself, in 1990 Cook followed Hadfield's example and bought a steel casting subsidiary in Ohio, as a way of breaking into the Sheffield firm's best export market. Based in Toledo, the acquisition proved a disaster. Union and labour problems, the poor quality of American technology, and the problems of operating overseas (as Cook put it, the fate of the United States company could be summed up in the phrase: 'While the cat's away, the mice will play'), led to the loss of $20 million.

This was the only blemish on what has been an unexpectedly successful record for a Sheffield steel casting firm. By 1993 Cook's operated seven subsidiaries around the country (with its main base in Sheffield); it employed about 2,500 workers (some 750 in the city); and sales had reached £100 million a year, with a peak of £130 million in early March 1991 (see Table 11.2). Within a decade or so it had emerged as Europe's largest steel caster and in the early 1990s was maintaining this position in the face of the United Kingdom's dwindling engineering base, high energy costs and

---

[6] Monopolies & Mergers Commission, *William Cook plc Acquisitions: A Report on the Mergers Situation.* Cm. 1196 (1990).

Table 11.2. *William Cook PLC: Financial results,*
1981–1992

	Sales (£000)	Pre-tax profit (£000)	Return on capital (%)
1981	4,073	138	6
1982	3,959	178	7
1983	5,178	344	13
1984	5,961	575	19
1985	7,110	459	13
1986	10,361	1,201	31
1987	25,200	1,464	13
1988	43,281	1,705	13
1989	58,984	5,055	27
1990	112,349	9,518	30
1991	133,220	12,178	34
1992	111,225	4,763	14
1993	100,509	3,854	13

Source: William Cook PLC, *Annual Reports*.

Andrew Cook's favourite *bête noire*, the subsidies handed out to European steel casting concerns.

Though the industry had been considerably reduced, Cook had preserved what had once been one of the mainstays of the Sheffield steel trade. All those products that had launched the fortunes of the old market leaders—Hadfields, Edgar Allen, and Osborn—were now made by William Cook. In Sheffield itself were made the castings for mines and quarries, construction and earth-moving—some still manufactured in Hadfield manganese steel (an alloy which has never been bettered for work-hardening)—all cast in three automated foundries using the green-sand, no-bake, and shell moulding processes. Holbrook Precision Castings provided small, high-integrity close-tolerance castings, up to 25 kgs. and needing little additional finishing. Fluids-handling, pump valve, and the food industries are all served with castings made by the lost-wax, investment, Shaw, and shell processes.[7] The large foundry at Penistone meanwhile catered for the higher specification market, including power-generation, offshore, nuclear, and turbine fields. Andrew Cook reckoned he had spent £20 million in modernization, whilst continuing to run things as a 'one-man band' with the majority shareholding. Why had he been successful, where others had failed? The slump, which threatened

[7] For a description of casting processes, see William Alexander and Arthur Street, *Metals in the Service of Man* (London, 9th edn., 1989). The Shaw process was developed in the mid-1950s at Darwins and is still used worldwide.

Cook's survival, was the turning point. According to Andrew Cook, this had thinned out the numerous powerful Sheffield steel castings companies, which were hindering rationalization. Once Cook had solved its own internal problems (the work of the financial director, Kevin Musgrove, providing a critical input), and became more powerful, its market position as a quoted company allowed it to raise the money necessary for expansion.

Outside forgings and castings, general engineering steels were now largely the province of UES (United Engineering Steels), the rump of the old United Steel companies. Here the reshufflings of British Steel and the Phoenix schemes had created the largest capacity in Western Europe for producing engineering steels (which according to UES's wide definition included alloy billets, bars, and rods for those uses, including free-cutting steels). In 1992 UES's estimated production of 1.3 million tonnes placed it some way ahead of its leading European competitors, such as Ascometal in France and Saarstahl in Germany (though both of these were members of one group—Unisor-Sacilor).

Producing steel, however, was not UES's problem; selling it was. In the early 1990s, under its chief executive Graham Mackenzie, the company's strategy was to expand through product-led growth into higher-value sectors, exploiting its position as the lowest cost base in Europe.[8] Mackenzie, an ex-TI board member who was director of its specialized engineering and tube divisions and had been involved with Sir Christopher Lewington in TI's globalization, arrived in Sheffield in 1989 as a successor to John Pennington and felt as if he had 'stepped back five or ten years'. Some of the old production-led philosophies still lingered at UES into the 1980s and 1990s. Mackenzie remembered that there were still steel shortages in the 1960s, even into the 1970s. 'It was then a major culture shock to discover that customers could buy elsewhere. It was also an education for customers themselves, who believed they could not get steel abroad.' With this legacy, UES's task as Mackenzie saw it was to retain its share of the home market, partly through a significant move into steel stockholding. Abroad, UES intended to internationalize in Europe, trying to capitalize on its advantages in lead-free cutting materials and in some sections of the forging market, such as in complex, safety-critical components. Its major target was to be the second source-supplier (after the domestic leader) in foreign markets: and, in fact, UES had succeeded in raising its export level from 30 per cent to a little under 40 per cent.

But business strategies, no matter how sophisticated, mean little without the bedrock demand for engineering steels. As Fig. 11.2 shows, this fell during the 1970s and then levelled off during the 1980s (at about a

[8] I am grateful to Graham Mackenzie and Ralph Beaumont for discussing UES's development with me, during interviews, 22 Mar. 1993.

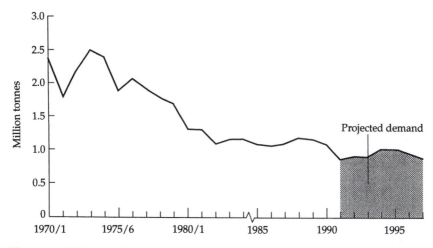

Fig. 11.2. *UK demand for engineering steels. Courtesy UES*

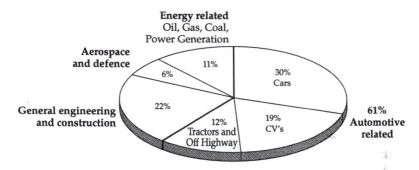

Fig. 11.3. *United Engineering Steels: estimate of end-use market sectors. Courtesy UES*

million tonnes), before suddenly beginning to decline again in the early 1990s as another recession began to bite. Partly this reflected demand from the automotive sector, which accounted for a massive 61 per cent of UES's sales (see Fig. 11.3).[9] There had been an increase in the number of vehicles produced, but this was offset by the steady reduction of steel used in them. It also reflected rising scrap prices, which jumped 60 per cent in one year in 1993–4. A major consideration was high energy costs, a crucial factor to firms such as UES, whose bills for powering its electric arcs, continuous casting plant, and rolling mills are enormous—running into millions of pounds each year. However, after the privatization of the

---

[9] Information courtesy of UES. See also *Minutes of Evidence taken Before the Trade and Industry Committee: Enquiry into the Motor Components Industry* (London, 1987). Memo submitted by UES (M66), 25 Mar. 1987, 247–60.

electricity industry in 1990 power costs have soared between 20 and 30 per cent, giving British industry the highest energy costs in Europe. The structure of the new privatized electricity industry—a duopoly in the place of the old monopoly, with a notably weak regulatory body—had little support from Sheffield steelmakers, who felt that no account had been taken of the big consumers.

In Europe, overcapacity was once more a problem in the depths of the recession in the early 1990s. At UES, alongside falling demand and rising costs, this produced the predictable result: diminishing profits and the constant task of reducing capacity. With capital of over £400 million, UES's pre-tax profits struggled to rise much above £50 million at the end of the 1980s; and by the recession of the early 1990s the company went into the red. It sold its steel castings interests, Lloyd's, to William Cook and closed the Brymbo Steel Works, measures which were associated with a trend which saw an increasing proportion of the country's alloy steels melted in South Yorkshire after 1985 (see Fig. 10.4). Only two out of the three electric furnaces at Aldwarke were expected to operate in the long-term; and at Stocksbridge all the investment was to go into one furnace. 'More capacity will come out', predicted Mackenzie in March 1993, 'and in employment the inexorable decline will continue.' This was fulfilled in September 1993 when UES's Templeborough site in Rotherham was closed with the loss of over 260 jobs.[10] Mackenzie left in the aftermath of the closure. Gone too was its glossy annual report.

Despite the problems of UES in the bulk area of special steel production, it is interesting to note that even in the 1980s and early 1990s, the strategies that had earned the old crucible steelmakers their first fortunes in the trade—in particular the identification of specific niches in the market, which could be secured by high quality and customer service—could still bring success. Some companies have attacked the market for new superalloys, with a strategy aimed at exploiting the latest developments in aerospace; others have been able to progress with more traditional special steels that rely on older markets. The tool steelmakers Barworth & Flockton and Sanderson Kayser illustrate the latter; Ross & Catherall is a prime example of the former.

Ross & Catherall was founded in 1936 as Ross & Co. (Foundry) Ltd., in Forge Lane, Killamarsh, a small town about fifteen miles to the south-east of Sheffield.[11] Initially, it supplied castings for magnets for a single customer, Marrison & Catherall Ltd., but under Norman Ross, its works

---

[10] 'UES Rationalises in a Tough Year', *Steel Times*, 222 (Feb. 1994), 61.

[11] This account draws on Thomas Mackie, 'A Case Study of the Evolution of the Ross Catherall Group plc and the Role of the Entrepreneur' (Sheffield Hallam University BA, 1990). Quotations, unless attributed to Mackie, are from my interview with Desmond Mawson, 25 Mar. 1992.

manager, it began supplying engineering and automobile castings. The firm prospered, though it was an unremarkable performer: by 1960 it had about forty workers, turnover was £175,000, and the return on sales a mere 5 per cent.

In 1961 a new general manager, Desmond Mawson, joined the firm. Mawson was a qualified physicist, who after the war had been introduced to the Jessop's research director, Donald Oliver, who was looking for recruits to work on magnetic research. Mawson joined Jessop's in 1947 as a technologist, but he later moved into sales. As he watched Jessop's develop in the boom of the 1950s, he became increasingly critical of its business strategy, especially its heavy spending on basic research, which Mawson believed was too high. Mawson recalls: 'Jessop's had to come up with a winner every five years. G18B and H46 kept the company going for 20 years, but they failed to come up with anything after that.' This was particularly damaging, because Mawson felt that Jessop's also suffered from what many critics have cited as a prime British business failing: it neglected marketing and commercial business and, despite its success in advanced research, was weak on production research. 'Jessop's had the world's worst delivery record in the 1950s', argues Mawson, 'twelve to eighteen months was quite usual and they were worse than any of the others. It was considered a privilege to have an order accepted.' Mawson promised himself that 'if ever I run a company I won't make the same mistakes with delivery'.

At Mawson's insistence Ross moved into a new product—air-melt remelting stock to foundries producing castings by the lost-wax process. Air-melt was a specialist electric melting technique, with close control of the melting and casting process, and it allowed the company to expand. According to a business study of the company: 'Mawson was the architect of the company's progression and the sole motivational force.'[12] He targeted two main markets: barstock and castings for aero-engine components (especially Rolls-Royce's); and alloys for turbo-chargers in automobiles (where the firm's high-quality nickel-based superalloys were used for rotor castings and wheels).

The company had two competitors—Jessop Saville and G. L. Willan—but Mawson (who has described himself as 'fanatical about customer service') soon established the firm as an accredited Rolls-Royce supplier in 1963. This enhanced the firm's reputation and enabled it also to supply Rolls-Royce subcontractors. At this time, Jessop's were beginning to flounder; while Willan's were more interested in general steel castings and their rather poor quality and service had dented their reputation with Rolls-Royce. Fortuitously, therefore, there were no significant barriers to

---

[12] Mackie, 'Case Study', 5.

Mawson entering these new markets. Between 1962 and 1967 sales grew from £192,270 to over £1 million, with the return on sales increasing from about 11 to 28 per cent.

In 1968 Ross & Catherall Ltd. was formed, with a major shareholder named Whiteley and Mawson as managing director. Mawson saw further opportunities in the expanding market for aero-engine components made by vacuum-melting, so in 1968 Ross & Catherall spent £25,000 on a vacuum-melting furnace and again won Rolls-Royce approval (even though the latter had advised Mawson against entering this market). Willan's was reluctant to become tied to Rolls-Royce; while another competitor, Union Carbide, proved unable to meet the quality requirements. The result was that Ross & Catherall secured a stranglehold in vacuum-melted products.

The early 1970s were eventful, with the Rolls-Royce bankruptcy in 1971 creating waves for Ross & Catherall, who were owed £250,000 by the engine-maker. But the Killamarsh firm maintained deliveries and was eventually repaid. In 1972 Mawson invested £600,000 in another vacuum furnace, and a second large furnace was installed in 1976, making it the largest supplier of remelted alloys in Europe. Between 1968 and 1980 sales increased from about £1 million to over £18 million; profits (which were largely in vacuum-melted alloys) increased from about £200,000 to nearly £4 million; and the return on sales was about 20 per cent. Mawson had generated this growth simply by ploughing back, without any borrowing, and the company never had any debts.

In the 1980s Mawson confirmed Ross & Catherall's position as a high-technology metals and materials producer with further acquisitions. In the recession of 1980–1 Mawson bought Trucast Ltd. on the Isle of Wight for £1.8 million as a captive market for alloys, especially for automobile turbochargers. This helped the firm weather the drop in aerospace orders. Mawson, however, commissioned a third vacuum furnace, ready for the upturn in demand, which duly came in 1984. In 1986 he added Certified Alloy Products in Long Beach, California, to the group to gain access to the United States aero-engine market. In 1988 PCC Ceramics, a company manufacturing preformed ceramic cores at Denby, near Derby, was bought for £2 million.

In 1985 Mawson became chairman, combining the post with that of chief executive when the firm became a holding company, the Ross Catherall Group PLC, three years later. In this period he maintained the company's growth and matched the profitability of previous years. Between 1981 and 1988 turnover increased from £16 million to £33 million; profit grew from about £4 million to nearly £6 million; and the return on sales was maintained at about 20 per cent, with reserves up from £4 million to £13 million. Ninety per cent of Ross & Catherall's capital was owned by four family trusts and one financial institution (3i). In 1989 3i persuaded Mawson and the trustees to float the firm, which boosted its authorized capital from £5.5 million to £47.8 million. Almost immediately, however, Vickers offered to take the firm over for £108 million. Mawson, now aged 65, and wishing to preserve the company from hostile predators, recommended acceptance of the offer. Now a millionaire, he was briefly appointed to the main Vickers' board until he retired in December 1991. By any standards, it was a remarkable success story: a company employing about a hundred in his early days had now become worldwide group with 800 to 900 workers (about 200 of whom were at Killamarsh).

Ross & Catherall was a relatively innovative firm, becoming a market leader in an industry that was relatively new to the Sheffield region. However, not every successful firm attempted this strategy: some preferred to follow a more hallowed Sheffield route by continuing to produce tool and high-speed steels and to fill small, specialized niches in the market. Such a firm was the Barworth Steelworks, the small crucible steelmaker founded in the 1920s.[13] In the post-war boom Barworth's had expanded under the direction of Reg Hulley, a metallurgist from Hadfields and Thomas Turton, who had joined as partner in 1945. He pursued a policy of steady acquisitions, buying first in 1949 the Fulwood Tool Co., a manufacturer of tool bits and ground flat stock; and then in 1951 the United Kingdom branch of the Czech firm Poldi, tool steel factors. In 1958 Hulley added three companies to his group: G. & J. Hall, an engineers' small tools manufacturers, then at Hereford Street; Flockton Tompkin, the tool steelmakers (which had been founded in 1866 by J. B. Tompkin) in Burgess Road; and Henry Stones Ltd. (a subsidiary of Flockton Tompkin), which made files at John Street. In 1960 the group was restructured as Barworth Holdings and almost immediately the steel companies were moved to an integrated site at Ecclesfield, about eight miles to the north of Sheffield. There the firm built a melting shop and heat-treatment plant, with reeling and centreless grinding and warehouse and despatch facilities. In 1962 the offices were moved to Ecclesfield, too, preparatory to the various parts forming one company—Barworth Flockton Ltd.—in 1968. By then, Donvale Steels Ltd. had joined the group, largely as a company specializing in export sales.

In 1970 G. & J. Hall moved to Burgess Road and expanded; and in the following year the steel division grew further by buying from Beardshaw's the forgers Henry Eadon & Sons Ltd., in Hillsborough. Finally, in 1975 a rolling mill was acquired from Kenyon Bros. During this period Noel Edwards, Hulley's son-in-law, joined the business, working first with Flockton Tompkin and then with Hall's on the sales side. Ac-

---

[13] This account is based on interviews with Noel Edwards, 2 May, 22 Oct. 1991.

cording to Edwards, Hulley was an expert on tool steelmaking, but there were management difficulties in organizing the firm's operations. In 1980 the family trustees, concerned at the firm's losses, gave Edwards the task of reorganizing the management. He immediately turned the company around, doing little to alter the basic direction of Reg Hulley (who was now 78 years old), but relying far more on a policy of steady investment that was based, mostly, on the group's own resources. He also ended some of the management overlaps and gave the firm a stronger central direction. Acquisitions, apart from the tool steel firm, Ledingham's, ceased.

Between 1979 and 1980 expansion began at Ecclesfield, with the installation of a Davy-Loewy press and a GFM machine. In the early 1980s, in the aftermath of the Warner Report on the Sheffield tool steel industry, Stanley Speight, the head of the Neepsend group, approached Edwards with an offer to sell its loss-maker Moss & Gamble, provided Barworth Flockton took over Neepsend's steel interests centred around Jonas & Colver. So Edwards bought Moss & Gamble for £200,000—'a bargain', as he describes it—along with the customers and stock of Jonas & Colver. Edwards is critical of the way some family managers ran the old tool steel firms: owners did not visit their works frequently enough, they seemed to have little idea of what was available in government subsidies, and their accounting was primitive. 'Often', he has said, 'the problems in the industry were due to bad family management—they did not know what their costs were.'

The business, which continued operating as a holding company under the family (Edwards' son, Richard, joining the business in 1986), was located on three main sites: the tool and high-speed steelmaking at Barworth Flockton Ltd., Ecclesfield, with 150 hands; the steel forging at Moss & Gamble Bros. on Penistone Road, employing forty; and engineers' tools production at G. & J. Hall in Attercliffe, with eighty workers. The organization was exactly like the old nineteenth-century Sheffield firms and was based on the same philosophy: independence and total control. Edwards had little taste for the recommendations of Sir Frederick Warner. When asked whether a chance was missed when the tool steel firms did not merge in the 1980s, he answers:

I couldn't see this super tool steel company actually being formed, since it would have involved *successful* family companies being broken up. Hulley had tried to build up an *integrated* steelworks, family-owned, and he did not want to give it up by merging with other companies. Instead we have pursued a strategy of being a very good *niche* producer.

Barworth Flockton usually sells about 1,600 bar tonnes each year as a minimum (though it has 2,000 tonnes a year melting capacity), of which two-thirds is tool steel, and the rest high-speed steel. In addition, the company do a good trade in hire-work—processing some 4,000 tonnes per annum for other companies—a practice which has somehow managed to survive in Sheffield almost since steelmaking began and which contributes a third of turnover. Occasionally for the cheaper grades, billet is bought in from outside. On its own terms, Edwards' policy has so far been successful. Whilst almost all the other tool steel firms have closed, Barworth Flockton have prospered. In 1979 group turnover was over £5.5 million; by 1991 it had increased to £15 million (with £9 million from the steel division); and by 1991 the firm employed about 282. In 1994 it invested £4.5 million in a new GFM rolling mill plant from Austria.

Whether Edwards' policy can survive until the end of the 1990s remains to be seen: one critic has described the firm's policy as simply one of retrenchment and Edwards himself admits concern at the steady erosion of the country's engineering base. However, he is not entirely alone. Sanderson Kayser have been pursuing a similar strategy for over two hundred years in Attercliffe and are still doing so. Most of its business is still in the 'very special steels'—tool and high-speed steel—though even with its more standard steels, it still offers something extra. The cost of the material is modest, but Sanderson Kayser gets a return by virtue of giving a service. 'Everybody's steel is that little bit different', explains the managing director, 'The facilities of engineers are adapted to that particular analysis and are reluctant to change unless there is something equally good.'[14]

The company still draws its strength from two things: it is the only integrated (*pace* the split site on Darnall and Newhall Roads) tool and high-speed steelmaker left in Sheffield itself; and it can still rely on a relatively large market for good-quality tool steel, which will always be required wherever products need to be drilled, punched, drawn, and stamped. In 1991 United Kingdom tool steel distribution still accounted for a quarter of Sanderson Kayser's market; and special steels sold direct some 16 per cent. In segmental saws, it was still the only manufacturer in the United Kingdom producing the total product; it was the only machine-knife maker in the country to produce its own steel; the only maker of silicon-iron; the principal supplier of material for punches; and virtually the only maker of injector pins for diesel engines. Since 1979 it has been owned by GEI International, which has led it perhaps to take a wider view of the industry than does Barworth Flockton. Its managers have been in favour of rationalization in the tool steel industry, indeed one stated in 1991 that the industry had been in need of proper rationalization for fifteen years—one that paid attention, not only to the production side (as

[14] I am grateful to Terry Worrall, Nigel Dick, and Bernard Callan for making available to me their expert knowledge of Sanderson Kayser.

Warner had done), but also to marketing. Warner, for example, had not addressed the problem of brand loyalty, on which it should have been possible to capitalize. The result, Sanderson Kayser believed, was that 'several firms were operating at less than efficient operating levels, which has allowed foreign competition to gain almost a stranglehold in the UK'. But this rationalization can hardly take place now, for the simple reason that there are so few firms left to merge their interests.

On the processing side of the steel industry, where firms did not melt their own steel (such as in wire manufacture), Arthur Lee & Sons still pressed ahead under family ownership in the 1980s. At the helm was Peter Lee, the great-grandson of the founder, who became chairman and managing director in 1979. Its strong balance sheet and careful financial controls ensured its survival, but competition from the cheaper end of the market gradually chipped away at its market share. The manufacture of certain types of wire—such as stainless and carbon steel—was phased out, to be replaced by precision stainless strip and a move into steel stockholding (which accounted for about a third of turnover by 1986). These were common-sense responses to competition in products that were now being produced quite cheaply worldwide—though Peter Lee did try one unexpected move in 1983 when he diversified into plastics by buying subsidiaries in Leicester and Mitcham. The move, looked upon askance by some of the Sheffield steel community, did not produce any dramatic changes in Arthur Lee's business. By the end of the 1980s, the limits of family ownership were being reached by Lee's, not because of poor leadership, but simply because certain products were best left to integrated companies that both made and finished steel. An example was the Europeanization of bright bar, which meant that Lee's Bright Bar division became a loss-maker and had to be sold to UES in 1992. As it was Lee's biggest subsidiary and one of its original businesses, it was a symbolic event. Employment at the company fell from about 1,500 to under 900 at a stroke. In 1993 Arthur Lee was taken over by the Leeds firm Carlco Engineering, and the Lee family departed. It was the end for another family name that had been around in Sheffield for over a hundred years.

Perhaps the biggest blow to Sheffield's reputation as a Steel City was the loss after the 1960s of its position as a major manufacturer of cutlery. This in some ways has injured Sheffield's pride more than the decline of the steel industry, since its defeat at the hands of foreign competition has been the more prominent, having taken place before Sheffielders' eyes in everyday household goods, and has been more complete. After the 1960s, Sheffield would continually plead that its products were of superior quality and better value than the competition—but the evidence in kitchens and on dining tables told a different story.

In evaluating the performance of Sheffield cutlery firms, one must carefully differentiate long-term trends in the industry from factors specific to individual firms or areas. Historically, Sheffield's forte was producing a wide range of product types of high quality . But most of us no longer work the land, hook stones from horses' hooves, go hunting, tackle desperadoes, wet-shave our chins, cut our quill pens, or even sharpen our pencils. Our everyday eating practices have changed, too, and the introduction of frozen, convenience, and fast foods has diminished the demand for traditional steel cutlery, in favour of plastics. We repair our shoes less and most of our clothes are mass-produced by automated machines—trends that have destroyed the business in trade knives and other products, such as scissors. Nowadays the bulk of the market is in table cutlery and kitchen knives, which account for about 70 per cent of United Kingdom sales (with table cutlery accounting for over half the market). Apart from the occasional wedding gift, consumers no longer buy sets of cutlery and have become relatively indifferent to quality as cutlery has become an increasingly mundane and uniform item of mass production. In these circumstances, cost has become the primary consideration, rendering Sheffield particularly vulnerable to imports.

Far Eastern competition in cutlery was already apparent by the late 1950s, particularly overseas. Wostenholm's managing director wrote home from Canada in 1958 that: 'The market is absolutely swamped with Japanese and German cutlery.'[15] Soon it was not only Sheffield's export markets which were inundated. Import penetration of the United Kingdom cutlery market gathered pace in the 1960s, but in the 1970s it became a deluge which swept away much of the Sheffield cutlery industry. By the mid-1970s, imports of cutlery surpassed the product value of domestic manufactures; and foreign products as a percentage of United Kingdom market value stayed at well over 50 per cent in the 1980s.[16] In some branches of the cutlery trade, such as stainless steel flatware, imports had soared to over 90 per cent in the 1970s. The number of workers in the industry fell steadily from nearly 12,000 in 1960 to 7,800 in 1971; by 1980 it was down to around 5,000, and estimates of the 1994 workforce put the total at not much above 2,000, and it is still falling. This was the period which saw the virtual extinction of the old-time craftsmen, as the newspapers in the 1970s and 1980s recorded the deaths of the last hand-forger, the last Bowie-knife maker, and the last scissor-hardener.

[15] SCL Wostenholm Records. S. Fowler to Wostenholm, 12 May 1958.

[16] Eric Williams, 'Low Cost Imports from the Far East have Decimated Sheffield Trade', *Tableware International* (Nov./Dec. 1975); Business & Market Research PLC, *The UK Market for Domestic Tableware* (1988); Keynote Publications, *Cutlery: An Industry Sector Overview* (London, 1988).

Inevitably, there was a string of casualties among the famous firms. The two biggest at the end of the 1950s were Viners and Richards. Viners, which was by far the largest company in the industry after 1960, with 530 workers and over £12 million sales, had prospered partly by importing low-priced cutlery through its Hong Kong subsidiary—not a popular policy in Sheffield. But this did little to save the firm in the long-term and it crashed in 1982. Richards declined after the post-war boom and, though its guiding hand, Wilhelm Muller, was able to buy up Wostenholm's in 1975 (which had meanwhile absorbed Joseph Rodgers) and eventually retire with a fortune, the company ended in the hands of the American firm Imperial-Schrade. They closed Richards in 1983, selling its famous trade marks on to other firms. By then the number of Sheffield cutlery firms had thinned considerably. A London Business School study in 1985 found only a couple of firms concentrating in the cutlery and silverware segments of the market—Oneida Silversmith (a United States company) and Terence Mason Investments—and a handful of old family firms, such as Arthur Price (much of whose production was based in Birmingham), Parkin Silversmiths, and Frank Cobb.[17] By the early 1990s some of these firms, such as Cobb, had closed; others were fighting for their survival in yet another recession.[18] In 1993 there were about twenty-four firms active: half of these were independent and a quarter family-owned.[19] There were only two little mesters active—Stan Shaw and Graham Clayton—producing hand-crafted pocket-knives.

By the 1990s, the reaction in Sheffield to the steady dribble of bankruptcies and closures had become one of resignation—a feeling that it was inevitable in the face of cutlery produced by 'slave-labour' in the Far East. There was something in this view: but was the *extent* of Sheffield cutlery decline inevitable? Not all imported products have come from the Far East and not all are at the low-priced end of the market. At time of writing, for example, it was possible to buy in Sheffield, as elsewhere, 'Swiss Army' knives by Victorinox, Sabatier Kitchen knives from France, and butchers' knives by the German Henckels firm. These companies have based their appeal on either innovative engineering, shrewd marketing, or both. For some reason, Sheffield companies failed to develop similar strategies.

Here the weaknesses specific to particular firms and to Sheffield need reviewing. The fragmented structure of the industry has already been highlighted. There were still about 275 cutlery manufacturers in Sheffield in the 1960s, and although the number of cutlery firms was under 200 by

[17] Robert M. Grant and Stephen Downing, 'The UK Cutlery Industry 1974–1982: A Study of Structural Adjustment, Business Strategies and Firm Performance', unpublished London Business School Study, May 1985.

[18] 'Cutlers Fight to Survive', *Sheffield Star*, 11 Mar. 1991.

[19] W. B. Spiers, 'Billy Ibberson Cutlery Research Project', unpublished Sheffield University Management School study, 17 Dec. 1993.

the mid-1970s and was declining rapidly, the survivors showed no real urgency to unite. The outwork system still flourished: indeed, even in the 1990s there was a handful of little mesters still plying their trade in backstreet workshops that had changed little since Victorian times.[20] Another feature of the trade had not changed either: its conservatism, when faced with technological change and the need to invest.

Before 1914 critics, such as Godfrey Lloyd and others, highlighted the technological and social progressiveness of German and American cutlers, when compared with Sheffield. In the early 1990s, such views have been restated. A recent study of the Tsubame cutlery industry has contrasted Sheffield's failure with Japanese success in the post-war period. Despite the fact that the Tsubame industry was highly fragmented (there were almost 2,500 firms and households in operation in 1980) and did not have a low-wage economy, it steadily increased market share at home and abroad (in the 1980s Japan was the front-ranking foreign exporter to the United States). The reason? Largely, it appears, because of 'longstanding differences in entrepreneurial attitudes and policies, especially with respect to innovation'.[21] It has been said that whereas Sheffield sought market share, not by innovation, but by minimizing costs in training, wages, and mechanization, Tsubame constantly upgraded its equipment-base with the installation of automatic grinding machines (after 1966) and semi-automatic equipment (after 1976). There is much truth in this view and it accords with even more recent evidence, which points to a lack of skilled workers in Sheffield, rather than the surplus one would perhaps expect in a declining industry. The Sheffield cutlery industry *has* been conservative. Certainly, it is difficult, even looking back over fifty years, to find a single example of real innovation in the industry.[22] Particularly depressing has been its inability to capitalize on its past successes. The Swiss Army knife, for example, is really only a cheap, if well-engineered, copy of the magnificent multi-blade knives at which Sheffield cutlers excelled in the nineteenth century. The fact that the Swiss have been left to dominate the market points to the continuing failure of Sheffield cutlery to utilize mass-production techniques (a failure highlighted earlier in this book) and modern marketing methods. Typically, too, it has even failed to make the most of the very few traditional cutlers left in the industry.[23]

[20] C. Jenkins and S. McClarence, *On the Knife Edge* (Sheffield, 1989).

[21] R. Hayter and J. Patchell, 'Different Trajectories in the Social Divisions of Labour: The Cutlery Industry in Sheffield, England, and Tsubame, Japan', *Urban Studies*, 30 (1993), 1427–45, 1441.

[22] In the early 1900s, George Jowitt had introduced the artificial grinding wheel (instead of the silicosis-inducing sandstone), but this had originated in America. More innovative was the electric etching technique for marking cutlery, introduced by the Sheffield firm Morgan Fairest Ltd. in about 1932. However, this was an engineering firm. See *Histories of Famous Firms* (1958), 12–13.

[23] G. Tweedale, *Stan Shaw: Master Cutler* (Sheffield, 1993).

One might say that, had the industry been more progressive, then at least *some* firms might have prospered, even if the general trend was contraction. We do not need to apply a counterfactual argument here, because, rather conveniently, there was such a firm—Richardson Sheffield. Since the 1960s, this company has been that rare thing in Steel City— a world-class cutlery manufacturer—a fact which has made it a favourite among business analysts.[24] Richardson Sheffield was founded in 1839 as a small cutlery workshop and was incorporated as Westall Richardson in 1929, operating as a typical family cutlery business. In 1956, Regent, an American cutlery firm, bought a half-share in Richardson, intending to use it as a source for knife blades. It needed substantial investment in machinery to bring the firm up to scratch, something which launched Richardson on its road to success and also led the American interests to acquire the remaining shareholding by 1960. In 1986 the Americans sold the business to McPherson's Ltd., the leading Australian manufacturer of kitchen knives and cutlery, which had diverse interests in publishing and engineering.

Under both American and Australian ownership, Richardson had an important element of continuity in the presence of Bryan Upton, who had joined the company as a progress chaser in 1959 and was managing director after 1966 (becoming chairman of Richardson Sheffield in 1988). Under his direction, the company made two key decisions: in 1966 it began making complete kitchen knives; and in 1979–80 it introduced its well-known Laser knife. Underlying these decisions was a policy of concentrating on increasing the efficiency of its manufacturing operations through process innovation and cost saving. Recalled Upton: 'When I took over in 1966, we were manufacturing blades in such antiquated methods, you wouldn't have believed it. In 1966, the chairman and I put our heads together and realised that we would be out of business in ten years if we carried on like that. There were plenty of guys in the Far East developing automated methods of production that would kill us.'[25] Upton and his engineers began building their own automated machines, then applied flow-production ideas and eventually computers to reduce their costs further. Meanwhile, they abandoned one of the time-honoured traditions in Sheffield cutlery—piecework—in favour of hourly wages, which cut supervision, yet allowed greater control of the manufacturing system.

[24] The following section draws on Robert M. Grant, 'The Richardson Sheffield Story: A British Winner', London Business School, Case Series No. 2 (Feb. 1988). See also Paul Geroski and Anastassios Vlassopoulos, 'A Market Leader in a Declining Industry: Richardson Sheffield', *Economic Journal*, 8 (1990), 15–18, which evidently also draws on Grant, although for some reason without credit. I am grateful to Ian Penwald for updating my information on Richardson.

[25] Grant, 'Richardson', 10.

Better manufacturing techniques, in turn, paved the way for Richardson Sheffield's major breakthrough in product development—the Laser knife. This was a mixture of clever technology—the Laser knife was designed never to need sharpening, due to its optimum angle of edge and minute serrations—and even better marketing. The success of this product appears to have owed as much to the inspired linking of the high-technology word 'Laser' with the Richardson Sheffield brand, as to any radical innovation in cutting. Most customers are actually unsure of why the knives are so named, many believing that they are somehow sharpened by laser (actually the beam only checks the angle of edge). No matter. Richardson Sheffield used the Laser knife to expand its sales and marketing operations. With a good product, an unprecedented 25-year guarantee and an evocative brand name, it set out to capture a large share of the kitchen knife market by paying careful attention to all the things that Sheffield firms had so often neglected: styling and packaging, custom-labelling for large department stores, and speed of delivery.

The results were dramatic. In the early 1970s, its turnover had been £0.5 million; by 1987 it was over £12 million; and by 1993 it had reached about £25 million. The return on capital had been consistently good, rising to about 25 per cent in the early 1980s after the introduction of the Laser knife (with all the profits being reinvested in the business—an unusual policy in a Sheffield cutlery firm). In the 1980s the firm had also bought Elford Plastics Ltd., in order to secure supplies for knife handles, and also purchased one of the nine Sabatier professional knife manufacturers. By 1993 Richardson Sheffield had won 55 per cent of the United Kingdom market in kitchen knives and about 9 per cent of the market in Europe, where it had sales offices in Germany, Italy, and Scandinavia. In 1994 the firm (which employed about 500) launched a new range of knives edged with titanium carbo-nitride, the result of collaboration with Sheffield Hallam University. It was also linked with materials research at Sheffield University through a £1 million government-sponsored project. This was a remarkable performance in an industry which had seen output and employment shrink; moreover, Richardson Sheffield's success was 'almost entirely attributable to its own efforts'.[26] Or at least, its own efforts alongside those of its American and Australian owners, who provided critical inputs. Perhaps that is why Richardson Sheffield has been more successful than any other firm—it is not entirely a Sheffield firm at all!

What of the tool sector? This had held up slightly better than the cutlery industry, as perhaps one would expect. Its record of innovation was superior and it tended to be less conservative. Sheffield remained the centre of the United Kingdom hand tool industry into the 1990s

---

[26] Ibid. 22.

employing over 36 per cent of the national workforce, and three of the largest United Kingdom hand tool companies—James Neill, Stanley, and Record—had their headquarters there. Sheffield-owned companies manufacturing both in the city and elsewhere were responsible for approximately two-thirds of the country's output in about 1990.[27] The industrial side of the tool business has declined—for example, bulldozers and earth-moving equipment have reduced the demand for sledge hammers, shovels, and picks—but this has been offset by the growth of the DIY market and the corresponding growth of superstores. Some Sheffield makers have even exploited the EIY (enjoy it yourself) market, as retired people or the unemployed have taken up craft hobbies.[28]

As with cutlery, in tool manufacture high production volumes linked to low costs necessitated investment in automatic, semi-automatic, and computerized production. At firms such as Stanley, by the 1990s most production was highly mechanized, from the initial basic preparation of raw materials, such as the machining of plane bases, right through to assembly and packing. Robots were increasingly used on repetitive tasks, especially to ensure highly accurate tolerances. Meanwhile, the old Sheffield hand tool craftsmen had mostly retired or died out. For example, Ernest Nutbrown, the last hand-cutter of files, who worked at the Globe Works at V. S. Brown's, retired in 1980.

But overall the picture is mixed. While Sheffield has consolidated its position nationwide, generally the hand tool industry has been in long-term decline, despite a growing world demand for tools. Employment in Sheffield has fallen from about 8,000 in 1971 to 3,650 in 1989. Meanwhile, after 1982 the United Kingdom began running an annual trade deficit in hand tools, which has increased every year.

In tools, there were few major success stories to parallel those of Richardson, even though some companies maintained their position. The larger firms eschewed a strategy of core growth, in favour of one of acquisitions. Stanley acquired the Surform range of products in 1962, then bought Rabone Chesterman in 1989, and Mosley-Stone (a Leeds and Manchester paint-brushes and decorators' equipment manufacturers) in 1991. Stanley still had its headquarters in New Britain, Connecticut, and operated worldwide with 18,000 employees (about a thousand of whom worked in and around Sheffield). Neill's became one of the largest hand tool manufacturing businesses in the world in the 1970s, when it purchased a number of companies, including John Shaw, the owner of the Britool business in Wolverhampton; Moore & Wright, an old Sheffield specialist in tools and measuring equipment; and Elliott Lucas, the

---

[27] 'Sheffield Hand Tool Sector: Decline Through Acquisition', in *Sheffield Economic Bulletin* (Dept. of Employment, Sheffield City Council, Summer 1992), 38–43.
[28] A. Iles, *Memories of a Sheffield Tool Maker* (Mendham, NJ, 1993).

Cannock plier makers. In 1985, relatively late, Neill's moved into the DIY market with a major diversification—the purchase of Spear & Jackson.

It has been suggested that once the merger movement in the tool industry has reached its maximum extent, the market leaders will begin looking abroad for acquisitions. Or maybe they will be taken over themselves by foreign groups—as was the Sheffield Twist Drill & Steel Co. by SKF in 1975. This created the world's largest manufacturer of high-speed steel cutting tools, but the holding company was located in Gothenburg in Sweden.

Generally—and it has been a feature running through this study—the engineering tools and hand tools sector performed better than the city's much-vaunted cutlery industry. How much longer it would continue to hold its place internationally remained questionable in 1994.

Epilogue: Steel City and United Kingdom Industrial Decline

> without steel there could be no Sheffield.
>
> *Sheffield Replanned* (Sheffield Town Planning Committee, 1945).

In about 1844, many years after Benjamin Huntsman's death, a visitor to Sheffield had stood and watched the crucible teemers at work, when the industry was getting into full swing. He later wrote that:

no description can give an adequate idea of the scene which is presented. The terrible yawning mouth over which the first man hovers, the glowing mass which he draws forth, the intense whiteness of the liquid steel as it flows into the mould, the profusion of delicate greenish sparks which shoot forth during the pouring—all form a spectacle which, once seen, will not be soon forgotten.[1]

Visitors touring a major Sheffield steelworks in 1993—some 250 years after Huntsman's discovery of the crucible steel process—usually have much the same feelings, even though the whole scale of operations has changed. Modern melting shops, such as those for stainless steel production at Shepcote Lane, can be overpowering to the uninitiated both in size, heat, and noise. To feel the air and the walkways vibrate with the deafening crackle of a 130-tonne electric arc furnace is to feel something of the awe with which spectators viewed the doings of the crucible men. At places such as Shepcote Lane, one is struck by the immense size of operations, by the intense heat, by the feeling of danger as huge vessels of molten steel are swung from place to place and as giant red-hot slabs shoot along rollers or are squeezed back and forth between huge presses. One is struck too by the remarkable absence of human activity. In fact, the melters and other workers have become bit players, reduced to minor walk-on-parts against a giant industrial set: they can be glimpsed occasionally in the cab of an overhead crane, at computer consoles in the control room, or more adventurously performing obscure tasks around the furnaces themselves.

The sights at the melting shop at Shepcote Lane can give rise to some conflicting impressions of Steel City, since they take place in an area whose most marked characteristic appears to be one of catastrophic

---

[1] 'A Day at the Fitzalan Steel and File-Works, Sheffield', *The Penny Magazine*, 13 (30 Mar. 1844), 121–8.

decline. A mile or so from Shepcote Lane is the beginning of the industrial wasteland of the Don Valley and the ruins of the old steel firms. Within the former nineteenth-century heartland of steel, in the Don valley, the only companies of any real size in the early 1990s were William Cook and Sheffield Forgemasters. Sanderson Kayser still flew the flag for the old Sheffield tool steel industry, but nearly all the other tool steelmakers had gone, the battle with the Austrians, Swedes, and other European producers long since lost. It looked questionable whether the Sheffield high-speed steel industry would survive to celebrate its own centenary in the year 2000. In specialist alloys, high-quality stainless steels, and castings, a scattering of small, sometimes privately-owned, firms survived, but in the early 1990s many of them were drastically cutting their operations. Usually they were invisible to the ordinary Sheffielder, since they were located outside the city centre or even further afield at Rotherham. To most, steel was a thing of the past, and many Sheffielders believed, perhaps understandably, that steelmaking had ended in the city.

In the 1980s, Sheffield had begun discarding its old Steel City image—something which necessitated a radically new outlook and was closely linked with major changes in local government. Sheffield in the 1970s has been described as a 'traditional, Labour-controlled local authority, confident of its service provision, and a touch parochial and complacent about it too'.[2] Popularly known as the 'Socialist Republic of South Yorkshire', its campaigns for cheap bus fares and its close identification with working-class interests made it an emblem for the Left in British politics. The Sheffield business community then played little part in local affairs: it had its own network of social contacts through the Chamber of Commerce and the Cutlers' Company, and had no direct linkages with the local political world of mainly Labour city councillors.

But the decline of steel was linked with a political transformation, which saw a marked shift in the relationship between central and local government. By the mid-1980s, the Conservative party under Margaret Thatcher was intent on reducing the powers of local authorities and eliminating socialism as a political force, a course which inevitably led to confrontation with Sheffield city council. Opposition to the corporatism of both the Labour and Conservative parties briefly intensified left-wing influence in the city council, one manifestation of which was the creation of a new employment department and committee—a body which initially rejected any involvement by the business community as it pursued its aims of regenerating the local economy according to the tenets of industrial democracy and workers' rights. But after the council had been de-

---

[2] Patrick Seyd, 'The Political Management of Decline 1973–1993', in C. Binfield *et al.*, *The History of the City of Sheffield 1843–1993* (Sheffield, 1993), i. 151–85, 154, which provides an excellent overview.

feated by central government over the rate-capping issue, attitudes changed. Suddenly a partnership developed between senior city councillors and a leading group of local businessmen, who had become active and prominent in the Chamber of Commerce. Economic decline, allied with pressure from central government, prompted an intermingling of Labour ideals with the new Conservative ideology of enterprise, which (as we have seen from the development of Sheffield Forgemasters and William Cook) was beginning to permeate the depressed local economy. Significantly, though, the business group did not include any representatives from the leading steel and engineering firms. Instead, newer industries in the area began supplying the great and good: men such as Norman Adsetts, the chairman of Sheffield Insulations Group.

The first outcome of this new partnership was the Sheffield Economic Regeneration Committee, established in 1986, a public and private sector collaboration which aimed at restoring the economic health of the area, especially in the lower Don Valley. The socialism of the city council (if such it ever was) was soon jettisoned; no more May Day red flags over the Town Hall, no nuclear-free zones or twinning with Chinese and Russian cities. Instead, there was talk of a 'board of directors' for the city and the 'fostering of confidence and pride by local businesses in their city'. This collaboration provided the framework for the next step: the creation of the Urban Development Corporation for the lower Don Valley, which came into being in March 1988 with a £50 million grant from central government. A promotional campaign now began attracting new industry, investment, and employment to the city. The first results were a city-centre Sheffield Science Park, for encouraging high-technology industry; and a Cultural Industries Quarter, where much of the city's media, design, and music industry is based.

Whilst it searched for alternatives to steel, Sheffield became something of a regional centre, attracting many London-based insurance and government groups. It looked to conferences and tourism for jobs and for the first time began exploiting its natural situation in the heart of some of the most beautiful scenery in Britain. Leisure and sport became an industry, rather than simply a relaxation. In the late 1980s, Sheffield embarked on an ambitious £100 million programme to establish itself as a major sports and cultural centre. Giant sports stadia, Olympic-standard swimming pools, and athletic tracks suddenly sprouted from the ruins of the steelworks in the Don Valley. Major sporting events were drawn to the city, so that if a young person was asked to describe Sheffield today they would be more likely to mention snooker or the World Student Games (staged there for the first time in 1991) than steel. Other signs-of-the-times have appeared, such as Meadowhall—one of the largest shopping areas in Europe—on the site of Hadfields old East Hecla works. It is probably not a development which the old steelmakers would have understood or approved.

As Sheffield sheds its parochialism (there are even plans for an airport in the Don Valley) and turns its back on its Steel City image, the long-term impact of this reorientation on the political and social structure remains to be seen. As yet only a start has been made. Regeneration of the economy will require more than service and leisure industries—the problem of industrial Britain in microcosm. Can the attempt at regeneration succeed? Indeed, is it possible—as is often the implied intention of such schemes— to find a replacement for an industry such as steel? Perhaps a closer look at the extent of steel's decline and the possible causes may set these questions in context.

First, we need to understand that, just as the decline of the United Kingdom economy is only relative (since clearly the average person is better off than at the end of the Second World War), so the decline of Sheffield steel is not absolute. Steel City may have been overtaken in output by countries such as Brazil, Italy, Japan, and Spain, but in production and technology the picture is not entirely gloomy. In and around Sheffield in 1993 were some of the most advanced and productive steel melting facilities in the world, which were concentrated at four main sites. In Sheffield were the plants of Sheffield Forgemasters and Avesta Steel Stainless (the former British Steel works at Shepcote Lane); and in Rotherham and Stocksbridge were those of United Engineering Steels. At Stocksbridge two large electric furnaces of 100-tonnes and 150-tonnes capacity—a far cry from the 10-ton units installed during the last War— produced steel at a rate and in qualities undreamt of by Huntsman. The plant (which consumed £1 million in electricity per month!) was capable of producing half a million tonnes of liquid steel per year, a considerable achievement in view of the complexity of the product mix and an average order size of 15 tonnes, as well as the demand for such high quality. At UES's Aldwarke melting facility, in 1993 a £9 million investment pro- gramme saw the installation of a new 165-tonne electric arc furnace—one of the largest in Europe.

In fact, in the 1980s Sheffield was melting more steel than it had in the Second World War and early 1950s, and with a far smaller workforce— one of the results of the marked rise in the productivity of British steel- workers in the 1980s. The qualities of special steels for critical applications in aerospace and nuclear engineering had continued their steady march, aided by the research facilities at Swinden Laboratories. Technical pro- gress and carefully targeted marketing had tapped new growth areas in automobile, constructional, and offshore structural steels. In the 1980s, for example, considerable progress was made in so-called high-strength low alloy (HSLA) steels (an important development in metallurgy, based

Table 12.1. *Turnover of the top twenty Sheffield companies, 1993*

Company	Turnover (£m.)
Hepworth [refractories, plumbing]	661.3
Stocksbridge Engineering Steels	327.7
TWIL	285.3
Avesta Steel Stainless	No data
SKF Investments	167.7
Davy McKee (Sheffield)	152.1
T. C. Harrison [motor dealers]	151.1
William Cook	133.2
Henry Boot [construction, civil engineers]	131.0
Sheffield Forgemasters	130.5
Hartons Group [plastics distributors]	128.8
Sheffield Insulations [insulation distributors]	127.0
Arthur Lee	105.6
Aurora	86.0
Wards Brewery	81.3
Tinsley Wire (Sheffield)	80.0
Thorntons [confectionery]	79.9
Stanley	79.0
James Neill (Holdings)	77.8
Cantors [furniture retailers]	57.0

Source: Business North: Sheffield Centenary Business Survey (Jan./Feb. 1993), 42.

on research conducted in Sheffield in the 1960s), used in bridges, high-rise buildings, and oil and gas pipelines. Stainless steel had also found new mass markets: in beer barrels and cans, in offshore oil platforms, and in automobile exhausts.[3]

In turnover, Sheffield companies involved in steel and its allied trades (including engineering) still accounted for a surprising proportion of the city's industrial base in 1993. As Table 12.1 indicates, well over half the top twenty Sheffield companies were either in steel or broadly related industries.[4] This may, of course, reflect industrial weakness rather than strength; nevertheless, the fact remains that the steel industry's contribution to the local economy was, in the early 1990s at least, a vital one.

Only when we turn to employment is any dramatic decline evident. Table 12.2 shows the employment profile of the leading steel firms in the

[3] Bernard Argent, 'Materials Research in Sheffield', *Metals and Materials*, 6 (July 1990), 431–5; F. Fitzgerald, 'Steel—Technical Achievements and Challenges', ibid. 7 (June 1991), 378–87; D. Dulieu and T. Gladman, 'The Future for Alloy Steels', *Steel Times*, 212 (Dec. 1984), 574–82.

[4] This statement is made without picking over the listing too much, since some are holding companies for production elsewhere. For another listing of top firms in Sheffield only, see *Sheffield Telegraph*, 20 Aug. 1993.

Table 12.2. *Leading Sheffield steel producers, January 1993*

Company	Employees
Avesta Steel Stainless	2,500
Rotherham Engineering Steels	2,300
Sheffield Forgemasters	2,000
Stocksbridge Engineering Steels	1,750
William Cook	750
Barworth Holdings	450
Sanderson Kayser	300
Ross & Catherall	200

Note: Cook and Ross & Catherall figures refer to the Sheffield workforce only: total group figures for these companies were 2,556 and 850 respectively.

Sources: Company and personal information; *Sheffield Telegraph*, 20 Aug. 1993; 'Sheffield Centenary Business Survey', *Business North* (Jan./Feb. 1993).

Sheffield region in 1993. It bears little resemblance to the situation in 1914 (Table 3.4), either in terms of numbers employed or company names. The crisis in the 1970s and 1980s had finally cracked the old Victorian structure, which had survived very much unchanged until 1960 (although that characteristic split between the bulk special steel producers and the smaller, specialist firms, can just about be discerned).

The decline in the workforce, partly the inevitable price of technological advance, had enormous social repercussions. Working in a steelworks may have been hell—hot, dusty, and dangerous—but the job also bought a career, good wages, respect, and a social life.[5] In the tool steel sector, the number of workers fell from 20,000 in 1970 to 1,200 in 1991. On a broader front, employment in the South Yorkshire steel industry (Sheffield and Rotherham combined) fell from about 60,000 in 1971, to about 43,000 in 1979, and to approximately 16,000 in 1987. By 1994 the total had fallen below 10,000. Even as this book was being completed, further reductions took place in the aftermath of the worst economic recession for sixty years. For example, the closure of UES's Templeborough site in 1993 had trimmed over 250 from its workforce at a stroke. Avesta Sheffield, which had been formed in 1992 as a defensive merger by the leading Swedish producer of stainless steel and British Steel Stainless, lost £50 million in its first year of operations, £8.3 million in the next, and in 1994 was planning redundancies in both Sheffield and Sweden.

---

[5] Geoffrey Beattie, *Survivors of Steel City: A Portrait of Sheffield* (London, 1986).

By 1993, even the biggest steel firms employed far fewer than the leaders in the service sector: these were Sheffield City Council with 27,000 employees and Sheffield Health Authority with 12,800. Even Meadowhall shopping mall, with 7,000 workers, was a bigger employer than any local steel company. By the 1990s, two-thirds of employment in Sheffield was in the service sector and only one-quarter in the manufacturing sector. Not surprisingly, it has been said that by the late 1980s, Sheffield and Rotherham had 'virtually lost their distinctive character as industrial centres, as far as their labour employment was concerned'.[6]

What factors underlay this situation? Was it merely the case that Sheffield, as perhaps the United Kingdom itself, was undergoing a necessary structural shift from manufacturing to services—not unusual in the modern era and hardly surprising in a region that was one of the first to reach industrial maturity. Or did the decline of Sheffield steel show something far more worrying: a sudden loss of entrepreneurial spirit, a bias against industry, a failure to modernize the educational and industrial base?

Finding the reasons for the loss of Sheffield's dominance in steel is almost as difficult as explaining the underperformance of the United Kingdom economy generally. Almost everyone—both industrialists and members of the public—have their own ideas on where Sheffield went wrong. During the research for this book, I often asked the Sheffield steelmaking community for their own views on this matter. Many criticized the Government: for failing to take a strong line on foreign dumping, for creating an awkward public/private interface, for burdening the industry with inflated energy costs and high exchange rates, and for refusing to support independent sector programmes of rationalization. But most agreed that the industry had shortcomings, despite its superb record in steel production and research: arrogance towards Far Eastern competitors, parochialism, outdated sales techniques, tardiness in investing, and reluctance to merge fragmented steel interests. They tended to see the decline as being rooted in fairly recent times—the period after the 1960s—though in cutlery most agreed the downturn occurred somewhat sooner, in the 1950s. These were typical statements:[7]

Sheffield did not lose its way due to the failure to research: the basic problem was far too many producers.

We were too slow getting the tool steel companies together.

Most Sheffield firms went bust, not because they did not invest, but because they invested on borrowed money with high interest charges.

---

[6] S. Pollard, 'Labour', in Binfield, *History*, ii. 260–78, 278.

[7] Comments from interviews conducted by the author during 1991–3, with individuals cited in the note on sources.

The death of Sheffield was in the death of the Birmingham car industry. As soon as we started importing steel and cars, it was downhill.

In the 1970s there were too many powerful influences in the Sheffield steel industry—they could never agree.

We were slow in modernizing—but not as slow as the Americans.

I blame the decline and cessation of steel production in Sheffield on nationalization and takeover by City financiers who thought there were gold ingots under steel; and were wrong.

Sheffield was complacent and reluctant to change. It had been protected by two world wars.

Sheffield was fundamentally an armaments industry.

It was the stunning commercial blows of the 1970s, by foreign companies who themselves could make little claim to viable steel operation, that brought the tool steel industry to its sorry state.

Business historians and economists, with their longer perspectives, have not surprisingly looked for the roots of failure much deeper in the past—in the late nineteenth century, for example, when Britain was caught and surpassed by her rivals; or in the inter-war years, when steelmakers failed to relocate and invest; or in a more sophisticated and complex mix of factors—the quality of entrepreneurship, the organization of management, and even in society's social and economic beliefs.[8]

In Sheffield's case, perhaps a logical approach would be to analyse how its competitive advantage has changed since its nineteenth-century heyday. In Chapter 1, that competitive advantage was attributed to a series of determinants—factor conditions, demand, the existence of related industries, and company strategy and structure—which interacted in a dynamic way. It follows that: 'National competitive advantage in an industry is lost . . . when [these] conditions . . . no longer support and stimulate investment and innovation to match the industry's evolving structure.'[9] Once this happens, decline is hard to arrest since the various factors are interrelated, creating a vicious circle. Competitive advantage, no matter how extensive, begins to unravel. How did this happen in Sheffield?

The key to Sheffield's success, in both steel and cutlery, was its rich generation of factor conditions, especially in human resources. It was the incredible skill in a whole range of industries—from clay-pot-making to working silver, from forging giant ingots to assembling tiny pocket-knives—that underlay the growth of Steel City. Cutlery was the first big

---

[8] The literature by economists and historians on the subject of Britain's industrial decline is already extensive. David Coates, *The Question of UK Decline: The Economy, State and Society* (London, 1994), gives an excellent introduction.

[9] M. E. Porter, *The Competitive Advantage of Nations* (London, 1990), 170.

Sheffield industry to be de-skilled, a process that was already under way in the nineteenth century in America and Germany and was well advanced in Sheffield before the Second World War. In steel, however, scientific advances and educational developments were successfully grafted on to the traditional local skills, which allowed Sheffield to keep competition at bay, helped considerably by the fact that the higher reaches of steelmaking remained highly dependent on skill until well after the Second World War. However, in the late 1950s and 1960s, the new precision steelmaking technologies and the development of computerized control and metallurgical analysis heralded the start of a new era. Continuous casting and secondary steelmaking techniques greatly boosted product output and quality. They also took steel melting out of the hands of the furnace operators, and broke the hold of the small firms.

This has had enormous implications for Sheffield. Special steelmaking is still 'high-technology', but the thrust of the industry now lies in a different direction. Improvements in alloy steels have become incremental, as major discoveries have dried up, and special steel has become more production-driven. The old division between special and bulk steels has, in fact, become blurred. Many bulk steels are now 'special' in some way; while even some of the highest qualities of alloy steels have succumbed to large-scale production. For over 200 years, Sheffield had been able to retain a competitive edge on the basis that tool steel and alloys could only be produced in small quantities and by specialist producers. That era had almost ended.

With even special steels subject to the laws of the market, steelmaking was able to take root almost anywhere: it became global, moving to areas of cheap labour, low scrap costs, and expanding consumer industries. In this global marketplace, there was still room for the niche producer, but the industry was typified mostly by its high capital investment costs—a far cry from the days when a Sheffielder could hire a furnace and a few hands and launch a business. As alloy steelmaking moved into mass production, it suffered the fate of all such technologies: it ended in a familiar cycle of cut-throat competition, over-production, and then capacity reduction. Special steels had become simply part of the product cycle. In the information age, steel technology was no longer regarded with awe, but almost with contempt—so much so that a firm like William Cook, which produced steel castings by processes that in the nineteenth century would have been regarded as miraculous, could be described in 1992 by one leading business journal as 'a low-technology metal-basher'.[10]

Sheffield's older factor conditions had also dated and offered little defence. The region's natural advantages, such as water-power, no longer

---

[10] *Financial Times*, 22 May 1992.

provided the energy for the steel mills. Steel City's situation on the South Yorkshire coalfield was now irrelevant, which was perhaps as well, since in the 1990s the coal industry was withering away. Refractories were still important in steelmaking and there were still a few large local firms, such as Dyson's: but this yielded little competitive advantage to the leading steel companies.

What of the demand for Sheffield steel in the 1990s and beyond? How did that compare with the past? In some respects, the future demand for steel and alloys did not look too bad. Steel was still a crucial material and the available resources of iron oxide were immense, and it was economic (compared with other products such as aluminium) to produce. In 1993 it appeared that it would have no serious competitor, for the next fifty years at least, for its role as a key component in economic infrastructures. But for Sheffield the picture looked more problematical. Steel demand in the industrialized countries was expected at best to stagnate or decline slightly in the 1990s, partly as the result of the more efficient use of steel, improvement in the quality and strength of steel products, the need to meet tougher environmental standards, and steel's replacement by competing materials. Although some analysts predicted that alloy steel production in the United Kingdom would grow, this outcome depended on Britain remaining a manufacturing nation with some degree of economic growth.[11]

But the 1980s, like the previous decade, had seen a further divergence between Britain's manufacturing and services sectors in both output and employment and increasing import penetration. Incredibly, despite the windfall of North Sea oil, Britain had a slower rate of growth in the 1980s than comparable periods before—this despite the much-vaunted supply-side miracle of the Conservative Government. Actually, the Government, until as late as 1985 (if not later), continued to display an extreme lack of concern regarding the performance of the country's manufacturing sector—even at times (as when criticizing the conclusions of the House of Lords Select Committee on Overseas Trade) questioning whether, and to what degree, manufacturing actually mattered.[12] Between 1985 and 1993 the Government could claim very few successes in its manufacturing policy, except perhaps in attracting multinationals (especially Japanese ones) to invest in Britain's increasingly low-wage and deregulated economy. Astonishing as it would have seemed only a generation before, by 1993 the United Kingdom was about to complete a comprehensive shutdown of its coal-mining capacity (a policy that would add to the negative influences on the Sheffield steel industry), and it had sold its last

[11] Dulieu and Gladman, 'Alloy Steels'.

[12] John Wells, 'Uneven Development and De-industrialisation since 1979', in Francis Green (ed.), *The Restructuring of the UK Economy* (Hemel Hempstead, 1989), 25–64.

indigenous car manufacturer. The one industry that did perform well, through high government defence spending, was aerospace: but in the age of electronics, this sector was no longer a major market for the steel producer. What demand existed was as likely to be satisfied by imports of alloy steels as by Sheffield: these had risen almost every year until 1990 (see Table 10.2).

The market for Sheffield steel and tools has altered profoundly compared with that of the nineteenth century. Whole areas of demand for tool steels in engineering and agriculture have simply disappeared with improvements in technology or social changes; and a vast array of tools, trade implements, and pocket-knives have also become a thing of the past. Two examples will suffice. The market for tool steel has been greatly reduced by carbides, which offer a superior performance. In the surface machining of, say, a 500-mm. long and 100-mm. diameter round steel bar, Mushet tool steel in 1900 would have taken about 100 minutes to do the job; with high-speed steel, this was reduced to about 30 minutes; and the first carbide tools did the work in 6 minutes. With modern coated-carbide inserts, the job takes only 1 minute.[13] Such machining processes have also made filing increasingly redundant, consigning to oblivion a whole Sheffield industry. This was a trade which had employed over 6,000 in the nineteenth century, when the file-cutters could provide an extraordinary 10,000 variations on the length, cut, and shape of files. In the 1990s consumers would no longer be able to choose from such delightfully named implements as bastards, fish-backs, horse-rasps, rifflers, and bellied three-squares.

The demise of these numerous small industries has had a far-reaching impact. Any visitor to Sheffield in 1993 will not be surprised to learn that the complex texture of related industries in the city, described in Chapter 1, no longer exists. Of the sixty or so trades listed in Table 1.1, very few survive. They have fallen victim to either technological change (Sheffield Plate), or foreign competition (cutlery), or have become obsolete (candlesticks). Cutlery and tool manufacture have ceased to be major consumers of special steels—indeed some of the raw material is now imported. Most of the biggest steelworks are now fully integrated operations, destroying forever that characteristic hive of converters, forgers, furnace-builders, engineers, and the numerous other support trades. Particularly significant has been the decline of the engineering sector, whose experience has paralleled that of steel. Rio Tinto Zinc took over the complex rag-bag empire of Thos. W. Ward and then dismantled it in the 1980s, leaving behind only the huge and empty Albion Works on Savile Street and a number of tiny manufacturing fragments (such as Ward Hi-Tech, which

---

[13] Sandvik AB, *Transformation: Sandvik 1862–1987* (Sandviken, 1987).

now imports Far Eastern computer machine-tools). Davy McKee had maintained a significant presence in the city, but by the early 1990s it had been absorbed by the London-based Trafalgar House group, and contraction in Sheffield was soon under way, exacerbated by Davy's problems with North Sea oil contracts. Of profound importance to Sheffield has been the unravelling of the cluster of related industries in Rotherham, Leeds, Derby, Manchester, and Birmingham. Inevitably, the scenario of decline has been much the same here, too, in electrical, railway, coal, agricultural, and motor-transport engineering—all former consumers of Sheffield special steels.

Also gone was the old structure of the Sheffield steel industry itself—fragmented, independent, and family-owned. It had been mostly replaced by large-scale businesses run as public companies, with professional managers and technologists, sometimes controlled from abroad. The nineteenth-century outlook of the industry, which was based largely on local talent and capital, had been destroyed. The traditional strategies, which relied on quality and an ancient name and mark, were no longer relevant. Special steelmaking now had all the hallmarks of a mature technology, in which standardization was widespread and high quality was taken for granted. In many Sheffield products, it was now difficult to sell other than on price, and though the city still traded on its distinguished name, the days when it meant something had gone.

When one looks at this stripping away of Sheffield's advantages, the decline of Steel City seems mostly inevitable. The strategies of business leaders might have slowed the decline, but they could hardly have arrested it. Too many factors were beyond their control. Coal, scrap, and electricity were all subject to price fluctuations and the industry had enormous fixed capital costs. Indeed, in some ways the situation in 1993 was exactly perhaps as one would have expected: a high-technology industry had ended in the hands of a small but extremely efficient band of workers and managers. And it would continue to decline or progress according to the demands of steel consumers.

Did any historical factors, though, accelerate this decline—perhaps even initiate it? What of the views of business historians summarized in the prologue on the structure, strategy, and performance of the British steel industry? One fashionable subject of debate amongst business historians has been the so-called 'entrepreneurial failure' of British businessmen, especially in the period between 1890 and 1914. Linked to this theme have been doubts about the role of the family firm, the poor commitment to science-based technology, and the antiquated structure of British industry. It has even been suggested that the British do not really like manufacturing at all.

This book demonstrates the difficulty of applying these ideas and theories to specific cases. The charge of entrepreneurial failure is difficult to sustain for much of Sheffield's steel history—which may come as a surprise to those nurtured on accounts of American, German, and Japanese steelmaking supremacy. But it should not be, when one considers the major technological advances and where they came from. Certainly as regards the late nineteenth century, the idea of entrepreneurial failure could usefully be discarded. Sheffield business leaders were at their peak at the precise moment when, it is said, British steel was in decline. In any case, proving a causal link between entrepreneurial performance and the decline of Sheffield is a dubious exercise. Have the enormous changes over the last 250 years, and especially the industry's precipitous decline since the 1960s, happened simply because one generation of businessmen was better than another? It seems unlikely. In fact, the careers of men such as Andrew Cook, Des Mawson, and Philip Wright show that Sheffield can still produce high-calibre management if conditions are right. Another point must also be considered. Until well after the Second World War, Sheffield drew not only on the managers at the top, but also on the skills of its workforce. Harry Brearley went so far as to say that the whole edifice of Sheffield steel and its reputation as the premier steel centre were based on the skills of the ordinary workmen. We need not accept Brearley's argument in its entirety to see that there is a good deal of truth in this view. To overemphasize entrepreneurship may give a misleading impression of Sheffield's industrial history: the steel entrepreneurs were only part of a team, and steel was only one industry among many in Sheffield.

Such warped views of the evolution of the British steel industry only arose because writers had focused far too long on the bulk steels, where it was easy to suggest that 'first movers' such as America and Germany were so much more efficient and progressive than the United Kingdom. However, this was not the technological leading edge of the steel industry—that lay in special steelmaking, where Sheffield excelled. In the appliance of science, Sheffield did far better than America, which concentrated its efforts on bulk production, and also surpassed Germany before 1914.[14] Naturally, it is difficult to assess the degree of parity with the efforts of other countries, because little work has been done on the history of their special steelmaking technology, too. How big and successful was Krupp's research department, for example? We simply do not know in detail. But it does seem likely that, even if the laboratories of Hadfields and Firth-Brown were smaller than their German and American counterparts, they punched more heavily than their weight. The evidence strongly supports Sidney Pollard's view that British economic

---

[14] There have been few studies of R&D in the US steel industry, but see Janet F. Knoedler, 'Market Structure, Industrial Research and Consumers of Innovation: Forging Backward Linkages to Research in the Turn-of-the-Century US Steel Industry', *Business History Review*, 67 (Spring 1993), 98–139.

decline in certain areas before 1914 has been greatly exaggerated.[15] In Sheffield's case, at least, R&D and industrial education were not backward. And this strong research effort continued up to the 1960s. Of course, one might argue that Sheffield was merely the exception to the rule: however, any theories of decline that cannot find room for the world's most renowned steelmaking centre will never be entirely persuasive.

This is not to say that Sheffield had no weaknesses. After a dynamic performance in America in the early nineteenth century, marketing was sometimes less a success story than steel manufacture—a weakness perhaps stemming from an ingrained parochialism. The way in which the Germans infused vitality into Sheffield steelmaking and marketing in the late nineteenth century, which this study has highlighted, does perhaps suggest that there was some room for improvement in the town's business performance (though it could also be argued that Sheffield created the opportunities that allowed these immigrants to prosper). Sheffield's individualism also had its negative side. The complacency which flowered in the sellers' market in the 1950s had its roots in the nineteenth century, when a dominant position allowed Sheffielders to believe that the world could teach them little about steelmaking. The liking for independence also meant that often companies were slow to merge their interests, when it would have been logical to do so.

The industry was also severely distorted by the demand for armaments. The late nineteenth-century arms race and the two world wars had a profound impact on Steel City. Often in its history, Sheffield steel *was* 'fundamentally' an armaments industry. Economists and historians have disagreed on the precise long-term impact of the war economy on United Kingdom industry; however, the Sheffield experience does show many of the adverse effects of an over-commitment to armaments. Much of the layout and strategies of the big Sheffield firms were dictated purely by arms considerations. At the same time, wartime demands prevented vital organizational adjustments at key moments in Sheffield's history. If one is looking for crucial events and periods of decline in Sheffield steel, then in the huge expansion in orders during the Second World War, which enabled firms to avoid coming to terms with the full consequences of the First, followed by the boom of the 1950s, lay the seedbed for many of the problems after the 1960s.

Another criticism of Steel City may be made: that for too long it believed its destiny was to produce steel and cutlery—a belief which made eventual restructuring slower and more difficult than it might have been. It was the depression of the 1930s which first forced Sheffield to consider seriously a future without such a vast steel trade—when it was recognized

---

[15] S. Pollard, *Britain's Prime and Britain's Decline* (London, 1989).

that armaments was a 'dead industry', and that what was required was 'not reorganisation . . . but new industries'.[16] But any thought of broadening the local economic base was promptly forgotten as rearmament got under way. In 1945, there were briefly fears that an overreliance on steel was unwise, but those too were blotted out in the 1950s. When contraction of the industry began in earnest after the 1960s, Sheffield was no better prepared for it than it had been thirty years earlier. The initial response of the city council was not an attempt to attract new industries, but a misguided hope that steel could be revitalized.[17] Meanwhile, the newspapers still contained much talk of Sheffield 'fighting back' in cutlery and of regaining its old position. When it was finally realized that the days of Sheffield as a Steel City were numbered, the next move was sudden and ill-advised: an expensive foray into the World Student Games. The roots of this blunder lay in the inability to plan properly for the day when steel would no longer be the leading sector.

However, any overall assessment needs to balance criticism with a judgement as to what it was reasonable to expect a single city to achieve. All things considered, Sheffield's performance in steel and tool manufacture must be regarded as outstanding. One could emphasize many facets of that performance—research, production, and individual genius—but perhaps the most telling was the ability of Sheffield to maintain a front-ranking position in the industry with very few marked advantages. In the nineteenth century it had none of America's assets—a huge internal market, wonderful resources of high-grade iron ore and coal, a protective tariff, foreign capital, and a supply of hapless immigrant labour it could ruthlessly exploit in the steel mills. Japan, it is true, has also recently become highly successful with very few natural resources. But Sheffield did not benefit, as did Japan, from an incisive Government industrial policy, initially backed by overseas capital.[18] The contrast could hardly be greater between Japan's deliberate cultivation of the steel industry's resources to maximize competitive advantage, and—for example—the United Kingdom Government's belated support for the nationalized industry after 1967 (in which Sheffield was a side issue). A similar disparity is apparent when we compare Austrian, Swedish, German, and Spanish support for their indigenous tool steel producers with official policy in the United Kingdom: while overseas manufacturers were subsidized, the

---

[16] 'A Publicity Campaign for Sheffield', *SDT*, 30 Dec. 1932.

[17] See Sheffield City Council Employment Dept. booklets: *Steel in Crisis* (1984); *The Uncertain Future of Special Steels* (1987).

[18] See generally Etsuo Abe and Toshitaka Suzuki, *Changing Patterns of International Rivalry: Some Lessons from the Steel Industry* (Tokyo, 1991). On Japan, see Patricia O'Brien, 'Industry Structure as Competitive Advantage: The History of Japan's Post-war Steel Industry', *Business History*, 34 (Jan. 1992), 128–59; Seiichiro Yonekura, *The Japanese Iron and Steel Industry 1850–1990: Continuity and Discontinuity* (London, 1994).

British Government from the 1970s consistently undermined the Sheffield tool steel industry with the high value of the pound, energy prices that ran ahead of inflation, steel nationalization, and a lack of action against subsidized imports—all against a background of declining shipbuilding and engineering.

One interesting feature of Sheffield's success was that it drew heavily from the legacy of the small family firm. As one local writer stated: 'It was the personally-owned business, in which the son succeeded father as a matter of course, on which Sheffield's industrial strength was founded and developed.'[19] This runs counter to the big-business recipe for success that has become popular with some American business historians, such as Alfred Chandler.[20] Of course, one might argue that the survival in South Yorkshire of a few large firms, such as UES—which also happens to have originated from the most progressive steel company (United Steel)—confirms the wisdom of the belief that industrial success depends upon American-style corporatism. However, this view becomes more superficial the more one looks at it. The development of Sheffield steel does not really correspond to a Chandler-style framework. This was simply because for most of the period up to the 1950s, special steelmaking was not usually a large-scale activity. It stemmed from a different ethos of small-scale manufacture in which the local entrepreneur, tailoring his production to suit a specific niche, was supreme. The individualist approach has proved as successful and enduring in Sheffield as any of the strategies pursued by big United Kingdom and foreign steel corporations: it flourished in the 1740s when Benjamin Huntsman began melting crucible steel; it remained successful in the 1990s at firms such as Ross Catherall. This world of the special steelmaker—with its crucibles, relatively small electric furnaces, and commitment to added-value, high-technology, specialist products—may be unrecognizable to economic historians who have become accustomed to a historical landscape dominated by the likes of Andrew Carnegie and US Steel. But they should not underestimate the contribution made by specialist firms in Sheffield or elsewhere. In fact, it is the small (often privately owned) companies that have proved the most fertile breeding ground for innovations in steel technology. Sheffield's development of alloy steels shows that beyond doubt. Even after the 1950s, when some of the special steels succumbed to mass production, major advances originated in the small firms. In the early history of continuous casting, for example, most of the key innovations occurred in the small plants of the special steelmakers, where flexibility and the need to assure survival provided the stimulus.

---

[19] *SDT*, 20 Nov. 1941. Obit. of J. S. Tyzack.

[20] A. D. Chandler, *Scale and Scope* (Cambridge, Mass., 1990). See also B. Elbaum and W. Lazonick, *The Decline of the British Economy* (Oxford, 1986).

The recent trend towards flexibility in production through so-called 'mini-mills' has underlined the importance of relatively small-scale production.[21]

The idea of successful businesses functioning by a 'visible hand', with dynamic entrepreneurs pulling the strings of the corporate economy, does not really fit the Sheffield experience at all. This book has shown why. Steel City was a highly complex industrial community, with dozens of different industries, scores of firms, and a myriad of interconnecting links. Moreover, the structure was very deep-rooted, stretching back hundreds of years. Steven Tolliday, writing about the inter-war British steel industry, has described how even the biggest firms were hamstrung by competitive restraints and intrafirm institutions. He neatly reverses Chandler's classic formula for the evolution of big business and argues that in the United Kingdom it was the industrial structure which determined the strategies of business leaders, not vice versa.[22] This conclusion could be applied with even greater force to Sheffield. Any attempt to modernize the industry after 1918 inevitably came up against not only the highly fragmented structure of the industry itself and the individualism of steelmasters, but also generations of historical traditions, workshop practices, and social attitudes. In that sense, critics of British business performance, such as Bernard Elbaum and William Lazonick, are right to stress institutional rigidities as a possible reason for British business failure—though whether Sheffield steelmakers should be criticized for failing to free themselves from such constraints is debatable. Complicating Sheffield's problems was a factor usually absent in most historical discussions—the role of demand-side forces in hindering the introduction of mass-production technologies and large-scale corporate enterprise. Sheffield steel itself was continually responding to a highly diverse domestic demand from industries such as engineering and tools, which had similarly deep roots. In these circumstances, which did not exist to the same degree in markets such as America, it is little wonder that rationalization took so long. Only in the 1960s, when many of the institutional and demand restraints were removed, could proper modernization be achieved. In any case, it is doubtful whether the route favoured by most critics of the British steel industry—one which led towards large-scale mergers and big plants—was really the best for Sheffield. Its steelmakers may be criticized for their preference for individualism in recent decades, but for much of Steel City's history one suspects that they got the balance

---

[21] For historical accounts of continuous casting and mini-mills, see Bruce Seely (ed.), *Encyclopedia of American Business History and Biography: The Iron and Steel Industry in the Twentieth Century* (Columbia, SC, 1994).

[22] S. Tolliday, *Business, Banking and Politics: The Case of British Steel, 1918–1939* (Cambridge, Mass., 1987), 159.

about right. Certainly, the misguided expansion of the British Steel Corporation in the early 1970s shows only too well the kind of strategic mistakes that could be made by trying to think too big.

Some historians have seized on the success of the small firm in Sheffield (and the weaknesses of Chandler's arguments) to suggest that small-scale manufacture points the way to the future regeneration of the area.[23] That idea has its merits, but is not entirely convincing, either. Sheffield included both big and small firms in its heyday; and in the last thirty years most special steelmaking has had to become bigger to succeed. Arguing that 'small is beautiful' in Sheffield, even for the period between 1880 and 1930, also ignores the historical experience of that quintessential small Sheffield industry—cutlery. This industry shows again how difficult it can be to apply generalizations in industrial history, even those that concern industries in broadly the same product area within *one* locality. The Sheffield industry (and within that term we can also include some tool trades, such as files) was a classic example of British business failure. There were one or two bright spots—stainless steel in the 1920s, the performance of Richards and Richardson Sheffield in more recent times— but basically the picture is one of almost unrelieved decline from the industry's peak in the 1870s. This is all the more astonishing, because it occurred in a city with such a superb record in steel manufacture.

Why? It is not an easy question to answer. Perhaps part of the problem lay, ironically, in the cutlers' commitment to high quality. Their superb hand-forged cutlery led them to believe that perfection had been attained in the late nineteenth century and that they should remain tied to the old methods. They were not to know that in the twentieth century quality would not always be a primary consideration of buyers. In steel, however, the commitment to quality led in a more positive direction, towards new horizons in alloy steels. Also significant was the fact that steel and cutlery occupied very different social and economic worlds, which rarely mixed industrially. Only Sir Frederick Mappin and Sir Albert Hobson seem to have bridged the divide, by occupying managerial posts in both sectors. Cutlery was also far less cosmopolitan than steel. There were no Germans here to provide entrepreneurial talent until the 1930s, when they had a predictably galvanic effect. Cutlery was also not habituated to change, like steel—a fact noted by contemporaries. The Master Cutler, W. H. Ellis, at the exhibition of German cutlery at Cutlers' Hall in 1915, remarked that in contrast to Sheffield cutlers the steelmakers had advanced 'by developing their works to meet ever changing needs, and by the readiness and courage of workmen to undertake work of a constantly heavier description . . . [and] . . . they had reorganised to produce what the consumer

---

[23] Roger Lloyd-Jones, Mervyn Lewis, and Van Gore, 'Sheffield History Proves Small is Beautiful', *Guardian*, 7 Feb. 1994.

required, and to meet what might be called the change of fashion'.[24] This never happened to the same extent in cutlery. The only way to succeed in Sheffield cutlery, it seems, was to stand outside the culture. Thus, of the two most dynamic firms in the twentieth century, one was German (Richards) and the other a multinational (Richardson Sheffield). Of the latter's success, it has been said that 'a key factor must be Richardson's distancing itself from the rest of the Sheffield cutlery trade'.[25] This also may explain why the Sheffield tool firms, being more closely allied with steel than with cutlery, have had a much better record.

The history of both Sheffield cutlery and steel suggests that what matters is not how big or small firms are, but the kind of overall economic system in which business operates. This entails a much wider view of entrepreneurship and the business environment, with all that implies in terms of factors of production, structure, and social attitudes. This book, written from the perspective of business strategy and technology, suggests that Sheffield steel is best viewed historically as a geographical grouping—a cluster—which created distinctive opportunities for individuals, firms, and groups of firms, with complex linkages to other industries and areas. More detail could be provided on this cluster—this 'huge workshop for steel goods', as it was described earlier—and the way in which it networked with other sectors in the United Kingdom economy: indeed, there are many aspects of South Yorkshire industry about which we need to know more. But enough has been said to show why Sheffield will find replacing steel so difficult. It was never one industry, but many, which evolved from an economic system which had been many centuries in the making; and although Government arms orders had helped the process, the creation of Steel City was largely unplanned—indeed, who in 1743 could have predicted the rise of such a massive industry in such an unlikely locality? This is not a reassuring conclusion for industry planners or for business historians keen to apply their knowledge to the problem of regeneration. We do not even know whether in the present era of information technologies future industrial systems will operate in such dense manufacturing centres or follow a different pattern.

What is certain is that Sheffield's network of steel-related industries produced something unique. To be sure, one can point to other nineteenth-century steel centres, such as Pittsburgh, which to a certain extent mirror Sheffield's spread and complexity within a relatively concentrated locality. More recently, some European clusters—such as the Lumezzane valley in northern Italy—have become successful in metal manufacture by drawing on the potential created by the distinctive relationships existing

---

[24] 'Germans and the Cutlery Trade', *SI*, 20 Mar. 1915.

[25] Robert M. Grant, 'The Richardson Sheffield Story: A British Winner', London Business School, Case Series No. 2 (Feb. 1988), 29.

between groups of firms.[26] In computer-related technologies, California's Silicon Valley and Greater Boston's Route 128 have become the most spectacularly successful of all industrial concentrations. But none of the foreign metal-working clusters ever quite emulated the wide range of industries in Sheffield nor the richness and depth of its historical tradition; while it will be many years before we know whether the computer clusters have proved as enduring as Steel City. For over 200 years after the discovery of crucible steelmaking, Sheffield was the leading special steel and toolmaking centre in the world, maintaining its position by a strategy that focused on high-technology, added-value, specialist products, and combining this with an unceasing effort to innovate and upgrade factors of production. That is not a bad record for any industry; nor a bad example for a Government apparently drawn increasingly towards a low-wage, deregulated, service-oriented economy.

[26] John Kay, *Foundations of Corporate Success: How Business Strategies Add Value* (Oxford, 1993), 67–8.

PRIMARY SOURCES

When I first began work on the Sheffield steel industry towards the end of the 1970s, primary source material on the city's steel firms was relatively scarce. The nineteenth-century scene was reasonably well covered in Sheffield City Library Archives with the minute books, letters, and annual reports of some of the tool steel and cutlery firms, such as Allen, Balfour, Marsh Bros., and Spear & Jackson; but records for some of the city's biggest companies and its holdings for the twentieth century were patchy.[1] The archives of firms such as Hadfields and Firth-Brown still lay locked away in obscure parts of their old steelworks. Elsewhere, the records of the big three—Vickers, Brown, and Cammell—were either not easily accessible or unknown to historians.

During the late 1980s and early 1990s, this picture has changed dramatically. The decline of British industry has meant a windfall for the business historian, as the demise of the old smokestack industries has filled archives to bursting-point. Vickers deposited its company papers—mostly on microfilm, alas, but well catalogued—in Cambridge University Library. The nineteenth-century Charles Cammell records surfaced at the Cammell-Laird shipyard in Birkenhead (and were lodged at Birkenhead Town Hall); and the John Brown papers were released to historians, while being retained at the head office of the firm (now part of the Trafalgar Group) at Paddington, London. The Cammell and Brown papers consist mostly of detailed minute books and annual reports, surviving in a complete run from their registration as limited companies in 1864.

The rapid decline of Steel City has made Sheffield City Library Archives into the largest repository in Britain (and probably the world) for records on the steel industry and its related trades. The avalanche began in the mid-1980s with the timely rescue of the records of Hadfields Ltd., which contained not only what was left of Sir Robert Hadfield's personal papers, but also much of interest concerning the twentieth-century history of the company. This was soon supplemented by material from some of the failed mergers of the post-1970 period, such as the Aurora tool steel group. The collapse of Aurora also unearthed several interesting finds from the nineteenth and early twentieth century for firms such as Huntsman, Darwins, and J. H. Andrew. Material from some of the biggest steel firms followed. The closure of the English Steel Corporation resulted in a large run of records, perhaps the most interesting of which (for the writing of this study) was a complete set of over a hundred directors' reports covering the period between 1928 and the mid-1930s and charting the

---

[1] SCL, *Catalogue of Business and Industrial Records* (1977).

birth of the Corporation. Perhaps the largest hoard of all—the Firth-Brown collection—was deposited with SCL Archives in 1993. It contained not only scores of box-files for every directors' meeting between the 1930s and 1970s, but also the detailed Thomas Firth & Sons' directors' minute books from 1888.

Cutlery—often poorly-served by business records, due to the small-scale nature of much of the industry—also benefited from some notable accessions. Sometimes these came from some surprising locations. The archive of George Wostenholm & Son had, it transpired, been shipped to Atlanta, Georgia, in the early 1970s by an antique cutlery dealer. In the 1980s, this collection was transferred by Emory University to Sheffield Archives and, dovetailing perfectly with previous accessions of Wostenholm material, it now forms what is probably the largest group of cutlery business records anywhere.

Not all the sources for this book were so conveniently located. The nationalization of the steel industry had meant that records relating to British Steel Corporation companies—which included Samuel Fox and the Rotherham-based constituents of United Steel (notably Steel, Peech, & Tozer)—had been dispersed. Most of these company papers (mainly minute books) were located at the British Steel Regional Record Centre, Middlesborough. (However, at the time of writing these records, too, are being transferred to Sheffield City Archives.)

If the quantity of this manuscript material has presented problems to often poorly resourced archive staff in cataloguing, it has also brought a conundrum for the historian. Put simply, it is impossible for the lone researcher to read it all. The Firth-Brown records, which became access-ible only towards the end of the research for this book, are an example. They proved far too voluminous to read in their entirety. In short, much remains to be done on the industrial history of Sheffield using these sources. In fact, many of the records in SCL Archives on industries as diverse as coal-mining, iron, engineering, silver plate, refractories, glass, pottery, and gas utilities are still largely unexplored.

The period after the 1950s presented other difficulties. Aside from the thirty-year rule for public records, many business records (even if they have been deposited in Sheffield Archives) remain 'closed' for some years. The decline of Steel City and the lessening importance of steel have also meant that it is reported less frequently in the newspapers and trade journals and in far less detail. I have therefore used a much broader brush for recent decades and supplemented printed sources with oral history. Despite their obvious drawbacks, interviews with Sheffield's leading steelmakers have been indispensable for insights into the history of the industry during contemporary times.

With the exception of Stocksbridge Engineering Steels, nearly all the information offices and public relations departments of the leading companies proved willing to help with either interviews or works visits. A few business leaders and technologists declined (or ignored) my requests for an interview, but the following went out of their way to help: Bernard Argent (Sheffield University), Bill Bailey (Jessop), Mark Balfour (Balfour Darwin), Robert T. Bavister (Fox), Ralph Beaumont (UES), Rennie Bell (Firth-Brown), Ian Blakey (BISPA), Malcolm Brand (Sheffield Forgemasters), Derek Bray (British Steel Stainless), Bernard Callan (Sanderson Kayser), John Chesters (United Steel), Bernard Connolly (ESC), Andrew Cook (William Cook), Bryan Cookson (River Don Castings), Bernard Cotton (Osborn), Harry Cowlishaw (ESC), Robson Davies (Aurora), Nigel Dick (Sanderson Kayser), the late Richard Doncaster (Doncaster), Noel Edwards (Barworth Flockton), Geoffrey Fisher (ESC), Frank Fitzgerald (Swinden Laboratories), Sam Gillott (Gillott), David Grieves (British Steel), Norman Hanlon (Hadfields), Donald Hardwick (Firth-Brown), Gordon Harrison (Carr), George Holst (Arthur Lee), Tom Kilpatrick (United Steel), Peter Lee (Arthur Lee), Jim Lessells (Swinden Laboratories), Kenneth Lewis (British Steel), Geoffrey Lucas (Firth-Brown), Graham Mackenzie (UES), Jack Machin (ESC), Des Mawson (Ross Catherall), John Monks (Darwins), Douglas Oldham (ESC), Brian Pickering (United Steel), Gordon Polson (Firth Vickers), William D. Pugh (ESC), David Rea (BISPA), Lord Riverdale (Balfour), Jim Russell (ESC), the late Frank Saniter (United Steel), Stan Shaw (Ibberson and Wostenholm), the late Marjorie Sheard (Hadfields), Stanley Speight (Neepsend), Eric Stubbs (Senior), John Trueman (Firth Vickers), Tom Waddington (ESC), Denis Ward (Hadfields), Terry Worrall (Sanderson Kayser), and Bob Young (Gillott).[2]

[2] My interview notes with the above individuals and a print-out of data on Sheffield's leading entrepreneurs and steel firms between about 1850 and 1993 (containing a fuller list of references than appear in this book) will be deposited with SCL Local Studies Department.

SECONDARY SOURCES

Theses and Unpublished Papers

'Ambrose Shardlow & Co. Ltd'. Typescript, n.d., in SCL.

DANIELLS, L., 'Metropolis of Steel'. Typescript in SCL.

GARLICK, P., 'The Sheffield Cutlery and Allied Trades and Their Markets in the 18th and 19th Centuries' (Sheffield University MA, 1951).

GRANT, R. M., 'The Richardson Sheffield Story: A British Winner', London Business School, Case Series No. 2 (Feb. 1988).

—— and DOWNING, S., 'The UK Cutlery Industry 1974–1982: A Study of Structural Adjustment, Business Strategies and Firm Performance', unpublished London Business School Study, May 1985.

HARVEY, P., 'Sheffield Obituary'. Typescript in SCL.

HEWITT, E. C., 'Organisational Developments at Darnall', typescript, Nov. 1990. Courtesy Davy McKee.

LEDBETTER, R. M., 'Sheffield's Industrial History from about 1700, with Special Reference to the Abbeydale Works' (Sheffield University MA, 1971).

LEWIS, M. J., 'The Growth and Development of Sheffield's Industrial Structure, 1880–1930' (Sheffield Hallam University Ph.D., 1989).

MACKIE, T., 'A Case Study of the Evolution of the Ross Catherall Group plc and the Role of the Entrepreneur' (Sheffield Hallam University BA, 1990).

Montague, Loebl, Stanley & Co., *Special Steels* (April, 1976). Copy in SCL Local Studies.

NEWTON, L., 'The Finance of Manufacturing Industry in the Sheffield Area, *c*.1850–*c*.1885' (Leicester University Ph.D., 1993).

SPALDING, C. W., 'Tubes of Steel: Being the History of Howell & Co., Sheffield Tube Works, 1865–1971' (*c*.1971), typescript in SCL.

SPIERS, W. B., 'Billy Ibberson Cutlery Research Project', unpublished Sheffield University Management School study, 17 Dec. 1993.

TAYLOR, S., 'Tradition and Change: The Sheffield Cutlery Trades 1870–1914' (Sheffield University Ph.D., 1988).

TIFFANY, P. A., 'Industrial Research at the United States Steel Corporation, 1901–1929', unpublished paper presented to 29th annual meeting of the Society for the History of Technology, 25 Oct. 1986.

TIMMINS, J. G., 'The Commercial Development of the Sheffield Crucible Steel Industry' (Sheffield University MA, 1976).

WARNER, F., 'An Enquiry into the Special Steels Industry' (July 1981).

WHITE, A. P., 'Formation and Development of Middle-Class Urban Culture and Politics: Sheffield 1825–1880' (Leeds Ph.D., 1990).

Newspapers and Professional Journals

British Steelmaker
Brown Bayley's Journal

Daily Telegraph
The Director
The Economist
Edgar Allen News
Engineer
Engineering
Implement & Machinery Review
Investors' Guardian
Iron & Coal Trades Review
Ironmaking & Steelmaking
Ironmonger
Journal of the Iron & Steel Institute
Management Today
Metallurgia
Metal Bulletin Monthly
Metals & Materials
Penny Magazine
Quality
Sheffield Daily Telegraph
Sheffield Independent
Sheffield Mercury
Sheffield Times
South Yorkshire Topic
Steel Times
Stock Exchange Yearbook
The Times
The Times Engineering Supplement

Books and Pamphlets

(Place of publication is London, unless stated)

ABE, E., and SUZUKI, T., *Changing Patterns of International Rivalry: Some Lessons from the Steel Industry* (Tokyo, 1991).

ABROMEIT, H., *British Steel: An Industry Between the State and Private Sector* (Leamington, 1986).

ADAMS, R. B., *King C. Gillette: The Man and His Wonderful Shaving Device* (Boston, 1978).

ADAMS, W., VOYLES, J. B., and MOSS, T., *The Antique Bowie Knife Book* (Conyers, Georgia, 1990).

ALEXANDER, W., and STREET, A., *Metals in the Service of Man*, 9th edn., (1989).

ALLEN, T., *A New and Complete History of the County of Yorkshire*, 3 vols. (1831) .

ANDREWS, C. R., *The Story of Wortley Ironworks*, 2nd edn. (Nottingham, 1956).

ANDREWS, P. W. S., and BRUNNER, E., *Capital Development in Steel* (Oxford, 1951).

Annual Statistics (published variously by Iron and Steel Board, BISF, BSC, Iron and Steel Statistics Bureau).

Arsenal of the World (Sheffield, 1918).

ASHTON, T. S., *An Eighteenth Century Industrialist: Peter Stubs of Warrington, 1756–1806* (Manchester, 1939).
—— *Iron and Steel in the Industrial Revolution*, 2nd edn. (Manchester, 1951).
ASHURST, D., *The History of South Yorkshire Glass* (Sheffield, 1993).
AUSTIN, J., and FORD, M., *Steel Town: Dronfield and Wilson Cammell 1873–1883* (Sheffield, 1983).
BACON, R., and ELTIS, W. A., *Britain's Economic Problem: Too Few Producers* (1976).
Balfour, Arthur & Co., *A Centenary: 1865–1965* (Nottingham, 1967).
BALLARD, J., *England in 1815 as Seen by a Young Boston Merchant* (Boston, 1913).
BAMBERY, A., *Old Sheffield Plate* (Aylesbury, 1988).
BARNETT, C., *The Audit of War* (1986).
BARRACLOUGH, K. C., *Steelmaking Before Bessemer: Blister Steel; Crucible Steel*, 2 vols. (1984).
—— *Steelmaking 1850–1900* (1990).
BEATTIE, G., *Survivors of Steel City: A Portrait of Sheffield* (1986).
BENNION, E., *Antique Medical Instruments* (1979).
BENSON, J., and NEVILLE, R. G. (eds.), *Studies in the Yorkshire Coal Industry* (Manchester, 1976).
BESSEMER, H., *An Autobiography* (1905).
BINFIELD, C., CHILDS, R., HARPER, G., HEY, D., MARTIN, D., and TWEEDALE, G. (eds.), *The History of the City of Sheffield, 1843–1993*, 3 vols. (Sheffield, 1993).
BIRCH, A., *The Economic History of the British Iron and Steel Industry 1784–1879* (1967).
BIRD-DAVIS, C. H., *Sketches and Illustrations of the Iron, Steel & Allied Trades: Souvenir of the Iron & Steel Institute Meeting, Buxton, September 1910* (1910).
BLACKABY, F. T. (ed.), *De-industrialization* (1978).
Board of Trade, Committee on Industry and Trade (Balfour Committee), *Minutes of Evidence; Survey of the Metal Industries* (1927–8).
Board of Trade, Safeguarding of Industries, *Report* (1925), Cmd. 2540.
BOOTH, G., *Diamonds in Brown Paper: The Colourful Lives and Hard Times of Sheffield's Famous Buffer Lasses* (Sheffield, 1988).
BOSWELL, J., *Business Policies in the Making* (1983).
BRADBURY, F., *History of Old Sheffield Plate* (London, 1912).
BREARLEY, H., *Steel-Makers* (1933).
—— *Knotted String* (1941).
—— *Talks about Steelmaking* (Cleveland, Ohio, 1946).
—— *Stainless Pioneer* (Sheffield, 1988).
British Association Handbook & Guide to Sheffield (Sheffield, 1910).
British Industry and Commerce (1967).
British Iron & Steel Federation, *Tool Steels* (1954).
—— *The Steel Industry: The Stage I Report of the Development Co-ordinating Committee of the British Iron and Steel Federation* (1966).
British Steel Stainless, *75 Years of Stainless Steel, 1913–1988* (Sheffield, 1988).
BRITTAIN, F., *Address . . . on the Results of Foreign Tariffs, Especially with Reference to Sheffield* (Sheffield, 1875).
—— *British Trade and Foreign Competition* (1877).

Brown, John & Co. Ltd., *John Brown & Company Ltd.: Atlas Works, Sheffield; Shipyard and Engineering Works, Clydebank* (1903).

—— *John Brown & Co. Ltd., 1864–1924* (Sheffield, 1924).

Brown Bayleys Ltd., *Brown Bayleys 1871–1971* (Sheffield, 1971).

—— *Brown Bayleys: A Story of Development* (n.d.).

BURK, K., *The First Privatisation: The Politicians, the City, and the Denationalisation of Steel* (1988).

BURN, D. L., *The Economic History of Steelmaking 1867–1939* (Cambridge, 1940).

—— *The Steel Industry, 1939–1959: A Study in Competition and Planning* (Cambridge, 1961).

Business & Market Research, *The UK Market for Domestic Tableware* (1988).

BUXTON, N. K., and ALDCROFT, D. H. (eds.), *British Industry Between the Wars* (1979).

CALLAN, G. B., *400 Years of Iron and Steel* (Sheffield, 1971).

—— *Secrets of Sheffield Steelmakers* (Sheffield, 1993).

The Century's Progress (1893).

CARPENTER, E., *My Days and Dreams* (1916).

CARR, J. C., and TAPLIN, W., *A History of the British Steel Industry* (Oxford, 1962).

CHANDLER, A. D., *The Visible Hand: The Managerial Revolution in American Business* (Cambridge, Mass., 1977).

—— *Scale and Scope: The Dynamics of Industrial Capitalism* (Cambridge, Mass., 1990).

CHAPMAN, A. W., *The Story of a Modern University: a History of the University of Sheffield* (Oxford, 1955).

CHURCH, R., *Herbert Austin* (1979).

COATES, D., *The Question of UK Decline: The Economy, State and Society* (Hemel Hempstead, 1994).

COWARD, H., *Reminiscences of Henry Coward* (1919).

CROSSLEY, D., CASS, N., FLAVELL, N., and TURNER, C. (eds.), *Water Power on the Sheffield Rivers* (Sheffield, 1989).

DAVENPORT-HINES, R. P. T., *Dudley Docker: The Life and Times of a Trade Warrior* (Cambridge, 1984).

—— 'The British Marketing of Armaments, 1885–1914', in Davenport-Hines (ed.), *Markets and Bagmen: Studies in the History of Marketing and British Industrial Performance, 1830–1939* (Aldershot, 1986).

DAVID, A. B., and DREYFUS, M. S., *The Finest Instruments Ever Made* (Arlington, Mass., 1986).

DAY, J., and TYLECOTE, R. F., *The Industrial Revolution in Metals* (1991).

DEFOE, D., *A Tour Through the Whole Island of Great Britain* (1724–6).

DINTENFASS, M., *The Decline of Industrial Britain, 1870–1980* (1992).

DISRAELI, B., *Sybil* (1845).

Dixon, James & Sons Ltd., *Centenary Souvenir* (Sheffield, 1905).

DUDLEY, G. F., and RICHARDSON, J. J., *Politics and Steel in Britain, 1967–1988: The Life and Times of the British Steel Corporation* (Aldershot, 1990).

EATON, R., *The Ultimate Brace: A Unique Product of Victorian Sheffield* (Hunstanton, 1989).

ELBAUM, B., and LAZONICK, W. (eds.), *The Decline of the British Economy* (Oxford, 1986).

ERICKSON, C. J., *British Industrialists: Steel and Hosiery 1850–1950* (Cambridge, 1959).

EVANS, H., *Vickers: Against the Odds 1956–1977* (1978).

Firth, Thos. & Sons Ltd., *Modern Projectile Factories of Thomas Firth & Sons Ltd.* (1912).

Firth-Brown Ltd., *The Staybrite Book* (Sheffield, 1934).

GATTY, A., *Sheffield Past and Present* (Sheffield, 1873).

Gillott, Joseph & Sons, *The Gillotts of Sheffield* (Sheffield, 1951).

GORDON, R. B., and MALONE, P. M., *The Texture of Industry* (New York, 1994).

GRANT, A., *Steel and Ships: The History of John Brown's* (1950).

GRAY, R. D., *Alloys and Automobiles: The Life of Elwood Haynes* (Indianapolis, 1979).

GRINYER, P. H., and SPENDER, J. C., *Turnaround: The Fall and Rise of the Newton Chambers Group* (1979).

Great Industries of Great Britain (1886).

Griffith's Guide to the Iron Trade of Great Britain (1867: repr. Newton Abbot, 1967).

HADFIELD, R. A., *The Work and Position of the Metallurgical Chemist* (Sheffield, 1921).

HALLAM, D. J., *The First 200 Years: A Short History of Rabone Chesterman Ltd.* (Birmingham, 1984).

HAMILTON, J., *The Misses Vickers* (Sheffield, 1984).

HATFIELD, J., and HATFIELD, J., *The Oldest Sheffield Plater* (Huddersfield, 1974).

HATFIELD, W. H., *The Application of Science to the Steel Industry* (Cleveland, Ohio, 1928).

—— 'Stainless Steel', paper read before the Institution of Production Engineers, Sheffield Section, 7 Oct. 1935. Pamphlet in SCL.

—— *Sheffield Burns* (Sheffield, 1943).

HAWKINS, R., 'The Distribution of Crucible Steel Furnaces in Sheffield' (SCL Information Sheet, 2nd edn., 1973).

HEAL, D. W., *The Steel Industry in Postwar Britain* (Newton Abbot, 1974).

HEY, D., *Packmen, Carriers and Packhorse Roads: Trade and Communication in North Derbyshire and South Yorkshire* (Leicester, 1980).

—— *The Fiery Blades of Hallamshire: Sheffield and Its Neighbourhood, 1660–1740* (Leicester, 1991).

HIGHAM, N., *A Very Scientific Gentleman: The Major Achievements of Henry Clifton Sorby* (1963).

HINTON, J., *The First Shop Stewards' Movement* (1973).

Histories of Famous Firms (1957–8).

HOERR, J. P., *And the Wolf Finally Came: The Decline of the American Steel Industry* (Pittsburgh, 1988).

HOGAN, W. T., *Economic History of the Iron and Steel Industry in the United States*, 5 vols. (Lexington, Mass., 1971).

HOLLAND, G. C., *The Vital Statistics of Sheffield* (Sheffield, 1843).

HOLLAND, J., *Tour of the Don* (1837).

HOPKINS, E., *Birmingham: The First Manufacturing Town in the World* (1989).

HOUSLEY, H., *Grinders and Buffers: A Boyhood in the Sheffield Cutlery Industry* (Sheffield, 1988).

HUDSON, R., and SADLER, D., *The Uncertain Future of Special Steels: Trends in the Sheffield, UK and European Special Steels Industries* (Sheffield, 1987).

HUME, J. R., and MOSS, M., *Beardmore: The History of a Scottish Industrial Giant* (1979).

HUNTER, J., *Hallamshire: The History and Topography of the Parish of Sheffield in the County of York*. Rev. edn. by Arthur Gatty (Sheffield, 1869).

ILES, A., *Memories of a Sheffield Tool Maker* (Mendham, NJ, 1993).

Industrial Sheffield and Rotherham: The Official Handbook of the Sheffield and Rotherham Chambers of Commerce (1919).

Industries of Sheffield and District (Sheffield, 1905).

INGHAM, J. N., *Making Iron and Steel: Independent Mills in Pittsburgh, 1820–1920* (Columbus, Ohio, 1991).

IRVINE, K. J., 'Swinden Laboratories: 50 Years of Steel Research' (Rotherham, privately published, 1984).

JEANS, J. S., *Steel: Its History, Manufacture, Properties and Uses* (1880).

JENKINS, C., and McCLARENCE, S., *On the Knife Edge* (Sheffield, 1989).

JEREMY, D. J., and SHAW, C. (eds.), *Dictionary of Business Biography*, 5 vols. (1984–6).

JEREMY, D. J., and TWEEDALE, G., *Dictionary of 20th-Century Business Leaders* (1994).

Jessop, William & Sons, *Visit to a Steelworks* (Sheffield, 1913).

JONES, G. (ed.), *British Multinationals* (1986).

JONES, J., and JONES, M., *'A Most Enterprising Thing'* (Chapeltown, 1993).

KANIGEL, R., *One Best Way: Frederick Winslow Taylor and the Making of the 20th Century* (forthcoming).

KAY, J., *Foundations of Corporate Success* (Oxford, 1993).

KEANE, J., *Six Months in Mecca* (1881).

KEELING, B., *World Steel: A New Assessment of Trends and Prospects*, The Economist Intelligence Unit Special Report No. 1124 (1988).

KENWORTHY, J., *The Early History of Stocksbridge and District*, 2 vols. (Deepcar, 1915).

Kenyon, John & Co., *Bi-Centenary Celebration, 1710–1910* (Sheffield, 1910).

Keynote Publications, *Cutlery: An Industry Sector Overview* (London, 1988).

KOHN, F., *Iron and Steel Manufacture* (1869).

KRUMHOLZ, P. L., *A History of Shaving and Razors* (Bartonville, Ill., 1987).

LANDES, D. S., *The Unbound Prometheus* (Cambridge, 1970).

Laycock Engineering Ltd., *Laycock Centenary 1880–1980* (1980).

LEADER, R. E., *The Sheffield Banking Company Ltd.: An Historical Sketch, 1831–1916* (Sheffield, 1916).

Lee, Arthur & Sons, *Lee Steel 1874–1974* (Sheffield, 1974).

LEVINE, A. L., *Industrial Retardation in Britain, 1880–1914* (1967).

LEVINE, B., *Levine's Guide to Knives and their Values*, 2nd edn. (Northbrook, Ill., 1993).

LINTON, D. L. (ed.), *Sheffield and Its Region: A Scientific and Historical Survey* (Sheffield, 1956).

LLOYD, G. I. H., *The Cutlery Trades: An Historical Essay in the Economics of Small-Scale Production* (1913).

LUCAS, G., and POLLOCK, J. F., *Gas Turbine Materials* (1957).

McCLOSKEY, D. M., *Economic Maturity and Entrepreneurial Decline: British Iron and Steel, 1870–1913* (Cambridge, 1973).

Market Research Inco Europe Ltd., *Stainless Steel Statistics; Post-war Historical Series* (1977).

Marples, William Ltd., *Price List of American Tools and Hardware* (1909), repr. with an intro. by K. D. Roberts (1980).

MARSHALL, A., *Principles of Economics* (1890), 8th edn. (1964).

Men of the Period (1896).

MENSFORTH, E., *Family Engineers* (1981).

MERRILL, J., *A Hundred Years of History: Lockwood & Carlisle Ltd 1876–1976* (Sheffield, 1976).

Minutes of Evidence taken Before the Trade and Industry Committee: Enquiry into the Motor Components Industry (1987).

Monopolies & Mergers Commission, *William Cook plc Acquisitions: A Report on the Mergers Situation*, Cm. 1196 (1990).

MONYPENNY, J. H. G., *Stainless Steel and Iron*, 2nd edn. (1931).

Mosely Industrial Commission to the United States of America (Manchester, 1903).

MYERS, S., *Cars from Sheffield: The Rise and Fall of the Sheffield Motor Industry, 1900–1930* (Sheffield, 1986).

Nether Edge Neighbourhood Group, *They Lived in Sharrow and Nether Edge* (Sheffield, 1988).

Official Illustrated Guide to the Great Northern Railway (c.1857).

OSBORN, F. M., *The Story of the Mushets* (1952).

OVENDEN, K., *The Politics of Steel* (1978).

PARSONS, C. S., *New Hampshire Clocks and Clockmakers* (Exeter, NH, 1976).

Pawson & Brailsford's Illustrated Guide to Sheffield and Neighbourhood (Sheffield, 1862, 1879).

PAYNE, P. L., *Colvilles and the Scottish Steel Industry* (Oxford, 1979).

—— *British Entrepreneurship in the Nineteenth Century*, 2nd edn. (1988).

PEACH, L. G., *The Company of Cutlers in Hallamshire in the County of York, 1906–1956* (Sheffield, 1960).

PERRET, J.-J., *Mémoire sur L'Acier, Dans Lequel on Traite des Différentes Qualités de ce Métal, de la Forge, du Bon Emploi et de la Trempe* (Paris, 1779).

PIKE, W. T., *Sheffield at the Opening of the 20th Century* (Brighton, 1901).

PIORE, M. J., and SABEL, C. F., *The Second Industrial Divide* (New York, 1984).

POLLARD, S., *Three Centuries of Sheffield Steel: The Story of a Family Business* (Sheffield, 1954).

—— *A History of Labour in Sheffield* (Liverpool, 1959).

—— (ed.), *The Sheffield Outrages* (Bath, 1971).

—— *Britain's Prime and Britain's Decline* (1989).

—— *The Development of the British Economy, 1914–1990*, 4th edn. (1992).

PORTER, M. E., *The Competitive Advantage of Nations* (1990).

Pryor, Edward & Son Ltd., *Making a Mark*, 6th edn. (Sheffield, 1957).

PYBUS, S., *'Damned Bad Place, Sheffield'* (Sheffield, 1994).

RAMSAY, T., *The Picture of Sheffield* (Sheffield, 1824).

The Record of Davy Bros. Ltd. in the World War, 1914–1918 (Sheffield, 1918).

REES, D. M., *Yorkshire Craftsmen at Work* (Clapham, 1981).

Reports of Artisans Selected by a Committee Appointed by the Council of the Society of Arts to Visit the Paris Universal Exhibition 1867 (1867).

REUTTER, M., *Sparrows Point: Making Steel—The Rise and Ruin of American Industrial Might* (New York, 1988).

Rodgers, Joseph & Sons, *Under Five Sovereigns* (Sheffield, 1911).

ROLT, L. T. C., *Tools for the Job* (1965).

Rotherham Borough Council, *A Lifetime in Steel: A Pictorial History of Iron and Steelmaking in Rotherham* (1987).

Royal Commission on the Private Manufacture of and Trading in Arms. Cmd. 5292. Minutes of Evidence (1935–6).

Ruskin Gallery, *The Cutting Edge: An Exhibition of Sheffield Tools* (Sheffield, 1992).

SALAMAN, R. A., *Dictionary of Tools Used in the Woodworking and Allied Trades 1700–1900* (1975).

—— *Dictionary of Leather-Working Tools c.1700–1950, and the Tools of the Allied Trades* (1986).

SAMPSON, A., *The Arms Bazaar* (1977).

Sandvik AB, *Transformation: Sandvik 1862–1987* (Sandviken, 1987).

SCHMOLLER, T., *Sheffield Papermakers: Three Centuries of Papermaking in the Sheffield Area* (Wylam, 1992).

SCOTT, J. D., *Vickers: A History* (1962).

SCRANTON, P., *Figured Tapestry: Production, Markets, and Power in Philadelphia Textiles, 1885–1941* (New York, 1989).

SEEBOHM, H., *On the Manufacture of Crucible Cast Steel* (Sheffield, 1884).

SEED, T. A., *Pioneers for a Century, 1852–1952: The Growth and Achievement of Samuel Osborn & Co. Ltd.* (Sheffield, 1952).

SEELY, B. (ed.), *Encyclopedia of American Business History and Biography: Iron and Steel in the Twentieth Century* (Columbia, SC, 1994).

SETH-SMITH, M., *200 Years of Richard Johnson & Nephew* (Manchester, 1973).

Sheffield City Council, *Sheffield Replanned* (Sheffield, 1945).

—— *Sheffield and Rotherham Steel Industry Study* (Sheffield, 1980).

—— *Steel in Crisis: Alternatives to Government Policy and the Decline in South Yorkshire's Steel Industry* (Sheffield, 1984).

Sheffield and Rotherham Bank: A Banking Bicentenary, 1792–1992 (Sheffield, 1992).

Sheffield and Rotherham Up-to-Date (Sheffield, 1897).

SHELDON, J., *The Founders and Builders of Stocksbridge Works* (Stocksbridge, 1922).

SIMONS, E. N., *Steel Files: Their Manufacture and Application* (1947).

——, *Lockwood & Carlisle Ltd of Sheffield: A Chapter of Marine History* (Sheffield, 1962).

Skelton, C. T. & Co., *Announcing One Hundred Years of Progress, 1855–1955* (Sheffield, 1955).

SMITH, C. S., *A History of Metallography* (Chicago, 1960).

SMITH, D., *Conflict and Compromise: Class Formation in English Society, 1830–1914* (1982).

SMITH, J., *Explanation or Key, to the Various Manufactories of Sheffield, with Engravings of Each Article*, ed. J. S. Kebabien (Vermont, 1975).

SMITH, P., and MOYLE, N., *Lock, Stock and Barrel: Sheffield Craftsmanship in Shooting Accessories* (Sheffield, 1991).

Souvenir of the Master Cutlership of Henry Hall Bedford JP, 1907–8 (Sheffield, 1907).

STAINTON, J. H., *The Making of Sheffield 1865–1914* (Sheffield, 1924).

STANSFIELD, H., *Samuel Fox & Co. Ltd. 1842–1967* (Stocksbridge, 1967).

Stead, J. & Co., *Steady Progress for Half a Century, 1901–1951* (Sheffield, 1951).

Swann-Morton Ltd., *The First Fifty Years* (Sheffield, 1982).

TAYLOR, W., *The Sheffield Horn Industry* (Sheffield, 1927).

THOMPSON, P., *Sharing Success: The Story of NFC* (1990).

TIFFANY, P., *The Decline of American Steel: How Management, Labor and the Government Went Wrong* (New York, 1988).

TIMMINS, J. G., *Workers in Metal Since 1784: A History of W. & G. Sissons* (Sheffield, 1984).

TOLLIDAY, S., *Business, Banking and Politics: The Case of British Steel, 1918–1939* (Cambridge, Mass., 1987).

Turner, Thomas, & Wingfield Rowbotham, *Handicrafts that Survive: Centenary Souvenir 1802–1902* (Sheffield, 1902).

TREBILCOCK, C., *The Vickers Brothers: Armaments and Enterprise 1854–1914* (1977).

TWEEDALE, G., *Giants of Sheffield Steel* (Sheffield, 1986).

—— *Sheffield Steel and America: A Century of Commercial and Technological Interdependence, 1830–1930* (Cambridge, 1987).

—— *Stan Shaw: Master Cutler* (Sheffield, 1993).

TWIL: Fifty Years On (Sheffield, 1983).

Ward, Thos. Ltd., *Outline of Progress: Commemorating 75 Years Industrial Service* (Sheffield, 1962).

WARREN, K., *The British Iron and Sheet Steel Industry since 1840* (1970).

—— *Armstrongs of Elswick* (1989).

WENGENROTH, U., *Enterprise and Technology: The German and British Steel Industries, 1865–1895* (Cambridge, 1993).

WHITE, W., *A Month in Yorkshire*, 5th edn. (1879).

WHITTLE, F., *Jet: the Story of a Pioneer* (1953).

WILSON, R. E., *Two Hundred Precious Metal Years: A History of the Sheffield Smelting Co. Ltd., 1760–1960* (1960).

WREGE, C. D., and GREENWOOD, R. D., *Frederick W. Taylor: The Father of Scientific Management* (Homewood, Ill., 1990), 9–29.

WRIGHT, F., *Stanley 1936–1986* (Sheffield, 1986).

—— *James Neill: A Century of Quality and Service 1889–1989* (Sheffield, 1989).

YONEKURA, S., *The Japanese Iron and Steel Industry 1850–1990: Continuity and Discontinuity* (1994).

Articles

ALDCROFT, D. H., 'The Entrepreneur and the British Economy, 1870–1914', *Economic History Review*, 17 (Aug. 1964).

BARRACLOUGH, K. C., 'Sheffield and the Development of Stainless Steel', *Ironmaking and Steelmaking*, 16 (1989).

BERG, M., 'Small-Producer Capitalism in Eighteenth-Century England', *Business History*, 35 (Jan. 1993).

CALLAN, G. B. (ed.), 'Two Hundred Years of Special Steel', *The Sanderson Kayser Magazine*, 2 (1976).

DAVENPORT-HINES, R. P. T., 'The British Marketing of Armaments, 1885–1914', in Davenport-Hines (ed.), *Markets and Bagmen: Studies in the History of Marketing and British Industrial Performance, 1830–1939* (Aldershot, 1986).

DAVENPORT-HINES, R. P. T., 'Vickers as a Multinational', in Geoffrey Jones (ed.), *British Multinationals* (Aldershot, 1986).

DESCH, C. H., 'The Steel Industry of South Yorkshire: A Regional Study', Paper read to the Sociological Society, 24 Jan. 1922. Pamphlet in SCL.

DONCASTER, R. T., 'Daniel Doncaster & Sons and the Poppet Valve Trade', *The Cutting Edge: Magazine of the Sheffield Trades Historical Society*, 7 (1991).

GEROSKI, P., and VLASSOPOULOS, A., 'A Market Leader in a Declining Industry: Richardson Sheffield', *Economic Journal*, 8 (1990).

HADFIELD, R. A., ELLIOT, T. G., and WILLEY, G. B., 'The Development and Use of the Microscope in Steelworks', repr. from *Journal of the Microscopical Society* (June 1925).

HANNAH, L., 'Scale and Scope: Towards a European Visible Hand?', *Business History*, 33 (Apr. 1991).

HAWLEY, K., 'The Ledgers of John Littlewood, Sheffield Edge Tool Makers, 1900–1909', *Tools and Trades*, 7 (1992).

HAYTER, R., and PATCHELL, J., 'Different Trajectories in the Social Divisions of Labour: The Cutlery Industry in Sheffield, England, and Tsubame, Japan', *Urban Studies*, 30 (1993).

HIGGINS, D., and TWEEDALE, G., 'Asset or Liability?: Trademarks in the Sheffield Cutlery and Tool Trades', *Business History* (forthcoming).

KNOEDLER, J. F., 'Market Structure, Industrial Research and Consumers of Innovation: Forging Backward Linkages to Research in the Turn-of-the-Century US Steel Industry', *Business History Review*, 67 (Spring 1993).

MUSSON, A. E., 'The Engineering Industry', in Roy Church (ed.), *The Dynamics of Victorian Business* (London, 1980).

O'BRIEN, P., 'Industry Structure as Competitive Advantage: The History of Japan's Post-War Steel Industry', *Business History*, 34 (Jan. 1992).

PALMER, H. J., 'Cutlery and Cutlers at Sheffield', *The English Illustrated Magazine* (Aug. 1884).

PEATMAN, J., 'The Abbeydale Industrial Hamlet: History and Restoration', *Industrial Archaeology Review*, 11 (Spring 1989).

POTTER, J., 'Atlantic Economy, 1815–1860: The USA and the Industrial Revolution in Britain', in L. S. Pressnell (ed.), *Studies in the Industrial Revolution. Studies Presented to T. S. Ashton* (1960).

ROSENBERG, N., 'Technological Change in the Machine Tool Industry', 1840–1910', *Journal of Economic History*, 23 (1963).

SABEL, C., and ZEITLIN, J., 'Historical Alternatives to Mass Production: Politics, Markets and Technology in Nineteenth-Century Industrialization', *Past and Present*, 108 (1985).

SANDERSON, M., 'The Professor as Industrial Consultant: Oliver Arnold and the British Steel Industry, 1900–14', *Economic History Review*, 31, 2nd ser. (Nov. 1978).

SANDFORD, J., 'Hardmetal: The History to 1950', *JHMS* 19 (1985).

SAUL, S. B., 'The Market and the Development of the Mechanical Engineering Industries in Britain, 1860–1914', in Saul (ed.), *Technological Change: The United States and Britain in the Nineteenth Century* (1970).

SCHOLEY, R., 'European Steel: What Future?', *Ironmaking and Steelmaking*, 14 (1987).

Sheffield City Council, 'Sheffield Hand Tool Sector: Decline Through Acquisition', in *Sheffield Economic Bulletin* (Dept. of Employment, Sheffield City Council, Summer 1992).

TAYLOR, M., 'The Sheffield Steel Inquiry of 1869', *THAS* 15 (1989).

TEMIN, P., 'The Relative Decline of the British Steel Industry, 1880–1913', in Henry Rosovsky (ed.), *Industrialization in Two Systems* (New York, 1966).

TIMMINS, J. G., 'Concentration and Integration in the Sheffield Crucible Steel Industry', *Business History*, 24 (Mar. 1982).

TOWNSEND, H., 'The Structure and Problems of the Sheffield Cutlery Trade', *District Bank Review* (1954).

TRUEMAN, J., 'The Initiation and Growth of High Alloy (Stainless) Steel Production', *JHMS* 19 (1985).

TWEEDALE, G., 'Transatlantic Specialty Steels: Sheffield High-Grade Steel Firms and the USA, 1860–1940', in Jones (ed.), *British Multinationals* (Aldershot, 1986).

—— 'Business and Investment Strategies in the Inter-War British Steel Industry: A Case Study of Hadfields Ltd. and Bean Cars, *Business History*, 29 (Jan. 1987).

—— 'Science, Innovation and the "Rule of Thumb": The Development of British Metallurgy to 1945', in J. Liebenau (ed.), *The Challenge of New Technology* (Aldershot, 1988).

—— 'The Beginnings of Electro-Metallurgy in Britain: A Note on the Career of Robert S. Hutton', *JHMS* 25 (1991), 72–7.

—— 'The Razor Blade King of Sheffield: The Forgotten Career of Paul Kuehnrich', *THAS* 16 (1991).

—— 'The Metallurgist as Entrepreneur: The Career of Sir Robert Hadfield', *JHMS* 26 (1992).

—— 'Strategies for Decline: George Wostenholm & Son and the Sheffield Cutlery Industry', *THAS* 17 (1993).

—— 'Pioneering in Steel Casting: A Steel Melter's Reminiscences, *c*.1856–70s', *JHMS* (forthcoming).

—— 'Industry and De-industrialisation in the 1970s', in R. Coopey and N. Woodward (eds.), *The Troubled Economy* (1995).

WARREN, K., 'The Sheffield Rail Trade: An Episode in the Locational History of the British Steel Industry', *Institute of British Geographers' Transactions*, 34 (1964).

VOYLES, J. B., 'The Decline and Fall of the Sheffield Empire', in K. Warner (ed.), *Knives '86* (Northbrook, Ill. 1985).

WELLS, J., 'Uneven Development and Deindustrialisation in the UK since 1979', in Francis Green (ed.), *The Restructuring of the UK Economy* (Hemel Hempstead, 1989).

WILKINS, M., 'The Neglected Intangible Asset: The Influence of the Trade Mark on the Rise of the Modern Corporation', *Business History*, 34 (Jan. 1992).

WILLIAMS, E., 'Low Cost Imports from the Far East have Decimated Sheffield Trade', *Tableware International* (Nov./Dec. 1975).

WOLF, M. M., 'History of Continuous Casting', in *Steelmaking in the 20th Century: From Black Magic to Technology* (Warrendale, Pa., Iron & Steel Society, 1992).

INDEX